Expert Data Modeling with Power BI

Second Edition

Enrich and optimize your data models to get the best out of Power BI for reporting and business needs

Soheil Bakhshi

BIRMINGHAM—MUMBAI

Expert Data Modeling with Power BI
Second Edition

Copyright © 2023 Packt Publishing

All rights reserved. No part of this book may be reproduced, stored in a retrieval system, or transmitted in any form or by any means, without the prior written permission of the publisher, except in the case of brief quotations embedded in critical articles or reviews.

Every effort has been made in the preparation of this book to ensure the accuracy of the information presented. However, the information contained in this book is sold without warranty, either express or implied. Neither the author nor Packt Publishing or its dealers and distributors, will be held liable for any damages caused or alleged to have been caused directly or indirectly by this book.

Packt Publishing has endeavored to provide trademark information about all of the companies and products mentioned in this book by the appropriate use of capitals. However, Packt Publishing cannot guarantee the accuracy of this information.

Senior Publishing Product Manager: Devika Battike
Acquisition Editor – Peer Reviews: Gaurav Gavas
Project Editor: Namrata Katare
Content Development Editor: Rebecca Robinson
Copy Editor: Safis Editing
Technical Editor: Aneri Patel
Proofreader: Safis Editing
Indexer: Manju Arasan
Presentation Designer: Ganesh Bhadwalkar
Developer Relations Marketing Executive: Monika Sangwan

First published: May 2021
Second edition: April 2023

Production reference: 2080523

Published by Packt Publishing Ltd.
Livery Place
35 Livery Street
Birmingham
B3 2PB, UK.
ISBN: 978-1-80324-624-6

www.packt.com

I dedicate this book to my lovely wife, Elica Mehr, and our precious daughter, Avina. Without their unconditional support, none of this would have been possible. I also owe this success to my parents, who always believed in me and encouraged me to follow my dreams.

Foreword

I am delighted to introduce the new edition of this book by Soheil, an MVP and Power BI expert. This book is a comprehensive guide for anyone who wants to learn Power BI through practical exercises. It covers a wide range of topics, from data modeling and visualization to advanced features and best practices. Whether a beginner or an expert, you will find something useful and interesting in this book. Power BI is the leading platform and tool for enterprise and self-service BI. It is powerful, flexible, and easy to use. This new edition has been updated to reflect the latest changes and developments in Power BI. Some chapters have been completely revamped, and three new chapters have been added to cover new topics. You will learn how to deal with some data warehousing concepts in Power BI, such as SCDs and degenerate dimensions, how to use dataflows to create reusable curated data, and how to leverage DirectQuery to Power BI Datasets and Analysis Services in Composite Models. You will also discover new options, features, and DAX functions that can enhance your data analysis and reporting. This book is designed to help you learn by example. Every concept is explained using clear and concise examples that you can follow along. You will also find tips and tricks to save you time and effort. I highly recommend this book to anyone who wants to master Power BI and gain valuable insights from their data.

Christian Wade

Principal Program Manager, Microsoft

Contributors

About the author

Soheil Bakhshi is the founder of Data Vizioner, a Microsoft Data Platform MVP, an expert in data analytics, an author, a blogger, and a speaker. He is the author of *Expert Data Modeling with Power BI* and the *Power BI for Intermediates* e-book. Soheil has over 20 years of experience in data analysis and is a thought leader in the industry, working as a consultant, trainer, and solution architect for various clients across different industries. He is passionate about data and analytics and enjoys learning new technologies and techniques to deliver innovative solutions.

About the reviewers

Ana María Bisbé York is a BI consultant and trainer with more than 25 years of industry experience, from developing desktop solutions in FoxPro to data analysis and BI consulting and training. She has a degree in Economic Cybernetics from Moscow's State University of Management in the former USSR, and a Master's degree in BI from the University of Alcala, Spain. She is currently an independent consultant specializing in the data world on Microsoft technologies, including modeling and data analysis with SQL Server BI, Excel BI, Azure ML, R, and Power BI.

Ana is a Microsoft Data Platform MVP and Microsoft Partner in Power BI, as well as a LinkedIn Learning trainer and author of *Curso Power BI* (Spanish) with ANAYA. She is often a speaker, organizer, or attendee at various technical events and forums.

She was awarded the *Teckfluencer* award by *Globant Award Spain* in 2022.

I am grateful to all the people who have contributed to my professional and personal training.

Thank you to my family for their patience and support.

Ahmed Oyelowo is a Microsoft-certified Power BI data analyst associate and Microsoft-certified Azure enterprise data analyst who has developed cutting-edge BI and data analysis solutions for various corporate clients. Having started his career in banking, Ahmed moved on to consulting, where he gained data analysis and training experience. He has over 6 years of experience in delivering data analysis training and solutions and is currently a managing partner and the lead trainer and consultant at Foresight BI & Analytics Global Solutions.

Ahmed is a 3-time recipient of the prestigious Microsoft Most Valuable Professional (MVP) award under the Data Platform category for his technical contributions to Power BI communities. He is also a Microsoft Certified Trainer and has taught various data analysis and Power BI courses—his Power BI course on Udemy has been taken by over 80,000 students in less than 3 years, and has been tagged as a *Best Seller* by Udemy on several occasions.

My sincere appreciation to my Creator for the gift of all required to complete this review. I must also thank my dearest wife, Kafayat Oyelowo, and my lovely daughter, Yusraa Oyelowo, for their support and understanding while I was spending time away reviewing the best Power BI book for Power BI developers.

Finally, to the author, Soheil Bakshi (MVP), and Packt Publishing for the opportunity to review (I say again) the best Power BI book for Power BI developers.

Anil Maharjan is a Microsoft Data Platform MVP. He has a BE in Computer Engineering and Data Science Specialization from Coursera, Johns Hopkins University and over 12 years of development and implementation experience in the healthcare data analytics and telecommunication industries as a BI developer, database consultant, senior BI engineer, and senior data engineer.

He is a frequent blogger and speaker at local SQL Server user groups and Power BI user groups, in addition to speaking at SQL Saturday, Data and BI Summit 2018 (Dublin), Microsoft Ignite 2019 (Singapore), Power Platform Summit 2019 (Australia), and other SQL and Power BI events. He is also the user group leader of the Nepal Power BI user group, and was a program committee member for PASS Summit 2014 and DATA and BI Summit 2018 (Dublin) and a committee track leader for Power Platform Summit 2019 (Australia).

Anil is the author of the popular *Power BI MVP* Book, and blogs at anilmaharjanonbi.wordpress.com.

I am extremely grateful to my parents and family for their love, prayers, and care, and their sacrifices to educate and prepare me for my future. I am very much thankful to my wife and daughter for their love, understanding, and support. Special thanks to my wife Deepa for suggesting I review this book, and for her love and support.

Join us on Discord!

Join The Big Data and Analytics Community on the Packt Discord Server!

Hang out with 558 other members and enjoy free voice and text chat.

https://packt.link/ips2H

Table of Contents

Preface — xxi

Section I: Data Modeling in Power BI

Chapter 1: Introduction to Data Modeling in Power BI — 1

Understanding the Power BI layers — 2
    The data preparation layer (Power Query) • 3
    The data model layer • 3
        The Data view • 4
        The Model view • 6
    The data visualization layer • 6
        The Report view • 6
    How data flows in Power BI • 7

What data modeling means in Power BI — 9
    Semantic model • 9
    Building an efficient data model in Power BI • 10
    Star schema (dimensional modeling) and snowflaking • 11
        Transactional modeling versus star schema modeling • 11
        Snowflaking • 14
        Understanding denormalization • 14

Power BI licensing considerations — 22
    Maximum size of an individual dataset • 23
    Incremental data load • 23
    Hybrid tables • 23
    Calculation groups • 23
    Shared datasets • 24
    Power BI Dataflows • 25

Power BI Datamarts • 25
The iterative data modeling approach 25
  Conducting discovery workshops • 26
  Data preparation based on the business logic • 26
  Data modeling • 27
  Testing the logic • 27
  Demonstrating the business logic in basic data visualizations • 27
  Thinking like a professional data modeler • 27
Summary 28

Chapter 2: Data Analysis eXpressions and Data Modeling   29

Understanding virtual tables 29
  Creating calculated tables • 30
  Visually displaying the results of virtual tables • 35
    Creating calculated tables in Power BI Desktop • 35
    Using DAX Studio • 36
  Understanding relationships in virtual tables • 37
Time intelligence and data modeling 48
  Detecting valid dates in the date dimension • 48
  Period-over-period calculations • 56
    Implementing dynamic measure selection with Fields Parameters • 63
  Generating the Date dimension with DAX • 66
    Marking a Date table as a date table • 69
  Creating a time dimension with DAX • 74
Summary 76

Section II: Data Preparation in Query Editor

Chapter 3: Data Preparation in Power Query Editor   81

Introducing the Power Query M formula language in Power BI 81
  Power Query is CaSe-SeNsItIvE • 82
  Queries • 83
  Expressions • 83
  Values • 83
    Primitive values • 84
    Structured values • 84

Types • 89
- Primitive types • 89
- Custom types • 90

Introduction to Power Query Editor 90

Queries pane • 92
- Tables • 92
- Custom functions • 92
- Query parameters • 92
- Constant values • 92
- Groups • 93

Query Settings pane • 94
- Query Properties • 95
- Applied Steps • 97

Data View pane • 99

Status bar • 101

Advanced Editor • 102

Introduction to Power Query features for data modelers 103

Column quality • 104

Column distribution • 107

Column profile • 110

Understanding query parameters 111

Understanding custom functions 118

Recursive functions • 124

Summary 126

Chapter 4: Getting Data from Various Sources — 127

Getting data from common data sources 127

Folders • 128

CSV/TEXT/TSV • 134

Excel • 140
- Excel file stored in local drive • 140
- Excel file stored in SharePoint Online • 147

Power BI datasets • 152

Power BI dataflows • 160

Power BI Datamarts • 162

SQL Server • 164

SQL Server Analysis Services and Azure Analysis Services • 167

    SSAS multidimensional/tabular • 167
    AAS • 169
  OData feed • 170
  Dataverse • 173
Understanding data source certification 174
  Bronze • 175
  Silver • 175
  Gold/Platinum • 175
Working with connection modes 175
  Data Import • 176
    Applications • 176
    Limitations • 176
  DirectQuery • 177
    Applications • 177
    Limitations • 177
  Connect Live • 177
    Applications • 178
    Limitations • 178
Working with storage modes 178
Understanding dataset storage modes 179
Summary 180

Chapter 5: Common Data Preparation Steps   181

Data type conversion 183
Splitting a column by delimiter 191
Merging columns 194
Adding a custom column 196
Adding a column from examples 199
Duplicating a column 201
Filtering rows 204
Working with Group By 207
Appending queries 210
Merging queries 215
Duplicating and referencing queries 218
Replacing values 219
Extracting numbers from text 222
Dealing with Date, DateTime, and DateTimeZone 225

Pivoting tables 230
Summary 236

Chapter 6: Star Schema Preparation in Power Query Editor 237

Identifying dimensions and facts 237
  Understanding business requirements • 238
    Number of tables in the data source • 238
    The linkages between existing tables • 239
    Finding the lowest required grain of Date and Time • 240
  Defining dimensions and facts • 242
    Determining the potential dimensions • 243
    Determining the potential facts • 243
Creating Dimension tables 246
  Geography • 247
  Sales order • 250
  Product • 252
  Currency • 256
  Customer • 256
  Sales Demographic • 260
  Date • 262
  Time • 265
  Creating Date and Time dimensions – Power Query versus DAX • 267
Creating fact tables 268
Summary 276

Chapter 7: Data Preparation Common Best Practices 279

Consider loading a proportion of data 280
Appreciate case sensitivity in Power Query 283
Be mindful of query folding and its impact on data refresh 283
  Understanding query folding • 283
  DirectQuery and Dual storage modes and query folding • 284
  Data sources and query folding • 284
  Indications for query folding • 285
  Query folding best practices • 285
    Using SQL statements • 286
    Push the data preparation to the source system when possible • 291
    Disabling View Native Query does not necessarily mean a transformation step is not folded • 292

Organize queries in the Power Query Editor 294
Follow data type conversion best practices 296
    Data type conversion can affect data modeling • 296
    Avoid having columns with any data type • 304
    Include the data type conversion in the step when possible • 305
    Consider having only one data type conversion step • 306
Optimize query size 307
    Remove unnecessary columns and rows • 308
    Summarization (Group by) • 308
    Disabling query load • 309
Use query parameters 309
    Parameterizing connections • 309
    Restricting the row counts in development for large tables • 309
Define key columns in queries 312
Use naming conventions 313
Summary 314

Section III: Data Modeling

Chapter 8: Data Modeling Components   317

Data modeling in Power BI Desktop 317
Understanding tables 318
    Table properties • 319
    Featured tables • 322
    Calculated tables • 323
Understanding fields 329
    Data types • 329
    Custom formatting • 331
    Columns • 334
        Calculated columns • 334
        Grouping and binning columns • 334
        Column properties • 337
    Hierarchies • 342
    Measures • 343
        Implicit measures • 344
        Explicit measures • 346
        Textual measures • 346

Using relationships 348

    Primary keys/foreign keys • 350

    Handling composite keys • 350

    Relationship cardinalities • 355

        One-to-one relationships • 355

        One to many relationships • 355

        Many to many relationships • 355

    Filter propagation behavior • 358

    Bidirectional relationships • 360

Summary 363

Chapter 9: Star Schema and Data Modeling Common Best Practices   365

Dealing with many-to-many relationships 365

    Many-to-many relationships using a bridge table • 369

    Hiding the bridge table • 376

Avoiding bidirectional relationships 376

Dealing with inactive relationships 379

    Reachability via multiple filter paths • 380

    Multiple direct relationships between two tables • 381

Using configuration tables 384

    Segmentation • 384

    Dynamic color coding with measures • 386

Avoiding calculated columns when possible 391

Organizing the model 394

    Hiding insignificant model objects • 395

        Hiding unused fields and tables • 395

        Hiding key columns • 397

        Hiding implicit measures • 398

        Hiding columns used in hierarchies when possible • 398

    Creating measure tables • 398

    Using folders • 402

        Creating a folder in multiple tables in one go • 403

        Placing a measure in various folders • 404

        Creating subfolders • 405

Reducing model size by disabling auto date/time 406

Summary 410

Section IV: Advanced Data Modeling

Chapter 10: Advanced Data Modeling Techniques   413

Using aggregations 413

   Implementing aggregations for non-DirectQuery data sources • 414

      Implementing aggregation at the Date level • 415

      Implementing aggregation at the Year and Month level • 421

   Using Agg Awareness • 426

      Creating an aggregation table • 429

      Loading tables in DirectQuery mode • 430

      Creating relationships • 432

      Setting the aggregation table and its related dimensions' storage mode • 433

      Managing aggregation • 435

      Testing the aggregation • 438

   Implementing multiple aggregations • 446

   Important notes about aggregations • 449

Incremental refresh and hybrid tables 450

   Configuring incremental refresh policy and hybrid table in Power BI Desktop • 451

   Testing the incremental refresh • 458

   Important notes about incremental refresh and hybrid tables • 462

Parent-Child hierarchies 463

   Identify the depth of the hierarchy • 465

   Creating hierarchy levels • 467

Implementing roleplaying dimensions 471

Using calculation groups 474

   Requirements • 474

   Terminology • 475

   Implementing calculation groups to handle time intelligence • 475

   Testing calculation groups • 482

      Fixing the format string issue • 482

   DAX functions for calculation groups • 484

Summary 485

Chapter 11: Row-Level and Object-Level Security   487

What RLS and OLS mean in data modeling 488

   Terminology • 488

  Roles • 488

  Rules • 489

  Enhanced row-level security editor • 491

  Validating roles • 491

 Assigning members to roles in the Power BI Service • 493

 Assigning members to roles in Power BI Report Server • 494

RLS implementation flow 495

Common RLS implementation approaches 496

 Static RLS implementation • 496

 Dynamic RLS implementation • 503

  Restricting unauthorized users from accessing data • 503

  Managers can access their team members' data in parent-child hierarchies • 506

  Getting the user's login data from another source • 512

Introduction to OLS 519

 OLS implementation flow • 519

OLS implementation 520

 Validating roles • 522

 Assigning members and validating roles in the Power BI Service • 524

 RLS and OLS implementation in a single model • 524

 Considerations in using RLS and OLS • 527

Summary 529

Chapter 12: Dealing with More Advanced Data Warehousing Concepts in Power BI   531

Dealing with SCDs 531

 SCD type zero (SCD 0) • 534

 SCD type 1 (SCD 1) • 534

 SCD type 2 (SCD 2) • 544

Dealing with degenerate dimensions 549

Summary 552

Chapter 13: Introduction to Dataflows   553

Introduction to Dataflows 553

 Scenarios for using Dataflows • 554

 Dataflow terminology • 555

 Create Dataflows • 555

  Create new entities • 557

Create linked tables from other Dataflows • 563

Create computed entities • 565

Configure incremental data refresh in Dataflows • 567

Export/import Dataflows • 569

Export Dataflows • 569

Import Dataflows • 570

No-code/low-code experience • 570

Query plans in Dataflows • 573

Summary 575

Chapter 14: DirectQuery Connections to Power BI Datasets and Analysis Services in Composite Models   577

Introduction to composite models 577

Enabling DirectQuery for live connections 578

Allow DirectQuery connections to Power BI datasets in the Power BI service • 578

New terminologies 579

Chaining • 579

Chain length • 580

RLS in composite models with DirectQuery to Power BI datasets 586

Setting dataset permissions for contributors (report writers) 592

Summary 593

Chapter 15: New Options, Features, and DAX Functions   595

Field parameters 595

Introduction to Power BI Datamarts 601

What is a Datamart? • 601

What is Power BI Datamarts? • 602

Demystifying Power BI Datamart misunderstandings • 603

The Datamart Editor • 604

Create a simple Power BI Datamart • 605

Load the data into the Datamart • 605

Build the data model in Datamarts • 608

Analyze Datamarts in the Datamart Editor • 610

Analyze Datamarts in SQL client tools • 618

RLS in Datamarts • 620

New DAX functions 624

NETWORKDAYS() • 625

EVALUATEANDLOG() • 626
Window functions • 630
    PARTITIONBY() • 631
    ORDERBY() • 632
    INDEX() • 632
    OFFSET() • 639
    WINDOW() • 640

Summary 645

Other Books You May Enjoy   649

Index   653

Preface

Nowadays, information is easily accessible via the Internet. A quick search of "What is Power BI?" results in millions of websites and articles about the topic. Here is a condensed definition of Power BI:

Power BI is the data platform subset of a larger **Software as a Service (SaaS)** platform called **Power Platform,** offered by Microsoft.

To better understand the preceding definition, we need to know what data platform and SaaS applications are.

A data platform is a comprehensive software framework designed to store, manage, integrate, analyze, and visualize large volumes of data from various sources in a secure, reliable, and scalable manner, enabling organizations to gain insights, make data-driven decisions, and improve their operations and customer experiences. Power BI has all the characteristics of a data platform.

A SaaS application is a subscription-based software solution fully hosted in the cloud that organizations rent and use via the Internet. Power BI is a SaaS application that is subscription-based and fully hosted in Microsoft's cloud system. It offers various subscription plans, each with its own features, limitations, and toolsets.

It is critical to understand that the core of a data platform is the data itself. Spending time and money on a data platform is worth nothing without paying attention to how the data is stored, prepared, and modeled for analysis. The Power BI platform provides the required tools for that, and we need to have the knowledge to effectively and efficiently use those tools to establish the foundations of our data platform successfully.

This book will guide you to understand the ins and outs of data modeling and the required data preparations. This book teaches you how to connect to multiple data sources, understand the data and its interrelationships, and reshape it to create efficient data models. You will also learn about data exploration and navigation techniques to identify new metrics and perform custom calculations using various data modeling techniques. As you advance through the chapters, the book will demonstrate how to create full-fledged data models, enabling you to develop efficient and performant DAX code with new data modeling features. The book uses various real-world scenarios to ensure you learn practical techniques to solve business challenges by building optimal data models and being flexible in changing existing ones to meet evolving business requirements.

Finally, you'll learn how to use some new and advanced modeling features to enhance your data models to carry out a wide variety of complex tasks. By the end of this book, you will have gained the skills to structure data from multiple sources in different ways and create optimized data models that support reporting and data analytics requirements.

Who this book is for

If you are a Power BI user who wants to learn how to design and build effective data models for your reports and dashboards, this book is for you. Whether you are a beginner or an advanced user, you will find practical and useful tips and techniques to improve your data modeling skills and solve common challenges. You will also learn how to apply best practices and optimize your data model performance. This book is suitable for anyone who works with data and wants to leverage the power of Power BI to create insightful and interactive data visualizations. This book is also ideal for data analysts, business analysts, and BI professionals who have a basic understanding of Power BI and want to learn advanced data modeling techniques to design scalable and optimized data models for their business needs. Additionally, the book may also be beneficial to database developers and data engineers who want to learn how to integrate Power BI into their data architecture and create efficient data models for their organization.

What this book covers

Chapter 1, *Introduction to Data Modeling in Power BI*, briefly describes different functionalities of Power BI and why data modeling is important. This chapter also reveals some important notes to be considered around Power BI licensing, which could potentially affect your data model. This chapter introduces an iterative data modeling approach, which guarantees an agile Power BI implementation.

Chapter 2, *Data Analysis eXpressions and Data Modeling*, does not discuss DAX in detail, as in *Part 3* and *4* of this book DAX is heavily used to solve different data modeling challenges. Therefore, we'll only focus on the DAX functionalities that are harder to understand and are very relevant to data modeling. This chapter starts with a quick introduction to DAX, then we jump straight into virtual tables and time intelligence functionalities and their applications in real-world scenarios.

Chapter 3, *Data Preparation in Power Query Editor*, quickly explains the components of Power Query and their application. It expresses the importance of creating query parameters and user-defined functions along with real-world use cases and scenarios to demonstrate how powerful they are in building much more flexible and maintainable models.

Chapter 4, *Getting Data from Various Sources*, explains how to get data from different data sources that are more commonly used in Power BI. Then, the importance of data source certification is explained, which helps you set your expectations on the type of data you're going to deal with. This is especially helpful in estimating data modeling efforts. Different connection modes are also explained in this chapter.

Chapter 5, *Common Data Preparation Steps*, explains common data preparation steps along with real-world hands-on scenarios. A combination of what you have learned so far in this book and the steps discussed in this chapter gives you a strong foundation to go on to the next chapters and build your data models more efficiently.

By learning these functionalities, you can deal with a lot of different scenarios to implement different data models.

Chapter 6, *Star Schema Preparation in Power Query Editor*, explains how to prepare your queries based on the star schema data modeling approach with real-life scenarios. The Power Query M language will be heavily used in this chapter, so you will learn how to deal with real-world challenges along the way. As you have already learned common data preparation steps in the previous chapter, the majority of Power Query scenarios explained in this chapter will be easier to implement. You'll also learn how to build dimension tables and fact tables, and how to denormalize your queries when needed.

Chapter 7, *Data Preparation Common Best Practices*, explains common best practices in data preparation. Following these practices will help you build more efficient data models that are easier to maintain and more flexible to make changes to. By following these practices, you can also avoid common mistakes, which can make your life much easier.

Chapter 8, *Data Modeling Components*, explains data modeling components from a Power BI perspective, along with real file examples. In this chapter, we heavily use DAX when applicable, so having a basic understanding of DAX is essential. We also have a complete star schema model in Power BI. The concept of config tables is covered, which unlocks a lot of possibilities for handling more complex business logic in the data model. The chapter ends with data modeling naming conventions.

Chapter 9, *Star Schema and Data Modeling Common Best Practices*, explains common data modeling best practices to help you make better decisions while building your data model to prevent facing some known issues down the road. For instance, dealing with data type issues in key columns that are used in relationships is somewhat time-consuming to identify, but it's very easy to prevent. So, knowing data modeling best practices helps you save a lot of maintenance time and consequently saves you money.

Chapter 10, *Advanced Data Modeling Techniques*, explains special modeling techniques that solve special business requirements. A good data modeler is one who is always open to new challenges. You may face some of the advanced business requirements discussed in this chapter or you may face something different but similar. The message we want to send in this chapter is to think freely when dealing with new business challenges and try to be innovative to get the best results.

Chapter 11, *Row-Level and Object-Level Security*, explains how to implement Row-Level Security (RLS) and Object-Level Security (OLS) in a Power BI data model. Dealing with RLS and OLS can be complex, and knowing how to deal with different situations requires deep knowledge of data modeling and filter propagation concepts. Our aim in this chapter is to transfer that knowledge to you so you can design and implement high-performing and low-maintenance data models.

Chapter 12, *Dealing with More Advanced Data Warehousing Concepts in Power BI*, explains two concepts coming from data warehousing, **Slowly Changing Dimensions** (**SCDs**) and degenerate dimensions. This chapter also demonstrates when and how we can implement these concepts in a Power BI data model.

Chapter 13, *Introduction to Dataflows*, briefly introduces Dataflows, another available feature in Power BI. This chapter is designed to cover the basics and help you to build robust building blocks for your learning journey. This chapter also explains how to export/import Dataflows, and how the no-code/low-code experience and query plan work in Dataflows.

Chapter 14, DirectQuery Connections to Power BI Datasets and Analysis Services in Composite Models, introduces new terminologies related to composite models and discusses how to resolve more complex scenarios with fewer issues. This chapter also covers RLS challenges in composite models with DirectQuery connections to either a Power BI dataset or Azure Analysis Services and explains the challenges around setting dataset permissions for contributors after RLS is created.

Chapter 15, New Options, Features, and DAX Functions, introduces field parameters, Power BI Datamarts, and some new DAX functions. One of the main features is Field Parameters, which allow developers to create dynamic reports where users can switch between different fields using a slicer. Additionally, the chapter introduces Power BI Datamarts, a subject-oriented subset of a data warehouse focusing on a particular business unit, department, subject area, or business functionality. This chapter also explains how RLS Power BI Datamarts are implemented. The chapter also highlights new DAX functions, including `NETWORKDAYS()` and `EVALUATEANDLOG()`, and window functions such as `INDEX()`, `OFFSET()`, and `WINDOW()`.

To get the most out of this book

You will need to download and install the latest version of Power BI Desktop. All expressions have been tested in the March 2023 release of Power BI Desktop and should work in the later versions released on later dates. Power BI Desktop is a free application that lets you connect to various data sources, transform and model data, create visualizations, and share your work by publishing to the Power BI service. You can get Power BI Desktop in two ways:

- As a Windows app from the Microsoft Store
- As an executable desktop application downloadable directly from the Power BI website

In addition to Power BI Desktop, you will need to install and use DAX Studio, Tabular Editor, SQL **Server Management Studio** SSMS, and DAX Debug Output. All of these applications are free of charge. Here are the minimum requirements for the required applications to work properly:

Power BI Desktop:

- Hardware: A **Personal Computer** (**PC**) with at least a 1-Gigahertz (GHz) 64-bit (x64) processor, 2 GB of RAM, and 1 GB of available disk space. At least 1440x900 or 1600x900 (16:9) resolution is required. Lower resolutions such as 1024x768 or 1280x800 aren't supported because some controls (such as closing the startup screens) display beyond those resolutions. For optimal performance, having 8 GB of RAM and a 64-bit processor is recommended.
- Software: Install the latest version of Power BI Desktop from the Microsoft Store or the Power BI website on a Windows machine with Windows 8.1 or Windows Server 2012 R2 or later. You need to have .NET Framework 4.6.2 or higher and the Microsoft Edge browser (Internet Explorer is no longer supported). Power BI Desktop automatically installs WebView2. It is recommended to use a client version of Windows, such as Windows 10, instead of Windows Server. Power BI Desktop doesn't support Internet Explorer Enhanced Security Configuration.

- Security: You need to have a valid Power BI account to sign in to Power BI Desktop and publish reports. You also need to have permission to access the data sources and services that you want to use in your reports.

The following are download links for Power BI Desktop:

- Power BI Desktop from the Microsoft Store: https://aka.ms/pbidesktopstore
- Power BI Desktop from the web: https://www.microsoft.com/en-us/download/details.aspx?id=58494

You can sign up for a Power BI Service as an individual. Read more here: https://learn.microsoft.com/en-us/power-bi/fundamentals/service-self-service-signup-for-power-bi?WT.mc_id=DP-MVP-5003466.

Since January 31, 2021, Power BI Desktop is no longer supported on Windows 7.

Tabular Editor:

Tabular Editor is a powerful tool to create and manage tabular models in Microsoft Analysis Services and Power BI. The vendor, Kapacity, currently offers the tool in two flavours, Tabular Editor 2.x, which is the free version, and Tabular Editor 3.x, which is the commercial paid version. In this book, we use the free version. The following are the minimum requirements for running Tabular Editor:

- Hardware: A Windows PC with at least 4 GB of RAM and 100 MB of free disk space.
- Software: Windows 7, Windows 8, Windows 10 (recommended), Windows Server 2016, Windows Server 2019 or newer, and .NET Framework 4.6 or later. Microsoft Analysis Services client libraries (installed by default with SQL Server Management Studio or Visual Studio) are also required.
- Security: Administrator rights on the PC where Tabular Editor is installed or run. Read and write permissions on the tabular model that you want to edit are also required.

You can download Tabular Editor 2.x from here: https://github.com/TabularEditor/TabularEditor/releases/.

DAX Studio:

DAX Studio is a free, powerful tool from SQLBI for analyzing and optimizing DAX queries. It can connect to various data sources, such as Power BI, SQL Server Analysis Services Tabular Models, Azure Analysis Services, and Power Pivot. To use DAX Studio effectively, you need to meet some hardware, software, and security requirements as follows:

- Hardware: A Windows PC with a minimum of 4 GB of RAM and 100 MB of disk space.
- Software: Windows 7, Windows 8, Windows 10 (recommended), .NET Framework 4.7.1 or later, and Office primary interop assemblies are required. Office 2016 and later should have this enabled by default.

- Security: DAX Studio requires administrator privileges to install and update unless its portable version is used. It also requires access to the data sources that you want to connect to.

You can download DAX Studio from here: `https://daxstudio.org/downloads/`.

SQL Server Management Studio (SSMS):

SQL Server Management Studio (SSMS) is a **Graphical User Interface (GUI)** tool for developing, managing, and administrating SQL Server databases and servers. You can use SSMS to create and modify database objects, run queries and scripts, monitor performance and activity, configure security and backup options, and more. SSMS is a free and downloadable offering from Microsoft that works with any edition of SQL Server. SSMS can also be used to run DAX queries when connected to an instance of **SQL Server Analysis Services (SSAS)** Tabular Models, **Azure Analysis Services (AAS)**, or a premium Power BI dataset via XMLA endpoints. The following are the prerequisites to run SSMS efficiently throughout this book:

- Hardware: A Windows PC with at least a 1.8 GHz or faster x86 (Intel, AMD) processor (dual-core or better recommended), 2 GB of RAM is required (4 GB of RAM recommended), and 2.5 GB is the minimum if run on a **Virtual Machine (VM)**. It also requires a minimum of 2 GB of available space (up to 10 GB).
- Software: Windows 10 (64-bit) version 1607 (10.0.14393) or later, Windows 11 (64-bit), Windows Server 2016 (64-bit), Windows Server 2019 (64-bit), or Windows Server 2022 (64-bit).
- Security: SSMS requires administrator privileges to install.

SSMS is available to download from here: `https://learn.microsoft.com/en-us/sql/ssms/download-sql-server-management-studio-ssms?view=sql-server-ver16&WT.mc_id=DP-MVP-5003466`.

DAX Debug Output:

DAX Debug Output is a free community tool that allows developers to view the results of DAX expressions run in Power BI Desktop. This can help troubleshoot and optimize complex DAX formulas and measures. This tool is currently in public preview and the developer has not released much information about its system requirements yet. It currently works with the Power BI Desktop August 2022 release or later. DAX Debug Output is available to download from here: `https://github.com/pbidax/DAXDebugOutput/releases/tag/v0.1.0-beta`.

If you are using the digital version of this book, we advise that you type the code yourself or access the code via the GitHub repository (link available in the next section). Doing so will help you avoid any potential errors related to the copying and pasting of code.

Download the example code files

The code bundle for the book is hosted on GitHub at `https://github.com/PacktPublishing/Expert-Data-Modeling-with-Power-BI-Second-Edition`. We also have other code bundles from our rich catalog of books and videos available at `https://github.com/PacktPublishing/`. Check them out!

Download the color images

We also provide a PDF file that has color images of the screenshots/diagrams used in this book. You can download it here: https://packt.link/XAVMa.

Conventions used

There are a number of text conventions used throughout this book.

`CodeInText`: Indicates code words in text, database table names, folder names, filenames, file extensions, pathnames, dummy URLs, user input, and Twitter handles. For example: "Open the `Adventure Works, Internet Sales.pbix file`."

A block of code is set as follows:

```
Sequential Numbers =
SELECTCOLUMNS(
    GENERATESERIES(1, 20, 1)
    , "ID"
    , [Value]
)
```

Bold: Indicates a new term, an important word, or words that you see on the screen. For instance, words in menus or dialog boxes appear in the text like this. For example: "Click **New table** from the **Modeling** tab."

Warnings or important notes appear like this.

Tips and tricks appear like this.

Get in touch

Feedback from our readers is always welcome.

General feedback: Email `feedback@packtpub.com` and mention the book's title in the subject of your message. If you have questions about any aspect of this book, please email us at `questions@packtpub.com`.

Errata: Although we have taken every care to ensure the accuracy of our content, mistakes do happen. If you have found a mistake in this book, we would be grateful if you reported this to us. Please visit `http://www.packtpub.com/submit-errata`, click **Submit Errata**, and fill in the form.

Piracy: If you come across any illegal copies of our works in any form on the internet, we would be grateful if you would provide us with the location address or website name. Please contact us at copyright@packtpub.com with a link to the material.

If you are interested in becoming an author: If there is a topic that you have expertise in and you are interested in either writing or contributing to a book, please visit http://authors.packtpub.com.

Share your thoughts

Once you've read *Expert Data Modeling with Power BI, Second Edition*, we'd love to hear your thoughts! Scan the QR code below to go straight to the Amazon review page for this book and share your feedback.

https://packt.link/r/1803246243

Your review is important to us and the tech community and will help us make sure we're delivering excellent quality content.

Download a free PDF copy of this book

Thanks for purchasing this book!

Do you like to read on the go but are unable to carry your print books everywhere? Is your eBook purchase not compatible with the device of your choice?

Don't worry, now with every Packt book you get a DRM-free PDF version of that book at no cost.

Read anywhere, any place, on any device. Search, copy, and paste code from your favorite technical books directly into your application.

The perks don't stop there, you can get exclusive access to discounts, newsletters, and great free content in your inbox daily

Follow these simple steps to get the benefits:

1. Scan the QR code or visit the link below

https://packt.link/free-ebook/9781803246246

2. Submit your proof of purchase
3. That's it! We'll send your free PDF and other benefits to your email directly

Section 1
Data Modeling in Power BI

In this section, we quickly introduce data modeling in Power BI from a general point of view. We assume you know what Power Query is, what DAX is, and that you know the basic concepts of the star schema. In this section, you will learn about virtual tables and time intelligence functionalities in DAX and how you can implement a powerful model with real-world scenarios.

This section comprises the following chapters:

- *Chapter 1, Introduction to Data Modeling in Power BI*
- *Chapter 2, Data Analysis eXpressions and Data Modeling*

1
Introduction to Data Modeling in Power BI

Power BI is not just a reporting tool to build sophisticated reports; it is a platform that supplies a wide range of features from data preparation to data modeling and visualization. It is also a very well-designed ecosystem, giving a variety of users the ability to contribute to their organization's data analysis journey in many ways, from sharing datasets, reports, and dashboards to using their mobile phones to add some comments to a report, ask questions, and circulate it back to the relevant people. All of this is only possible if we take the correct steps in building our Power BI ecosystem. A very eye-catching and beautiful report is worth nothing if it shows incorrect figures or if the report is too slow to render, so the user does not have the appetite to use it.

One of the most critical aspects of building a good Power BI ecosystem is to get the data right. In real-world scenarios, you usually get data from various data sources. Getting data from the data sources and then preparing it are just the beginning. Then, you need to develop a well-designed data model that guarantees you always represent the correct figures supporting the business logic, leading to well-performing related reports.

In this chapter, we start learning about the different Power BI layers and how data flows between the different layers to be able to fix any potential issues more efficiently. Then, we study one of the essential aspects of Power BI implementation, data modeling. You learn more about the data modeling feature availabilities and limitations under various Power BI licensing plans. Finally, we discuss the iterative data modeling approach and its different phases.

This chapter covers the following main sections:

- Power BI Desktop layers
- What data modeling means in Power BI
- Power BI licensing considerations for data modeling
- The iterative data modeling approach

Understanding the Power BI layers

As stated before, Power BI is not just a reporting tool. As this book focuses on data modeling, we will not spend much time explaining the tool itself; instead, we cover some concepts that should be pointed out. When we talk about data modeling in Power BI, we refer to Power BI Desktop as a development tool. You can think of Power BI Desktop like Visual Studio when developing an **SQL Server Analysis Services (SSAS)** Tabular model. Power BI Desktop is a free tool offered by Microsoft that can be downloaded from `https://powerbi.microsoft.com/en-us/downloads/`.

This book refers to Power BI Desktop when mentioning Power BI unless stated otherwise.

The following illustration shows a straightforward process we usually go through while building a report in Power BI Desktop:

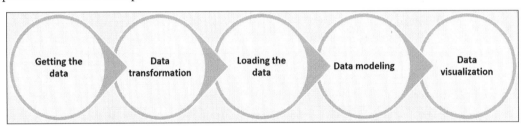

Figure 1.1: Building a new report process in Power BI

We use different conceptual layers of Power BI to go through the preceding processes. The following image shows where to access these layers in Power BI Desktop:

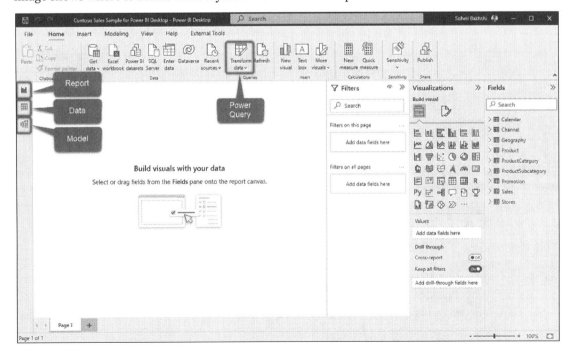

Figure 1.2: Power BI layers

Chapter 1

Let us discuss each point in detail:

- The **Power Query** (data preparation) layer
- The **Model** layer (data model)
- The **Report** layer (data visualization)

> The **Data** tab shown in the preceding image is where we can see the actual data loaded into the data model, so it is not considered a layer in Power BI Desktop.

> To follow the following exercises, download the `Microsoft Contoso Sales` sample for Power BI Desktop from https://www.microsoft.com/en-us/download/confirmation.aspx?id=46801.

The data preparation layer (Power Query)

In this layer, we get the data from various data sources, transform and cleanse that data, and make it available for the next layer. This is the first layer that touches the data, so it is an essential part of the data journey in Power BI. In the Power Query layer, we decide which queries load data into the data model and which ones take care of data transformation and data cleansing without loading the data into the data model:

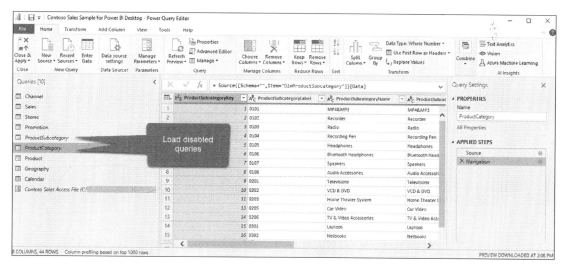

Figure 1.3: Power Query

The data model layer

This layer has two views, the **Data** view and the **Model** view. In the **Data** view, we see the data being loaded; in the **Model** view, we see the data model, including the tables and their relationships.

The Data view

After finishing the data preparation in the Power Query layer, we load the data into the data model layer. We can see the underlying data in our data model using the **Data** view. Depending on the connection mode, the **Data** view may or may not show the underlying data. We can take actions such as creating calculated tables, calculated columns, and measures or copying data from tables within the **Data** view.

All objects we create using DAX (measures, calculated columns, and so on) are a part of our data model.

The following screenshot shows the **Data** view in Power BI Desktop when the storage mode of the **Sales** table is **Import**:

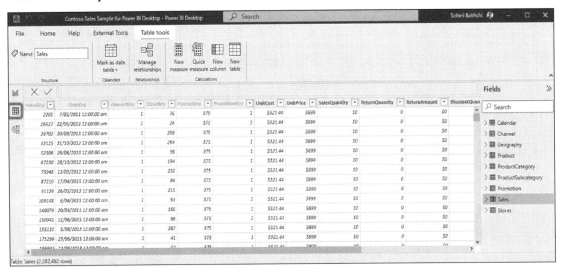

Figure 1.4: Data view; storage mode: Import

If the table's storage mode is **DirectQuery**, then the **Data** view does not show the underlying data, as the following image illustrates:

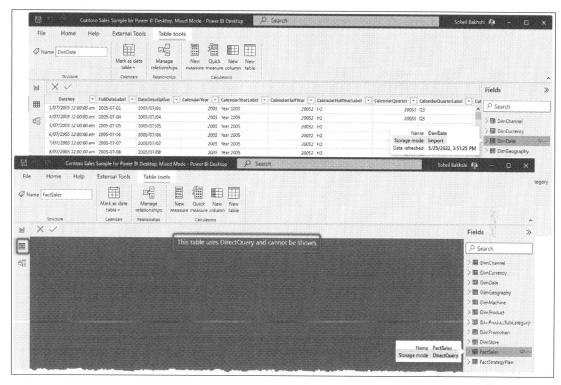

Figure 1.5: Data view; storage mode: DirectQuery

The Model view

As its name implies, the **Model** view is where we stitch all the pieces together. We can see the current relationships between the tables, create new relationships, format fields, define synonyms, and show and hide fields in the **Model** view. The following image shows the **Model** view of the **Contoso Sales Sample** when we selected the **Store** table:

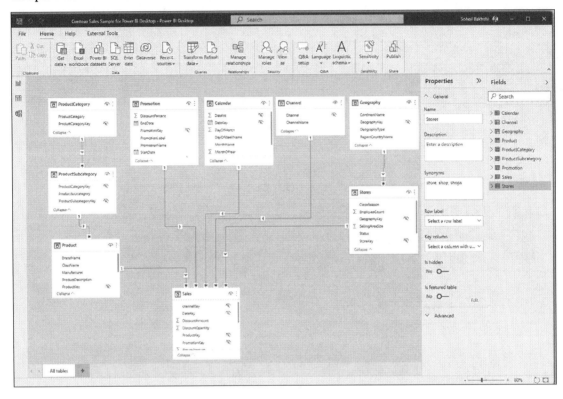

Figure 1.6: Model view

The data visualization layer

In this layer, we bring the data to life by making meaningful and professional-looking data visualizations. The data visualization layer is accessible via the **Report** view, the default view in Power BI Desktop.

The Report view

In the **Report** view, we can build storytelling visualizations to help businesses make data-driven decisions. We can also create analytical calculations with DAX, such as calculated tables, calculated columns, and measures from the **Fields** pane in the **Report** view, but this does not mean those objects are a part of the data visualization layer. Indeed, they are a part of the data model layer.

The following image shows the **Report** view of the **Sales & Returns Sample**:

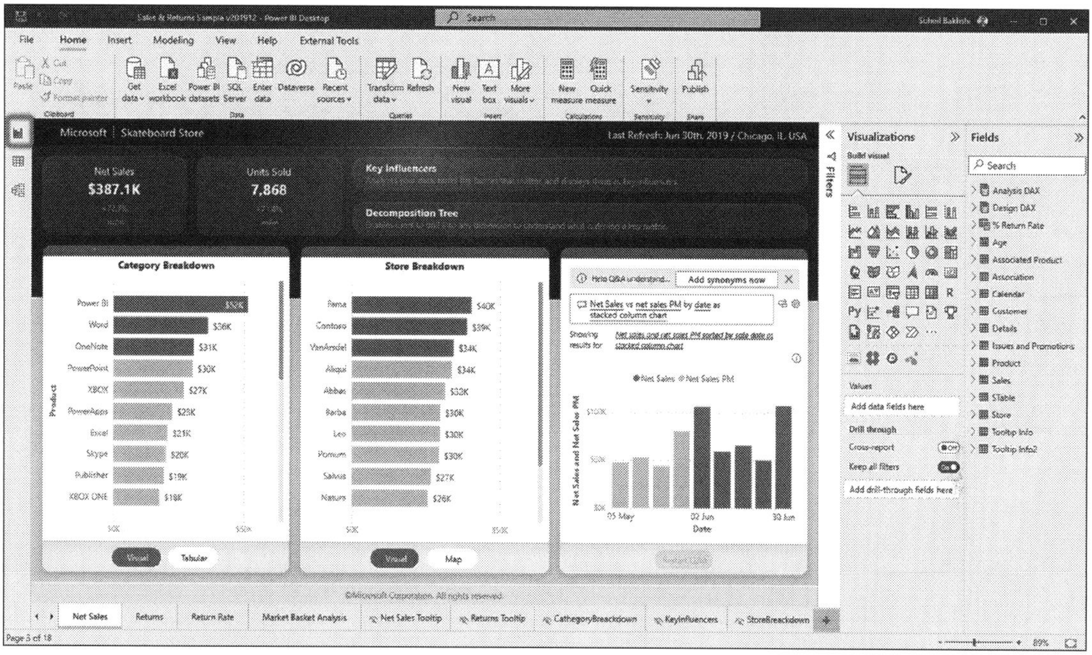

Figure 1.7: The Report view

To load the preceding view, download the `Sales & Returns sample.pbix` file from `https://docs.microsoft.com/en-us/power-bi/create-reports/sample-datasets#sales--returns-sample-pbix-file`.

How data flows in Power BI

Understanding how data flows during its journey in Power BI is vital. For instance, when we face an issue with some calculations in a report, we know how to analyze the root cause and trace the issue back to an actionable point. When we find an incorrect value in a line chart, and the line chart uses a measure dependent on a calculated column, we know that we do not find that calculated column in Power Query. The reason is that the objects we create in the data model are *not* accessible in Power Query. So, in that sense, we never look for a measure in the Power Query layer. We also do not expect to use custom functions created within Power Query in the data model layer. We discuss custom functions in the *Custom Functions* section of *Chapter 3, Data Preparation in Power Query Editor*.

The following image shows the flow of data between different layers in Power BI:

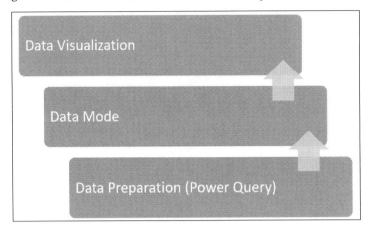

Figure 1.8: The flow of data in Power BI

To understand the flow of data better, let us go through a scenario.

In a Power BI report, the developer has defined a **query parameter**. The parameter has a list of capital letters, E, O, and P. There is also a **Product** query in Power Query holding descriptive information about the product. The parameter filters the **Product Name** column. Therefore, when the developer selects E from the parameter, the **Product** query filters the results showing only the products whose name starts with E. The *connection mode* is **Import**.

We put a **Table** visual on the report canvas with the **Product Name** column. Can we add a **Slicer** visual to the report canvas showing the parameter's values, so the end user changes the values in the **Slicer** and sees the changes in the **Table** visual?

To answer the question, we need to think about Power BI layers. Let us do some analysis:

- The query parameters are defined in the data preparation layer in Power Query.
- Filtering a query is also a transformation step in Power Query, which changes the result sets of the query. Therefore, when we import the data into the data model, the result sets do *not* change unless we change the parameter's values, which changes the result sets of the **Product** query and imports the new result sets to the data model.
- By default, query parameter's values are not loaded into the data model unless the developer sets **Enable load**. Setting **Enable load** only loads the selected values from the parameters list and not the whole list.
- We refer to the data visualization layer when we talk about a **Slicer** visual. This means that the **Slicer** can only access the data loaded into the data model.

So, the answer is *no*. After importing the curated data into the data model, it is accessible to the data visualization layer.

Now that we understand the flow of data in Power BI, it is time to learn more about data modeling in Power BI.

What data modeling means in Power BI

Data modeling is undoubtedly one of the most important parts of Power BI development. It is crucial to understand the purpose of data modeling in Power BI from data models in transactional systems. In a transactional system, the goal is to have a model optimized for recording transactional data. Nevertheless, a well-designed data model in Power BI must be optimized for querying the data and reducing the dataset size by aggregating the data.

In reality, not everyone has the luxury of having a data warehouse, so it is a vital skill to know how to create a data model in Power BI. While it is very tempting to get all the data from various data sources and import it to Power BI, answering business questions can quickly translate to complex queries that take a long time to process, which is not ideal. The best practice is to avoid importing everything from the data sources into Power BI and solving the related problems later such as performance issues, data model complexities, and having unnecessarily large data models. Instead, it is wise to get the data model right to precisely answer business-driven questions in the most performant way. When modeling data in Power BI, we must build a data model based on the business logic. So, we may need to join different tables and aggregate the data to a level that answers all business-driven questions, which can be tricky when we have data from various data sources of different grains.

Therefore, we need to transform and reshape the data in Power Query before loading it into the data model. After cutting all the noise from the data, we have a clean, easy-to-understand, and easy-to-work-with data model.

Semantic model

Power BI inherits its characteristics from **Power Pivot** and SSAS Tabular. Both of them use the **xVelocity engine**, an updated version of the VertiPaq engine designed for in-memory data analysis. The **xVelocity engine** leverages column store indexing and consists of semantic model objects such as tables, relationships, hierarchies, and measures stored in memory. All of this means that we would expect tremendous performance gains over highly compressed data, right? Well, it depends. We can expect fast and responsive reports if we efficiently transform and model the data supporting the business logic. Conceptually, the data model in Power BI is a semantic model. Let us untangle this a bit.

A semantic model is a unified data model that provides business contexts to data. The semantic model can be accessed from various data visualization tools, such as Excel, without further transformation. When we publish a **Power BI report file** (**PBIX**) to the Power BI Service, the service stores the report in two separate objects. The transformation steps and the data model are stored as a `Dataset` object and the report as a `Report` object. A dataset in the Power BI Service is indeed our semantic model. We can connect to the datasets from Power BI Desktop, analyze the datasets in Excel, or use third-party tools such as Tableau. The latter requires an **XMLA endpoint** connection to a Power BI Premium dataset.

We will not cover the details of XMLA endpoints in this book. You can read more about XMLA endpoints here: https://docs.microsoft.com/en-us/power-bi/enterprise/service-premium-connect-tools?WT.mc_id=DP-MVP-5003466.

Building an efficient data model in Power BI

An efficient data model is easy to understand and easy to maintain. At the same time, it must answer all data-driven questions the business may ask. Let us analyze the preceding sentence. An efficient model must do the following:

- Perform well (be fast)
- Be business-driven
- Decrease the complexity of the required DAX expressions (easy to understand)
- Low maintenance (low cost)

Let us look at the preceding points with a scenario.

We are tasked to create a report on top of the following three different data sources:

- An OData data source with 15 tables. The tables have between 50 and 250 columns.
- An Excel file with 20 sheets with interdependencies and many formulas.
- A data warehouse hosted in SQL Server. The data comes from five dimensions and two fact tables:
    - Within those five dimensions is a **Date** and a **Time** dimension. The grain of the **Time** dimension is the hour and minute.
    - Each of the fact tables has between 50 and 200 million rows. From a **Date** and **Time** perspective, the grain of both fact tables is the day, hour, and minute.
    - The organization owns Power BI Pro licenses.

Before getting the data from the source systems, there are essential points in the preceding scenario, and many points are unclear at this stage.

Let us analyze the scenario, along with some related questions we might ask the business to optimize the performance of the report and avoid customer dissatisfaction:

- **OData**: OData is an online data source, so it could be slow to load the data.
- The tables are wide, which can potentially impact the performance.
    1. Do we need to import all the columns from those 15 tables?
    2. Do we also need to import all data, or is just a portion of the data enough? For example, if the data source contains 10 years of data, does the business need to analyze all the historical data, or does bringing 1 or 2 years of data fit the purpose?
- The organization owns Power BI Pro licenses, so a 1 GB file size limit applies.
- **Excel**: Excel files with many formulas can be tricky data sources.
    1. Does the business require you to analyze all the data contained in the 20 sheets? We may be able to exclude some of those sheets.
    2. How often are the formulas edited? This is critical as modifying the formulas can easily break the data processing in Power Query and generate errors. It is best to replicate the Excel formulas in Power BI and load the raw data from Excel before the formulas are applied.

- **Data warehouse in SQL Server**: It is beneficial to have a data warehouse as a source system, as data warehouses typically have a much better structure from an analytical viewpoint. In our scenario, the finest grain of both fact tables is down to a minute, which can quickly become an issue. Remember, we have Power BI Pro licenses, so we are limited to a 1 GB file size only.
    1. Does the business need to analyze all the metrics down to the minute, or is day-level enough?
    2. Is the business required to analyze the whole history, or is bringing a portion of the data enough?

We now have a handful of questions to ask. One common question on the list is about the necessity of analyzing all the historical data. What if the business needs to analyze the whole history? In that case, we should consider using some advanced modeling techniques such as composite models and aggregations.

On the bright side, the fact that we already have five dimensions in the data warehouse might become handy. We might reuse those dimensions with minimal changes in our data model. So, it is wise to look at the other data sources and find commonalities in the data patterns.

We may come up with some more legitimate points and questions later. The takeaway is that we have to *talk to the business* and *ask questions* before starting the job. It is a big mistake to start getting data from the source systems before framing the questions around the business processes, requirements, and technology limitations. There are also other points we need to think about from a project management perspective, which are beyond the scope of this book.

The following are initial points to take into account for building an efficient data model:

- We must ask questions to avoid confusion and potential future reworks.
- We need to understand the technical limitations and come up with solutions.
- We have to have a good understanding of data modeling to look for common data patterns to prevent overlaps.

At this point, you may think, "OK, but how can we get there?" This book aims to cover all the preceding points and more. The rest is about you and how you apply your learning to your daily Power BI challenges. The section explains the star schema and snowflaking.

Star schema (dimensional modeling) and snowflaking

First things first, the **star schema** and **dimensional modeling** are the same things. In Power BI data modeling, the term *star schema* is more commonly used. The following sections are generic reminders about some star schema concepts.

Transactional modeling versus star schema modeling

In transactional systems, the main goal is improving the solution's performance in creating new records and updating/deleting existing ones. So, when designing transactional systems, it is essential to go through the normalization process to decrease data redundancy and increase data entry performance by breaking the tables down into master-detail tables.

But the goal of a business analysis system is very different. In a business analysis solution, we need a data model optimized for querying in the most performant way.

Let us continue with a scenario. Suppose we have a transactional retail system for an international retail shop. We have hundreds of transactions every second from different parts of the world. The company owners want to see the total sales in the past 6 months.

This calculation sounds easy. It is just a simple SUM of sales. But wait, we have hundreds of transactions every second, right? If we have 100 transactions per second, then we have 8,640,000 transactions a day. So, for 6 months of data, we have more than 1.5 billion rows. Therefore, a simple SUM of sales takes a reasonable amount of time to process.

Now, the business raises a new request. The company owners now want to see the total sales in the past 6 months by country and city. They simply want to know what the best-selling cities are.

We need to add another condition to our simple SUM calculation, which translates into a join to the geography table. For those coming from a relational database design background, it is trivial that joins are relatively expensive operations. This scenario can go on and on. So, you can imagine how quickly a simple scenario turns into a rather tricky situation.

In the star schema, however, we already joined all those tables based on business entities. We aggregated and loaded the data into denormalized tables. In the preceding scenario, the business is not interested in seeing every transaction at the second level. So, summarizing the data at the *day* level decreases the row count from 1.5 billion to approximately 18,000 rows for the 6 months. Now you can imagine how fast the summation would run over 18,000 instead of 1.5 billion rows.

The idea of the star schema is to keep all numeric values in separate tables called **fact tables** and put all descriptive information into other tables called **dimension tables**. Usually, the fact tables are surrounded by dimensions explaining the facts. A data model with a fact table in the middle surrounded by dimensions looks like a star, which is why this modeling approach is called a star schema.

 This book generally uses **Adventure Works DW** data, a renowned Microsoft sample dataset, unless stated otherwise. Adventure Works is an imaginary international bike shop selling products online and in their retail shops.

The following figure shows **Internet Sales** in a star schema shape:

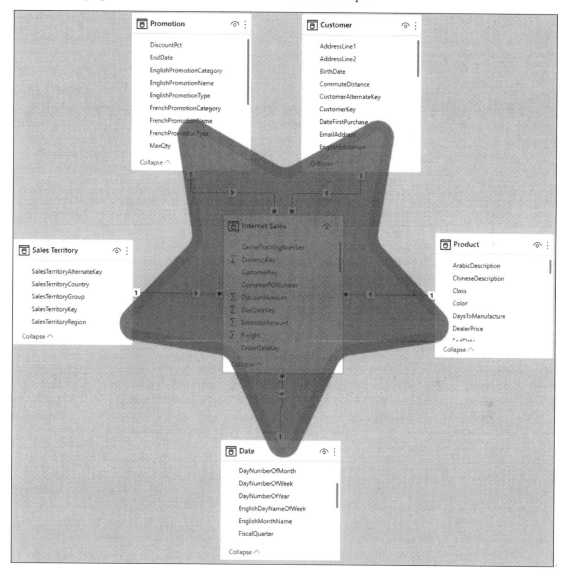

Figure 1.9: Internet Sales star schema

Snowflaking

Snowflaking is when we do not have a perfect star schema when dimension tables surround the fact tables. In some cases, we have some levels of descriptions stored in different tables. Therefore, some dimensions in the model are linked to other tables describing the dimensions in more detail. Snowflaking is normalizing the dimension tables. In some cases, snowflaking is inevitable; nevertheless, the general rule of thumb in data modeling in Power BI (when following a star schema) is to avoid snowflaking as much as possible to have a simpler and more performant model. The following figure shows snowflaking in Adventure Works **Internet Sales**:

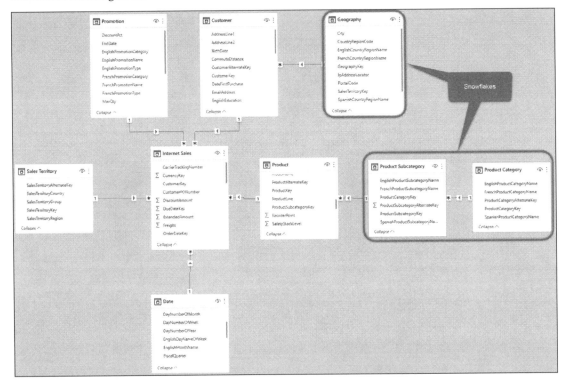

Figure 1.10: Adventure Works, Internet Sales snowflakes

We could avoid the **Product Category** and **Product Subcategory** snowflakes in the preceding model by denormalizing them into the **Product** table. The following section explains denormalization.

Understanding denormalization

In real-world scenarios, not everyone has the luxury of having a pre-built data warehouse designed in a star schema. In reality, snowflakes in data warehouse designs are inevitable. The data models are usually connected to various data sources, including transactional database systems and non-transactional data sources such as Excel files and CSV files. So, we almost always need to denormalize the model to a certain degree. Depending on the business requirements, we may have some normalization along with some denormalization. The reality is that there is no specific rule for the level of normalization and denormalization. The general rule of thumb is denormalizing the model, so each dimension describes all the related details as much as possible.

Chapter 1

In the preceding example from **Adventure Works DW**, we have snowflakes of **Product Category** and **Product Subcategory** that can be denormalized into the **Product** dimension.

Let us go through a hands-on exercise.

Go through the following steps to denormalize the **Product Category** and **Product Subcategory** into the **Product** dimension.

You need to download the Adventure Works, Internet Sales.pbix file from here:

https://github.com/PacktPublishing/Expert-Data-Modeling-with-Power-BI-Second-Edition/blob/28e2af1762336ab5236a3b3961c41e9020de8200/Samples/Chapter%2001/Adventure%20Works,%20Internet%20Sales.pbix

You also need to download the Excel file used as the data source in the PBIX file from here:

https://github.com/PacktPublishing/Expert-Data-Modeling-with-Power-BI-Second-Edition/blob/28e2af1762336ab5236a3b3961c41e9020de8200/Samples/AdventureWorksDW(xlsx)/AdventureWorksDW2017.xlsx

Before we start, let us set up the sample file first. Open the Adventure Works, Internet Sales.pbix file, then change the **Adventure Works DW Excel Path** parameter as follows:

a. Click the **Transform data** drop down button.
b. Click **Edit parameters**.
c. Enter the path for the .save location of the AdventureWorksDW2017.xlsx file.
d. Click **OK**.

The following image illustrates the preceding steps:

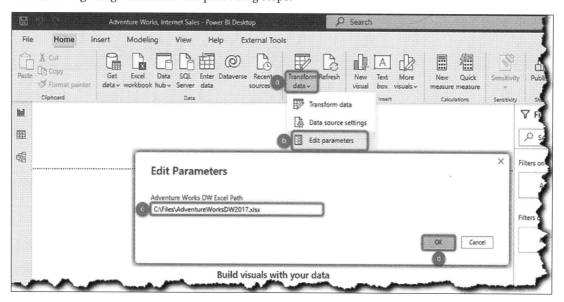

Figure 1.11: Setting up the Adventure Works, Internet Sales.pbix sample file

After changing the values of the parameter, we have to **Apply changes**.

Figure 1.12: Applying changes after changing the parameter value

The preceding process reloads the data from the Excel file.

Now that we have correctly set up the sample file, follow these steps:

1. Click **Transform data** in the **Home** tab of the **Queries** section.
2. Click the **Product** query.
3. Click **Merge Queries** in the **Home** tab of the **Combine** section.
4. Select **Product Subcategory** from the drop-down list.
5. Click **ProductSubcategoryKey** in the **Product** table.
6. Click **ProductSubcategoryKey** in the **Product Subcategory** table.
7. Select **Left Outer (all from first matching from the second)** from the **Join Kind** drop-down.
8. Click **OK**.

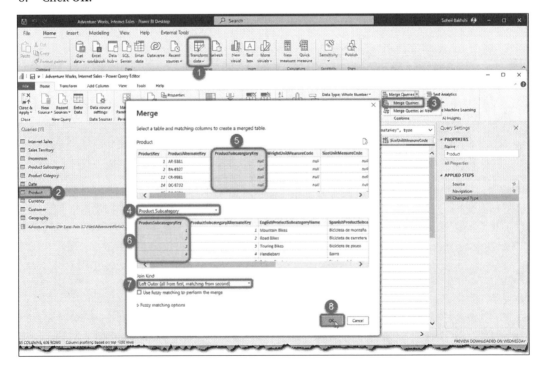

Figure 1.13: Merging Product and Product Subcategory

This adds a new step named **Merged Queries**. As you can see, the values of this column are all **Table**. This type of column is called a **Structured Column**. The merging step creates a new structured column named **Product Subcategory**:

You will learn more about structured columns in *Chapter 3, Data Preparation in Power Query Editor*.

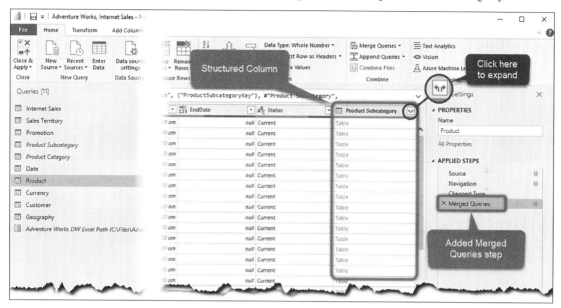

Figure 1.14: Merging the Product and Product Subcategory tables

Now let us look at how to expand a structured column in the Query Editor:

1. Click the **Expand** button to expand the **Product Subcategory** column.
2. Select **ProductCategoryKey**.
3. Select the **EnglishProductSubcategoryName** columns and unselect the rest.
4. Unselect **Use original column name as prefix**.
5. Click **OK**.

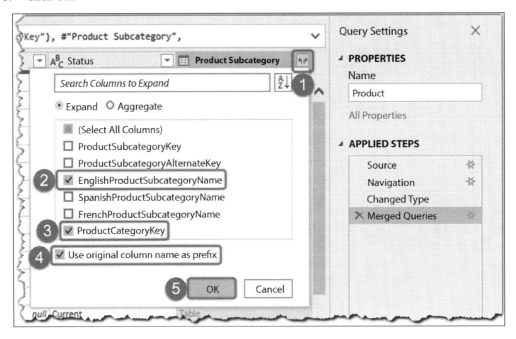

Figure 1.15: Expanding Structured Column in the Query Editor

So far, we have added the **EnglishProductSubcategoryName** and **ProductCategoryKey** columns from the **Product Subcategory** query to the **Product** query. The next step is to add **EnglishProductCategoryName** from the **Product Category** query. To do so, we need to merge the **Product** query with **Product Category**:

1. Click **Merge Queries** again.
2. Select **Product Category** from the drop-down list.
3. Select **ProductCategoryKey** from the **Product** table.
4. Select **ProductCategoryKey** from the **Product Category** table.
5. Select **Left Outer (all from first matching from second)**.
6. Click **OK**:

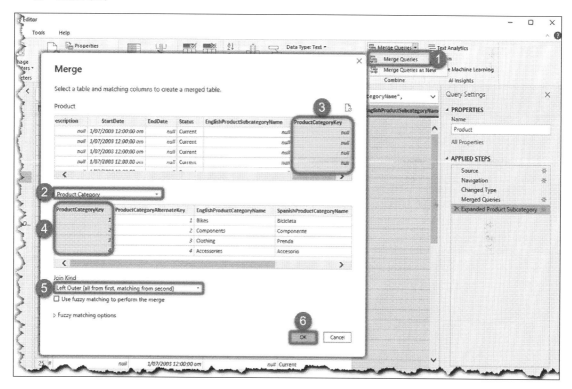

Figure 1.16: Merging Product and Product Category

This adds a new structured column named **Product Category**. We now need to do the following:

1. Expand the new column.
2. Pick **EnglishProductCategoryName** from the list.
3. Unselect **Use original column name as prefix**.
4. Click **OK**:

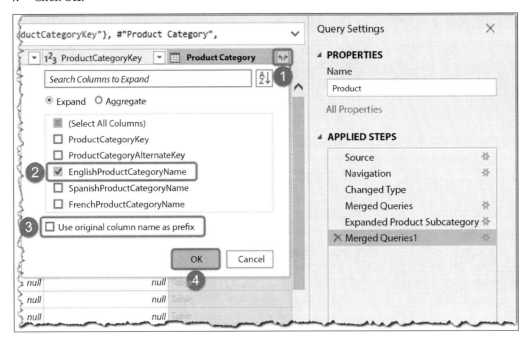

Figure 1.17: Merging Product and Product Category

So far, we moved the **EnglishProductCategoryName** into the **Product** table. Therefore, the **ProductCategoryKey** column is no longer needed. So, the next step is removing the **ProductCategoryKey** column as we no longer need it. To do so, follow these steps:

1. Click on the **ProductCategoryKey** column.
2. Click the **Remove Columns** button in the **Managed Column** section of the **Home** tab:

Chapter 1

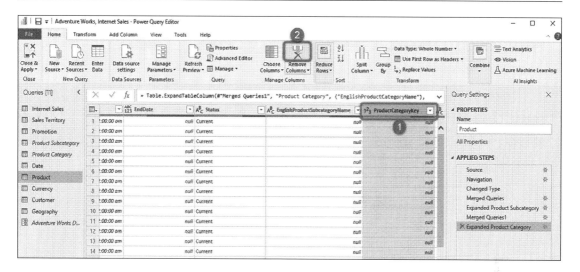

Figure 1.18: Removing a column in the Query Editor

We have merged the **Product Category** and **Product Subcategory** snowflakes with the **Product** query. So, we successfully denormalized the snowflakes.

The very last step is to unload both the **Product Category** and **Product Subcategory** queries:

1. Right-click on each query.
2. Untick **Enable load** from the menu.
3. Click **Continue** on the **Possible Data Loss Warning** pop-up message:

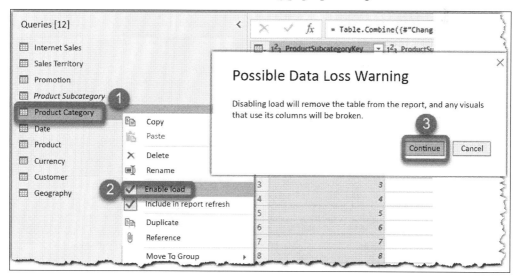

Figure 1.19: Unloading queries in the Query Editor

Now we need to import the data into the data model by clicking **Close & Apply**:

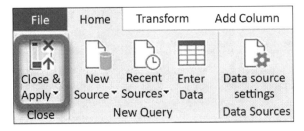

Figure 1.20: Importing data into the data model

We have now achieved what we were after: we denormalized the **Product Category** and **Product Subcategory** tables, so instead of loading those two tables, we now have **EnglishProductCategoryName** and **EnglishProductSubcategoryName** as new columns in the **Product** table. So the data model is simpler now, and we load less data, leading to better performance.

Job done!

Power BI licensing considerations

At this point, you may be wondering how Power BI licensing affects data modeling. It does, as each licensing tier comes with a set of features that can potentially affect the data modeling. Nevertheless, regardless of the licensing tier, Power BI Desktop is free. This section explains some licensing considerations related to data modeling.

The following table is a simplified version of the Power BI feature comparisons published on the Microsoft website separately based on different licenses:

Power BI License	Maximum Size of Individual Dataset	Incremental Data Load	Hybrid Tables	Calculation Groups	Shared Datasets	Power BI Dataflows	Power BI Datamarts
Free	1	No	No	Yes	No	No	No
Professional	1	Yes	No	Yes	Yes	Yes	No
Power BI Report Server	2	Yes	No	Yes	N/A	N/A	N/A
Embedded EM1/A1	3	Yes	Yes	Yes	Yes	Yes	Yes
Embedded EM2/A2	5	Yes	Yes	Yes	Yes	Yes	Yes
Embedded EM3/A3	10	Yes	Yes	Yes	Yes	Yes	Yes
Premium P1/A4	25	Yes	Yes	Yes	Yes	Yes	Yes
Premium P2/A5	50	Yes	Yes	Yes	Yes	Yes	Yes
Premium P3/A6	100	Yes	Yes	Yes	Yes	Yes	Yes
Premium P4	200	Yes	Yes	Yes	Yes	Yes	Yes
Premium P5	400	Yes	Yes	Yes	Yes	Yes	Yes
Premium Per User (PPU)	100	Yes	Yes	Yes	Yes	Yes	Yes

Figure 1.21: A simplified version of Power BI feature comparisons

The following few sections briefly explain each feature.

Maximum size of an individual dataset

As the preceding table shows, we are limited to 1 GB for each dataset published to the Power BI Service under Free or Professional licensing. Therefore, managing the file size is quite important. There are several ways to keep the file size just below the limit, as follows:

- Import the necessary columns only.
- Import just a portion of data when possible. Explain the technology limitation to the business and ask whether you can filter out some data. For instance, the business may not need to analyze 10 years of data, so filter older data in Power Query.
- Use aggregations. In many cases, you may have the data stored in the source at a very low granularity. However, the business requires data analysis on a higher grain. Therefore, you can aggregate the data to a higher granularity, then import it into the data model. For instance, you may have data stored at a minute level. At the same time, the business only needs to analyze that data at the day level.
- Consider disabling the auto date/time settings in Power BI Desktop.
- Consider optimizing the data types.

We cover all the preceding points in the upcoming chapters.

Incremental data load

One of the most remarkable features available in Power BI is the ability to set up incremental data loads. Incremental data loading in Power BI is inherited from SSAS to work with large models. Power BI does not truncate the dataset and re-import all the data from scratch when the incremental data load is set up correctly. Instead, it only imports the data that has been changed since the last data refresh. Therefore, incremental data load can significantly improve the data refresh performance and decrease the processing load on the Power BI tenant. Incremental data load is available in both Professional and Premium licenses.

Hybrid tables

Microsoft announced a new feature in December 2021 called **Hybrid tables**, which takes the incremental data refresh capability to the next level. A hybrid table is a regular table with incremental data refresh where the table has one or more partitions in **Import mode** and another (the last partition) in **DirectQuery mode**. Therefore, we get all the performance benefits of the two worlds; the historical data is imported into the dataset and is available in memory, while we also have the real-time data in place as the last partition is in DirectQuery mode to the source system. The hybrid table capability is only available in Premium licenses.

Calculation groups

Calculation groups are similar to *calculated members* in **Multi-Dimensional eXpressions (MDX)** in **SQL Server Analysis Services Multi-Dimensional (SSAS MD)**. Calculation groups were initially introduced in SSAS Tabular 2019. They are also available in **Azure Analysis Services (AAS)** and all Power BI licensing tiers.

It is a common scenario that we create (or already have) some base measures in the Power BI model. We then create multiple time intelligence measures on top of those base measures. Suppose we have three measures, as follows:

- `Product cost = SUM('Internet Sales'[TotalProductCost])`
- `Order quantity = SUM('Internet Sales'[OrderQuantity])`
- `Internet sales = SUM('Internet Sales'[SalesAmount])`

Imagine a scenario when the business requires the following time intelligence calculations on top of the preceding measures:

- Year to date
- Quarter to date
- Month to date
- Last year to date
- Last quarter to date
- Last month to date
- Year over year
- Quarter over quarter
- Month over month

We have nine calculations to be built on top of the three measures in our model. Hence, we have *9 x 3 = 27* measures to build in our model. You can imagine how quickly the number of measures can increase in the model, so do not get surprised if someone says they have hundreds of measures in their Power BI model.

Another common scenario is when we have multiple currencies. Without calculation groups, we need to convert the values into strings and use the `FORMAT()` function in DAX to represent the numbers in the currency format. Now, if you think about the latter point, combined with time intelligence functions, you see how serious the issue can get very quickly.

Calculation groups solve those sorts of problems. We cover calculation groups in *Chapter 10, Advanced Data Modeling Techniques*.

Shared datasets

As the name implies, a shared dataset is used across various reports in a *workspace* within the Power BI Service. Therefore, it is only available in the Power BI Professional and Power BI Premium licenses. This feature is quite crucial to data modelers. It provides more flexibility in creating a generic dataset, covering the business requirements in a single dataset instead of having several datasets that may share many commonalities.

Power BI Dataflows

Dataflows, also called Power Query Online, provide a centralized data preparation mechanism in the Power BI Service that other people across the organization can take advantage of. Like using Power Query in Power BI Desktop for data preparation, we can prepare, cleanse, and transform the data in dataflows. Unlike Power Query queries in Power BI Desktop that are isolated within a dataset after being published to the Power BI Service, with dataflows, we can share all data preparations, cleansing, and transformation processes across the organization.

We can create Power BI dataflows inside a workspace, which is available to Professional and Premium users. We cover Power BI dataflows in *Chapter 13, Introduction to Dataflows*.

Power BI Datamarts

The **Datamart** capability is a new feature announced in May 2022. The primary purpose of datamarts is to enable organizations to build self-service, no-code/low-code analytical solutions connecting to multiple data sources, creating **ETL** (**Extraction, Transformation, and Load**) pipelines with Power Query, and then loading the data into an **Azure SQL Database**. The datamart capability is currently available for Premium users only. We cover the datamarts capability in *Chapter 15, New Options, Features, and DAX Functions*.

We discussed the Power BI licensing considerations for data modeling in Power BI; the following chapter describes the iterative approach to data modeling.

The iterative data modeling approach

Data modeling is usually an ongoing process. We talk to the business to understand their requirements and then apply the business logic to the model. In many cases, we build the data visualizations and then find that we get better results if we make changes to our model. In many other cases, the business logic applied to the model is not what the business needs. This is a typical comment that many of us get from the business after the first few iterations:

This looks really nice, but unfortunately, it is not what we want.

So, taking advantage of an agile approach would be genuinely beneficial for Power BI development. Here is the iterative approach to follow in Power BI development:

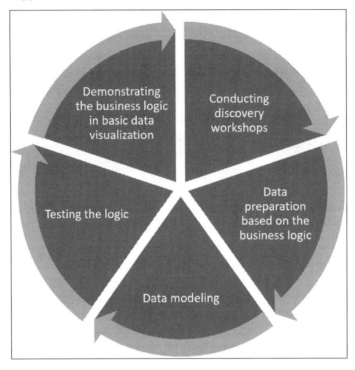

Figure 1.22: The iterative data modeling approach

The following few sections describe the pillars of the preceding approach.

Conducting discovery workshops

The Power BI development process starts with gathering information from the business by conducting discovery workshops to understand the requirements better. A business analyst may take care of this step in the real world, and many Power BI users are indeed business analysts. Whether we are business analysts or not, we are data modelers, so we need to analyze the information we receive from the business. We have to ask relevant questions that lead us toward various design possibilities. We have to identify potential risks, limitations, and associated costs and discuss them with the customer. After we get the answers, we can confidently take the next steps to design a data model that best covers the business requirements, mitigates the risks, and aligns with the technology limitations well.

Data preparation based on the business logic

We have a lot on our plate by now. We must get the data from multiple sources and go through the data preparation steps. Now that we have learned a lot about business logic, we can take the proper data preparation steps. For instance, if the business needs to connect to an OData data source and get a list of the columns required, we can prepare the data more efficiently with all the design risks and technology limitations in mind. After consciously preparing the data, we go to the next step, data modeling.

Data modeling

If we properly go through the previous steps, we can build the model more efficiently. We need to think about the analytical side of things while considering all the business requirements, design possibilities, risks, and technology limitations. For instance, if the business cannot tolerate data latency longer than 5 minutes, we may need to consider using DirectQuery. Using DirectQuery comes with some limitations and performance risks. So, we must consider the design approach that satisfies the business requirements the most. We cover DirectQuery in *Chapter 4, Getting Data from Various Sources*, in the *Dataset storage modes* section.

Testing the logic

One of the most trivial and yet most important steps in data modeling is testing all the business logic we implement to meet the requirements. Not only do we need to test the figures to ensure the results are accurate, but we also need to test the solution from a performance and user experience perspective. Be prepared for tons of mixed feedback and sometimes strong criticism from the end users, especially when we think everything is OK.

Demonstrating the business logic in basic data visualizations

As we are modeling the data, we do not need to worry about data visualization. Confirming with the business **SMEs (Subject Matter Experts)** is the fastest way to ensure all the reporting logic is correct. The fastest way to get confirmation from SMEs is to demonstrate the logic in the simplest possible way, such as using table and matrix visuals and some slicers on the page. When demonstrating the solution to SMEs, do not forget to highlight that the visualization is only to confirm the reporting logic with them and not the actual product delivery. In the real world, we have many new discussions and surprises during the demonstration sessions, which usually means we are at the beginning of the second iteration, so we start gathering information about the required changes and the new requirements, if any.

We gradually become professional data modelers as we go through the preceding steps several times. This book also follows an iterative approach, so we go back and forth between different chapters to cover some scenarios.

In the next section, we quickly cover how professional data modelers think.

Thinking like a professional data modeler

None of us become a professional in something overnight. We make many mistakes, and we learn from them. Professionalism comes with experience. To get the experience, we need to practice and practice a lot. Let me share a short back story about myself. Back in the day, in the late 90s, I was working on transactional database systems. So it is essential to know how to normalize the data model to the **third normal form**.

In some cases, we normalize the model to the **Boyce-Codd normal form**. I carried out many projects, faced challenges, and made many mistakes, but I learned from those mistakes. Gradually, I could visualize the data model to the second or, sometimes, even the third normal form in my mind while I was in the discovery sessions with the customer.

Regardless of their usage, all data modeling approaches that I had a chance to work with or read about are based on relational models, such as transactional models, star schema, Inmon, and data vaults. They are all based on relational data modeling. Data modeling in Power BI is no different. Some professional data modelers can visualize the data model in their minds from their first discovery sessions with the customer. But as mentioned, this capability comes with experience.

Once we have enough experience in data modeling, we ask more relevant questions from the SMEs. We already know about successful practices, the challenges, and the pitfalls, so we can quickly recognize similar situations. Therefore, we can avoid many future changes by asking more relevant questions early. Moreover, we can also give the customer some new ideas to solve other problems they may face down the road. Usually, the business requirements change during the project's lifetime. So, we are not surprised when those changes happen.

Summary

This chapter discussed the different layers of Power BI and what is accessible in which layer. Therefore, when we face an issue, we know exactly where we should look to fix the problem. Then, we discussed making a semantic layer when building a data model in Power BI. We also discussed some star schema and snowflaking concepts essential to an efficient data model. We then covered different Power BI licensing considerations and how they can affect our data modeling. Lastly, we looked at the data modeling iterative approach to deliver a precise and reliable data model that solves many problems that the report writers may face down the road.

The next chapter looks at DAX and data modeling. We discuss a somewhat confusing topic, virtual tables. We also look into time intelligence scenarios that help with many data modeling tasks.

Join us on Discord!

Join The Big Data and Analytics Community on the Packt Discord Server!

Hang out with 558 other members and enjoy free voice and text chat.

`https://packt.link/ips2H`

2

Data Analysis eXpressions and Data Modeling

The previous chapter discussed that Power BI has different layers: data preparation, data modeling, and data visualization. This chapter discusses **Data Analysis eXpressions** (**DAX**), and their relationship to data modeling. Although data modeling and DAX are connected such that you cannot imagine one without the other, our goal in this book is not to focus only on DAX. Data modeling encompasses much broader concepts, while DAX is the expression language developers must use to implement business logic in the data model. We assume that you have an intermediate level of knowledge of DAX; therefore, we do not cover basic DAX concepts in this book such as DAX syntax. Instead, we focus on more advanced ones with hands-on scenarios.

This chapter covers the following topics:

- Understanding virtual tables
- Understanding relationships in virtual tables
- Time intelligence

Understanding virtual tables

The concept of **virtual tables** in DAX is somewhat confusing and misunderstood, yet it is one of the most powerful and important concepts in DAX. When we talk about virtual tables, we refer to in-memory tables that we build using certain DAX functions or constructors. The data in a virtual table is either derived from the data within the data model or the data we construct for specific purposes.

Remember, whenever we use a DAX function that results in a table of values, we are creating a virtual table.

At this point, you may ask, *so when I use a DAX function to create a calculated table, am I creating a virtual table?* The answer is *it depends*. If you simply use a set of DAX functions that generate data or selectively load data from other tables into a calculated table, the answer is *no*: you have not created any virtual tables.

Nevertheless, when generating or loading the data from other tables, taking some table operations, and loading the results into a calculated table, we have probably created a virtual table first and then populated the calculated table with the results. As the name implies, virtual tables are not physically stored in the model. Therefore, we cannot see them, but they exist in memory as we create them within our calculations. Hence, they are only accessible within that calculation, not from other calculations or other parts of our data model. If you come from a SQL development background, you can think of DAX virtual tables as subqueries in SQL.

Is this still confusing? Let's continue with some hands-on scenarios.

Creating calculated tables

We want to create a calculated table and name it **Sequential Numbers** with an **ID** column. The **ID** column values are sequential numbers between 1 and 20, increasing by one step in each row:

1. Open a new Power BI Desktop instance.
2. Click **New table** from the **Modeling** tab:

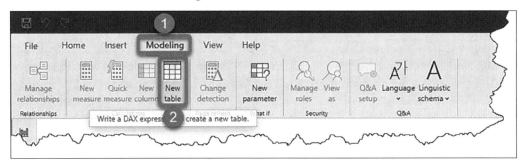

Figure 2.1: Creating a calculated table in Power BI

3. Type the following DAX expression, and then press *Enter*:

```
Sequential Numbers = GENERATESERIES(1, 20, 1)
```

This creates a calculated table named **Sequential Numbers**, as illustrated here, but the column name is **Value**, not **ID**:

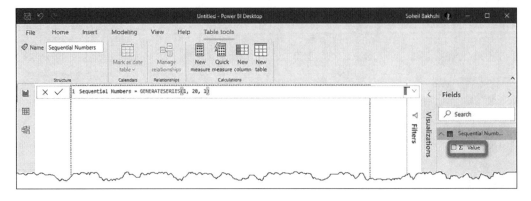

Figure 2.2: Using the GENERATESERIES() function to create a calculated table

The `GENERATESERIES()` function generates values for us. The output is a desirable table, but we need to do one last operation to rename the **Values** column to **ID**.

4. Replace the previous expression with the following expression, and then press *Enter*:

```
Sequential Numbers = 
SELECTCOLUMNS(
    GENERATESERIES(1, 20, 1)
    , "ID"
    , [Value]
)
```

The following figure shows the results of the preceding calculation:

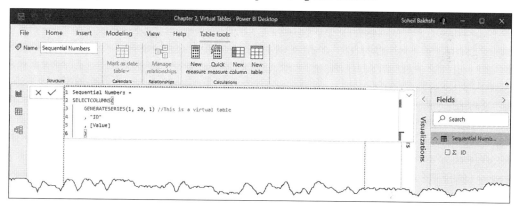

Figure 2.3: The calculated table and virtual table

We first created a virtual table with a **Value** column in the preceding code. Then, we renamed the **Value** column to **ID**, and finally, we populated a calculated table with the results.

In the preceding scenario, we used a virtual table to create a calculated table. In the following scenario, we will demonstrate the usage of virtual tables for a measure.

Let's take a step further with a more complex scenario.

Download the `Chapter 2, Virtual Tables 02, Adventure Works, Internet Sales.pbix` sample from the following URL:

https://github.com/PacktPublishing/Expert-Data-Modeling-with-Power-BI-Second-Edition/blob/main/Samples/Chapter%2002/Chapter%202%2C%20Virtual%20Tables%2002%2C%20Adventure%20Works%2C%20Internet%20Sales.pbix

Create a measure in the **Internet Sales** table to calculate the quantities ordered for products when their list price is higher than $1,000. Name the measure **Orders with List Price Bigger than or Equal to $1,000**:

GOOD PRACTICE

Always create a new measure by right-clicking on the desired table from the **Fields** pane and clicking **New measure**. This way, you can be sure that you have created the measure in the desired table. If you use the **New measure** button from the **Home** tab from the ribbon, the new measure will be created in a table that you previously focused on. Suppose there is no table selected (focused on)—in that case, the new measure will be created in the first table available in your data model, which is not ideal.

1. Right-click on the **Internet Sales** table.
2. Click **New measure**.
3. Type the following DAX expression and press *Enter*:

```
Orders with List Price Bigger than or Equal to $1,000 =
CALCULATE(
    SUM('Internet Sales'[OrderQuantity])
        , FILTER('Product' //Virtual table start
            , 'Product'[List Price]>=1000
            ) //Virtual table end
)
```

The following figure shows the preceding expression in Power BI Desktop:

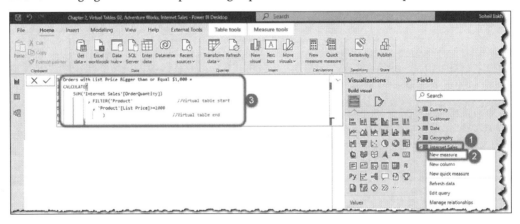

Figure 2.4: Calculating orders with a list price bigger than or equal to $1,000

Let's analyze the preceding calculation:

- We created a virtual table using the `FILTER()` function on top of the **Product** table to get only the products with a List Price value bigger than or equal to $1,000. All columns from the **Product** tables are available in this virtual table, which lives in memory. It is only available within the **Orders with List Price Bigger than or Equal to $1,000** measure and nowhere else in the data model.

- The SUM() function then calculates the summation of the OrderQuantity from the **Internet Sales** table.

To use the preceding measure, put a table visual on a report page. Select **Product Name** from the **Product** table, and then select the **Orders with List Price Bigger, or Equal to $1,000** measure. The result looks like the following figure:

Product Name	Orders with List Price Bigger than or Equal $1,000
Mountain-100 Black, 38	49
Mountain-100 Black, 42	45
Mountain-100 Black, 44	60
Mountain-100 Black, 48	57
Mountain-100 Silver, 38	58
Mountain-100 Silver, 42	42
Mountain-100 Silver, 44	49
Mountain-100 Silver, 48	36
Mountain-200 Black, 38	582
Mountain-200 Black, 42	614
Mountain-200 Black, 46	620
Mountain-200 Silver, 38	596

Figure 2.5: Orders with a list price bigger than or equal to $1,000 by product

Let's take another step forward and look at a more complex scenario.

Using the same sample file used in the previous scenario, create a measure in the **Internet Sales** table to calculate order quantities containing more than 4 products with a list price bigger than $1,000. Name the measure **Order Qty for Customers Buying More than 4 Products with List Price Bigger Than $1,000**.

To solve this scenario, we need to create a virtual table of customers with more than 4 orders for products that cost more than $1,000. The following code will take care of that:

```
Order Qty for Customers Buying More than 4 Product with List Price Bigger Than
$1,000 =
SUMX(
    FILTER(
        VALUES(Customer[CustomerKey]) //Virtual table
        , [Orders with List Price Bigger than or Equal $1,000] > 4
    )
    , [Orders with List Price Bigger than or Equal $1,000]
)
```

Analyzing the preceding calculation helps us to understand the power of virtual tables much better:

- The virtual table here has only one column, which is **CustomerKey**. Remember, this column is only accessible within the current calculation.
- Then, we use the `FILTER()` function to filter the results of `VALUES()` to only show customer keys that have more than 4 orders for products with a list price of more than $1,000.
- Last, we sum all those quantities for the results of `FILTER()`.

We can now put a table visual on the report page, and then select **First Name** and **Last Name** from the **Customer** table and the new measure we just created. The following figure shows the customers who ordered more than 4 items that cost more than $1,000:

First Name	Last Name	Order Qty for Customers Buying More than 4 Product with List Proce Bigger Than $1,000
Adriana	Gonzalez	5
Brad	She	5
Brandi	Gill	5
Francisco	Sara	5
Janet	Munoz	5
Kaitlyn	Henderson	5
Margaret	He	5
Maurice	Shan	6
Nichole	Nara	5
Randall	Dominguez	5
Rosa	Hu	5
Total		**56**

Figure 2.6: The Order Qty for Customers Buying More than 4 Products with List Price Bigger Than $1,000 by Customer table

As stated earlier, we can use all DAX functions that return a table value to create virtual tables. However, the functions in the following table are the most common ones:

ADDCOLUMNS()	CALENDARAUTO()	FILTERS()	SELECTCOLUMNS()	VALUES()
ADDMISSINGITEMS()	CALCULATETABLE()	GENERATESERIES()	SUMMARIZE()	Table Constructor {}
ALL()	CROSSJOIN()	INTERSECT()	SUMMARIZECOLUMNS()	
ALLEXCEPT()	DATATABLE()	NATURALINNERJOIN()	TOPN()	
ALLSELECTED()	DISTINCT()	NATURALLEFTOUTERJOIN()	TREATAS()	
CALENDAR()	EXCEPT()	RELATEDTABLE()	UNION()	

Figure 2.7: Commonly used functions

The virtual tables are only available in memory. Moreover, they are not visible in the model view in Power BI Desktop. Therefore, they are a bit hard to understand. However, there are still some ways that you can test the virtual tables and visually see the results, which we cover in the next section.

Visually displaying the results of virtual tables

In this section, we explain how you can see the results of **virtual tables**. It is always good to observe the outputs of the virtual table rather than only internalizing the results in our minds. In this section, we look at two different ways to see a virtual table's results.

Creating calculated tables in Power BI Desktop

You can create calculated tables in Power BI Desktop with the function (or functions) you used to create the virtual tables.

We will use the second scenario discussed in this chapter to see how this works:

1. In Power BI Desktop, click **New Table** from the **Modeling** tab.
2. Copy and paste the virtual table's DAX expression below. Use **Test Virtual Table** as the name for the new calculated table, and then press *Enter*:

   ```
   Test Virtual Table =
   FILTER('Product'//Virtual table start
           , 'Product'[List Price]>=1000
               ) //Virtual table end
   ```

3. Click the **Data** tab from the left pane.
4. Select **Test Virtual Table** from the **Fields** pane to see the results.

As you can see, all columns from the **Product** table are available. However, there are only 126 rows loaded into this table, which are the products with a **List Price** value bigger than or equal to 1000. The original **Product** table has 606 rows:

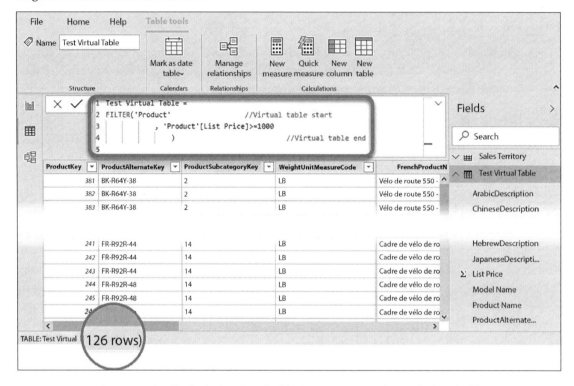

Figure 2.8: Visually displaying virtual tables in a Power BI Desktop calculated table

Using DAX Studio

DAX Studio is one of the most popular third-party tools, created by the amazing team at SQLBI, available to download for free. You can get it from the tool's official website (https://daxstudio.org/). You can easily use DAX Studio to see the results of your virtual tables. First of all, you need to open your Power BI file (*.pbix) before you can connect to it from DAX Studio. Open DAX Studio and follow these steps:

1. Click **PBI/SSDT Model**.
2. Select the desired Power BI Desktop instance.
3. Type in the EVALUATE statement, and then copy and paste the **Virtual Table** part of the calculation onto a new line:

```
FILTER('Product' //Virtual table start
        , 'Product'[List Price]>=1000
            ) //Virtual table end
```

4. Press *F5* or click the **Run** button to run the query:

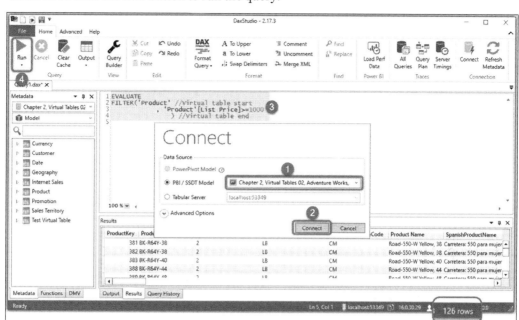

Figure 2.9: Running virtual table expressions in DAX Studio

 In DAX Studio, you can run DAX queries, which must start with the EVALUATE statement.

Understanding relationships in virtual tables

When we think about tables in relational systems, we usually think about tables and their relationships. So far, we have learned about virtual tables. Now let us think about the relationships between virtual tables and other tables (either physical tables available in the data model or other virtual tables). As stated earlier, we create a virtual table by generating it, constructing it, or deriving it from an existing table within the data model. Moreover, there are some cases where we can create more than one virtual table to calculate results. When it comes to virtual tables, there are two types of relationships:

- Suppose a virtual table has been derived from an existing physical table in the data model. There is a relationship between the virtual table and the original physical table, which is the so-called **lineage**.

- In some cases, we create more than one virtual table in a calculation. Then, we create relationships between those virtual tables programmatically. In some other cases, we might need to replace an existing relationship with a new one. This type of relationship is called a **virtual relationship**.

Either way, the relationship is not a physical relationship within the data model. It is created within the calculation itself and resides in memory for the duration that the calculation runs. Therefore, understanding virtual relationships is crucial. So, let's go through a hands-on scenario.

A business requires you to calculate the average product standard cost by **Product Category**, **Product Subcategory**, and **Product**.

To go through this scenario, open the sample file: Chapter 2, Virtual Tables 03, Avg Product Standard Cost.pbix. Look at the data model. It is pretty simple. It consists of only two tables, **Product** and **Internet Sales**. As you can see, we can use the **ProductStandardCost** column from the **Internet Sales** table in our measure. The following figure shows the data model:

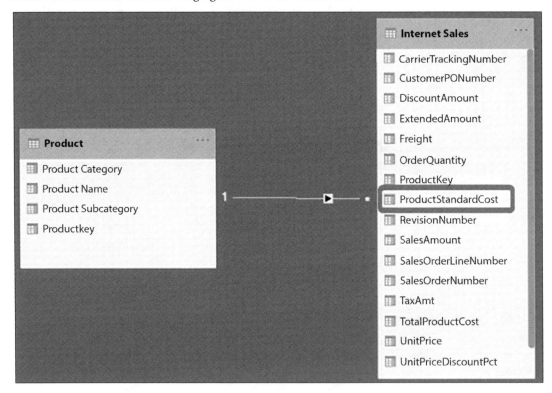

Figure 2.10: Product and Internet Sales

The next step is to create a measure to calculate the average product standard cost:

```
Avg. Product Standard Costs = 
AVERAGE('Internet Sales'[ProductStandardCost])
```

Let's test the created measure with the following steps:

1. Put a matrix visual on the report canvas.
2. Put the **Product Category**, **Product Subcategory**, and **Product** columns from the **Product** table into the **Rows** section of the matrix visual.
3. Put the **Avg. Product Standard Costs** measure in the **Values** section of the matrix.

The following screenshot illustrates the steps:

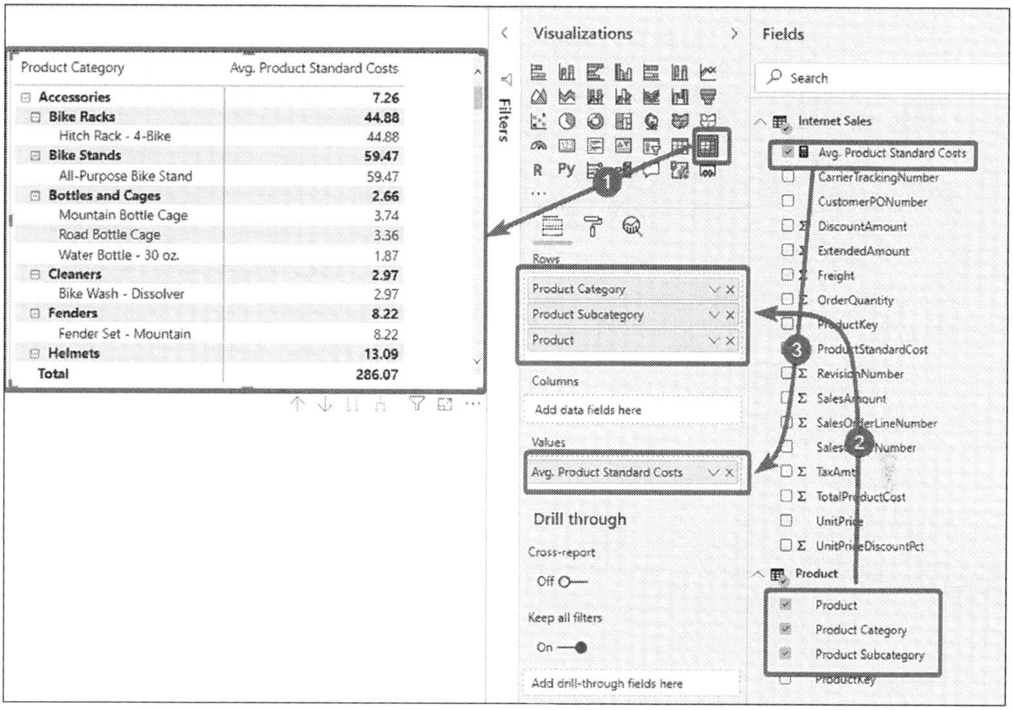

Figure 2.11: Visualizing Avg. Product Standard Costs by Product Category, Product Subcategory, and Product

Easy! But let's have a more thorough look at the underlying data to ensure the calculation is correct. Click **Data View** from the left pane in Power BI Desktop, and then click the **Internet Sales** table.

As you can see in the following figure, there is a **ProductStandardCost** value for each transaction. In other words, we considered all product costs from when the supplier supplies the item until the item comes off the shelf:

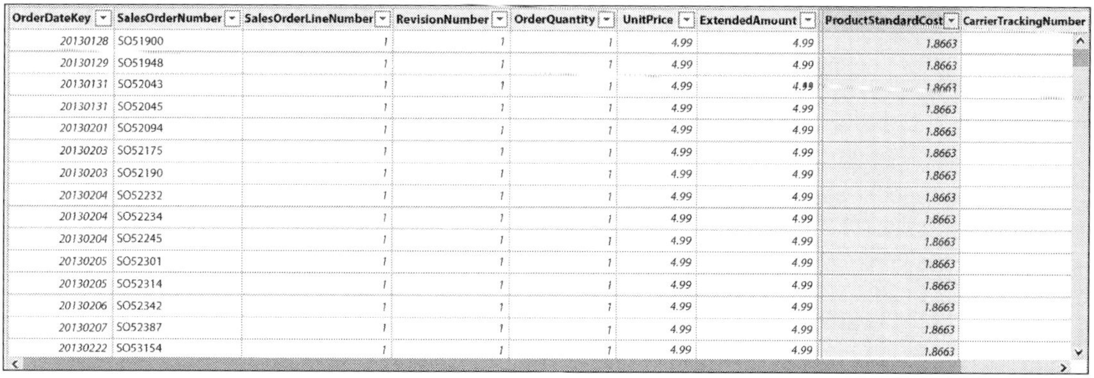

OrderDateKey	SalesOrderNumber	SalesOrderLineNumber	RevisionNumber	OrderQuantity	UnitPrice	ExtendedAmount	ProductStandardCost	CarrierTrackingNumber
20130128	SO51900	1	1	1	4.99	4.99	1.8663	
20130129	SO51948	1	1	1	4.99	4.99	1.8663	
20130131	SO52043	1	1	1	4.99	4.99	1.8663	
20130131	SO52045	1	1	1	4.99	4.99	1.8663	
20130201	SO52094	1	1	1	4.99	4.99	1.8663	
20130203	SO52175	1	1	1	4.99	4.99	1.8663	
20130203	SO52190	1	1	1	4.99	4.99	1.8663	
20130204	SO52232	1	1	1	4.99	4.99	1.8663	
20130204	SO52234	1	1	1	4.99	4.99	1.8663	
20130204	SO52245	1	1	1	4.99	4.99	1.8663	
20130205	SO52301	1	1	1	4.99	4.99	1.8663	
20130205	SO52314	1	1	1	4.99	4.99	1.8663	
20130206	SO52342	1	1	1	4.99	4.99	1.8663	
20130207	SO52387	1	1	1	4.99	4.99	1.8663	
20130222	SO53154	1	1	1	4.99	4.99	1.8663	

Figure 2.12: Each transaction has a value for ProductStandardCost

The product costs are usually variable, and they change over time. So, it is crucial to know if that is the case in our scenario. If so, then the preceding calculation is correct.

Now let's make the scenario a bit more challenging. To confirm whether our understanding of the requirements is correct, we ask the business to confirm whether they calculate all costs for an item until it sells. In that case, we need to keep the product cost in the **Internet Sales** table.

The response from the business is that they need to show the current product standard cost for an item before it goes on the shelf. In other words, there is just one flat rate for the standard cost associated with each product. So, in this specific scenario, we do not need to keep the history of the costs in the **ProductStandardCost** column in the **Internet Sales** table. Instead, we have to move the **ProductStandardCost** column to the **Product** table.

Therefore, the preceding calculation is incorrect. By moving the **ProductStandardCost** column into the **Product** table, there is only one product standard cost associated with each product. This is how data modeling can help to decrease the level of complexity of our DAX expressions. But to demonstrate the virtual tables, we create another measure and analyze the results. Before creating the measure, let's review our requirements once again.

We need to get the average of the product standard cost by **Product Category**, **Product Subcategory**, and **Product**. Each product has only one current product standard cost. Therefore, we can create a virtual table with the **ProductKey** column and the **ProductStandardCost** column side by side. Note that the two columns come from different tables. However, since there is a physical relationship between the two tables already, we can easily have the two columns side by side in a single virtual table.

The following measure caters to the preceding requirements:

```
Avg. Product Standard Costs Correct = 
AVERAGEX(
    SUMMARIZE (
        'Internet Sales'
        , 'Product'[ProductKey]
        , 'Internet Sales'[ProductStandardCost]
    )
        , 'Internet Sales'[ProductStandardCost]
)
```

We can now add the new measure to the matrix visual we previously put on the report canvas to see both measures. This way, we quickly show the differences between the two calculations. The totals especially show a big difference between the two. The following image shows the differences:

Product Category	Avg. Product Standard Costs	Avg. Product Standard Costs Correct
⊟ **Accessories**	7.26	12.02
⊞ Bike Racks	44.88	44.88
⊞ Bike Stands	59.47	59.47
⊞ Bottles and Cages	2.66	2.99
⊞ Cleaners	2.97	2.97
⊞ Fenders	8.22	8.22
⊞ Helmets	13.09	13.09
⊞ Hydration Packs	20.57	20.57
⊞ Tires and Tubes	5.30	7.29
⊟ **Bikes**	1,105.71	918.41
⊞ Mountain Bikes	1,094.39	1,004.64
⊞ Road Bikes	1,113.45	881.46
⊞ Touring Bikes	1,102.87	885.93
⊟ **Clothing**	22.34	25.56
⊞ Caps	6.92	6.92
⊞ Gloves	9.16	9.16
⊞ Jerseys	39.97	40.03
⊞ Shorts	26.18	26.18
⊞ Socks	3.36	3.36
⊞ Vests	23.75	23.75
Total	286.07	679.19

Figure 2.13: Comparing two measures created for Avg. Product Standard Costs

Let's analyze the preceding measure to see how it works.

The AVERAGEX() function is an iterator function that iterates through all the rows of its table argument to calculate its expression argument. Here is where we created the virtual table using the SUMMARIZE() function.

As you can see in the following figure, we created a virtual table on top of the **Internet Sales** table. We get the **ProductStandardCost** values grouped by **ProductKey** from the **Product** table:

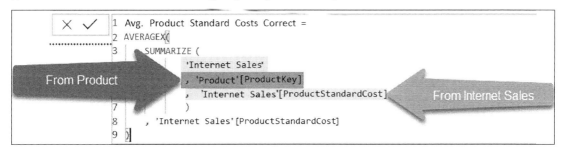

Figure 2.14: A virtual table created on top of two tables

How is that possible? Here is how it works.

As mentioned earlier, the AVERAGEX() function is an iterator function. It goes through each row of the virtual table created by the SUMMARIZE() function. The SUMMARIZE() function gets the values of the **ProductStandardCost** column from the **Internet Sales** table grouped by related **ProductKey** instances from the **Product** table via the existing relationship between the two tables. When we run the SUMMARIZE() part of the preceding calculation in DAX Studio, we see that SUMMARIZE() retrieves only 158 rows, while the **Internet Sales** table has more than 60,000 rows. The reason is the existing relationship between the **Internet Sales** table and the **Product** table.

The following figure shows the results of running the SUMMARIZE() section of the preceding calculation in DAX Studio:

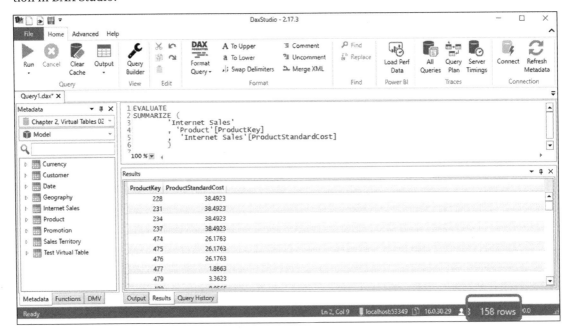

Figure 2.15: Results of running the SUMMARIZE() part of the calculation in DAX Studio

So far, so good.

The other point to note is that we created a virtual table inside a measure. When we put the **Product Category**, **Product Subcategory**, and **Product** columns into the matrix visual, they show the correct values for the **Avg. Product Standard Costs Correct** measure. We did not physically create any relationships between **Internet Sales** and the virtual table created by the SUMMARIZE() function. How come we get the correct results?

The lineage between the derived virtual table and the original physical table is the answer. The virtual table inherits the relationship with the **Internet Sales** table from the **Product** table. In other words, the virtual table has a one-to-one virtual relationship with the **Product** table through **ProductKey**. Hence, when we put the **Product Category**, **Product Subcategory**, and **Product** columns into the matrix visual, the filters propagate to the **Product** table and the **Internet Sales** table. The following figure illustrates how the virtual table relates to the **Product** table and the **Internet Sales** table:

 Neither the virtual table nor any virtual relationships are visible in the data model. The following figure is for illustration only.

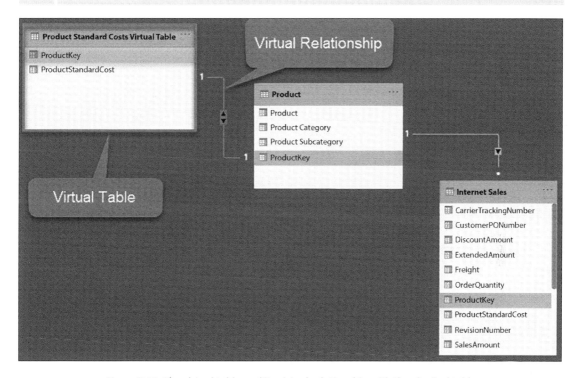

Figure 2.16: The virtual table and its virtual relationship with the physical table

Using virtual tables is an effective technique we can use on many occasions. A great example is when there is no relationship between two tables, and we cannot create a physical relationship between the two as the relationship is only legitimate in some business cases.

Let's look at more complex scenarios with multiple virtual tables with inter-virtual relationships. The business needs to calculate **Internet Sales** in USD. At the same time, there are several values in the **Internet Sales** table in other currencies. We use the `Chapter 2, Virtual Tables 04, Virtual Relationships.pbix` file for this scenario.

The model contains an **Exchange Rates** table. As per the scenario, the base currency is USD. That is why the **AverageRate** column is always 1 when **Currency** is USD. In other words, the **Exchange Rates** table contains all currency ratings for each day compared to USD. The following figure shows the **Exchange Rates** data:

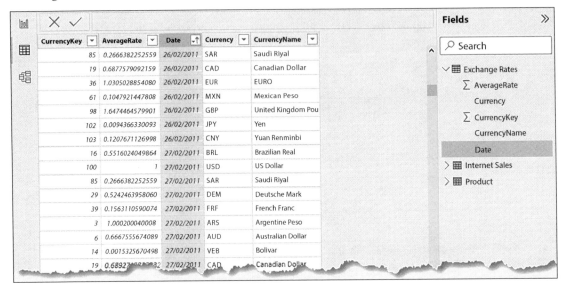

Figure 2.17: Exchange Rates data

To better understand the scenario, let's look at the **Internet Sales** and **Exchange Rates** data side by side, as shown in the following figure:

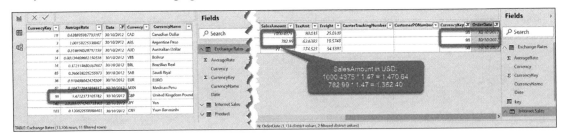

Figure 2.18: Calculating internet sales in USD

To calculate the internet sales in USD for a specific date, we need to find the relevant **CurrencyKey** for that specific date in the **Exchange Rates** table, then multiply the value of **SalesAmount** from the **Internet Sales** table by the value of **AverageRate** from the **Exchange Rates** table.

The following measure caters to that:

```
Internet Sales USD =
SUMX(
    NATURALINNERJOIN (
        SELECTCOLUMNS(
```

```
                            'Internet Sales'
    , "CurrencyKeyJoin", 'Internet Sales'[CurrencyKey] * 1
                    , "DateJoin", 'Internet Sales'[OrderDate] + 0
                    , "ProductKey", 'Internet Sales'[ProductKey]
                    , "SalesOrderLineNumber", 'Internet
    Sales'[SalesOrderLineNumber]
                    , "SalesOrderNumber", 'Internet Sales'[SalesOrderNumber]
                    , "SalesAmount", 'Internet Sales'[SalesAmount]
                    )
            , SELECTCOLUMNS (
                'Exchange Rates'
                , "CurrencyKeyJoin", 'Exchange Rates'[CurrencyKey] * 1
                , "DateJoin", 'Exchange Rates'[Date] + 0
                , "AverageRate", 'Exchange Rates'[AverageRate]
            )
        )
    , [AverageRate] * [SalesAmount]
    )
```

The following figure shows how the preceding calculation works:

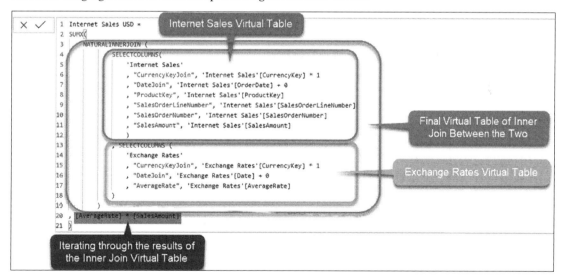

Figure 2.19: How Internet Sales USD works

Looking at the **Exchange Rates** table, we see that the combination of the values of the **CurrencyKey** and **Date** columns ensures the uniqueness of the rows.

As the preceding figure shows, we first create two virtual tables. We join those two virtual tables using two columns, the **CurrencyKeyJoin** and **DateJoin** columns. If you look at the construction of the two columns, you see the following:

- We added 0 days to `'Internet Sales'[OrderDate]` to construct **DateJoin** for the virtual table derived from the **Internet Sales** table. We did the same to `'Exchange Rates'[Date]` to construct **DateJoin** for the virtual table derived from the **Exchange Rates** table.
- We multiplied **CurrencyKey** by 1 to construct the **CurrencyKeyJoin** column in both virtual tables.

At this stage, you may ask why we need to do any of this. The reason is purely to make the `NATURALINNERJOIN()` function work. The `NATURALINNERJOIN()` function, as its name implies, performs an inner join of a table with another table using the same column names with the same data type and the same lineage.

We want to perform an inner join between the two virtual tables based on the following columns:

- `'Internet Sales'[OrderDate]` → `'Exchange Rates'[Date]`
- `'Internet Sales'[CurrencyKey]` → `'Exchange Rates'[CurrencyKey]`

The first requirement for the `NATURALINNERJOIN()` function is to have the same column names in both joining tables. To meet that requirement, we renamed both the **OrderDate** column from the **Internet Sales** table and the **Date** column from the **Exchange Rates** table to **DateJoin**.

The second requirement is that the columns participating in the join must have the same data type. We already meet this requirement.

The last requirement, which is the most confusing one yet, is that the columns contributing to the join must have the same lineage if there is a physical relationship between the two tables. If there is no physical relationship between the tables, the columns participating in the join must not have lineage to any physical columns within the data model. Therefore, we need to break the lineage of the join columns. Otherwise, the `NATURALINNERJOIN()` function does not work. We need to use an expression rather than an actual column name to break the lineage. Therefore, we add 0 days to `'Internet Sales'[OrderDate]` and multiply `'Exchange Rates'[CurrencyKey]` by 1 to break the lineage of those two columns.

Finally, we have the desired result set, so we can multiply `[SalesAmount]` by `[AverageRate]` to get the sales amount in USD.

The following figure shows the **Internet Sales** (without considering the exchange rates) and **Internet Sales USD** measures side by side:

Product Category	Internet Sales	Internet Sales USD
⊟ **Accessories**	**700,759.96**	**$640,920.11**
All-Purpose Bike Stand	39,591.00	$35,628.69
Bike Wash - Dissolver	7,218.60	$6,352.51
Fender Set - Mountain	46,619.58	$41,974.10
Hitch Rack - 4-Bike	39,360.00	$35,934.55
HL Mountain Tire	48,860.00	$42,839.80
HL Road Tire	27,970.80	$24,531.24
Hydration Pack - 70 oz.	40,307.67	$35,307.84
LL Mountain Tire	21,541.38	$19,092.44
LL Road Tire	22,435.56	$21,492.01
ML Mountain Tire	34,818.39	$31,580.66
ML Road Tire	23,140.74	$20,554.35
Mountain Bottle Cage	20,229.75	$18,814.51
Mountain Tire Tube	15,444.05	$13,759.74
Patch Kit/8 Patches	7,307.39	$6,595.31
Road Bottle Cage	15,390.88	$13,953.77
Total	**29,358,677.22**	**$26,054,827.45**

Figure 2.20: Visualizing Internet Sales and Internet Sales USD side by side in a matrix visual

 In virtual tables, we can join two tables using multiple columns.

We created the **Internet Sales USD** measure to demonstrate how virtual tables, virtual relationships, and lineage work. But keep in mind that in real-world scenarios the best practice is to move the **AverageRate** column to the **Internet Sales** table when possible. In our example, it is easily possible by merging the **Internet Sales** table with the **Exchange Rates** table in Power Query Editor to get the **AverageRate** column into **Internet Sales**.

Considering the following notes is advised while approaching tasks like the one we have looked at in this section:

- The best practice is to implement business logic in the source system when possible. If we cannot take care of the business logic at the source, then try to solve the issue(s) in Power Query Editor. If the logic is too complex to implement in Power Query Editor, look at the data model and investigate the possibilities for creating physical relationships rather than virtual ones. For instance, in the **Exchange Rates** scenario, we can move the rates for each transaction to the **Internet Sales** table without changing the granularity of **Internet Sales**.

- Review the business logic and look for any conformities of using the same virtual tables. If you are likely to use the same virtual table(s) multiple times, try creating either physical or calculated tables that can be used across the data model.
- Virtual tables and virtual relationships are potent tools to have in your toolbelt, yet they are costly. When used on large amounts of data, you may not get good performance out of your virtual tables.

So far, we have looked at virtual tables, how they work through relationships, and how we can leverage their power in our model. In the next section, we look at **time intelligence** in data modeling.

Time intelligence and data modeling

Time intelligence is one of the most powerful and commonly used functionalities in Power BI. For those coming from a SQL development background, it is pretty clear how hard it is to build time intelligence analysis in a relational database system such as SQL Server. These complex calculations are easily accessible in Power BI using just a handful of time intelligence functions. This section briefly looks at the common challenges of working with time intelligence functions in Power BI.

There are currently 35 time intelligence functions available in Power BI. You can find the complete list of functions on the Microsoft website: `https://docs.microsoft.com/en-us/dax/time-intelligence-functions-dax?WT.mc_id=DP-MVP-5003466`.

Detecting valid dates in the date dimension

When dealing with periodic calculations in time intelligence, it is often hard to just get valid dates to show in the visuals.

Let's have a look at how to do this with a scenario.

A business needs to see the following calculations:

- Internet Sales Month to Date (MTD)
- Internet Sales Last Month to Date (LMTD)
- Internet Sales Year to Date (YTD)
- Internet Sales Last Year to Date (LYTD)
- Internet Sales Last Year Month to Date (LY MTD)

Writing the preceding measures is super easy using the existing DAX functions. The calculations are as follows.

To calculate MTD, use the following DAX expressions:

```
Internet Sales MTD =
TOTALMTD(
    [Internet Sales]
    , 'Date'[Full Date]
)
```

Use the following DAX expressions to calculate LMTD:

```
Internet Sales LMTD =
TOTALMTD(
    [Internet Sales]
    , DATEADD('Date'[Full Date], -1, MONTH)
)
```

Use the following DAX expressions to calculate YTD:

```
Internet Sales YTD =
TOTALYTD(
    [Internet Sales]
    , 'Date'[Full Date]
)
```

Use the following DAX expressions to calculate LYTD:

```
Internet Sales LYTD =
TOTALYTD (
    [Internet Sales]
    , DATEADD('Date'[Full Date], -1, YEAR)
)
```

Finally, use the following DAX expressions to calculate LY MTD:

```
Internet Sales LY MTD =
TOTALMTD(
    [Internet Sales]
    , SAMEPERIODLASTYEAR('Date'[Full Date])
)
```

The SAMEPERIODLASTYEAR('Date'[Full Date]) and DATEADD('Date'[Full Date], -1, YEAR) act the same. We used different functions to demonstrate the possibilities.

We can then put a table visual on the report canvas to show the calculations side by side with **Full Date** from the **Date** table. Everything looks good unless we sort the **Full Date** column in descending order, which is when we realize that there is an issue. We get null values for the **Internet Sales**, **Internet Sales MTD**, and **Internet Sales LMTD** measures for many dates. We are also getting a lot of duplicate values for the **Internet Sales YTD** measure.

The following figure illustrates the results:

Full Date	Internet Sales	Internet Sales MTD	Internet Sales LMTD	Internet Sales YTD	Internet Sales LYTD	Internet Sales LY MTD
31/12/2014				45,694.72	16,351,550.34	1,874,360.29
30/12/2014				45,694.72	16,349,753.51	1,872,563.46
29/12/2014				45,694.72	16,348,239.22	1,871,049.17
28/12/2014				45,694.72	16,346,404.43	1,869,214.38
27/12/2014				45,694.72	16,298,029.10	1,820,839.05
26/12/2014				45,694.72	16,237,069.32	1,759,879.27
25/12/2014				45,694.72	16,158,162.73	1,680,972.68
24/12/2014				45,694.72	16,100,081.95	1,622,891.90
23/12/2014				45,694.72	16,030,548.31	1,553,358.26
22/12/2014				45,694.72	15,953,633.70	1,476,443.65
21/12/2014				45,694.72	15,887,711.51	1,410,521.46
20/12/2014				45,694.72	15,838,919.73	1,361,729.68
19/12/2014				45,694.72	15,772,150.34	1,294,960.29
18/12/2014				45,694.72	15,689,030.88	1,211,840.83
17/12/2014				45,694.72	15,621,755.41	1,144,565.36
16/12/2014				45,694.72	15,549,742.27	1,072,552.22
15/12/2014				45,694.72	15,491,654.78	1,014,464.73
14/12/2014				45,694.72	15,420,654.38	943,464.33
13/12/2014				45,694.72	15,362,190.34	885,000.29
12/12/2014				45,694.72	15,296,625.96	819,435.91
11/12/2014				45,694.72	15,200,014.35	722,824.30
10/12/2014				45,694.72	15,142,292.49	665,102.44
9/12/2014				45,694.72	15,087,238.76	610,048.71
8/12/2014				45,694.72	15,007,394.58	530,204.53
7/12/2014				45,694.72	14,949,089.82	471,899.77
6/12/2014				45,694.72	14,885,605.61	408,415.56
5/12/2014				45,694.72	14,823,418.61	346,228.56
4/12/2014				45,694.72	14,734,321.19	257,131.14
3/12/2014				45,694.72	14,651,472.92	174,282.87
2/12/2014				45,694.72	14,585,185.26	107,995.21
1/12/2014				45,694.72	14,535,718.65	58,528.60
30/11/2014				45,694.72	14,477,190.05	1,780,920.06
29/11/2014				45,694.72	14,441,694.02	1,745,424.03
Total	29,358,677.22			45,694.72	16,351,550.34	1,874,360.29

Figure 2.21: Future date-related issues in the periodic time intelligence calculations

This is indeed an expected behavior. We must cover all dates from 1st January to 31st December in the date dimension. So, we expect null values for future dates for the **Internet Sales, Internet Sales MTD,** and **Internet Sales LMTD** measures and duplicate values for the **Internet Sales YTD** measure. The following figure shows more results by scrolling down the table visual. We can see that the last date with a valid transaction is **28/01/2014**, which means all the preceding measures must finish their calculations by that date:

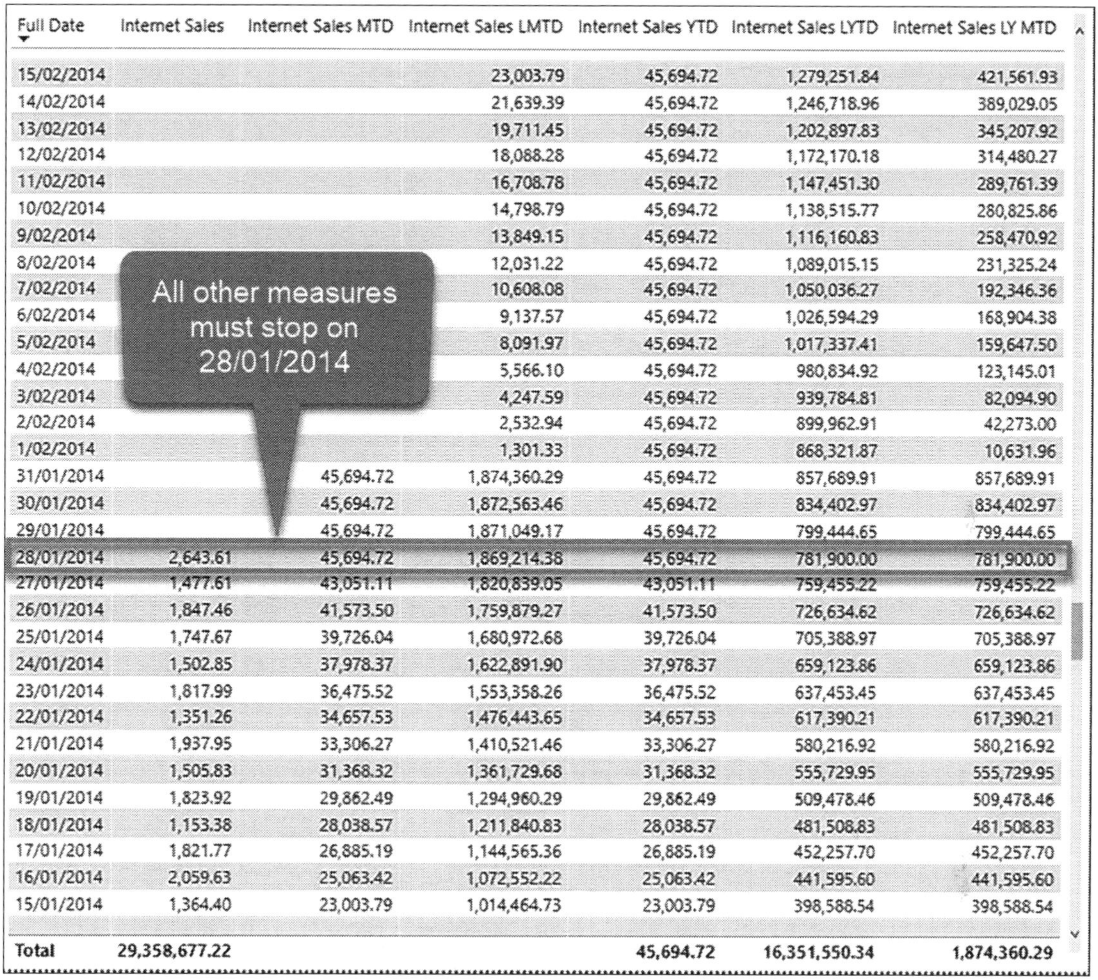

Full Date	Internet Sales	Internet Sales MTD	Internet Sales LMTD	Internet Sales YTD	Internet Sales LYTD	Internet Sales LY MTD
15/02/2014			23,003.79	45,694.72	1,279,251.84	421,561.93
14/02/2014			21,639.39	45,694.72	1,246,718.96	389,029.05
13/02/2014			19,711.45	45,694.72	1,202,897.83	345,207.92
12/02/2014			18,088.28	45,694.72	1,172,170.18	314,480.27
11/02/2014			16,708.78	45,694.72	1,147,451.30	289,761.39
10/02/2014			14,798.79	45,694.72	1,138,515.77	280,825.86
9/02/2014			13,849.15	45,694.72	1,116,160.83	258,470.92
8/02/2014			12,031.22	45,694.72	1,089,015.15	231,325.24
7/02/2014			10,608.08	45,694.72	1,050,036.27	192,346.36
6/02/2014			9,137.57	45,694.72	1,026,594.29	168,904.38
5/02/2014			8,091.97	45,694.72	1,017,337.41	159,647.50
4/02/2014			5,566.10	45,694.72	980,834.92	123,145.01
3/02/2014			4,247.59	45,694.72	939,784.81	82,094.90
2/02/2014			2,532.94	45,694.72	899,962.91	42,273.00
1/02/2014			1,301.33	45,694.72	868,321.87	10,631.96
31/01/2014		45,694.72	1,874,360.29	45,694.72	857,689.91	857,689.91
30/01/2014		45,694.72	1,872,563.46	45,694.72	834,402.97	834,402.97
29/01/2014		45,694.72	1,871,049.17	45,694.72	799,444.65	799,444.65
28/01/2014	2,643.61	45,694.72	1,869,214.38	45,694.72	781,900.00	781,900.00
27/01/2014	1,477.61	43,051.11	1,820,839.05	43,051.11	759,455.22	759,455.22
26/01/2014	1,847.46	41,573.50	1,759,879.27	41,573.50	726,634.62	726,634.62
25/01/2014	1,747.67	39,726.04	1,680,972.68	39,726.04	705,388.97	705,388.97
24/01/2014	1,502.85	37,978.37	1,622,891.90	37,978.37	659,123.86	659,123.86
23/01/2014	1,817.99	36,475.52	1,553,358.26	36,475.52	637,453.45	637,453.45
22/01/2014	1,351.26	34,657.53	1,476,443.65	34,657.53	617,390.21	617,390.21
21/01/2014	1,937.95	33,306.27	1,410,521.46	33,306.27	580,216.92	580,216.92
20/01/2014	1,505.83	31,368.32	1,361,729.68	31,368.32	555,729.95	555,729.95
19/01/2014	1,823.92	29,862.49	1,294,960.29	29,862.49	509,478.46	509,478.46
18/01/2014	1,153.38	28,038.57	1,211,840.83	28,038.57	481,508.83	481,508.83
17/01/2014	1,821.77	26,885.19	1,144,565.36	26,885.19	452,257.70	452,257.70
16/01/2014	2,059.63	25,063.42	1,072,552.22	25,063.42	441,595.60	441,595.60
15/01/2014	1,364.40	23,003.79	1,014,464.73	23,003.79	398,588.54	398,588.54
Total	29,358,677.22			45,694.72	16,351,550.34	1,874,360.29

All other measures must stop on 28/01/2014

Figure 2.22: The last valid date is 28/01/2014

One way of solving the issue is to return BLANK() for the invalid dates. The following calculation shows the Internet Sales MTD Blanking Invalid Dates measure, which returns null if there is no transaction for a particular date:

```
Internet Sales MTD Blanking Invalid Dates =
VAR lastorderDate = MAX('Internet Sales'[OrderDateKey])
RETURN
IF(
    MAX('Date'[DateKey]) <= lastorderDate
    , TOTALMTD(
        [Internet Sales]
        , 'Date'[Full Date]
    )
)
```

What we are doing in the preceding measure is simple. We get the maximum of **OrderDateKey** from the **Internet Sales** table, and then we add a condition that if an **OrderDateKey** value does not exist, we return a blank; otherwise, we return the `TOTALMTD()` calculation.

The following figure shows the results of the `Internet Sales MTD Blanking Invalid Dates` measure:

Full Date	Internet Sales	Internet Sales MTD Blanking Invalid Dates
28/01/2014	2,643.61	45,694.72
27/01/2014	1,477.61	43,051.11
26/01/2014	1,847.46	41,573.50
25/01/2014	1,747.67	39,726.04
24/01/2014	1,502.85	37,978.37
23/01/2014	1,817.99	36,475.52
22/01/2014	1,351.26	34,657.53
21/01/2014	1,937.95	33,306.27
20/01/2014	1,505.83	31,368.32
19/01/2014	1,823.92	29,862.49
18/01/2014	1,153.38	28,038.57
Total	**29,358,677.22**	

Figure 2.23: Internet Sales MTD Blanking Invalid Dates

While this calculation may work for some scenarios, it is not a correct calculation in some other scenarios, such as ours. Looking more precisely at the results reveals an issue. The following figure reveals the problem:

Full Date	Internet Sales	Internet Sales MTD Blanking Invalid Dates
7/02/2011	21,088.06	119,199.78
8/02/2011	17,891.35	137,091.13
9/02/2011	21,469.62	158,560.75
10/02/2011	11,929.73	170,490.48
11/02/2011	14,313.08	184,803.56
12/02/2011	21,113.06	205,916.62
14/02/2011	3,578.27	209,494.89
15/02/2011	21,266.34	230,761.23
16/02/2011	17,109.47	247,870.70
17/02/2011	21.266.34	269,137.04
18/02/2011	28,016.32	297,153.36
Total	**29,358,677.22**	

(13/02/2011 is missing)

Figure 2.24: Missing dates as a result of blanking invalid dates

The other way to overcome the issue is to create a flag column in the **Date** table to validate each date value in the **Date** table. It shows TRUE when the **DateKey** value is between the minimum and maximum of the **OrderDateKey** values. We can create the new column either in Power Query Editor or as a calculated column using DAX. From a performance and data compression viewpoint, creating a calculated column with DAX is ideal in terms of performance. The column's data type is Boolean; therefore, its cardinality is low. Hence, the xVelocity engine perfectly compresses the data.

The following calculation creates a new calculated column:

```
IsValidDate =
    AND('Date'[DateKey] >= MIN('Internet Sales'[OrderDateKey])
        , 'Date'[DateKey] <= MAX('Internet Sales'[OrderDateKey])
    )
```

Now we have two options:

- We can simply use the **IsValidDate** calculated column as a visual filter. In this case, we do not need to change the DAX expressions of the original measures. The following figure shows the results in a table visual:

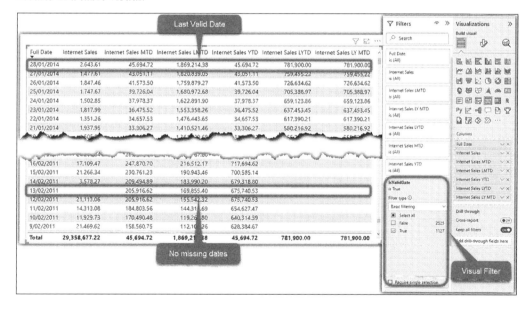

Figure 2.25: Using the IsValidDate calculated column under Filters

- We can add the **IsValidDate** column to all measures. In this case, we need to filter the results of the periodic functions by **IsValidDate** when **IsValidDate** returns TRUE().

Use the following DAX expressions to calculate Internet Sales MTD with Valid Dates:

```
Internet Sales MTD with Valid Dates =
TOTALMTD(
    [Internet Sales]
    , CALCULATETABLE(
        VALUES('Date'[Full Date])
        , 'Date'[IsValidDate] = TRUE()
    )
)
```

Use the following DAX expressions to calculate Internet Sales LMTD with Valid Dates:

```
Internet Sales LMTD with Valid Dates =
TOTALMTD(
    [Internet Sales]
    , DATEADD(
        CALCULATETABLE(
                VALUES('Date'[Full Date])
                , 'Date'[IsValidDate] = TRUE()
            )
        , -1
        , MONTH
    )
)
```

Use the following DAX expressions to calculate Internet Sales YTD with Valid Dates:

```
Internet Sales YTD with Valid Dates =
CALCULATE(
    TOTALYTD(
        [Internet Sales]
        , CALCULATETABLE(
                VALUES('Date'[Full Date])
                , 'Date'[IsValidDate] = TRUE()
            )
        )
)
```

Use the following DAX expressions to calculate Internet Sales LYTD with Valid Dates:

```
Internet Sales LYTD with Valid Dates =
TOTALYTD (
    [Internet Sales]
    , DATEADD(
```

```
                CALCULATETABLE(
                    VALUES('Date'[Full Date])
                    , 'Date'[IsValidDate] = true()
                )
                , -1
                , YEAR
            )
        )
```

And finally, use the following DAX expressions to calculate `Internet Sales LY MTD with Valid Dates`:

```
Internet Sales LY MTD with Valid Dates =
TOTALMTD(
    [Internet Sales]
    , SAMEPERIODLASTYEAR(
        CALCULATETABLE(
            VALUES('Date'[Full Date])
            , 'Date'[IsValidDate] = TRUE()
        )
    )
)
```

The following figure shows the results of putting the preceding measures in a table visual without filtering the visual with the **IsValidDate** column:

Full Date	Internet Sales	Internet Sales MTD with Valid Dates	Internet Sales LMTD with Valid Dates	Internet Sales YTD with Valid Dates	Internet Sales LYTD with Valid Dates	Internet Sales LY MTD with Valid Dates
28/01/2014	2,643.61	$45,694.72	$1,869,214.38	45,694.72	781,900.00	781,900.00
27/01/2014	1,477.61	$43,051.11	$1,820,839.05	43,051.11	759,455.22	759,455.22
26/01/2014	1,847.46	$41,573.50	$1,759,879.27	41,573.50	726,634.62	726,634.62
25/01/2014	1,747.67	$39,726.04	$1,680,972.68	39,726.04	705,388.97	705,388.97
24/01/2014	1,502.85	$37,978.37	$1,622,891.90	37,978.37	659,123.86	659,123.86
23/01/2014	1,817.99	$36,475.52	$1,553,358.26	36,475.52	637,453.45	637,453.45
22/01/2014	1,351.26	$34,657.53	$1,476,443.65	34,657.53	617,390.21	617,390.21
21/01/2014	1,937.95	$33,306.27	$1,410,521.46	33,306.27	580,216.92	580,216.92
20/01/2014	1,505.03	$31,368.32	$1,361,729.68	31,368.32	555,729.95	555,729.95
19/01/2014	1,823.92	$29,862.49	$1,294,960.29	29,862.49	509,478.46	509,478.46
18/01/2014	1,153.38	$28,038.57	$1,211,840.83	28,038.57	481,508.83	481,508.83
17/01/2014	1,821.77	$26,885.19	$1,144,565.36	26,885.19	452,257.70	452,257.70
16/01/2014	2,059.63	$25,063.42	$1,072,552.22	25,063.42	441,595.60	441,595.60
15/01/2014	1,364.40	$23,003.79	$1,014,464.73	23,003.79	398,588.54	398,588.54
14/01/2014	1,927.94	$21,639.39	$943,464.33	21,639.39	380,848.06	380,848.06
13/01/2014	1,623.17	$19,711.45	$885,000.29	19,711.45	363,983.89	363,983.89
12/01/2014	1,379.50	$18,088.28	$819,435.91	18,088.28	334,651.83	334,651.83
Total	29,358,677.22	$45,694.72	$1,869,214.38	45,694.72	781,900.00	781,900.00

Figure 2.26: Periodic calculations with improved measures

This method also fixes the issue of showing invalid dates when we use the **Full Date** column in a slicer visual. It is much nicer if we only show the valid dates in the slicer. The following figure illustrates a slicer visual showing **Full Range Dates** ranges from the **Date** table, side by side with another slicer visual showing **Valid Dates Only**:

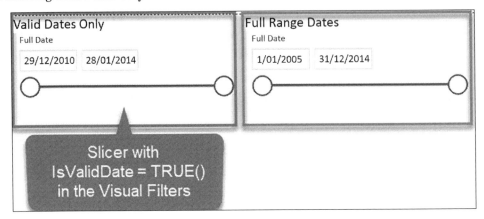

Figure 2.27: The date slicer filtered by IsValidDate

In the preceding image, we used the **IsValidDate** flag column to filter the values of the left slicer.

Period-over-period calculations

In many cases, businesses need period-over-period calculations, such as year-over-year and month-over-month calculations. Period-over-period calculations can vary from business to business, but the principles remain the same. This section has a broader focus. The scenario we use in this section is based on a real-world and highly demanded business requirement: dynamic measure selection. In this section, we learn how to use the out-of-the-box features available in Power BI Desktop to solve some data visualization challenges. In May 2022, Microsoft announced a new feature called Fields Parameters.

Let's move forward with the dynamic measure selection scenario. The business requires you to analyze the **Internet Sales** over different periods as follows:

- Month-over-month internet sales variance
- Year-over-year internet sales variance

In the report, the user should be able to select between the preceding measures dynamically with the following conditions:

- The report contains only one area chart.
- The report enables the users to choose between year-over-year or month-over-month calculations. The year-over-year calculation compares **Internet Sales** values by **Internet Sales Last Year** (**LY**). Month-over-month compares **Internet Sales** values by **Internet Sales Last Month** (**LM**).
- The following formulas show the required equation to calculate period-over-period variance:

```
Internet Sales MoM Variance = Internet Sales - Internet Sales LM
Internet Sales YoY Variance = Internet Sales - Internet Sales LY
```

- According to the scenario, the business needs to calculate the **Internet Sales Month-over-Month (MoM) variance** and **Internet Sales Year-over-Year (YoY) variance**. The Internet Sales measure already exists, so we need to create two new measures, Internet Sales LM and Internet Sales LY.

The measures are as follows:

```
Internet Sales LM =
CALCULATE(
        [Internet Sales]
        , DATEADD('Date'[Full Date], -1, MONTH)
)
Internet Sales LY =
CALCULATE(
        [Internet Sales]
        , SAMEPERIODLASTYEAR('Date'[Full Date])
)
```

Before implementing the scenario, let's look at the **Internet Sales** and **Internet Sales LM** measures side by side to understand how to implement **Internet Sales MoM Variance**. The following figure shows the two measures side by side in a table visual:

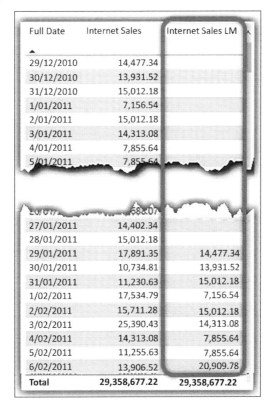

Figure 2.28: There are blank values for the last month

The preceding figure shows the issue immediately. **Internet Sales LM** returns null values for the first 28 rows as the first transaction started on **29/12/2010**.

Let us create a measure based on the scenario's formulas and see what can go wrong:

```
Internet Sales MoM Variance = [Internet Sales] - [Internet Sales LM]
```

Now put the new measure into the table visual. The following figure shows the results:

Full Date	Internet Sales	Internet Sales LM	Internet Sales MoM Variance
29/12/2010	14,477.34		14,477.34
30/12/2010	13,931.52		13,931.52
31/12/2010	15,012.18		15,012.18
1/01/2011	7,156.54		7,156.54
2/01/2011	15,012.18		15,012.18
3/01/2011	14,313.08		14,313.08
4/01/2011	7,855.64		7,855.64
5/01/2011	7,855.64		7,855.64
6/01/2011	20,909.78		20,909.78
7/01/2011	10,556.53		10,556.53
8/01/2011	14,313.08		14,313.08
23/01/2011	17,534.79		17,534.79
24/01/2011	28,041.32		28,041.32
25/01/2011	19,785.36		19,785.36
26/01/2011	17,688.07		17,688.07
27/01/2011	14,402.34		14,402.34
28/01/2011	15,012.18		15,012.18
29/01/2011	17,891.35	14,477.34	3,414.01
30/01/2011	10,734.81	13,931.52	-3,196.71
Total	29,358,677.22	29,358,677.22	0.00

Figure 2.29: The variance values for the first 28 rows do not make sense

As you see, the variance values start to make sense only after **28/01/2011**. It is trivial to understand the reason. There were no sales in the past 28 days, so we have to cut off those values. One of the first solutions that may come to mind is eliminating null values for **Internet Sales LM**. The measure looks as follows:

```
Internet Sales MoM Variance Incorrect =
IF(
    NOT(ISBLANK([Internet Sales LM]))
    , [Internet Sales] - [Internet Sales LM]
)
```

In the preceding calculation, we say that if **Internet Sales LM** is not blank, get the variance; otherwise, show blank.

But there is a problem with the calculation. The following figure shows the issue:

Full Date	Internet Sales	Internet Sales LM	Internet Sales Mom Variance Incorrect
17/02/2011	21,266.34	11,255.63	10,010.71
18/02/2011	28,016.32	14,313.08	13,703.24
19/02/2011	17,688.07	38,241.29	-20,553.22
20/02/2011	10,531.53	15,012.18	-4,480.65
21/02/2011	28,968.70	10,734.81	18,233.89
22/02/2011	7,652.36	11,433.91	-3,781.55
23/02/2011	24,691.33	17,534.79	7,156.54
24/02/2011	7,156.54	28,041.32	-20,884.78
25/02/2011	7,156.54	19,785.36	-12,628.82
26/02/2011	19,785.36	17,688.07	2,097.29
27/02/2011	24,691.33	14,402.34	10,288.99
28/02/2011	20,859.78	15,012.18	5,847.60
1/03/2011	14,313.08	17,534.79	-3,221.71
2/03/2011	35,782.70	15,711.28	20,071.42
3/03/2011	11,433.91	25,390.43	-13,956.52
4/03/2011	21,119.06	14,313.08	799.98
5/03/2011	10,734.81	11,255.63	-520.82
6/03/2011	22,168.72	13,906.52	8,262.20
7/03/2011	15,012.18	21,088.06	-6,075.88
8/03/2011	10,734.81	17,891.35	-7,156.54
9/03/2011	24,463.05	21,469.62	2,993.43
10/03/2011	10,734.81	11,929.73	-1,194.92
11/03/2011		14,313	-14,313.08
12/03/2011	6,978.26	21,113.06	-14,134.80
13/03/2011	8,351.46		
14/03/2011	17,891.35	3,578.27	14,313.08
15/03/2011	14,313.08	21,266.34	-6,953.26
16/03/2011	15,012.18	17,109.47	-2,097.29
17/03/2011	13,956.52	21,266.34	-7,309.82
18/03/2011	17,891.35	28,016.32	-10,124.97
19/03/2011	25,568.71	17,688.07	7,880.64
20/03/2011	7,156.54	10,531.53	-3,374.99
21/03/2011	22,307.98	28,968.70	-6,660.72
Total	29,358,677.22	29,358,677.22	0.00

Callouts: "There are no sales on 13/02/2011" and "The variance should be 8,351.46"

Figure 2.30: The calculation results in incorrect variance values when there are no sales in a particular day

There is also another issue with the preceding calculation. The calculation shows the last month's sales for future dates, which is incorrect. We can see the issue when we sort the results by **Full Date** in descending order. *Figure 2.31* illustrates the problem:

Full Date ▼	Internet Sales	Internet Sales LM	Internet Sales MoM Variance Incorrect
28/02/2014		2,643.61	-2,643.61
27/02/2014		1,477.61	-1,477.61
26/02/2014		1,847.46	-1,847.46
25/02/2014		1,747.67	-1,747.67
24/02/2014		1,502.85	-1,502.85
23/02/2014		1,817.99	-1,817.99
22/02/2014		1,351.26	-1,351.26
21/02/2014		1,937.95	-1,937.95
20/02/2014		1,505.83	-1,505.83
19/02/2014		1,823.92	-1,823.92
18/02/2014		1,153.38	-1,153.38
17/02/2014		1,821.77	-1,821.77
16/02/2014		2,059.63	-2,059.63
15/02/2014		1,364.40	-1,364.40
14/02/2014		1,927.94	-1,927.94
13/02/2014		1,623.17	-1,623.17
12/02/2014		1,379.50	-1,379.50
11/02/2014		1,909.99	-1,909.99
10/02/2014		949.64	-949.64
9/02/2014		1,817.93	-1,817.93
8/02/2014		1,423.14	-1,423.14
7/02/2014		1,470.51	-1,470.51
6/02/2014		1,045.60	-1,045.60
5/02/2014		2,525.87	-2,525.87
4/02/2014		1,318.51	-1,318.51
3/02/2014		1,714.65	-1,714.65
2/02/2014		1,231.61	-1,231.61
1/02/2014		1,301.33	-1,301.33
31/01/2014		1,796.83	-1,796.83
30/01/2014		1,514.29	-1,514.29
29/01/2014		1,834.79	-1,834.79
28/01/2014	2,643.61	48,375.33	-45,731.72
27/01/2014	1,477.61	60,959.78	-59,482.17
Total	29,358,677.22	29,358,677.22	0.00

Figure 2.31: Future dates show up for Internet Sales LM. The calculation must stop at the last valid date with internet sales

Two failures in a calculation are enough to prompt us to come up with a better solution. The following calculation resolves the issues:

```
Internet Sales MOM Variance =
VAR firstValidDateWithSalesLM = FIRSTNONBLANK(ALL('Date'[Full Date]), [Internet
Sales LM])
VAR lastValidDateWithSalesLM = LASTNONBLANK(ALL('Date'[Full Date]), [Internet
Sales])
RETURN
    SUMX(
        FILTER(
            VALUES('Date'[Full Date])
            , 'Date'[Full Date] >= firstValidDateWithSalesLM
                && 'Date'[Full Date] <= lastValidDateWithSalesLM
        )
        , [Internet Sales] - [Internet Sales LM]
    )
```

Let's see how the preceding calculation works.

- The firstValidDateWithSalesLM variable calculates the first non-blank date from the **Date** table hosting the Internet Sales LM measure.
- The lastValidDateWithSalesLM variable calculates the last non-blank date from the **Date** table containing the Internet Sales measure.
- In FILTER(), we generate a virtual table, getting the valid dates that fall between the firstValidDateWithSalesLM and LastValidDateWithSalesLM.
- At last, the SUMX() function iterates through the rows of the virtual table, calculating the variance.

The preceding logic guarantees that we only get valid values for the valid date range. The valid date range starts from the first date with a transaction for **Internet Sales LM** and goes up to the last date with a transaction for **Internet Sales**.

The following figure shows the results:

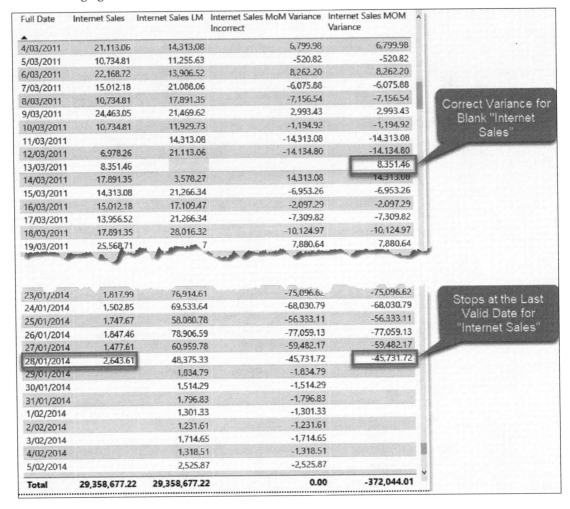

Figure 2.32: The correct calculation shows the correct results when Internet Sales LM is blank and stops the calculation at the last date with an Internet Sales value

Now that we know the logic, we can create the other measure, `Internet Sales LY`, as follows:

```
Internet Sales YoY Variance =
VAR firstValidDateWithSalesLY = FIRSTNONBLANK(ALL('Date'[Full Date]), [Internet Sales LY])
VAR lastValidDateWithSalesLY = LASTNONBLANK(ALL('Date'[Full Date]), [Internet Sales])
RETURN
    SUMX(
        FILTER(
            VALUES('Date'[Full Date])
```

```
                , 'Date'[Full Date] >= firstValidDateWithSalesLY
                    && 'Date'[Full Date] <= lastValidDateWithSalesLY
            )
            , [Internet Sales] - [Internet Sales LY])
```

So far, we have sorted out the initial measures; we can now implement the rest of the scenario using the **Fields Parameters** feature.

Implementing dynamic measure selection with Fields Parameters

Microsoft announced a new feature in May 2022 for Power BI Desktop, making dynamic field selection, such as dynamic measure selection and dynamic column selection, much more manageable. So we can use the Fields Parameters to implement the *period-over-period* challenge in a more manageable way. When we talk about *period-over-period* calculations, the period is the dynamic part of the equation, such as Year-over-Year, Month-over-Month, Week-over-Week, and so on. Our scenario requires **Internet Sales YoY Variance** and **Internet Sales MoM Variance**. So when the end users ask a question about *Internet Sales Variance period-over-period*, they are referring to either of the preceding measures.

Let us revisit the scenario conditions:

- The report contains only one area chart.
- The report enables the users to choose between year-over-year or month-over-month calculations.

Before we start implementing the solution, let us raise some notes:

- The Fields Parameters are different from the **Query Parameters**. The Fields Parameters are accessible from the data model, but the Query Parameters are accessible within the **Power Query Editor**.
- Implementing dynamic measure selection is not the only use case for the Fields Parameters. This section discusses this use case to solve the scenario. We look into the Fields Parameters in more detail in *Chapter 15, New Options, Features, and DAX Functions*.

Let us use the Fields Parameters to implement the scenario by following these steps (sample file: Chapter 2, Time Intelligence.pbix):

1. Click the **New parameter** button from the **Modeling** tab on the ribbon
2. Click the **Fields** option
3. Enter **Internet Sales Variance PoP** for the **Name**
4. Expand the **Internet Sales** table
5. Tick the **Internet Sales MoM Variance** and the **Internet Sales MoM Variance** measures from the **Fields** section
6. Leave the **Add slicer to this page** option ticked
7. Click the **Create** button

The following image shows the preceding steps:

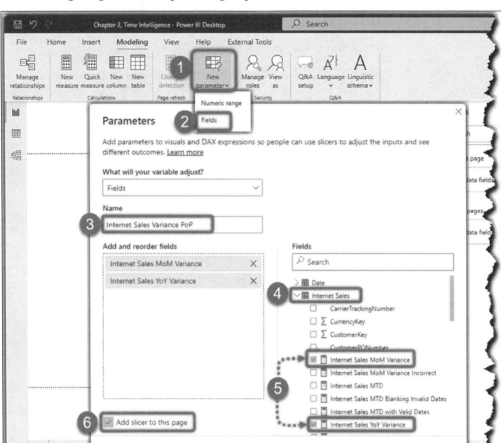

Figure 2.33: Implementing dynamic measure selection with Fields Parameters

Going through the preceding steps makes the following changes:

- Creates a new **Calculated Table** named **Internet Sales Variance PoP** containing the following three columns:
    - Internet Sales Variance PoP
    - Internet Sales Variance PoP Fields
    - Internet Sales Variance PoP Order
- Adds a **Slicer** to the page

We can also see the DAX expressions that Power BI has automatically generated to create the new calculated table, as illustrated in the following image:

Figure 2.34: The changes defining Fields Parameters make

So far, we have created the required Fields Parameters. Let us finish the implementation of the scenario by following these steps:

8. Put an area chart on the report page
9. Put the **Full Date** column from the **Date** table to the *x axis*
10. Put the **Internet Sales Variance PoP** column from the **Internet Sales Variance** PoP table to the *y axis*

As the following image illustrates, the chart shows both **Internet Sales MoM Variance** and **Internet Sales YoY Variance** measures. So the user can select either measure to show on the chart, select both, or select none. But the scenario requires the user always to select only one measure. The following steps show how we achieve this:

11. Select the Slicer
12. Click the Format visual tab from the Visualizations pane
13. Expand the Slicer settings
14. Toggle on the **Single select** option from the **Selection** section

Now, the user can select the desired measure to show on the **area chart**. The following image shows the preceding steps:

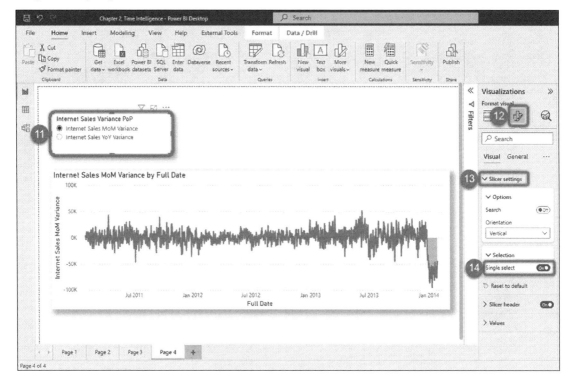

Figure 2.35: Changing the Slicer selection option to Single select

So far, we have overcome a few scenarios related to time intelligence. We learned how to create measures that calculate the metrics more accurately by considering valid date ranges. We also implemented dynamic measure selection. The next section discusses generating a **Date** dimension using DAX.

Generating the Date dimension with DAX

Thinking about a data model without any date values is unrealistic. In many cases, multiple dates describe a single fact. Moreover, we usually need to analyze facts using multiple date elements, such as the year, quarter, month, financial year, public holidays, and so on. In addition, the time intelligence functions in DAX perform the best with a **Date** table. Therefore, having a **Date** table in any model is inevitable. This section describes creating a **Date** table in Power BI using DAX.

Before we begin, take note of the following considerations:

- If a **Date** table is already available in the source system, we do not need to create another using DAX. It is best to avoid creating multiple **Date** tables unless we have a firm justification to do so.
- The **Date** table must have at least one column with the `Date` or `DateTime` data type.
- The column containing the date values must be at day granularity (not year/month).

- The **Date** column must start from 1st January of the starting year and go up to 31st December of the ending year.
- The date range in the **Date** table must be continuous, so there are no gaps between the dates.

It is a good practice to ask the business to provide the date range they would like to cover. We can find the start date from the data model by looking at the fact tables to find the minimum date. But the end date is usually not that simple. So we have to ask the business to understand the date-related requirements. Some prefer the end date to be the 31st December in the current year, while others require a broader date range.

The following two DAX functions can help us to identify the date range:

- `CALENDARAUTO()`: Searches across the data model, among all columns with `Date` or `DateTime` data types, and finds the minimum and maximum dates. Finally, it generates one column named **Date**, which starts on 1st January as the first date and finishes on 31st December as the last date. This is quite handy, but you need to be careful. It also considers the *date of birth* or *deceased date*, which may result in irrelevant dates in the model. If the data contains an unknown date from the past (01/01/1900) and an unknown date from the future (31/12/9999), the `CALENDARAUTO()` function also considers those dates, resulting in an unnecessarily large **Date** table. Therefore, we have to tailor the results.
- `CALENDAR()`: Accepts a start date and an end date. Both the start and end dates must be in either `Date` or `DateTime` data types. Like `CALENDARAUTO()`, the `CALENDAR()` function also generates a **Date** column containing date values. But unlike `CALENDARAUTO()`, it does not automatically start from 1st January of the start date, and it does not finish by 31st December of the end date. Remember, the date dimension needs to start from 1st January of the starting year and finish by 31st December of the ending year. Therefore, we need to adjust the results.

As mentioned earlier, if, for any reason, we cannot get the start year and end year from the business, then we need to use one of the preceding DAX functions. This can be laborious if we use the `CALENDAR()` function and have many **Date** or **DateTime** columns across the model. Therefore, we can always use the `CALENDARAUTO()` function, which automatically generates the date based on all **Date** or **DateTime** columns across the model. However, we need to review the results. While using the `CALENDARAUTO()` or `CALENDAR()` functions works, there are other points to consider before creating a **Date** table using DAX. Many Power BI developers create a new calculated table with either of the preceding functions and then add calculated columns. While this method works, it is not ideal. The reason is that we are creating a few calculated columns. The calculated columns are generated on the fly. Whether we use them in the visuals or not, the data gets loaded into memory at creation time, and we need to close the Power BI file to release the allocated memory.

On the other hand, calculated tables interact differently with memory. The calculated tables are also created on the fly. However, the data is not loaded into the memory unless we use the columns in a visual. So, it is best practice to add the required columns in the **Date** table within the DAX expression to create the calculated table, rather than creating the calculated table and adding those columns as calculated columns later.

The following DAX expressions generate a basic **Date** table using `CALENDARAUTO()`:

```
Date =
VAR firstOrderDate = MIN('Internet Sales'[OrderDate])
VAR lastOrderDate = MAX('Internet Sales'[OrderDate])
RETURN
ADDCOLUMNS(
    SELECTCOLUMNS(
            CALENDARAUTO()
            , "Full Date"
            , [Date]
            )
    , "DateKey", VALUE(FORMAT([Full Date], "yyyyMMdd"))
    , "Quarter", CONCATENATE("Q ", QUARTER([Full Date]))
    , "Month", FORMAT([Full Date], "MMMM")
    , "Month Short", FORMAT([Full Date], "MMM")
    , "MonthOrder", MONTH([Full Date])
    , "Week", CONCATENATE("Wk ", WEEKNUM([Full Date]))
    , "Day", FORMAT([Full Date], "dddd")
    , "Day Short", FORMAT([Full Date], "ddd")
    , "Day of Month", DAY([Full Date])
    , "DayOrder", WEEKDAY([Full Date], 2) //First day is Monday
    , "Year Month", FORMAT([Full Date], "yyyy-MM")
    , "IsValidDate", AND([Full Date] >= firstOrderDate, [Full Date] <= lastOrderDate)
)
```

The following figure shows the results of running the preceding code:

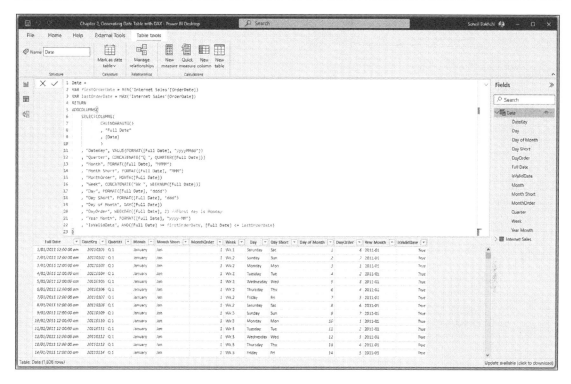

Figure 2.36: Creating a Date table with DAX

The preceding DAX expression uses the `CALENDARAUTO()` function, which automatically generates date ranges from the *1st January* of the minimum date value and *31st December* of the maximum date value across the entire data model. We then used the `SELECTCOLUMNS()` function to name the [Date] column Full Date. We finally used the `ADDCOLUMNS()` function to add some other date-related columns. The firstOrderDate and lastOrderDate are two variables to get the minimum and maximum of **OrderDate**, which later are used for creating the **IsValidDate** column.

Marking a Date table as a date table

So far, we have discussed the importance of having a **Date** table in our model and looked at some related scenarios. This section explains an essential aspect of the **Date** dimension. As discussed in the previous section, time intelligence functions work best with a **Date** table. In many cases, we only keep the date keys in the fact tables. These date keys are then used in the relationship between the fact tables and the **Date** dimension. To ensure the time intelligence functions work correctly, we need to set a unique identifier column with either the Date or DateTime data type within the **Date** table. We need the unique identifier when setting the **Mark as Date Table** configuration. Marking a **Date** table as containing dates is super easy. Let us see in a scenario what happens if we do not mark the **Date** table as a Date table.

For this scenario, we use the Chapter 2, Mark Date as Date Table Before.pbix and Chapter 2, Mark Date as Date Table After.pbix sample files.

In this scenario, the business needs to analyze the following measures within a **calendar hierarchy**:

- Internet Sales MTD
- Internet Sales YTD
- Internet Sales LMTD
- Internet Sales LYTD

The calendar hierarchy holds the following levels:

- Year
- Month
- Full Date

> The relationship between **Internet Sales** and the **Date** table is created between **OrderDateKey** from **Internet Sales** and **DateKey** from the **Date** table. Both **OrderDateKey** and **DateKey** are in the Number data type (integer).

The DAX expressions for the preceding measures are as follows:

Use the following DAX expressions to calculate Internet Sales MTD:

```
Internet Sales MTD = 
TOTALMTD(
        [Internet Sales]
        , 'Date'[Full Date]
        )
```

Use the following DAX expressions to calculate Internet Sales YTD:

```
Internet Sales YTD = 
TOTALYTD(
        [Internet Sales]
        , 'Date'[Full Date])
```

Use the following DAX expressions to calculate Internet Sales LMTD:

```
Internet Sales LMTD= 
TOTALMTD(
        [Internet Sales]
        , DATEADD('Date'[Full Date], -1, MONTH)
        )
```

Use the following DAX expressions to calculate `Internet Sales LYTD`:

```
Internet Sales LYTD =
TOTALYTD(
        [Internet Sales]
        , SAMEPERIODLASTYEAR('Date'[Full Date])
)
```

We put a table visual on the report canvas and use the preceding measures adjacent to the `Internet Sales` measure. The following figure shows the results:

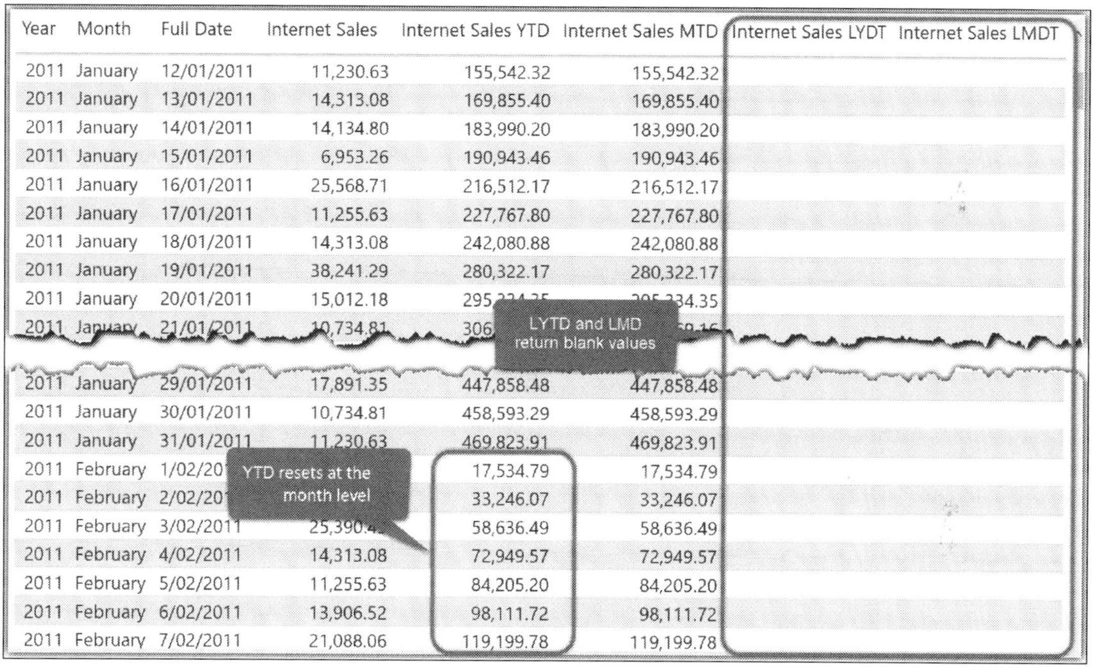

Year	Month	Full Date	Internet Sales	Internet Sales YTD	Internet Sales MTD	Internet Sales LYDT	Internet Sales LMDT
2011	January	12/01/2011	11,230.63	155,542.32	155,542.32		
2011	January	13/01/2011	14,313.08	169,855.40	169,855.40		
2011	January	14/01/2011	14,134.80	183,990.20	183,990.20		
2011	January	15/01/2011	6,953.26	190,943.46	190,943.46		
2011	January	16/01/2011	25,568.71	216,512.17	216,512.17		
2011	January	17/01/2011	11,255.63	227,767.80	227,767.80		
2011	January	18/01/2011	14,313.08	242,080.88	242,080.88		
2011	January	19/01/2011	38,241.29	280,322.17	280,322.17		
2011	January	20/01/2011	15,012.18	295,334.35	295,334.35		
2011	January	21/01/2011	10,734.81	306,069.16	306,069.16		
...							
2011	January	29/01/2011	17,891.35	447,858.48	447,858.48		
2011	January	30/01/2011	10,734.81	458,593.29	458,593.29		
2011	January	31/01/2011	11,230.63	469,823.91	469,823.91		
2011	February	1/02/2011		17,534.79	17,534.79		
2011	February	2/02/2011		33,246.07	33,246.07		
2011	February	3/02/2011	25,390.4	58,636.49	58,636.49		
2011	February	4/02/2011	14,313.08	72,949.57	72,949.57		
2011	February	5/02/2011	11,255.63	84,205.20	84,205.20		
2011	February	6/02/2011	13,906.52	98,111.72	98,111.72		
2011	February	7/02/2011	21,088.06	119,199.78	119,199.78		

(Annotations on figure: "LYTD and LMD return blank values"; "YTD resets at the month level")

Figure 2.37: Our time intelligence functions do not work correctly

As *Figure 2.37* shows, the time intelligence functions do not work correctly. One way to fix the issue is to add `ALL('Date')` to all calculations, and everything works as expected.

Use the following DAX expressions to calculate `Internet Sales MTD`:

```
Internet Sales MTD =
TOTALMTD(
        [Internet Sales]
        , 'Date'[Full Date]
        , ALL('Date')
)
```

Use the following DAX expressions to calculate Internet Sales YTD:

```
Internet Sales YTD =
TOTALYTD(
        [Internet Sales]
        , 'Date'[Full Date]
        , ALL('Date')
        )
```

Use the following DAX expressions to calculate Internet Sales LMTD:

```
Internet Sales LMTD =
TOTALYTD(
        [Internet Sales]
        , DATEADD('Date'[Full Date], -1, MONTH)
        , ALL('Date')
)
```

Use the following DAX expressions to calculate Internet Sales LYTD:

```
Internet Sales LYTD =
TOTALYTD(
        [Internet Sales]
        , SAMEPERIODLASTYEAR('Date'[Full Date])
        , ALL('Date'))
```

The following figure shows the new results:

Year	Month	Full Date	Internet Sales	Internet Sales YTD	Internet Sales MTD	Internet Sales LYDT	Internet Sales LMDT
2010	December	29/12/2010	14,477.34	14,477.34	14,477.34		
2010	December	30/12/2010	13,931.52	28,408.86	28,408.86		
2010	December	31/12/2010	15,012.18	43,421.04	43,421.04		
2011	January	1/01/2011	7,156.54	7,156.54	7,156.54		
2011	January	2/01/2011	15,012.18	22,168.72	22,168.72		
2011	January	3/01/2011	14,313.08	36,481.80	36,481.80		
2011	January	4/01/2011	7,855.64	44,337.44	44,337.44		
2011	January	5/01/2011	7,855.64	52,193.07	52,193.07		
2011	January	6/01/2011	20,909.78	73,102.85	73,102.85		
2011	January	7/01/2011	10,556.53	83,659.38	83,659.38		
2011	January	8/01/2011	14,313.08	97,972.46	97,972.46		
2011	January	9/01/2011	14,134.80	112,107.26	112,107.26		
2011	January	10/01/2011	7,156.54	119,263.80	119,263.80		
2011	January	11/01/2011	25,047.89	144,311.69	144,311.69		
2011	January	12/01/2011	11,230.63	155,542.32	155,542.32		
2011	January	27/01/2011	14,402.34	414,954.95	414,954.95		
2011	January	28/01/2011	15,012.18	429,967.13	429,967.13		
2011	January	29/01/2011	17,891.35	447,858.48	447,858.48		14,477.34
2011	January	30/01/2011	10,734.81	458,593.29	458,593.29		28,408.86
2011	January	31/01/2011	11,230.63	469,823.91	469,823.91		43,421.04
2011	February	1/02/2011	17,534.79	487,358.70	17,534.79		7,156.54
2011	February	2/02/2011	15,711.28	503,069.98	33,246.07		22,168.72
2011	February	3/02/2011	25,390.43	528,460.41	58,636.49		36,481.80
Total			29,358,677.22	45,694.72		16,351,550.34	

Figure 2.38: Resolving the incorrect time intelligence calculations by adding ALL('Date') to all expressions

As the preceding image shows, we now get the correct values. But the best way to resolve the issue is to mark the **Date** table as a **Date** table and specify **Full Date** as the unique date identifier. There are a few ways to do this; here, we show one of them:

1. Right-click the **Date** table from the **Fields** pane.
2. Click **Mark as date table|Mark as date table**.
3. Select a column of either the Date or DateTime data type.

4. Click **OK**:

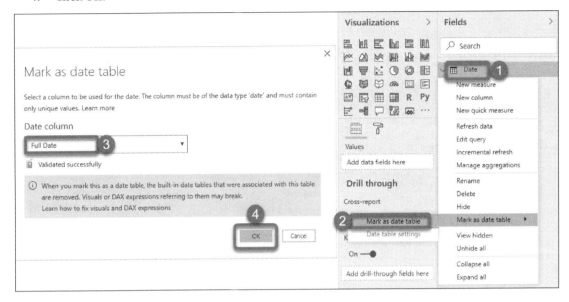

Figure 2.39: Marking Date as the date table

After setting the **Date** table as the **Date** table, we do not need to add ALL('Date') to the time intelligence calculations. All the time intelligence functions now work as expected. You can check the final results in the Chapter 2, Mark Date as Date Table After.pbix sample file.

Creating a time dimension with DAX

So far, we have discussed the importance of having a **Date** table in our data model. But what if we need to analyze the data at the time level, such as at the minute level? This means that the granularity of the fact table would be at the minute level. Suppose we store the data in the transactional database at the second level. In that case, we must aggregate that data to the minute level in the data model. It is crucial to consider the fact table's granularity in the first steps of the data modeling process.

In most cases, if not all cases, it is better to have a separate **Time** table. We also need to have a **TimeKey** or **Time** column in the fact table to create a relationship between the **Time** table and the fact table. This section explains a simple way to create a **Time** table using DAX.

The sample files required in this section are Chapter 2, Generating Time Table.pbix and its source FactInternetSales in Time Level.xlsx.

Let us discuss this scenario further. A business stores all **Internet Sales** transactions at the second level. The business needs to analyze the business metrics in different time buckets, 5 Min, 15 Min, 30 Min, 45 Min, and 60 Min. We are required to resolve this challenge only by using DAX.

Looking at the sample data, we see an **OrderDateTime** column of the DateTime data type in the **Internet Sales** table. As mentioned in the scenario, the granularity is down to the second level. To solve this challenge in DAX, we have to add a calculated column to **Internet Sales** to take the **Time** part of **OrderDateTime**. We use the following DAX expression to create the new calculated column:

```
Order Time = TIMEVALUE(FORMAT([OrderDateTime], "hh:mm:ss"))
```

Chapter 2

This column participates in the relationship between the **Time** table and the **Internet Sales** table.

We also need to create a calculated table with DAX that has a **Time** column at second granularity. The following expressions create the **Time** table, including the time buckets and the **Time** column at second granularity, which is required by the business:

```
Time =
SELECTCOLUMNS(
    GENERATESERIES(1/86400, 1, TIME(0, 0, 1))
    , "Time", [Value]
    , "Hour", HOUR ( [Value] )
    , "Minute", MINUTE ( [Value] )
    , "5 Min",  TIME(HOUR([Value]), FLOOR(MINUTE([Value])/5, 1) * 5, 0) + TIME(0, 5, 0)
    , "15 Min", TIME(HOUR([Value]), FLOOR(MINUTE([Value])/15, 1) * 15, 0) + TIME(0, 15, 0)
    , "30 Min", TIME(HOUR([Value]), FLOOR(MINUTE([Value])/30, 1) * 30, 0) + TIME(0, 30, 0)
    , "45 Min", TIME(HOUR([Value]), FLOOR(MINUTE([Value])/45, 1) * 45, 0) + TIME(0, 45, 0)
    , "60 Min", TIME(HOUR([Value]), FLOOR(MINUTE([Value])/60, 1) * 60, 0) + TIME(0, 60, 0)
)
```

The next step is to format all **DateTime** columns as **Time**. The following figure shows the results of running the preceding DAX expressions:

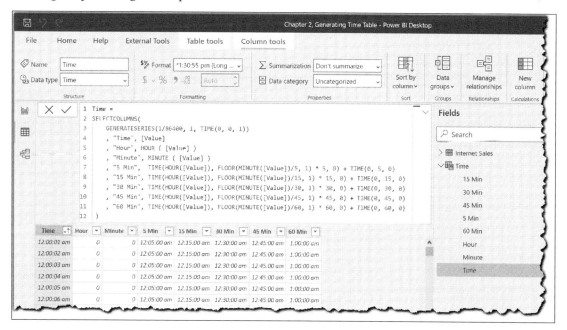

Figure 2.40: Generating a Time table with DAX

The preceding figure shows the results sorted by the **Time** column in ascending order.

The next step is to create a relationship between the **Order Time** column from the **Internet Sales** table and from the **Time** table.

The following figure shows how we can add some area charts to the report canvas and visualize **Internet Sales** by different time buckets:

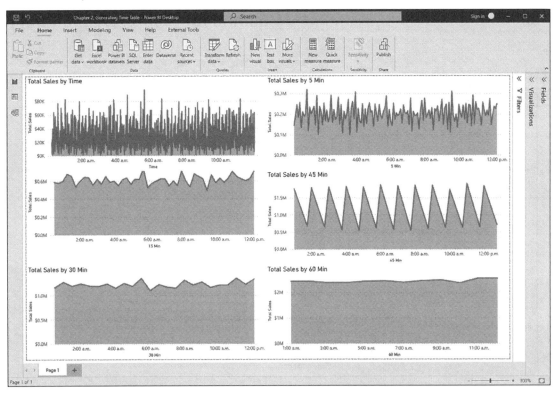

Figure 2.41: Visualizing Internet Sales by different time buckets

The best practice is to move all data transformations, such as generating **Date** or **Time** tables, to the source system as much as possible. If that is not an option for any reason, then it is best to take care of the transformations in Power Query Editor.

Summary

In this chapter, we discussed different aspects of DAX and how it can affect our data modeling. We looked at some real-world scenarios and challenges and how to solve them with DAX.

In the next chapter, we look at the Power Query (M) expression language in more detail. We also go through some hands-on scenarios and prepare a star schema in Power Query step by step.

Join us on Discord!

Join The Big Data and Analytics Community on the Packt Discord Server!

Hang out with 558 other members and enjoy free voice and text chat.

`https://packt.link/ips2H`

Section 2

Data Preparation in Query Editor

In this section, you will learn how to prepare efficient data models in Query Editor. This section is all about transitioning from theory to reality. It will explain one of the most important aspects of data modeling, which is data preparation.

Not everyone has the luxury of having a pre-built data warehouse; therefore, it is important to know how to build dimensions and facts in Query Editor. Power BI leverages the power of Power Query in Query Editor, so this chapter quickly introduces the Power Query language from a data modeling perspective and then explains how to make all components needed in the star schema available for use in the data model layer in Power BI.

We will explain different techniques in data modeling along with real-world, hands-on scenarios. We will also discuss common pitfalls that can easily turn building a simple report into a nightmare and ways to avoid falling into those traps.

This section comprises the following chapters:

- *Chapter 3, Data Preparation in Power Query Editor*
- *Chapter 4, Getting Data from Various Sources*
- *Chapter 5, Common Data Preparation Steps*
- *Chapter 6, Star Schema Preparation in Power Query Editor*
- *Chapter 7, Data Preparation Common Best Practices*

3
Data Preparation in Power Query Editor

In the previous chapters, we discussed various layers in Power BI and went through some scenarios. By now, we know Power BI is not only a reporting tool. Power BI is indeed a sophisticated all-round **Business Intelligence** (**BI**) technology, with the flexibility to be used as a self-service BI tool that supports many BI aspects such as **Extract, Transform, and Load** (**ETL**) processes, data modeling, data analysis, and data visualization. As a powerful BI tool, Power BI is improving every day, which is fantastic. Microsoft's Power BI development team constantly brings new ideas to this technology to make it even more powerful. Data preparation and ETL activities are the BI areas in which Power BI is great for using the **Power Query Editor** in Power BI Desktop. **Power Query Editor** is the dedicated tool in Power BI to write Power Query expressions. Power Query is available in Excel and a few other Microsoft data platform products. This chapter looks at the **Power Query** formula language, also known as the M formula language, in more detail. In this chapter, we learn about the following topics:

- Introducing the Power Query M formula language in Power BI
- Introducing Power Query Editor
- Introducing Power Query features for data modelers
- Understanding query parameters
- Understanding custom functions

We use some hands-on, real-world scenarios to see the concepts in action.

Introducing the Power Query M formula language in Power BI

Power Query is a data preparation technology offering from Microsoft to connect to many different data sources from various technologies, enabling businesses to integrate data, transform it, make it available for analysis, and get meaningful insights from it. Power Query can currently connect to many data sources.

It also provides a **custom connectors software development kit** (**SDK**) that third parties can use to create their data connectors. Power Query was initially introduced as an Excel add-in that quickly became a vital part of the Microsoft data platform for data preparation and transformation.

Power Query is currently integrated with a few Microsoft products such as **Dataverse** (also known as **Common Data Service** (**CDS**)), **SQL Server Analysis Services Tabular models** (**SSAS Tabular**), **SQL Server Integration Services** (**SSIS**), **Azure Data Factory** (**ADF**), and **Azure Analysis Services** (**AAS**), as well as Power BI and Excel. Therefore, learning about Power Query helps data professionals to support data preparation in multiple technologies. You can find the full list of Microsoft products and services using Power Query from the Microsoft official website via this link:

https://docs.microsoft.com/en-us/power-query/power-query-what-is-power-query?WT.mc_id=DP-MVP-5003466#where-can-you-use-power-query

Power Query M is a formula language capable of connecting to various data sources to mix and match the data between those data sources, which then loads into a single dataset. In this section, we introduce Power Query M.

Power Query is CaSe-SeNsItIvE

While Power Query is a *case-sensitive* language, **Data Analysis Expressions** (**DAX**) is not, which may confuse some developers. Power Query and DAX are different worlds that came together in Power BI to take care of different aspects of working with data. Not only is Power Query case-sensitive in terms of syntax, but it is also case-sensitive when interacting with data. For instance, we get an error message if we run the following function:

```
datetime.localnow()
```

This is because the following is the correct syntax:

```
DateTime.LocalNow()
```

Ignoring Power Query's case sensitivity in data interactions can become an issue that is hard and time-consuming to identify. A real-world example is when we get **globally unique identifier** (**GUID**) values from a data source containing lowercase characters. Then, we get some other GUID values from another data source with uppercase characters. When we match the values in Power Query to merge two queries, we do not get any matching values. But if we turn the lowercase GUID into uppercase, the values match.

Comparing two string values with different character cases in Power Query does not raise any errors. The data mashup engine simply compares the two values and returns *false* because the two strings are not the same. So there are no errors to raise; however, the result is incorrect.

For example, the following two GUID values are not equal in Power Query, while they are equal in DAX:

```
D5E99E0E-0737-45B2-B62A-4170B3FEFC0E
d5e99e0e-0737-45b2-b62a-4170b3fefc0e
```

Queries

In Power Query, a query contains **expressions**, **variables**, and **values** encapsulated by `let` and `in` statements. A `let` and `in` statement block is structured as follows:

```
let
    Variablename = expression1,
    #"Variable name" = expression2
in
    #"Variable name"
```

As the preceding structure shows, we can have spaces in the variable names. However, we need to encapsulate the variable name using a number sign (#) followed by quotation marks—for example, **#"Variable Name"**. By defining a variable in a query, we create a **query formula step** in Power Query. Query formula steps can reference any previous steps. Lastly, the query output is the variable that comes straight after the `in` statement. Each step must end with a comma, except the last step before the `in` statement.

Expressions

In Power Query, an expression is a formula that results in values. For instance, the following image shows some expressions and their resulting values:

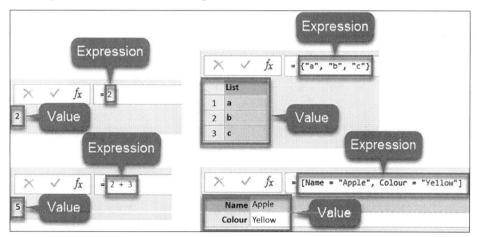

Figure 3.1: Expressions and their values

Values

As mentioned earlier, values are the results of expressions. For instance, in the top left of *Figure 3.1*, the expression is 2, resulting in 2 as a constant value.

In Power Query, values fall into two general categories: **primitive values** and **structured values**.

Primitive values

A primitive value is a constant value such as a number, a text, a null, and so on. For instance, 123 is a primitive **number** value, while "123" (including quotation marks) is a primitive **text** value.

Structured values

Structured values contain either primitive values or other structured values. There are four kinds of structured values: **list**, **record**, **table**, and **function** values:

- **List value**: A list is a sequence of values shown in only one column. We can define a list value using curly brackets {}. For instance, we can create a list of lowercase English letters using {"a".."z"} or a list of numbers between 1 and 10 by using {1..10}. The following image shows the list of English letters from *a* to *z*:

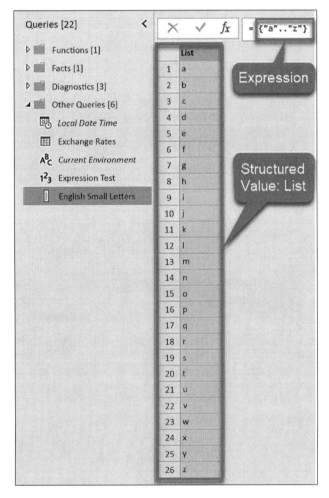

Figure 3.2: Defining a list of lowercase English letters

- **Record value:** A record is a set of fields that make up a row of data. To create a record, we use brackets []. Inside the brackets, we mention the *field name* and an *equal sign* followed by the field's *value*. We separate different fields and their values using a comma, as follows:

    ```
    [
        First Name = "Soheil"
        , Last Name = "Bakhshi"
        , Occupation = "Consultant"
    ]
    ```

The following image shows the expression and the values:

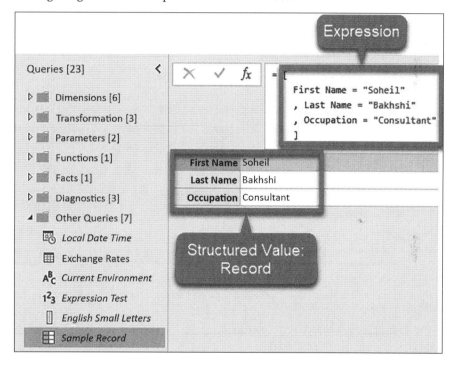

Figure 3.3: Defining a record in Power Query

 When defining a record, we do not need to put the field names in quotation marks.

As illustrated in the previous image, records are shown vertically.

As stated before, a structured value can contain other structured values. The following expression produces a record value containing a list value that holds primitive values:

```
[
    Name = {"Soheil", "John"}
]
```

The following image shows the result (a record value containing list values):

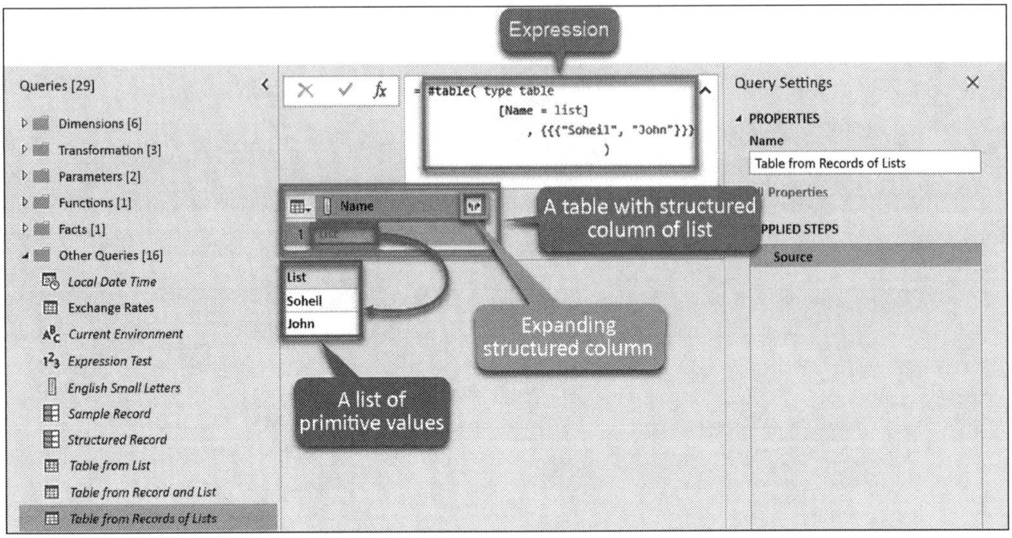

Figure 3.4: A structured value containing other structures' values

- **Table value:** A table is a set of values organized into columns and rows. Each column must have a name. There are several ways to create a table using various Power Query functions. Nevertheless, we can construct a table from lists or records. *Figure 3.5* shows two ways to construct a table, using the #table keyword shown in the next code snippet:

    1. Here is the first way to construct a table:

       ```
       #table( {"ID", "Fruit Name"}, {{1, "Apple"}, {2, "Orange"}, {3, "Banana"}})
       ```

    2. Here is the second way to construct a table:

       ```
       #table( type table [ID = number, Fruit Name = text], {{1, "Apple"}, {2, "Orange"}, {3, "Banana"}} )
       ```

The following image shows the results:

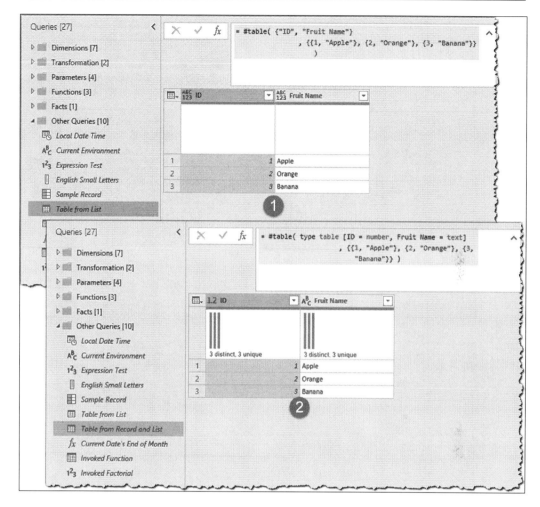

Figure 3.5: Constructing a table in Power Query

As you can see in the preceding image, we defined the column data types in the second construct, while in the first one, the column types are **any**.

The following expression produces a table value holding two lists. Each list contains primitive values:

```
#table( type table
        [Name = list]
            , {{{"Soheil", "John"}}}
            )
```

We can expand a structured column to get its primitive values, as illustrated in the following image:

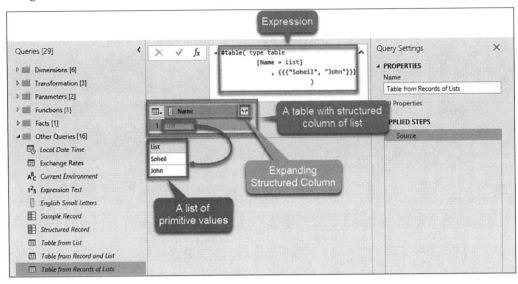

Figure 3.6: Table with a structured column

The following image shows the result after expanding the structured column to new rows:

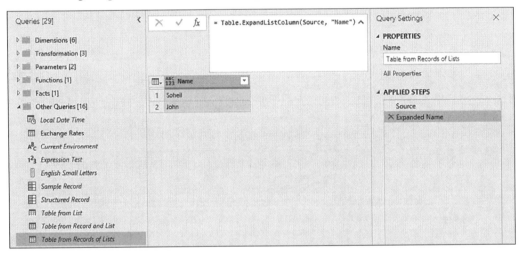

Figure 3.7: Table with an expanded structured column

- **Function value**: A function is a value that accepts input parameters and produces a result. To create a function, we put the list of *parameters* (if any) in *parentheses*, followed by the output *data type*. We use the *goes-to symbol* (=>), followed by the *function's definition*.

For instance, the following function calculates the end-of-month date for the current date:

```
()as date => Date.EndOfMonth(Date.From(DateTime.LocalNow()))
```

The preceding function does not have any input parameters but produces an output.

The following image shows a function invocation without parameters that returns the end-of-month date for the current date (today's date):

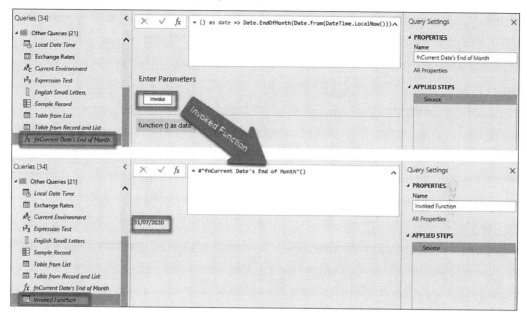

Figure 3.8: Invoking a custom function

Types

In Power Query, values have types. A **type value** classifies other values. There are two general categories for types: **primitive types** and **custom types**.

Primitive types

A value can have a primitive type, as follows:

- `binary`
- `date`
- `datetime`
- `datetimezone`
- `duration`
- `list`
- `logical`
- `null`
- `number`
- `record`
- `text`
- `time`

- type
- function
- table
- any
- none

In the preceding list, the any type is an interesting one. All other Power Query types are compatible with the any type. However, we cannot say a value is of type any.

Using the is operation, we can check if a value's type is compatible with the specified **primitive** type. For instance, the following expression returns `false` as "1" is of type text, not number:

```
"1" is number
```

But the following expression returns `true`:

```
1 is number
```

Custom types

Custom types are types we can create. For instance, the following expression defines a custom type of a list of numbers:

```
type { number }
```

Power Query does not check values against custom types.

Introduction to Power Query Editor

In Power BI Desktop, Power Query is available within **Power Query Editor**. There are several ways to access **Power Query Editor**, outlined as follows:

- Click the **Transform data** button from the **Home** tab, as illustrated in the following image:

Figure 3.9: Opening Power Query Editor from the ribbon in Power BI

- We can navigate directly to a specific table query in **Power Query Editor** by right-clicking the desired table from the **Fields** pane and then clicking **Edit query**, as shown in the following image:

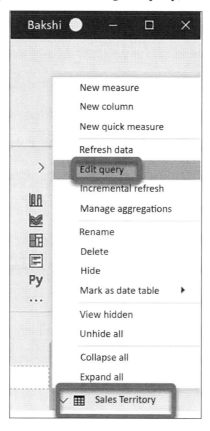

Figure 3.10: Navigating directly to a specific underlying query in Power Query Editor

Power Query Editor has the following sections:

1. The **Ribbon** bar
2. The **Queries** pane
3. The **Query Settings** pane
4. The **Data View** pane
5. The **Status** bar

The following image shows the preceding sections:

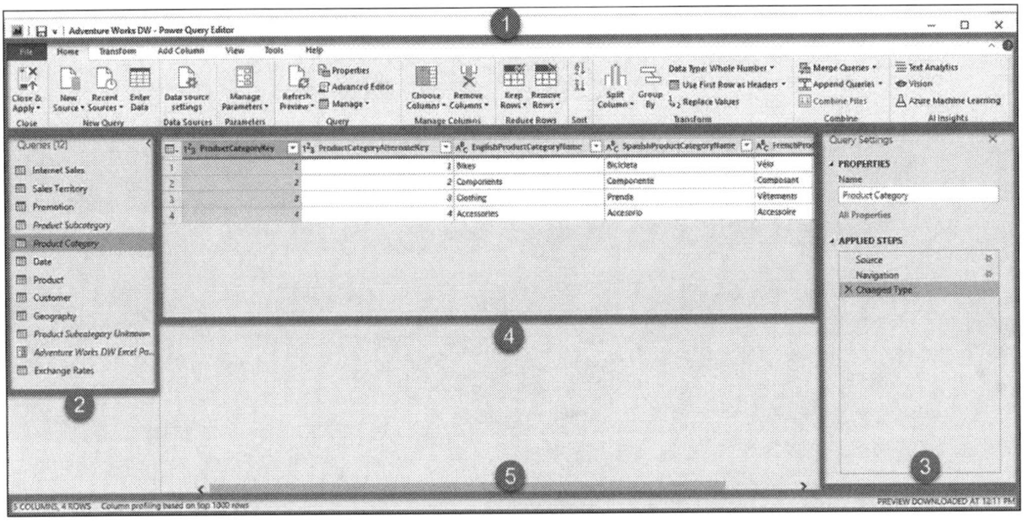

Figure 3.11: Sections of Power Query Editor

The following sections go through some features and tools available in **Power Query Editor** related to data modeling.

Queries pane

This section shows all active and inactive queries and groups. The queries include tables, lists, records, custom functions, parameters, and constant values. In the next few sections, we discuss those.

Tables

A table query includes tables from the data sources, tables created within Power BI using **Enter Data**, constructed tables, and tables that reference other table queries. The icon for tables is ▦.

Custom functions

The function queries are the functions we create within **Power Query Editor**. We can invoke and reuse custom functions in other queries. The icon for custom functions is fx.

Query parameters

With query parameters, we can parameterize various parts of our queries that must be hardcoded otherwise. We can find the query parameters in the **Queries** pane with this icon: ▤.

Constant values

In some cases, we may have a query with a constant result that includes text, datetime, date, datetimezone, and so on. We can quickly recognize queries with constant output from their icon depending on the resulting data type. For instance, if the query output is datetime, then the query icon would be 📅, or if the output is text, then the iconography would be A^B_C.

Chapter 3

Groups

We can organize the **Queries** pane by grouping queries as follows:

- Select relevant tables to group by pressing and keeping the *Ctrl* key on your keyboard and clicking the desired tables from the **Queries** pane.
- Right-click on the mouse and select **Move To Group**.
- Click **New Group...** from the context menu.

The following image shows the preceding steps to group selected tables:

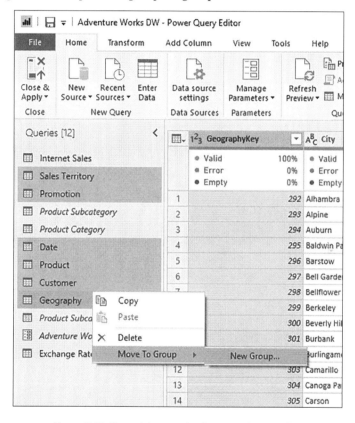

Figure 3.12: Organizing queries in Power Query Editor

It is good practice to organize the queries, especially in larger models that may have many queries referencing other queries.

The following image illustrates what organized queries may look like:

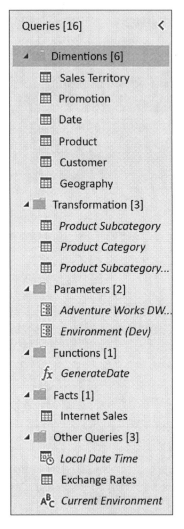

Figure 3.13: Organized queries in Power Query Editor

Query Settings pane

This pane, located on the right side of the **Power Query Editor** window, contains all query properties and all transformation steps applied to the selected query (from the **Queries** pane). The **Query Settings** pane disappears if the selected query is a query parameter.

The **Query Settings** pane has two parts: **PROPERTIES** and **APPLIED STEPS**, as illustrated in the following image:

Chapter 3

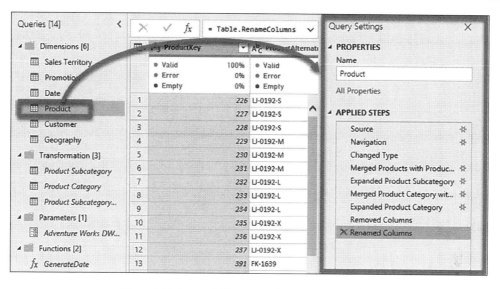

Figure 3.14: Query Settings pane in Power Query Editor

Query Properties

We can rename a selected query by typing a new name in the **Name** textbox. We can also set some other properties by clicking **All Properties**, as shown in the following image:

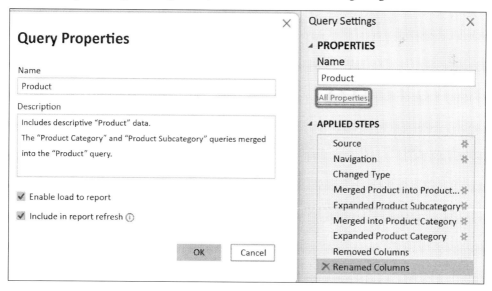

Figure 3.15: Query Properties from the Query Settings pane

Here is what we can see in the preceding image:

- **Name:** This is, again, the query name.
- **Description:** We can type in some descriptions for the query. This is useful as it can help us with documentation.

- **Enable load to report:** When enabled, data will be loaded into the data model from the source system(s). As you see in *Figure 3.15*, we merged the **Product** query with two other queries. Each query may come from a different data source. When this option is disabled, data will not be loaded into the data model. However, if other queries reference this query, data will flow through all the transformation steps applied to this query.
- **Include in report refresh:** In some cases, we need data to be loaded into the model just once, so we do not need to include the query in the report refresh. When this option is enabled, the query gets refreshed whenever the data model is refreshed. We can refresh the data model from Power BI Desktop by clicking the **Refresh** button, or after publishing the report to the Power BI Service, we refresh the data from there. Either way, if this option is disabled for a query, the query is no longer included in future data refreshes.

> The **Include in report refresh** option is dependent upon the **Enable load to report** option. Therefore, if **Enable load to report** is disabled, **Include in report refresh** is also disabled.
>
> It is a common technique used in more complex scenarios to disable **Enable load to report** for the queries created as transformation queries.

As the following image shows, we can also access the query properties as well as the **Enable load** and **Include in report refresh** settings from the **Queries** pane by right-clicking a query:

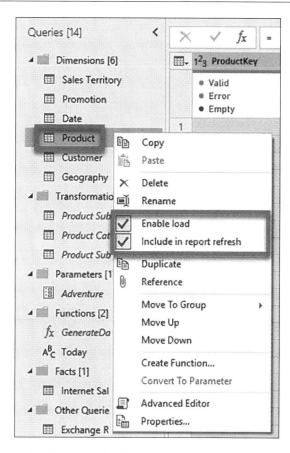

Figure 3.16: Accessing Enable load and Include in report refresh settings from the Queries pane

Applied Steps

The **Applied Steps** contain the transformation steps applied to the selected query in sequential order. Each step usually references its previous step, but it is not always the case. We might create some steps referring to one of the previous steps or not referring to any steps at all. For example, we may want to take some operations over the current date. So we use the `DateTime.LocalNow()` function in a step without referring to any previous steps. The following options are available when right-clicking each transformation:

- **Edit Settings**: This option is enabled if there is a UI available for the selected transformation step.
- **Rename**: It is good to give each transformation step a meaningful name so we can quickly recognize what each step does. Use this option to rename the selected transformation step.
- **Delete**: Use this option to delete the selected transformation step.
- **Delete Until End**: Deletes the selected transformation step and all its following steps.
- **Insert Step After**: Inserts a new step after the selected step.
- **Move before**: Moves up the selected step.
- **Move after**: Moves down the selected step.

- **Extract Previous:** Creates a new query by moving all previous steps to the selected one and references the new query in the current query while keeping the selected step and all its following steps in the current query.
- **View Native Query:** When we connect to a relational database such as a SQL Server instance, Power Query tries to translate the expressions into the native query language supported by the source system, which is T-SQL for a SQL Server data source. This option is enabled if Power Query can translate the selected transformation step into the native query language. If the source system does not have any query languages or Power Query cannot translate the step into the native query language, then this option is disabled. We discuss the query folding concept in detail in *Chapter 7, Data Preparation Common Best Practices*.
- **Diagnose:** We can diagnose a query for performance tuning, analyzing query folding, and more. We look at query diagnostics in *Chapter 7, Data Preparation Common Best Practices*, in more detail.
- **Properties:** We can use this option to add some descriptions to the selected transformation step to explain what it does and how it works in more detail.

The following image shows the preceding options:

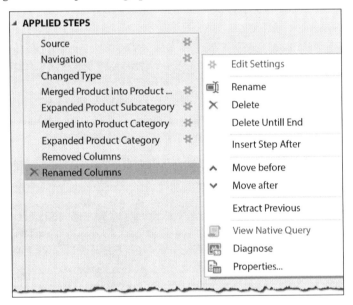

Figure 3.17: The context menu options when right-clicking a transformation step from the APPLIED STEPS pane

So far, we have looked at the **Query Settings** pane in detail. The next section explains the **Data View** pane.

Data View pane

The **Data View** pane is in the center of **Power Query Editor**. When selecting a query from the **Queries** pane, depending on the type of the selected query, we see one of the following:

- A table with its underlying data when the selected query is a table, as shown in the following image:

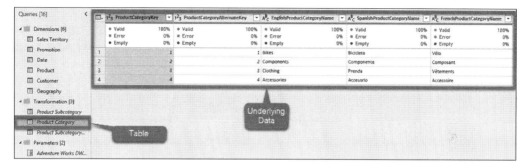

Figure 3.18: The Data View pane when the selected query from the Queries pane is a table

- **Enter Parameters**, to invoke a function when the selected query is a custom function, as shown in the following image:

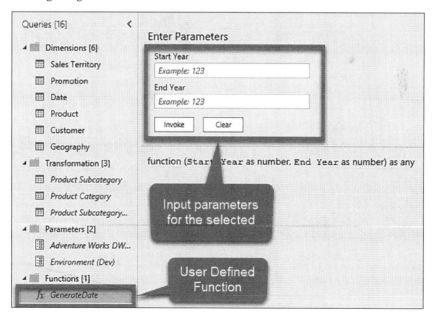

Figure 3.19: Data View pane when selecting a custom function from the Queries pane

- The results of the selected query. The following image shows the **Data View** pane when the selected query retrieves the local date and time:

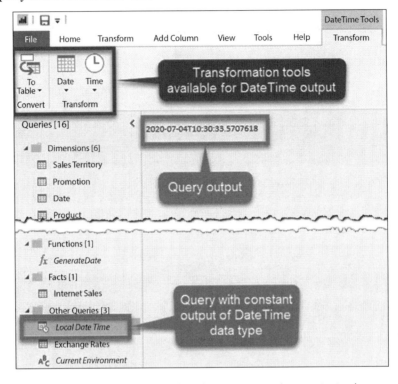

Figure 3.20: Data View pane when the query output is a constant value

Depending on the data type of the query results, different transformation tools appear in the ribbon bar. *Figure 3.21* shows the results of a query that references the **Environment** parameter, which is a query parameter. So, the result of the **Current Environment** query varies depending on the values selected in the **Environment** query parameter.

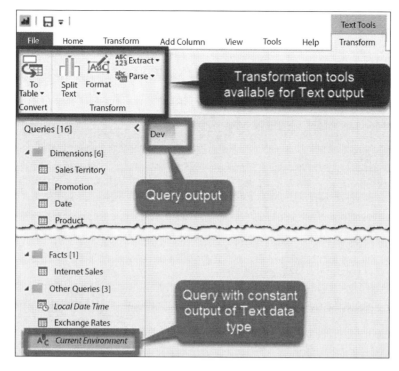

Figure 3.21: Transformation tools available for a query resulting in a Text value

As we can see, the transformation tools available in *Figure 3.20* and *Figure 3.21* are different.

Status bar

At the bottom of **Power Query Editor**, we have a status bar that includes some information about the selected query from the **Queries** pane, as shown in the following image:

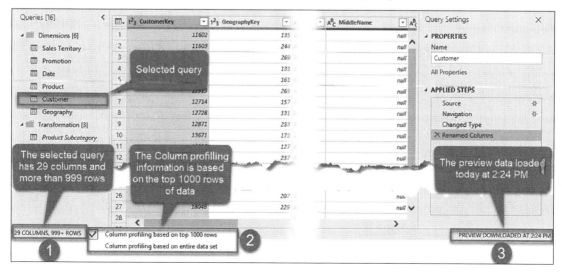

Figure 3.22: Status bar in Power Query Editor

In the preceding image, we can see the following features:

1. Number of columns: We can quickly get a sense of how wide the table is.
2. Number of rows contributing to **Column profiling**: This enables us to indicate whether the profiling information provided is trustworthy. In some cases, the **Column profiling** setting shows incorrect information when calculated based on **1000** rows (which is the default setting).
3. When the data preview refreshed.

Advanced Editor

The **Advanced Editor** contains all expressions related to the selected query. We may use the **Advanced Editor** to create a new query or modify an existing query. The **Advanced Editor** is accessible from various places in **Power Query Editor**, as shown in *Figure 3.23*.

To use the **Advanced Editor**, proceed as follows:

1. Select a query from the **Queries** pane.
2. Either click on **Advanced Editor** from the **Home** tab on the ribbon or right-click the query and select **Advanced Editor** from the context menu. The following image illustrates both options:

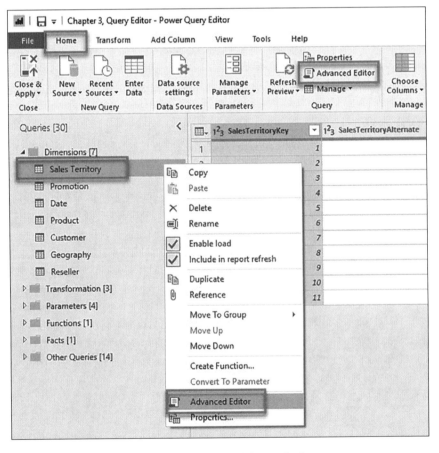

Figure 3.23: Opening the Advanced Editor

Introduction to Power Query features for data modelers

This section looks at some features currently available within **Power Query Editor** that help data modelers identify and fix errors quickly. Data modelers can understand data quality, statistics, and data distribution within a column (not the overall dataset). For instance, a data modeler can quickly see a column's cardinality, how many empty values a column has, and so forth.

As previously mentioned, the information provided by the **Column quality**, **Column distribution**, and **Column profile** features is calculated based on the top **1000** rows of data (by default), which sometimes leads to false information. It is good practice to set **Column profile** to get calculated based on the entire dataset for smaller amounts of data. However, this approach may take a while to load the column profiling information for larger amounts of data, so be careful while changing this setting if you are dealing with large tables.

To change the preceding setting from the status bar, proceed as follows:

1. Click the **Column profiling based on top 1000 rows** dropdown.
2. Select **Column profiling based on entire data set**.

The following image illustrates how to do this:

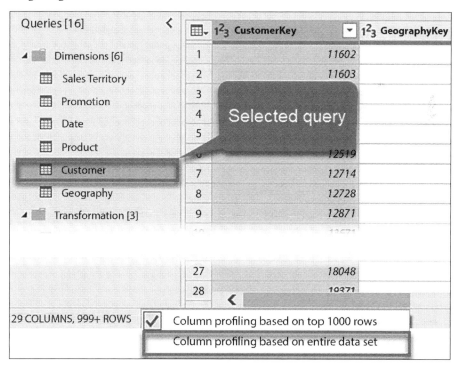

Figure 3.24: Setting column profiling to be calculated based on the entire dataset

Let us have a closer look at these features. The next section explains the **Column quality** feature in Power Query Editor.

Column quality

In **Power Query Editor**, a green bar under each column title briefly shows the column's data quality. This green bar is called the **Data Quality Bar**. A flyout menu reveals more data quality information when we hover over it. The following image shows the data quality of the **Size** column from the **Product** table:

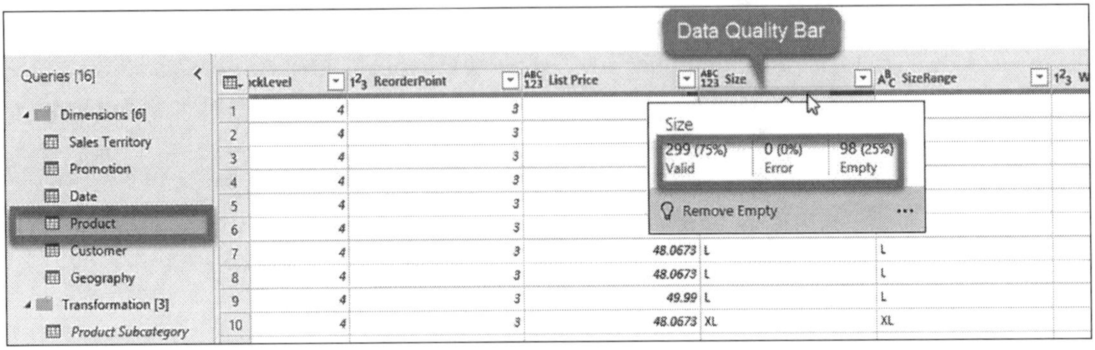

Figure 3.25: Data Quality Bar in Power Query Editor

While this is an excellent feature, it is still hard to efficiently get a sense of the data quality. There is another feature available in **Power Query Editor** called **Column quality**. The following steps show how to enable the **Column quality** feature:

1. In **Power Query Editor**, navigate to the **View** tab.
2. Check **Column quality**.
3. More details are shown in a flyout menu by hovering over the **Column quality** box for each column.

As illustrated in the following image, we can quickly validate columns' values and identify errors (if any), the percentage of valid values, and empty values with the **Column quality** feature. This is very useful for identifying errors. We can also use this feature to identify columns with many empty values so that we can potentially remove them later:

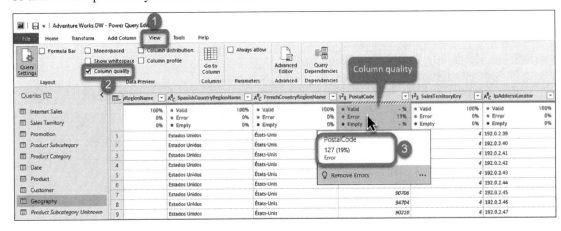

Figure 3.26: Enabling Column quality in Power Query Editor

We can also take some actions from the flyout menu by clicking the ellipsis button at the bottom right of the flyout menu, as shown in the following image:

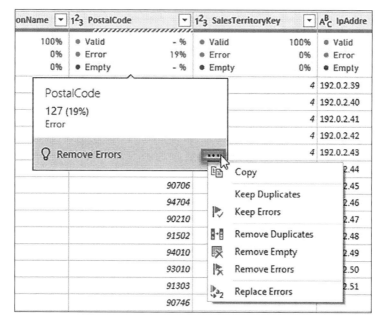

Figure 3.27: Available options from the Column quality box flyout menu

The preceding image shows that we can copy the data quality, which can be helpful for documentation. We can also take some actions on errors from the flyout menu, such as removing any errors. It is better to review and fix errors wherever possible, but we only tend to remove errors where necessary.

There are other use cases for the **Column quality** feature helping us in real-world scenarios.

We want to remove all columns from the **Customer** table with less than 10% valid data. We use the Chapter 3, Query Editor.pbix file for this scenario, available here: https://github.com/PacktPublishing/Expert-Data-Modeling-with-Power-BI-Second-Edition/blob/a39dd14eeac3fdceafd3daf4a45909f6693d68b6/Source%20Code/Chapter%2003/Chapter%203,%20Query%20Editor.pbix

After opening the Chapter 3, Query Editor.pbix file, we head to the **Power Query Editor** where we look at the **Quality** box of all columns. We quickly understand that we can remove the following columns:

1. Title
2. **Suffix**
3. **AddressLine2**

The following image shows that the preceding columns contain a lot of empty values:

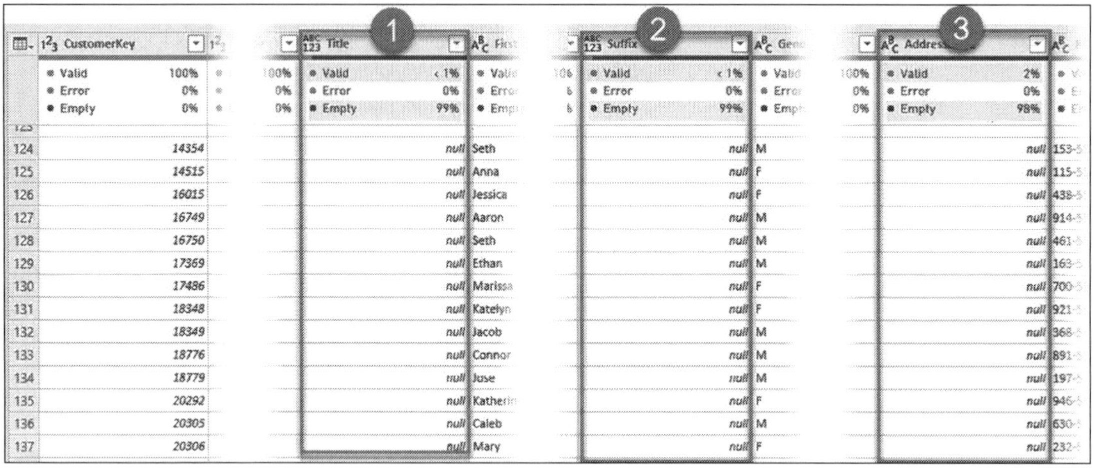

Figure 3.28: Using Column quality to identify columns with less than 10% valid data

We can remove those columns by following these steps:

1. Click the **Home** tab.
2. Click the **Choose Columns** button.
3. Uncheck the preceding columns.
4. Click **OK**.

The following image shows the preceding steps:

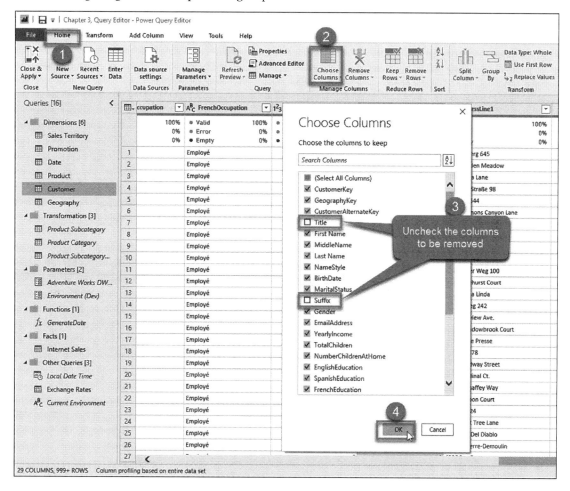

Figure 3.29: Removing columns

Column distribution

Column distribution is another feature that provides more information about the data distribution and distinct and unique values. The **Column distribution** information helps data modelers with the cardinality of a column. **Column cardinality** is an essential topic in data modeling, especially for memory management and data compression.

The general rule of thumb is that we want to get lower cardinality. When the xVelocity engine loads data into the data model, it better compresses the low-cardinality data. Therefore, the columns with lower cardinality have fewer (or no) unique values.

By using the **Column distribution** feature, we can decide whether we load a column into the model or not. Removing unnecessary columns can potentially help us with file-size optimization and performance tuning.

To enable the **Column distribution** feature, click the corresponding feature from the **View** tab, as shown in the following image:

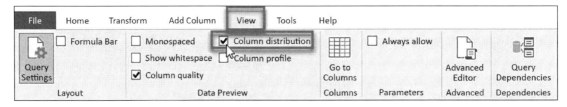

Figure 3.30: Enabling the Column distribution feature from Power Query Editor

After enabling this feature, a new box is added under the **Column quality** box visualizing the column distribution. If you hover over the **Distribution Box**, a flyout menu shows some more information about the column distribution, as depicted in the following image:

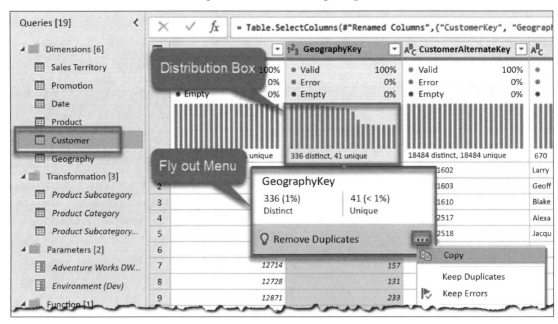

Figure 3.31: Distribution box flyout menu

We can copy the distribution data from the flyout menu and take other appropriate actions, as shown in the preceding image.

Let's look at the **Column distribution** feature in action with a real-world scenario.

Look at the **Customer** table in the Chapter 3, Query Editor.pbix file. The **Customer** table is wide and tall. To optimize the file size and memory consumption, we want to nominate some columns for removal and discuss it with the business:

1. Select the **Customer** table from **Queries**.
2. Set **Column profiling** to be calculated based on the entire dataset.
3. Quickly scan through the **Column Distribution** boxes of the columns to identify high cardinality columns.

These are the columns with high cardinality:

- **CustomerKey**
- **CustomerAlternateKey**
- **EmailAddress**
- **Phone**

These columns are highlighted in the following image:

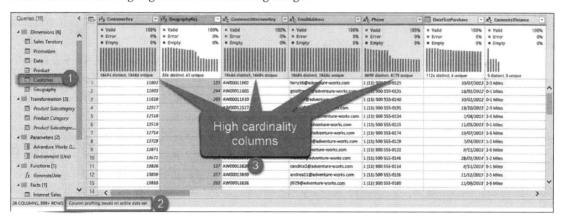

Figure 3.32: Identifying high-cardinality columns in the Customer table

The **CustomerKey** column is not a candidate for removal as it participates in the relationship between the **Internet Sales** and **Customer** tables in the data model. We can remove the **CustomerAlternateKey** column. This is an excessive column with very high cardinality (100% unique values), and it also does not add any value from a data analysis point of view. The two other columns are excellent candidates to discuss with the business to see if we can remove them from the **Customer** table.

If we remove all three columns, we can reduce the file size from 2,485 **kilobytes** (**KB**) to 1,975 KB. This is a significant saving in storage, especially in larger data models.

Column profile

So far, we have looked at the **Column quality** and **Column distribution** features. We can also enable the **Column profile** feature to see more information about a selected column's values. To enable this feature, tick the **Column profile** box under the **View** tab, as illustrated in the following image:

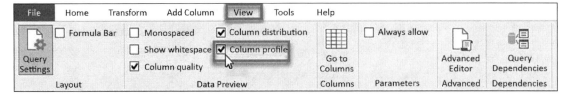

Figure 3.33: Enabling Column profile from Power Query Editor

As the preceding image shows, we can see **Column statistics** and **Value Distribution** by enabling the **Column profile** feature. We can hover over the values to see the count number of that value and its percentage in a flyout menu. We can also take some actions on the selected value by clicking the ellipsis button at the flyout menu's bottom right, as illustrated in the following image:

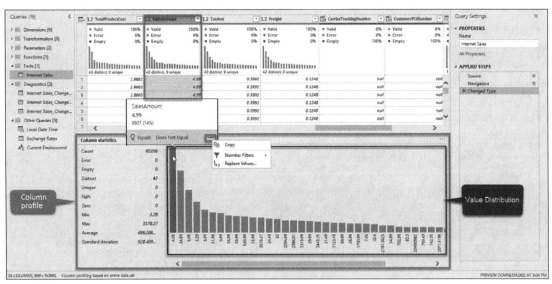

Figure 3.34: Column profile

So far, we have discussed how the Power Query formula language works and how to use **Power Query Editor** in Power BI. We have also looked at some features that can help us with our data modeling. The following section explains a crucial topic: query parameters.

Understanding query parameters

One of the most valuable features is the ability to define **query parameters**. We can then use defined query parameters in various cases. For instance, we can create a query referencing a parameter to retrieve data from different datasets, or we can parameterize filter rows. With query parameters, we can parameterize the following:

- Data Source
- Filter Rows
- Keep Rows
- Remove Rows
- Replace Rows

In addition, we can load the parameters' values into the data model to reference them from measures, calculated columns, calculated tables, and report elements if necessary.

We can easily define a query parameter from **Power Query Editor**, as follows:

1. Click **Manage Parameters**.
2. Click **New**.
3. Enter a name.
4. Type in an informative description that helps the user understand the parameter's purpose.
5. Checking the **Required** box makes the parameter mandatory.
6. Select a type from the drop-down list.
7. Select a value from the **Suggested Values** drop-down list.
8. Depending on the suggested values selected in the previous step, you may need to enter some values (this is shown in *Figure 3.35*). If you selected **Query** from the **Suggested Values** drop-down list, we need to select a query in this step.
9. Again, depending on the selected suggested values, we may/may not see the default value. If we selected **List of values**, we need to pick a default value.
10. Pick or enter a value for **Current Value**.
11. Click **OK**.

The preceding steps are illustrated in the following image:

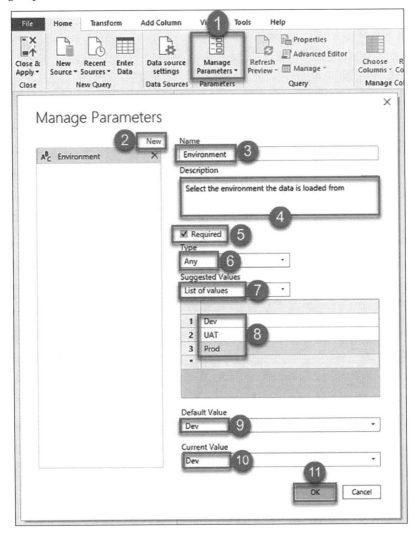

Figure 3.35: Defining a new query parameter

 It is best practice to avoid hardcoding the data sources by parameterizing them. Some organizations consider their data source names and connection strings as sensitive data. They only allow PBIT files to be shared within the organization or with third-party tools, as PBIT files do not contain data. So, if the data sources are not parameterized, they can reveal server names, folder paths, SharePoint **Uniform Resource Locators** (**URLs**), and so on. Using query parameters with **Suggested Values** of **Any** value makes perfect sense to avoid data leakage.

The number of use cases for query parameters is quite vast. Let's look at a real-world scenario when using query parameters comes in handy.

In this scenario, we want to parameterize the data sources. Parameterizing a data source is helpful. One of the most significant benefits of parameterizing data sources is avoiding hardcoding the server names, database names, files, folder paths, and so on.

The business has a specific BI governance framework requiring separate **Development (Dev)**, **User Acceptance Testing (UAT)**, and **Production (Prod)** environments. The business wants us to produce a sales analysis report on top of the enterprise data warehouse in SQL Server. We have three different servers, one for each environment, hosting the data warehouse. While a Power BI report is in the development phase, it must connect to the Dev server to get the data from the Dev database. When the report is ready for testing in the UAT environment, we must switch both the server and the database to the UAT environment. When the UAT people have done their testing, and the report is ready to go live, we need to switch the server and the database again to point to the Prod environment. To implement this scenario, we need to define two query parameters. One keeps the server names, and the other keeps the database names. Then, we set all relevant queries to use those query parameters. It is much easier to implement such a scenario if we use the query parameters from the beginning of the project. The process is easy even if there is currently an existing Power BI report, and we must parameterize the data sources. Once we set it, we do not need to change any code in the future to switch between different environments. Let's create a new query parameter as follows:

1. In **Power Query Editor**, click **Manage Parameters**.
2. Click **New**.
3. Enter the parameter name as Server Name.
4. Type in a description.
5. Check the **Required** field
6. Select the **Type** as **Text** from the drop-down list.
7. Select **List of values** from the **Suggested Values** drop-down list.
8. Enter the server names in the list.
9. Select **devsqlsrv01\edw** as the **Default Value**.
10. Pick **devsqlsrv01\edw** again as the **Current Value**.
11. Click **OK**.

The following image highlights the preceding steps:

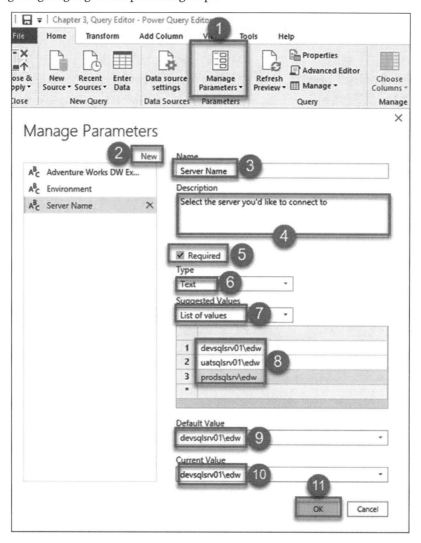

Figure 3.36: Creating a query parameter holding the server names for different environments

We must go through the same steps to create another query parameter for the database names. We can skip this step if the database names are the same. The following image shows the other parameter we created for the database names:

Chapter 3

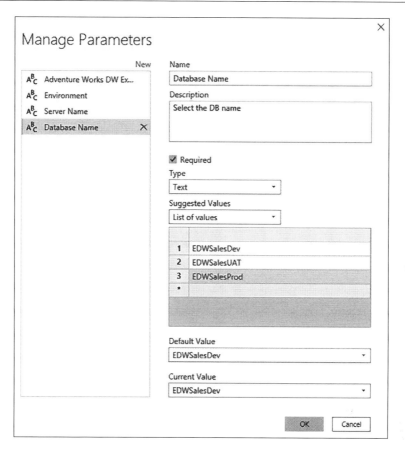

Figure 3.37: Creating a query parameter holding the database names for different environments

If we already have some queries, then we need to modify the data sources as follows:

1. Click a query to parameterize.
2. Click the gear icon of the first step, **Source**.
3. Select **Parameter** from the **Server** dropdown.
4. Select the **Server Name** parameter from the **Server parameters** dropdown.
5. Select **Parameter** again from the **Database** dropdown.
6. Select the **Database Name** parameter from the **database parameters** dropdown.
7. Click **OK**.

The preceding steps are highlighted in the following image:

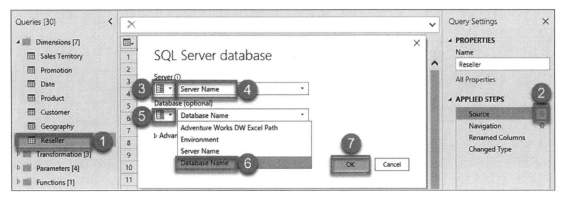

Figure 3.38: Parameterizing a data source

We need to go through similar steps to parameterize other queries. After finishing the parameterization, we only need to change the parameters' values whenever we want to switch the data sources. To do so from **Power Query Editor**, proceed as follows:

1. Click the **Manage Parameters** drop-down button.
2. Click **Edit Parameters**.
3. Select the UAT **Server Name**.
4. Select the UAT **Database Name**.
5. Click **OK**.

The following image highlights the preceding steps:

Chapter 3

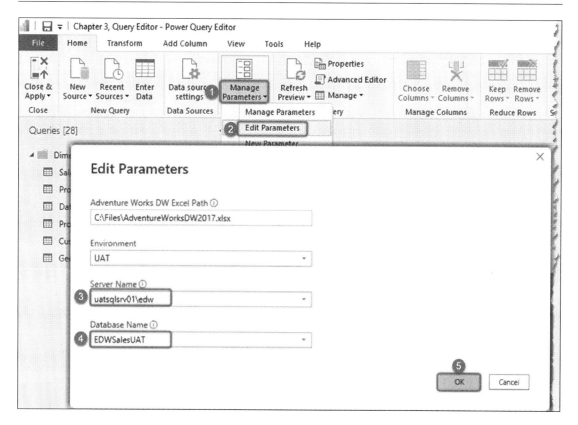

Figure 3.39: Changing query parameters' values from Power Query Editor

After clicking the **Close & Apply** button, the data gets loaded from the selected server and database.

We can also change the parameters' values from the main Power BI Desktop window as follows:

1. Click the **Transform data** drop-down button.
2. Click **Edit parameters**.
3. Select the UAT **Server Name**.
4. Select the UAT **Database Name**.
5. Click **OK**.

The following image shows the preceding steps:

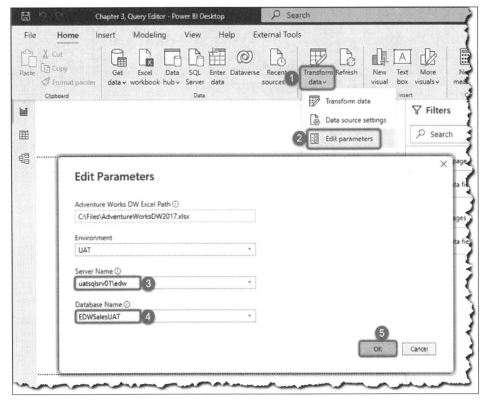

Figure 3.40: Changing query parameters' values from the main Power BI Desktop window

Understanding custom functions

In many cases, we are in a situation where we require repetitive transformation logic. In such cases, creating a **custom function** that takes care of all the calculation logic needed makes sense. After defining the custom function, we invoke it many times. As stated in the *Introducing the Power Query M formula language in Power BI* section, under *Function value*, we create a custom function by putting the parameters (if any) and their data type in parentheses, along with the output data type and the goes-to symbol =>, followed by the definition of the function.

The following example shows a straightforward form of a custom function that gets a date input and adds one day to it:

```
SimpleFunction = (DateValue as date) as date =>
Date.AddDays(DateValue, 1)
```

We can invoke the preceding function as follows:

```
SimpleFunction(#date(2020,1,1))
```

The result of invoking the function is 2/01/2020.

We can define a custom function as an inline custom function and invoke it within a single query in the **Advanced Editor**. The following image shows how we use the preceding code to define SimpleFunction as an inline custom function and invoke the function within the same query:

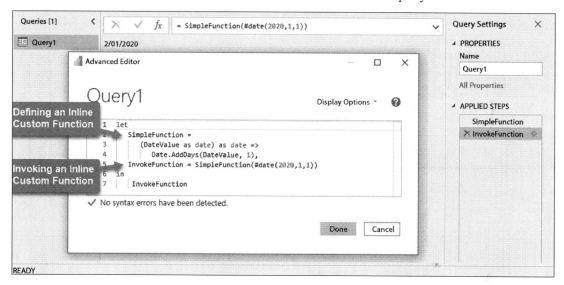

Figure 3.41: Defining and invoking inline custom functions

There are cases where custom functions can help with automating manual and time-consuming development tasks. The following real-world scenario shows how we can save development time using custom functions.

We are tasked to build a data model on top of 100 tables with the following characteristics:

- Each table has between 20 and 150 columns.
- The column names are in camel case without spaces, which is not user friendly.

We have two options after connecting to the data source in the Power Query Editor:

- Manually renaming all columns.
- Find a way to rename all columns in one go per table.

While we repeat the second option for each table, we still save much development time by renaming each table's columns in a single step. We create a custom function to rename all columns and invoke the function in each table.

Let us look at the original column names in one table. The following image shows the original column names of the **Product** table, which are not user-friendly. Note that the status bar shows the number of columns in the table. In this case, the **Product** table has 37 columns. So, it would be very time-consuming if we wanted to rename every column manually to make them more readable:

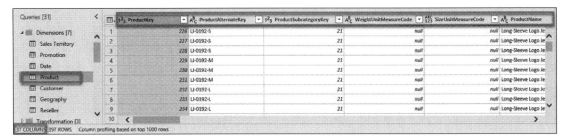

Figure 3.42: Original column names in the Product table

In this scenario, splitting the column names when the character case transitions from lowercase to uppercase would be enough.

Follow these steps to create the custom function:

1. In **Power Query Editor**, create a blank query by clicking the **New Source** drop-down button and selecting **Blank Query**, as illustrated in the following image:

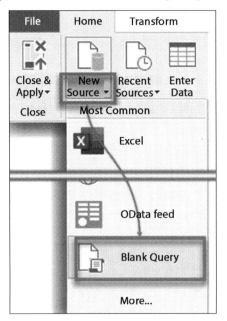

Figure 3.43: Creating a blank query from Power Query Editor

2. Open **Advanced Editor**.

3. Copy and paste the expressions shown next, in *Step 4*, in the **Advanced Editor**, and click **OK**.
4. Rename the query to fnRenameColumns, as shown in the following code snippet:

```
let
    fnRename = (ColumnName as text) as text =>
        let
            SplitColumnName = Splitter.SplitTextByCharacterTransition({"a".."z"}, {"A".."Z"})(ColumnName)
        in
        Text.Combine(SplitColumnName, " ")
in
    fnRename
```

The following image shows what the created function looks like in **Power Query Editor**:

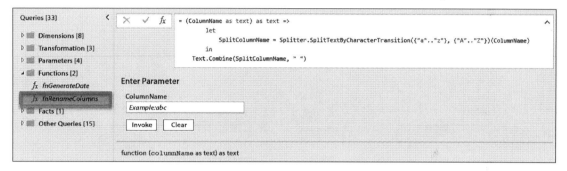

Figure 3.44: Creating a custom function

The preceding function accepts text values and works as follows:

- Whenever a case transition from lowercase to uppercase happens, it splits the text value into a list of texts.
- It combines the split text putting a space between the split parts.

To understand how the preceding custom function works, we need to read the documentation of the Splitter.SplitTextByCharacterTransition() function on the Microsoft Docs website: https://docs.microsoft.com/en-us/powerquery-m/splitter-splittextbycharactertransition?WT.mc_id=DP-MVP-5003466

Note that the Splitter.SplitTextByCharacterTransition() function returns a function, therefore the Splitter.SplitTextByCharacterTransition({"a".."z"}, {"A".."Z"})(ColumnName) part of the preceding expression applies the SplitTextByCharacterTransition function to the function's input parameter, which is ColumnName, resulting in a list of texts.

So far, we have created the fnRenameColumns custom function. Now we invoke it in the **Product** table as follows:

1. Enable **Formula Bar** if it is not enabled already from the **View** tab, as shown in the following image:

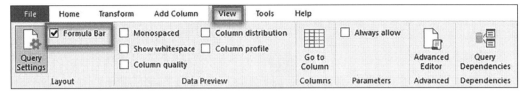

Figure 3.45: Enabling the Formula Bar option in Power Query Editor

2. Select the **Product** table from the **Queries** pane.
3. Click the **Add Step** button (***fx***) from the **Formula Bar** to add a new step. This is quite handy as it shows the last step name, which we use next. The following image shows what the newly added step looks like:

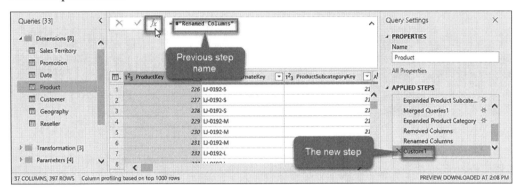

Figure 3.46: Adding a new step from the Formula Bar

4. We now use the Table.TransformColumnNames() function, which transforms column names of a given table by a given name-generator function. This table comes from the previous step, and the name-generator function is the fnRenameColumns function we created earlier. So, the function looks like this:

```
Table.TransformColumnNames(#"Renamed Columns", fnRenameColumns)
```

5. After committing this step, all columns in the **Product** table are immediately renamed.

The following image shows the results:

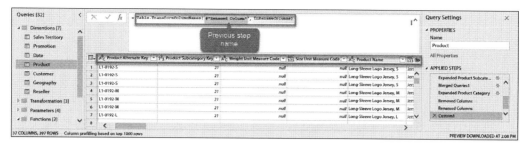

Figure 3.47: Renaming all columns at once

6. The last step is to rename the new step to something more meaningful. To do so, right-click the step and click **Rename** from the context menu, and type in a new name, as shown in the following image:

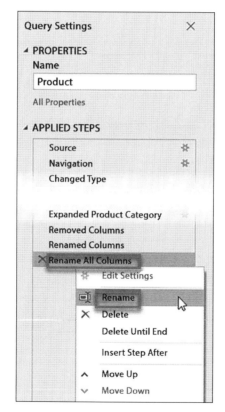

Figure 3.48: Renaming a query step

In this section, we learned how to define and invoke custom functions. We usually invoke the custom function in other custom functions or queries. But it is not always the case. The next section explains custom functions that invoke themselves. Let us see how they work.

Recursive functions

A recursive function is when we invoke a function within the function itself. **Factorial** is a mathematical calculation that multiplies all positive whole numbers from any chosen number down to 1. In mathematics, an exclamation mark shows a factorial calculation (for example, n!). The following formula shows the mathematical calculation of **Factorial**:

$$n! = n * (n - 1)!$$

As the preceding calculation suggests, a **Factorial** calculation is a recursive calculation. In a **Factorial** calculation, we can choose a positive integer (an integer larger than *0*) when *0* is an exception; if *0* is chosen, then the result is *1*. Here are some examples to make the **Factorial** calculation clearer:

```
10! = 10 * 9 * 8 * 7 * 6 * 5 * 4 * 3 * 2 * 1 =  3,628,800
5! = 5 * 4 * 3 * 2 * 1 = 120
1! = 1
0! = 1
```

We need to use an @ operator to reference the function within itself. For example, the following function calculates the factorial of a numeric input value:

```
let
    Factorial =
        (ValidNumber as number) as number =>
            if ValidNumber < 0
            then error "Negative numbers are not allowed to calculate Factorial. Please select a positive number."
            else
                if ValidNumber = 0
                then 1
                else ValidNumber * @Factorial(ValidNumber - 1)
in
    Factorial
```

We return 1 if the input is 0; otherwise, we calculate the **Factorial** recursively.

Did you notice the error part of the code? We can use the error keyword to raise a custom error message. So in the preceding code, we check if the input value is invalid, then we raise a custom error message. The following image shows the result of invoking a **Factorial** function with an invalid number:

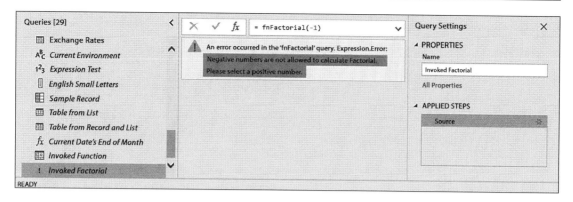

Figure 3.49: Raising an error when invoking a Factorial function with an invalid value

There are cases when we do not want to raise any error messages even if the input is not valid. Instead, we want to show a constant value. The following code shows another version of the Factorial function checking if the input value is a positive value, then it calculates the factorial, otherwise, it returns -1:

```
let
    Factorial =
        (ValidNumber as number) as number =>
            if Number.Sign(ValidNumber) = 1
            then
                if ValidNumber = 0
                then 1
                else ValidNumber * @Factorial(ValidNumber - 1)
            else -1
in
    Factorial
```

The following image shows the result of invoking a Factorial function to calculate 10!:

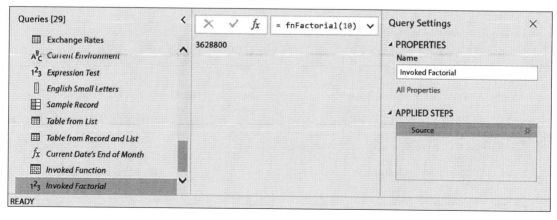

Figure 3.50: The result of invoking a Factorial function to calculate 10!

Summary

This chapter introduced different aspects of the Power Query M formula language and looked at how we can use **Power Query Editor**. We also looked at real-world scenarios and challenges that can directly affect our productivity and learned how to manage our data preparation step more efficiently.

The next chapter discusses getting data from various data sources, connection modes, and how they affect our data modeling.

Join us on Discord!

Join The Big Data and Analytics Community on the Packt Discord Server!

Hang out with 558 other members and enjoy free voice and text chat.

https://packt.link/ips2H

4

Getting Data from Various Sources

In previous chapters, we discussed some aspects of data modeling, including various layers in Power BI, how the data flows between different layers, virtual tables in **Data Analysis eXpressions** (**DAX**), and how they relate to data modeling. We also discussed leveraging query parameters and creating custom functions in the Power Query Editor with the Power Query formula language.

This chapter discusses getting data from various sources and describes some known challenges and common pitfalls in getting data from some sources. We also discuss data source certification and different connection modes to various data sources.

In this chapter, you will learn about the following topics:

- Getting data from common data sources
- Understanding data source certification
- Working with connection modes
- Working with storage modes
- Understanding dataset storage modes

Getting data from common data sources

With Power BI, we can connect to many different data sources. In this section, we look at some common data sources that we can use in Power BI. We also look at common pitfalls when connecting to those data sources. But before we start, let us take a moment to discuss a common misunderstanding among many Power BI developers and users on what *get data* means. When we say *get data*, we refer to connecting to a data source from the **Power Query Editor**, regardless of the data source type. Then, we create some transformation steps to prepare the data to be imported into the data model.

While working in the **Power Query Editor**, we have not imported any data into the data model unless we click the **Close and Apply** button from the **Home** tab on the ribbon bar (or by clicking the **Apply** drop-down button). After clicking the **Close and Apply** button, data gets imported into the data model. At this point, you may ask: *what is the data shown in the Data preview in the Power Query Editor?* The answer is that the data shown in the **Data preview** is only sample data imported from the source system to show how the different transformation steps affect the data. Therefore, we technically connect to the data source and take some transformation steps. When the **Data Import** process starts, it goes through all the transformation steps before landing in the data model.

Now that we know what *get data* means, it is time to discuss the common data sources.

Folders

Getting data from a **folder** is one of the most common scenarios when dealing with file-based data sources. The folder we intend to get data from can contain a mix of different file types, such as **Excel, Access, Comma-Separated Values (CSV), Portable Document Format (PDF), JavaScript Object Notation (JSON)**, a **text** file **(TXT)**, and so on. The data structure can also be different, making it more complex than it looks. One of the most powerful features of the folder connector in Power Query is its ability to automatically retrieve all the files in the source folder, including the subfolders. While this is useful in many cases, it can be an issue when we do not want to combine the files stored in subfolders. In that case, we can filter the results based on the **Folder Path** column to exclude the unwanted data stored in subfolders.

Let us look at the **Folder** data source with a scenario. One of the most common scenarios is when we have to analyze the data from multiple Excel files stored in a folder.

In this scenario, the business needs to analyze the data stored in files exported from an **Enterprise Resource Planning (ERP)** system in a folder using an **Extract, Transform, and Load (ETL)** tool. The ETL tool generates various file formats as outputs. However, the business only needs to analyze the data from the Excel files. The ETL process archives old data in an **Archive** folder. We must import the data from the Excel files stored in the **Excel** folder, excluding the files stored in the **Archive** folder. The following image shows the folder's structure:

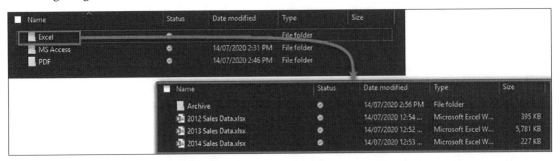

Figure 4.1: The Excel folder includes an Archive folder that must be excluded from the data model

To achieve our goal, we go through the following steps:

1. In Power BI Desktop, click the **Get data** button.

2. From **All**, click **Folder**.
3. Click **Connect**.
4. Click **Browse...** and navigate to the corresponding folder.
5. Click **OK**.
6. Click **Transform Data**.

The following image highlights the preceding steps:

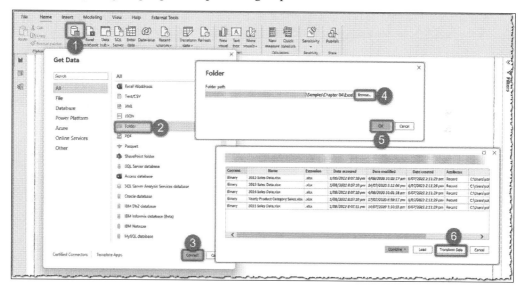

Figure 4.2: Getting data from the folder

The folder structure illustrated in *Figure 4.1* shows that only three Excel files are to be analyzed in the source folder, but *Figure 4.2* shows four files; so we filter the results by the **Folder Path** column, as the following image shows:

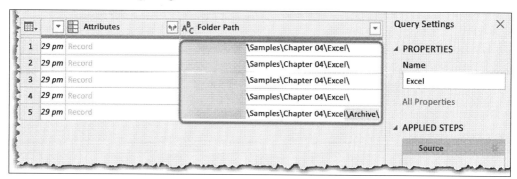

Figure 4.3: Filtering the results based on the Folder Path column

The following steps explain how to filter the results:

7. Click on the filter dropdown.
8. Hover over **Text Filters**.
9. Click **Does Not Contain…**.
10. In the **Filter Rows** window, type in `Archive` as that is the subfolder containing data that we want to exclude from the data model.
11. Click the **OK** button.

The following image highlights the preceding steps:

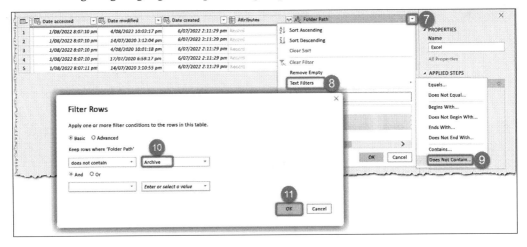

Figure 4.4: Eliminating the Archive folder

So far, we have got the correct files in the query results. The last step is to combine the contents of the Excel files. To do so, follow these steps:

12. Click the **Combine Files** button on the **Content** column to open the **Combine Files** window, as shown in the following image:

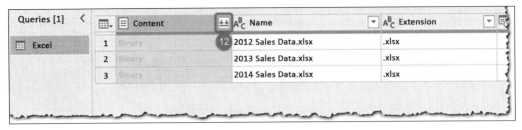

Figure 4.5: Combining files from the column

In the **Combine Files** window, we have the choice to select a sample file. Power BI uses the sample file to create a custom function on the fly to navigate through all Excel files. From here, we have the following two options:

- Selecting a table (if any) or a sheet listed under **Parameter1**
- Right-clicking **Parameter1** and then clicking **Transform Data**

Dealing with data stored in tables is usually more straightforward than dealing with sheets.

13. Click the **Sales_Data** table.
14. Click **OK**.

The preceding steps are highlighted in the following image:

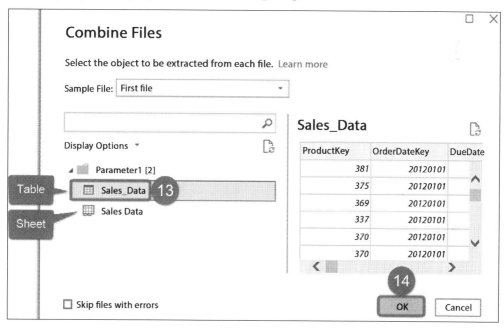

Figure 4.6: Navigating the Excel files to be combined

The preceding steps result in the creation of four new queries in the Power Query Editor, as shown in the following image:

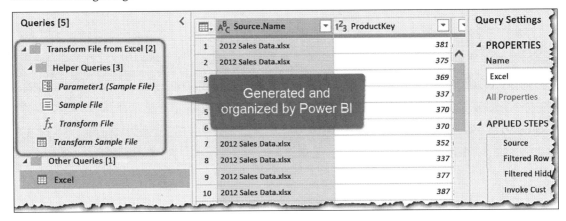

Figure 4.7: Queries and folders automatically created to combine the files

Let us look at the new four queries automatically generated by the **Power Query Editor**:

- **Parameter1**: A **Binary** query parameter used in the **Transform File** custom function and the **Transform Sample File** query.
- **Sample File**: This is our original query with one more step in navigating to the first Excel workbook.
- **Transform File**: A custom function accepting **Parameter1** as an input parameter. Then, based on our choice in *step 13*, it navigates through the Excel file, reading the data from a sheet or a table (in our case, it is a table).
- **Transform Sample File**: A sample query to open the Excel file using **Parameter1**. The sample query is disabled to load into the data model.

In some cases, we need to keep some files' metadata, such as **Date created** (which you can see in *Figure 4.8*). The **Attribute** column is a structured column of records keeping more metadata. We leave this to you to investigate further. But for this scenario, we would like to keep the **Date created** column for future reference. We now need to modify an automatically created step as follows:

1. Click the gear icon on the right side of the **Removed Other Columns1** step.
2. Tick the **Date created** column.
3. Click **OK**.

The following image highlights the preceding steps:

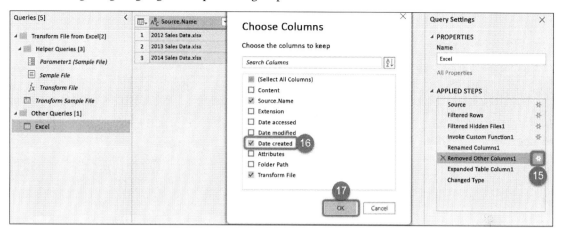

Figure 4.8: Modifying the automatically created steps to keep some columns

We have successfully combined data from multiple Excel files stored in a folder. As the following image shows, we can quickly determine which row is loaded from which Excel file. We also see when that Excel file was created, which is handy for support people in the future. A good use case for keeping the **Source.Name** and **Date created** columns is to track the errors and find out which Excel file is troublesome:

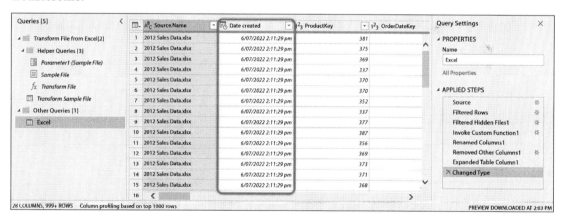

Figure 4.9: The results of combining Excel files stored in a folder

Finally, we rename the **Excel** table to **Sales**.

CSV/TEXT/TSV

While there is a dedicated connector for CSV and TXT files in Power BI, no specific connectors support **tab-separated values** (**TSV**) files. This section looks at these three file types using an example scenario.

In the previous sections of this chapter, we managed to import sales data stored in a folder. Now, the business receives some data dumps stored in various formats. We have **Product** data in CSV format, **Product Subcategory** data in TSV format, and **Product Category** data in .txt format. We need to import the data from the files into Power BI. We use the Chapter 4, Get Data From Various Sources.pbix sample file:

https://github.com/PacktPublishing/Expert-Data-Modeling-with-Power-BI-Second-Edition/blob/ea3530461d68ff6b08af69d1acdbc4c26204a63c/Samples/Chapter%2004/Chapter%204,%20Get%20Data%20From%20Various%20Sources.pbix

The following image shows the files to import to Power BI:

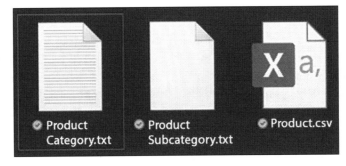

Figure 4.10: The CSV, TXT, and TSV files to be imported to Power BI

We start by getting data from the **Product Category** file, as follows:

1. In **Power Query Editor**, click the **New Source** drop-down button.
2. Click **Text/CSV**.
3. Navigate to the folder holding sample files and select the **Product Category.txt** file.
4. Click **Open**.
5. Power BI correctly detected the **File Origin** and the **Delimiter**, so click **OK**.

Chapter 4

The following image shows the preceding steps:

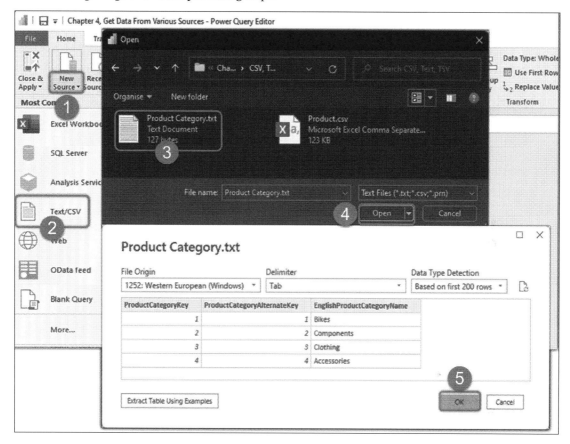

Figure 4.11: Getting data from a Txt file

We are successfully connected to the **Product Category.txt** file from the **Power Query Editor**.

The next step is to get the **Product Subcategory** data stored in a TSV file. As mentioned earlier, there are currently no dedicated connectors for TSV files in Power BI. Nevertheless, that does not mean we cannot get data from TSV files. As the name suggests, TSV files are used for storing tab-delimited data in text format. Therefore, we must get the TSV files using the **Text/CSV** connector. To do this, proceed as follows:

1. Click the **New Source** drop-down button again.
2. Click **Text/CSV**.
3. Navigate to the folder holding sample files, and select **All files (*.*)** from the file type dropdown.
4. The `Product Subcategory.tsv` file shows up; select this file.
5. Click **Open**.
6. Power BI correctly detected the **File Origin** and the **Delimiter**, so click **OK**.

The preceding steps are highlighted in the following image:

Figure 4.12: Getting data from a TSV file

So far, we got data from text-based data sources in the TXT and TSV file formats, and everything went smoothly. But this is not always the case. In reality, we may face many issues when dealing with uncurated file-based data sources. Let us look at one of the most common challenges we may face while dealing with text-based data. Now that we have the **Product Category** and **Product Subcategory** data, it is time to move forward and get the **Product** data stored in CSV format. To get the data from a CSV file, we use the same TXT/CSV connector used in the previous parts to get the data from *.txt, so we do not have to repeat the steps.

The quality bar of the **ProductKey** column in *Figure 4.13* reveals some errors in that column. However, the **Product** table has only 607 rows, as shown in the status bar. Note that an error has occurred within the sample data. Occasionally, errors might not be evident until we import the data into the data model. In our case, we can scroll down through the data preview to find the erroneous cell in row 204. The **ProductKey** value is 226 in the last row before the error happens.

We click on the erroneous cell to see the error message.

Looking at the data more thoroughly reveals some other issues as follows:

- Incorrect date value in the **ProductAlternateKey** column.
- Incorrect data type for the **ProductSubcategoryKey** column.
- Incorrect date value in the **ProductSubcategoryKey** column. The values must be number types.

While we can remove the errors in some cases, in our case, the data shows up in an incorrect column. The following image illustrates the issues:

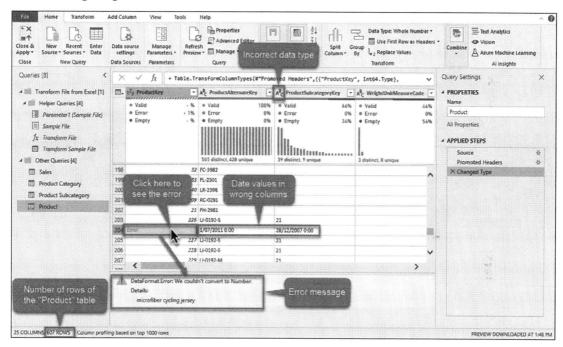

Figure 4.13: Getting data from CSV-produced errors

Let us have a look at the data in more detail. While we have only 607 rows of data, it makes sense to open the CSV file in a text editor such as *Notepad++*.

You can download Notepad++ for free from here: https://notepad-plus-plus.org/downloads/.

In Notepad++, enable **Show All Characters**, and then search the file for where the **ProductKey** value is 226. So, it is now more obvious what has happened. A **carriage return** (CR) and a **line feed** (LF) appear within the text.

When we investigate more, it turns out that the **EnglishProductDescription** column contains **(CR)** and **(LF)** characters. This issue can happen when the user presses the *Enter* key from the keyboard while typing the product description in the source system. Then, the data is exported from the source system into CSV. This issue may happen in any other column with type text. Some other issues in the data shown in the following image are not trivial when we look at the data. Those issues did not produce any errors in the **Power Query Editor** either, so they can be difficult to spot. However, they will cause some issues when we reconcile the data later:

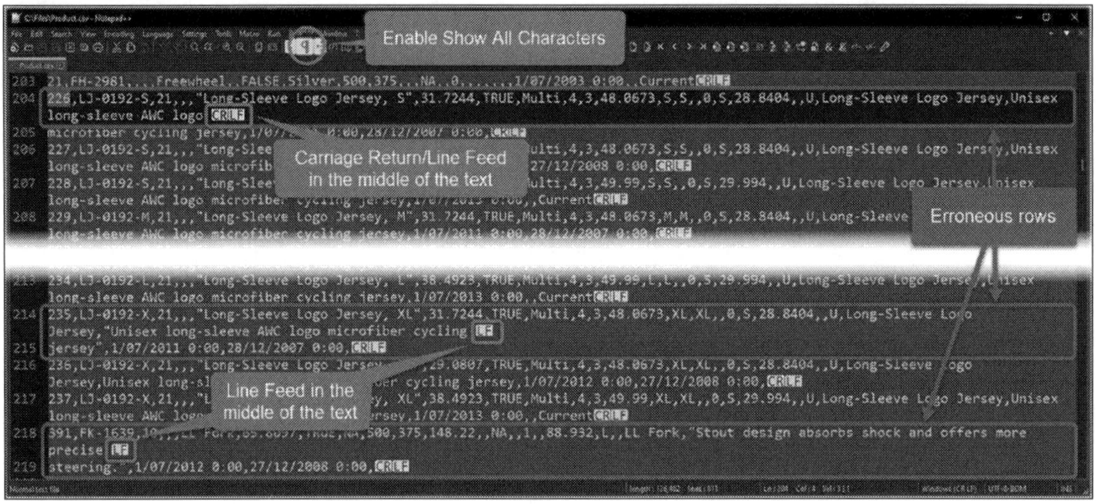

Figure 4.14: The Product.csv file opened in Notepad++ reveals some issues

While we already found the culprit, the same issue might have happened in other parts of the data where it is not that obvious. The easiest way to deal with the issue is to fix it in the source, but in our case, we only have access to the data exported to **CSV** format and not to the source system. Therefore, we have to fix the issue in Power Query. We may think we could replace the **(CR)/(LF)** characters with a blank. But the reality is that the **(CR)/(LF)** characters represent a new row of data. Therefore, we cannot simply replace these with a blank and expect to get the issue sorted.

Luckily, in our case, the issue is not that complex to fix. Looking at the erroneous rows, we can see that there was always a space character before the **(CR)/(LF)** characters. This is also the case with the **(LF)** character. To fix the issue, we first need to get the text and fix the issues before we transform it into the table. While we can fix the issue that way, what if it happens again in the future in some other CSV files? In *Chapter 3, Data Preparation in Power Query Editor*, we learned how to create a custom function. To solve the issue we face in the current scenario, we need a custom function that does the following:

1. Accepts a file path as a text value.
2. Opens the file as text.
3. Replaces all occurrences of **(CR)(LF)** (read Space, Carriage Return, Line Feed) with an empty string ("").
4. In the text results of the previous step, it replaces all occurrences of **(LF)** (read Space, Line Feed) with an empty string ("").

Chapter 4

5. Transforms text in to binary.
6. Opens the result of the previous step as CSV.
7. Promotes the first row as a header.
8. Changes the column types.

With the following expression, we can create a custom function ticking the required boxes:

```
// fnTextCleaner
(FilePath as text) as table =>
let
    Source = File.Contents(FilePath),
    GetText = Text.FromBinary(Source),
    ReplaceCarriageReturn = Text.Replace(GetText, " #(cr,lf)", ""),
    ReplaceLineBreaks = Text.Replace(ReplaceCarriageReturn, " #(lf)", ""),
    TextToBinary = Text.ToBinary(ReplaceLineBreaks),
    #"Imported CSV" = Csv.Document(TextToBinary,[Delimiter=",", Columns=25, Encoding=1252, QuoteStyle=QuoteStyle.None]),
    #"Promoted Headers" = Table.PromoteHeaders(#"Imported CSV", [PromoteAllScalars=true]),
    #"Changed Type" = Table.TransformColumnTypes(#"Promoted Headers",{{"ProductKey", Int64.Type}, {"ProductAlternateKey", type text}, {"ProductSubcategoryKey", type number}, {"WeightUnitMeasureCode", type text}, {"SizeUnitMeasureCode", type text}, {"EnglishProductName", type text}, {"StandardCost", type text}, {"FinishedGoodsFlag", type logical}, {"Color", type text}, {"SafetyStockLevel", Int64.Type}, {"ReorderPoint", Int64.Type}, {"ListPrice", type text}, {"Size", type text}, {"SizeRange", type text}, {"Weight", type text}, {"DaysToManufacture", Int64.Type}, {"ProductLine", type text}, {"DealerPrice", type text}, {"Class", type text}, {"Style", type text}, {"ModelName", type text}, {"EnglishDescription", type text}, {"StartDate", type datetime}, {"EndDate", type datetime}, {"Status", type text}})
in
    #"Changed Type"
```

To create a custom function, we need to create a new blank query, open the **Advanced Editor**, then copy and paste the preceding scripts into the **Advanced Query**. We then rename the query to fnTextCleaner. We can then simply invoke the function with the Product.csv file to fix the issue, as follows:

1. Select the fnTextCleaner function from the **Queries** pane.
2. Type in the file path you stored the Product.csv file in.
3. Click **Invoke**.
4. This creates a new query named **Invoked Function**.
5. Rename the query as Product.

The preceding steps are highlighted in the following image:

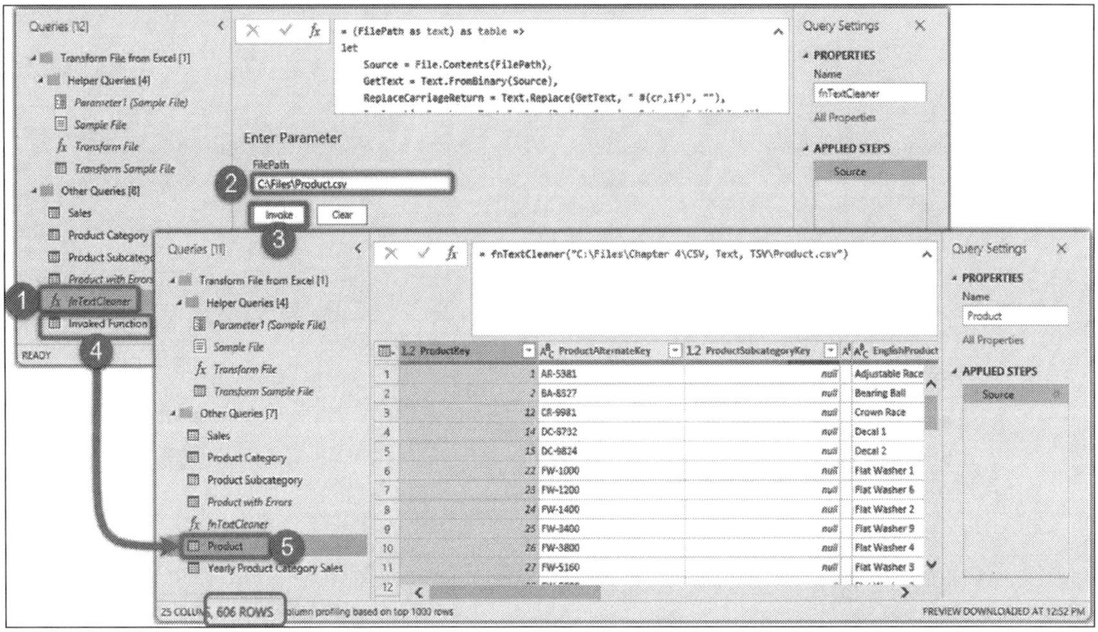

Figure 4.15: Invoking the fnTextCleaner function to fix the text issues in the Product.csv file

As shown in the preceding image, we now get **606** rows, which is correct.

Excel

Excel is one of the most popular data sources used in Power BI. Power BI has a dedicated connector for Excel, but depending on where the Excel file is stored, we may need to use a **Web** connector, which is not as straightforward as it looks. Regardless of the method used to connect to an Excel file, working with Excel data sources is not always that simple. This section explains two of the most common scenarios for connecting to an Excel file: an Excel file stored on a local drive and an Excel file stored in SharePoint Online.

Excel file stored in local drive

In reality, there are many cases where we get an Excel file full of formulas referencing tables, columns, or cells from other worksheets or even from other workbooks. In those cases, we may face some issues and get errors generated by the formulas.

In other scenarios, we get Excel files full of pivot tables with several dimensions. Power BI follows relational data modeling consisting of tables, and tables contain columns, so dealing with multi-dimensional pivot tables is not always straightforward.

Chapter 4

Another common issue with Excel sources is merging cells, which leads to missing data in Power BI. You may think of other complex scenarios that make dealing with Excel data even more challenging. This section looks at one of the most common scenarios: an Excel file containing a pivot table. The `Yearly Product Category Sales.xlsx` file is a sample Excel file we use in this scenario. The following image shows the contents of this sample file:

	A	B	C	D	E	F	G	H
1					Year			
2	Category	Subcategory	2010	2011	2012	2013	2014	Grand Total
3		Bike Racks				$ 36,960.00	$ 2,400.00	$ 39,360.00
4		Bike Stands			$ 159.00	$ 37,683.00	$ 1,749.00	$ 39,591.00
5		Bottles and Cages			$ 280.62	$ 55,008.82	$ 1,508.75	$ 56,798.19
6	Accessories	Cleaners				$ 6,908.55	$ 310.05	$ 7,218.60
7		Fenders			$ 109.90	$ 44,443.56	$ 2,066.12	$ 46,619.58
8		Helmets			$ 909.74	$ 216,028.26	$ 8,397.60	$ 225,335.60
9		Hydration Packs			$ 109.98	$ 38,932.92	$ 1,264.77	$ 40,307.67
10		Tires and Tubes			$ 577.84	$ 232,276.42	$12,675.06	$ 245,529.32
11		Mountain Bikes	$16,974.95	$1,332,364.80	$2,263,420.53	$ 6,339,999.28		$ 9,952,759.56
12	Bikes	Road Bikes	$26,446.09	$5,743,161.12	$3,554,883.93	$ 5,196,092.90		$14,520,584.04
13		Touring Bikes			$ 21,390.87	$ 3,823,410.18		$ 3,844,801.05
14		Caps			$ 71.92	$ 18,870.01	$ 746.17	$ 19,688.10
15		Gloves			$ 73.47	$ 33,379.87	$ 1,567.36	$ 35,020.70
16	Clothing	Jerseys			$ 415.92	$ 165,574.11	$ 6,960.65	$ 172,950.68
17		Shorts				$ 67,400.37	$ 3,919.44	$ 71,319.81
18		Socks			$ 17.98	$ 4,863.59	$ 224.75	$ 5,106.32
19		Vests			$ 63.50	$ 33,718.50	$ 1,905.00	$ 35,687.00
20	Grand Total		$43,421.04	$7,075,525.93	$5,842,485.20	$16,351,550.34	$45,694.72	$29,358,677.22

Yearly Product Category Sales

Figure 4.16: Yearly Product Category Sales data stored in Excel

The aim is to load the preceding pivot table into Power BI as follows:

1. In the **Power Query Editor**, click the **New Source** drop-down button.
2. Click **Excel**.
3. Navigate to the folder containing the Excel file and select the Excel file.
4. Click **Open**.
5. Select the `Yearly Product Category Sales.xls` sheet.
6. Click **OK**.

The preceding steps are highlighted in the following image:

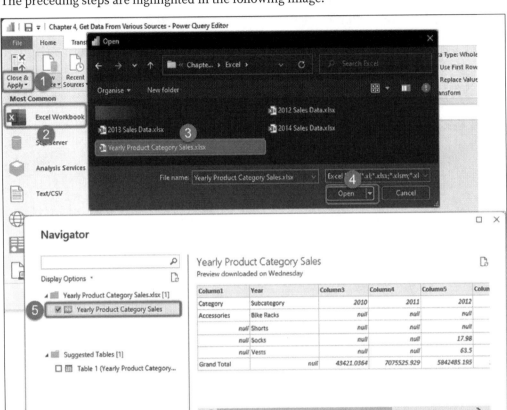

Figure 4.17: Getting data from Excel

Figure 4.17 shows that Power BI has already created some steps. With the following steps, we can turn the pivot table into a regular table:

- The **Changed Type** step is not necessary, so we can remove it.
- We have to remove the **Grand Total** column appearing in **Column8** and the **Grand Total** row appearing in *row 19*.
- We must fill in the missing data in **Column1**.
- The column headers of the first two columns appear in the data. We need to promote them as column headers.
- The year values must be shown in a column.

The preceding points are explained in the following image:

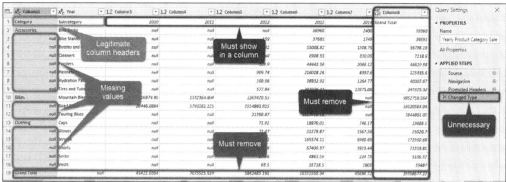

Figure 4.18: Transforming a pivot table

Follow these next steps to fix the preceding issues one by one:

7. Remove the **Change Type** step.
8. Click the **Column8** column.
9. Click the **Remove Columns** button from the **Home** tab, as shown in the following image:

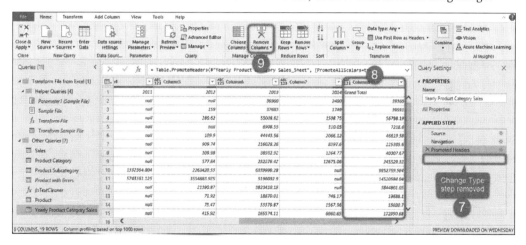

Figure 4.19: The excessive step and column removed

We remove the **Grand Total** row with the following steps:

10. Click the **Remove Rows** button from the **Home** tab and click **Remove Bottom Rows**.
11. Type **1** in the **Number of rows** textbox.
12. Click **OK**.

The preceding steps are highlighted in the following image:

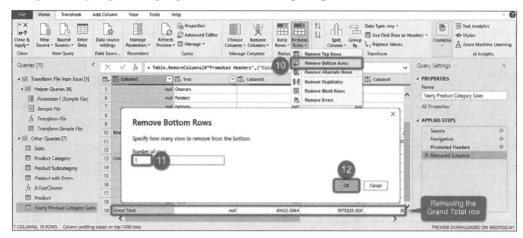

Figure 4.20: Removing the bottom row

Follow these steps to fill in the missing items in **Column1**:

13. Click **Column1**.
14. Click the **Fill** button, then click **Down**.

The preceding steps are highlighted in the following image:

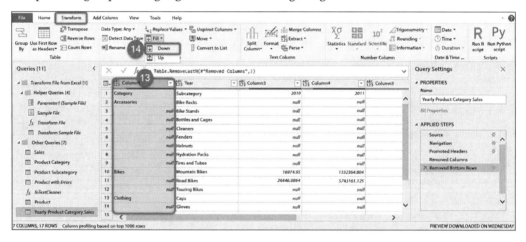

Figure 4.21: Filling in the missing values

The next step is to promote the column headers so that the **Category**, **Subcategory**, and **Year** numbers turn into column headers. Proceed as follows:

15. Click **Use First Row as Headers** from the **Home** tab.

The following image shows the preceding step. Note the results of the previous step to fill in the missing values:

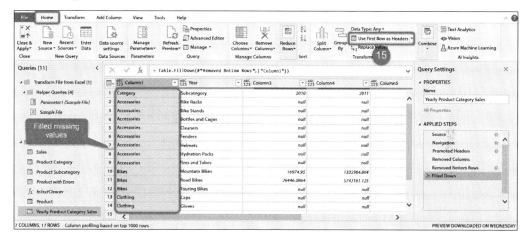

Figure 4.22: Using the first row as a header

We now need to move the year numbers from the column headers to the columns. But the earlier step also added a **Changed Type** step that is still unnecessary, so we also need to remove that by unpivoting the columns with year-number headers. The following steps take care of that:

16. Remove the **Changed Type** step by selecting it and clicking the X icon.
17. Select all columns with a year number by pressing and holding the *Ctrl* key on your keyboard and clicking the columns.

 You can select all columns between the first and last click by pressing and holding the *Shift* key on your keyboard, selecting the first column, and then selecting the last column.

18. Right-click on any column header and click **Unpivot Columns** from the context menu.

The preceding steps are highlighted in the following image:

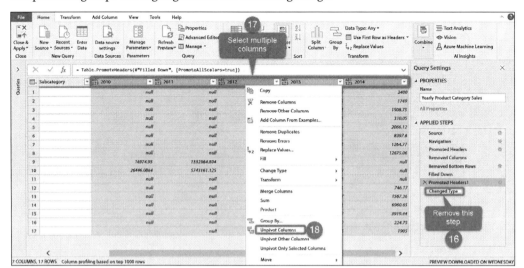

Figure 4.23: Removing unnecessary steps and unpivoting columns

The very last steps are listed here:

19. Rename the **Attribute** column to **Year** and rename **Value** to **Sales**.
20. Change all column types by selecting all columns.
21. Click the **Detect Data Type** button from the **Transform** tab, as shown in the following image:

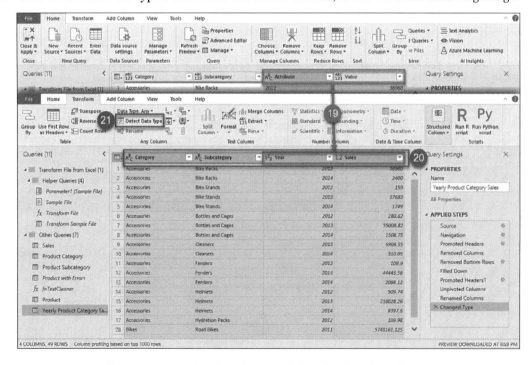

Figure 4.24: Renaming the columns and changing the columns' types

This section dealt with a real-world challenge when working with Excel files. We look at other common data sources in the next few sections.

Excel file stored in SharePoint Online

As stated earlier, the method of connecting to an Excel file varies based on where the Excel file is stored. A common way of storing Excel files is SharePoint Online. This section explains two methods to connect to an Excel file on SharePoint Online. The same approaches would work for Excel files stored in OneDrive for Business.

Method 1: Getting the Excel file path from the Excel desktop app

This method requires having an Excel windows application installed on our machine. In this method, we open the Excel files stored in SharePoint Online in the Excel Desktop App and get the file path from there.

In SharePoint Online, go to the desired document library, then follow these steps:

1. Select the Excel file
2. Click the **Open** button
3. Click **Open in app**

   The following image shows the preceding steps:

   Figure 4.25: Opening the Excel file from SharePoint Online in Excel Desktop App

   This opens the Excel file in the Excel Desktop application. In Excel, follow these steps:

4. Click the **File** menu
5. Click **Info**
6. Click the **Copy path** button

The following image shows the preceding steps:

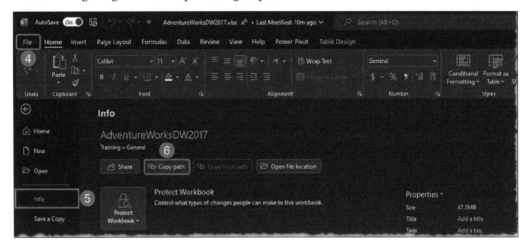

Figure 4.26: Copying Excel path from Excel Desktop App

So far, we have got the Excel file path. The next step is to get data from the copied path in Power BI Desktop.

Open Power BI Desktop and follow these steps:

7. Click **Get data**
8. Click **Web**:

Figure 4.27: Getting data from Excel stored in SharePoint Online in Power BI Desktop

Chapter 4

9. Paste the path we copied from Excel into the **URL** textbox
10. Delete the ?web=1 part from the end of the copied path
11. Click **OK**

The following image shows the preceding steps:

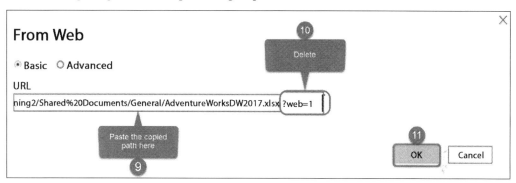

Figure 4.28: Modifying the path copied from Excel to get the data in Power BI Desktop

We get the following error if we miss *step 10*, as shown in the following image:

Details: "The input URL is invalid. Please provide a URL to the file path on SharePoint up to the file name only (with no query or fragment part)."

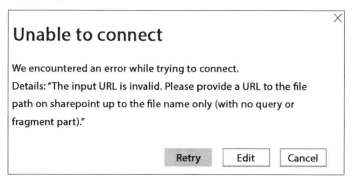

Figure 4.29: An error is raised if we forget to take out the query part from the file path

12. From the **access web content** page, click **Organizational account**
13. Click **Sign in** and pass your credentials
14. Click **Connect**

The following image shows the preceding steps:

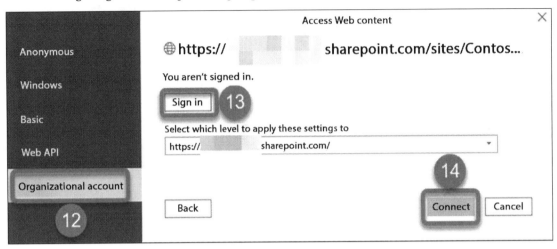

Figure 4.30: Passing credentials for an organizational account to access Excel data from SharePoint Online in Power BI Desktop

Now you can select tables for sheets and start building your reports in Power BI Desktop, as the following image shows:

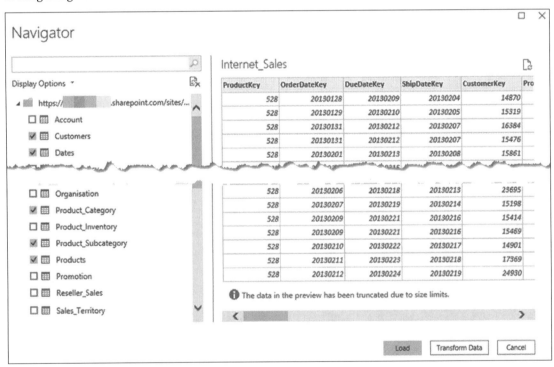

Figure 4.31: Navigating the Excel data stored in SharePoint Online

Chapter 4

Method 1: Getting the excel file path directly from SharePoint

In SharePoint Online, we can get the file path directly from the file details, so this method works for all types of files such as CSV, Excel, and so on. The following steps show how to get the file path in SharePoint Online:

1. Select the Excel file
2. Click the ellipsis button
3. Click **Details**
4. In the **Details** pane, scroll down to find the **Path** section
5. Click the **Copy Direct Link** button

The following image shows the preceding steps:

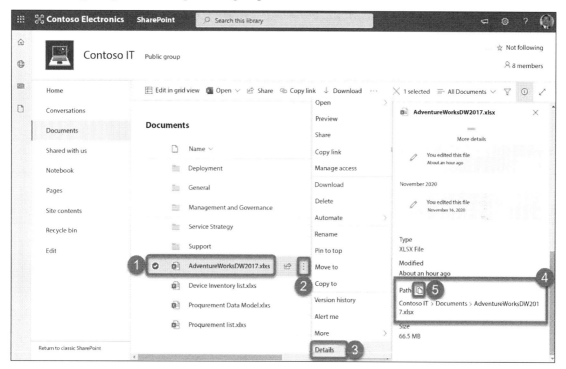

Figure 4.32: Copying a direct file link from File Details in SharePoint Online

In Power BI Desktop, just click **Get data**, then select **Web**, and paste the link in the **URL** textbox as the following image shows:

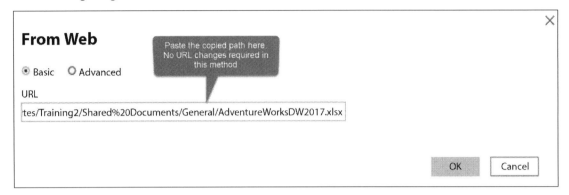

Figure 4.33: Getting data from Excel hosted in SharePoint Online with a direct link

The following list shows the benefits of this method over the first method:

- It requires fewer clicks to get the direct link
- The direct link does not have any query parts, so we do not need to modify the link
- The whole process is easier to remember

The next section explains connecting to Power BI datasets.

Power BI datasets

Considering the increasing demand for team working and collaboration, using Power BI datasets is becoming more and more popular. When we create a data model in Power BI Desktop and publish it to a Power BI Service workspace, the underlying transformation pipelines in Power Query and the data model turn into a dataset. Then, we make the datasets available across the organization. This is an efficient method of collaboration in large Power BI projects. The data modelers create the models and publish them to the service, and the report writers make thin reports on top of the available shared datasets.

 Shared Power BI datasets are not available in the Power BI free licensing plan. The reason is that accessing Workspaces requires a Pro license; therefore, accessing any objects contained in the Workspaces requires a Pro license.

With the Power BI dataset connector, we can Connect Live to a Power BI dataset from Power BI Desktop. In that case, Power BI Desktop becomes a data visualization tool. So, the Power Query editor is not accessible anymore, and the model view is in view mode only. Therefore, any changes in the data model must be applied to the dataset by the data modelers. The reason is that the dataset contains the data model separate from the report. However, we have the option to turn the connection type from **Connect Live** to **DirectQuery**.

When we Connect Live to a dataset, we cannot make any changes to the data model, but we can create report-level measures within Power BI Desktop. The report-level measures are only available within their containing report. Therefore, they are inaccessible from other datasets or reports.

In contrast, if we turn the Power BI dataset connection to **DirectQuery**, we can leverage all the data modeling features such as creating calculated columns, calculated tables, and measures. In this case, Power Query Editor does not show any tables as the actual tables are contained in the connected dataset in Power BI.

 In the *Working with connection modes* section, we discuss different connection modes.

The following steps show the process of connecting to a Power BI dataset in Connect Live mode:

1. Click the **Data hub** drop-down button from the **Home** tab.
2. Click **Power BI datasets**.
3. Select the desired dataset.
4. Click **Connect**.

The following image illustrates the preceding steps:

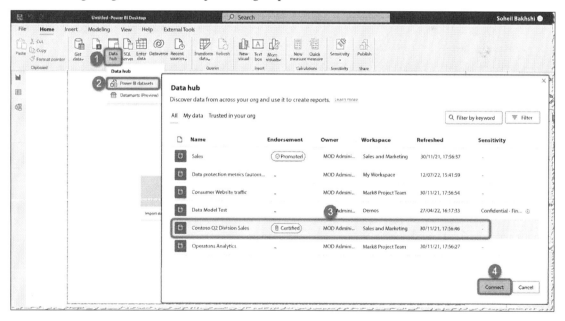

Figure 4.34: Connecting to a Power BI dataset

Alternatively, we can click the **Get Data** drop-down button and click the **Power BI datasets** button from the **Data** section of the **Home** tab, as shown in the following image:

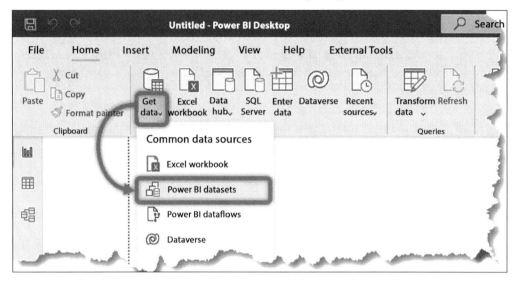

Figure 4.35: The Power BI datasets button from the Home tab

After we connect live to a dataset, only reporting features are available in Power BI Desktop, as outlined here:

1. All tools from the **Modeling** tab are disabled except the **New measure**, the **Quick measure**, and the **Make Changes to this model** tools.
2. The **Data** tab disappears from the left pane, while the **Report** and **Modeling** tabs are still enabled. We will look at the **Modeling** tab later in this section.
3. The status bar shows that we are connected live to the dataset, along with the option to **Make changes to this model**.

Chapter 4

The following image shows the tooling changes in Power BI Desktop after connecting to a Power BI dataset:

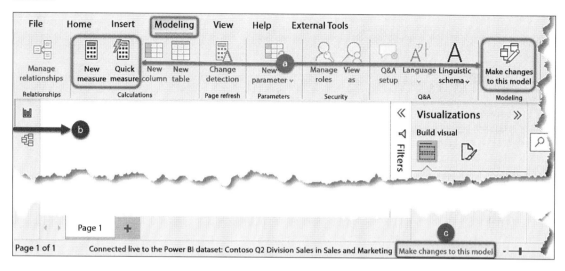

Figure 4.36: Power BI Desktop tooling changes after connecting to a Power BI dataset

As we see in the preceding image, the **Model** view is still accessible from the left pane. If we click the **Model** view, we can see all the tables and their relationships, which is very handy for better understanding the underlying data model. The following image shows the **Model** view:

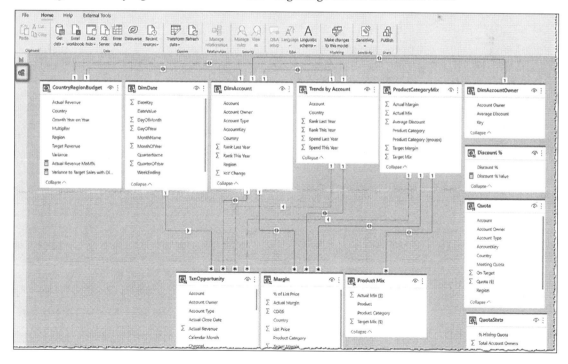

Figure 4.37: The underlying data model of a connected Power BI dataset

We can create new layouts on top of the model, as shown in the following image:

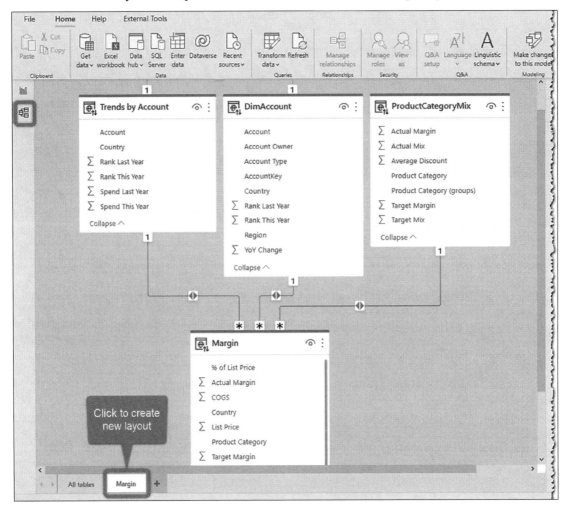

Figure 4.38: Creating new layouts in the data model

Note that the icon is used for the tables in Connect Live.

There is one more point to note: we can only see and access the datasets from workspaces that have **Admin, Member,** or **Contributor** permissions.

Chapter 4

The other method to connect to a dataset is to turn the connection into DirectQuery mode. This has been made possible by the **DirectQuery for PBI datasets and AS** feature currently in public preview. Follow these steps to enable it:

1. Click **File**
2. Click **Options and settings**
3. Click **Options**
4. From the **GLOBAL** section, click **Preview features**
5. Tick the **DirectQuery for PBI datasets and AS** feature
6. Click **OK**

The following image shows the preceding steps:

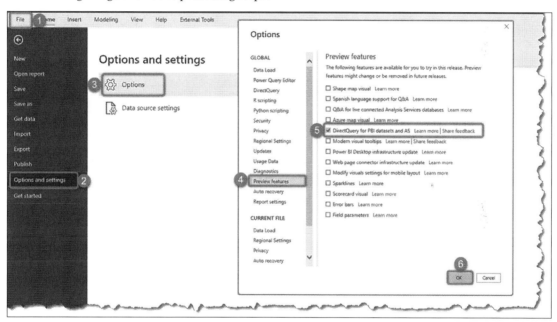

Figure 4.39: Enabling the DirectQuery for PBI datasets and AS preview feature

Now that we have enabled the **DirectQuery for PBI datasets and AS** preview feature, we have various options to connect to a dataset in DirectQuery mode. We have to first connect to the dataset in Connect Live mode, then turn Connect Live to DirectQuery as follows:

1. Click the **Make changes to this model** button from the **Modeling** tab on the ribbon.
2. Click the **Make changes to this model** link from the status bar.
3. From the **Model** view, click the **Make changes to this model** button from the **Home** tab on the ribbon.
4. After performing the preceding steps, a warning message appears; click the **Add a local model** button.

The following image shows the preceding options:

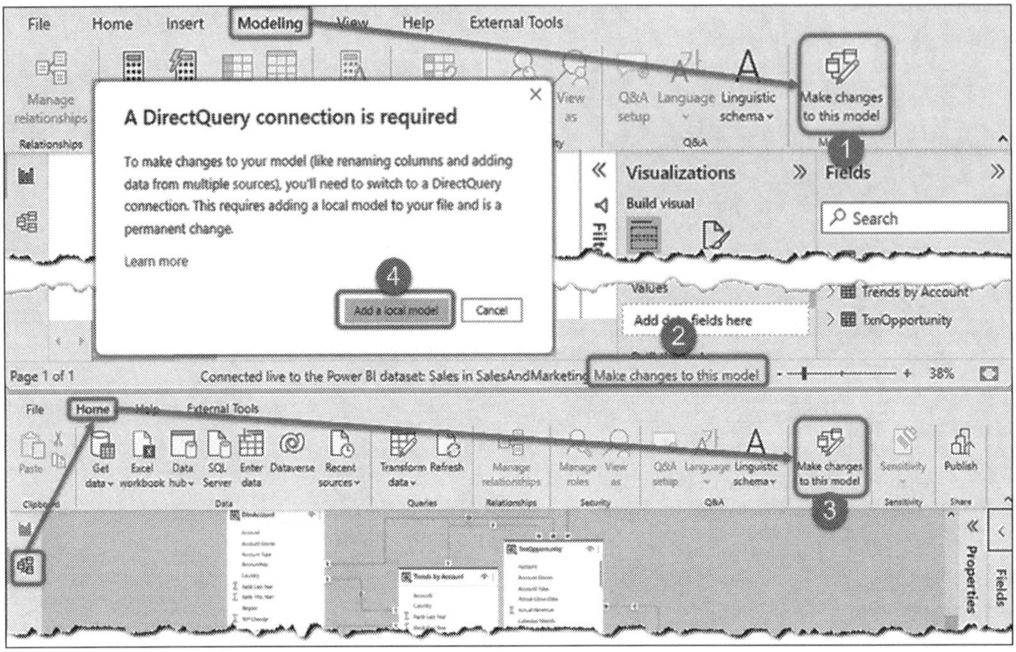

Figure 4.40: Switching the Connect Live connection to a dataset to DirectQuery

5. Keep all the tables selected and tick the **Include tables added later** option.
6. Click the **Submit** button.

The following image shows the preceding steps:

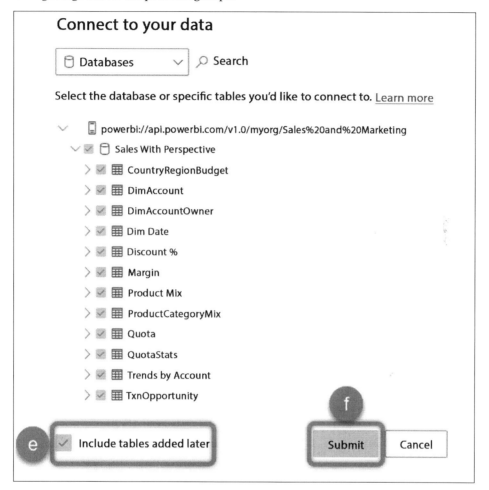

Figure 4.41: Selecting tables to be included in the DirectQuery mode

We can modify the data model after switching the connection to DirectQuery. We can also get data from various sources to create a Composite mode. We discuss this in more detail in *Chapter 14, DirectQuery Connections to Power BI Datasets and Analysis Services in Composite Models*.

The model looks like the following image after switching to DirectQuery:

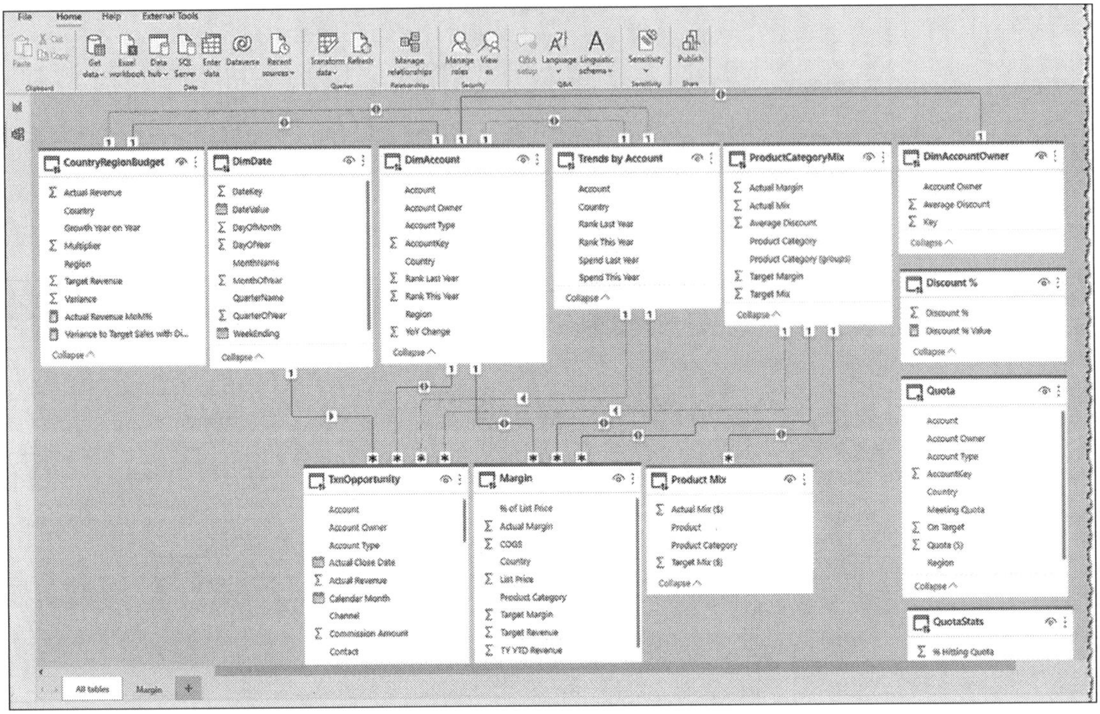

Figure 4.42: The data model after switching to DirectQuery mode

Note that the tables' icon has now changed from ⊞ to ⊟.

Power BI dataflows

A Power BI dataflow is the cloud experience for Power Query in the Power BI Service, and provides organizations with endless self-service data preparation. Creating a dataflow and making it available across the organization increases reusability and improves development efficiency. There is a dedicated connection for dataflows available in Power BI Desktop.

> **DirectQuery** to dataflows is only available on the dataflows created in a workspace backed by either a Premium Capacity or **Premium Per User (PPU)** license.

Before connecting to a dataflow from Power BI Desktop, we must log into Power BI Service from the desktop. The following steps explain how to connect to an existing dataflow:

1. Click the **Get data** dropdown.
2. Click **Power BI dataflows**.
3. A list of all dataflows available to you shows up in the **Navigator** window. Expand the desired workspace.

Chapter 4

4. Expand the dataflow model.
5. Select a table.
6. Click **Load**.

The preceding steps are highlighted in the following image:

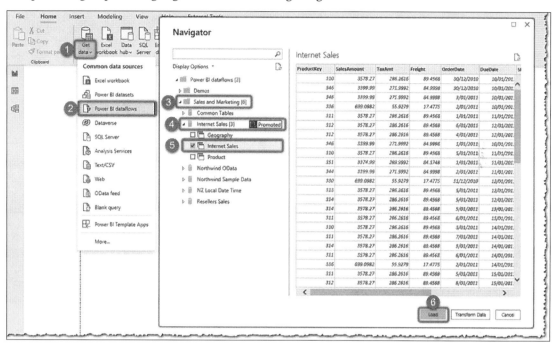

Figure 4.43: Getting data from Power BI dataflows

At this point, if we meet the requirements, Power BI prompts us to select the storage mode from either **Import** or **DirectQuery** mode, as the following image shows:

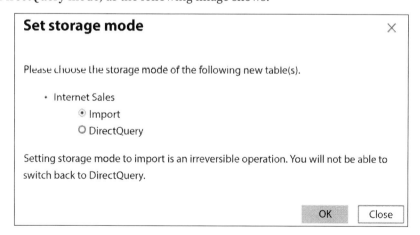

Figure 4.44: Selecting the storage mode when connecting to a Power BI dataflow

We should meet the following requirements to enable the DirectQuery mode in the Power BI dataflow connections:

1. The dataflow must be in a Premium workspace
2. The **Enhanced compute engine** must be turned on as follows:
    a. In Power BI Service, click the ellipsis button of the desired dataflow
    b. Click **Settings**
    c. Expand the **Enhanced compute engine settings** option
    d. Click **On**
    e. Click **Apply**

The following image shows the preceding steps:

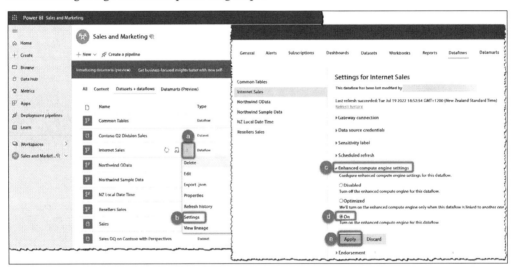

Figure 4.45: Turning on the Enhanced compute engine on a Power BI dataflow

3. Refresh the dataflow after turning the **Enhanced compute engine settings** on

Now that we meet the requirements, we can connect to a dataflow from Power BI Desktop in DirectQuery mode.

Power BI Datamarts

The term **Datamart** is related to data warehousing where users have access to relevant and business-centric data, while a data warehouse is usually enterprise-wide, covering a broad range of historical and current data.

Microsoft introduced Datamart capability for Power BI Premium licenses in May 2022, enabling organizations to leverage governed and secure self-service data transformation without seeing the IT team as a bottleneck in the data migration processes. Organizations traditionally have an IT team taking care of the data migration and transformation from the source systems into central storage.

This process is usually complex, cumbersome, and time-consuming, leading the business teams to see the IT team as a bottleneck. In response, business users started building their own data stores using local SQL Server instances, Excel files, SharePoint site, or Microsoft Access files to cover their requirements. This resulted in a lack of governance and data leakage, resulting in serious security breaches that are often very hard and costly to fix.

With the new datamarts feature, users can connect to various supported data sources and migrate and transform the data into a fully managed Azure SQL database. Power BI automatically creates a dataset connected to the datamart, which is used to connect to the datamart. We cover the datamarts in detail in *Chapter 15, New Options, Features, and DAX Functions*.

Follow these steps to connect to an existing datamart from Power BI Desktop:

1. Click the **Data hub** drop-down button from the **Home** tab
2. Click **Datamarts**
3. Select the datamart
4. Click **Connect**

The following image shows the preceding steps:

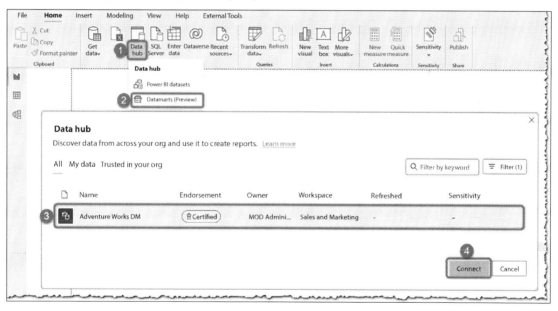

Figure 4.46: Connecting to a Datamart from Power BI Desktop

As the following image shows, we are indeed connected live to the dataset automatically created by Power BI on top of the datamart.

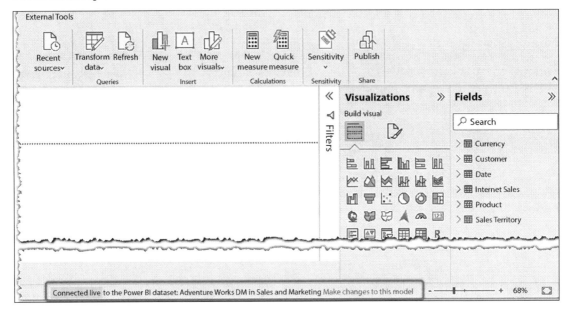

Figure 4.47: Connect Live to a Power BI dataset linked to a datamart

SQL Server

SQL Server is one of the most common data sources for Power BI. When connecting to a SQL Server database, we have two options: importing the data into the data model or connecting to the database in DirectQuery mode. This chapter discusses the connection modes in later sections. Follow these steps to get data from a SQL Server data source:

1. Click the **SQL Server** button from the **Home** tab.
2. Enter the **Server** name.
3. We may want to enter the **Database name (optional)** depending on our scenario.
4. We can either select **Import** or **DirectQuery**.
5. Again, depending on our scenario, we may want to enter **Transact-SQL (T-SQL)** statements. To do so, click to expand the **Advanced options**.
6. Leave the **Include relationship columns** option ticked (untick this option to stop Power BI from detecting related tables when selecting a table from the **Navigator** page and clicking the **Select Related Tables** option).
7. Leave the **Navigate using full hierarchy** option unticked (tick this option if you would like to see the navigation based on database schemas).

8. If you have **High Availability (HA)** settings on the SQL Server instance, then tick the **Enable SQL Server Failover support** item; otherwise, leave it unticked.
9. Click **OK**.

The preceding steps are highlighted in the following image:

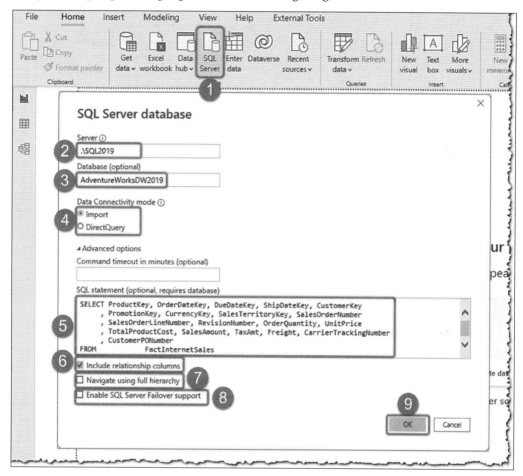

Figure 4.48: Getting data from SQL Server

10. Tick a desired table from the list. This option is only available if we do not enter T-SQL statements.
11. Click the **Select Related Tables** button.
12. Depending on what you need to do next, you can either click the **Load** button to load the data into the data model or click the **Transform Data** button, which navigates you to the **Power Query Editor**.

The preceding steps are highlighted in the following image:

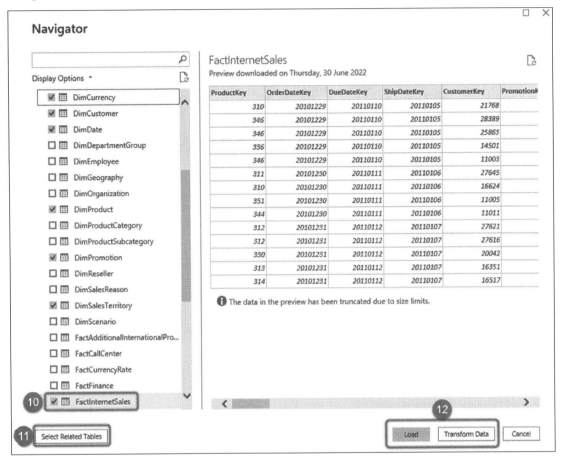

Figure 4.49: Selecting a table and related tables from the Navigator window

 As shown in *step 5* in *Figure 4.48*, typing T-SQL statements disables query folding in Power Query, which potentially causes some performance degradation during the data refresh. However, there is a technique with which we can enforce query folding when using T-SQL statements. *Chapter 7, Data Preparation Common Best Practices*, discusses more details in the *Query folding best practices* section.

SQL Server Analysis Services and Azure Analysis Services

SQL Server Analysis Services (SSAS) has two different technologies, multi-dimensional models and tabular models. **Azure Analysis Services (AAS)** is a **Platform-as-a-Service (PaaS)** version of the tabular model in Azure. A dedicated connection connects to both types of on-premises versions of SSAS, and another dedicated connector supports AAS. When connecting from Power BI Desktop to SSAS or AAS, we have three connection types: **Connect Live**, **Import**, and **DirectQuery**. Power BI Desktop becomes a reporting tool if we select the **Connect Live** option. In that case, the report does not include the data model. When we Connect Live to an on-premises SSAS, an AAS, or a Power BI dataset, we create a **thin report**. So, a thin report is a report without the data model attached. In any thin report, we can create **report-level measures**. The report-level measures are only available within the report itself; therefore, they are not accessible within the underlying data model.

It is best to avoid using the **Import** mode when connecting to either SSAS or AAS. When we create a model in Power BI, we create a semantic model. Importing SSAS or AAS data into a Power BI model means creating a new semantic model on top of an existing one, which is not ideal. Therefore, it is best to avoid this method unless we have a strong justification.

In December 2020, Microsoft announced a new version of composite models where we can turn a Connect Live connection into an AAS or a Power BI dataset into a **DirectQuery** one. Later in 2022, Microsoft expanded this feature to support SSAS Tabular 2022. Therefore, we can now connect to multiple AAS, SSAS tabular, or Power BI datasets to build a single source of truth within an enterprise-grade semantic layer in Power BI. We cover composite models with live connection in *Chapter 14, DirectQuery Connections to Power BI Datasets and Analysis Services in Composite Models*.

SSAS multidimensional/tabular

To connect to an instance of SSAS, follow these steps:

1. Click the **Get data** dropdown.
2. Click **Analysis Services**.
3. Enter the **Server** name.
4. Enter the **Database** name (optional).
5. Select the connection mode; if you select **Import**, you could write **Multi-dimensional Expressions (MDX)** or **DAX** expressions to get a result set.
6. Click **OK**.

The preceding steps are highlighted in the following image:

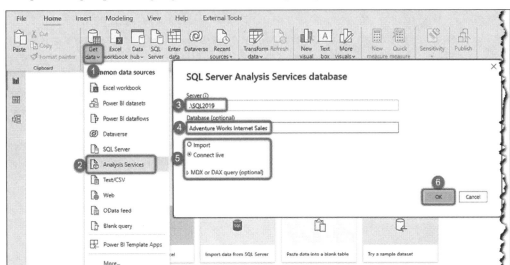

Figure 4.50: Connecting to SSAS

7. Select the model.
8. Click **OK**.

The preceding steps are highlighted in the following image:

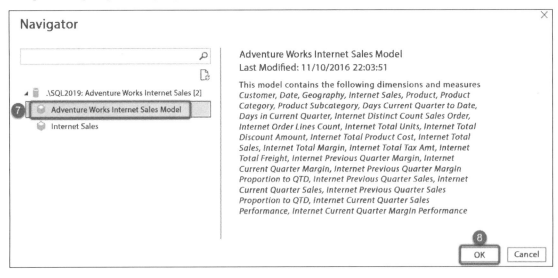

Figure 4.51: Connecting to the model

AAS

Connecting to an instance of AAS is similar to connecting to an instance of SSAS. The only difference is that this time, we use its dedicated connector. We can find the **Azure Analysis Services database** connector under the **Azure** folder from the **Get Data** window, as shown in the following image, so we will not go through the steps again:

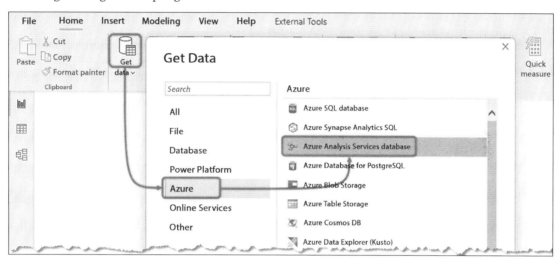

Figure 4.52: Connecting to an AAS tabular model

An extra option available on the **Azure portal** for AAS databases is downloading the PBIX file directly from the Azure portal. The downloaded PBIX file contains the connection to the desired model in AAS. The following steps explain how to do this:

1. After logging in to the Azure portal, navigate to your instance of AAS, then click **Overview**.
2. Find the model you want to connect to and click the ellipsis button on the right.
3. Click **Open in Power BI Desktop**.

The following image shows the preceding steps:

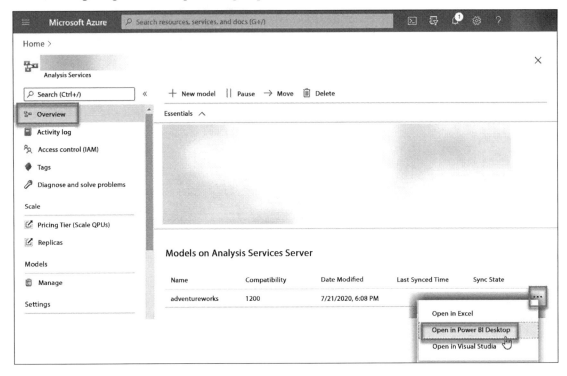

Figure 4.53: Opening the AAS model in Power BI Desktop from the Azure portal

When opening the downloaded file in Power BI Desktop, it is *connected live* to our AAS model.

OData feed

The **Open Data Protocol** (**OData**) is another common data source used in Power BI. Many web services support OData, which is one of the reasons this type of data source is quite common. If the source system accessible via an OData connection is a **Customer Relationship Management** (**CRM**) or an **Enterprise Resource Planning** (**ERP**) system, the underlying data model contains many tables with many columns. In some cases, we have to deal with wide tables with more than 200 columns; therefore, a good understanding of the underlying data model is essential. In this section, we describe how to connect to the underlying data model of Microsoft's **Project Web App** (**PWA**), as follows:

1. In Power BI Desktop, click the **Get data** drop-down button.
2. Click **OData feed**.

Chapter 4

3. Enter your PWA **Uniform Resource Locator (URL)**. It must look like this: `https://Your_Tenant.sharepoint.com/sites/pwa/_api/`.
4. Click **OK**.
5. Click **Organizational account**.
6. Click the **Sign in** button, then pass your credentials.
7. Click **Connect**.

   The following image shows the preceding steps:

   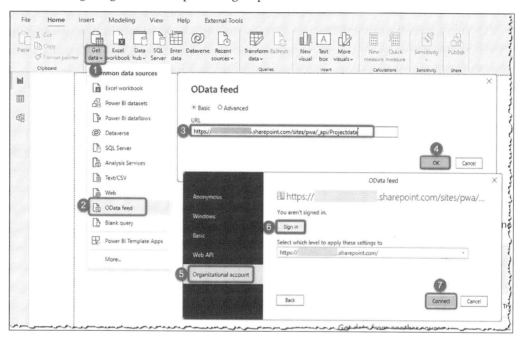

   Figure 4.54: Connecting to OData feed

8. Select the desired tables; in our sample, we selected the **Projects** table.
9. Click either **Load** or **Transform Data**; we selected the **Transform Data** option.

The preceding steps are highlighted in the following image:

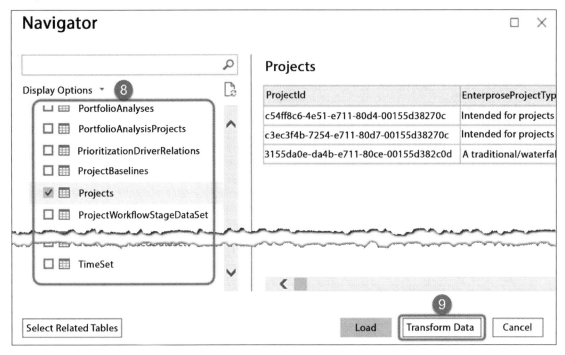

Figure 4.55: Selecting tables from the Navigator page

As shown in the following image, the **Projects** table has 131 columns:

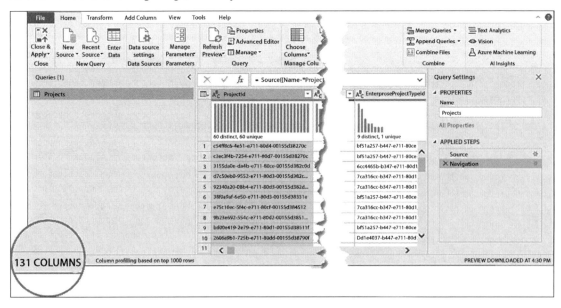

Figure 4.56: The Projects table from the PWA data source in Power Query

We usually do not require the loading of all columns into the data model. Therefore, having a good understanding of the underlying database structure is essential. If we do not know much about the underlying data source, it is wise to involve **subject-matter experts** (**SMEs**). They can help identify the more relevant columns in the business.

Dataverse

Microsoft Dataverse, formerly named **Common Data Services** (**CDS**), is a data service and application platform supporting multiple connected applications and processes under the Microsoft Power Platform umbrella. Dataverse provides a cloud-based central repository for Power Platform solutions such as **PowerApps, Power Automate, Power Virtual Agent,** and **Power Pages**. We can also integrate **Dynamic 365** (**D365**) solutions such as **Business Central** (**BC**) with Dataverse.

Follow these steps to connect to Dataverse:

1. Click the **Dataverse** button from **Home**
2. Click **Sign in**
3. Pass your credentials and click **Connect**
4. Expand the desired environment
5. Select the desired table
6. Depending on what you want to do next, click **Load** or **Transform Data**
7. Select the connection type (**Import** or **DirectQuery**)
8. Click **OK**

The following image shows the preceding steps:

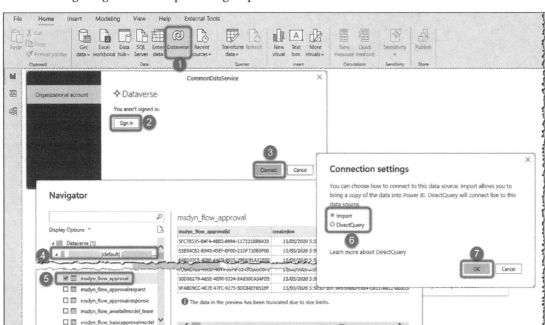

Figure 4.57: Connecting to Dataverse

To learn more about Dataverse, visit the following page in the Microsoft documentation:

https://docs.microsoft.com/en-nz/power-apps/maker/data-platform/data-platform-intro?WT.mc_id=DP-MVP-5003466

Understanding data source certification

While data source certification leans toward Power BI governance, it is crucial to understand what it is and how it affects data modelers. The data source certification is more about the quality of data and assessing the level of trust we can build upon the data available in different data sources. With data source certification, we group our data sources into three (or more) categories. Different organizations use different terminology to refer to the quality of their data. This section uses the Bronze, Silver, and Gold/Platinum categories, indicating the quality of data contained in the data sources. You may use different terms in your data source certification.

This section does not explain the steps and processes of data source certification as it is beyond the scope of this book.

Bronze

The **Bronze** data sources contain uncurated data. The data has never been thoroughly quality-controlled. While the data source may have valuable data, it may have some duplication or incorrect data. The other factor we may consider is the location where the data is stored and not the quality of the data itself; for example, when we store Excel files in a personal OneDrive or Google Drive storage. Bronze data sources are typically copied or exported from the web or other source systems. Sometimes, SMEs store and analyze the data in untrusted storage systems that the organization does not manage; the data is also not in the best shape for consumption in analytical tools such as Power BI. The most common data sources include Excel, CSV, and TXT files. Many organizations strictly ban Bronze data sources as the contained data cannot be trusted and is prone to breach governance policies. The maintenance costs associated with analyzing the Bronze data source are often relatively high. When dealing with Bronze data, we usually expect more complex data preparation and higher maintenance costs when estimating the development effort.

Silver

The **Silver** category is semi-curated data, and the organization manages the storage. While there might still be some data quality issues here and there, the data can be used in analytical tools to gain insights. Nevertheless, the data preparation costs are reasonable as the data is not in its best shape. The most common data sources categorized as Silver are transactional data sources stored by different technologies in different locations. These can typically be transactional databases hosted in SQL Server or Oracle or Excel files stored in SharePoint or OneDrive for Business. Some organizations even consider some of their data warehouses as Silver data sources, so it depends on how we define the boundaries.

Gold/Platinum

Gold or **Platinum** data sources are fully curated from both a data and business perspective. Data quality issues are minimal. The data is in its best possible shape to be analyzed and visualized in analytical and reporting tools such as Power BI. Typical Gold data sources can be semantic models hosted in SSAS, either multi-dimensional or tabular models, **SAP Business Warehouse** (**SAP BW**), data warehouses, and so on. When we deal with a Gold/Platinum data source, we are more confident that the data is correct. We expect almost zero data preparation and data modeling efforts from a development perspective.

Working with connection modes

When we connect to a data source, the query connection mode falls into one of the following three different categories:

- Data Import
- DirectQuery
- Connect Live

Every query connecting to one or more data sources in the **Power Query Editor** has one of the preceding connection modes, except Connect Live. When the connection mode is Connect Live, a Power BI model cannot currently connect to more than one instance of SSAS or AAS, or a Power BI dataset. As mentioned earlier, in December 2020, Microsoft released the preview of the new version of the composite models in which we can connect to multiple Power BI Datasets or AAS/SSAS tabular 2022 models when using the DirectQuery mode. We discuss composite models in more detail in *Chapter 14, DirectQuery Connections to Power BI Datasets and Analysis Services in Composite Models*.

This section looks at the connection modes, their applications, and their limitations.

Data Import

This is the most common connection mode in Power BI Desktop. It is the only option in many connections, such as file-based connections. As its name suggests, the **Data Import** mode imports the data from the source(s) into the Power BI data model. The data is already prepared and transformed in the Power Query layer; then, it is imported into the data model. We can refresh the data manually within Power BI Desktop or automatically after publishing it to the Power BI Service.

Applications

The main application for the **Data Import** mode consolidates data from different sources into a single source of truth. In addition, it gives us data modeling capabilities to create a semantic model in Power BI. We can frequently refresh the data throughout the day. All that goodness comes with some limitations, as outlined next.

Limitations

The Power BI datasets in **Data Import** mode have limited storage sizes and automatic data refreshes based on the licensing tier.

Storage per dataset is limited to the following:

- 1 GB per dataset under the **free** and **Pro** licensing plans
- 100 GB for datasets published to workspaces backed with a **PPU** capacity
- 400 GB for datasets published to workspaces backed with a **Premium** capacity

Depending on our licensing tier, we can currently schedule the data refreshes from the Power BI Service with the following restrictions:

- Once a day for the free licensing plan
- Up to 8 times a day for Power BI Pro
- Up to 48 times a day for Power BI Premium and PPU

With the preceding restrictions in mind, if real-time or near real-time data analytics is required, this mode may not be ideal.

DirectQuery

While **Data Import** is the most common connection mode, for some data sources, an alternative approach is to connect directly to the data source using **DirectQuery**. When a connection is in DirectQuery mode, it does not import the data into the model. Instead, it fires multiple concurrent queries back to the data source, which can be a relational database data source, to get the results.

Applications

This connection mode is ideal for supporting real-time data processing scenarios with minimal data latency when the data is stored in a relational database. The other applications are when the 1-GB file size limit is insufficient due to a large amount of data in the data source or when we must implement row-level security at the sources for security reasons. While, in DirectQuery mode, we do not import any data into a data model, we still can create a data model with some limitations.

Limitations

Generally speaking, queries in DirectQuery mode are not as performant as similar queries in **Import** mode. DirectQuery fires concurrent queries back to the source systems. So, performance issues can lead to timeouts if the source database system is not strong enough to handle many concurrent queries (or if it is not well configured). In that case, the underlying data model and, consequently, the reports may fail.

We can expect poor performance if the queries in DirectQuery mode are complex. The other drawback is when many concurrent users run the same report, leading to even more concurrent query executions against the source systems.

Moreover, there are a few limitations with **DirectQuery**, making this connection mode even more complex to use. For instance, some Power Query functions are not available in DirectQuery mode. DirectQuery is also limited to retrieving 1 million rows for the cloud sources and 4 megabytes (MB) of data per row for an on-premises data source, or a maximum of *16 MB for the entire visual* under the Power BI Pro license. The maximum row limit for Power BI Premium can be set under the **admin-set** limit.

Therefore, it is essential to undertake thorough investigations before using **DirectQuery**.

Connect Live

Connect Live mode is used when the report is connected to any of the following data sources:

- A Power BI dataset
- An SSAS instance, either multi-dimensional or tabular
- An instance of AAS

Connect Live is the recommended connection mode for Power BI reporting in an enterprise **business intelligence** (BI) solution. In this connection mode, all business logic is captured in the semantic model and made available for all reporting tools within the Power BI dataset or SAAS or AAS instance we are connecting to. In this mode, the data model and its data are kept in the source, so we do not import any data into Power BI.

Applications

This is the desired connection mode when the source system is a Power BI dataset, an instance of AAS, or a tabular/multidimensional instance of SSAS.

Limitations

Power BI becomes a reporting tool when we use the Connect Live mode. Therefore, no Power Query or data modeling capabilities are available under this connection model, but we can still see the underlying data model in Power BI Desktop. Moreover, we can create report-level measures when connecting live to an SSAS tabular model (this is not applicable when connecting live to an SSAS multidimensional model). While we can see Power BI Desktop's underlying data model, we cannot make any changes to it. As all the data processing is done in the AAS or SSAS instance, the SSAS instance must have enough resources to respond efficiently to concurrent users.

Working with storage modes

In the previous section, we discussed various connection modes for the queries from a Power Query perspective. This section looks at different storage modes that apply to tables after the data is loaded into a data model or connected to a data source. Every table in a Power BI data model has a storage mode property that shows if the data is cached or not. There are three types of storage modes, as outlined next:

- **Import**: This means the data is cached in the memory. Therefore, all queries over a table with this storage mode get the results from the cached data.
- **DirectQuery**: The data is not cached; therefore, all queries fire back to the source system.
- **Dual**: The tables in this mode can get data from the cache or the source system. For instance, depending on the level of detail into which the user drills down in an aggregation setup, the query results may come from the cached data or directly from the source. We discuss aggregations in *Chapter 9, Star Schema and Data Modeling Common Best Practices*.

 All DirectQuery limitations described in the *Working with connection modes* section also apply to the tables in the **Dual** storage model setting.

We can see or change the storage mode property from the **Model** view from the left pane of Power BI Desktop, as follows:

1. Click the **Model** view.
2. Select a table from the **Fields** pane.
3. Expand **Advanced** from the **Properties** pane.
4. Select a **Storage mode** from the drop-down list.

The preceding steps are highlighted in the following image:

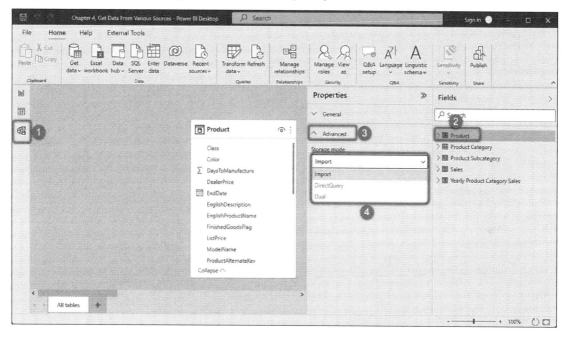

Figure 4.58: Changing the table's Storage mode property

 We cannot change a table's storage mode from **Import** mode to either **DirectQuery** or **Dual** mode because of the features that are not available in DirectQuery mode.

This section discussed the storage modes of tables. In the next section, we learn about dataset storage modes.

Understanding dataset storage modes

As you may have already guessed, dataset storage modes refer to whether the data in a dataset is cached in memory or not. With that in mind, from a dataset perspective, there are three different modes, as outlined next:

- **Import:** When the whole data is cached in memory. In this mode, all tables are in the **Import** storage mode setting.
- **DirectQuery:** When the data is not cached in memory. In this mode, all tables are in the **DirectQuery** storage mode setting.
- **Composite** (**Mixed**): When a portion of data is cached in memory, while the rest is not. In this mode, some tables are in the **Import** storage mode setting; other tables are in **DirectQuery** storage mode or the **Dual** storage mode setting.

To see and edit the dataset storage modes in Power BI Desktop, look at the right side of the status bar, as shown in the following image:

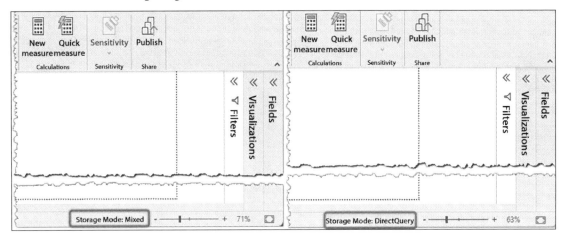

Figure 4.59: Identifying dataset storage modes in Power BI Desktop

Dataset storage mode is an essential point to consider at the beginning of the project. We must ensure that the dataset storage mode used in our Power BI model covers all the business needs. The dataset storage mode has a direct effect on our Power BI architecture. For instance, if a business requires minimal data latency or even real-time data analysis, **DirectQuery** would be a potential choice.

Summary

In this chapter, we learned how to work with the most common data sources supported in Power BI, such as folders, CSV, Excel, Power BI datasets, Power BI dataflows, SQL Server SSAS instances, and an OData feed, with some challenging real-world scenarios. We also went through data source certifications and discussed why it is essential to know which data source certification level we are dealing with. We then looked at connection, storage, and dataset modes and how different they are. It is worthwhile emphasizing the importance of understanding different connection modes, storage modes, and dataset modes as they directly affect our data modeling and overall Power BI architecture.

In the next chapter, we look at common data preparation steps in the **Power Query Editor** and real-world scenarios.

Join us on Discord!

Join The Big Data and Analytics Community on the Packt Discord Server!

Hang out with 558 other members and enjoy free voice and text chat.

`https://packt.link/ips2H`

5

Common Data Preparation Steps

In the previous chapter, we discussed some data sources that are frequently used in Power BI. We also covered data source certifications and the differences between various connection modes, storage modes, and dataset modes. This chapter looks at common data preparation steps such as table, text, `Date`, `DateTime`, and `DateTimeZone` manipulations.

We look at each of these by providing real-world scenarios that can help deal with real daily data preparation challenges. In Power Query Editor, the data preparation activities are categorized into three separate tabs, as shown in the following screenshot:

1. **Home:** Contains more generic actions, such as creating a new query, creating or managing query parameters, and performing common data preparation steps such as split column, Group By, and more.
2. **Transform:** Contains more transformation functionalities that can be performed through the UI.
3. **Add Column:** Contains data preparation steps related to adding a new column through the UI:

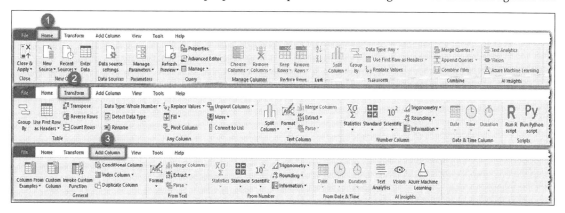

Figure 5.1: Data preparation functionalities available via Power Query Editor UI

The following few sections describe some of the functionalities available under the tabs shown in the preceding image and some that are not available through the UI but are commonly used during the data preparation phase.

This chapter starts with the *Chapter 5, Common Data Preparation Steps*, `Raw.pbix` sample file. Moving forward, we'll continue developing this file. To use the sample file, open it in Power BI Desktop, then change the values of the following query parameters to point to your local copy of the sample source files:

- Adventure Works DW Excel path to point to `AdventureWorksDW2017.xlsx`
- Internet Sales in Time Excel path to point to `Internet Sales in Time Level.xlsx`

Ensure you apply the changes from the yellow warning message appearing under the ribbon bar.

You can find the source code and sample files from GitHub via the following link:

`https://github.com/PacktPublishing/Expert-Data-Modeling-with-Power-BI-Second-Edition/tree/main/Samples/Chapter%2005`

In Power BI, we can get data from various sources in different formats. Regardless of the format of the data source, the quality of the data is important. In some cases, we must deal with already transformed data, but in reality, there are many more cases where we need to transform the data and prepare it for analysis in the data model. A prevalent example is when the data source is a pivot table in Excel or CSV. Therefore, we must prepare the data before loading it into the data model. This chapter takes a closer look at the most used data transformations and data manipulation functionalities in Power Query, including the following:

- Data type conversion
- Splitting a column by delimiter
- Merging a column
- Adding a custom column
- Adding a column from examples
- Duplicating a column
- Filtering rows
- Working with Group By
- Appending queries
- Merging queries
- Duplicating and referencing queries
- Replacing values
- Extracting numbers from text
- Dealing with Date, DateTime, and DateTimeZone
- Pivoting tables

While unpivoting tables is also a common transformation, we do not cover it in this chapter, as we already discussed it in *Chapter 4, Getting Data from Various Sources*, in the *Excel* section.

Let us look at them in more detail.

Data type conversion

Data type conversion is one of the most common steps in Power Query, yet it is one of the most important ones that can become tricky if not managed well. One cool feature of Power BI, if enabled, is to detect data types automatically. While this is a handy feature in many cases, it can be the root cause of some issues down the road. The critical point to note is how Power BI automatically detects data types. Power BI automatically detects column data types based on the first few hundred rows; that is where things may go wrong, as the data types are not detected based on the whole dataset. Instead, the data types are detected based on the part loaded for preview. In most cases, we deal with data type conversion in table values. Either we use Power Query Editor UI or manually write the expressions; here, we use the following function:

```
Table.TransformColumnTypes(Table as table, TypeTransformations as list,
 optional Culture as nullable text)
```

In the `Table.TransformColumnTypes()` function, we have the following:

- `Table` is usually the result of the previous step.
- `TypeTransformations` accepts a list of column names, along with their corresponding data type.
- `Culture` is optional and nullable text such as `en-NZ` specifying the culture.

We already discussed the types available in Power Query in *Chapter 3, Data Preparation in Power Query Editor*, in the *Introduction to Power Query (M) Formula Language in Power BI* section, in the *Types* subsection. The following table shows the types, along with the syntax we can use to specify the data types:

Type Kind	Type Representation	Specifying Type Syntax 1	Specifying Type Syntax 2
binary	Binary	type binary	Binary.Type
date	Date	type date	Date.Type
datetime	Date/Time	type datetime	DateTime.Type
datetimezone	Date/Time/Zone	type datetimezone	DateTimeZone.Type
duration	Duration	type duration	Duration.Type
list	List	type list	List.Type
logical	Logical	type logical	Logical.Type
null	Null	type null	Null.Type
number	Whole Number	-	Int64.Type
number	Decimal Number	type number	Int64.Type
number	Fixed Decimal Number	-	Currency.Type
number	Percentage	-	Percentage.Type
record	Record	type record	Record.Type
text	Text	type text	Text.Type
time	Time	type time	Time.Type
type	Type	type type	Type.Type
function	Function	type function	Function.Type
table	Table	type table	Table.Type
any	Any	type any	Any.Type
none	None	type none	None.Type

Table 5.1: Power Query types, their representation, and their syntax

Let's look at this in more detail with a scenario.

Imagine that we received the Chapter 5, Common Data Preparation Steps, Raw.pbix file built by someone else, and we have to develop a report. Bear in mind the following considerations:

- We already know the previous developer connected to the source Excel files.
- We have loaded the data into the data model without making any changes in Power Query.
- We have created some relationships in the data model.
- The developer noted that the **PostalCode** column from the **Geography** table contains many *blank* values that do not match the source Excel file.
- The developer also noticed that the results are odd when using the **Date** column from the **Date** table and the **Internet Sales** measure on a table visual.

We want to investigate and fix the issues. Let us open the Chapter 5, Common Data Preparation Steps, Raw.pbix file, and go through the following steps:

1. Open **Power Query Editor** and select the **Geography** table from the **Queries** pane.
2. When we created the sample file, we did not change the data types. The last step is automatically created, and the data types are automatically detected.
3. Scroll the **Data** view to the right. Here, we can see that the **Column Quality** bar of the **PostalCode** column turned red, which means there is an error in the sample data (the top 1,000 rows).
4. Scroll down a bit in the **Data** view to find an erroneous cell. Click a cell that's producing an error to see the error message.
5. As the following screenshot shows, the error is caused by an incorrect data type conversion:

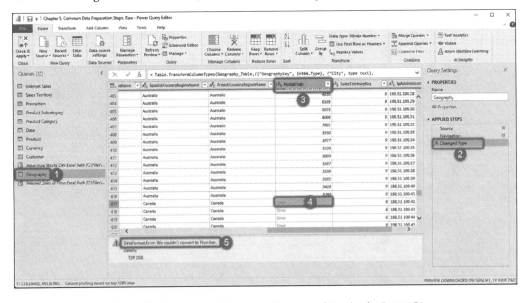

Figure 5.2: Errors caused by wrong data type detection by Power BI

Fixing the issue is straightforward. Here, we must set the **PostalCode** column data type to **Text**, which is the correct data type.

6. Click the column type indicator button.
7. Click **Text**.
8. Click the **Replace current** button on the **Change Column Type** message:

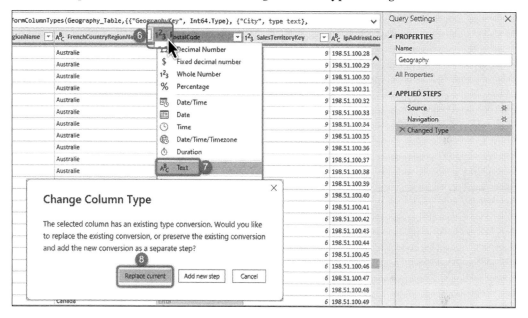

Figure 5.3: Changing a column data type

As shown in *step 8*, we do not get a new step in **APPLIED STEPS**, but the issue is resolved. In the following screenshot, **Column distribution** shows no indication of any issues anymore:

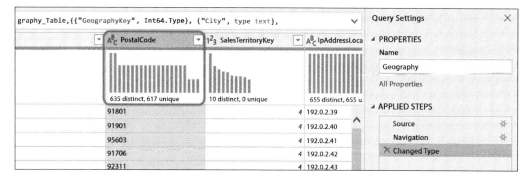

Figure 5.4: Data type conversion issue resolved

In the preceding example, we quickly found and fixed the issue. But in many cases, data conversion issues and their fixes are not as trivial, even when we do not use the automatic data type detection feature. Let's apply the changes, save the file as a new file, and name it Chapter 5, Common Data Preparation Steps, Fixed PostCode.pbix.

Now, click the **Data** view on Power BI Desktop, navigate to the **Geography** table, and look at the **PostalCode** column's data to ensure the changes we made so far fixed that issue. The following image shows the results:

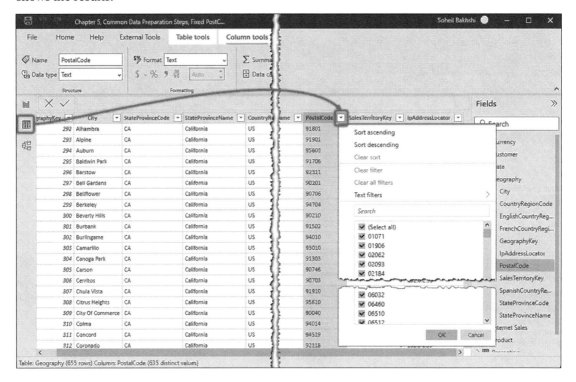

Figure 5.5: Confirming that the blank postalCode issue is resolved

As the preceding image shows, the **PostalCode** column no longer contains *blank* values.

Now that we've solved the first issue, let us focus on the next issue, which is incorrect results when using the **Date** column from the **Date** table and the **Internet Sales** measure on a table visual.

To reproduce the issue, we put a table visual on the report canvas, select the **Date** column from the **Date** table and the **Internet Sales** measure, and the issue quickly appears. As shown in the following image, the results do not look to be correct:

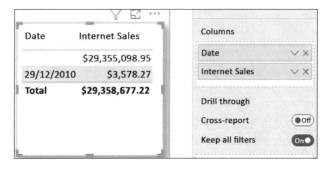

Figure 5.6: The Internet Sales measure shows values for only one date

In cases like this, a few things may have gone wrong, leading to incorrect results. So, we usually go through some initial checks to narrow down the possibilities and find the issue's root cause(s). The following are some of them:

- We review the **Model** tab from the left pane to review the relationships.
- If the relationship between the two tables is **one-to-many**, then we check for *blank* values in the related column participating in the *many* side of the relationship from the **Data** tab.
- We check that the data types of the related columns match.

As the following image shows, the **Date** column from the **Date** table and the **OrderDateTime** column in the **Internet Sales** table participate in a **one-to-many** relationship between the **Date** and **Internet Sales** tables:

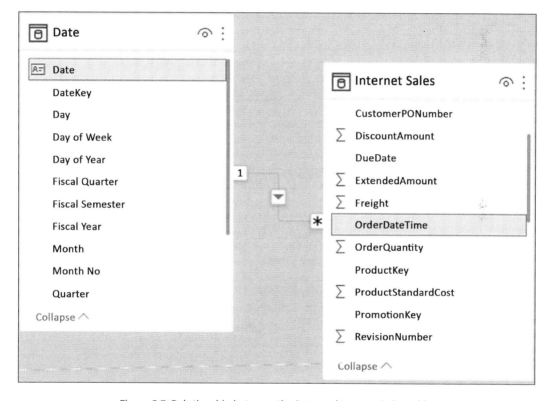

Figure 5.7: Relationship between the Date and Internet Sales tables

So, the next step is to check for blank values in the **OrderDateTime** column from the **Internet Sales** table. As the following image shows, there are no blank values in the **OrderDateTime** column:

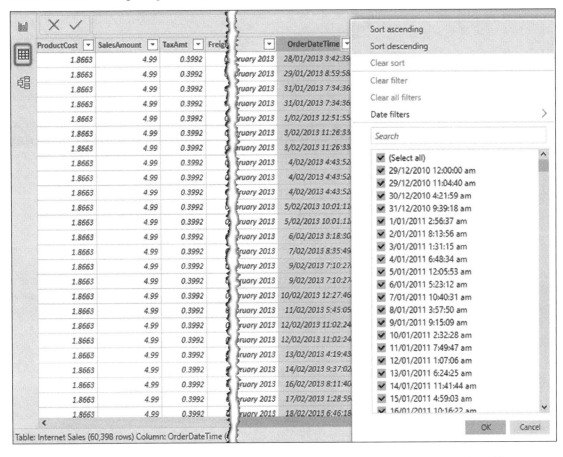

Figure 5.8: No blank values in the OrderDateTime column from the Internet Sales table

So, the next thing to ensure is that the data type of the **Date** column from the **Date** table and the **OrderDateTime** column in the **Internet Sales** table match. We can check the columns' data types from various places in the Power BI Desktop. Here is one of them:

1. Click the **Report** tab.
2. Select the column from the **Fields** pane.
3. See the **data type** from the **Column tools** tab on the ribbon.

The following image shows the preceding steps:

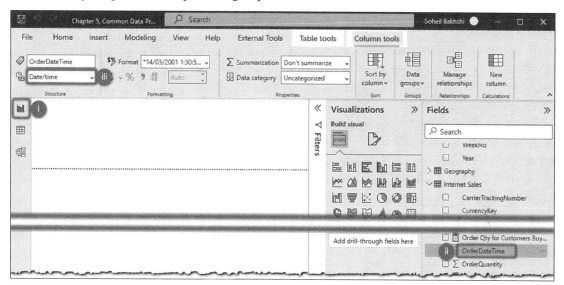

Figure 5.9: Checking a column's data type in Power BI Desktop

Looking at the data types of the **OrderDateTime** column in **Internet Sales** and the **Date** column in the **Date** table reveals that the data type of the **Date** column is **Date**, while the data type of the **OrderDateTime** column is **Date/Time**. Those data types are compatible from a data modeling perspective. Nevertheless, the data in the **OrderDateTime** column has a time element. Therefore, the only matching values from the **OrderDateTime** column are those with a time element of **12:00:00 AM**. To ensure this is right, we can do a quick test.

We can put a table on the reporting canvas showing the **Date** column from the **Date** table and the **OrderDateTime** column from the **Internet Sales** table side by side.

The following screenshot shows the results:

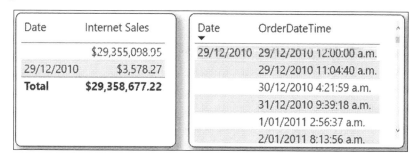

Figure 5.10: Date and OrderDateTime do not match

As you can see, there is only one match between the two columns. Now that we have identified the issue, the only step we need to take is to convert the **OrderDateTime** column's data type from **DateTime** to **Date**:

1. Open Power Query Editor and select the **Internet Sales** table from the **Queries** pane.
2. Right-click the **OrderDateTime** column.
3. Click **Date** from the context menu under the **Change Type** submenu.
4. Click the **Replace current** button
5. Click **Close & Apply** to apply the changes to the data model:

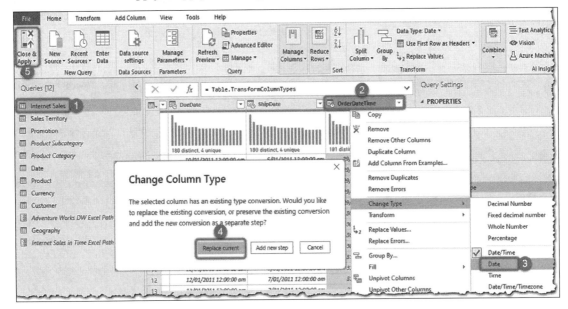

Figure 5.11: Changing the column's data type from DateTime to Date

Now, let's switch to the **Report** view and see the results. As shown in the following screenshot, the issue has been resolved:

Date	Internet Sales
29/12/2010	$14,477.34
30/12/2010	$13,931.52
31/12/2010	$15,012.18
1/01/2011	$7,156.54
2/01/2011	$15,012.18
3/01/2011	$14,313.08
4/01/2011	$7,855.64
5/01/2011	$7,855.64
6/01/2011	$20,909.78
Total	**$29,358,677.22**

Figure 5.12: The correct results after changing the OrderDateTime column's data type from DateTime to Date

As the preceding sample clearly shows, selecting an incorrect data type can significantly affect our data model. So, the critical point is that the key columns in both tables that are used in a relationship must contain the same data type. Save the file as a new file and name it Chapter 5, Common Data Preparation Steps, Fixed OrderDateTime Data Type.pbix.

The preceding scenario emphasized the importance of paying attention to the data type conversion in Power Query. We look at some other common data preparation steps in the following few sections.

Splitting a column by delimiter

One of the most common transformation steps in Power Query is **Split Column by Delimiter**. There are many use cases for this transformation. The following are some of the use cases:

- Splitting **First Name**, **Middle Name**, and **Last Name** from a **Full Name** column
- Splitting date, time, and time zone elements from DateTimeZone values into separate columns
- Splitting comma-delimited values into separate columns

Let us move forward with a scenario. In the previous section's scenario, we converted the **OrderDateTime** column's type to **Date**. In this scenario, the business needs to analyze the **Internet Sales** data at both the **Date** and **Time** levels. There are many techniques we can use to satisfy this new requirement, such as the following:

- Creating a new **Time** table, which can be done either using DAX (we discussed this in *Chapter 2, Data Analysis eXpressions and Data Modeling*, in the *Creating a Time dimension with DAX* section) or within Power Query Editor
- Splitting the **OrderDateTime** column into two columns—one **Date** column and one **Time** column
- Creating a relationship between the **Time** and the **Internet Sales** tables

We'll only look at the second option in this scenario: splitting the **OrderDateTime** column by a delimiter. In the previous scenario, we converted the **OrderDateTime** column into **Date**. So, for this scenario, we pick the Chapter 5, Common Data Preparation Steps, Fixed PostCode.pbix sample file containing the transformation steps before changing the data types of the **OrderDateTime** column into **Date**. Download the sample file from here:

https://github.com/PacktPublishing/Expert-Data-Modeling-with-Power-BI-Second-Edition/blob/9d6388ffe6e83586a02de81ff959e04c31dbf1da/Samples/Chapter%2005/Chapter%205,%20Common%20Data%20Preparation%20Steps,%20Split%20Column%20By%20Delimiter.pbix

Once downloaded, take the following steps:

1. In **Power Query Editor**, select the **Internet Sales** table from the left pane.
2. Select the **OrderDateTime** column.
3. Click the **Split Column** drop-down button from the **Transform** tab. We have a few splitting options here.
4. Click **By Delimiter**.
5. Select **Space** from the **Select or enter delimiter** drop-down list.
6. Tick the **Left-most delimiter** option.

7. **Quote Character** does not consider the delimiter when it appears within the quote character. The default is a *quotation mark (double quote)*. Leave it as is.
8. Click **OK**.

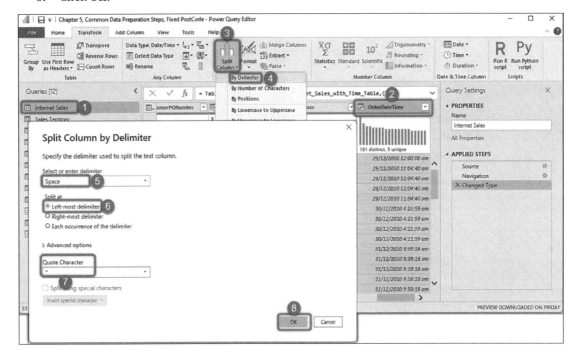

Figure 5.13: Splitting a column by delimiter

So far, we've added a new transformation step named **Split Column by Delimiter** to split the **OrderDateTime** column into two columns named (by default) **OrderDateTime.1** and **OrderDateTime.2**. The following screenshot illustrates the results:

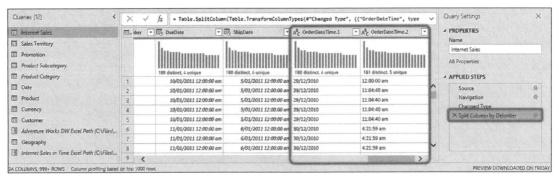

Figure 5.14: Split column creates two new columns called OrderDateTime.1 and OrderDateTime.2

The new columns' names are not user-friendly, so we should rename them.

> **GOOD PRACTICE**
>
> Avoid creating excessive transformation steps when possible. More transformation steps translate into more data processing time and extra load on the Power Query engine.

With the preceding note in mind, we do not rename the two new columns as a new step. Instead, we change the Power Query expression of the **Split Column by Delimiter** step. There are two ways to do so.

The first option is to change the expressions from **Advanced Editor**, as shown in the following image:

1. Click **Advanced Editor** from the **Home** tab on the ribbon bar.
2. Find the #"Split Column by Delimiter" step.
3. Change the column names.
4. Click **Done**:

Figure 5.15: Changing the default column names of the splitter columns from the Advanced Editor

The second option is to change the expressions from the **Formula Bar**, as shown in the following screenshot:

1. Click the **Split Column by Delimiter** step from **APPLIED STEPS**.
2. Click the down arrow on the **Formula Bar** to expand it.
3. Change the names of the columns.
4. Click the **Submit** (✓) button:

Figure 5.16: Changing the default column names of the splitter columns from the Formula Bar

The last thing we need to do is change the **OrderDate** column's data types to **Date** and the **OrderTime** column to **Time**. We can now apply the changes and save the file as a new file: Chapter 5, Common Data Preparation Steps, Split Column By Delimiter.pbix.

Merging columns

A typical transformation under the **Add Column** category is **Merge Columns**. There are many use cases where we need to merge different columns, such as merging **First Name**, **Middle Name**, and **Last Name** to create a **Full Name** column or merging a multipart address like (**AddressLine1** or **AddressLine2**) to get an **Address** column containing the full address. Another common use case is to merge multiple columns to create a unique ID column. Let's continue with an example from the Chapter 5, Common Data Preparation Steps, Split Column By Delimiter.pbix sample file. You can download the file from here:

https://github.com/PacktPublishing/Expert-Data-Modeling-with-Power-BI-Second-Edition/blob/9d6388ffe6e83586a02de81ff959e04c31dbf1da/Samples/Chapter%2005/Chapter%205,%20Common%20Data%20Preparation%20Steps,%20Split%20Column%20By%20Delimiter.pbix

After opening the file, head to Power Query Editor and follow these steps:

1. Select the **Customer** table from the **Queries** pane of **Power Query Editor**.
2. Select the **First Name**, **Middle Name**, and **Last Name** columns.
3. Right-click one of the selected columns and click **Merge Columns**. Alternatively, we can click the **Merge Column** button from the **Transform** tab (shown in yellow in the following image).
4. Select **Space** from the **Separator** dropdown.
5. Type **Full Name** into the **New column name** text box.
6. Click **OK**.

Chapter 5

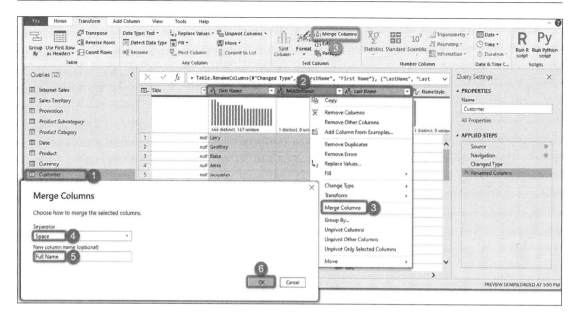

Figure 5.17: Merge Columns popup

After merging the three columns into one column, the output looks as follows:

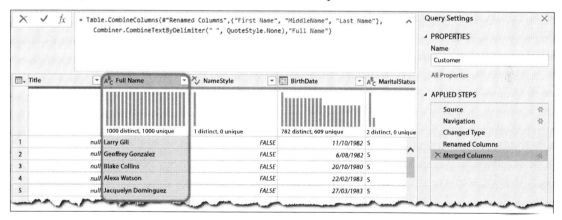

Figure 5.18: The three selected columns merged into one single column named Full Name

We successfully merged the **First Name**, **Middle Name**, and **Last Name** columns into a **Full Name** column. Save the file as a new file named Chapter 5, Common Data Preparation Steps, Merged Columns. pbix.

Adding a custom column

Adding a new column is one of the most common steps during data preparation. There are countless scenarios where we need to add a new column, such as adding some new analytical equations as a new column, creating data clusters in a new column, adding an index column as a new column, or using some **machine learning** (ML) and **artificial intelligence** (AI) algorithms. You may also have many other scenarios in mind. Whether we use Power Query Editor UI or manually write the Power Query expressions, we must add a custom column using the following function:

```
Table.AddColumn(Table as table, NewColumnName as text, ColumnGenerator as
function, optional ColumnType as nullable type)
```

In the `Table.AddColumn()` function, we have the following:

- `Table`: This is the input table value, the result of the previous step, or other queries that provide table output.
- `NewColumnName`: The new column name.
- `ColumnGenerator`: The expressions we use to create a new column.
- `ColumnType`: Specifying the data type of the new column is an optional operand, but it is handy. More on this later in this section.

Let us continue with a scenario. In the Chapter 5, Common Data Preparation Steps, Merged Columns. pbix sample file, we need to add a column to the **Customer** table to show if the customer's annual income is below or above the overall average income. To do so, we need to calculate the average annual income first. We have the annual income of all customers captured in the **YearlyIncome** column. To calculate the average income, we must reference the **YearlyIncome** column and calculate the average. We can reference a column within the current table by referencing the step's name and the column's name. So, in our case, because we want to get the average of **YearlyIncome**, the Power Query expression looks like this:

```
List.Average(#"Merged Columns"[YearlyIncome])
```

In the preceding expression, `#"Merged Columns"` is the name of the previous step. The result of referencing a column supplies a list of values, so by using the `List.Average(as list, optional precision as nullable number)` function, we can get the average of the values of a list. In our example, this is the **YearlyIncome** column.

Let us add a new custom column by following these steps:

1. Select the **Customer** table from the **Queries** pane.
2. Click the **Custom Column** button from the **Add Column** tab of the ribbon.
3. Type in a name for the new column.
4. Type in the expression shown in the following line of code:

   ```
   if [YearlyIncome] <= List.Average(#"Merged Columns"[YearlyIncome]) then
   true else false
   ```

5. Click **OK**:

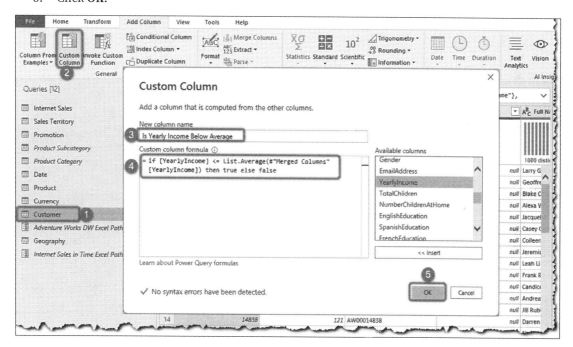

Figure 5.19: Adding a new custom column

In the preceding screenshot, we are specifying the operands of the Table.AddColumn() function within Power Query Editor UI, so:

- Number 3 is the NewColumnName operand
- Number 4 is the ColumnGenerator operand

The preceding steps result in a new custom column with TRUE or FALSE values indicating whether the customer's yearly income is below the average of all customers' yearly income. The following screenshot shows the results of the preceding steps:

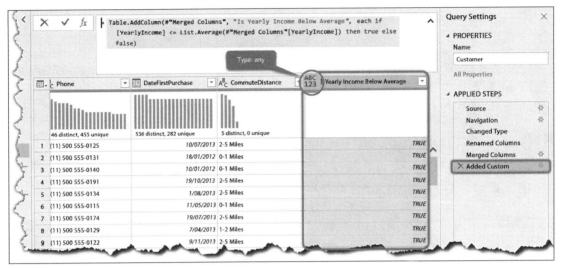

Figure 5.20: Result of adding a new custom column

As you can see, the new column's data type is **any**, while we expect the output to be **logical**. So, here, we have two options. Most developers do the most trivial step by adding another **Changed Type** step to convert the new column into **logical**, which is not a good practice. What if we need to add some more custom columns? Will we add a **Changed Type** step after every new custom column? No, we do not need to add any extra steps after adding a new custom column. The second option is to use the ColumnType optional operand of the Table.AddColumn() function. The following expression shows the ColumnType optional operand within the Table.AddColumn() function:

```
Table.AddColumn(#"Merged Columns", "Is Yearly Income Below Average", each if
[YearlyIncome] <= List.Average(#"Merged Columns"[YearlyIncome]) then true else
false, type logical)
```

The output now looks as follows, without us adding any new steps:

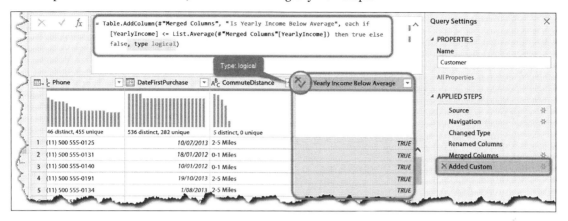

Figure 5.21: Specifying the data type of the new custom column

We can use this column in our data model and data visualizations later to analyze the data relevant to the customers' yearly income. Save the file as Chapter 5, Common Data Preparation Steps, Added Custom Columns.pbix.

Adding a column from examples

Adding a column from examples is a brilliant feature of Power Query. It not only helps speed up the development process but also helps developers learn Power Query. The idea is that we can create a new column from sample data by entering the expected values in a sample column. Power Query then guesses what sort of transformation we are after and generates the expressions needed to achieve the results we entered manually. We can create new columns from selected columns or all columns. Let us have a quick look at this feature by example.

Using the Chapter 5, Common Data Preparation Steps, Added Custom Columns.pbix sample file from the previous section, we want to extract the usernames of the customers from their **EmailAddress** column, while the email structure is UserName@adventure-works.com, from the **Customer** table.

You can download the sample file from here:

https://github.com/PacktPublishing/Expert-Data-Modeling-with-Power-BI-Second-Edition/blob/9d6388ffe6e83586a02de81ff959e04c31dbf1da/Samples/Chapter%2005/Chapter%205,%20Common%20Data%20Preparation%20Steps,%20Added%20Custom%20Columns.pbix

The following steps show how we can achieve this by adding a column from examples from Power Query Editor:

1. Select the **Customer** table from the **Queries** pane.
2. Select the **EmailAddress** column.
3. Click the **Column From Examples** drop-down button from the **Add Columns** tab of the ribbon.
4. Click the **From Selection** option:

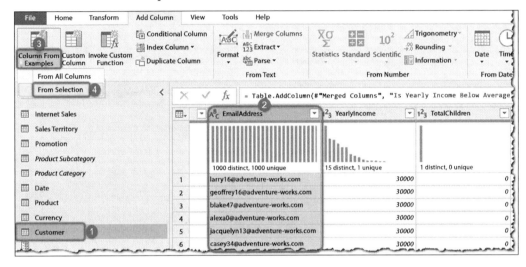

Figure 5.22: Adding a column from examples

5. Type in some expected results by double-clicking a cell and typing in a value, as shown here:

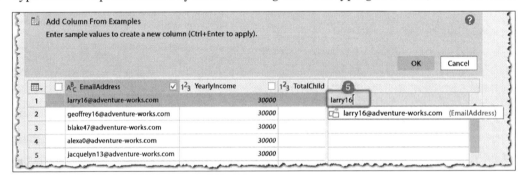

Figure 5.23: Entering example values

6. Press *Enter* on your keyboard. At this point, if Power Query correctly guesses what we are after, we can enter a name for the new column. Otherwise, we must continue entering more examples to help Power Query make a better guess.
7. Click **OK**.

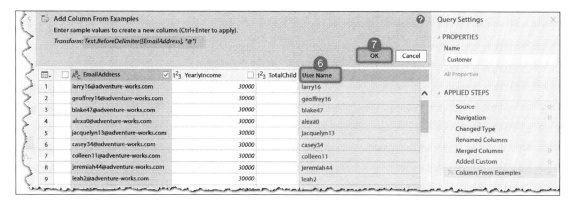

Figure 5.24: Naming the new column and confirming the new column from an example

Note the section highlighted in the preceding image. We can learn how to write Power Query expressions by looking at the Power Query expressions appearing in the highlighted section. Let us apply the changes and save the file as a new file: Chapter 5, Common Data Preparation Steps, Added Column from Example.pbix.

One of the drawbacks of this method is that it only allows us to enter the example for a couple of rows, which does not make the best pattern for Power Query to guess what we are after. The other downside is that Power Query cannot guess the logic of the entered examples in complex cases. Therefore, it does not work properly.

Duplicating a column

Another common transformation step under the **Add Column** tab is duplicating a column. In many scenarios, we want to duplicate a column, such as keeping the original column available in our model while needing to transform it into a new column. Let us revisit the scenario that we looked at earlier in this chapter in the *Splitting a column by delimiter* section. In that scenario, we split the **OrderDateTime** column from the **Internet Sales** table into two columns, **Order Date** and **Order Time**. In this section, we do the same thing, but this time we duplicate the **OrderDateTime** column instead of splitting it. We use the Chapter 5, Common Data Preparation Steps, Fixed PostCode.pbix sample file that can be downloaded from here: https://github.com/PacktPublishing/Expert-Data-Modeling-with-Power-BI-Second-Edition/blob/main/Samples/Chapter%205/Chapter%205,%20Common%20Data%20Preparation%20Steps,%20Fixed%20PostCode.pbix.

After opening the sample file, open Power Query Editor and follow these steps:

1. Select the **Internet Sales** table from the **Queries** pane.
2. Select the **OrderDateTime** column.

3. Click the **Duplicate Column** button from the **Add Column** tab of the ribbon (the duplicate column can also be accessed by right-clicking the column):

Figure 5.25: Selecting and duplicating a column

4. Click the **OrderDateTime** column.
5. From the **Transform** tab, click the **Date** dropdown from the **Date and Time Column** section.
6. Click the **Date Only** option:

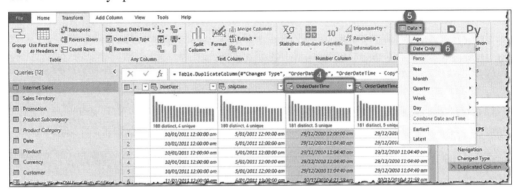

Figure 5.26: Transforming OrderDateTime to Date

7. Click the **OrderDateTime - Copy** column.
8. Click the **Time** dropdown from the **Date and Time Column** section.
9. Click the **Time Only** option:

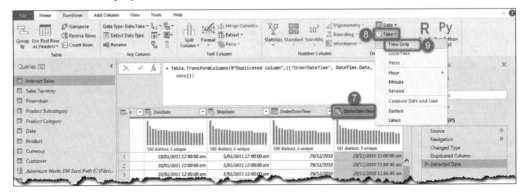

Figure 5.27: Transforming OrderDateTime – Copy to Time

10. Rename the **OrderDateTime** column to **Order Date** and rename the **OrderDateTime – Copy** column to **Order Time**:

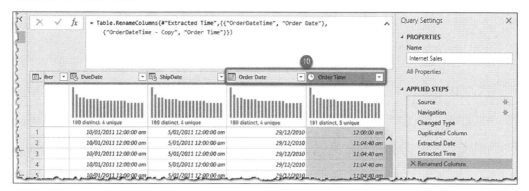

Figure 5.28: Renaming the columns

Apply the changes and save the file as a new file named Chapter 5, Common Data Preparation Steps, Duplicated Columns.pbix.

We could rename the **OrderDateTime - Copy** column in **Duplicated Column** by changing the expression of the **Duplicated Column** step from the following expression:

```
Table.DuplicateColumn(Internet_Sales_with_Time_Table, "OrderDateTime", 
"OrderDateTime - Copy")
```

To this one:

```
Table.DuplicateColumn(Internet_Sales_with_Time_Table, "OrderDateTime", "Order 
Time")
```

However, since we also need to rename the OrderDateTime column, it makes sense to rename both columns in a separate step.

 This approach has an advantage over the previous approach, where we *Split a column by delimiter*. In the first approach, the Split Column breaks the query folding when the query is connected to a relational database such as SQL Server. But in the second approach, the query folds to the Extracted Date. But the Extracted Time stops the query folding. There are a few approaches to overcoming the unfoldable step, but they are out of the scope of this section. We discuss the query folding concept in detail in *Chapter 7, Data Preparation Common Best Practices*.

Filtering rows

The other common transformation is **filtering rows**. There are many use cases where we may want to restrict the results by specific values. For instance, we may want to filter the Product table to show the products with a **Status** of **Current**. Filtering the rows based on columns' values is very simple. We have to select the desired column, click the arrow down button (▼) from the column's caption, and select the values we want to use to filter the rows. The following image shows the preceding use case:

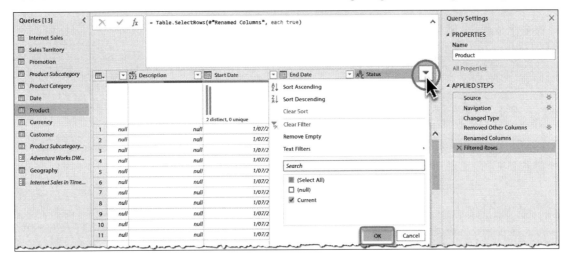

Figure 5.29: Filtering rows

While this is a straightforward step, not all filtering use cases are simple, such as when we do not have specific values to filter the rows upon. Instead, the business provides a list specifying the values to use in the filters. Let us look at this with a scenario.

The business provides a list of **Approved Product Subcategories** every season in Excel format. We need to filter the **Product** table on the **Product Subcategory** column by the **Approved Product Subcategories** column from the **Approved Subcategories** table. To simplify this scenario, we use the Chapter 5, Common Data Preparation Steps, Dynamic Filtering, Base.pbix sample file containing the **Approved Subcategories** query connected to the Approved Subcategories List.xlsx source file. You can download the sample file from here:

https://github.com/PacktPublishing/Expert-Data-Modeling-with-Power-BI-Second-Edition/blob/9d6388ffe6e83586a02de81ff959e04c31dbf1da/Samples/Chapter%2005/Chapter%205,%20Common%20Data%20Preparation%20Steps,%20Dynamic%20Filtering,%20Base.pbix

... and the source Excel file from here:

https://github.com/PacktPublishing/Expert-Data-Modeling-with-Power-BI-Second-Edition/blob/9d6388ffe6e83586a02de81ff959e04c31dbf1da/Samples/Chapter%2005/Approved%20Subcategories%20List.xlsx

After opening the file, in Power Query Editor, change the value of the **Approved Subcategories List** path parameter to point to the Approved Subcategories List.xlsx Excel file on your local machine.

The following image shows the contents of the **Approved Subcategories** query in Power Query Editor:

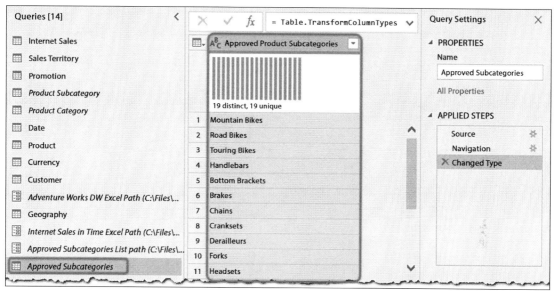

Figure 5.30: Approved Subcategories

Filtering a column by the values of a column from another table is simple. We only need to know how to reference a column from another table. To reference a column from another table, we need to have the query name followed by the column name in brackets, as shown in the following expression:

```
#"Query_Name"[Column_Name]
```

The result of the preceding structure is a **list** value. In our scenario, the **Approved Product Subcategories** column from the **Approved Subcategories** table filters the **Product Subcategory** column from the **Product** table. So, we use the `List.Contains(list, values)` function to get the matching values with the following structure:

```
List.Contains(#"Referenced_Table"[Referenced_Column], [Column_to_be_Filtered])
```

So, the `List.Contains()` function in our scenario looks like the following expression:

```
List.Contains(#"Approved Subcategories"[Approved Product Subcategories],
[Product Subcategory])
```

We use Power Query Editor UI to filter the **Product Subcategory** column from the **Product** table with a dummy value. Then, we replace that value in the code with the `List.Contains()` function. Follow these steps to get this done:

1. Select the **Product** table from the **Queries** pane.
2. Filter the **Product Subcategory** column by any value; we used **Bike Racks** in the filter.

3. Click **OK**:

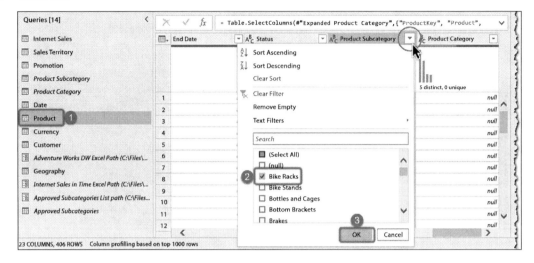

Figure 5.31: Filtering the rows of the Product table by a value of the Product Subcategory column

The following is the Power Query expression that the UI generates:

```
= Table.SelectRows(#"Removed Other Columns", each ([Product Subcategory] = "Bike Racks"))
```

As shown in the following screenshot, the generated expression looks like this:

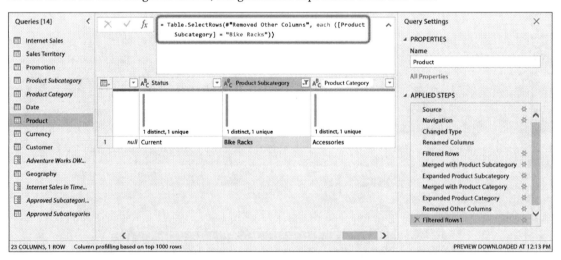

Figure 5.32: Power Query expression generated by Power Query Editor UI

The `Table.SelectRows(table, condition)` function accepts a table, which is the previous step, named `#"Removed Other Columns"`, and a condition called `each ([Product Subcategory] = "Bike Racks")`. So, here is how we read the preceding code in natural English.

Select rows from the #"Removed Other Columns" step where each value in the **Product Subcategory** column is "Bike Racks". We want to change the preceding code to select rows from the #"Removed Other Columns" step where **each** value in the **Product Subcategory** column is contained in the **Approved Product Subcategories** column from the **Approved Subcategories** table.

Now, let's continue. We want to change the condition parameter of the Table.SelectRows(table, condition) function from ([Product Subcategory] = "Bike Racks") to List.Contains(#"Approved Subcategories"[Approved Product Subcategories], [Product Subcategory]), as shown here:

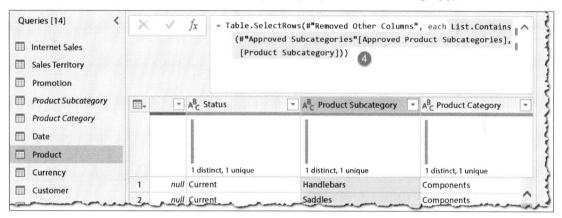

Figure 5.33: Changing the condition of the Table.SelectRows function

The **Product** table is now being filtered by the values of the **Approved Product Subcategories** column from the **Approved Subcategories** table.

Let us save the file as a new file: *Chapter 5*, Common Data Preparation Steps, Dynamic Filtering, Applied Filter.pbix.

Working with Group By

One of the most valuable and advanced techniques in data modeling is creating summary tables. In many scenarios, using this method is very beneficial. We can use this method to manage our Power BI file's size and improve performance and memory consumption. Summarization is a known technique in data warehousing where we change the granularity of a fact table to a higher grain. But in Power Query, there are other cases where we can use the **Group By** functionality to cleanse the data. From a data modeling point of view, we summarize a table by grouping it into descriptive columns and aggregating the numeric values.

Let us go through a scenario and see how the **Group By** functionality works.

In this section, we use the Chapter 5, Common Data Preparation Steps, Fixed OrderDateTime Data Type.pbix sample file that we created before. You can download the file from here:

https://github.com/PacktPublishing/Expert-Data-Modeling-with-Power-BI-Second-Edition/blob/9d6388ffe6e83586a02de81ff959e04c31dbf1da/Samples/Chapter%2005/Chapter%205,%20Common%20Data%20Preparation%20Steps,%20Fixed%20OrderDateTime%20Data%20Type.pbix

We want to summarize the **Internet Sales** table into a new **Internet Sales Summary** table with the following conditions:

- Group by **ProductKey**
- Group by **OrderDateTime**
- Sum of **SalesAmount**
- Count of **Internet Sales**
- Average of **OrderQuantity**
- Sum of **TaxAmt**
- Average of **TotalProductCost**

After opening the sample file, open Power Query Editor and follow these steps:

1. Right-click on the **Internet Sales** table.
2. Click **Reference**:

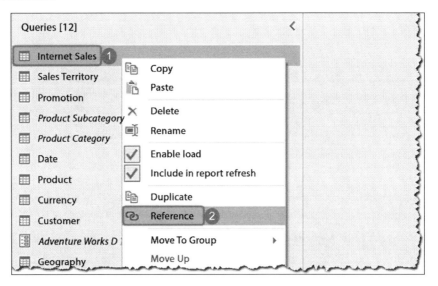

Figure 5.34: Referencing the Internet Sales table

3. Rename the new query to **Internet Sales Summary**.
4. Select the **ProductKey** and **OrderDateTime** columns participating in the Group By action.
5. Click the **Group By** button from the **Transform** tab of the ribbon.
6. Type in Sales for **New column name**, select the **Sum** operation, and select the **SalesAmount** column.
7. Click the **Add aggregation** button.
8. Repeat *steps 4* to *7* to add the other aggregations.
9. Click **OK**.

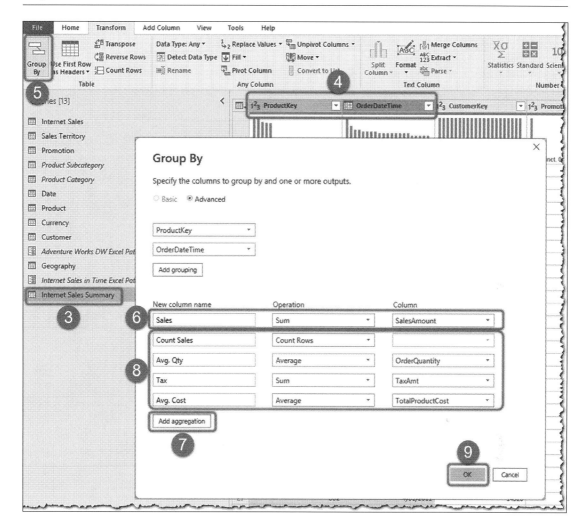

Figure 5.35: Group By columns in Power Query

The result of the preceding operation looks as follows:

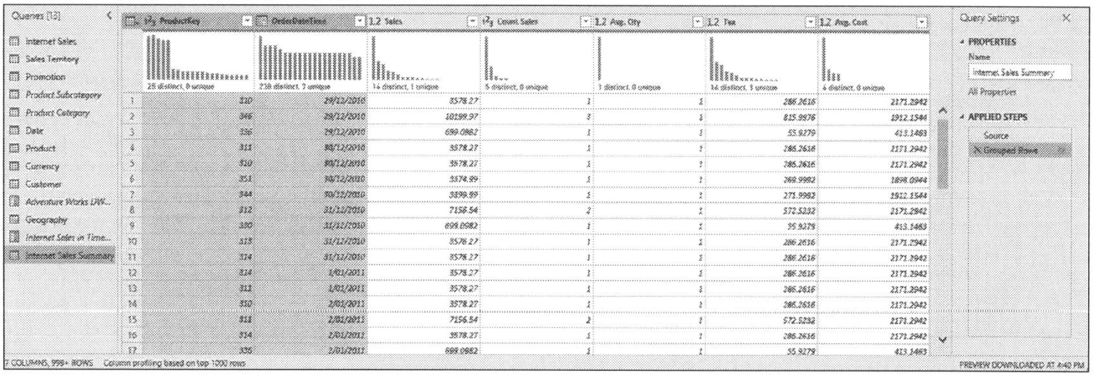

Figure 5.36: Result of the Group By operation

Apply the changes and save the file as a new file: Chapter 5, Common Data Preparation Steps, Group By.pbix.

Usually, the summary table has much fewer rows than the original table. In some cases, due to business requirements, we must unload the original table from the data model and only use the summary table.

In our sample, the granularity of the **Internet Sales Summary** table is **Product** and **Date**, containing **23,797** rows, while the **Internet Sales** table has **60,398** rows. The following image shows the number of rows in both tables from the **Data** view:

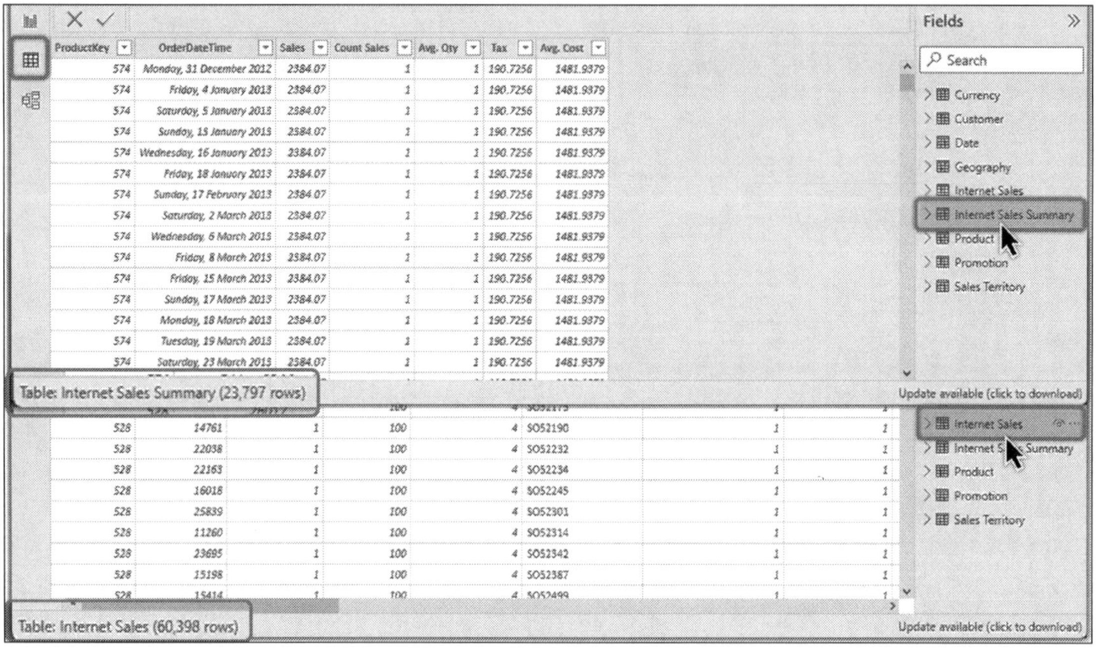

Figure 5.37: The Internet Sales Summary table content

So if we create the relationships between the **Product** table and the **Date** table, we can analyze the **Sales** data by **Product** and **Date** over a much smaller table, which translates to better performance.

Appending queries

There are some scenarios where we get the data with the same structure from different sources, and we want to consolidate it into a single table. In those cases, we need to append the queries. We have two options to append the queries:

- Append the queries to the first query
- Append the queries as a new query

The latter is prevalent when we follow ETL best practices. We unload all the queries, append them as a new query, and load the new query into the data model. Therefore, the unloaded queries work as ETL pipelines. However, it does not mean that the first option is not applicable.

Suppose we have a simple business requirement that can be achieved by appending two or more queries to the first query. In that case, use the first option instead. The critical point to note when we append queries is that the `Table.Combine(tables as list, optional columns as any)` function accepts a list of tables. If the column names in the tables are the same, it appends the data with the same column name, regardless of the columns' data types. Therefore, if we have two tables and both tables have a **Column1** column, then the data of those two columns, regardless of their data types, gets appended with the same column name.

If the data types do not match, the appended column data type is **any**. Remember, Power Query is case-sensitive. Therefore, if we have the **column1** column in **Table1** and the **Column1** column in **Table2**, the column names are different when we append the two tables. So, after appending, we have a table with both **column1** and **Column1** columns. Let us look at an example.

For this example, we use the `Chapter 5, Common Data Preparation Steps, Append Queries.pbix` sample file, which contains sales data for different years in different file formats. You can download the sample file and its source data from here:

`https://github.com/PacktPublishing/Expert-Data-Modeling-with-Power-BI-Second-Edition/blob/9d6388ffe6e83586a02de81ff959e04c31dbf1da/Samples/Chapter%2005/Chapter%205,%20Common%20Data%20Preparation%20Steps,%20Append%20Queries.pbix`

We can always find the data sources used in Power BI Desktop by following these steps:

1. Click the **Transform data** dropdown.
2. Click **Data source settings**.

As shown in the following image, we have three separate queries for each year's sales data, which can change by selecting each file and clicking the **Change Source...** button:

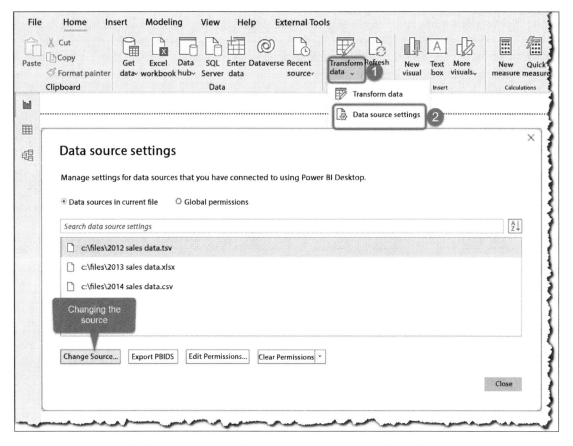

Figure 5.38: Sales data spread across three separate queries coming from different data sources

Change the source files to the downloaded source files on your local drive. After closing the **Data source settings** dialog box, a warning appears, as illustrated in the following image. Click **Apply changes**:

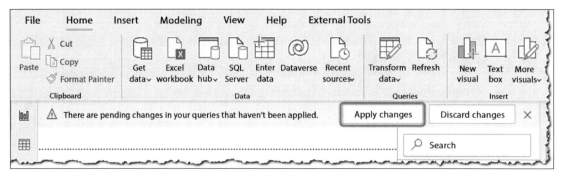

Figure 5.39: Applying changes after changing the source files in Power BI Desktop

In this scenario, we want to consolidate the queries into a single **Sales** query. To do so, follow these steps in Power Query Editor:

1. Select the 2012 **Sales Data** query from the **Queries** pane.
2. Click the **Append Queries** drop-down button from the **Home** tab of the ribbon.
3. Click **Append Queries as New**.
4. Click **Three or more tables**.
5. Select **2013 Sales Data** and **2014 Sales Data** from the **Available tables** list.
6. Click the **Add >>** button.
7. Click **OK**:

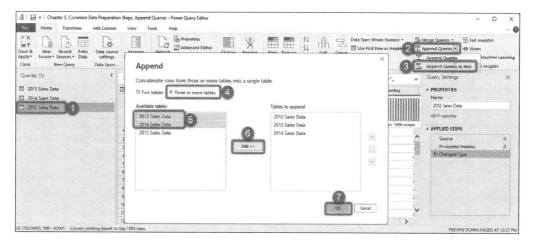

Figure 5.40: Appending queries as a new query

The preceding steps create a new query named **Append1**.

8. Rename the query to **Sales**.
9. Unload all the queries that we appended by right-clicking on 2012 **Sales Data**.

10. Untick the **Enable load** option as shown in the following image:

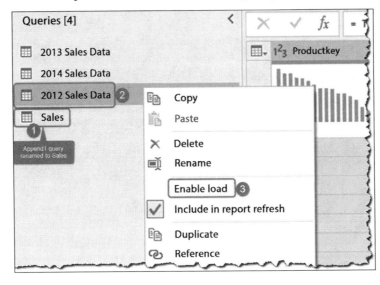

Figure 5.41: Renaming the Append1 query and unloading the original queries

Repeat the preceding process to disable loading for the **2013 Sales Data** and **2014 Sales Data**.

The results of the preceding steps raise an issue with the data. The following screenshot highlights this issue:

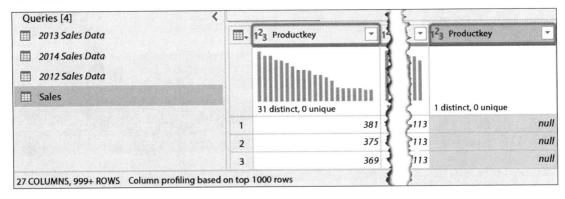

Figure 5.42: There are two ProductKey columns as a result of the case sensitivity of Power Query

As shown in the preceding image, there are two **Product Key** columns—**ProductKey** and **Productkey**. This is a result of Power Query's case sensitivity. So, we need to rename one of those columns from the sourcing query. Looking at these queries reveals that the **Productkey** column comes from the 2012 **Sales Data** query, while the other two queries contain **ProductKey**. We leave this issue for you to fix.

Merging queries

Another common data transformation operation is merging queries. The merge queries functionality is useful when you want to denormalize snowflakes absorbing the data stored in different tables into one table. When using the UI in Power Query, depending on the selected matching type, Power Query uses one of the following functions behind the scenes:

- `Table.NestedJoin()`
- `Table.FuzzyNestedJoin()`

The following image shows the relevant UI:

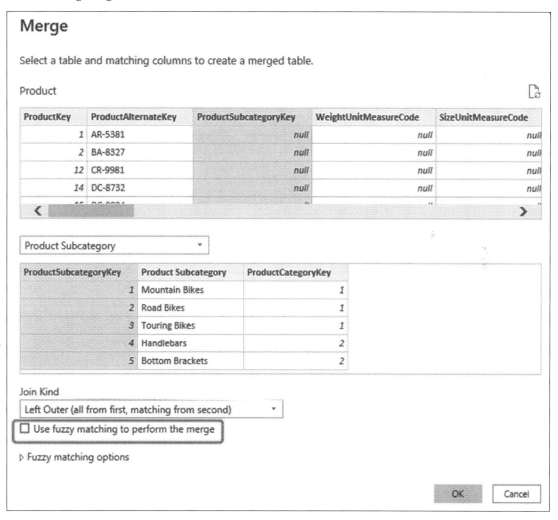

Figure 5.43: Merging queries via the UI uses different Power Query functions, depending on the matching type

If we do not tick the **Use fuzzy matching to perform the merge** box, Power Query generates the following function:

```
Table.NestedJoin(
    FirstTable as table
    , KeyColumnofFirstTable as any
    , SecondTable as any
    , KeyColumnofSecondTable as any
    , NewColumnName as text
    , optional JoinKind as nullable JoinKind.Type
)
```

Otherwise, Power Query generates the following:

```
Table.FuzzyNestedJoin(
    FirstTable as table
    , KeyColumnofFirstTable as any
    , SecondTable as table
    , KeyColumnofSecondTable as any
    , NewColumnName as text
    , optional JoinKind as nullable JoinKind.Type
    , optional JoinOptions as nullable record
)
```

In both preceding functions, the join kind is optional, with **Left Outer** as the default if not specified. We can choose to use numeric enumerations to specify the join kind or explicitly mention the join kind. The following table shows the join kinds and their respective enumerations:

Join Kind	Enumeration
JoinKind.Inner	0
JoinKind.LeftOuter	1
JoinKind.RightOuter	2
JoinKind.FullOuter	3
JoinKind.LeftAnti	4
JoinKind.RightAnti	5

Table 5.2: Power Query join kinds in Merge Queries

A difference between the `Table.NestedJoin()` function and the `Table.FuzzyNestedJoin()` function is that the `Table.NestedJoin()` function uses the equality of the key columns' values, while the `Table.FuzzyNestedJoin()` function uses text similarities in the key columns.

IMPORTANT NOTE FOR MERGING TWO QUERIES

Merge queries allows composite keys in the merging tables; therefore, we can select multiple columns while selecting the key columns of the first and the second table.

There are six different join types. Therefore, we must understand how the join types are different and which join types suit the purpose.

In this section, we focus on the join kinds and how they are different:

- **Inner:** Joins two queries based on the matching values of the key columns from both tables participating in the join operation.
- **LeftOuter:** Joins two queries based on all values of the key columns from the first table and matches the values of the key columns from the second table.
- **RightOuter:** Joins two queries based on all the values of the key columns from the second table and matches the values of the key columns from the first table.
- **FullOuter:** Joins two queries based on all the values of the key columns from both tables participating in the join operation.
- **LeftAnti:** Joins two queries based on all the values of the key columns from the first table that do not have any matching values in the key columns from the second table.
- **RightAnti:** Joins two queries based on all the values of the key columns from the second table that do not have any matching values in the key columns from the first table.

Let's use a graphical representation of different joins to understand this:

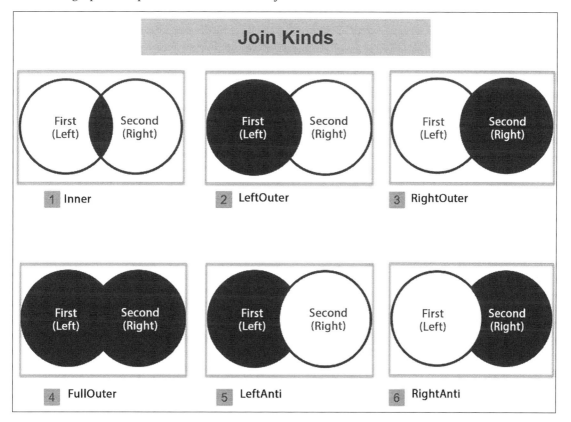

Figure 5.44: Different join kinds

Please refer to *Chapter 1*, *Introduction to Data Modeling in Power BI*, in the *Snowflaking* section, for an example scenario where we denormalized the **Product Subcategory** and **Product Category** tables into the **Product** table.

Duplicating and referencing queries

Duplicating and referencing queries are somehow similar. We duplicate a query when we need to have all the transformation steps we already took on the original query. At the same time, we want to change those steps or add more transformation steps. In that case, we must change the original query's nature, translating it so that it has a different meaning from a business point of view. But when we reference a query, we are referencing the final results of the query. Therefore, we do not get the transformation steps in the new query (the referencing query). Referencing a query is a common way to break down the transformation activities. This is the preferred way of preparing the data for most **Extract, Transformation, and Load** (**ETL**) experts and data warehousing professionals. In that sense, we can do the following:

- We have base queries connected to the source system that resembles the **Extract** part of the ETL process.
- We reference the base queries and go through the **Transformation** steps of the ETL process.
- Finally, we reference the transformation queries to prepare our Star Schema. This is the **Load** part of the ETL process.

In the preceding approach, we unload all the queries for the first two points as they are our transformation steps, so we only enable data loading for the queries of the **Load** part (the last point). Duplicating and referencing a query is simple; right-click a desired query from the **Queries** pane and click either **Duplicate** or **Reference**, as shown in the following screenshot:

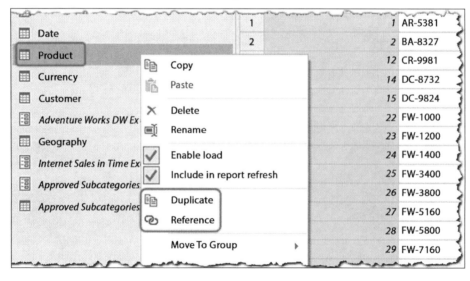

Figure 5.45: Referencing or duplicating a query

When we reference a query, we must be vigilant about making changes to the base query. Any changes to the base query may break the referencing query or queries.

When the base query is loaded into the data model, if we make changes to it and load the data into the data model, the base query and all the queries referencing it will be refreshed. However, this is not the case when we duplicate queries. The duplicated query is independent of its base query.

So far, we've looked at the most common table manipulations in Power Query. In the next section, we'll look at common text manipulations.

Replacing values

In data cleansing, replacing values is one of the most common transformation activities. A simple example is when we have a description column in the source system containing free text, and we want to replace some parts of the description with something else.

Power Query Editor UI uses the `Table.ReplaceValue(table as table, OldValue as any, NewValue as any, Replacer as function, columnsToSearch as list)` function behind the scenes to replace a value in a table. If we want to replace the value of a **List**, it uses the `List.ReplaceValue(list as list, OldValue as any, NewValue as any, Replacer as function)` function. Depending on the value's data type, the **Replacer** function can be either `Replacer.ReplaceText` or `Replacer.ReplaceValue`. The difference between the two is that we can use `Replacer.ReplaceText` to replace text values, while we can use `Replacer.ReplaceValue` to replace any values. For instance, if we want to replace semicolons with colons in a text column, we take the following steps from the UI:

1. Click a column whose values we want to be replaced.
2. Click **Replace Values** from the **Transform** tab.
3. Depending on the data type of the selected column, more options are available to us under **Advanced options**, such as **Replace using special characters**.
4. Type ; into the **Value To Find** text box.
5. Type , into the **Replace With** text box.
6. Click **OK**:

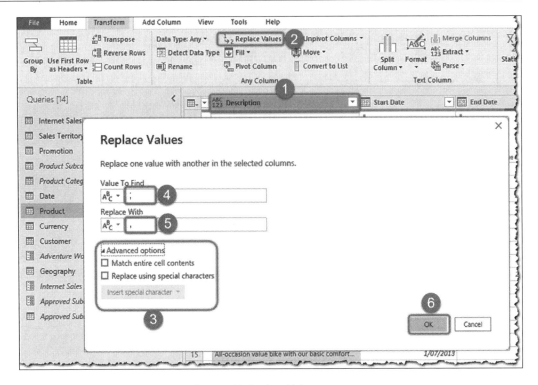

Figure 5.46: Replace Values popup

However, in most real-world cases, we face more challenging scenarios. Let us continue with a scenario.

The business wants to show product descriptions in a table visualization. There are some long descriptions. The business wants to cut off excessive text in the Description column from the Product table when the description's length is greater than 30 characters and show "..." at the end of the description. These three dots indicate that the text values in the **Description** columns are truncated. We use the Chapter 5, Common Data Preparation Steps, Raw.pbix sample file for this scenario. You can download the file from here:

https://github.com/PacktPublishing/Expert-Data-Modeling-with-Power-BI-Second-Edition/blob/9d6388ffe6e83586a02de81ff959e04c31dbf1da/Samples/Chapter%2005/Chapter%205,%20Common%20Data%20Preparation%20Steps,%20Raw.pbix

The following steps show how to use Power Query Editor UI to generate the preliminary expression and how we change it to achieve our goal:

1. Select the **Product** query.
2. Select the **Description** column.
3. Click the **Replace Values** button from the **Transform** tab of the ribbon.

4. Type in dummy values in both the **Value To Find** and **Replace With** text boxes.
5. Click **OK**:

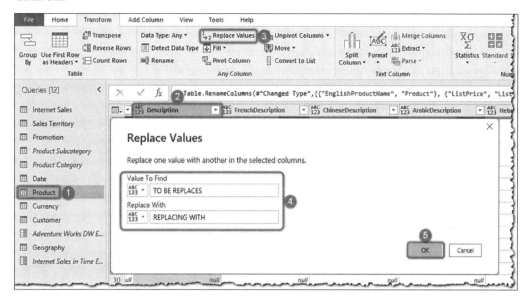

Figure 5.47: Replacing a dummy value

6. In the generated expression, replace the **TO BE REPLACED** string with the following expression:

   ```
   each if Text.Length([Description]) > 30 then [Description] else ""
   ```

7. Replace **REPLACING WITH** with the following expression:

   ```
   each Text.Start([Description], 30) & "..."
   ```

8. Click the **Submit** (✔) button.

The overall expression must look like this:

```
= Table.ReplaceValue(#"Renamed Columns", each if Text.Length([Description])
> 30 then [Description] else "",each Text.Start([Description], 30) &
"...",Replacer.ReplaceValue,{"Description"})
```

The preceding code block returns the following output:

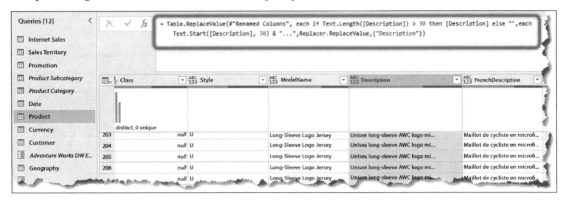

Figure 5.48: Cutting off the values in the Description column that are longer than 30 characters

Apply the changes and save the file as a new file: Chapter 5, Common Data Preparation Steps, Replaced Values.pbix.

Replacing values is a widespread transformation step with many use cases, such as replacing values based on another column, values from a previous step, or even values from another query. So it is down to the developer's creativity and the nature of the challenge to replace values efficiently.

Extracting numbers from text

Another common data preparation step is when we need to extract a number from text values. An excellent example is when we want to extract a flat number or a ZIP code from an address. Other examples include extracting the numeric part of a sales order number or cleaning full names of typos, such as when some names contain numbers. We will continue using the Chapter 5, Common Data Preparation Steps, Replaced Values.pbix sample file from the previous section. In our scenario, we want to add two new columns to the **Customer** table, as follows:

- Extract **Flat Number** as a new column from **AddressLine1**.
- Extract the rest of the address, **Street Name**, as a new column.

As the following image shows, the AddressLine1 column contains the flat number in different parts of the address; therefore, splitting by transitioning from digit to non-digit would not work:

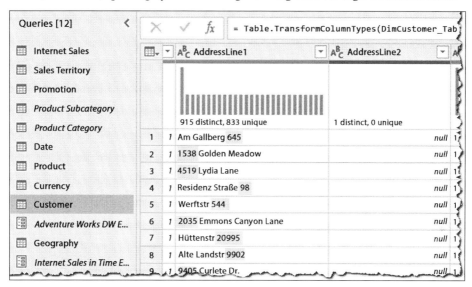

Figure 5.49: Flat numbers appear in different places in AddressLine1

To achieve our goal, we need to extract the numbers from text. To do so, we use the `Text.Select(Text as nullable text, SelectChars as any)` function. Follow these steps in Power Query Editor:

1. Select the **Customer** query.
2. Click the **Custom Column** button from the **Add Column** tab of the ribbon.
3. Type in **Flat Number** as **New column name**.
4. Type in the following expression:

    ```
    Text.Select([AddressLine1], {"0".."9"})
    ```

5. Click **OK**.

The following screenshot shows the preceding steps:

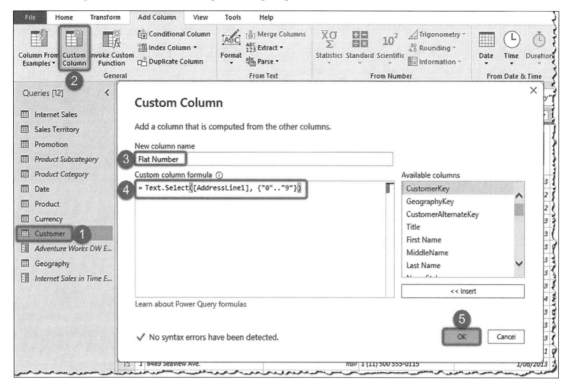

Figure 5.50: Extracting Flat Number from Address as a new column

Now, we use the same function with a different character list to extract the street name from **AddressLine1**, as follows:

1. Click the **Custom Column** button again to add a new column.
2. Type in **Street Name** as **New column name**.
3. Type in the following expression:

   ```
   Text.Select([AddressLine1], {"a".."z", "A".."Z", " ", "."})
   ```

4. Click **OK**.

The preceding expression keeps all small and capital letters, the space character, and the dot character dropping any other characters. The following screenshot shows the results:

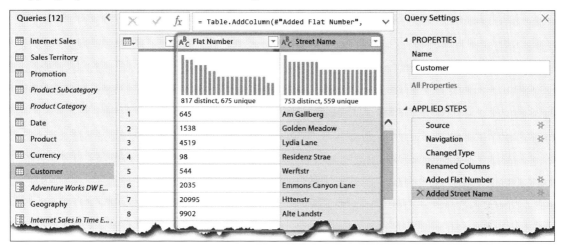

Figure 5.51: The Flat Number and Street Name columns added to the Customer table

Apply changes and save the file as Chapter 5, Common Data Preparation Steps, Extracting Numbers From Text.pbix.

As the preceding image shows, we renamed the last two steps to have more meaningful step names. You may have already noticed that the data type of both columns is text. As we discussed in the *Adding a custom column* section, it is better to specify the new column's data within the Table.AddColumn() function.

Dealing with Date, DateTime, and DateTimeZone

Generating date, datetime, and datetimezone values in Power Query is simple. We just need to use one of the following three functions:

1. To generate date values, we can use the following command:

   ```
   #date(year as number, month as number, day as number)
   ```

2. To generate datetime values, we can use the following command:

   ```
   #datetime(year as number, month as number, day as number, hour as number,
   minute as number, second as number)
   ```

3. To generate datetimezone values, we can use the following command:

   ```
   #datetimezone(year as number, month as number, day as number, hour as
   number, minute as number, second as number, offsetHours as number,
   offsetMinutes as number)
   ```

The following code generates a record of the Date, DateTime, and DateTimeZone values:

```
let
    Source = [
    Date = #date(2020, 8, 9)
    , DateTime = #datetime(2020, 8, 9, 17, 0, 0)
    , DateTimeZone = #datetimezone(2020, 8, 9, 17, 0, 0, 12, 0)
    ]
in
    Source
```

The results of the preceding code are illustrated in the following image:

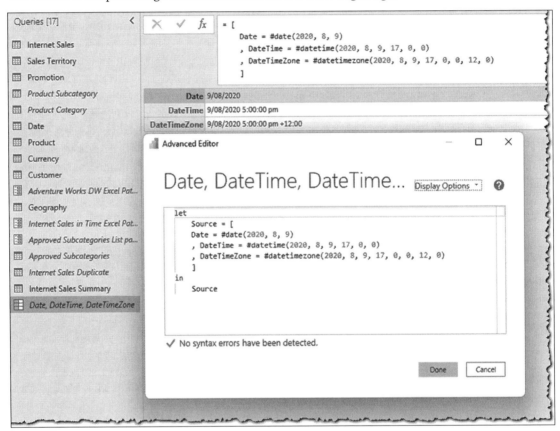

Figure 5.52: Generating Date, DateTime, and DateTimeZone values

A common use case is when we have **Smart Date Keys** and want to generate the corresponding dates or vice versa.

A **Smart Date Key** is an integer representation of a date value. Using a Smart Date Key is very common in data warehousing for saving storage and memory. So, the `20200809` integer value represents the `2020/08/09` date value. Therefore, if our source data comes from a data warehouse, we are likely to have Smart Date Keys in our tables.

Let us continue with a scenario. We have the date values in the **Internet Sales** table. We want to get the Smart Date Key of the **OrderDate** column as a new **OrderDateKey** column.

We use the `Chapter 5, Common Data Preparation Steps.pbix` sample file that can be downloaded from here:

https://github.com/PacktPublishing/Expert-Data-Modeling-with-Power-BI-Second-Edition/blob/9d6388ffe6e83586a02de81ff959e04c31dbf1da/Samples/Chapter%2005/Chapter%205,%20Common%20Data%20Preparation%20Steps.pbix

Follow these steps in Power Query Editor:

1. In the **Internet Sales** table, add a new column.
2. Name it **OrderDateKey**.
3. Use the following expression as our **Custom Column Formula**:

    ```
    Int64.From(Date.ToText([OrderDate], "yyyyMMdd"))
    ```

4. Click **OK**.
5. Add `Int64.Type` as the optional operand of the `Table.AddColumn()` function from the expression bar.

The following screenshot shows the preceding steps:

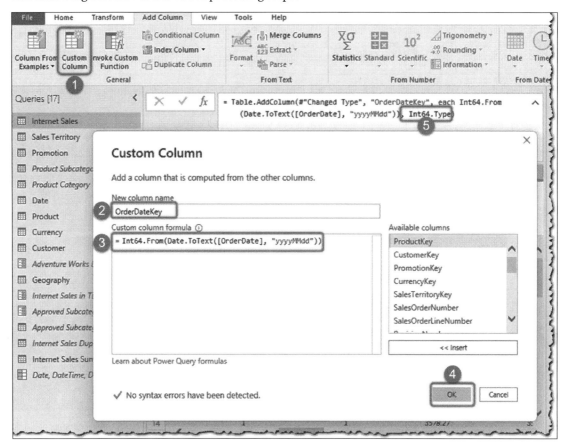

Figure 5.53: Adding OrderDateKey (Smart Date Key) as a new column

Another scenario that can happen from time to time is when we must represent the Date values in a different time zone. Let us go through this with a scenario.

The Date values in the OrderDateTime column in the **Internet Sales Date Time** table are stored in New Zealand's local date-time. The business must also show **OrderDateTime** in **Universal Time Co-ordinated** (**UTC**) too.

To achieve this, we need to add a new custom column by using the `DateTimeZone.ToUtc(DateTimeZone as nullable datetimezone)` function:

```
Table.AddColumn(#"Changed Type", "OrderDateTimeUTC", each DateTimeZone.
ToUtc(DateTimeZone.From([OrderDateTime])), DateTimeZone.Type)
```

The following screenshot shows the results of adding the new custom column:

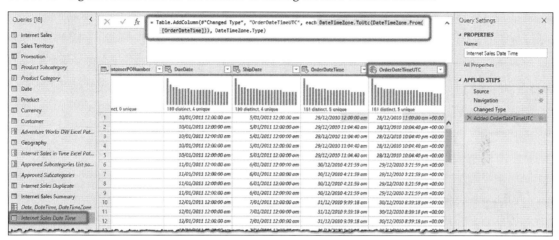

Figure 5.54: OrderDateTimeUTC custom column added

Note the highlighted values in the preceding screenshot. The difference between the two columns is 13 hours. When we look at the data, we see that OrderDateTimeUTC considered the daylight saving dates of my local machine. While I live in New Zealand, my local time difference between UTC time can be either 12 hours or 13 hours, depending on the date. If we use the `DateTimeZone.ToUtc()` function, while not specifying the time zone, the value converts into the DateTimeZone data type and then `DateTimeZone.ToUtc()` turns the values into UTC.

What if we have the values of the **OrderDateTime** column stored in UTC, but the business needs to see the data in our local date-time? We can use the `DateTimeZone.ToLocal(dateTimeZone as nullable datetimezone)` function. So, if we need to add a new column to show the UTC values in local time, then it looks like the following expression:

```
Table.AddColumn(#"Added OrderDateTimeUTC", "OrderDateTimeLocal", each
DateTimeZone.ToLocal([OrderDateTimeUTC]), type datetimezone)
```

The results are shown in the following image:

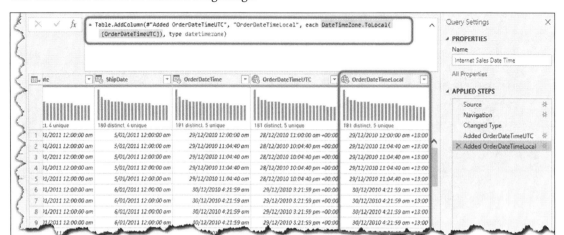

Figure 5.55: Adding a new custom column to show OrderDateTime values in local time from UTC values

Enable the **Internet Sales Date Time** query load, apply changes, and save the file.

Pivoting tables

Working with Pivot tables comes naturally for Power BI developers with an Excel background. The pivot table is a compelling and common functionality across many data analysis tools, including Power Query in Power BI. The pivoting functionality accepts a table, rotates the values of the selected other column as column headers, groups the unique values of all other columns, and calculates the aggregation of values of the selected column by the other columns. In other words, the pivot function aggregates the intersection of the column that represents column headers and all other columns in the table. When we pivot a table in Power Query, we use the following function:

```
Table.Pivot(table as table, pivotValues as list, attributeColumn as text,
valueColumn as text, optional aggregationFunction as nullable function)
```

In the preceding function:

- table is the function's input.
- pivotValues is a list of values of the column that rotates as column headers.
- attributeColumn is the column that the function aggregates the values upon.
- aggregationFunction is one of the available aggregation functions, including Count (all), Count (not blank), Minimum, Maximum, Median, Sum, Average, and Don't aggregate.

Let us have a look at it with an example. We use the Chapter 5, Common Data Preparation Steps, Pivot.
pbix sample file that can be downloaded from here:

https://github.com/PacktPublishing/Expert-Data-Modeling-with-Power-BI-Second-Edition/
blob/9d6388ffe6e83586a02de81ff959e04c31dbf1da/Samples/Chapter%2005/Chapter%205,%20
Common%20Data%20Preparation%20Steps,%20Pivot.pbix

We used the **Enter Data** capability in Power BI to manually enter some data for this exercise, as the following image shows:

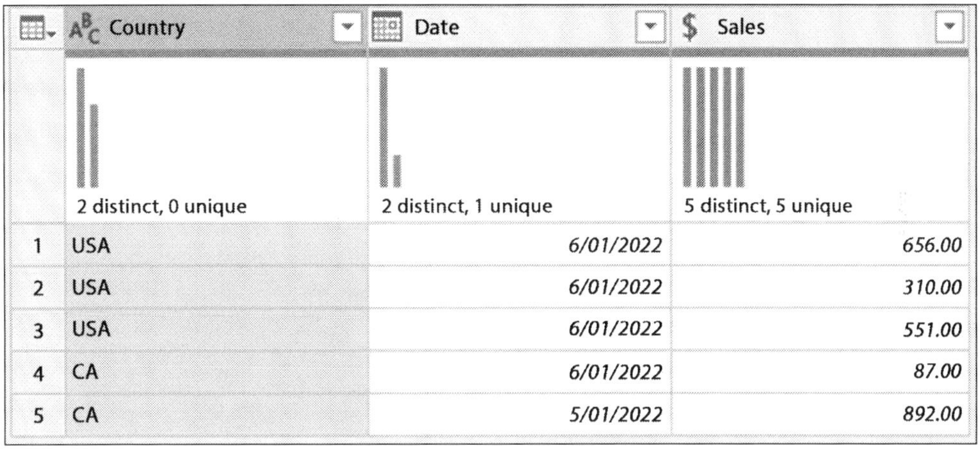

	Country	Date	Sales
	2 distinct, 0 unique	2 distinct, 1 unique	5 distinct, 5 unique
1	USA	6/01/2022	656.00
2	USA	6/01/2022	310.00
3	USA	6/01/2022	551.00
4	CA	6/01/2022	87.00
5	CA	5/01/2022	892.00

Figure 5.56: Sample data manually added in Power BI

As the preceding image shows, we have some country sales values by date. Let us say we want to pivot the country and get the sales values by date. Let us reference the original table to perform the pivot to keep the results as a separate query: **Pivot Country**. Follow these steps:

1. Select the **Pivot Country** query.
2. Select the **Country** column.
3. Click **Pivot Columns** from the **Transform** tab.
4. Select **Sales** from the **Values Column** dropdown.
5. Expand **Advanced options** to ensure the **Sum** aggregation is selected.
6. Click **OK**.

The following image shows the preceding steps:

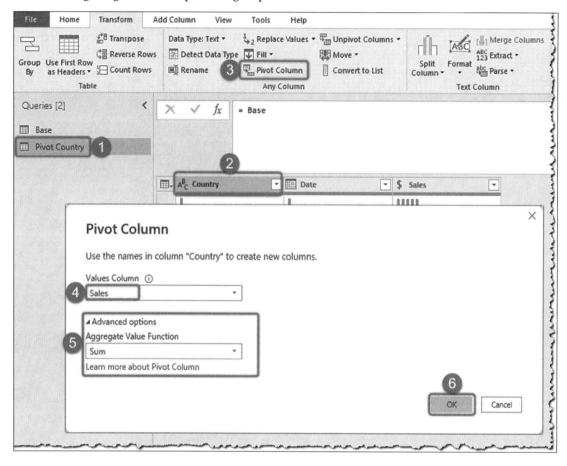

Figure 5.57: Pivoting Country Sales by Date

The following image shows the results of the preceding process:

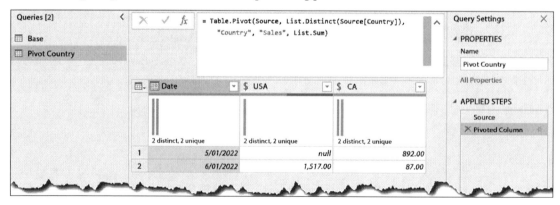

Figure 5.58: The results of pivoting

As mentioned before, **Don't aggregate** is also an option when pivoting a table, and it is when we do not enter the last operand of the `Table.Pivot()` function, which is the aggregation function. Let us see how it works. Again, we perform the pivot operation on a table referencing the **Base** table. This time, we want to pivot the **Date** column without aggregations on the **Sales** column. Follow these steps:

1. Select the **Pivot Date No Agg** table.
2. Select the **Date** column.
3. Click **Pivot Column** from the **Transform** tab.
4. Select **Sales** from **Valyes Column** dropdown.
5. Select **Don't Aggregate** from the **Avdanced options** drop down.
6. Click **OK**.

The following image shows the preceding steps:

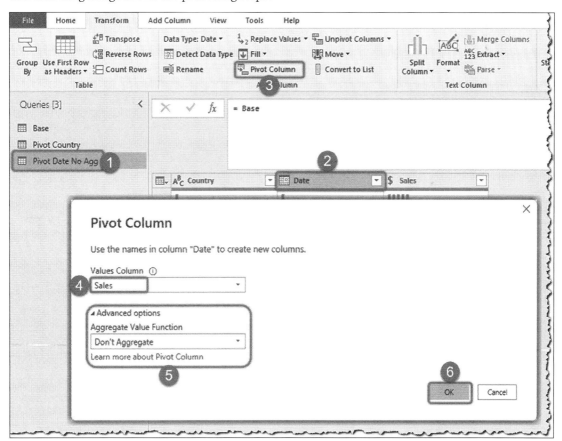

Figure 5.59: The results of pivoting Date by Sales values

As the following image shows, we are getting an error in the results:

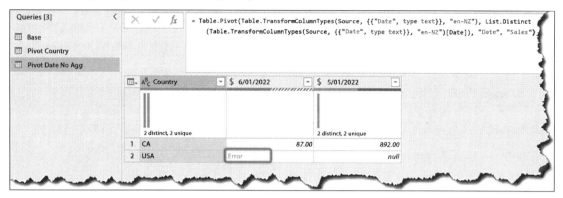

Figure 5.60: The results of pivoting Date by Sales values resulted in errors

Let us see the reason that we get the error. If we look at the data before pivoting, we see that the intersection of the **Date** and **Country** for the **Sales** values contains duplicates if we do not aggregate the data. The following image illustrates the issue:

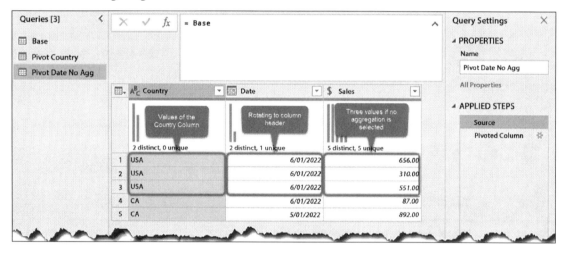

Figure 5.61: The results of pivoting Date by Sales values resulted in errors

As stated before, the pivot function aggregates the intersection of the column that represents column headers and all other columns in the table. So we just need to add a column that represents unique values for each row that forces the intersection of the pivoted column and all other columns to always have unique values. Therefore, adding an **Index Column** must resolve the issue. Follow these steps to add an **Index Column** before pivoting the table:

1. Select the previous step of the pivot column.
2. Click the **Index Column** dropdown from the **Add Column** tab.
3. Select **From 1**.
4. Click **Insert** when the **Insert Step** dialog box appears.

The following image shows the preceding steps:

Figure 5.62: Adding an Index Column

The preceding steps add a new **Index Column** to the table before the pivot happens, so now we expect to get the correct results when we click **Pivoted Column**, as the following image shows:

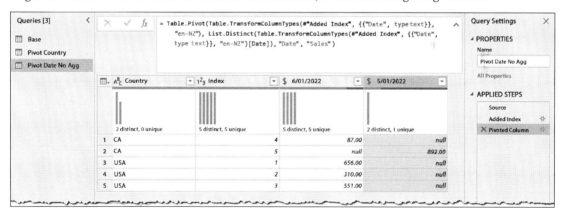

Figure 5.63: Pivoting without aggregation works after adding an Index Column

We can remove the **Index Column** later if necessary.

Summary

This chapter explained some common data preparation steps, which means we now know how data type conversion works and what can go wrong during this. We learned how to split a column, merge columns, add a custom column, and filter rows. We also learned how to use the Group By functionality in queries to create summarized tables. We also learned how to append queries and merge queries; we dealt with scenarios related to `Date`, `DateTime`, and `DateTimeZone`. Lastly, we solved some challenges while pivoting a table.

These skills give us firm ground to move on to the next chapter. In the next chapter, we learn how to prepare a Star Schema in Power Query Editor.

Join us on Discord!

Join The Big Data and Analytics Community on the Packt Discord Server!

Hang out with 558 other members and enjoy free voice and text chat.

`https://packt.link/ips2H`

6

Star Schema Preparation in Power Query Editor

In the previous chapter, we learned about some common data preparation steps, including data type conversions, split columns, merge columns, adding a custom column, and filtering rows. We also learned how to create summary tables using the Group By feature, appending data, merging queries, and pivoting tables.

This chapter uses many topics discussed in the past few chapters and helps you learn how to prepare a Star Schema in Power Query Editor. Data modeling in Power BI starts with preparing a Star Schema. In this chapter, we use the `Chapter 6, Sales Data.xlsx` file, which contains flattened data. You can download the file from here: `https://github.com/PacktPublishing/Expert-Data-Modeling-with-Power-BI-Second-Edition/blob/28e2af1762336ab5236a3b3961c41e9020de8200/Samples/Chapter%2006/Chapter%206,%20Sales%20Data.xlsx`.

A common daily scenario is that we get a set of files containing data exported from a source system, and we need to build a report to answer business questions. Therefore, having the required skills to build a Star Schema on top of a flat design becomes handy.

In this chapter, we cover the following topics:

- Identifying dimensions and facts
- Creating dimension tables
- Creating fact tables

Identifying dimensions and facts

When talking about a Star Schema, we automatically discuss **dimensions** and **facts**. In a Star Schema model, we usually keep all the numeric values in fact tables and put all the descriptive data in the dimension tables. But not all numeric values fall into fact tables. A typical example is Product Unit Price. If we need to do some calculations regarding the Product Unit Price, it is likely to be a part of our fact table; but if it filters or groups the data, it is a part of a dimension.

Designing a data model in a Star Schema is not possible unless we have a concrete understanding of the business requirements and a good level of understanding of the data.

Understanding business requirements

In this section, we will try to find the dimensions and facts based on the business requirements. We also discuss whether to create separate tables for them or not and why. In the following sections, we look at this in more detail and implement the required dimensions and facts.

Before continuing, let us connect to our sample file from Power Query Editor, as shown in the following image. In the past few chapters, we learned how to get the data from an Excel file; therefore, we will skip explaining the **Get Data** steps:

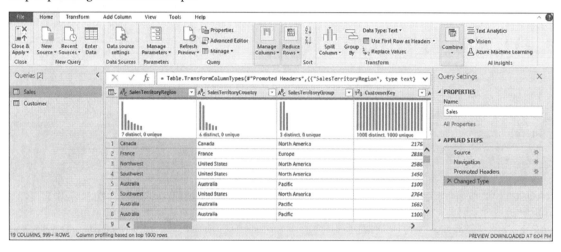

Figure 6.1: Power Query Editor connected to the Chapter 6, Sales Data.xlsx sample data

We must study the data by looking at the sample data itself as well as using Power Query Editor to find out the following:

- The number of tables in the data source
- The linkages between existing tables
- The lowest required grain of Date and Time

The preceding points are the most straightforward initial points we must raise with the business within the initial discovery workshops. These simple points help us understand the scale and complexity of the work. In the following few sections, we look at the preceding points in more detail.

Number of tables in the data source

Our sample file contains two sheets that translate into two **base tables: Sales** and **Customer**. We extract the dimensions and facts from the base tables; therefore, they will not be loaded into the model in their original shape. From a modeling perspective, there must be a linkage between the two tables, so we need to raise this with the business, study the data, and see if we can find the linkage(s). The names of the tables in the source system (an Excel file in our case) are highlighted in the following image:

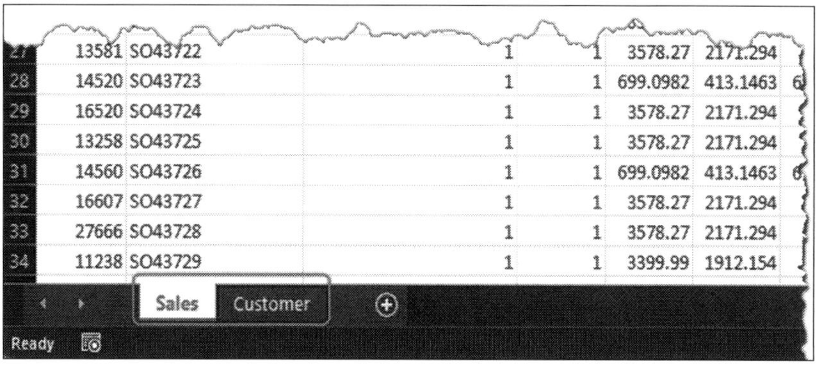

Figure 6.2: The Excel sample file contains two sheets that translate into two base tables in Power Query Editor

We have to be careful that the number of base tables does not trick us. These tables can be wide and tall, becoming multiple dimensions and fact tables once we prepare the Star Schema model data. Our sample only contains two base tables, which turn into five dimensions and one fact table once we prepare the data for a Star Schema.

The linkages between existing tables

The columns of the two tables are as follows:

- **Sales**: SalesTerritoryRegion, SalesTerritoryCountry, SalesTerritoryGroup, CustomerKey, SalesOrderNumber, SalesOrderLineNumber, OrderQuantity, ExtendedAmount, TotalProductCost, SalesAmount, TaxAmt, Freight, OrderDate, DueDate, ShipDate, Product, ProductCategory, ProductSubcategory, Currency
- **Customer**: CustomerKey, Title, FirstName, MiddleName, LastName, NameStyle, BirthDate, MaritalStatus, Suffix, Gender, EmailAddress, YearlyIncome, TotalChildren, NumberChildrenAtHome, EnglishEducation, EnglishOccupation, HouseOwnerFlag, NumberCarsOwned, AddressLine1, AddressLine2, Phone, DateFirstPurchase, CommuteDistance, City, StateProvinceCode, StateProvinceName, CountryRegionCode, EnglishCountryRegionName, PostalCode, SalesRegion, SalesCountry, SalesContinent

By studying the data, we understand that the **CustomerKey** column in both tables represents a linkage between them. But there are more. The following list shows some other potential linkages:

- The linkage between geographical data such as **Region**, **Country**, **Territory Group**, **State/Province**, **City**, **Address**, and **Postal Code**
- The linkage between product data such as **Product Category**, **Product Subcategory**, and **Product**
- The linkage between sales order data such as **Sales Order** and **Sales Order Line**
- The linkage between `Date` and `Time`, such as **Order Date**, **Due Date**, and **Ship Date**

Finding the lowest required grain of Date and Time

In most real-world cases, if not all, the business must analyze data over multiple dimensions such as **Product**, **Customer**, **Date** or **Time**, or both **Date** and **Time**. We must find the lowest grain of detail required to support the business requirements. You will often be faced with requirements such as:

As a Sales manager, I want to analyze sales data by branch, location, date, and time.

In the above user story, a fact is an event that the business wants to analyze. So, the sales are a fact. On the other hand, the dimensions are everything that the fact is analyzed by. So, in the preceding user story, **branch**, **location**, **date**, and **time** are the dimensions. We also have a **Person** dimension to cover the *sales manager*. While we identify the facts and dimensions, it is a crucial task to identify the granularity of the data, too. The granularity of the data, also called the grain, is not so evident at first look. For instance, in the preceding user story, at what level of detail must the sales data be analyzed for the following dimensions?

- Location: Continent, Country, City, County, Area, Postcode, and Street number
- Date: Year, Quarter, Month, Week, and Day
- Time: Hour, Minute, and Second

In real-world scenarios, especially in large projects, we have to ask relevant questions of the business to identify the grain. In small projects, we can identify the grain by carefully studying the data. Let us look at our scenario.

In our example, the business needs to analyze the data over both Date and Time. But we have to be more descriptive about the level of Date and Time that the business requires to analyze the data. By studying the data, we find out that both the **Sales** and **Customer** tables have columns with the Date or DateTime data types. The **Sales** table has three columns containing the DateTime data type. Power Query Editor automatically detects the columns' data types. Studying the data more precisely shows that the time element of the values in both DateTime columns is always **12:00:00 AM**. So, most probably, the data type of the **DueDate** and **ShipDate** columns is Date, not DateTime. This means that the only column with the DateTime data type is the **OrderDate** column. The following image shows that the data in the **OrderDate** column is stored in Seconds:

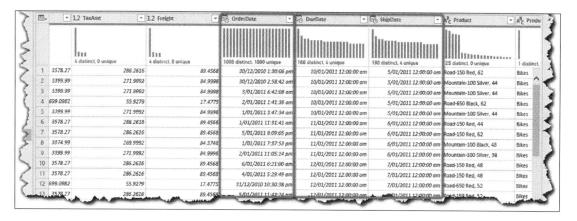

Figure 6.3: Columns with the Date and DateTime data types in the Sales table

So, the grain of the **OrderDate** column can be in Seconds. We save this question and confirm it with the business later.

Let's also look at the **Customer** table. The **Customer** table also has two columns with the Date data type, **BirthDate** and **DateFirstPurchase**, as shown in the following image:

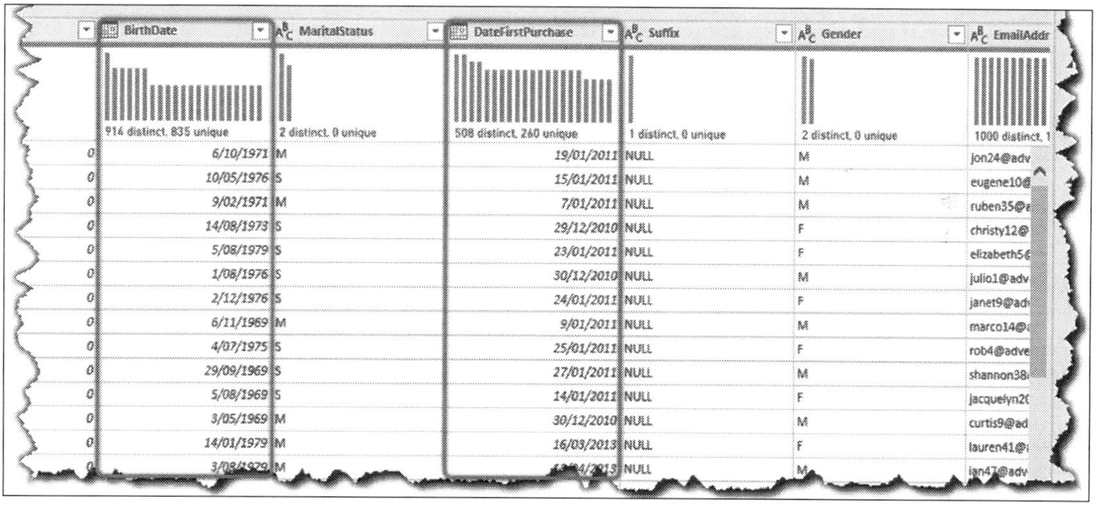

Figure 6.4: The Date column in the Customer table

As the next step in our discovery workshops, we must clarify the following points with the business:

- Do they need to analyze the data for customers' birth date?
- Do they need to have the **BirthDate** data at different date levels (Year, Quarter, Month, and so on)?
- Do they need to analyze the data for **DateFirstPurchase**?
- Do they need to show the **DateFirstPurchase** data at various date levels?
- What are the required levels of Date and Time for the **OrderDate** from the **Sales** table?
- What is the Date level for the **DueDate** and **ShipDate** columns from the **Sales** table?

In our imaginary discovery workshop, the business clarifies that they do not want to analyze the customers' birth dates or first purchase dates. We also discovered that they need to analyze **OrderDate** from the **Sales** table over Date at the Day level and over Time at the Minutes level. They also confirm that the **DueDate** and **ShipDate** from the **Sales** table are at the Day level.

With the preceding findings, it is clear that we need to create a Date dimension and a Time dimension.

The next step is identifying the dimensions, their granularity, and their facts.

Defining dimensions and facts

To identify the dimensions and the facts, we have to conduct requirement-gathering workshops with the business. We need to understand the business processes by asking WWWWWH questions; that is, *What, When, Where, Who, Why,* and *How*. This is a popular technique, also known as 5W–1H. The answers to these questions help us understand the business processes, which helps to identify the dimensions and facts. Let us have a look at some examples:

- The answer to the *What* question can be a product, item, service, and so on.
- The answer to the *When* question can be a date, time, or both and at what level, month, day, hour, minute, and so on.
- The answer to the *Where* question can be a physical location such as a store or warehouse, geographical location, and so on.

In the requirement-gathering workshops, we try to determine what describes the business and how the business measures itself. In our scenario, we imagine we have conducted several discovery workshops, and we found out the business requires the following sales data:

- Sales amount
- Quantity
- Costs (tax, freight, and so on)

The sales data must be analyzed by the following:

- Geography
- Sales order
- Product
- Currency

- Customer
- Sales demographic
- Date at the day level
- Time at the minute level

In the next few sections, we will determine our dimensions and facts.

Determining the potential dimensions

To identify the dimensions, we generally look for descriptive data. Let us look at our sample files based on our findings from the discovery workshops. In both the **Sales** and **Customer** tables, we can potentially create the following dimensions:

Potential Dimension	Derived From	Dimension Attributes
Geography	Sales	SalesTerritoryRegion, SalesTerritoryCountry, SalesTerritoryGroup
Sales Order	Sales	SalesOrderNumber, SalesOrderLineNumber
Product	Sales	ProductCategory, ProductSubcategory, Product
Currency	Sales	Currency
Customer	Customer	CustomerKey, Title, FirstName, MiddleName, LastName, NameStyle, BirthDate, MaritalStatus, Suffix, Gender, EmailAddress, YearlyIncome, TotalChildren, NumberChildrenAtHome, Education, Occupation, HouseOwnerFlag, NumberCarsOwned, AddressLine1, AddressLine2, Phone, DateFirstPurchase, CommuteDistance
Sales Demographic	Customer	City, StateProvinceCode, StateProvinceName, CountryRegionCode, CountryRegionName, PostalCode, SalesRegion, SalesCountry, SalesContinent

Figure 6.5: Potential dimensions derived from existing tables

Determining the potential facts

To identify the facts, we look at our findings from the discovery workshops. With our current knowledge of the business, we have an idea of our facts. Let us look at the data in Power Query Editor and find the columns with the Number data type. Nevertheless, not all the columns with the Number data type contain facts. Facts must make sense to the business processes identified in earlier steps. With that in mind, in our exercise, the following list shows the potential facts:

Potential Fact	Derived From	Fact Columns
Sales	Sales	OrderQuantity, ExtendedAmount, TotalProductCost, SalesAmount, TaxAmt, Freight

Figure 6.6: Potential facts derived from existing tables

In real-world scenarios, we conduct discovery workshops with **Subject Matter Experts (SMEs)** to identify the dimensions and facts. But it is also a common scenario when the business supplies a set of source files and asks us to create analytical reports.

Now that we have identified potential dimensions and facts, it is time to start preparing the Star Schema. The first step is unloading the **Sales** and **Customer** tables as their current flat shape is unsuitable for a Star Schema. We explained how to unload tables in *Chapter 1, Introduction to Data Modeling in Power BI*, in the *Understanding denormalization* section.

The next step to take is to change the columns' data types. If a **Changed Type** step is automatically added to **Applied Steps**, we inspect the detected data types to ensure the data types are correct. This is shown in the following image:

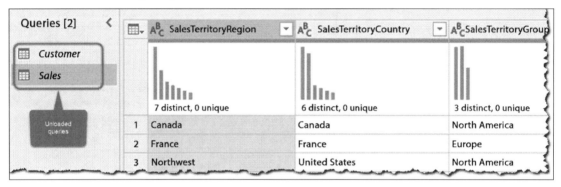

Figure 6.7: Both the Sales and Customer tables unloaded

Power Query automatically detects column headers and generates a **Changed Type** step for each table if the **Type Detection** setting is not **Never detect column types and headers for unstructured sources**. The **Type Detection** setting is configurable from Power Query Editor (or Power BI Desktop) from **Options and settings|Options**, under **Type Detection**.

The auto-detecting data type behavior of Power Query is also configurable at both the **Global** and **Current File** levels. By changing the settings under the **Global** section, the change applies to Power BI Desktop for the file and the future files opened in Power BI Desktop. But changing the settings under the **Current File** section applies only to the current file.

The following steps show how to change this setting at the **Global** level:

1. Click the **File** menu.
2. Click **Options and settings**.
3. Click **Options**.
4. Click **Data Load**.
5. Under **Type Detection**, you have the option to select one of the following:
    - Always detect column types and headers for unstructured sources
    - Detect column types and headers for unstructured sources according to each file's settings
    - Never detect column types and headers for unstructured sources:

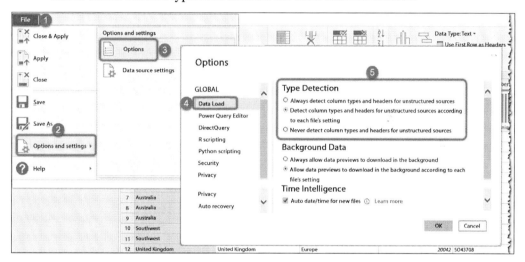

Figure 6.8: Changing the Type Detection configuration at the Global level

6. Click **Data Load** under the **CURRENT FILE** section.
7. Check/uncheck the **Detect column types and headers for unstructured sources** option:

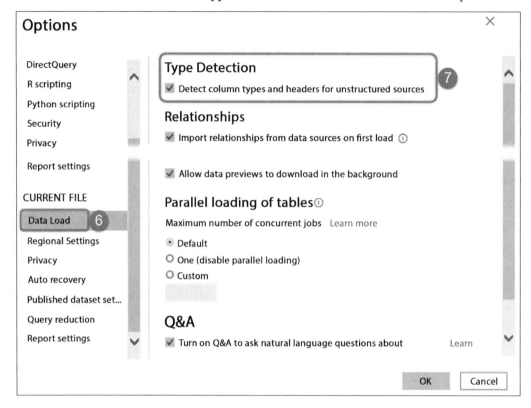

Figure 6.9: Changing the Type Detection configuration at the CURRENT FILE level

In this section, we identified potential dimensions and facts. In the next section, we look at how to create physical dimensions from the potential ones.

Creating Dimension tables

We should already be connected to the Chapter 6, Sales Data.xlsx file from Power Query Editor. In this section, we look at the necessity of creating the potential dimensions identified in the previous section. We first evaluate each dimension from a business requirement perspective. If we are convinced that the dimension is required, we create it.

Geography

The identified business requirements show that we must have a dimension keeping geographical data. When we look at the data, we can see geography-related columns in the **Sales** table. We can create a separate **Geography** dimension derived from the **Sales** table. However, this might not cover all business requirements.

As the following image shows, there are some geography-related columns in the **Customer** table. We must find commonalities in the data and think about the possibility of combining the data from both tables into a single **Geography** dimension. Using **Column Distribution** shows that the **CustomerKey** column is a **primary key** of the **Customer** table:

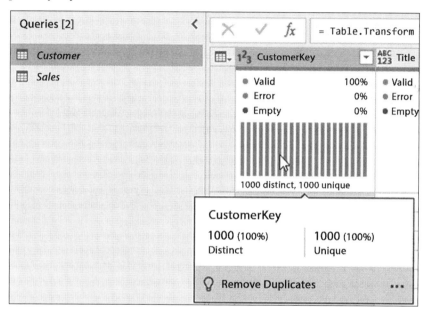

Figure 6.10: Column Distribution shows that CustomerKey is the primary key of the Customer table

Enabling and using **Column Distribution** was explained in *Chapter 3, Data Preparation in Power Query Editor*.

Looking at **Column Distribution** for the **SalesContinent, SalesCountry,** and **SalesRegion** columns from the **Customer** table and **SalesTerritoryGroup, SalesTerritoryCountry,** and **SalesTerritoryRegion** from the **Sales** table shows that the number of distinct values in each column from the **Customers** tables matches the number of distinct values in the corresponding column from the **Sales** table, as shown in the following image:

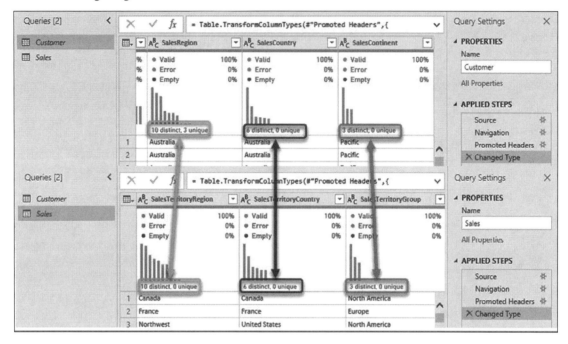

Figure 6.11: Comparing Column Distribution for geography-related columns from the Customer table and the Sales table

To ensure the values of the **SalesContinent, SalesCountry,** and **SalesRegion** columns from the **Customer** table and the **SalesTerritoryGroup, SalesTerritoryCountry,** and **SalesTerritoryRegion** columns from the **Sales** table match, we go through the following test process:

1. Reference the **Customer** table.
2. Rename the table to **CustomerGeoTest**.
3. Unload the table.
4. Keep the **SalesContinent, SalesCountry,** and **SalesRegion** columns by selecting **Remove Other Columns**.
5. Click the table icon from the top-left corner of the **Data View** pane and click **Remove Duplicates**. The following image shows the preceding steps:

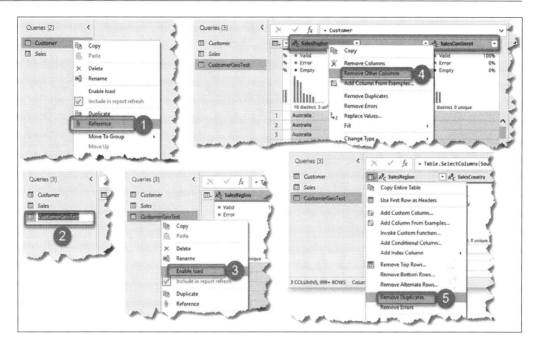

Figure 6.12: Steps required to reference the Customer table and remove duplicates

The results of the preceding steps are as follows:

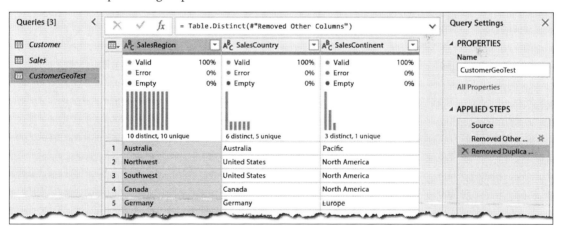

Figure 6.13: The results of referencing the Customer table and removing duplicates from the geography-related columns

We must go through the same process to remove the duplicates of the following columns from the **Sales** table:

- SalesTerritoryGroup
- SalesTerritoryCountry
- SalesTerritoryRegion

The following image shows the latter results next to the results of removing the duplicates of the **SalesContinent**, **SalesCountry**, and **SalesRegion** columns from the **Customer** table:

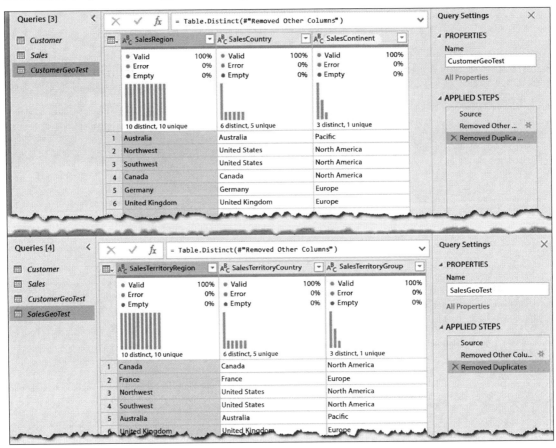

Figure 6.14: Comparing the results of the CustomerGeoTest table and the SalesGeoTest table

As the preceding screenshots show, the only difference between the two is the columns' sorting order, which is not essential. As a result of the preceding exercise, we do not need to create a **Geography** dimension as the **SalesTerritoryGroup**, **SalesTerritoryCountry**, and **SalesTerritoryRegion** columns from the **Sales** table are redundant compared to the **SalesContinent**, **SalesCountry**, and **SalesRegion** columns from the **Customer** table, while the geography-related columns in the **Customer** table provide a higher level of detail.

Sales order

In the **Sales** table, the **SalesOrderNumber** and **SalesOrderLineNumber** columns contain descriptive data for sales orders. Do we need to create a dimension for this? Let us look at the data:

1. Change **Column profiling** to **based on the entire data set**.
2. Looking at **Column Distribution** for both columns shows that **SalesOrderNumber** has 27,659 distinct values and that **SalesOrderLineNumber** has only 8 distinct values:

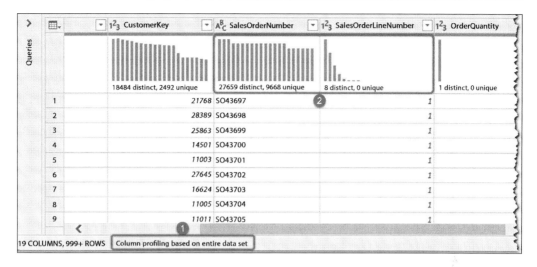

Figure 6.15: Looking at the Column Distribution data shows that there are a lot of distinct values in SalesOrderNumber

The **SalesOrderNumber** column contains many distinct values, which decreases the chance of creating a new **Sales Order** dimension being a good idea. So, we need to find more evidence to avoid creating the **Sales Order** dimension. If we merge the two columns, we get a better idea of the number of rows we get in the new dimension if we decide to create it.

3. Select both the **SalesOrderNumber** and **SalesOrderLineNumber** columns.
4. Click **Merge Columns** from the **Transformation** tab.
5. From the **Merge Columns** window, stick to the defaults and click **OK**:

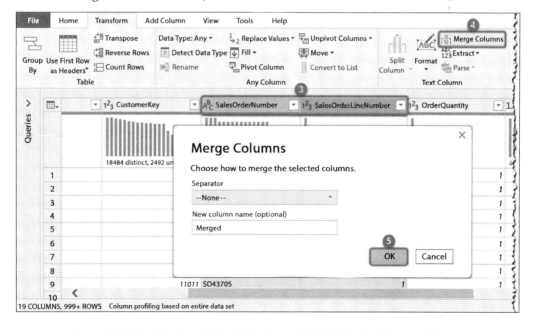

Figure 6.16: Merging the SalesOrderNumber and SalesOrderLineNumber columns

The new **Merged** column contains **60,398 distinct** and **60,398 unique values**, which means the combination of **SalesOrderNumber** and **SalesOrderLineNumber** is the **primary key** of the **Sales** table, as shown in the following image. Therefore, even if we create a separate dimension, we get the same number of rows as our fact table. Moreover, we cannot imagine any linkages to any other dimensions. Therefore, keeping those two columns in the **Sales** table is best. These dimensions cannot be moved out of the fact table because of their data characteristics. They also do not have any other attributes or meaningful links to other dimensions. These types of dimensions are called **degenerate dimensions**:

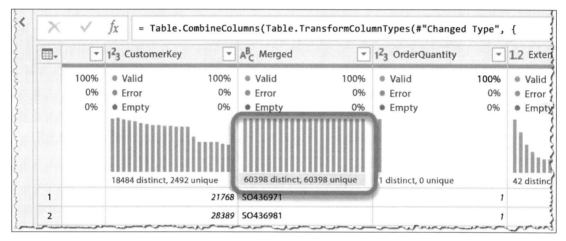

Figure 6.17: Merged column results

Now, we must remove the **Merged Column** step from **Applied Steps**.

Product

The Product dimension is the most obvious one, with three descriptive columns. We derive the Product dimension from the **Sales** table by referencing the **Sales** table. Then, we remove other columns to keep the **Product, ProductSubcategory**, and **ProductCategory** columns. As the next step, we must remove the duplicates from the **Product** table. Moreover, we need to generate a **ProductKey** column as the primary key of the **Product** table, which we will use in the data model later. Next, we merge the **Sales** table with the **Product** table to get a **ProductKey** in the **Sales** table. We also rename the columns to more user-friendly versions: **ProductSubcategory** to **Product Subcategory** and **ProductCategory** to **Product Category**.

 Moving forward, we reference the **Sales** table many times. Therefore, we rename the **Sales** table **Sales Base**.

The following steps show how to implement the preceding process in Power Query Editor:

1. Rename the **Sales** table **Sales Base**:

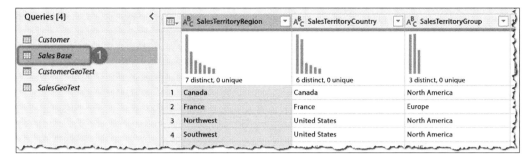

Figure 6.18: Renaming the Sales table Sales Base

2. **Reference** the **Sales Base** table:

Figure 6.19: Referencing the Sales Base table

3. **Rename** the referencing table **Product**.
4. Select the **ProductCategory**, **ProductSubcategory**, and **Product** columns, respectively.

Power Query places the sequence of the columns by order of our selection in *Step 4*.

5. Right-click one of the selected columns and click **Remove Other Columns**:

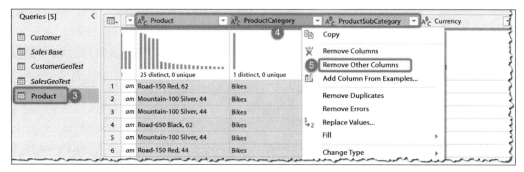

Figure 6.20: The Remove Other Columns option

6. Click the table button from the top-left corner of the **Data view** pane.
7. Click **Remove Duplicates**:

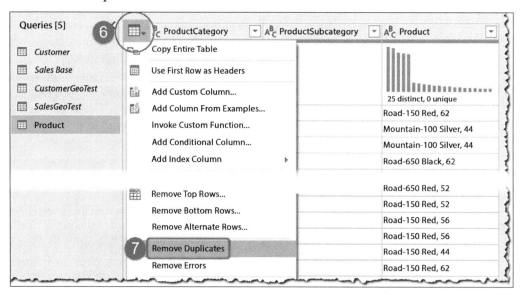

Figure 6.21: Removing duplicates from all rows

Remove Duplicates from the Power Query UI uses the `Table.Distinct(table as table)` function in the background. The `Table.Distinct()` function is equivalent to the `Table.AddKey(table as table, columns as list, isPrimary as logical)` function when the isPrimary operand is true. The `Table.AddKey()` function defines a column or multiple columns as the `primary key` columns for a table. But after loading the data into the data model, the xVelocity engine does not support **composite primary keys**.

Therefore, we have to add an index column to use as the primary key of the **Product** table. Follow these steps:

8. Click the **Add Column** tab from the ribbon.
9. Click the **Index Column** drop-down button.
10. Click **From 1**:

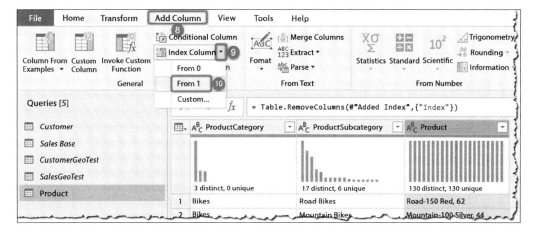

Figure 6.22: Adding an Index column with an index starting from 1

11. The default name for an index column is **Index**. We rename it to **ProductKey** by editing the Power Query expression generated in the **Added Index** step rather than renaming it from the UI that adds a new **Rename Column** step.

12. Click the **Added Index** step from **Applied Steps**. Then, from the formula bar, change **Index** to **ProductKey**, as shown in the following image:

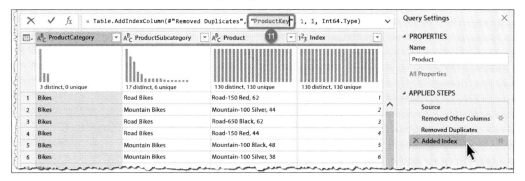

Figure 6.23: Changing the default index column's name

With that, we have created the **Product** dimension.

Currency

The **Currency** column in the **Sales Base** table holds the currency description for each transaction. So, by definition, it is a dimension. Let us raise the *Why* question here. Why do we need to create a separate table for **Currency**? We need to look at the situation more thoroughly to answer this question. The **column distribution** box, when set to work based on the entire dataset, shows that the **Currency** column's cardinality is low, with only 6 distinct values, as shown in the following image:

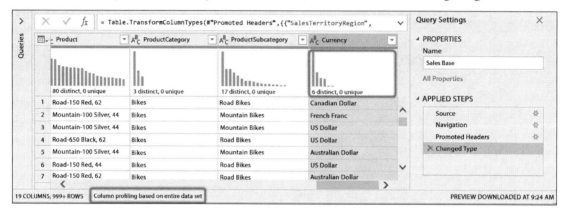

Figure 6.24: Column Distribution for the Currency column over the entire dataset

Since the `Columnstore` indexing in the **xVelocity** engine provides better data compression and performance over low cardinality columns, we can expect minimal or no sensible performance or storage gains by creating a new dimension table for **Currency** in our scenario. Besides, we do have other attributes providing more descriptions for currencies. Lastly, **Currency** does not have any meaningful linkages to other dimensions. As a result, we can keep the **Currency** column as a **degenerate dimension** in the fact table.

Let us move forward and look at the other potential dimensions.

Customer

We can derive the **Customer** table from the original **Customer** table from the source. To do this, we'll rename the original **Customer** table **Customer Base**.

Let us look at the **Sales Base** table to see how each row relates to the **Customer Base** table. The **Sales Base** table has a **CustomerKey** column. We set **Column profiling based on entire data set** to have a more realistic view of **CustomerKey**. The **Column Quality Box** of **CustomerKey** in the **Sales Base** table reveals that a customer key exists for every single sales transaction in the **Sales Base** table (0% **Empty**). The following image shows the **Column Quality Box** for the **CustomerKey** column in the **Sales Base** table:

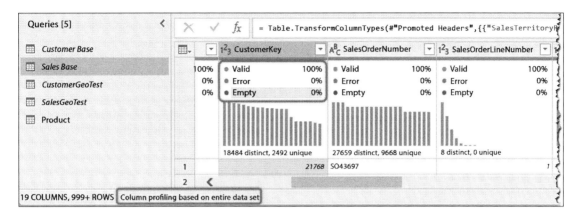

Figure 6.25: The Column Quality information shows 0% Empty for CustomerKey

Therefore, every row of the **Sales Base** table can relate to the descriptive data in the **Customer Base** table. To ensure that we can create the relationship between the two tables, we must ensure that the data type of **CustomerKey** column in both the **Sales Base** and **Customer Base** tables match. We also want the **CustomerKey** in the **Customer Base** table to be the primary key, meaning that the number of **distinct** and **unique** values must be the same. The following image shows that the data types of the **CustomerKey** column in both tables match and that **CustomerKey** in the **Customer Base** table is the primary key:

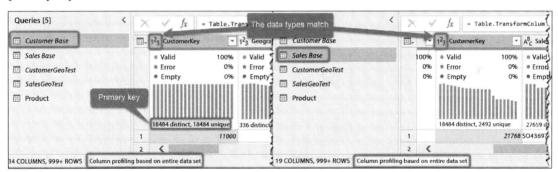

Figure 6.26: The data type of CustomerKey matches in both tables, and it is the primary key of the Customer Base table

Now that we have enough evidence that the **Customer** table is a dimension, let us create it by following these steps:

1. **Reference** the **Customer Base** table:

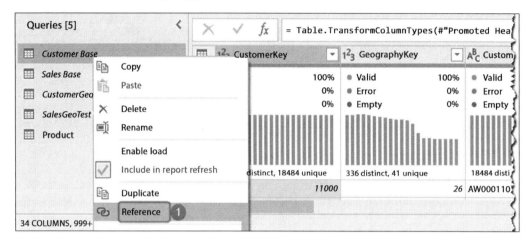

Figure 6.27: Referencing the Customer Base table

2. **Rename** the referencing table to **Customer**.

    We need to keep the following columns by removing the other columns; that is, **CustomerKey**, **Title**, **FirstName**, **MiddleName**, **LastName**, **NameStyle**, **BirthDate**, **MaritalStatus**, **Suffix**, **Gender**, **EmailAddress**, **YearlyIncome**, **TotalChildren**, **NumberChildrenAtHome**, **Education**, **Occupation**, **HouseOwnerFlag**, **NumberCarsOwned**, **AddressLine1**, **AddressLine2**, **Phone**, **DateFirstPurchase**, and **CommuteDistance**.

3. The simplest way to do so is to click **Choose Columns** from the **Home** tab.
4. Keep the preceding columns and deselect the rest.
5. Click **OK**:

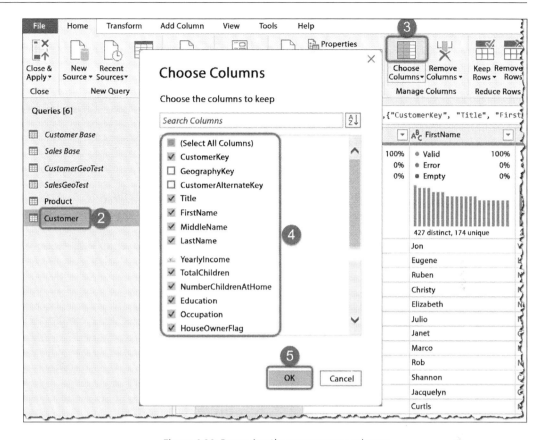

Figure 6.28: Removing the unnecessary columns

With that, we created the **Customer** dimension. Since the **Customer** dimension already has a primary key, **CustomerKey**, we do not need to take any more actions.

In the next section, we create a separate dimension containing geography-related data by referencing the **Customer Base** table; therefore, we do not need any geography-related columns in the **Customer** dimension.

Sales Demographic

We previously looked at creating a **Geography** dimension, which revealed that the geography columns in the **Customer Base** table could give us more details, which helps with creating more accurate analytical reports with lower granularity. Now, we'll create a new dimension to keep the **Sales Demographic** descriptions derived from **Customer Base**, as follows:

1. **Reference** the **Customer Base** table from Power Query Editor.
2. **Rename** the new table **Sales Demographic**.
3. Click the **Choose Columns** button from the **Home** tab.
4. Uncheck all the columns other than **City**, **StateProvinceCode**, **StateProvinceName**, **CountryRegionCode**, **CountryRegionName**, **PostalCode**, **SalesRegion**, **SalesCountry**, and **SalesContinent**.
5. Click **OK**:

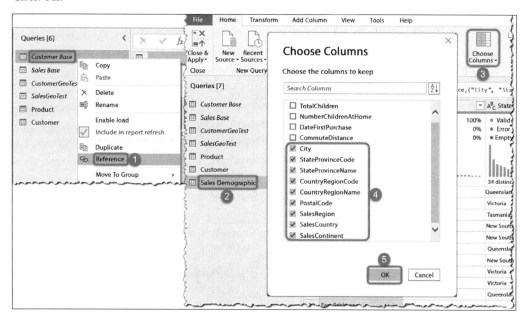

Figure 6.29: Referencing the Customer Base table to create a Sales Demographic table and keep the relevant columns

The data in the **CountryRegionName** and **SalesCountry** columns shows that the two columns contain the same data. Therefore, we need to remove one of them by double-clicking the **Remove Other Columns** step and unchecking the **CountryRegionName** column.

The next step is to remove the duplicate rows, which avoids getting any duplicate rows in the dimension in the future, even if there are currently no duplicate rows.

6. Select a column in the **Sales Demographic** table and press *Ctrl+A* on your keyboard to select all columns.

7. Click the **Remove Rows** option from the **Home** tab.
8. Click the **Remove Duplicates** option:

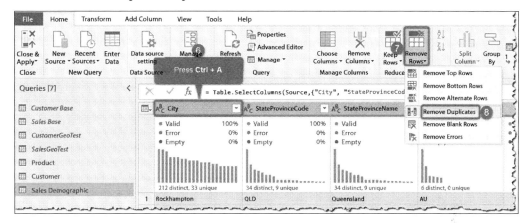

Figure 6.30: Removing duplicates from the Sales Demographic table

The next step is adding an **Index column** to create a **primary key** for the **Sales Demographic** dimension.

9. Click the **Index Column** drop-down button from the **Add Column** tab.
10. Click **From 1**:

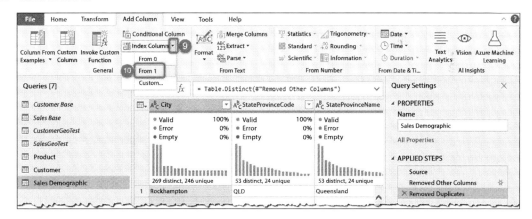

Figure 6.31: Adding an Index column to the Sales Demographic table

11. Replace **Index** with **SalesDemographicKey** from the formula bar.

12. Click the **Submit** button ✓:

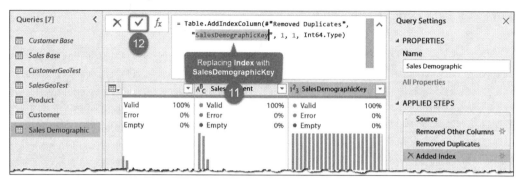

Figure 6.32: Replacing Index with SalesDemographicKey

So far, we have created all the potential dimensions derived from the **Sales Base** and **Customer Base** tables. As discussed earlier in this chapter, we also need to create a Date dimension and a Time dimension. We do so in the following sections.

Date

The outcomes of the discovery sessions with the business showed that we need to have Date and Time dimensions. We already discussed in *Chapter 2, Data Analysis eXpressions and Data Modeling*, that we can create the Date dimension using DAX. We also discussed the advantages and disadvantages of using the CALENDARAUTO() function in DAX. In this section, we will create a custom function in Power Query Editor to generate a simple Date dimension accepting two input parameters: Start Year and End Year. We invoke the custom function to generate a Date table starting from 1st Jan of Start Year and ending on 31st Dec of End Year.

The dates generated in the **Date** column are continuous and do not have any gaps between dates. The following steps show how to use the following expressions to create and invoke the custom function:

1. The custom function can be created by copying the following Power Query expression:

```
// fnGenerateDate
(#"Start Year" as number, #"End Year" as number) as table =>
    let
        GenerateDates = List.Dates(#date(#"Start Year",1,1), Duration.Days(Duration.From(#date(#"End Year", 12, 31) - #date(#"Start Year" - 1,12,31))), #duration(1,0,0,0) ),
        #"Converted to Table" = Table.TransformColumnTypes(Table.FromList(GenerateDates, Splitter.SplitByNothing(), {"Date"}), {"Date", Date.Type}),
        #"Added Custom" = Table.AddColumn(#"Converted to Table", "DateKey", each Int64.From(Text.Combine({Date.ToText([Date], "yyyy"), Date.ToText([Date], "MM"), Date.ToText([Date], "dd")})), Int64.Type),
```

```
        #"Year Column Added" = Table.AddColumn(#"Added Custom", "Year",
each Date.Year([Date]), Int64.Type),
        #"Quarter Column Added" = Table.AddColumn(#"Year Column Added",
"Quarter", each "Qtr "&Text.From(Date.QuarterOfYear([Date])) , Text.
Type),
        #"MonthOrder Column Added" = Table.AddColumn(#"Quarter Column
Added", "MonthOrder", each Date.ToText([Date], "MM"), Text.Type),
        #"Short Month Column Added" = Table.AddColumn(#"MonthOrder Column
Added", "Month Short", each Date.ToText([Date], "MMM"), Text.Type),
        #"Month Column Added" = Table.AddColumn(#"Short Month Column
Added", "Month", each Date.MonthName([Date]), Text.Type)
    in
        #"Month Column Added"
```

The preceding code is also available in this book's GitHub repository, in the Chapter 6, Generate Date Dimension.m file, via the following URL: https://github.com/PacktPublishing/Expert-Data-Modeling-with-Power-BI-Second-Edition/blob/0b26cc981f0448edfa108cf9f587cef439fb454b/Source%20Code/Chapter%2006/Chapter%206,%20Generate%20Date%20Dimension.m

2. In Power Query Editor, click the **New Source** drop-down button.
3. Click **Blank Query**.
4. **Rename** the new query from Query1 to fnGenerateDate.
5. Click the **Advanced Editor** button from the **Home** tab.
6. Delete the existing code and paste the expressions we copied in the first step.
7. Click **Done**:

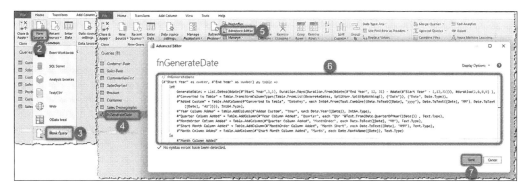

Figure 6.33: Creating the fnGenerateDate custom function in Power Query Editor

The preceding process creates the fnGenerateDate custom function in Power Query Editor. The next step is to invoke the function by entering the Start Year and End Year parameters. In real-world scenarios, we confirm the date range of the Date dimension with the business to ensure the Date dimension supports all current and future requirements.

Sometimes, we need to find the minimum and maximum dates of all the columns contributing to our data analysis with Date or DateTime data types. There are various ways to overcome those cases, such as the following:

- We can get the minimum and maximum dates by eyeballing the data if the dataset is small.
- We can sort each of the **OrderDate**, **DueDate**, and **ShipDate** values in ascending order to get the minimum dates, and then we can sort those columns in descending order to get the maximum dates.
- We can use the List.Min() function for each column to get the minimum dates. Then, using the List.Max() function for each column gives us the maximum dates.
- We can find the minimum and maximum dates using DAX.
- We can use the **Column profile** feature in Power Query Editor.

Now that we have the fnGenerateDate custom function handy, we pass the Start Date and End Date parameters and invoke it. Our sample's start and end years are 2010 and 2014, respectively. We invoke the fnGenerateDate function as follows:

8. Select the **fnGenerateDate** custom function from the **Queries** pane.
9. Type in 2010 for the **Start Year** parameter and 2014 for the **End Year** parameter.
10. Click **Invoke**:

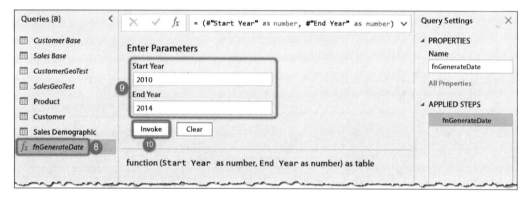

Figure 6.34: Invoking the fnGenerateDate function

Invoking the fnGenerateDate function creates a new table named **Invoked Function**. Rename it **Date**, as shown in the following image:

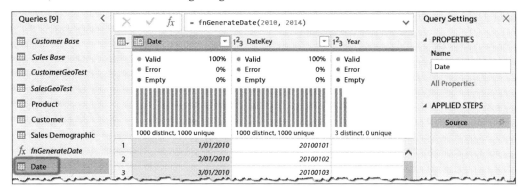

Figure 6.35: Renaming the invoked custom function Date

As a **Date** dimension is commonly used in Power BI, it is handy to have a custom function to reuse on other solutions if required.

So far, we have created the **Date** dimension. Next, we will create the **Time** dimension.

Time

The outcomes of the discovery sessions with the business showed that we need to have a **Time** dimension. In the previous section, we created a custom function to generate a **Date** dimension. In *Chapter 2, Data Analysis eXpressions and Data Modeling*, we discussed that we could use DAX to create the Time dimension. This section discusses creating the Time dimension in Power Query.

Creating the **Time** dimension provides the flexibility to analyze the data over time elements, such as hour, minute, and second, or time buckets such as 5 min, 15 min, 30 min, and so on.

The following Power Query expressions create a Time dimension with 5 min, 15 min, 30 min, 45 min, and 60 min time buckets:

```
let
Source = Table.FromList({1..86400}, Splitter.SplitByNothing()),
    #"Renamed Columns" = Table.RenameColumns(Source,{{"Column1", "ID"}}),
    #"Time Column Added" = Table.AddColumn(#"Renamed Columns", "Time", each
Time.From(#datetime(1970,1,1,0,0,0) + #duration(0,0,0,[ID]))),
    #"Hour Added" = Table.AddColumn(#"Time Column Added", "Hour", each Time.
Hour([Time])),
```

```
        #"Minute Added" = Table.AddColumn(#"Hour Added", "Minute", each Time.
Minute([Time])),
        #"5 Min Band Added" = Table.AddColumn(#"Minute Added", "5 Min Band", each
Time.From(#datetime(1970,1,1,0,0,0) + #duration(0, 0, Number.RoundDown(Time.
Minute([Time])/5) * 5, 0)) + #duration(0, 0, 5, 0)),
        #"15 Min Band Added" = Table.AddColumn(#"5 Min Band Added", "15 Min
Band", each Time.From(#datetime(1970,1,1,0,0,0) + #duration(0, 0, Number.
RoundDown(Time.Minute([Time])/15) * 15, 0)) + #duration(0, 0, 15, 0)),
        #"30 Min Band Added" = Table.AddColumn(#"15 Min Band Added", "30 Min
Band", each Time.From(#datetime(1970,1,1,0,0,0) + #duration(0, 0, Number.
RoundDown(Time.Minute([Time])/30) * 30, 0)) + #duration(0, 0, 30, 0)),
        #"45 Min Band Added" = Table.AddColumn(#"30 Min Band Added", "45 Min
Band", each Time.From(#datetime(1970,1,1,0,0,0) + #duration(0, 0, Number.
RoundDown(Time.Minute([Time])/45) * 45, 0)) + #duration(0, 0, 45, 0)),
        #"60 Min Band Added" = Table.AddColumn(#"45 Min Band Added", "60 Min
Band", each Time.From(#datetime(1970,1,1,0,0,0) + #duration(0, 0, Number.
RoundDown(Time.Minute([Time])/60) * 60, 0)) + #duration(0, 0, 60, 0)),
        #"Removed Other Columns" = Table.SelectColumns(#"60 Min Band
Added",{"Time", "Hour", "Minute", "5 Min Band", "15 Min Band", "30 Min Band",
"45 Min Band", "60 Min Band"}),
        #"Changed Type" = Table.TransformColumnTypes(#"Removed Other
Columns",{{"Time", type time}, {"Hour", Int64.Type}, {"Minute", Int64.Type},
{"5 Min Band", type time}, {"15 Min Band", type time}, {"30 Min Band", type
time}, {"45 Min Band", type time}, {"60 Min Band", type time}})
in
    #"Changed Type"
```

The preceding code is also available in this book's GitHub repository, in the Chapter 6, Generate Time Dimension.m file, via the following URL: https://github.com/PacktPublishing/Expert-Data-Modeling-with-Power-BI-Second-Edition/blob/0b26cc981f0448edfa108cf9f587cef439fb454b/Source%20Code/Chapter%2006/Chapter%206,%20Generate%20Time%20Dimension.m

With the preceding code handy, we only need to create a new **Blank Query**, rename it to **Time**, and copy and paste the preceding expressions into **Advanced Editor**, as shown in the following image:

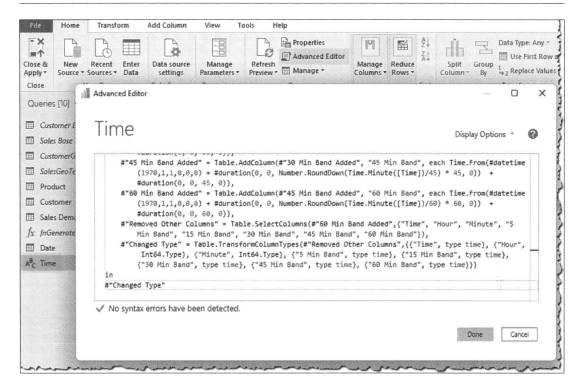

Figure 6.36: Creating the Time dimension in Power Query Editor

We created the **Date** and **Time** dimensions in Power Query in the last two sections. You may be wondering how this differs from creating those dimensions in DAX, which brings us to the next section.

Creating Date and Time dimensions — Power Query versus DAX

The last two sections discussed creating **Date** and **Time** dimensions in Power Query. As mentioned before, in *Chapter 2, Data Analysis eXpressions and Data Modeling*, we discussed creating the two dimensions using DAX. This section highlights the differences between these two approaches.

Generally speaking, once we have loaded the tables into the data model, both approaches would work and perform similarly. But some differences may make us pick one approach over the other, such as:

- We can create the **Date** and **Time** dimensions in Power Query by creating a custom function or a static query. We can reuse these queries to create **Power BI Dataflows** and make them available across the organization.

- If we need to use these tables in Power Query to expand the functionalities of other queries, for example, we may want to merge a query with **Date** or **Time**; having them defined in the data model using DAX makes them inaccessible in the Power Query layer.

- We can connect to public websites over the internet and mash up that data in Power Query if we need to consider local holidays in the **Date** table. This option is not available in DAX.
- If we need to consider all the columns with Date or DateTime data types across the data model, then using CALENDARAUTO() in DAX is super handy. A similar function does not currently exist in Power Query.
- Our knowledge of Power Query and DAX is also an essential factor to consider. Some of us are more comfortable with one language than the other.

Creating fact tables

Now that we have created all the dimensions, it is time to create a fact table that contains numeric values and the primary keys of the dimensions as foreign keys. The **Sales Base** and **Customer Base** data show that the **Sales Base** table holds many numeric values. Therefore, a fact table can be derived from the **Sales Base** table, which we name **Sales**, by following these steps:

1. **Reference** the **Sales Base** table and then rename the new table **Sales**.

    We want to get **ProductKey** from the **Product** table. To do so, we can merge the **Sales** table with the **Product** table.

2. Click **Merge Queries**.
3. Select the **ProductCategory**, **ProductSubcategory**, and **Product** columns, respectively.
4. Select the **Product** table from the drop-down list.
5. Again, select the **ProductCategory**, **ProductSubcategory**, and **Product** columns.
6. Select **Left outer (all from first, matching from second)** from the **Join Kind** drop-down list.
7. Click **OK**:

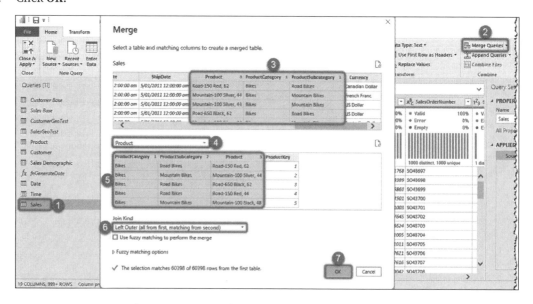

Figure 6.37: Merging the Sales table with the Product table

8. The preceding steps create a new structured column named **Product.1** and a new transformation step in **Applied Steps**. The default name for this step is **Merged Queries**. Rename it **Merged Sales with Product**.
9. Expand the **Product.1** column.
10. Check the **ProductKey** column (keep the rest unchecked).
11. Uncheck the **Use original column name as prefix** option.
12. Click **OK**:

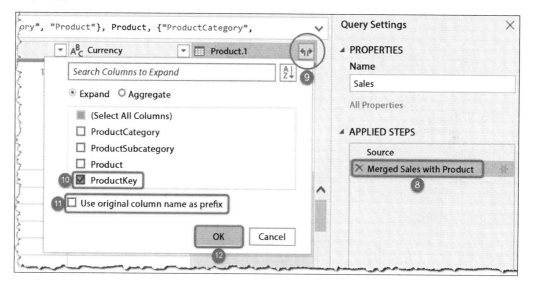

Figure 6.38: Expanding the Product.1 structured column

Now, we need to get **SalesDemographicKey** from the **Sales Demographic** table. The columns that make a unique identifier for each row in the **Sales Demographic** table are **SalesCountry**, **City**, **StateProvinceName**, and **PostalCode**. However, the **Sales** table does not contain all those columns. Besides, the **Sales Demographic** dimension is derived from the **Customer Base** table. Therefore, we have to merge the **Sales** table with the **Customer Base** table via the **CustomerKey** column and then merge it again with the **Sales Demographic** table to reach **SalesDemographicKey**.

13. From the **Applied Steps**, rename **Expanded Product.1** to **Expanded Product**.
14. Click **Merge Queries** again.
15. Select the **CustomerKey** column under the **Sales** section.
16. Select **Customer Base** from the drop-down list.
17. Select **CustomerKey**.

18. Select **Left Outer** for **Join Kind**.
19. Click **OK**:

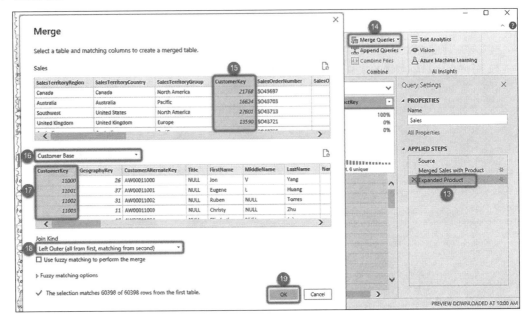

Figure 6.39: Merging the Sales table with Customer Base

This creates a new structured column named **Customer Base**. It also creates a new transformation step in **Applied Steps** named **Merged Queries**.

20. Rename this step **Merged Sales with Customer Base**.
21. Expand the **Customer Base** structured column.
22. Keep the **SalesCountry**, **City**, **StateProvinceName**, and **PostalCode** columns checked and uncheck the rest.
23. Uncheck the **Use original column name as prefix** option.
24. Click **OK**:

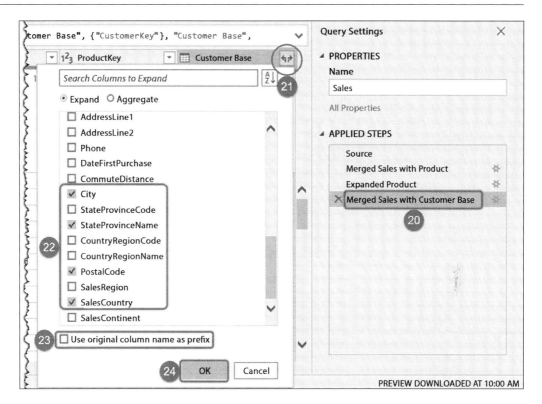

Figure 6.40: Expanding the Customer Base structured column

Now, we must merge the results with the **Sales Demographic** table and get the **SalesDemographicKey**.

25. After clicking **Merge Queries** again, select the **SalesCountry**, **City**, **StateProvinceName**, and **PostalCode** columns.
26. Select the **Sales Demographic** table from the dropdown.
27. Select the **SalesCountry**, **City**, **StateProvinceName**, and **PostalCode** columns, respectively. Remember, the sequence is important.

28. Keep **Join Kind** set to **Left Outer**.
29. Click **OK**:

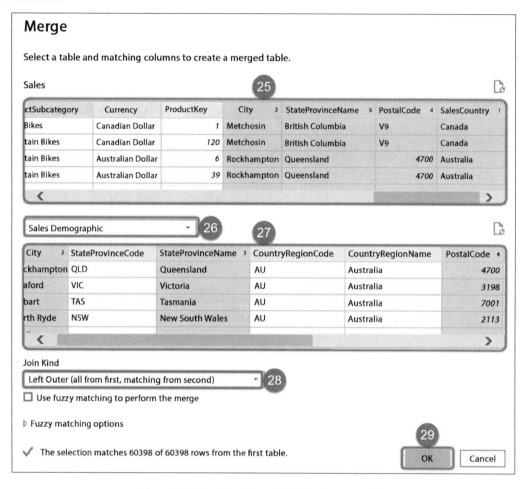

Figure 6.41: Merging Sales with Sales Demographic

This creates a new structured column named **Sales Demographic**. A new **Merged Queries** step is also created in **Applied Steps**.

30. Rename the **Merged Queries** step **Merged Sales with Sales Demographic**.
31. Expand the **Sales Demographic** structured column.
32. Uncheck all the columns except for the **SalesDemographicKey** column.

33. Uncheck the **Use original column name as prefix** option.
34. Click **OK**:

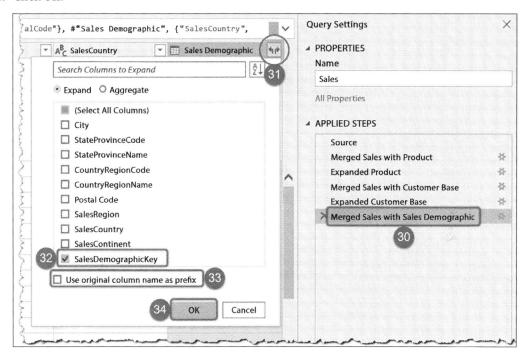

Figure 6.42: Merging Sales with Sales Demographic

So far, we have added **SalesDemographicKey** to the **Sales** table. Let us look at the columns in the **Sales** table with either Date or DateTime data types. The **Sales** table has three columns with the DateTime data type. Looking closer at the data shows that **OrderDate** is the only one with the DateTime data type, while the other two represent Date values (the Time part of all values is 12:00:00 AM). Therefore, it is better to convert the data type of those columns into Date. The **OrderDate** column represents both Date and Time. The remaining part is to split the Date and Time values into separate columns: **Order Date** and **Order Time**. These columns will be used in the data model relationships. Follow these steps to do so:

35. Select the **OrderDate** column.
36. Click the **Split Column** button from the **Home** tab of the ribbon.
37. Click **By Delimiter**.
38. Select **Space** as the delimiter.

39. Click **Left-most delimiter** for **Split at**.
40. Click **OK**:

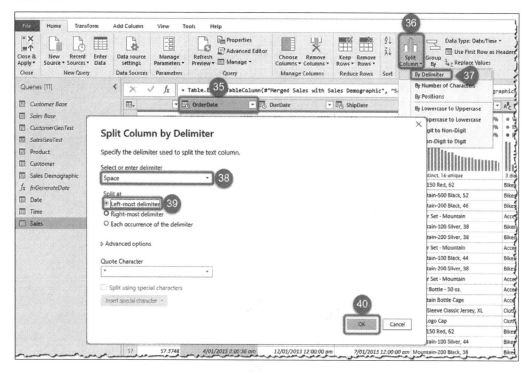

Figure 6.43: Splitting OrderDate by delimiter

41. Rename the **Split Column by Delimiter** step to **Split OrderDate by Delimiter** from **Applied Steps**.
42. From the formula bar, change **OrderDate.1** to **Order Date** and change **OrderDate.2** to **Order Time**. Then, submit these changes:

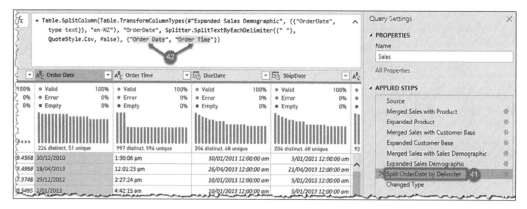

Figure 6.44: Changing the split column names from the formula bar

Power Query Editor automatically adds a **Changed Type** step if the **Type Detection** setting is set to detect the data types. Keep this step. Now, we need to change the data type of the **DueDate** and **ShipDate** columns from `DateTime` to `Date`.

43. Click the **Changed Type** step from the **Applied Step** pane.
44. Select both **DueDate** and **ShipDate**.
45. Click the **Data Type** drop-down button from the **Home** tab.
46. Select **Date**:

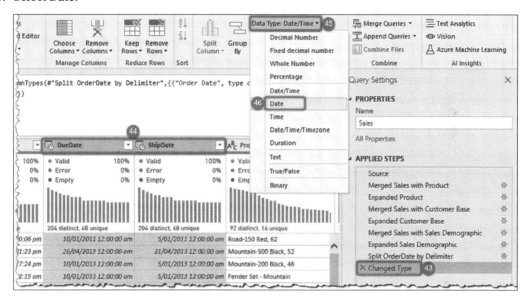

Figure 6.45: Changing the DueDate and ShipDate data types

So far, we have added all the key columns from the dimensions to the fact table, which will be used to create the relationships between the dimensions and the fact table in the data model layer. The only remaining piece of the puzzle is to clean up the **Sales** table by removing all the unnecessary columns.

47. Click the **Choose Column** button from the **Home** tab.
48. Keep the following columns checked and uncheck the rest; that is, **CustomerKey, SalesOrderNumber, SalesOrderLineNumber, OrderQuantity, ExtendedAmount, TotalProductCost, SalesAmount, TaxAmt, Freight, Order Date, Order Time, DueDate, ShipDate, Currency,** and **ProductKey**.

49. Click **OK**:

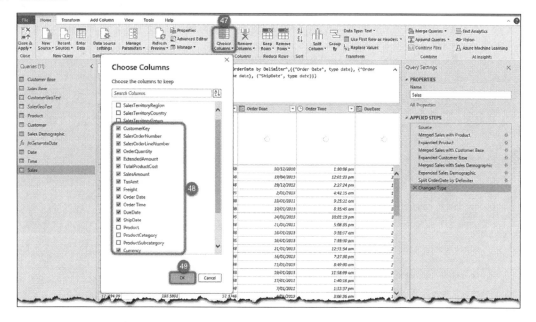

Figure 6.46: Removing unnecessary columns from the Fact table

The results of the preceding transformation steps show that the **Sales** fact table contains the following:

- The **OrderQuantity, ExtendedAmount, TotalProductCost, SalesAmount, TaxAmt,** and **Freight** columns, which are facts.
- **CustomerKey, Order Date, Order Time, DueDate, ShipDate, ProductKey,** and **SalesDemographicKey** are foreign keys that will be used in the data modeling layer to create relationships between the **Sales** table and its dimensions.
- **SalesOrderNumber, SalesOrderLineNumber,** and **Currency** are degenerated dimensions.

We have now successfully prepared the data supporting the Star Schema approach. We now apply the changes to load the data into the data model.

Summary

In this chapter, we prepared the data in a Star Schema, which has been optimized for data analysis and reporting purposes on top of a flat data structure. We identified potential dimensions and discussed the reasons for creating or not creating separate dimension tables. We then went through the transformation steps to create the justified dimension tables. Finally, we added all the dimension key columns to the fact table and removed all the unnecessary columns, which gave us a tidy fact table that only contained all the necessary columns.

The next chapter covers an exciting and rather important topic: *Data preparation common best practices*. By following these best practices, we can avoid a lot of reworks and maintenance costs.

Join us on Discord!

Join The Big Data and Analytics Community on the Packt Discord Server!

Hang out with 558 other members and enjoy free voice and text chat.

`https://packt.link/ips2H`

7

Data Preparation Common Best Practices

In the previous chapter, we connected to a flat data source, prepared the data with the star schema approach, and identified the dimensions and facts. In this chapter, we look at common data preparation best practices that help to avoid common pitfalls, having better-performing queries that are well organized and are cheaper to maintain by going through some general techniques and considerations in Power Query. We look at query folding and discuss its related best practices. We emphasize the importance of data conversion to avoid potential issues caused by inappropriate data conversions in the data model. We also discuss some query optimization techniques. Last but not least, we look at potential naming conventions essential for code consistency.

In this chapter, we discuss the following best practices:

- Consider loading a proportion of data
- Appreciate case sensitivity in Power Query
- Be mindful of query folding and its impact on data refresh
- Organize queries in the Power Query Editor
- Follow data type conversion best practices
- Optimize query size
- Use query parameters
- Define key columns in queries
- Use naming conventions

Following best practices guarantees that we avoid issues down the road that are hard to identify and hence expensive to rectify.

Consider loading a proportion of data

A general rule of thumb with all kinds of data sources is only to keep relevant columns during data preparation. We need to pay more attention to it when dealing with API-based data sources, as the available resources are usually pretty limited. For instance, when connecting to a data source stored in a SharePoint Online folder, we get throttled when we hit the 25 requests per second limit. Another common data source that we have to be more careful with is **Open Data Protocol** (**OData**). Microsoft invented OData, a commonly accepted method for creating and consuming REST APIs. Many **Enterprise Resource Planning** (**ERP**) systems are accessible via OData. When loading data via an OData connection into Power BI, it is essential to pay extra attention to the amount of data being loaded. In many cases, the underlying data model has wide tables with many columns containing metadata that is not necessarily needed.

Power BI reports brought production systems to their knees when developers initially tried to load all data from wide tables with more than 200 columns. So it is wise only to load the relevant columns into the data model. In some cases, we may also need to filter the data to load the part of it that matters the most to the business. Many API-based data sources like OData provide querying capabilities to call the required columns explicitly.

At this point, we may also need to involve **Subject Matter Experts** (**SMEs**) in the business who know the underlying data model quite well. The business sets the rules around the relevance of the data to analyze. If such a knowledgeable SME is not accessible, for us, the Power BI developers, it is important to know how large the data model we are connecting to is, how many tables are involved, and how many columns and rows they have. To do so, we can create a custom function to get the tables, how many columns and rows they have, and so on. The following custom function accepts an OData URL, and retrieves the table names, their column count, row count, the number of columns with decimal data, lists of decimal columns, the number of text columns, and lists of text columns:

```
//fnODataFeedAnalysis
(ODataFeed as text) as table =>
let
Source = OData.Feed(ODataFeed),
        FilterTables = Table.SelectRows(Source, each Type.Is(Value.
Type([Data]), Table.Type) = true),
    #"TableColumnCount Added" = Table.AddColumn(FilterTables, "Table Column 
Count", each Table.ColumnCount([Data]), Int64.Type),
    #"TableCountRows Added" = Table.AddColumn(#"TableColumnCount Added", "Table 
Row Count", each Table.RowCount([Data]), Int64.Type),
    #"NumberOfDecimalColumns Added" = Table.AddColumn(#"TableCountRows Added", 
"Number of Decimal Columns", each List.Count(Table.ColumnsOfType([Data], 
{Decimal.Type})), Int64.Type),
    #"ListOfDecimalColumns Added" = Table.AddColumn(#"NumberOfDecimalColumns 
Added", "List of Decimal Columns", each if [Number of Decimal Columns] = 0 then 
null else Table.ColumnsOfType([Data], {Decimal.Type})),
```

```
    #"NumberOfTextColumns Added" = Table.AddColumn(#"ListOfDecimalColumns
Added", "Number of Text Columns", each List.Count(Table.ColumnsOfType([Data],
{Text.Type})), Int64.Type),
    #"ListOfTextColumns Added" = Table.AddColumn(#"NumberOfTextColumns Added",
"List of Text Columns", each if [Number of Text Columns] = 0 then null else
Table.ColumnsOfType([Data], {Text.Type})),
    #"Sorted Rows" = Table.Sort(#"ListOfTextColumns Added",{{"Table Column
Count", Order.Descending}, {"Table Row Count", Order.Descending}}),
    #"Removed Other Columns" = Table.SelectColumns(#"Sorted Rows",{"Name",
"Table Column Count", "Table Row Count", "Number of Decimal Columns", "List of
Decimal Columns", "Number of Text Columns", "List of Text Columns"})
in
    #"Removed Other Columns"
```

To invoke the preceding custom function, we need to pass the OData URL to the preceding function, and it gives us a result set as follows:

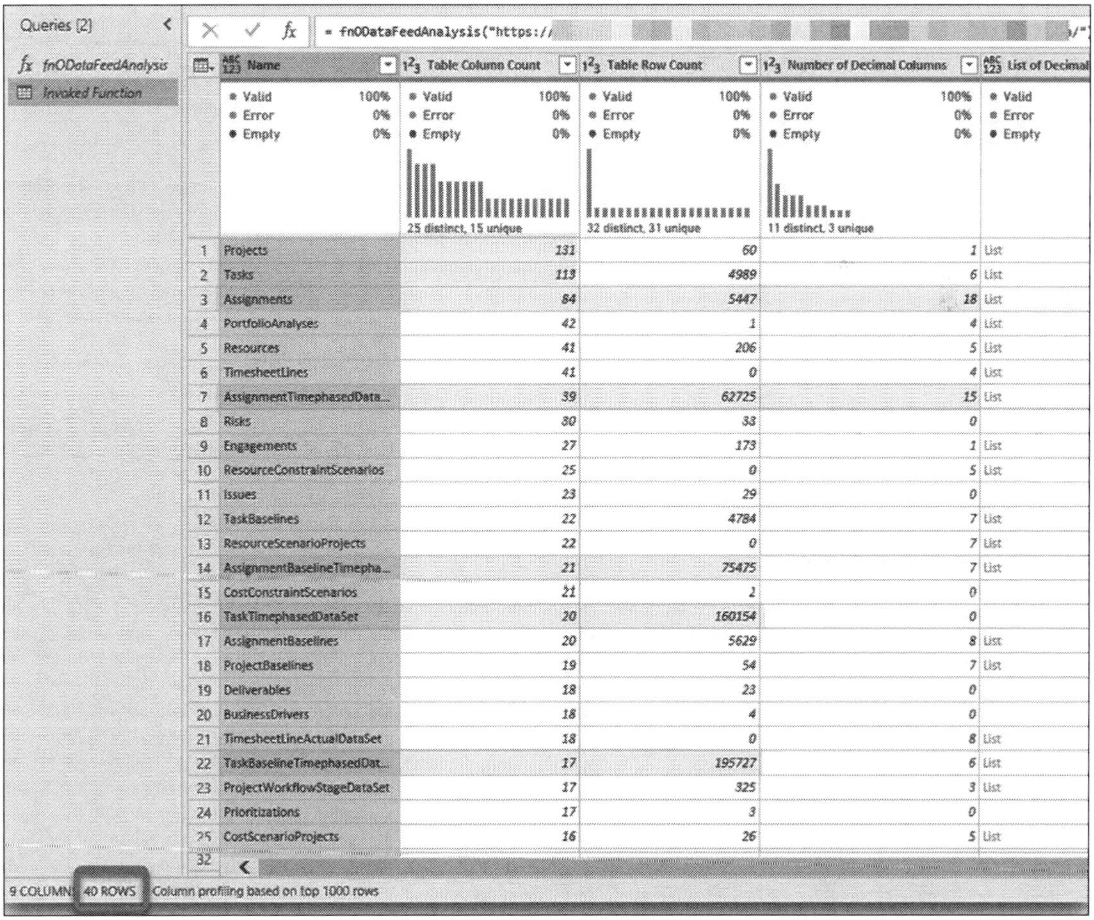

Figure 7.1: Invoked fnODataFeedAnalysis custom function

If you want to test the preceding custom function, you can use the Northwind test OData data source here: https://services.odata.org/Northwind/Northwind.svc/.

We invoked the fnODataFeedAnalysis custom function with the Microsoft Project Online OData URL. The function gets a list of all tables available in the OData data source and reveals the following information:

- **Name:** The names of the tables. As shown in *Figure 7.1*, the OData data source we connected to has 40 tables.
- **Table Column Count:** This shows the data source's number of columns, which is quite handy; we can quickly identify which tables are wide and need more attention. As shown in *Figure 7.1*, the top three tables with the highest number of columns are **Projects** with 131 columns, **Tasks** with 113 columns, and **Assignments** with 84 columns.
- **Table Row Count:** This shows the number of rows each table has. As illustrated in the figure, the **TaskBaselineTimephasedDataSet** table with 195,727 rows, the **TaskTimephasedDataSet** table with 160,154 rows, and the **AssignmentBaselineTimephasedDataSet** table with 75,475 rows are the top three tallest tables in the data source.
- **Number of Decimal Columns:** This shows the count of columns with the Decimal data type.
- **List of Decimal Columns:** Contains a list of columns with the Decimal data type. We can click on each cell to see the column names.
- **Number of Text Columns:** Shows the count of columns with the Text data type.
- **List of Text Columns:** Contains a list of columns with the Text data type.

The preceding points are essential. They show the number of columns of Decimal and Text data, which can consume too much memory if we do not handle them properly. By looking at the results of the preceding function, we can quickly find which tables need more attention in the data preparation, such as the tables that are wide and tall.

IMPORTANT NOTES ON USING THE FNODATAFEEDANALYSIS CUSTOM FUNCTION

If a table in your data source has millions of rows, then the #"TableCountRows Added" step can take a long time to get the row count of the table. In that case, you may want to remove the #"TableCountRows Added" step from the preceding query and use the rest.

Some OData feeds result in structured values. In those cases, we need to add some extra transformation steps to fnODataFeedAnalysis. But the current version of the function works with most OData feeds without any changes.

With some minor changes in the preceding function, we can make it work with many other data sources. For instance, we can change the connection from OData to SQL Server by changing the input parameter and the source line.

After we find the tables that are potentially problematic, we do the following:

- Eliminate all unnecessary columns.
- Filter the data to reduce the number of rows.
- We may consider changing the granularity of some tables by aggregating numeric values.
- The other crucial point is to treat the data types properly. We discuss it in the *Follow data type conversion best practices* section.

Appreciate case sensitivity in Power Query

As explained before, Power Query is case-sensitive. Case sensitivity is not just about the Power Query syntax; string data types in opposite cases are not equal in Power Query. So it is essential to pay attention to character cases when working with string data. When we mash up data from different sources, we often have GUIDs as key columns (either a primary or a foreign key). We get incorrect results if we compare the GUID values with different cases. For instance, in Power Query, the following values are not equal:

- C54FF8C6-4E51-E711-80D4-00155D38270C
- c54ff8c6-4e51-e711-80d4-00155d38270c

Therefore, if we merge two tables joining the key columns, we get weird results. It is also the case if we load the data into the data model and create a relationship between two tables with key columns in different character cases. The solution is simple; we only need to keep both key columns in the same character case using either the Text.Upper() or Text.Lower() functions in the Power Query Editor.

Be mindful of query folding and its impact on data refresh

Data modelers need to pay extra attention to query folding. Not only can query folding affect the performance of a data refresh but it can also hit resource utilization during the data refresh. Query folding is essential for the very same reason an incremental data refresh is, so if the refresh takes too long due to the queries not being folded, the incremental data refresh never happens. It is also crucial for the models in either DirectQuery or Dual storage mode as each transformation step must be folded. As query folding is a vital topic, it is good to spend some time to see what it is all about.

Understanding query folding

Query folding is simply the Power Query engine's capability to translate the transformation steps into the native query language. Therefore, based on the Power Query engine's capability, a query in the Power Query Editor may be fully folded or partially folded. For instance, we connect to a SQL Server database and take some transformation steps. The Power Query engine tries translating each transformation step into a corresponding function available in T-SQL. A query is fully folded when all query steps are translatable into T-SQL. If the Power Query engine cannot translate a step into T-SQL, the query is not folded anymore from that step onward, so the query is partially folded.

Here is the point: when the Power Query engine can fully fold a query, it passes the generated native query to the source system and gets the results back. On the contrary, when a query is partially folded, the Power Query engine sends the folded query parts back to the source system, gets the results back, and starts applying the unfolded transformation steps on our local machine itself. If the query is not folded at all, the Power Query engine itself must take care of all transformation steps.

DirectQuery and Dual storage modes and query folding

The concept of query folding in programming is called server-side/client-side data processing. A fully folded query is processed on the server, which is much more efficient when the query is partially or fully processed client-side.

Therefore, the queries in either DirectQuery or Dual storage modes must be fully folded; in other words, they must be translatable into the native query supported by the data source system. Hence, when we use a Power Query function that is not foldable in DirectQuery or Dual storage modes, we get the following warning, as also shown in *Figure 7.2*:

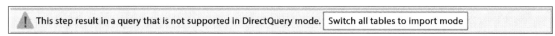

Figure 7.2: Switch all tables to Import mode warning in DirectQuery storage mode

Data sources and query folding

Most of the data sources that have a native query language support query folding, including the following:

- Relational databases that are supported in Power BI
- OData feeds
- SharePoint lists, which are basically OData feeds
- Microsoft Exchange
- Active Directory
- Microsoft Access

With that in mind, most file-based data sources, such as flat files, Excel files, blobs, and web data sources, do not support query folding.

If you do not have a data source that supports query folding but you want to learn how it works, download and install SQL Server 2019 from the following URL: https://www.microsoft.com/en-us/sql-server/sql-server-downloads.

Remember to download the Developer Edition. After you have downloaded and installed SQL Server 2019, you need a sample database. Microsoft provides a set of sample databases available for download from the following URL: https://learn.microsoft.com/en-us/sql/samples/adventureworks-install-configure?WT.mc_id=DP-MVP-5003466&view=sql-server-ver16&tabs=ssms.

Indications for query folding

Now that we know what query folding is, it would be good to determine when it happens and when it does not. The good news is that there are ways to indicate when a query is folded and when it is not. The indication can be noticeable depending on the storage mode and our transformation steps. We might need to take some steps to find out whether and when a query is folded.

As mentioned earlier, if the query's storage mode is DirectQuery or Dual, the query must be fully foldable. Otherwise, we get a warning message to change the storage mode to Data Import, which indicates that the query is not foldable. But if the storage mode is Data Import already, each step may or may not be folded. Generally, all query steps translated into the data source's native language are foldable.

If we map query folding to the SQL language, and if the query and its steps are translatable into a simple `SELECT` statement including `SELECT`, `WHERE`, `GROUP BY`, all `JOIN` types, aliasing (renaming columns), and `UNION ALL` (on the same source), then the query is foldable. With that in mind, we can also check query folding by right-clicking on each applied step and seeing whether the **View Native Query** option is enabled in the context menu or not. If **View Native Query** is enabled, then the step and all previous steps are certainly folded. Otherwise, the step we are at (or some previous steps) is probably not foldable. *Figure 7.3* shows a query on top of a SQL Server data source that is fully folded. We can click **View Native Query**, which is still enabled, to see the T-SQL translation of the current Power Query query:

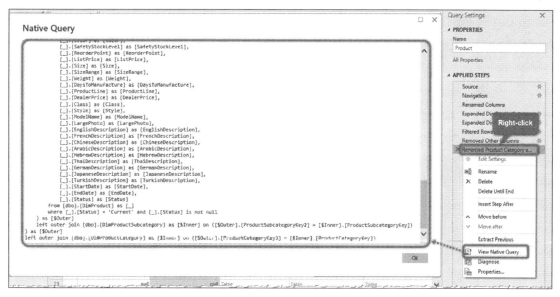

Figure 7.3: View Native Query in the Power Query Editor

Query folding best practices

So far, we have discussed the importance of query folding and how we can determine whether a query is fully folded or not. The general rule of thumb is to always try to have fully folded queries. But there are more best practices around query folding. Let us have a look at them.

Using SQL statements

When we connect to a SQL Server or a Dataverse data source, we can write T-SQL statements such as simple `SELECT` statements or execute stored procedures. The following screenshot shows the options available within the SQL Server connection:

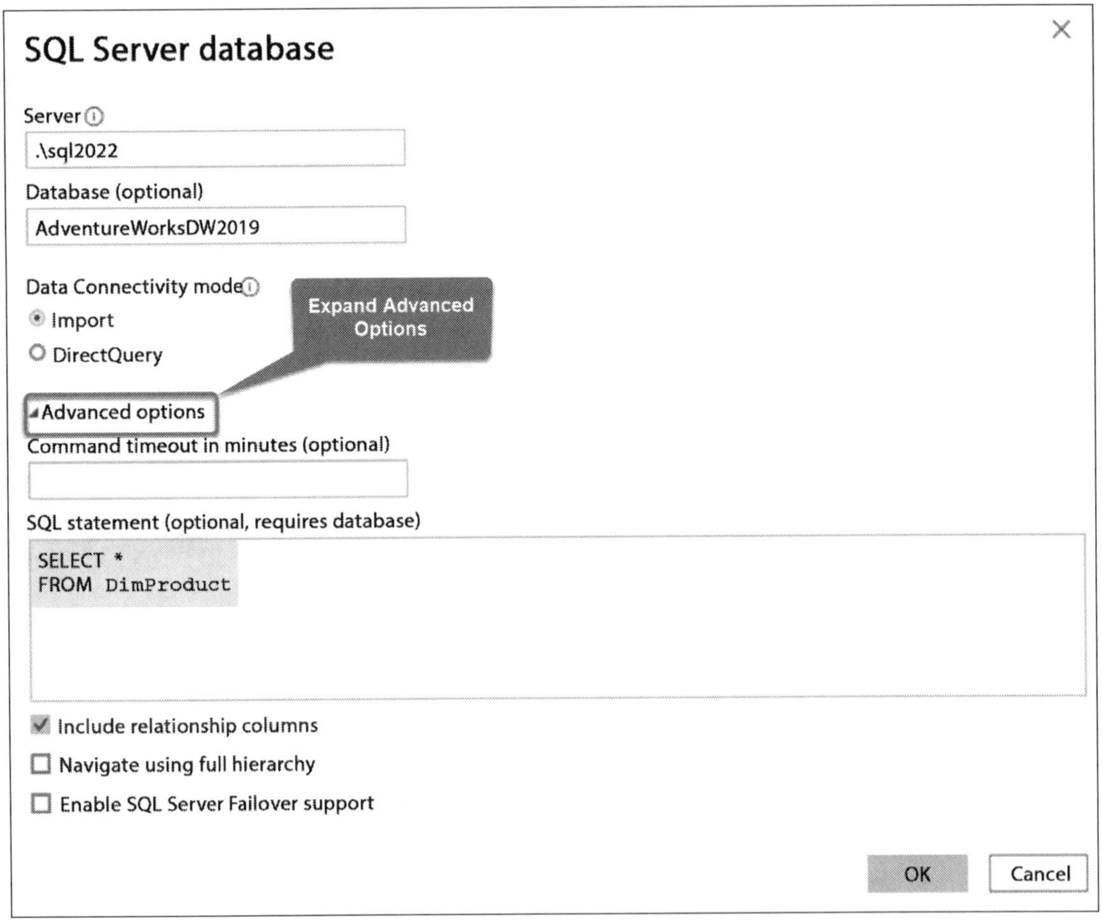

Figure 7.4: Using custom T-SQL statements when connecting to a SQL Server data source

When we use T-SQL statements, Power Query disables query folding, as shown in the following screenshot:

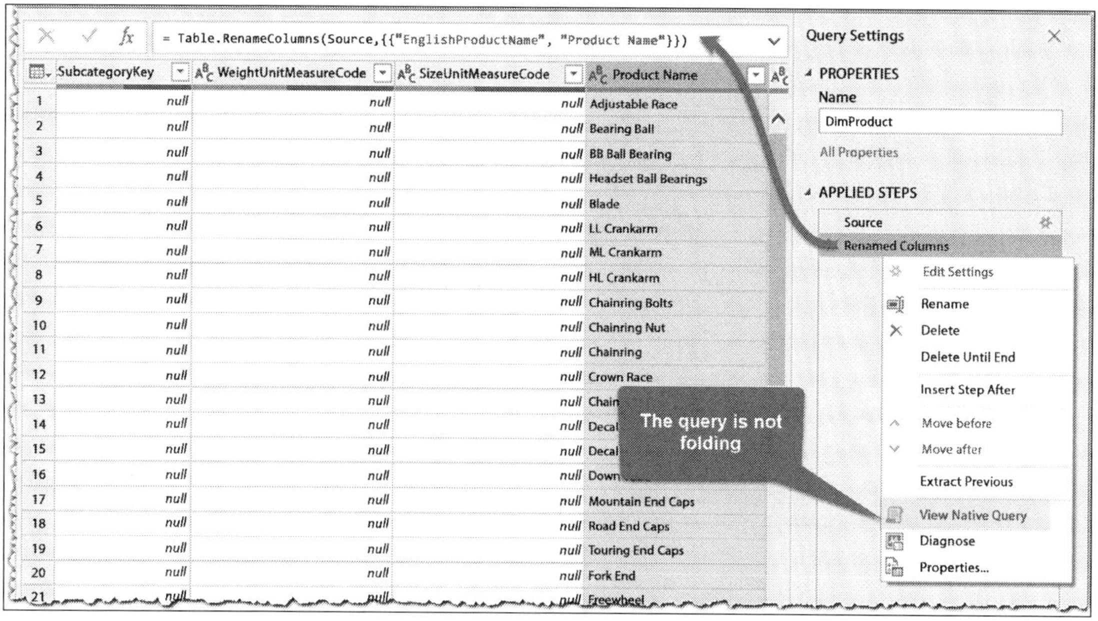

Figure 7.5: Query folding is disabled for custom T-SQL queries when connecting to SQL Server data sources

As mentioned before, it is best to take care of all possible transformation steps in the source, which translates to a SQL View in/out scenario. But if we do not have access to create a View in SQL Server, then we have to write a SQL statement to take care of all transformation steps, which in our simplistic scenario is renaming the **EnglishProductName** column to **Product Name**. In that case, we will have only one step in the **APPLIED STEPS** pane in the query editor.

Figure 7.6 shows the T-SQL version of the query shown in *Figure 7.5*:

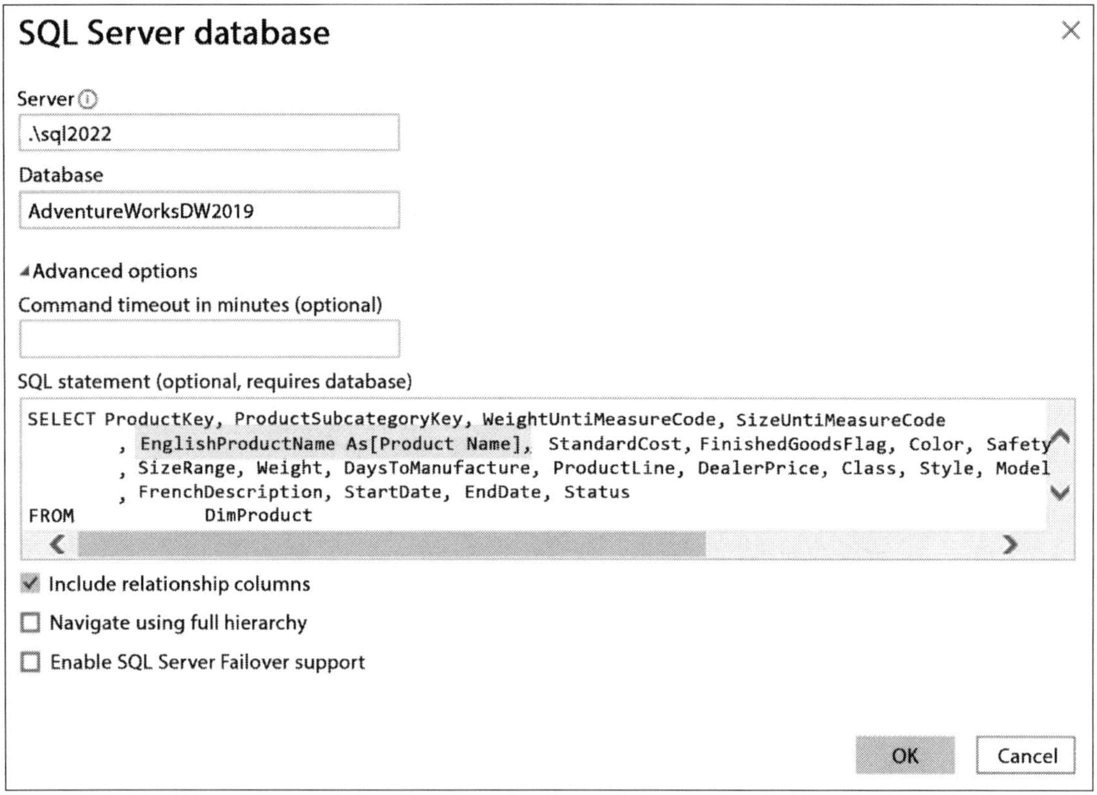

Figure 7.6: Taking care of transformation steps in T-SQL statements

As a general rule of thumb when writing T-SQL statements, we never use `SELECT *`.

Enabling folding for native queries

If you are not familiar enough with T-SQL to turn all Power Query transformation steps into their equivalents in T-SQL, you can enable folding for the native query using the `Value.NativeQuery()` function in Power Query. So, you can write a simple T-SQL query such as `SELECT * FROM Table_Name`, then enable folding for it, and implement the next transformation steps in Power Query. While this method works well, we still must ensure each step is actually folded. For the first time, Chris Webb uncovered the possibility of enabling folding for native queries by using the `Value.NativeQuery()` function on his following web log: https://blog.crossjoin.co.uk/2021/02/21/query-folding-on-sql-queries-in-power-query-using-value-nativequery-and-enablefoldingtrue/.

Here is how it works. Follow these steps to enable folding for the `SELECT * FROM DimProduct` T-SQL statement from the AdventureWorksDW2019 database:

Chapter 7

You can download the AdventureWorksDW2019 database from Microsoft's official website here: https://learn.microsoft.com/en-us/sql/samples/adventureworks-install-configure?view=sql-server-ver16&WT.mc_id=DP-MVP-5003466

1. In the Power Query Editor, use the **SQL Server** connector
2. Enter the **Server** name
3. Click **OK**

   The following screenshot shows the preceding steps:

   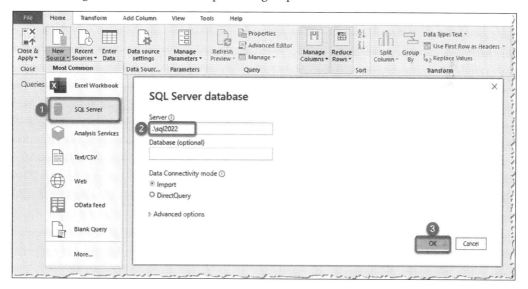

   Figure 7.7: Connecting to SQL Server from Power BI Desktop

4. Right-click the database
5. Select **Transform Data**

   The following screenshot shows the preceding steps:

   Figure 7.8: Transforming data at the database level

6. Click the *fx* button to create a new transformation step
7. Rename the new step to **SQL Folding**
8. Type in the Value.NativeQuery() function
9. Leave the previous step name as is
10. Type in the SELECT statement as a string in quotation marks
11. Pass null to the third operand
12. Pass [EnableFolding = true] to the fourth operand
13. Commit the changes

The following screenshot shows the preceding steps:

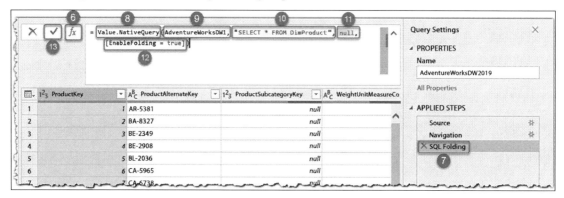

Figure 7.9: Enabling folding with the Value.NativeQuery() function

With the preceding steps, we successfully enabled folding for a native query. We can now add more transformation steps that support query folding such as renaming a column. The following screenshot shows that the native query is now enabled after renaming the **EnglishProductName** column to **Product Name**:

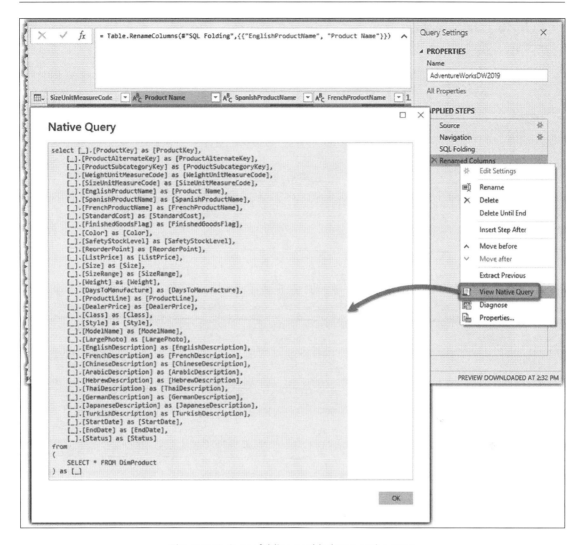

Figure 7.10: Query folding enabled on a native query

The next section explains another best practice: pushing the data preparation steps to the source system.

Push the data preparation to the source system when possible

It is advised to always push all the transformation steps to the source when possible. For instance, when we connect to a SQL Server data source, it is best to take care of all transformation steps on the SQL Server side by creating views, stored procedures, or tables that are populated by **Extract, Transform, and Load (ETL)** tools such as **SQL Server Integration Services (SSIS)** or **Azure Data Factory**.

Disabling View Native Query does not necessarily mean a transformation step is not folded

Investigating the foldability of a query or a transformation step is sometimes confusing. As mentioned earlier, an indication of a folded transformation step is to right-click a transformation step and see whether the **View Native Query** option is enabled within the context menu. But this is not true when we connect to relational databases. For instance, the combination of some transformation steps may disable **View Native Query** from the context menu. However, that step is folded back into the database. *Figure 7.11* shows a query connected to a SQL Server database. We added a simple **Kept First Rows** step to get the top 10 rows after changing the character case of the **CommuteDistance** column to uppercase. As the following screenshot shows, the **Uppercased Text** step folds, and we know that the **Kept First Rows** step translates to the TOP function in T-SQL, so it folds as well, but the **View Native Query** option from the context menu is disabled:

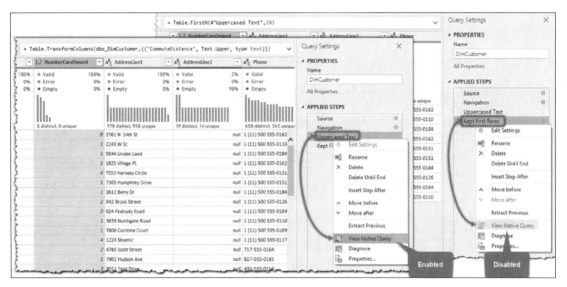

Figure 7.11: View Native Query disabled

However, it does not mean that the query is not folded. We can use the **Power Query Diagnostics** tool to see whether the query is folded back to the server or not. In this case, we want to diagnose a step. We can right-click on the **Kept First Rows** step from the **APPLIED STEPS** pane, then click **Diagnose**, as shown in the following screenshot:

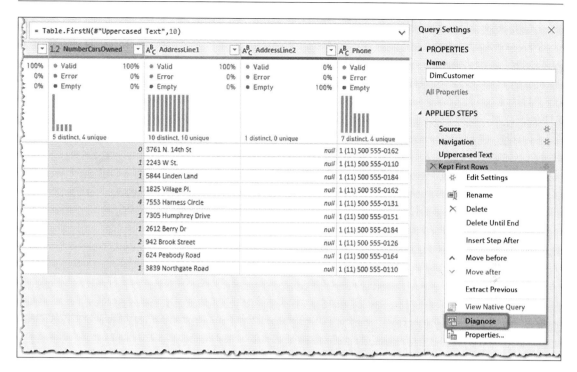

Figure 7.12: Diagnose step in Power Query Editor

This creates a **Diagnostics** folder in the **Queries** pane, including a couple of diagnostic queries. As *Figure 7.13* shows, there is a **Detailed** and an **Aggregated** query, which in our sample is named **DimCustomer_Kept First Rows_Aggregated**. For our sample, the **Aggregated** query gives us enough information. By clicking the **DimCustomer_Kept First Rows_Aggregated** query, we can see the diagnostic data:

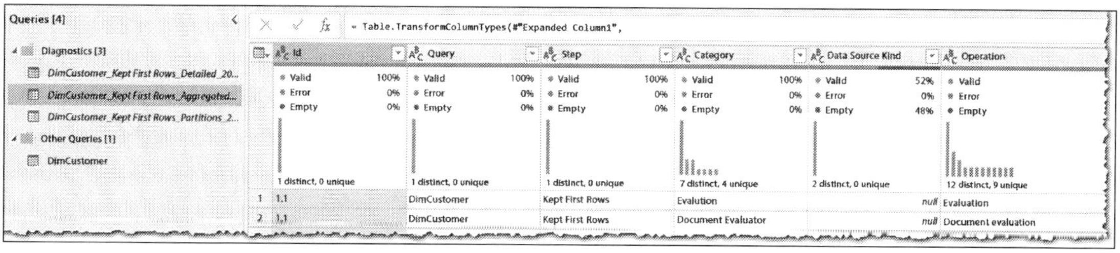

Figure 7.13: Aggregated diagnostic query

The diagnostic query provides a lot of information. But we are only interested in the **Data Source Query** column's values, which show the actual T-SQL that Power Query sends back to SQL Server. The last T-SQL query in the **Data Source Query** column is the query we are after. As the following screenshot shows, the query starts with **select top 10**, meaning the **Kept First Rows** step is also folded back to SQL Server.

This is quite important from a data modeling perspective to ensure building efficient and performant data preparation within the Power Query layer:

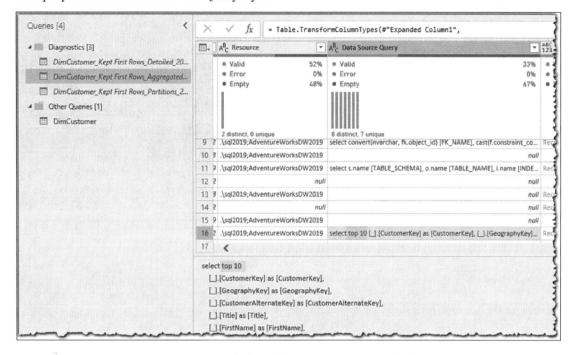

Figure 7.14: Query folded while View Native Query is disabled

Organize queries in the Power Query Editor

One of the aspects of a good development model in the software development world is to keep the code and objects organized, and Power BI development is not an exception. While this best practice is not directly relevant to data modeling, it is good to organize the queries from a maintenance perspective. Organizing queries is simple. Just follow these steps:

1. Select multiple queries from the **Queries** pane.
2. Right-click then hover over **Move to Group,** then click **New Group...**
3. Enter a name for the group.
4. Enter a relevant description for the group.
5. Click **OK**.

Chapter 7

The following screenshot shows the preceding steps:

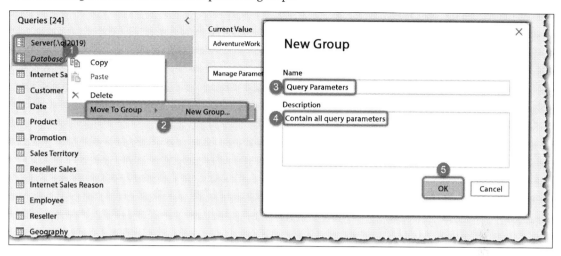

Figure 7.15: Grouping queries in the Power Query Editor

After grouping all queries, we have organized the **Queries** pane. This is handy, especially with larger models with many queries, as the following screenshot shows:

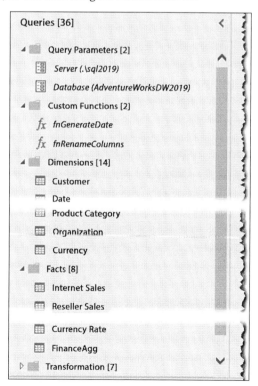

Figure 7.16: Organized queries in the Power Query Editor

When support specialists look at an organized instance of the Power Query Editor like the preceding example, they can quickly understand how the queries relate.

Follow data type conversion best practices

We previously discussed different Power Query types in *Chapter 3*, *Data Preparation in Power Query Editor*, in the *Introduction to Power Query (M)* section. In *Chapter 5*, *Common Data Preparation Steps*, we also discussed that data type conversion is one of the most common data preparation steps. In both chapters, we looked at different data types available in Power Query. So, as a data modeler, it is crucial to understand the importance of data type conversion. This section looks at some best practices for data conversion and how they can affect our data modeling.

Data type conversion can affect data modeling

As mentioned, we already discussed the data types in Power Query in *Chapter 3*, *Data Preparation in Power Query Editor*, and *Chapter 5*, *Common Data Preparation Steps*. However, briefly recalling some points in this section is worthwhile to emphasize the importance of understanding data types in Power Query. In Power Query, we have only one numeric data type: number. But wait, when selecting a numeric column in the Power Query Editor, in the **Transform** tab, there is a **Data Type** drop-down button showing four numeric data types, as the following screenshot shows:

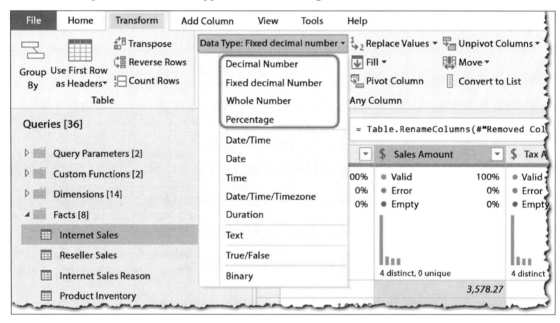

Figure 7.17: Data type presentations in the Power Query Editor

In Power Query formula language, there is just one numeric type, which is number. We specify it in the Power Query syntax as type number or Number.Type. The data types shown in the preceding screenshot are indeed not actual data types. They are data type presentations or data type **facets**. But in the Power Query data mashup engine, they are all of type number. Let us look at an example to see what this means.

The following expression creates a table with different numeric values:

```
#table({"Value"}
    , {
        {100}
        , {65565}
        , {-100000}
        , {-999.9999}
        , {0.001}
        , {10000000.0000001}
        , {999999999999999999.999999999999999999}
    }
)
```

The following screenshot shows the results of the preceding expression:

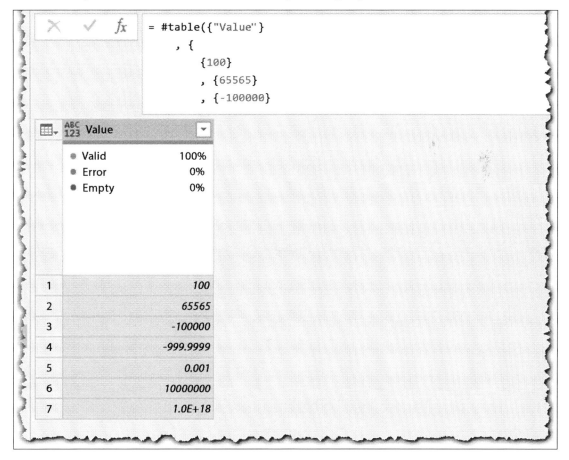

Figure 7.18: Numeric values in Power Query

Now we add a new column that shows the data type for each value. To do so, we can use the `Value.Type([Value])` function, which returns the type of each value of the **Value** column. The results are shown in the following screenshot:

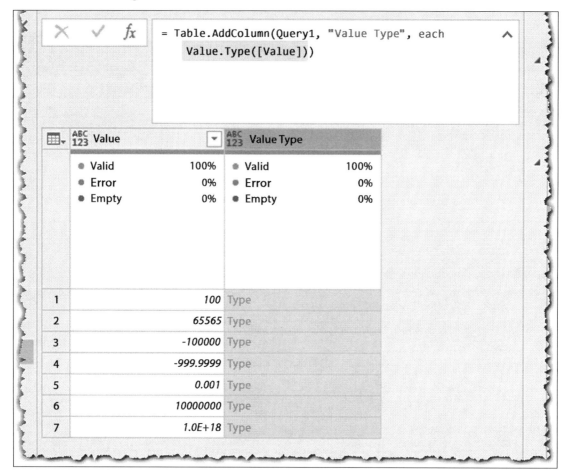

Figure 7.19: Getting a column's value types

To see the actual type, we have to click on each cell (not the values) of the **Value Type** column, as shown in the following screenshot:

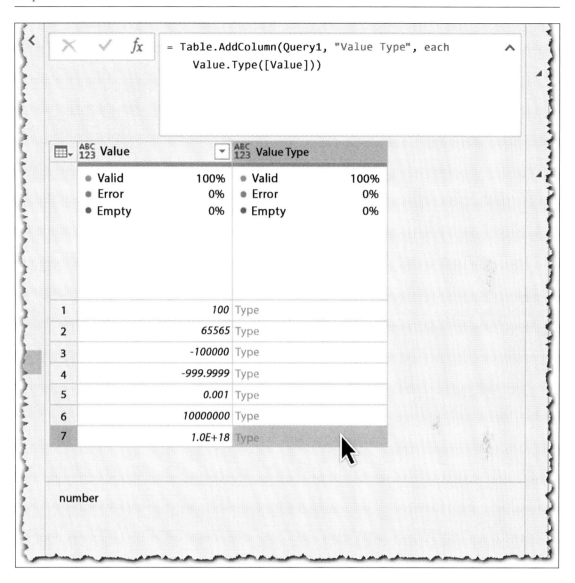

Figure 7.20: Click on a cell to see its type

While it is not ideal to click on every single cell to see the value's type, there is currently no function in Power Query that converts Type into Text. So, to show the type as text in the table, we have to use a simple trick. There is a function in Power Query that returns the table's metadata.

The function is Table.Schema(table as table). The function results in a table revealing information about the table used in the function, including column Name, TypeName, Kind, and so on. We want to show TypeName of the Value Type column. So, we only need to turn each value into a table using the Table.FromValue(value as any) function. We then get the values of the TypeName column from the output of the Table.Schema() function.

To do so, we add a new column to get textual values from TypeName. We name the new column Datatypes, and the expression is the following:

```
Table.Schema(
    Table.FromValue([Value])
    )[TypeName]{0}
```

The following screenshot shows the results:

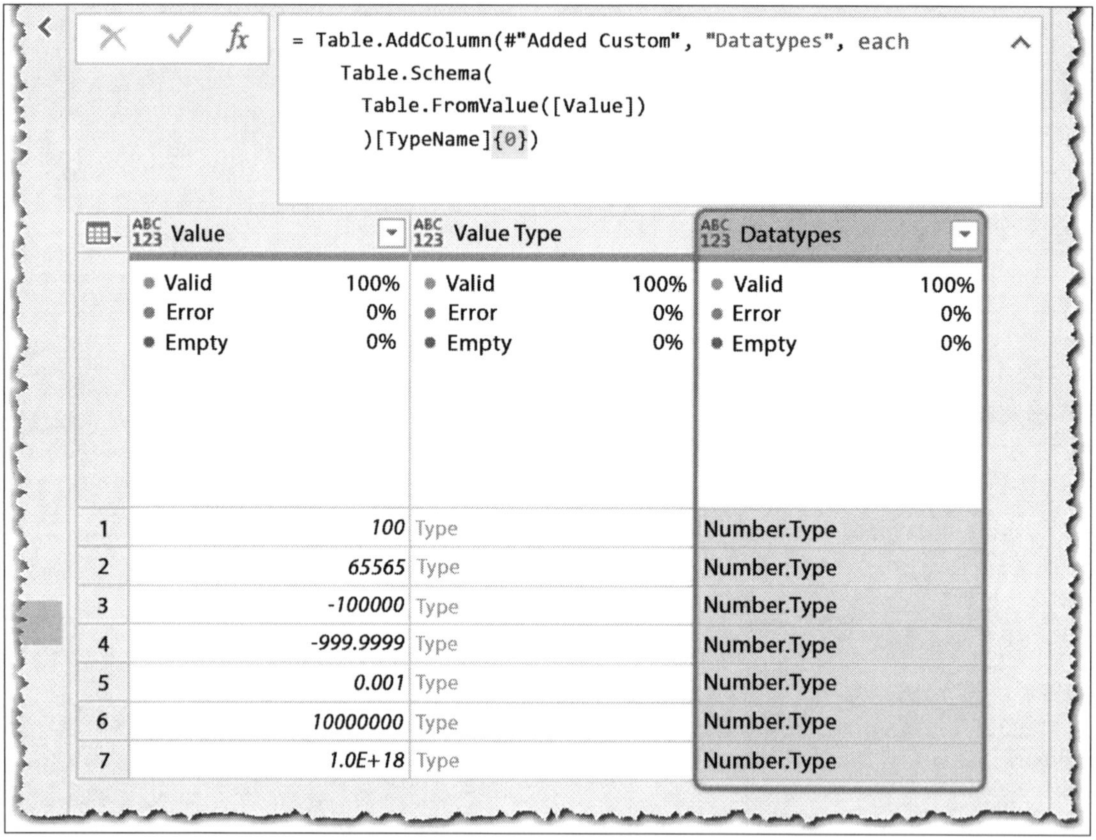

Figure 7.21: Power Query has only one numeric type, which is Number.Type

As the results show, all numeric values are of type Number.Type and how we present them in the Power Query Editor with different **facets** does not affect how the Power Query mashup engine treats those types. Here is the critical point: what happens after we load the data into the data model? Power BI uses the **xVelocity** in-memory data processing engine to process the data. The **xVelocity** engine uses columnstore indexing technology that compresses the data based on the cardinality of the column, which brings us to a critical point: although the Power Query engine treats all the numeric values as the type number, they get compressed differently depending on their column cardinality after loading the values in the Power BI model. Therefore, setting the correct type **facet** for each column is important.

Numeric values are one of the most common data types used in Power BI. Here is another example showing the differences between the four **number facets**. Run the following expression in a new blank query in the Power Query Editor:

```
// Decimal Numbers with 6 Decimal
let
    Source = List.Generate(()=> 0.000001, each _ <= 10, each _ + 0.000001 ),
    #"Converted to Table" = Table.FromList(Source, Splitter.SplitByNothing(), null, null, ExtraValues.Error),
    #"Renamed Columns" = Table.RenameColumns(#"Converted to Table",{{"Column1", "Source"}}),
    #"Duplicated Source Column as Decimal" = Table.DuplicateColumn(#"Renamed Columns", "Source", "Decimal", Decimal.Type),
    #"Duplicated Source Column as Fixed Decimal" = Table.DuplicateColumn(#"Duplicated Source Column as Decimal", "Source", "Fixed Decimal", Currency.Type),
    #"Duplicated Source Column as Percentage" = Table.DuplicateColumn(#"Duplicated Source Column as Fixed Decimal", "Source", "Percentage", Percentage.Type)
in
    #"Duplicated Source Column as Percentage"
```

The preceding expression creates 10 million rows of decimal values between 0 and 10. The resulting table has four columns containing the same data with different **facets**. The first column, **Source**, contains the values of type any, which translates to type text.

The remaining three columns are duplicated from the **Source** column with different **type number** facets, as follows:

- Decimal
- Fixed decimal
- Percentage

The following screenshot shows the resulting sample data of our expression in the Power Query Editor:

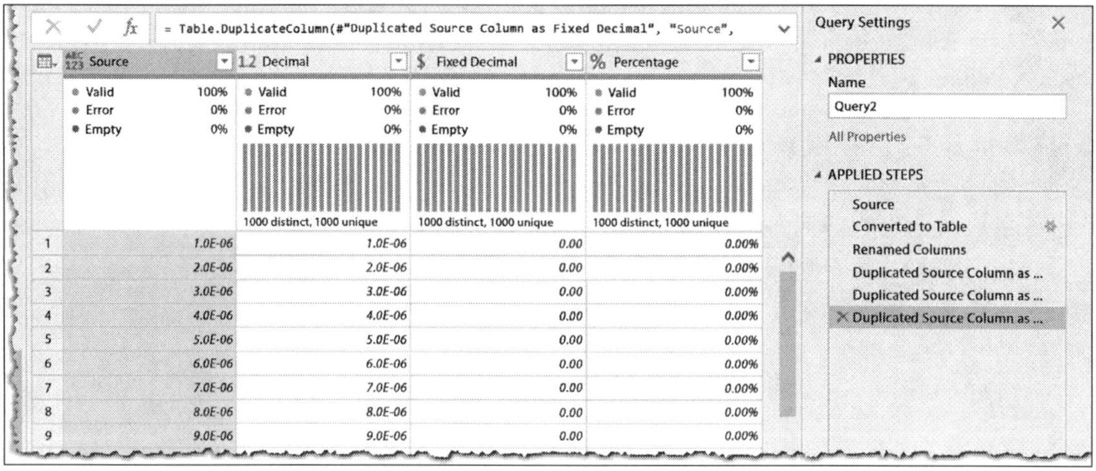

Figure 7.22: Numeric values with different type number facets

Now click **Close & Apply** from the **Home** tab of the Power Query Editor to import the data into the data model. At this point, we need to use a third-party community tool, **DAX Studio**, which can be downloaded from the following link: https://daxstudio.org/downloads/.

After downloading and installing, DAX Studio adds itself as an external tool in Power BI Desktop as the following screenshot shows:

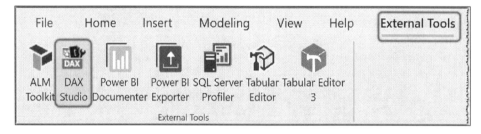

Figure 7.23: External Tools in Power BI Desktop

Click the **DAX Studio** button to open it; it automatically connects to the current Power BI Desktop model. Follow these steps:

1. Click the **Advanced** tab.
2. Click the **View Metrics** button.
3. Click **Columns** from the **VertiPaq Analyzer** section.
4. Look at the **Cardinality**, **Col Size**, and **% Table** columns.

The following screenshot shows the preceding steps:

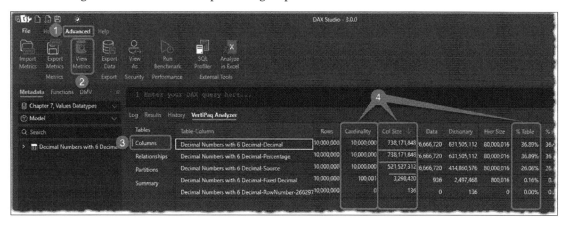

Figure 7.24: VertiPaq Analyzer Metrics in DAX Studio

The results show that the **Decimal** column and **Percentage** consumed the most significant part of the table's volume. Their cardinality is also much higher than the **Fixed Decimal** column. So here it is pretty clear why we should always use the `Fixed Decimal` data type (**facet**) for numeric values when possible.

> By default, the `Fixed Decimal` values translate to the `Currency` data type in DAX. So, we have to change their format if `Currency` is unsuitable for the column formatting.
>
> As the name suggests, `Fixed Decimal` has fixed four decimal points. Therefore, if the original value has more decimal digits after conversion into `Fixed Decimal`, the digits after the fourth decimal point are gone.

That is why the `Cardinality` column in VertiPaq Analyzer in DAX Studio shows much lower cardinality for the `Fixed Decimal` column (the column values only keep up to four decimal points, no more).

So, the message is always to use the data type that makes sense to the business and is efficient in the data model. Using VertiPaq Analyzer in DAX Studio is good for understanding the different aspects of the data model, including the column data types.

As a data modeler, it is essential to understand how the Power Query **types** and **facets** translate to DAX data types. Power Query and DAX are two different expression languages with their data types.

The following table shows the mapping between Power Query types and DAX data types:

Power Query Type Kind	Type Representation (Facet)	Mapping Datatype in DAX	xVelocity Internal Datatype
date	Date	Date/time	DateTime
datetime	Date/Time	Date/time	DateTime
datetimezone	Date/Time/Zone	Date/time	DateTime
duration	Duration	Decimal number	Double
logical	Logical	True/false	Boolean
number	Whole Number	Whole number	Int64
	Decimal Number	Decimal number	Double
	Fixed Decimal Number	Fixed decimal number	Decimal
	Percentage	Decimal number	Double
text	Text	Text	String
time	Time	Time	DateTime
any	Any	Text	String

Figure 7.25: Power Query to DAX data type mapping

As we see, the data type conversion can affect the data model's compression rate and performance. But that is not all. Having columns with any data type that is not converted into a more proper data type can cause some other implications, bringing us to the next section, *Avoid having columns with the any data type*.

Avoid having columns with any data type

As we explained in *Chapter 3, Data Preparation in Power Query Editor*, all data types in Power Query are compatible with the any data type. But, the xVelocity engine in the data model layer does not support the any data type. When the data is loaded into the data model, the any data type translates to text, which may or may not be correct. So, if the column contains integer values, but its data type is any, it turns into text when we load the data into the data model, and we all know that text consumes more memory than number. That is not the only downside. Refreshing a column with type any containing true/false values can result in unexpected behavior. This unexpected behavior is reported in the Power BI community, and Microsoft dedicated a subsection of its official Learn website to it explaining it as follows:

> When you create a report in Power BI Desktop that contains an ANY data type column, and that column contains TRUE or FALSE values, the values of that column can differ between Power BI Desktop and the Power BI Service after a refresh. In Power BI Desktop, the underlying engine converts the boolean values to strings, retaining TRUE or FALSE values. In the Power BI Service, the underlying engine converts the values to objects, and then converts the values to -1 or 0.
>
> Visuals created in Power BI Desktop using such columns may behave or appear as designed prior to a refresh event, but may change (due to TRUE/FALSE being converted to -1/0) after the refresh event.

You can find the article on the Microsoft Learn website here:

https://learn.microsoft.com/en-gb/power-bi/connect-data/refresh-troubleshooting-refresh-scenarios?WT.mc_id=DP-MVP-5003466

That is another piece of evidence to avoid having columns with the any data type.

Include the data type conversion in the step when possible

One of the crucial points some Power BI developers and data modelers miss is that some of the most used Power Query functions have an optional operand to force the type of a function's output. If we miss this point, we need to add at least one extra step for data type conversion; the more transformation steps, the slower the data refresh. The following functions have an optional columnType operand that we can use to force the output data type, which could potentially avoid adding extra steps for type conversion:

- Table.AddColumn(table as table, newColumnName as text, columnGenerator as function, optional columnType as nullable type)
- Table.DuplicateColumn(table as table, columnName as text, newColumnName as text, optional columnType as nullable type)
- Table.AddIndexColumn(table as table, newColumnName as text, optional initialValue as nullable number, optional increment as nullable number, optional columnType as nullable type)

For instance, I added four new columns, as the following screenshot shows, in four steps. Then, I added another step to change the type of the new columns in a single step:

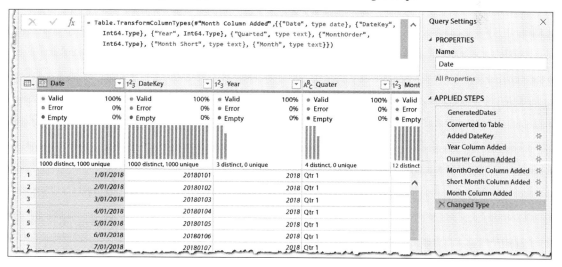

Figure 7.26: Added new column without adding the column data types to each transformation step

The DateKey Added expression looks like this:

```
Table.AddColumn(#"Converted to Table", "DateKey", each Int64.From(Text.Combine({Date.ToText([Date], "yyyy"), Date.ToText([Date], "MM"), Date.ToText([Date], "dd")})))
```

The following screenshot shows that the output type of the DateKey Added expression is **any**:

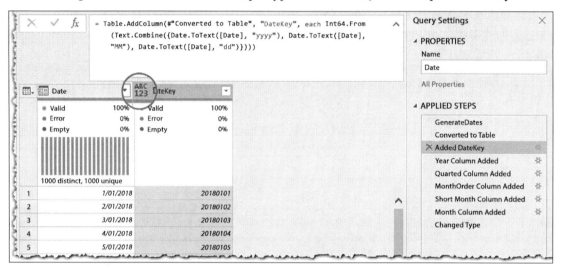

Figure 7.27: The type of the DateKey column is of type any

As explained earlier, the last operand of the Table.AddColumn() function in Power Query is columnType. So I can write the DateKey Added expression like the following expression instead:

```
Table.AddColumn(#"Converted to Table", "DateKey", each Int64.From(Text.Combine({Date.ToText([Date], "yyyy"), Date.ToText([Date], "MM"), Date.ToText([Date], "dd")})), Int64.Type)
```

With the preceding expression, I explicitly mentioned the type of output. Therefore, I can omit the **Changed Type** step by adding columnType to all other transformation steps.

Consider having only one data type conversion step

Having multiple data conversion steps is a habit many Power BI developers and data modelers have. It is a good idea to avoid this habit and add only one data type conversion step in the query when possible. The following screenshot shows a query in the Power Query Editor before and after consolidating all data conversion steps into one single step, while the results are the same:

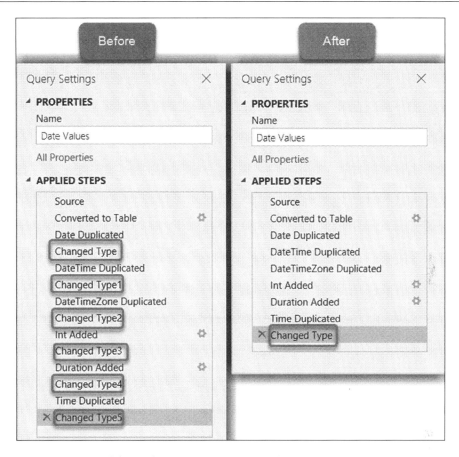

Figure 7.28: Consolidating data type conversion steps into one data type conversion step

As the preceding screenshot shows, we can omit excessive **Changed Type** steps by having only one **Changed Type** step as the last transformation step.

Optimize query size

This section discusses other data preparation best practices to improve our model. Optimizing queries' sizes can reduce the data refresh time. A model with an optimized size performs better after we import the data into the data model. In the following subsections, we look at some techniques that help us optimize queries.

Remove unnecessary columns and rows

In real-world scenarios, we might deal with large tables with hundreds of millions of rows and hundreds of columns. Some Power BI developers import all columns and rows from all data sources, resulting in poor-performing reports. As stated before, Power BI uses the **xVelocity** engine, which uses in-memory data processing for data analytics based on column cardinality. Therefore, fewer columns directly translate to less memory consumption and, as a result, a more performant data model. In many real-world scenarios, we need the business's approval to remove unwanted columns from tables.

Similarly, the number of rows directly impacts the data refresh and the data model performance. Another aspect that Power BI developers/modelers usually miss is forgetting the **Power BI Desktop Report** (**PBIX**)file size limitations. There are also some resource limitations on the Power BI Service. These limitations vary depending on the licensing plan we hold. So, creating reports by importing all the data from the data source into the Power BI models without being conscious of the size limitations is a bad idea, leading to an error complaining about exceeding the size limit. We discussed the different Power BI licensing models in *Chapter 1, Introduction to Data Modeling in Power BI*. The following table shows the PBIX file size limitations that apply to the licensing tier we hold:

Power BI License	Power BI Report (PBIX) File Size Limit
Free	Up to 1 GB
Pro	Up to 1 GB
Report Server	Up to 2 GB
P1/A4	Up to 3 GB
P2/A5	Up to 6 GB
P3/A6, P4/A7, and P5/A8	Up to 10 GB

Figure 7.29: PBIX file size limitations on Power BI Licenses

While Power BI Premium Capacity can support up to 400 GB of model size in the Power BI Service, the PBIX size limitations in the preceding table remain the same.

In many cases, we might not need to import the full history of data into the Power BI data model. So, be sure to find out the required amounts of data in information gathering workshops and filter out the unnecessary data.

Summarization (Group by)

In many instances, we need to create reports to show summarized data. So why do we need to import all the data in its lowest grain into the data model? One good reason is to build future-proof solutions that support as many business requirements as possible. We should endeavor to create centralized data models in Power BI serving multiple business processes. But creating centralized data models is not always that straightforward. One of the many reasons for that is the **PBIX file** limitation and the resource limitations in the Power BI Service. We discussed removing unnecessary columns and filtering rows as an efficient technique to optimize the model size.

Summarizing tables is another effective way of achieving model size optimization, leading to more performant data models. By summarizing the data, we change the granularity of the data to a higher level. So, the summarization level is another factor to identify in information gathering workshops with the business.

In Power Query, we use the Group by feature to summarize tables. You can study the Group by functionality in *Chapter 5, Common Data Preparation Steps*, in the *Common table manipulations* section. We revisit this technique in detail when discussing aggregations in *Chapter 10, Advanced Data Modeling Techniques*. But it was worth mentioning it as a data preparation best practice.

Disabling query load

Not everyone has the luxury of having a proper ETL and data warehouse, so they have to take care of the data transformation in Power Query. In such cases, it is a common practice to reference other queries. In most cases, the referenced queries are transformation hubs, and we do not need their data in the data model. Hence, we should consider disabling the query load from the Power Query Editor to avoid unnecessary data load. In *Chapter 3, Data Preparation in Power Query Editor*, in the *Query properties* section, we discussed disabling the query load.

Use query parameters

As we discussed in *Chapter 3, Data Preparation in Power Query Editor*, in the *Understanding query parameters* section, query parameters are one of the most valuable features of Power Query that can help us in many scenarios. The following sections explain some of them.

Parameterizing connections

It is best to parameterize all data source connections, especially if we have different environments. The parameterized connections become handy when configuring the deployment pipelines.

Restricting the row counts in development for large tables

Sometimes, we deal with large tables with several million rows, which can be time-consuming in development. Imagine a scenario in which we transform the data in Power Query Editor and then load it into the data model. If the table in the source system is large, it takes a long time to load the data into the data model, decreasing our productivity. In most cases, we do not need to load all the data into the data model during development. So, it is best to restrict the number of rows using query parameters so that we can work much quicker while in development. After publishing the data model in the Power BI Service, we change the query parameters to load all data. Let us quickly go through it. In this example, we use the AdventureWorksDW2017.xlsx sample file that you can download from here:

https://github.com/PacktPublishing/Expert-Data-Modeling-with-Power-BI-Second-Edition/tree/main/Samples/AdventureWorksDW(xlsx)

We want to restrict the row counts of the **Internet_Sales** table to 1,000 rows for development. We also want to be able to load all data when necessary. To do so, follow these steps:

1. In the Power Query Editor, get the **Internet_Sales** table data from the Excel file.

2. Create a parameter.
3. Name it RowCount.
4. Check **Required.**
5. For **Type,** select **Any.**
6. For **Suggested Values**, select **List of values.**
7. Type 1000 and All in the list.
8. Select 1000 for **Default Value.**
9. Select 1000 for **Current Value.**
10. Click **OK.**

The following screenshot shows the preceding steps:

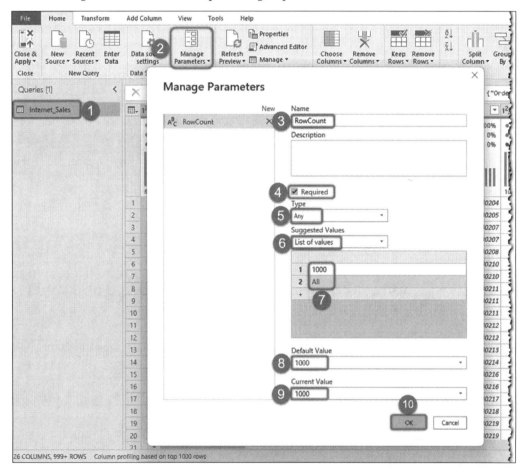

Figure 7.30: Creating a new parameter in the Power Query Editor

11. Select the **Internet_Sales** query.
12. Click the **Keep Rows** button.
13. Click the **Keep Top Rows** option.
14. Type a number in **Number of rows**.
15. Click **OK**.

The following screenshot shows the preceding steps:

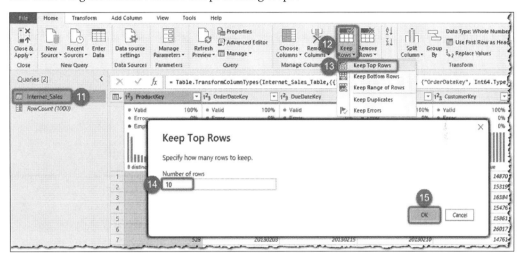

Figure 7.31: Keeping the top N rows

16. Replace the expression of the **Kept First Rows** step in the expression box with the following expression and commit the changes:

```
if Value.Is(RowCount, Number.Type)
    then Table.FirstN(#"Changed Type", RowCount)
    else #"Changed Type"
```

We can now load the data into the data model. After finishing the development, we change the parameter's value to **All** to load the entire data from the source into the data model.

The following screenshot shows the results.

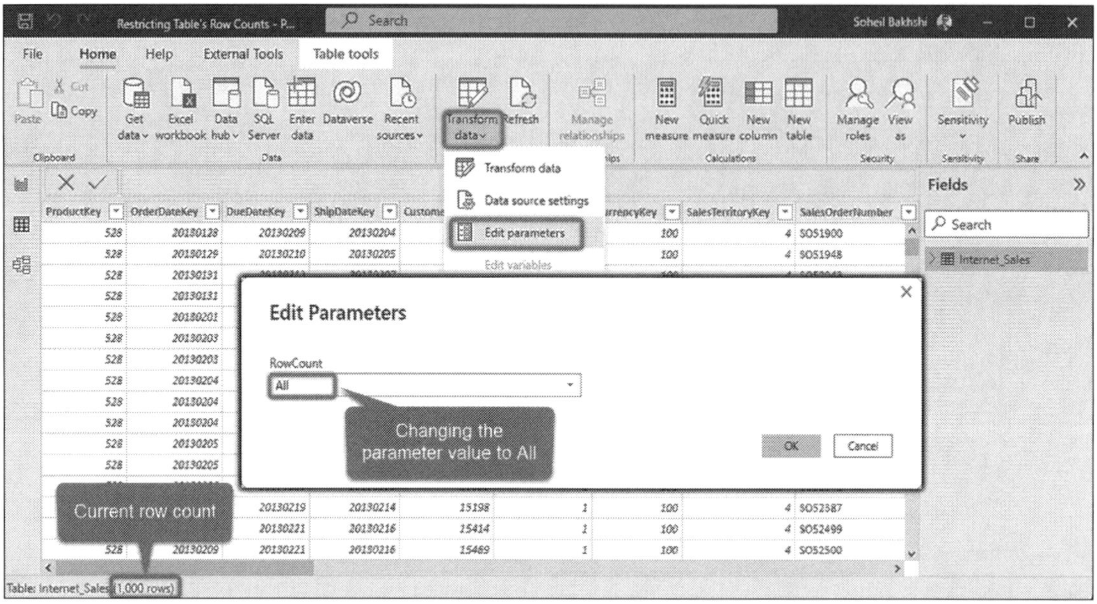

Figure 7.32: The results of restricting the row count of a table

Using query parameters in our Power Query implementations improves usability and helps build tidier and easier-to-maintain Power BI models.

Define key columns in queries

One of the most important aspects of a relational database is defining key columns. The key columns are the columns used to define a relationship between two tables. The key column(s) in a table guarantees the uniqueness of each row of data. The key column guaranteeing the uniqueness of each row within a table is the primary key. The primary key of a table appearing in another table is called a foreign key. In many cases, a single column does not guarantee the uniqueness of rows, but the so-called **Composite Key** does by considering multiple columns as key columns. The xVelocity engine in the data model layer, as we discuss in more detail in *Chapter 8, Data Modeling Components*, does not support composite keys, but the Power Query engine does. By defining the key columns in the Power Query Editor, we get some performance gains in refreshing the data, especially when merging two tables. We discussed merging tables in *Chapter 5, Common Data Preparation Steps*.

The Power Query engine uses the columns contributing to the join to find matches in the merging tables. Defining the primary key on one side of the join and the foreign key column on the other side helps the Power Query engine not to try to detect the primary keys and foreign keys internally; hence the join performance during the data refresh will be much better. The function to define the key columns in Power Query is `Table.AddKey(table as table, columns as list, isPrimary as logical)`. The Power Query UI in **Power BI Dataflows** has a **Mark as key** button on the ribbon to define the key columns, as shown in the following screenshot:

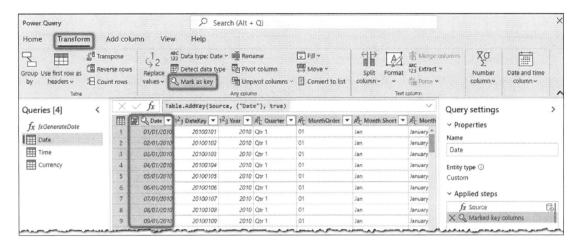

Figure 7.33: Mark as key in Power Query, in Power BI Dataflows

However, the Power Query Editor in the current version of Power BI Desktop (September 2022) still does not have the **Mark as key** button on the UI; therefore, we have to type the function. The following screenshot shows the scenario of defining a composite primary key in a table in the Power Query Editor in Power BI Desktop:

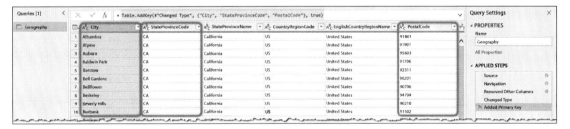

Figure 7.34: Defining composite key columns in the Power Query Editor

The key columns defined in the Power Query Editor are not recognizable in the data model layer as keys.

Use naming conventions

Having naming conventions for Power BI developers and data modelers is essential. It helps with solutions' consistency and makes the code more readable and more understandable for support specialists. It also sets common ground that everyone across the organization interacting with our Power BI solutions can benefit from.

Data sources do not necessarily have the most user-friendly object names. So, following a predefined naming convention during development is essential in helping the contributors understand the data model more efficiently and create new reports more confidently. The following naming conventions are suggested:

- Use camel case for object names, including table names, column names, and parameter names.
- Replace underscores, dashes, hyphens, or dots between the words with spaces.

- Remove prefixes and suffixes from table names (such as `DimDate` becoming `Date` or `FactSales` becoming `Sales`).
- Use the shortest and most self-explanatory names for queries and transformation steps.
- Rename the default transformation steps to something more meaningful.
- For custom functions, use the `fn` or `fx` prefix in the function name. Do not use any spaces in the name but keep the function name camel-cased, for example, `fnSampleCustomFunction`.
- When adding a new column supporting a specific calculation that will be **hidden** from the end user, use the `cal_` prefix in the column name so it can quickly be distinguished.
- Do not use acronyms in object names unless they make sense to the business. In some businesses (such as aviation), acronyms are widely used and are well understood by all end users. Therefore, in those cases, we always stick to the acronyms.
- Avoid using emojis in object names. We must not use emojis just because we can, and we think they look cool.
- Avoid using numbers in object names. In some cases, developers use a numeric value as a prefix for object names to sort. This is strongly against naming convention best practices.

You may have a more granular naming convention than the preceding list. However, if you do not have one, this can be a good starting point to think about the importance of having naming conventions in place.

Summary

This chapter discussed some of the most critical best practices for data preparation. We cannot cover all the best practices in a chapter or two, but we tried to cover some of the most important ones in this chapter. We learned how to optimize query sizes in Power Query and discussed how case sensitivity in Power Query could affect our data model. Going ahead, we learned the importance of query folding and how we can identify whether a query is folded. We then looked at some data type conversion best practices and how to reduce the number of steps by avoiding unnecessary steps and using query parameters. We then discussed the importance of having naming conventions.

In the next chapter, we will discuss data modeling components and building a star schema.

Join us on Discord!

Join The Big Data and Analytics Community on the Packt Discord Server!

Hang out with 558 other members and enjoy free voice and text chat.

`https://packt.link/ips2H`

Section 3

Data Modeling

Everything you have learned so far comes together in this section, in which we will build a well-designed data model in Power BI. While in the previous chapters you prepared the building blocks of your data model, it is now time to physically build the model with real-world hands-on scenarios.

The section starts with data modeling components from a Power BI point of view. Then the concept of granularity is discussed. This section also explains config tables and walks you through some scenarios in which you need to take advantage of them. This section ends with data modeling best practices.

This section comprises the following chapters:

- *Chapter 8, Data Modeling Components*
- *Chapter 9, Star Schema and Data Modeling Common Best Practices*

8

Data Modeling Components

In the previous chapter, we learned about some critical data preparation best practices, such as loading a proportion of data, removing unnecessary columns, and summarization to optimize our data model size. We also learned about query folding and how it can affect our data modeling in Power BI. We also looked at data type conversion and discussed the importance of selecting certain data types to keep our data model more optimized when we import the data into the data model; that brings us to this chapter. All our data preparation efforts pay off by having a cleaner data model that is easier to maintain and performs well. This chapter looks more closely at data modeling in Power BI by covering the following topics:

- Data modeling in Power BI Desktop
- Understanding tables
- Understanding fields
- Using relationships

We use the `Chapter 8, Data Modeling and Star Schema.pbix` sample file in this chapter. It is a copy of the sample file that resulted from our work in *Chapter 6, Star Schema Preparation in Power Query Editor*.

Data modeling in Power BI Desktop

The central premise for data modeling in Power BI Desktop is the **Model** tab in Power BI Desktop's main window. We can also create and edit calculation-based objects from the **Model** tab, such as creating a new calculated table, measure, or calculated column.

The following image shows the **Model** tab in Power BI Desktop:

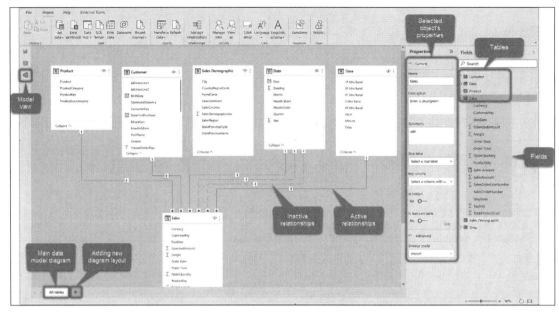

Figure 8.1: Model view tab in Power BI Desktop

The following sections discuss the modeling features currently available in Power BI Desktop. Then, we continue building the star schema we prepared in *Chapter 6, Star Schema Preparation in Power Query Editor*.

Understanding tables

From a data modeling perspective, tables are objects that contain related data by using columns and rows. In the Power Query Editor in Power BI, each query with **Enable load** activated becomes a table after loading into the data model.

Table properties

The table's properties show up in the **Properties** pane when clicking on a table from the **Model** view in Power BI Desktop, as shown in the following image:

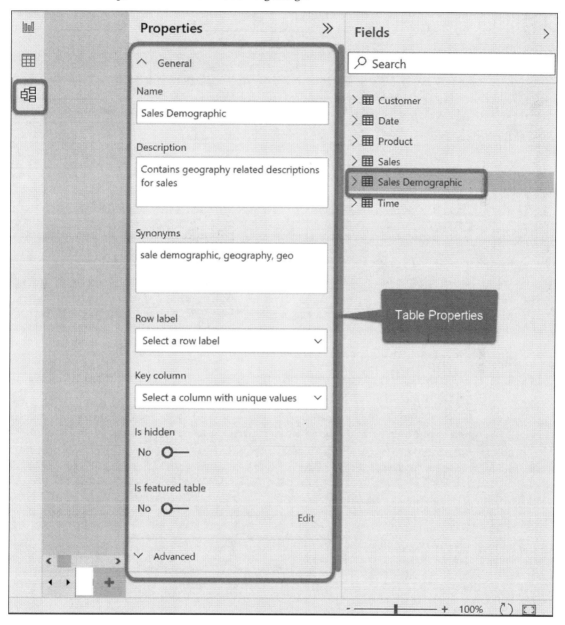

Figure 8.2: Table properties pane in the Model view

The following settings are currently available within the **Properties** pane. **General** includes the following general table properties:

- **Name:** The name of the table. We can rename a table from here.
- **Description:** We can write some descriptions about the table here. These descriptions show up in the **Data** view, as well as in the **Report** view, as shown in the following image:

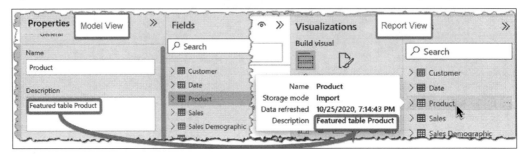

Figure 8.3: The table description shows up in the Report view when hovering over a table

We can also use the description for documentation purposes.

- **Synonyms:** Adding synonyms helps explicitly with Power BI's **Q&A** feature. The users usually use various terms to refer to the same thing. For instance, we have a table in the model named **Sales Demographic**. However, users may refer to it as **geography** or **geo**. So, we can add those phrases to the Synonyms box to help Q&A identify the Sales Demographic table if the user uses any of those phrases.
- **Row label:** This setting affects the data model in two ways, as follows:
    a. **Q&A:** This helps Q&A create more helpful visuals. A **Row label** defines which column best describes a single row of data. For instance, in the **Product** table, the row label is usually the **Product** (or **Product Name**) column. Therefore, Q&A treats the **Product** as a column instead of a table when the user asks for **Sales by product**. The following image shows the results of asking the **Sale by product as clustered column chart** question from Q&A:

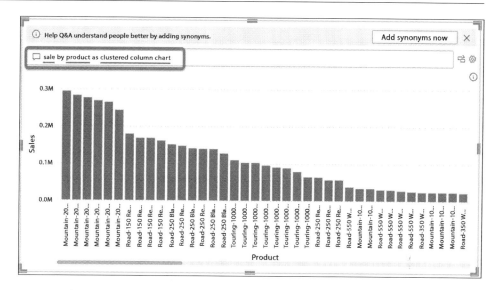

Figure 8.4: Row label from the table properties helps Q&A provide better results

    b. **Featured table**: When we set the table as a featured table in Power BI Desktop, the column selected as a **Row label** is used in Excel to identify the row quickly. More on this in the *Is featured table* bullet point.

- **Key column**: Provides a unique identifier for each table row. The **Key column** will then be used in Excel to link a cell's value to a corresponding row in the table.
- **Is hidden**: By toggling this setting to **Yes** or **No**, we can hide or unhide a table.
- **Is featured table**: With this setting, we can make a table a Featured Table, which makes the table's data accessible via Excel. After publishing the data model to the Power BI Service, only the specified users can access these featured tables. At the time of writing this book, the featured tables functionality is in public preview, so it may look slightly different in the version of Power BI Desktop you're currently using. In the meanwhile, let's look at the **Is featured table** setting. We'll look at the Featured Table concept in more detail in the next section. To configure this setting, we must toggle it to **Yes**. To turn this feature off if it is already on, we must toggle it to **No**. To edit the **Is featured table** setting, we can click the **Edit** hyperlink, which opens the **Setup this featured table** window.

In the following image, we set the **Product** table as a Featured Table by putting a short description in the **Description** text box, selecting the **Product** column as the **Row label**, and selecting the **ProductKey** column as the **Key column**:

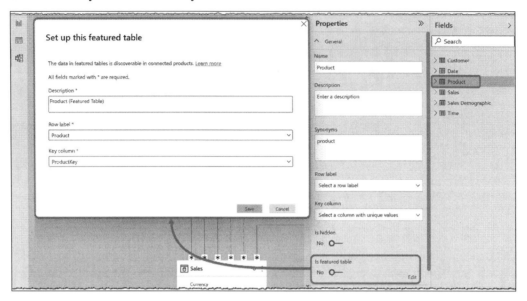

Figure 8.5: Setting up Featured Table from the Model view

- **Advanced**: The tables currently have only one advanced setting.
- **Storage mode**: This shows the storage mode of the table. We discussed the available storage modes in the *Storage modes* section of *Chapter 4, Getting Data from Various Sources*.

Featured tables

The concept of featured tables comes from the reusability mindset, where we take the prepared and already polished data across the organization in a secure way. The Power BI admins then have granular control of configuring or monitoring the featured table, who can publish or update the featured tables, or who, within the organization, can access the featured tables. In the previous section, we explained how to set the table as a featured table. After setting the table as a featured table from the **Model** view, the data (including measures held by a table) will be available in the **Data Types Gallery** in Excel after publishing the model to a modern **Workspace** in the Power BI Service.

The following image shows a new Excel file when the user types in a product name and then selects that **Product** from **Data Types Gallery** from the **Data** tab in Excel:

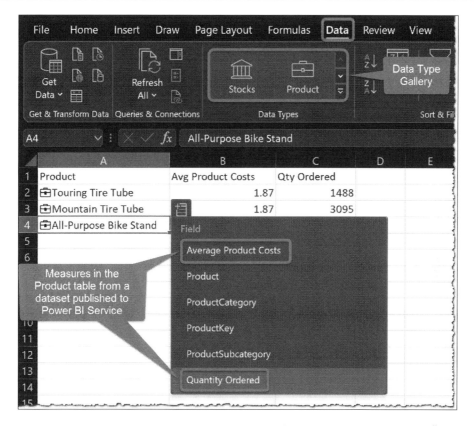

Figure 8.6: Getting Product data in Excel from the Product table

There are many benefits of setting the table as a featured table. Accessing and using featured tables in Excel is outside the scope of this book. You can learn more about using featured tables in Excel via the following link:

https://docs.microsoft.com/en-us/power-bi/collaborate-share/service-excel-featured-tables?WT.mc_id=5003466

Calculated tables

In Power BI Desktop, we can create new tables using DAX expressions. Calculated tables are physical tables that are generated as a result of using table functions or constructors in DAX. Unlike Virtual Tables, which we discussed in *Chapter 2*, *Data Analysis eXpressions and Data Modeling*, in the *Understanding virtual tables* section, calculated tables are much easier to work with as they are visually visible within the **Model** view in Power BI Desktop.

The following table shows the most common table functions in DAX that can be used to create a calculated table:

ADDCOLUMNS()	CALENDARAUTO()	FILTERS()	SELECTCOLUMNS()	VALUES()
ADDMISSINGITEMS()	CALCULATETABLE()	GENERATESERIES()	SUMMARIZE()	Table Constructor {}
ALL()	CROSSJOIN()	INTERSECT()	SUMMARIZECOLUMNS()	
ALLEXCEPT()	DATATABLE()	NATURAUNNERJOIN()	TOPN()	
ALLSELECTED()	DISTINCT()	NATURALLEFTOUTERJOIN()	TREATAS()	
CALENDAR()	EXCEPT()	RELATEDTABLE()	UNION()	

Figure 8.7: Most common table functions in DAX

We can create calculated tables in many scenarios, especially when the business needs to reuse the data contained in a calculated table in the future. Calculated tables become handy in many scenarios, such as creating summary tables based on the existing measures or creating **Date** or **Time** tables (when they do not exist in the data source). The data in calculated tables is already available in the data model, so refreshing the calculated tables does not take much time.

Data refresh is not available from the context menu when we right-click on a calculated table. The data is automatically populated when we refresh the underlying source tables. However, like any other physical tables, calculated tables consume some storage space. Hence, the data model's size in Power BI Desktop increases after creating calculated tables. Consequently, the dataset's size increases when we publish the model to the Power BI Service.

Creating a new calculated table now available in all views in Power BI Desktop including the **Model** view. To create a new calculated table from the **Model** view, click the **New Table** button from the **Calculations** section of the **Home** tab from the ribbon, as shown in the following image:

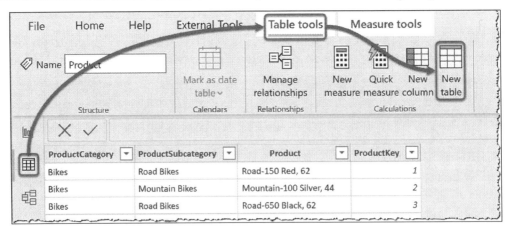

Figure 8.8: Creating a new calculated table from the Model view in Power BI Desktop

We can also create a new calculated table from the **Table Tools** tab from the **Data** view or from the **Modeling** tab of the **Report** view. The following image shows creating a new calculated table from the **Report** view:

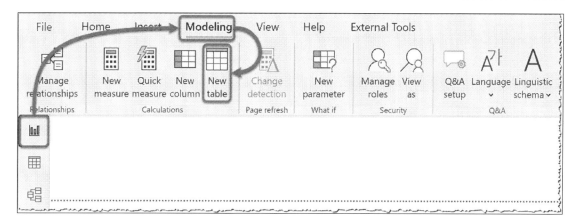

Figure 8.9: Creating a new calculated table from the Report view in Power BI Desktop

Look at the Chapter 8, Data Modelling and Star Schema.pbix sample file. The data model looks as follows:

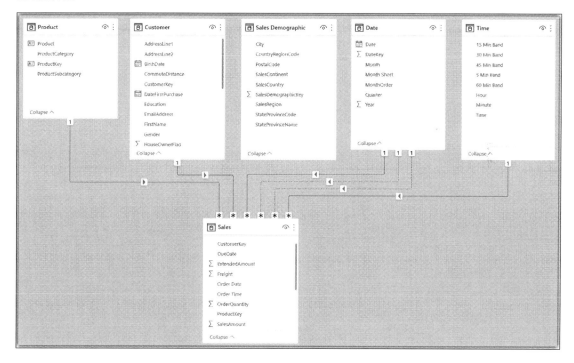

Figure 8.10: Sample Sales data model

With the preceding data model, we can analyze sales for many different business entities, such as **Sales** by **Product**, by **Customer**, by **Sales Demographics**, by **Date**, and by **Time**. Now, the business has a new requirement: getting the number of products sold to all customers with a yearly income greater than $100,000 at the year-month level. We can show these requirements in the data visualization layer. Still, the business would like to have the data as a summary table to analyze the data at higher levels and then reuse the data in different data visualizations.

The important points to note in this scenario are as follows:

- The business is only after the products that have been sold. Therefore, for each product from the **Product** table, there must be a **Sales Amount** within the **Sales** table.
- From the sold products, the business is only interested in the ones that the customers with a yearly income greater than $100,000 have bought.
- The results must be at the year-month level.
- The business requires the results as summary data so that they can analyze the data at a higher granularity.

We can use the following DAX expression to cater to that:

```
Sales for Customers with Yearly Income Greater Than $100,000 =
SUMMARIZECOLUMNS(
    'Product'[ProductKey]
    , 'Date'[Year-Month]
    , 'Customer'[CustomerKey]
    , DISTINCT('Product'[ProductKey])
    , FILTER(
        ALLNOBLANKROW('Customer'[CustomerKey], 'Customer'[YearlyIncome])
        , 'Customer'[YearlyIncome] >= 100000
        )
    , DISTINCT('Date'[Year-Month])
    , "Sales"
    , [Sales Amount]
)
```

The following image shows the results:

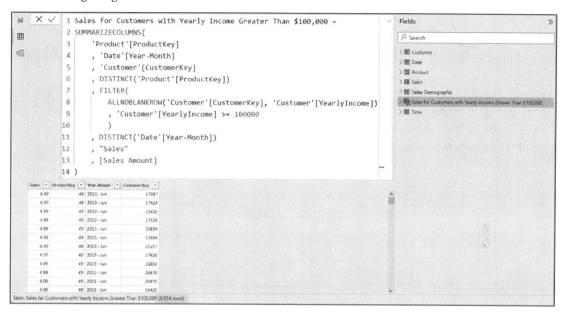

Figure 8.11: Calculated table showing sold products to customers with yearly income greater than $100,000

As the preceding image shows, the calculated table has four columns: **ProductKey**, **Year-month**, **CustomerKey**, and **Sales**.

When we create a calculated table derived from other tables in the data model, we might get a circular dependency error if we are not careful about the functions we used to create the calculated table. In that case, we cannot create any relationships between the calculated table and any tables it is derived from unless we change our choice of functions in the DAX expressions.

It is advised not to use calculated tables for any data transformation activities. We always move the data transformation logic to the source system when possible. Otherwise, we take care of the transformation in the Power Query layer.

Now, we can create the relationships between the new calculated table, the **Product** table, and the **Customer** table, as shown in the following image:

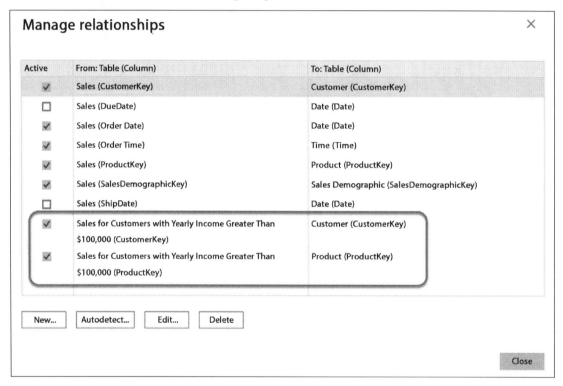

Figure 8.12: Creating relationships between the calculated table and the dimension tables

The business can now analyze the sales data based on the attributes of both the **Product** and **Customer** tables, but only for customers with an annual income greater than $100,000. This exercise can be an exciting analysis if you wish to target a specific group of customers and understand what products they spend their money on.

So far, we have learned about tables. Tables consist of fields. The next section explains fields in more detail.

Understanding fields

Fields in Power BI include columns and measures. We generally refer to both columns and measures when we talk about fields. For instance, when we talk about fields' data types, we refer to the data types for both columns and measures. The **Fields** term is used within Power BI Desktop in different views, so there is a **Fields** pane in the **Report** view, the **Data** view, and the **Model** view.

Data types

When we import data into the model, the model converts that data, in columns, into one of the Tabular Model data types. When we then use the model data in our calculations, the data is converted into a DAX data type for the duration of the calculation. The model data types are different from Power Query data types. For instance, in Power Query, we have DateTimeZone. However, the DateTimeZone data type does not exist in the data model, so it converts into DateTime when it loads into the model. The following table shows the different data types supported in the model, as well as DAX:

Data type in model	Data type in DAX	Description
Whole Number	Int64	Integer numbers between -9,223,372,036,854,775,808 (-2^63) and 9,223,372,036,854,775,807 (2^63-1).
Decimal Number	Double	Real numbers between negative values between -1.79E+308 and -2.23E-308 and positive values between 2.23E-308. and 1.79E+308. The number of digits after the decimal point is limited to 17 digits.
True/false	Boolen	Either a True or False value.
Text	String	A Unicode character data string in text format.
Date	DateTime	Shows the date part of DateTime values in the accepted date format. The default starting date in DAX is December 30,1899; however the official start date considered in calculations is March 1,1900.
Time	DateTime	Shows the time part of a DateTime values. If the date part is not specified in the source, then December 1, 1899 is considered as the date part.
Date/time	DateTime	Shows full DateTime values in accepted date/time format.
Fixed Decimal	Decimal	Currency data type allowing values between -922,337,203,685,477.5808 to 922,337,203,685,477.5807 with a fixed four digits after the decimal point.
N/A	Blank	A blank is a data type in DAX similar to null in SQL. We can create a blank by using the BLANK() function in DAX. To test for blanks we can use the ISBLANK() function.

Figure 8.13: Data types in DAX

In Power BI Desktop, the model data types are visible under the **Column tools** tab from the **Data** view or the **Report** view. The following image shows the data types from the **Column tools** tab within the **Data** view:

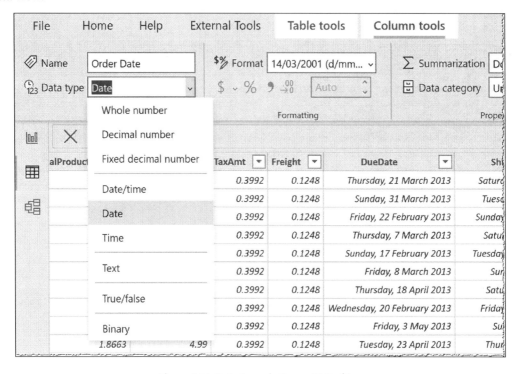

Figure 8.14: Data types in Power BI Desktop

While the binary data type is available in the **Data types** dropdown, Power BI does not support it in the data model. Hence, if we try to convert a column's data type to binary, we get an error message.

Power BI Desktop eliminates binary columns by default. Therefore, we should remove them from the Power Query Editor.

Power Query supports the binary type; therefore, converting the binary values into one of the supported tabular model data types is best.

We can implicitly define the data types for columns only. A measure's data types are automatically determined by the functions we use in DAX expressions.

When we use table functions in DAX, the result is a `Table` data type. We use this data type to create either virtual tables or calculated tables.

While Power Query supports the `DateTimeZone` type, it converts into `DateTime` without adjusting the zone when it loads into the data model. Therefore, we must consider the zone adjustments in the Power Query Editor before loading the data.

Power Query supports the `Duration` type, but when the data loads into the model, the duration values are converted into `Decimal` values.

We can `Add` and `Subtract` numeric values to/from `DateTime` values without raising any errors; for instance, DATE(2010, 1, 1) + 0.04167 = 1/01/2010 1:00:00 AM.

Custom formatting

Formatting is the way we garnish values. We only format values to make them more user-friendly and readable. Changing the value's formatting does not change its data type. Hence, it does not affect memory consumption or performance. Some data types support custom formatting.

The following table shows custom formatting for various supporting data types:

Datatype	Symbol	Description	Example
DateTime	d	Day number of the month without leading zero	FORMAT(CONVERT("2020/12/31 3:45:55", DATETIME) "dddd,mmm d yyyy h:mm:ss am/pm") returns Thursday, Dec 31 2020 3:45:55 am
	dd	Day number of the month with leading zero	
	w	Week number of the month without leading zero	
	ww	Week number of the month with leading zero	
	m	Month number of the year without leading zero	
	mm	Month number of the year with leading zero	
	mmm	Abbreviation of the month name	
	mmmm	Full mouth name	
	yy	Last two digit of year number	
	yyyy	Four-digit year number	
	h	Hour number of the day without leading zero (24-hour format without appended am/pm, 12-hour format with appended am/pm)	
	hh	Hour number of day with leading zero (24-hour format without appended am/pm, 12-hour format with appended am/pm)	
	n	Minute number of the hour without leading zero	
	nn	Minute number of the hour with leading zero	
	m	Minute number of the hour without leading zero if comes after h or hh	
	mm	Minute number of the hour with leading zero if comes after h or hh	
	s	Second number of the hour without leading zero	
	ss	Second number of the hour without leading zero	
	am/pm	Force the output to display the time in 12-hour format	

Numeric	0	Displays a digit or zero. If the number has fewer digits as the number of zeros in the format string, it puts leading or trailing zeros. If the number has more digits, it rounds the number to as the number of zeros in the format string.	FORMAT(0, "0,0") returns 00 FORMAT(0.1153, "0.00") returns 0.12 FORMAT(35.1113, "0,00.00") returns 035.11
	#	It works like the 0, but it displays a digit or nothing	FORMAT(0, "#,#") returns nothing FORMAT(0.1153, "#.##") returns .12 FORMAT(35.1113, "#,##.##") returns 35.11
	%	Displays the value in percentage by multiplying it by 100 and shows the % symbol where it appears in the format string	FORMAT(0.351156, "#,##.##0%") returns 35.116%
	$	Displays the dollar sign where it appears in the format string	FORMAT(-35.1156, "$#,##.##0") returns $35.116
	;	Section separator in the format string. Three sections are allowed in a format string if the semicolon is mentioned. If the format string has one section only, then the formatting applies to all values; otherwise, the first section applies to positive values, the second to negative values, and the third to zeros.	FORMAT(0.015, "$#,#.#0;;\Z\e\r\o") returns $.02 FORMAT(-0.015, "$#,0.#0;($#,0.#0);\Z\e\r\o") returns ($0.02) FORMAT(-0.015, "$#,0.0;($#,0.0);\Z\e\r\o") returns Zero
	()+-	Displays literal characters. This is normally used to show positive and negative values	FORMAT(-0.05, "$#,0.0;($#,0.0)") returns ($0.1)
	\	The backslash is the escape character in the format string. So, it displays the next character as literal. To show the backslash itself, we use \\ (backslash, backslash)	FORMAT(-0.01, "$#,0.0;($#,0.0);\n\i\l") returns nil

Figure 8.15: Custom formatting options

You can learn more about supported custom format syntax here: https://learn.microsoft.com/en-us/power-bi/create-reports/desktop-custom-format-strings?WT.mc_id=DP-MVP-5003466#supported-custom-format-syntax.

Columns

In Power BI, tables are created by a set of columns. These are either physical columns that come directly from the data source or are made by the developer or Power BI Desktop. In this section, we will look more closely at the different types of columns and column properties within the **Model** view in Power BI Desktop.

Calculated columns

Calculated columns are the columns that are not contained in the data source. We can create a calculated column in the data model using DAX expressions.

Power BI uses the xVelocity engine, Microsoft's proprietary in-memory data processing engine. The xVelocity engine uses ColumnStore indexing technology, which highly compresses the column's data based on the data's cardinality within that column. When we refresh a table's data, the engine compresses all columns' data and loads it into memory. This process applies to the physical columns that already exist in tables.

Power BI computes the calculated columns after loading the table (to which the calculated columns belong) into the model. When we refresh a table, the new data loads into the model, so the calculated columns' values are no longer valid. Therefore, the engine must recompute all the calculated columns. Moreover, the engine sequentially computes the calculated columns in a table. Thus, the calculated columns are not optimized and compressed as well as the physical ones.

Grouping and binning columns

In Power BI Desktop, we can create a grouping column on top of any columns. However, we can only create binning columns for the columns with numeric data types. Grouping and binning are two ways to manually group the values of a column. Grouping and binning come in handy when we need to group our data.

The grouping and binning features are not currently available in the **Model** view, so to create a new grouping or binning column, we need to switch to either the **Report** view or the **Data** view. Then, we must right-click on the desired column and select the **New group** option from the context menu. For instance, if we look at the **Product** table from our sample file, we can see, under the **ProductCategory** column, that the categories are **Accessories**, **Bikes**, and **Clothing**. Now, the business only needs to analyze its sales over two categories: **Bikes** and **Other**. There are many ways to answer this query, such as by creating a new column within the Power Query Editor. However, we want to look at the grouping feature by going through the following steps:

1. Click the **Data** view tab.
2. Right-click the **ProductCategory** column.
3. Click **New group**.
4. Enter **Bike Category** for **Name**.
5. Click **Bikes** from the **Ungrouped values** list.
6. Click the **Group** button.
7. Tick the **Include Other group** option.

8. Click **OK**.

The following image illustrates the preceding steps:

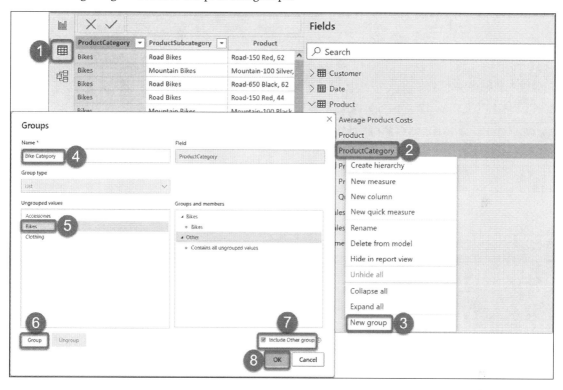

Figure 8.16: Creating a new Data Group

The preceding steps create a new **Data Group** column, as shown in the following image:

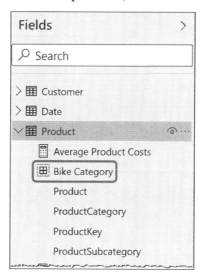

Figure 8.17: A new Data Group has been created

We can use this new **Data Group** in our data visualizations like any other columns.

Similar to creating a **Data Group** using the grouping, we can use the binning option for numeric columns.

An excellent example of binning the data in our sample is when the business must group the **SalesAmount** values from the **Sales** table when the bin (group) size for **SalesAmount** is **$1,000**.

The following steps show how to bin the values of **SalesAmount**:

1. Right-click the **SalesAmount** column from the **Sales** table.
2. Type in **Sales Amount Bins** for **Name**.
3. Stick to **Bin** via the **Group type** dropdown.
4. Make sure **Bin Type** is set to the **Size of bins**.
5. Enter **1000** for **Bin size**.
6. Click **OK**.

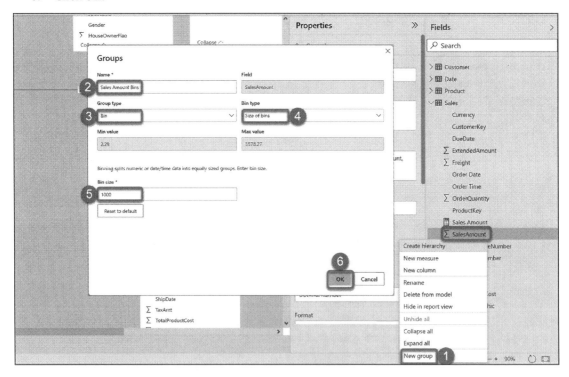

Figure 8.18: Creating Data Groups by binning the data

The preceding steps create a new numeric **Data Group** column with no summarization.

The following image shows a simple visualization detailing how grouping and binning can help us create storytelling visuals:

Figure 8.19: Using Data Groups for data visualization

In the preceding image, the user was interested in seeing sales analysis for all sales items smaller than **$1,000**. She clicked on the 0 bin from the right doughnut chart. This is how this simple activity reveals interesting information about our sales:

- In the right doughnut chart, we can see that **12.09%** of our total sales are from items cheaper than **$1,000**.
- The left doughnut chart shows that from that **12.09%** of total sales, **70.67%** comes from selling bikes, while **29.33%** comes from other categories.
- The column chart at the bottom of the report also reveals some exciting information. For example, we have **Road Bikes, Mountain Bikes,** and **Touring Bikes** that are cheaper than $1,000. From the items under $1,000 (**12.09%** of our total sales), our buyers bought under $1,000 worth of road bikes, **40.15%** of the under **$1,000** deals.

Column properties

The column properties are available within the **Model** view. We can see and change column properties by clicking on a column in the **Model** view via the **Properties** pane.

Depending on the data type of the selected column, we will see slightly different properties in the properties pane. For instance, the following image shows the column properties of the **Date** column from the **Date** table:

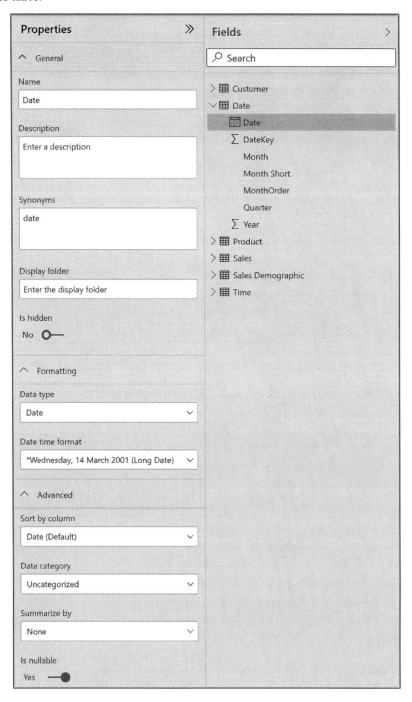

Figure 8.20: Column properties in the Model view

We can change a column's properties in bulk by pressing the *Ctrl* key on our keyboard and then clicking the columns via the **Properties** pane. Then, we can change the properties of the selected columns in bulk from the **Properties** pane.

The column properties include the following. **General** includes generic column properties, such as the following:

- **Name:** Contains the name of the column. We can rename a column by changing the value of its **Name** property.
- **Description:** Here, we can write a brief description of the column. The description of a column shows up when we hover over the column from the **Fields** pane in Power BI Desktop and the Power BI Service when the report is in **Edit** mode.
- **Synonyms:** We can enter some synonyms to help Q&A show more relevant information.
- **Display folder:** The display folder is also available for measures. We can organize our model by grouping relevant fields into display folders.

  We can group all the key columns in a folder by following these steps:

  1. Search for **key** in the search box in the **Model** view.
  2. Select multiple columns by pressing the *Ctrl* key on your keyboard and clicking each column.
  3. Enter **Key Columns** in the **Display folder** box of the **Properties** pane.

     The following image illustrates the preceding steps:

     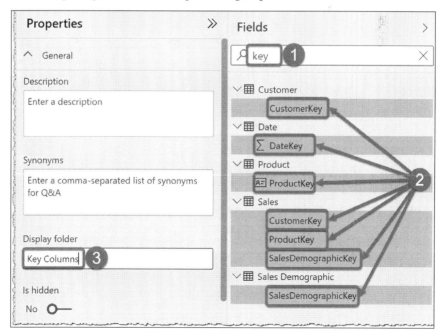

     Figure 8.21: Grouping columns with the Display folder option

The preceding steps create a **Key Columns** display folder in each table. The following image shows the new display folder:

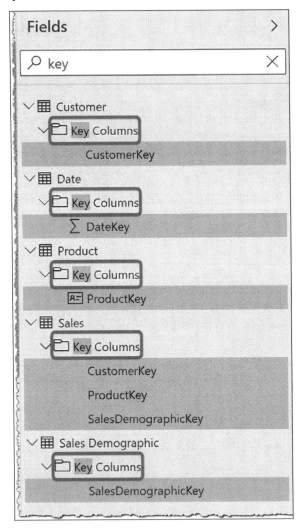

Figure 8.22: Display folders created in tables

We can also create nested folders by following the `Parent Folder\Child Folder` pattern. The following image shows an example of creating nested display folders:

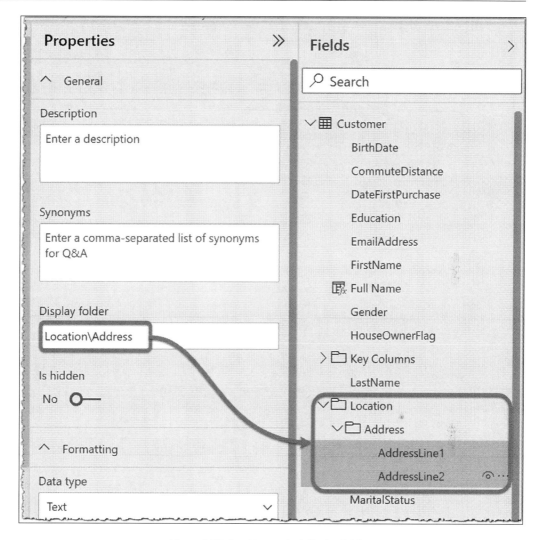

Figure 8.23: Creating nested display folders

Here is one property of **Fields**:

- **Is hidden:** We can hide a field by toggling this property to **Yes** or **No**.

  Formatting: This includes properties related to formatting a column. The formatting section varied based on the data type of the selected column, as follows:
  - **Data type:** We can change the data type of the selected columns by selecting a desired data type from the dropdown list.
  - **Format:** The format varies based on the data type, so we can pick a format that best suits our use case. We looked at custom formatting in detail in this chapter in the *Custom formatting* section.

Advanced: This includes more advanced column properties, as follows:

- **Sort by column**: We can set this property to sort a column by another; for example, we can sort the **Month** column by the **MonthOrder** column from the **Date** table.
- **Data category**: We can state the data category for the selected column by setting this property. This property tells Power BI how to treat the values in data visualization. For instance, we can set this property to **City** for the **City** column from the **Sales Demographic** table.
- **Summarize by**: This shows how we want to implicitly aggregate a column when we use it in our visuals. For instance, we might want to aggregate **ProductKey** to **COUNT** or **ProductKeys**. We can do this in DAX, but this is another way. We can set this property to **COUNT** for the **ProductKey** column from the **Product** table. When we use it in our visuals, it automatically shows the count of **ProductKeys**. The following image shows the card visual that we directly used for our **ProductKey** after setting its **Summarize by** property to **COUNT**:

Figure 8.24: Count of the ProductKey column by setting its Summarize by property

- **Is nullable**: We can set this property for the columns that are not supposed to have any null values, such as our primary keys. However, bear in mind that if we toggle this property to **No**, then if, in the future, there is a null value in the column, we get an error message while refreshing the data.

Hierarchies

Hierarchies are abstract objects in our model that show how different columns relate to each other from a hierarchical viewpoint. We can create hierarchies in the data model from the **Report** view, the **Data** view, or the **Model** view. To create a **Calendar hierarchy** in the **Date** table from the **Model** view, follow these steps:

1. Right-click the **Year** column.
2. Select the **Create hierarchy** option from the context menu.
3. From the **Properties** pane, change the **Name** value of the hierarchy to **Calendar Hierarchy**.
4. Select the **Month** and **Date** columns from the dropdown list from the **Hierarchy** section.
5. Click the **Apply Level Changes** button.

The following figure shows the preceding steps:

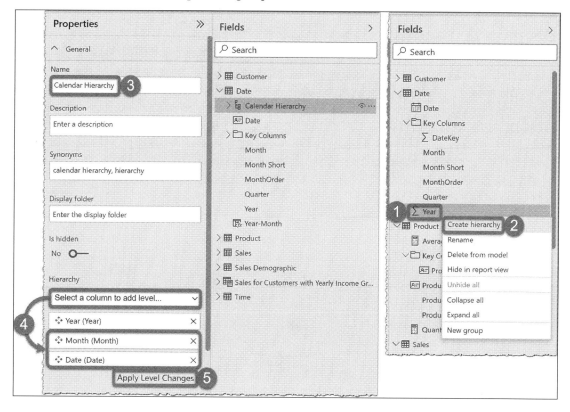

Figure 8.25: Creating a hierarchy from the Model view

As shown in the preceding image, some other properties are available for hierarchies that are similar to those available to columns, so we will skip explaining them again.

Measures

In data modeling, measures are calculations we create to help with data analysis. The results of these measures constantly change when we interact with the measures. This interaction with the measures can happen from the data visualization layer when we use the measures in visuals or within the data model when we use the measure to create other tabular objects such as calculated tables. We can create measures from the **Report** view or the **Data** view. Once we create the measures, we can set the measures' properties from the **Model** view. The properties for these measures are very similar to the column properties, so we will skip explaining them again. There are two types of measures in Power BI: *implicit* and *explicit*. Let's look at them in more detail.

Implicit measures

Implicit measures are abstract ones created when we use a column in a visual. Power BI automatically detects these implicit measures based on the column's data type when it is a numeric data type. We can quickly recognize these implicit measures by their ∑ icon from the **Fields** pane. If we set the **Summarize by** property of a numeric column (implicit measure), then we can use that column in a visual. This visual, by default, uses the selected aggregation within the **Summarize by** property. This means that if we set the **Summarize by** property of a column to **COUNT** when we use the column in a visual, the visual automatically uses the count of that column as a measure. In other words, implicit measures are the measures that we never create using DAX expressions. They are generated when we use them directly in our visuals. The following image shows the **Year** column being detected as an implicit measure. Therefore, when we use it on a table visual, the table automatically calculates the **SUM** value of **Year**, which is incorrect:

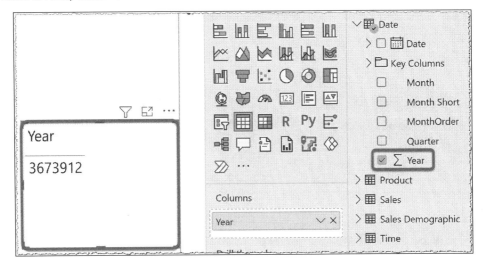

Figure 8.26: The Year column from the Date table detected as an implicit measure

While using implicit measures is very easy, we do not recommend using this feature. There are many reasons to avoid using implicit measures, some of which are as follows:

- In many cases, the columns detected as implicit measures do not contain additive values; therefore, a summation of those values is incorrect, such as in the **Year** example we looked at previously.
- Implicit measures are not reusable. They are created in the visualization layer and can only be used on the visuals.
- We do not have any control over the underlying expressions the visuals create.
- They are confusing and expensive to maintain.
- They are not compatible with some advanced data modeling techniques, such as **Calculation Groups**.

There are two ways we can disable implicit measures. The first method is to set the **Summarize by** property of the columns to **None**. We can quickly set this via the **Model** view by performing the following steps:

1. Click on a table from the **Fields** pane or the **Model** view.
2. Press *Ctrl+A* on your keyboard.
3. Right-click on a table.
4. Click the **Select columns** option from the context menu.
5. Expand the **Advanced** section of the **Properties** pane.
6. Select **None** from the dropdown list for the **Summarize by** property.

The following image illustrates the preceding steps:

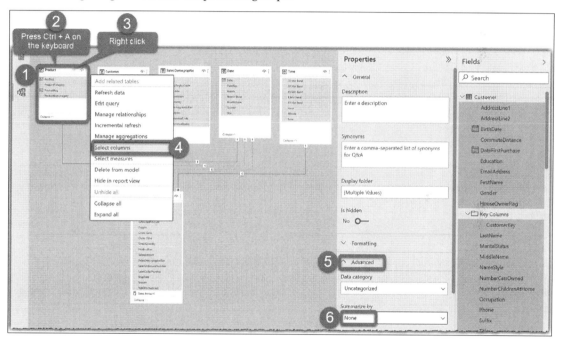

Figure 8.27: Setting the Summarize by property to None for all columns across the model

The second method is to disable the implicit measures using **Tabular Editor** across the entire model. This method prevents the model from detecting implicit measures; therefore, if we add more tables to our data model in the future, the model will not see any more implicit measures. **Tabular Editor** is an external tool that's widely used by the community. This setting is not available in Power BI Desktop at the time of writing. The following steps explain how to disable implicit measures from Tabular Editor:

1. Click the **External Tools** tab from the ribbon in Power BI Desktop.
2. If you installed the latest version of **Tabular Editor**, it would appear in **External Tool**. Click **Tabular Editor**.
3. In **Tabular Editor**, click **Model**.

4. Set the values of the **Discourage Implicit Measures** option to **True**.
5. Save the changes you made to the model:

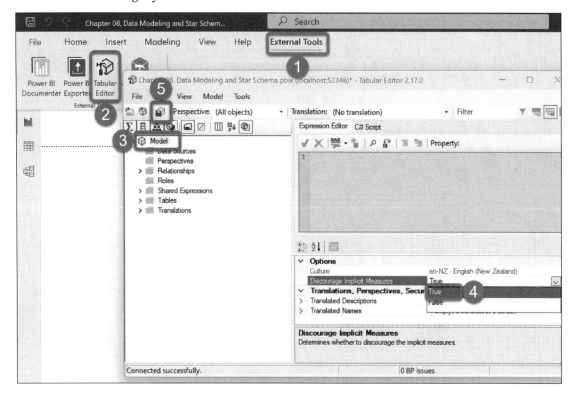

Figure 8.28: Discouraging implicit measures for the entire model in Tabular Editor

Now that we've saved the changes back to Power BI Desktop, close **Tabular Editor**, then refresh the model in Power BI Desktop to apply the changes properly.

Explicit measures

Explicit measures are the measures we create using DAX functions. There are endless use cases for measures. We can create measures to answer easy summation, complex time intelligence, and running total questions. We can create textual measures to make visual titles more dynamic. We can also create measures that will be used in conditional formatting to make the formatting more dynamic.

Textual measures

A textual measure is a measure that results in a textual value instead of a number. The concept of textual measures helps solve many data visualization scenarios. Here is a common scenario: the business needs to visualize the sales amount by product in a column chart. The color of the columns within the chart must change to red if the sales amount for that particular data point is below the average product sales.

Chapter 8

To solve this challenge, we need to create a textual measure such as the following:

```
Sales by Product Column Chart Colour =
    var avgSales = AVERAGEX(
                ALL('Product'[Product])
                , [Sales Amount]
            )
    return
    IF([Sales Amount] < avgSales, "Red")
```

Now, we must put a column chart on a report page and follow these steps:

1. Put the **Product** column from the **Product** table on **Axis**.
2. Put the **Sales Amount** measure on **Values**.
3. Click the **Format** tab from the **Visualizations** pane.
4. **Expand** the **Columns** section.
5. **Expand** the **Colors** dropdown.
6. Click the **fx** button.
7. Select the **Field value** from the **Format by** dropdown.
8. Select the **Sales by Product Column Chart Color** measure.
9. Click **OK**.

The following figure illustrates the preceding steps:

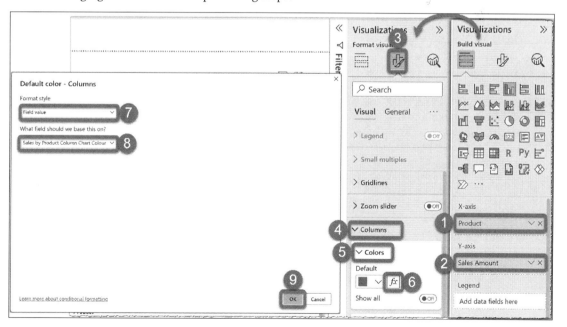

Figure 8.29: Using a textual measure to set the colors in a column chart dynamically

The following image shows the results:

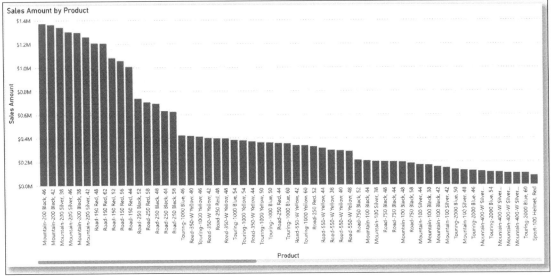

Figure 8.30: Conditionally formatted column chart using textual measures

Using relationships

When modeling relational data, a relationship describes the connection between two tables. For instance, our example shows a relationship between the **Customer** table and the **Sales** table. A customer can have multiple sales transactions in the **Sales** table. To create a relationship between the **Customer** and **Sales** tables, we must link **CustomerKey** from the **Customer** table to **CustomerKey** from the **Sales** table. This linkage enables Power BI to understand that each row of data in the **Customer** table can have one or more related rows in the **Sales** table.

To create relationships between tables in Power BI Desktop, we can either use the **Model** view to drag a column from a table and drop it to the relevant column from the other table or click the **Manage relationships** button from the ribbon. The **Manage relationships** button appears in several places in the ribbon.

The following image shows the **Manage relationship** window:

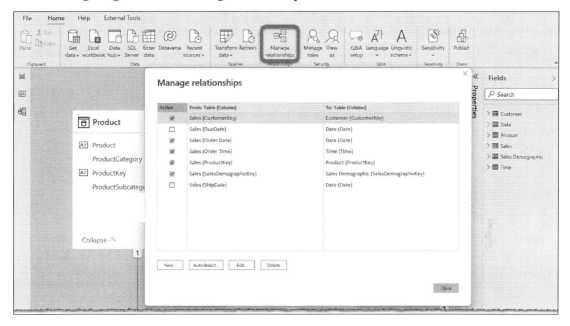

Figure 8.31: Manage relationships window in Power BI Desktop

When we create a relationship between two tables, we can see the relationship in the **Model** view, so the two tables are linked by either a solid line or a dotted line. A solid line represents an active relationship, while a dotted line represents an inactive relationship. The following image shows how the **Date** and **Sales** tables relate to each other:

Figure 8.32: Active and inactive relationships

Depending on the relationship cardinality, the relationship line starts or ends either with an asterisk (*) to show the *many* sides of the relationship or a one (1) indicating the *one* side of the relationship. There is also an arrow on every relationship, which shows the direction of filter propagation.

In the following sections, we'll discuss relationship cardinalities and filter propagation in more detail.

Primary keys/foreign keys

In relational data modeling, the tables may have a column (or a combination of columns) to guarantee the uniqueness of each row of data within that table. If each row in a table is not unique, then we have duplicate rows that we must take from them, either in the source systems or in the Power Query Editor. The column that guarantees the uniqueness of each row within a table is the **primary key** of that table. The primary key of a table cannot contain blank values. When the primary key of a table appears in a second table, it is, by definition, called a **foreign key**, but only if the data types of both columns are the same. Power BI Desktop currently does not force the same data type requirement. Therefore, we must be extra careful while creating relationships between two tables.

Handling composite keys

As we mentioned earlier, combining columns might guarantee each row's uniqueness. So, the primary key in such a table would be a composite key containing all the columns that make a row unique. In many relational database systems, including SQL Server, we can create multiple relationships between the two tables by connecting all the columns that contribute to the composite key. This is not legitimate in Power BI Desktop and all other Microsoft products using the Tabular model engine.

To fix this issue, we need to concatenate all the columns and create a new column that guarantees each row's uniqueness. We can either use the Power Query Editor to create this new column or DAX to create a calculated column, but the Power Query method is preferred. In *Chapter 6, Star Schema Preparation in Power Query Editor*, we learned how to do this in the *Creating dimensions Creating facts* sections. To remind you what we did and how it is relevant to handling composite keys, we'll quickly repeat the process here:

1. We created the **Product** dimension while keeping the descriptive values that describe a product derived from the **Sales Base** query.
2. We removed duplicate rows.
3. We identified the key columns that make each row of the **Product** table unique: **ProductCategory**, **ProductSubcategory**, and **Product**.
4. We added an **Index Column** starting from 1. This is where we handled the composite key. If we didn't add the index column, we had to figure out how to deal with the composite key later. To remind you again, the composite key in this scenario is a combination of the **ProductCategory**, **ProductSubcategory**, and **Product** columns; the new **ProductKey** column is the primary key of the **Product** table.
5. When we created the fact table later, we used the **ProductCategory**, **ProductSubcategory**, and **Product** columns from the **Product** table to merge the **Product** table into the **Sales** table. Then, we expanded the **Product structured** column from the **Sales** table by importing the **ProductKey** column from the **Product** table. **ProductKey** in the **Sales** table is now the foreign key.

Chapter 8

So, the value of taking the proper steps in the data preparation layer is, again, vital. Since we've already prepared the data to support an appropriate star schema in the data model, we do not need to deal with composite keys.

As we mentioned earlier, this is the Power Query method, but here is an example of how to deal with composite keys in the **Model** view. A good example of composite keys is the `Chapter 8, Adventure Works DW (with Exchange Rates).pbix` sample file. This file can be accessed on GitHub via the following link:

`https://github.com/PacktPublishing/Expert-Data-Modeling-with-Power-BI-Second-Edition/blob/2819fe0d48d8378aeb8064247fcbbcc90493cfea/Samples/Chapter%2008/Chapter%2008%2C%20Adventure%20Works%20DW%20(with%20Exchange%20Rates).pbix`

Here is a scenario: the **Internet Sales** table contains the sales amount in different currencies. The business would like to have internet sales in USD.

In the sample file, there is an **Exchange Rates** table with no relationship to any other tables.

The following image shows the **Internet Sales** layout of the underlying data model of the sample file:

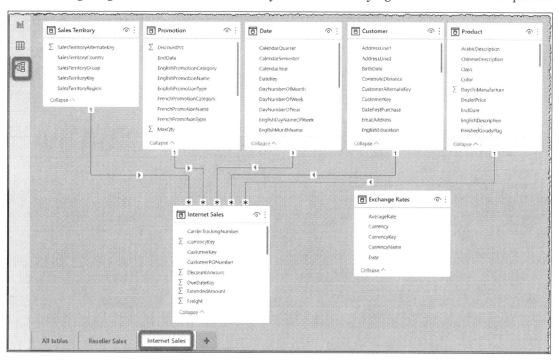

Figure 8.33: Internet Sales layout in the Model view

We solved the same problem in *Chapter 2, Data Analysis eXpressions and Data Modeling*, in the *Understanding relationships in virtual tables* section. We want to solve the problem by creating a relationship between the **Exchange Rates** table and the **Internet Sales** table.

If we look at the data in the **Exchange Rates** table, we can see that **CurrencyKey** is not the table's primary key, as it contains many duplicate values. The following image shows that the **Exchange Rates** table has **14,264 rows**, while the **CurrencyKey** column only has **14 distinct values**:

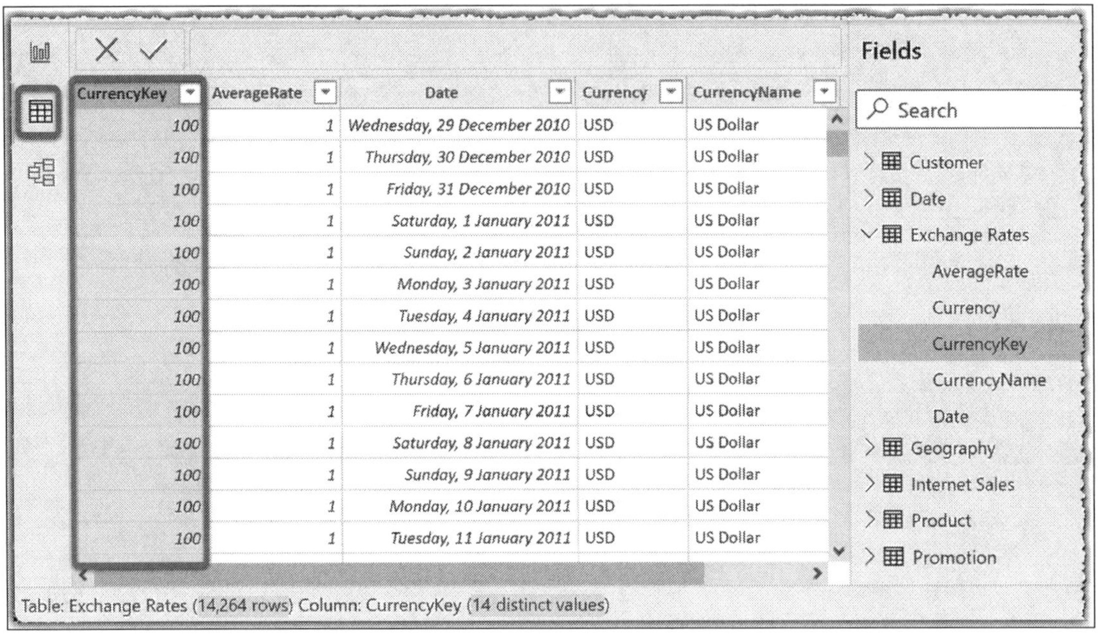

Figure 8.34: The CurrencyKey column is not the primary key for the Exchange Rates table

The **Date** column is also not the primary key in the **Exchange Rates** table. But combining both columns gives us a higher cardinality in the data. Concatenating **CurrencyKey** and **Date** creates a primary key for the **Exchange Rates** table. So, we can use the following DAX expression to create a new calculated column called **ExchKey** in the **Exchange Rates** table:

```
ExchKey = VALUE('Exchange Rates'[CurrencyKey] & FORMAT('Exchange Rates'[Date],
"yyyymmdd"))
```

The following image shows the cardinality of **ExchKey**:

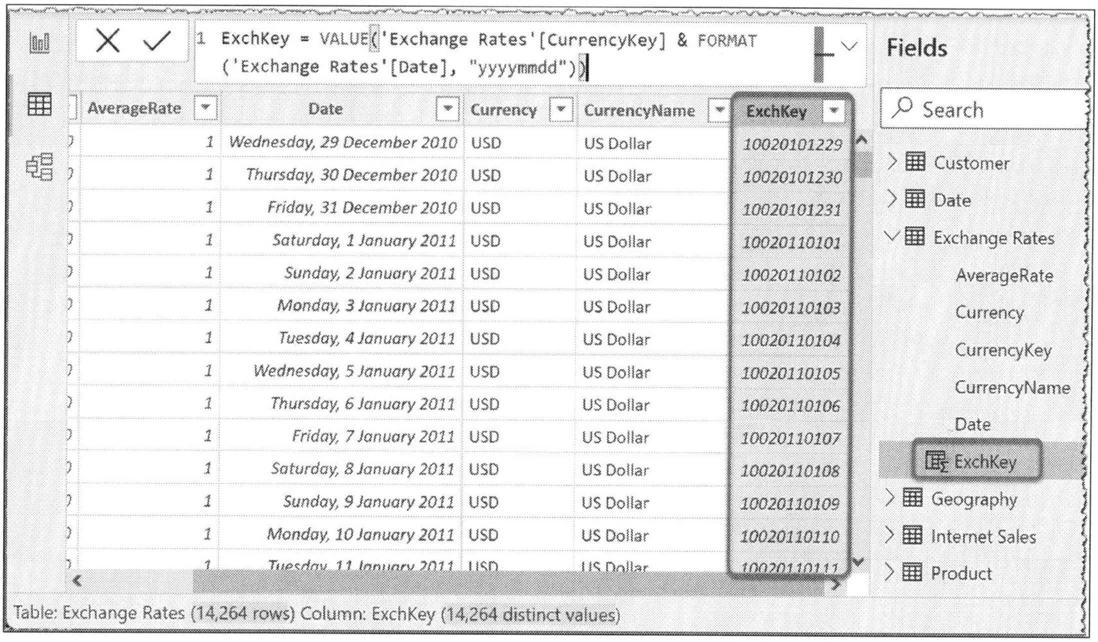

Figure 8.35: Adding a primary key to the Exchange Rates table

We must also create a corresponding foreign key column in the **Internet Sales** table. We can use the following DAX expressions to do so:

```
ExchKey = VALUE('Internet Sales'[CurrencyKey] & 'Internet Sales'[OrderDateKey])
```

Now, we will create a relationship between the **Exchange Rates** table and the **Internet Sales** table using the **ExchKey** column in both tables. Once this relationship has been created, we can create a new measure with a much simpler DAX expression than the one we used in *Chapter 2, Data Analysis eXpressions and Data Modeling*. We can use the following DAX expression to create the new measure:

```
Internet Sales in USD =
    SUMX(
        RELATEDTABLE('Exchange Rates')
        , [Internet Sales] * 'Exchange Rates'[AverageRate]
    )
```

If we use the **Internet Sales** and **Internet Sales in USD** measures side by side in a matrix visual, the results look as follows:

Product Category	Internet Sales	Internet Sales in USD
⊟ **Accessories**	**700,759.96**	**$640,920.111**
⊞ Bike Racks	39,360.00	$35,934.55
⊞ Bike Stands	39,591.00	$35,628.6896
⊞ Bottles and Cages	56,798.19	$52,340.3834
⊞ Cleaners	7,218.60	$6,352.5092
⊞ Fenders	46,619.58	$41,974.101
⊞ Helmets	225,335.60	$209,433.4812
⊞ Hydration Packs	40,307.67	$35,307.8438
⊞ Tires and Tubes	245,529.32	$223,948.5534
⊟ **Bikes**	**28,318,144.65**	**$25,107,749.7623**
⊞ Mountain Bikes	9,952,759.56	$8,954,853.1688
⊞ Road Bikes	14,520,584.04	$12,599,394.0018
⊞ Touring Bikes	3,844,801.05	$3,553,502.5943
⊟ **Clothing**	**339,772.61**	**$306,157.5785**
⊞ Caps	19,688.10	$18,674.1168
⊞ Gloves	35,020.70	$31,022.1741
⊞ Jerseys	172,950.68	$157,333.8088
⊞ Shorts	71,319.81	$62,692.697
⊞ Socks	5,106.32	$4,665.6082
⊞ Vests	35,687.00	$31,769.1769
Total	**29,358,677.22**	**$26,054,827.4537**

Figure 8.36: A new version of the Internet Sales in USD measure

The preceding scenario shows how data modeling can simplify our DAX expressions. Just as a reminder, here is the same measure that we created in *Chapter 2, Data Analysis eXpressions and Data Modeling*, without creating the relationship between the **Exchange Rates** table and the **Internet Sales** table:

```
Internet Sales USD =
SUMX(
    NATURALINNERJOIN (
        SELECTCOLUMNS(
            'Internet Sales'
, "CurrencyKeyJoin", 'Internet Sales'[CurrencyKey] * 1
            , "DateJoin", 'Internet Sales'[OrderDate] + 0
            , "ProductKey", 'Internet Sales'[ProductKey]
            , "SalesOrderLineNumber", 'Internet
Sales'[SalesOrderLineNumber]
            , "SalesOrderNumber", 'Internet Sales'[SalesOrderNumber]
            , "SalesAmount", 'Internet Sales'[SalesAmount]
        )
```

```
            , SELECTCOLUMNS (
                'Exchange Rates'
                , "CurrencyKeyJoin", 'Exchange Rates'[CurrencyKey] * 1
                , "DateJoin", 'Exchange Rates'[Date] + 0
                , "AverageRate", 'Exchange Rates'[AverageRate]
            )
        )
    , [AverageRate] * [SalesAmount]
)
```

Relationship cardinalities

In Power BI, we can create a relationship between two tables by linking a column from the first table to a column from the second table. There are three cardinalities of relationships in relational data modeling: **one to one, one to many** and **many to many**. This section will briefly look at each from a data modeling viewpoint in Power BI.

One-to-one relationships

A one-to-one relationship is when we create a relationship between two tables using the primary keys from both tables. Every row in the first table is related to zero or one from the second table. Therefore, the direction of filtering in a **one to one** relationship in Power BI is always **bidirectional**. When we have a **one to one** relationship, we can potentially combine the two tables into one table unless the business case we are working on dictates otherwise. We generally recommend avoiding **one to one** relationships when possible.

One to many relationships

A **one to many** relationship, the most common cardinality, is when each row of the first table is related to many rows of the second table. Power BI Desktop uses 1 - * to indicate a **one to many** relationship.

Many to many relationships

A **many to many** relationship is when a row from the first table is related to many rows of data in the second table and a row of data in the second table is related to many rows in the first table. While in a proper star schema, all relationships between dimensions tables and fact tables are **one to many**, the **many to many** relationship is still a legitimate cardinality relationship in Power BI. With **many to many** relationships, the necessity of having a primary table in tables participating in the relationship goes away. When we define a **many to many** relationship between two tables, the default behavior sets the filtering to bidirectional. But depending on the scenario, we can force the filtering direction to go in a single direction. Power BI uses * - * to indicate a **many to many** relationship.

An excellent example of a **many to many** relationship can be found in our sample file (`Chapter 8, Data Modelling and Star Schema.pbix`). This shows that the business needs to create analytical reports on top of the sales for the **Customers with Yearly Income Greater Than $100,000** summary table at higher granular levels such as **Quarter** or **Year**.

To allow the business to achieve this requirement, we need to create a relationship between the **Sales for Customers with Yearly Income Greater Than $100,000** table and the **Date** table using the **Year-Month** column in both tables. We set the **Cross filter direction** to **Single**, so the **Date** table filters the Sales for Customers with Yearly Income Greater Than $100,000 table. The following image shows the **Edit relationships** window upon creating the preceding relationship:

Figure 8.37: Creating a many-to-many relationship

As the preceding image shows, a warning message appears at the bottom of the **Edit relationships** window, explaining that the columns participating in a **many to many** relationship do not contain unique values. So, we must be cautious when using a **many to many** relationship unless we know what we are doing is correct.

The following image shows how we can visualize the data after creating the relationship:

Year	Month Short	Date	Sales
⊞ 2011			1,005,650.10
⊞ 2012			853,375.48
⊟ 2013	⊞ Jan		174,056.65
	⊞ Feb		95,510.06
	⊞ Mar		224,811.28
	⊞ Apr		160,332.28
	⊞ May		251,155.10
	⊞ Jun		280,168.62
	⊞ Jul		280,477.35
	⊞ Aug		296,024.60
	⊞ Sep		284,204.37
	⊞ Oct		292,203.92
	⊞ Nov		273,527.19
	⊞ Dec		331,138.01
	Total		2,943,609.43
⊟ 2014	⊟ Jan	1/01/2014	21,215.20	← Date level
		2/01/2014	21,215.20
		3/01/2014	21,215.20
		4/01/2014	21,215.20

Figure 8.38: Visualizing data from tables participating in a many-to-many relationship

It is essential to note the granularity of the data. As the preceding image shows, we can visualize the data at the **Year** and **Month** levels, but if we want to go one further down, the data still represents the **Year-Month** level. So, it is crucial to make the visualization available to the consumers at a correct level so that they do not get confused by seeing the data at an incorrect level of granularity.

> We suggest not using many-to-many cardinality in a relationship as it can dramatically elevate the level of model complexity, primarily when both tables participating in the relationship are also related to other tables. This situation can worsen if we set the cross-filter direction of the relationship to **Both**. As a result, we may potentially need to write more complex DAX expressions, which means we end up facing poor model performance. Instead, it is better to handle a many-to-many relationship using bridge tables. *Chapter 9, Star Schema and Data Modeling Common Best Practices,* will cover more on this.

Filter propagation behavior

Filter propagation is one of the most important concepts to understand when building a data model in Power BI Desktop. When we create a relationship between two tables, we are also filtering the data of one table by the data of another. We can see the direction of filter propagation in the **Model** view for each relationship. The following image shows the relationship between the **Product** and **Sales** tables and the direction of filtering the data:

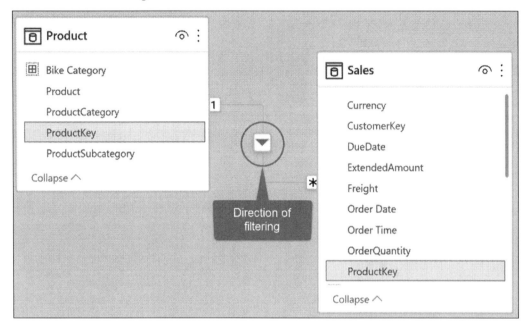

Figure 8.39: The direction of filtering the data via a relationship

The relationship shown in the preceding image indicates the following:

- Each row of data in the **Product** table (the 1 side of the relationship) is related to many rows of data in the **Sales** table (the * side of the relationship).
- If we filter a row of data in the **Product** table, the filter propagates through the relationship from the **Product** table to the **Sales** table.

The following image shows how the filter propagates from the **Product** table to the **Sales** table via the relationship between the two:

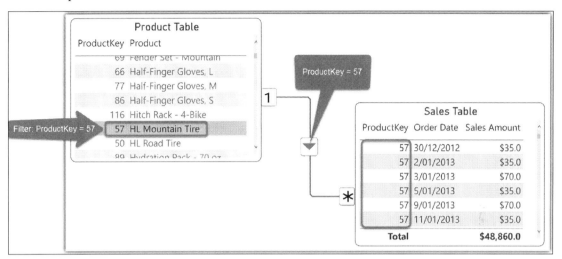

Figure 8.40: Filter propagation via a relationship

As the preceding image shows, when we click on a row of the **Product** table and select that **ProductKey** equalling 57, we are filtering the **Product** table and the **Sales** table through the relationship. Therefore, the **Sales** table shows only the rows of data where **ProductKey** equals 57. While the filter we put on **ProductKey** propagates from the **Product** table to the **Sales** table, it goes no further than the **Sales** table. This is because the **Sales** table does not have any relationships with any other tables, with the filter direction going from the **Sales** table to the other table. The following image shows how the filtering flows in our latter example:

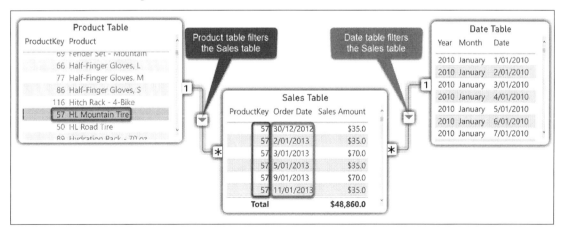

Figure 8.41: Filter propagation

As the preceding image shows, while the **Product** table and the **Date** table can filter the **Sales** table data, the filter does not flow in the opposite direction. Therefore, the **Sale** table can never filter the **Date** table with the relationships defined in the preceding model.

Bidirectional relationships

Now that we understand filter propagation, we can understand what a bidirectional relationship means and how it affects our data model. A relationship is bidirectional when we set its **Cross-filter direction** to **Both**. The ability to set the direction of filtering to both directions is a nice feature since it can help solve some data visualization challenges. An excellent example is when we use two slicers on the report page, one showing the **ProductCategory** column data and the other showing the **Full Name** data. The end user expects only relevant data in each slicer when selecting a value from the slicers. The following image shows the preceding scenario:

Figure 8.42: The Customer Name slicer filters the Sales data but not the Product Category data

As the preceding image illustrates, when the user selects a value from the **Customer Name** slicer, the filter propagates from the **Customer** table to the **Sales** table via the relationship between them. Therefore, the relevant data is shown in the table visual. So, we can see that Aaron Campbell bought some accessories and bikes here. Yet, the **Product Category** slicer still shows all the product categories in the data model.

The following image shows how the **Product**, **Customer**, and **Sales** tables relate to each other:

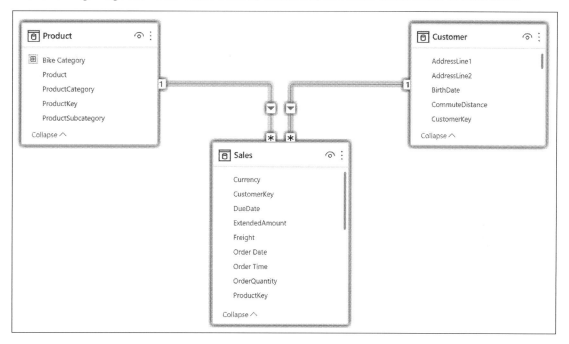

Figure 8.43: The relationships between the Product, Customer, and Sales tables

The end user expects only to see **Accessories** and **Bikes** in the **Product Category slicer**. One way to solve this issue is to set the relationship between the **Sales** table and the **Product** table to bidirectional by setting the relationship's **Cross-filter direction** to Both.

Follow these steps to change the **Cross-filter direction** to Both:

1. Switch to the **Model** view.
2. Double-click the relationship between the **Product** and **Sales** tables.
3. Set the **Cross-filter direction** to Both.
4. Click **OK**.

The following image shows the preceding steps:

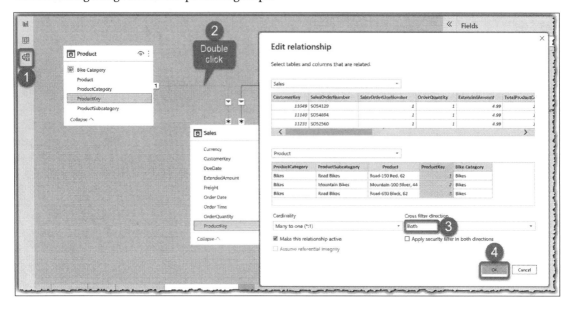

Figure 8.44: Making a relationship bidirectional

The following image shows how the relationship changed in the **Model** view:

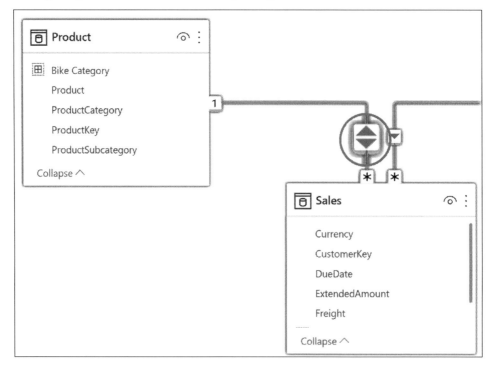

Figure 8.45: Visual representation of a bidirectional relationship

Now, when we go back to the **Report** view, we will see that making a relationship between the **Date** and **Sales** tables resolved this issue. The following image shows the results after making the relationship bidirectional:

Figure 8.46: The Customer Name slicer filters the Sales data and the Product Category data

Now, if the user selects a value from the **Product Category** slicer, the filter will propagate via the current relationship from the **Product** table to the **Sales** table. However, it will not propagate from the **Sales** table to the **Customer** table via the current relationship since the relationship between the **Sales** table and the **Customer** table is not bidirectional. So, we should also set the latter relationship to bidirectional.

The preceding scenario raises an important point: we may make all the model's relationships bidirectional. Using bidirectional relationships can be a killer, especially in larger data models with more complex relationships. Bidirectional relationships have adverse effects on model performance. It also elevates the complexity level of DAX expressions dramatically. We suggest avoiding bidirectional relationships as much as possible. There are more advanced techniques to solve similar scenarios to what we've covered in better ways without using bidirectional relationships, which we will cover in *Chapter 9, Star Schema and Data Modeling Common Best Practices*.

Summary

In this chapter, we learned about the data modeling components in Power BI Desktop. We learned about table and field properties; we looked at feature tables, how to make a table from our data model accessible across the organization, and how to build summary tables by creating calculated tables in DAX. We then dived deeper into one of the essential concepts in data modeling, which is relationships. We learned about different relationship cardinalities and filter propagation and also understood the concept of bidirectional relationships.

In the next chapter, *Star Schema and Data Modeling Common Best Practices*, we will look at many of the concepts we have learned about in this chapter in more detail.

Join us on Discord!

Join The Big Data and Analytics Community on the Packt Discord Server!

Hang out with 558 other members and enjoy free voice and text chat.

`https://packt.link/ips2H`

9

Star Schema and Data Modeling Common Best Practices

In the previous chapter, we learned about data modeling components in Power BI Desktop, including table and field properties. We also learned about featured tables and how they make dataset tables accessible across an organization. We then learned how to build summary tables with DAX. We also looked at the relationships in more detail; we learned about different relationship cardinalities, filter propagation, and bidirectional relationships. In this chapter, we look at some star schema and data modeling best practices, including the following:

- Dealing with many-to-many relationships
- Avoiding bidirectional relationships
- Dealing with inactive relationships
- Using configuration tables
- Avoiding calculated columns when possible
- Organizing the model
- Reducing model size by disabling auto date/time

In this chapter, we use the `Chapter 9, Star Schema and Data Modeling Common Best Practices.pbix` sample file to go through the scenarios which can be found here: https://github.com/PacktPublishing/Expert-Data-Modeling-with-Power-BI-Second-Edition/blob/28e2af1762336ab5236a3b3961c41e9020de8200/Samples/Chapter%2009/Chapter%209,%20Star%20Schema%20and%20Data%20Modelling%20Common%20Best%20Practices.pbix.

Dealing with many-to-many relationships

In the previous chapter, *Chapter 8*, *Data Modeling Components*, we discussed different relationship cardinalities. We went through some scenarios to understand one-to-one, one-to-many, and many-to-many relationships. We showed examples of creating a many-to-many relationship between two tables using non-key columns.

While creating a many-to-many relationship may work for smaller and less complex data models, it can cause severe issues and ambiguities in more complex models. In some cases, we may get incorrect results in totals; we might find some missing values or get poor performance in large models; while in other cases, we may find the many-to-many cardinality very useful.

The message here is that, depending on the business case, we may or may not use many-to-many cardinality; it depends on what works best for our model to satisfy the business requirements.

For instance, the many-to-many cardinality works perfectly fine in our scenario in *Chapter 8, Data Modeling Components*, in the *Many-to-many relationships* section. Just as a reminder, the scenario was that the business needed to create analytical sales reports for *Customers with Yearly Income Greater Than $100,000* from a summary table. We created a calculated table on the granularity of **Customer**, **Product**, and **Year-Month**. To enable the business to achieve the requirement, we needed to create a relationship between the **Sales for Customers with Yearly Income Greater Than $100,000** calculated table and the **Date** table using the **Year-Month** column on both sides. The following diagram shows the many-to-many cardinality relationship between the **Sales for Customers with Yearly Income Greater Than $100,000** table and the **Date** table via the **Year-Month** column:

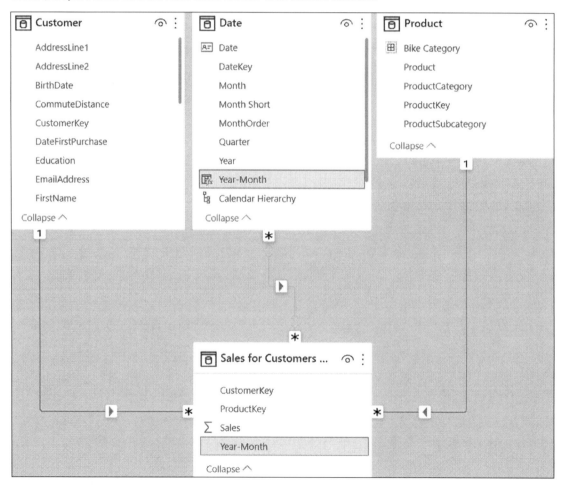

Figure 9.1: A many-to-many cardinality relationship

In the preceding model, the **Year-Month** column is not a key column in any of the tables participating in the relationship, which means the **Year-Month** column has duplicate values on both sides. As you may have noticed, the relationship between the **Sales for Customers with Yearly Income Greater Than $100,000** table and the **Date** table has a star (*) on both ends of the relationship, indicating the cardinality of the relationship is many-to-many. There is also a broken chain sign on both ends of the relationship, indicating the relationship's **evaluation** type is **limited**. Relationship evaluation relates to the cardinality of the relationship and the data sources of the two tables contributing to the relationship; therefore, it is not configurable. A relationship is either a **regular relationship** or a **limited relationship**.

A *regular* relationship is when the two related tables:

- Use the same storage mode: either in DirectQuery or Import.
- Have a relationship cardinality between the two tables of one-to-many, with which Power BI can determine that the "one" side of the relationship exists.

If the relationship between two tables does not meet any preceding conditions, then the relationship evaluation type is *limited*. A limited relationship is also referred to as a **weak relationship**. In other words, a *weak* relationship and a *limited* relationship are the same thing.

When we create a relationship between two tables using non-key columns, we create a many-to-many **cardinality** relationship. We insist on using the term *cardinality* for this kind of relationship to avoid confusing it with the **classic** many-to-many relationship. In relational data modeling, the many-to-many relationship is a conceptual relationship between two tables via a **bridge table**. In relational data modeling, we cannot create a physical many-to-many relationship between two tables. Instead, we create relationships between the primary key on one side of the relationship to the corresponding foreign key column on the many side of the relationship. Therefore, the only legitimate relationships from a relational data modeling viewpoint are *one-to-one* and *one-to-many* relationships. Hence, there is no many-to-many relationship kind.

Nevertheless, many business scenarios require many-to-many relationships. Consider banking: a customer can have many accounts, and an account can link to many customers when it is a joint account; or in an education system, a student can have multiple teachers, and a teacher can have many students.

The sample file we use in this chapter is `Chapter 9, Star Schema and Data Modelling Common Best Practices.pbix`.

Here is the scenario: the business wants to analyze the buying behavior of their online customers based on **Quantity Sold** over **Sales Reasons**. The following diagram shows the data model. Let's have a look at it:

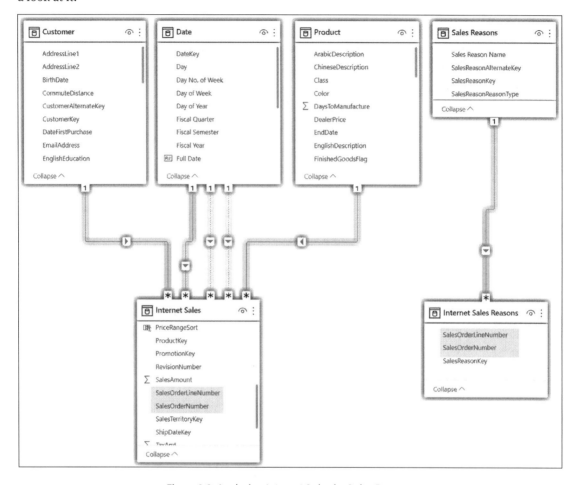

Figure 9.2: Analyzing Internet Sales by Sales Reasons

As the preceding diagram shows, the **Sales Reasons** table contains the descriptive data, and the **Internet Sales Reasons** table has a one-to-many relationship with the **Sales Reasons** table. The **Internet Sales Reasons** table contains three columns, the **SalesOrderLineNumber, SalesOrderNumber,** and **SalesReasonKey**, and it does not have any sales transactions. On the other hand, the **Customer** table has a one-to-many relationship with the **Internet Sales** table. The **Internet Sales** table keeps all sales transactions, where each row of data is unique for the combination of the **SalesOrderLineNumber** and the **SalesOrderNumber** columns. But there is currently no relationship between the **Customer** table and the **Sales Reasons** table. Each customer may have several reasons to buy products online, and each sales reason relates to many customers. Therefore, conceptually, there is a many-to-many relationship between the **Customer** and the **Sales Reason** tables. It is now time to refer back to the classic type of many-to-many relationship in relational data modeling.

As mentioned earlier, in relational data modeling, unlike in Power BI, we can only implement the many-to-many relationship using a bridge table regardless. The next section explains how to make the many-to-many relationship using a bridge table.

Many-to-many relationships using a bridge table

In relational data modeling, we put the primary keys of the two tables participating in the many-to-many relationship into an intermediary table, referred to as a *bridge* table. The bridge tables usually are available in the transactional source systems. For instance, there is always a many-to-many relationship between a customer and a product in a sales system. A customer can buy many products, and a product can end up in many customers' shopping carts. In the sales system, the cashiers scan the products' barcodes and the customers' loyalty cards so the system knows which customer bought which product.

Using the star schema approach, we spread the columns across **dimensions** and **facts** when we design a data warehouse. Therefore, in a sales data model (in a sales data warehouse), the **dimensions** surrounding a fact table have a many-to-many relationship via the **fact** table. So, in a sales data model designed in the Star Schema approach, the **Customer** and the **Product** tables contain *descriptive* values. Hence, they are **dimensions**. The **Sales** table, on the other hand, holds the foreign keys of the **Customer** and **Product** tables. It also keeps the **numeric** values related to sales transactions, such as sales amount, tax amount, ordered quantity, and so on. The **Sales** table is a *fact* table in the star schema approach.

The following diagram shows how the **Customer**, the **Product**, and the **Internet Sales** tables are related:

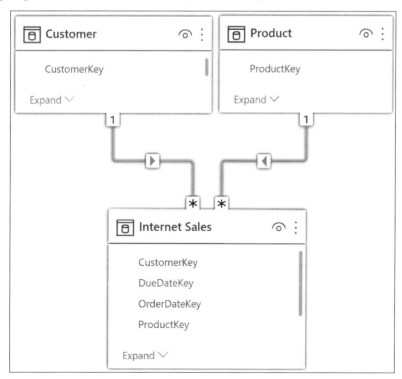

Figure 9.3: Relationships between Customer, Product, and Internet Sales

In the preceding data model, we have the following relationships:

- A one-to-many relationship between **Customer** and **Internet Sales**
- A one-to-many relationship between **Product** and **Internet Sales**
- A many-to-many relationship between **Customer** and **Product** (via the **Internet Sales** table)

The first two relationships are trivial, as we can visually see them in the data model. However, the latter is somewhat of a conceptual relationship handled by the **Internet Sales** table. From a Star Schema standpoint, we do not call the **Internet Sales** table a bridge table, but the principles remain the same. In data modeling using the Star Schema approach, a bridge table is created to manage many-to-many relationships. The many-to-many relationships usually happen between two or more dimensions. However, there are some cases when two fact tables contribute to a many-to-many relationship.

> In Star Schema, the fact tables containing the foreign keys of the dimensions without any other additive columns are called **factless fact** tables.

Our scenario already has a proper bridge table, the **Internet Sales Reasons** table, satisfying the many-to-many relationship between the **Customer** table and the **Sales Reasons** table. Therefore, we only need to create the relationship between the **Internet Sales** table and the **Internet Sales Reasons** table (the bridge). As the **xVelocity** engine does not support composite keys for creating physical relationships, we have to add a new column in both the **Internet Sales** and **Internet Sales Reasons** tables. The new column concatenates the **SalesOrderLineNumber** and **SalesOrderNumber** columns. We can create the new column either in Power Query or DAX. For simplicity, we create the calculated column using the following DAX expressions.

In the **Internet Sales** table, use the following DAX expression to create a new calculated column:

```
SalesReasonsID = 'Internet Sales'[SalesOrderNumber] & 'Internet Sales'[SalesOrderLineNumber]
```

In the **Internet Sales Reason** table, use the following DAX expression:

```
SalesReasonsID = 'Internet Sales Reasons'[SalesOrderNumber] & 'Internet Sales Reasons'[SalesOrderLineNumber]
```

After creating the **SalesReasonsID** column in both tables, we create a relationship between the two tables. The following image shows the **Create relationship** window, where we create a one-to-many relationship between the **Internet Sales** and the **Internet Sales Reasons** tables:

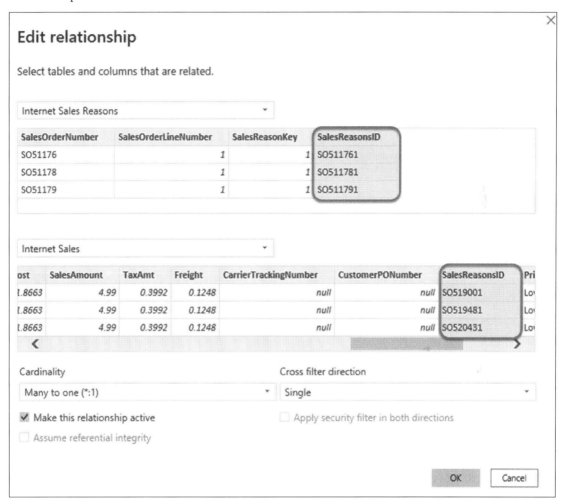

Figure 9.4: Creating a relationship between the Internet Sales and the Internet Sales Reasons tables

The following diagram shows our data model after creating the preceding relationship:

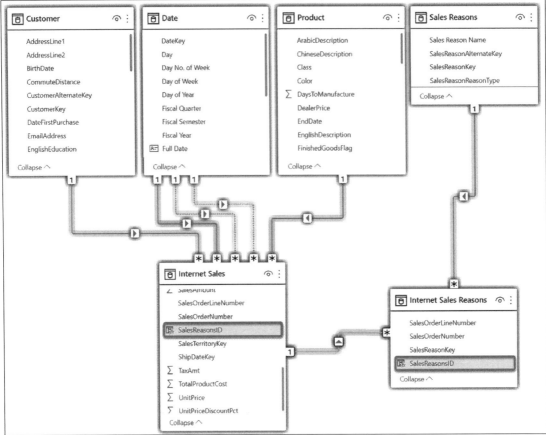

Figure 9.5: The data model after creating a new relationship between the two tables

From a data modeling perspective, there is now a many-to-many relationship between the **Internet Sales** table and the **Sales Reasons** table via the bridge (the **Internet Sales Reasons**) table. Consequently, the **Customer**, **Date**, and **Product** dimensions also have a many-to-many relationship with the **Sales Reason** table.

To visualize the data, we need to create two new measures, **Quantity Sold** and **Internet Sales Reasons**, with the following DAX expressions:

```
Quantity Sold = SUM('Internet Sales'[OrderQuantity])
Sales Reasons Count = COUNTROWS('Internet Sales Reasons')
```

Let's visualize the data and see how it works:

1. Put a **Matrix** visual on the reporting canvas.
2. Put the **Full Name** column from the **Customer** table on the **Rows**.
3. Put the **Product Name** from the **Product** table on the **Rows** under the **Full Name**.
4. Put the **Quantity Sold** measure on the **Values**.

So far, we have created a visual that shows the number of products each customer bought. The following image shows the preceding steps:

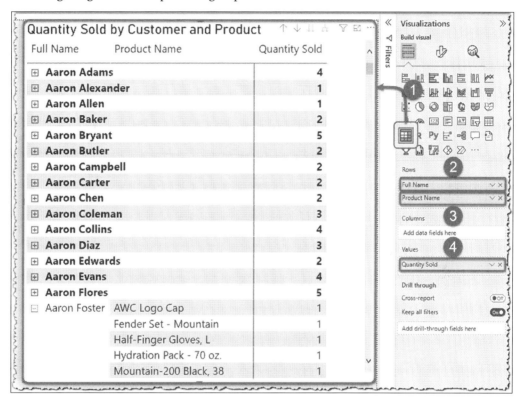

Figure 9.6: Visualizing Quantity Sold by customers' Full Name and Product Name in a matrix

5. Put another **Matrix** visual on the reporting canvas.
6. Put the **Product Name** column from the **Product** table on **Rows**.
7. Put the **Sales Reason Name** column from the **Sales Reasons** table on **Columns**.
8. Put the **Sales Reasons Count** measure on **Values**.

The following image shows the preceding steps:

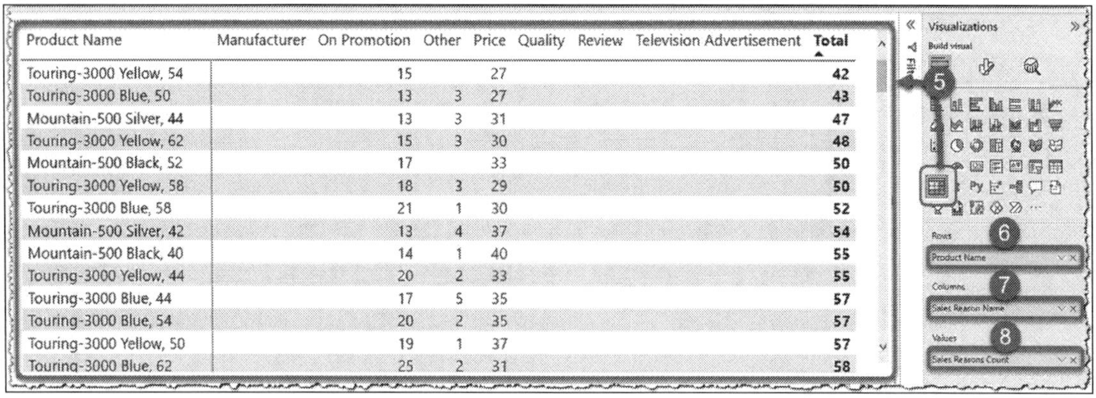

Product Name	Manufacturer	On Promotion	Other	Price	Quality	Review	Television Advertisement	Total
Touring-3000 Yellow, 54		15		27				42
Touring-3000 Blue, 50		13	3	27				43
Mountain-500 Silver, 44		13	3	31				47
Touring-3000 Yellow, 62		15	3	30				48
Mountain-500 Black, 52		17		33				50
Touring-3000 Yellow, 58		18	3	29				50
Touring-3000 Blue, 58		21	1	30				52
Mountain-500 Silver, 42		13	4	37				54
Mountain-500 Black, 40		14	1	40				55
Touring-3000 Yellow, 44		20	2	33				55
Touring-3000 Blue, 44		17	5	35				57
Touring-3000 Blue, 54		20	2	35				57
Touring-3000 Yellow, 50		19	1	37				57
Touring-3000 Blue, 62		25	2	31				58

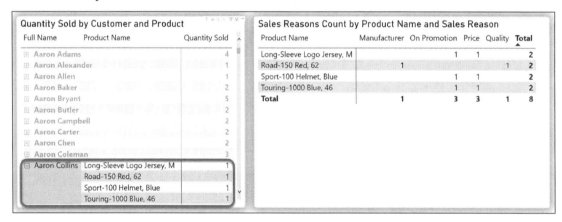

Figure 9.7: Visualizing Sales Reasons Count by Product Name and Sales Reason in a matrix

The preceding two visuals on a report page reveal the correlation between the products customers bought and the sales reasons for their purchases. The following image shows the correlation between Aaron Collins's purchases and the reasons for the sale:

Quantity Sold by Customer and Product

Full Name	Product Name	Quantity Sold
Aaron Adams		4
Aaron Alexander		1
Aaron Allen		1
Aaron Baker		2
Aaron Bryant		5
Aaron Butler		2
Aaron Campbell		2
Aaron Carter		2
Aaron Chen		2
Aaron Coleman		3
Aaron Collins	Long-Sleeve Logo Jersey, M	1
	Road-150 Red, 62	1
	Sport-100 Helmet, Blue	1
	Touring-1000 Blue, 46	1

Sales Reasons Count by Product Name and Sales Reason

Product Name	Manufacturer	On Promotion	Price	Quality	Total
Long-Sleeve Logo Jersey, M		1	1		2
Road-150 Red, 62	1			1	2
Sport-100 Helmet, Blue		1	1		2
Touring-1000 Blue, 46		1	1		2
Total	**1**	**3**	**3**	**1**	**8**

Figure 9.8: Analyzing customer purchases and sales reasons

As the preceding image shows, Aaron Collins has bought 4 items in total and he had 2 reasons for each purchase. For instance, he bought **Road-150 Red, 62** because of the **Manufacturer** and the product's **Quality**.

On the other hand, clicking the **Road-150 Red, 62** on the second matrix reveals that all customers spent their money for the same reasons: **Manufacturer** and **Quality**. The following image shows the results:

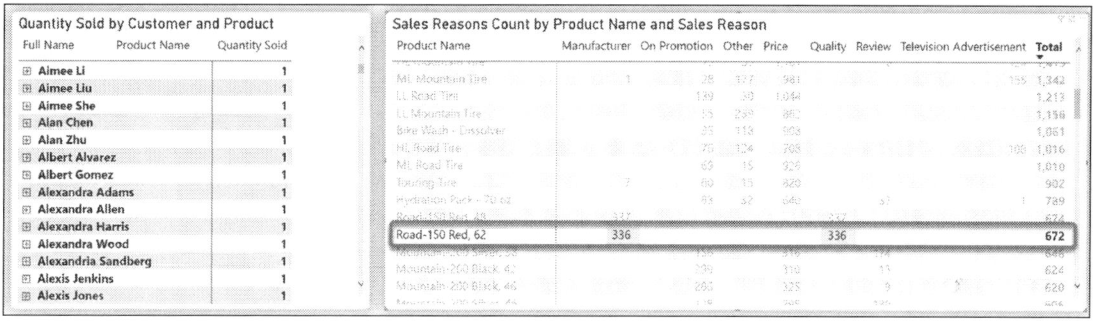

Figure 9.9: Analyzing customer purchases and sales reasons for a specific product

As you can see, the preceding analysis was made possible only by correctly handling the many-to-many relationship between the **Internet Sales** and **Sales Reasons** tables via the **Internet Sales Reasons** bridge table.

Hiding the bridge table

After implementing the many-to-many relationship in the data model, it is a good idea to hide the bridge table from the data model. We only have the bridge table in our data model as it carries the key columns of both tables participating in the many-to-many relationship. Hiding the bridge table also avoids confusion for other report creators who connect to our dataset to build the reports. To hide a table, we only need to switch to the **Model** view and click the hide/unhide (👁) button at the top right of the table. The following diagram shows the data model after hiding the **Internet Sales Reasons** table:

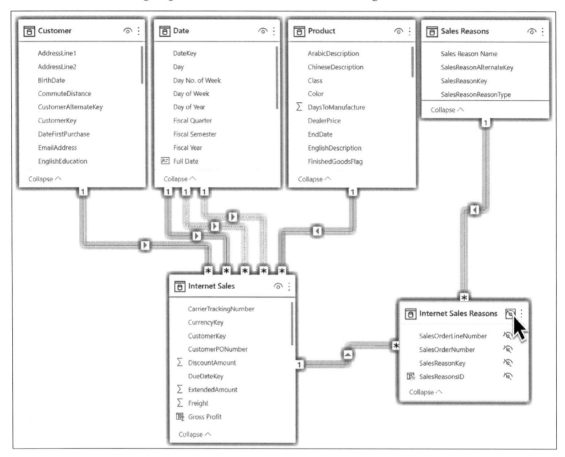

Figure 9.10: Hiding bridge tables from the Model view

Avoiding bidirectional relationships

One of the most misunderstood and somehow misused Power BI features in data modeling is setting the **Cross filter direction** to **Both**. This is widely known as a **bidirectional** relationship. There is nothing wrong with setting a relationship to bidirectional if we know what we are doing and are conscious of its effects on the data model. We have seen Power BI developers who have many bidirectional relationships in their model and consequently end up with many issues, such as getting unexpected results in their DAX calculations or being unable to create a new relationship due to ambiguity.

The reason that overusing bidirectional relationships increases the risk of having an ambiguous model is filter propagation. In *Chapter 8, Data Modeling Components*, we covered the concept of filter propagation and bidirectional relationships. We looked at a scenario where the developer needed to have two slicers on a report page, one for the product category and another for filtering the customers. It is a common scenario that developers set bidirectional relationships, which is no good. On many occasions, if not all, we can avoid bidirectional relationships. Depending on the scenario, we may use different techniques.

Let's look at the scenario we used in *Chapter 8, Data Modeling Components*, in the *Bidirectional relationships* section, again. We solve the scenario where we have two slicers on the report page without making a bidirectional relationship between the **Product** and **Sales** tables. We have a similar data model in this chapter's sample file in which we have **Customer**, **Product**, and **Internet Sales** tables, but this time, we do not make a bidirectional relationship between the **Product** and **Internet Sales** tables. The following diagram shows the data model:

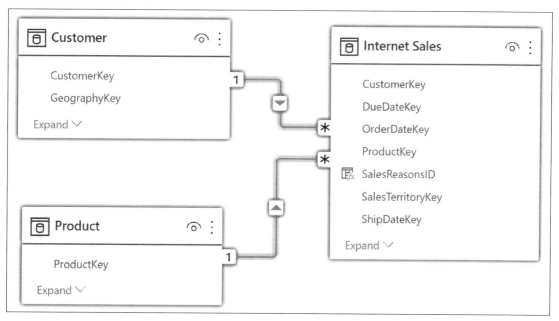

Figure 9.11: Internet Sales data model

The following diagram shows the reporting requirements:

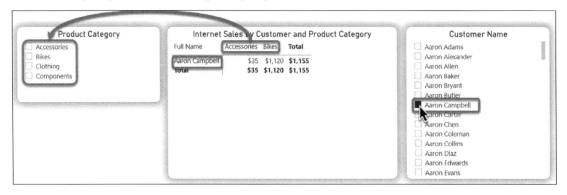

Figure 9.12: The Customer Name slicer filters the Sales data but not the Product Category data

As the preceding image shows, the **Customer Name** slicer filters **Internet Sales**. Still, the filter does not propagate to the **Product Category** table as the **Cross filter direction** of the one-to-many relationship between the **Product Category** table and the **Internet Sales** table is set to single; therefore, the filters flow from the **Product Category** table to the **Internet Sales** table but not the other way around. Similarly, the scenario also requires that the **Product Category** slicer filters the **Customer Name** slicer.

Let us solve the problem without making bidirectional relationships. The way to solve the scenario is to programmatically define the bidirectional relationships by using the CROSSFILTER() function in DAX. The following measure is a modified version of the **Internet Sales** measure, where we programmatically make the relationships between the **Product**, **Internet Sales**, and **Customer** tables to be bidirectional:

```
Internet Sales Bidirectional =
    CALCULATE(
        [Internet Sales]
        , CROSSFILTER(Customer[CustomerKey], 'Internet Sales'[CustomerKey], Both)
        , CROSSFILTER('Product'[ProductKey], 'Internet Sales'[ProductKey], Both)
        )
```

Now we add the new measure into the **visual filters** on both slicers and set the filter's **value** to **is not blank**. The following diagram shows the preceding process:

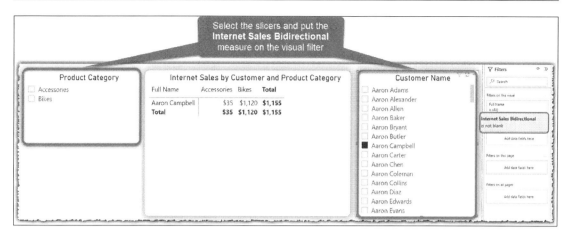

Figure 9.13: Using a measure in the visual filter for slicers

As the preceding diagram shows, the **Customer Name** slicer is successfully filtering the **Product Category** slicer and vice versa. The following steps show how it works on the **Customer Name** slicer; the same happens on the **Product Category** slicer:

1. The slicer gets the list of all customers from the **Full Name** column.
2. The visual filter kicks in and applies the filters. The **Internet Sales Bidirectional** measure used in the filter forces the slicer visual to run the measure and omit the blank values.
3. The **Internet Sales Bidirectional** measure forces the relationships between the **Product** table, the **Internet Sales** table, and the **Customer** table to be bidirectional for the duration that the measure runs.

If we do not select anything on the slicers, both slicers show the values having at least one row within the **Internet Sales** table.

The key message is to avoid bidirectional relationships as much as possible. In some cases, omitting the bidirectional relationship makes the DAX expressions too complex and hence not performant. We, as the data modelers, should decide which method works best in our scenarios.

Dealing with inactive relationships

In real-world scenarios, the data models can get very busy, especially when we are creating a data model to support enterprise BI; there are many instances where we have an inactive relationship in our data model. In many cases, there are two reasons that a relationship is inactive, as follows:

- The table with an inactive relationship is reachable via multiple filter paths.
- There are multiple direct relationships between two tables.

In both preceding cases, the xVelocity engine does not allow us to activate an inactive relationship to avoid ambiguity across the model.

Reachability via multiple filter paths

A multiple filter path between two tables means that the two tables are related and can be reached via other related tables. Therefore, the filter propagates from one table to another via multiple hops (relationships). The following diagram shows a data model with an inactive relationship:

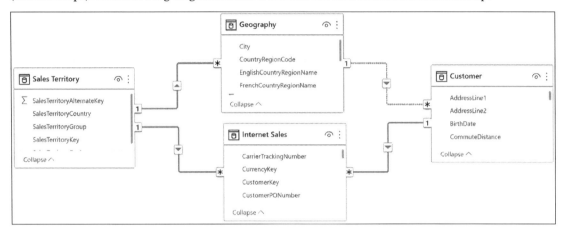

Figure 9.14: Inactive relationship due to multiple paths detected

As the preceding diagram shows, there is already a relationship between the **Sales Territory** table and the **Internet Sales** table. Power BI raises an error message, indicating that activating the relationship between the **Geography** table and **Customer** table will cause ambiguity between **Sales Territory** and **Internet Sales** if we attempt to activate the inactive relationship. The following diagram illustrates how the **Internet Sales** table would be reachable through multiple filter paths:

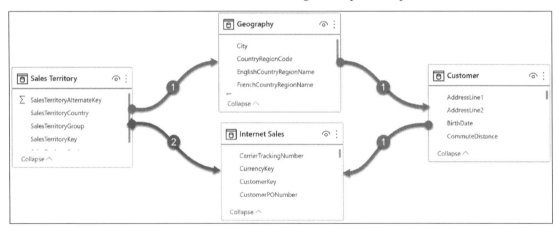

Figure 9.15: Internet Sales reachability through multiple paths

Looking at the preceding diagram shows how the **Internet Sales** table is reachable via two paths. The following steps show what happens when we put a filter on the **Sales Territory** table:

1. The filter propagates to the **Geography** table via the relationship between **Sales Territory** and **Geography**.
2. The filter then propagates to the **Customer** table through the relationship between **Geography** and **Customer**.
3. The filter propagates once more, reaching **Internet Sales** via the relationship between **Customer** and **Internet Sales**.

In the preceding image, the **Sales Territory** table and the **Internet Sales** table are related through two filter paths:

1. The path marked as *1*: an indirect filter path between **Sales Territory** and **Internet Sales**.
2. The path marked as *2* is a direct filter path via the relationship between the **Sales Territory** and the **Internet Sales** tables.

It is now clearer why the relationship between **Geography** and **Customer** is inactive.

Multiple direct relationships between two tables

The other common cause of having an inactive relationship is when there are multiple direct relationships between two tables, meaning that we can use each relationship for a different analytical calculation. The following diagram shows that the **Date** table is related to the **Internet Sales** table via several relationships:

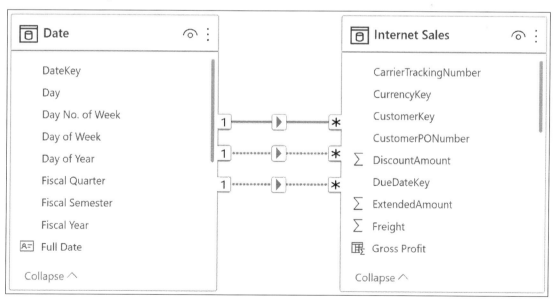

Figure 9.16: Two tables with multiple direct relationships

We can look at the **Manage relationships** window to see what those relationships are as shown in the following image:

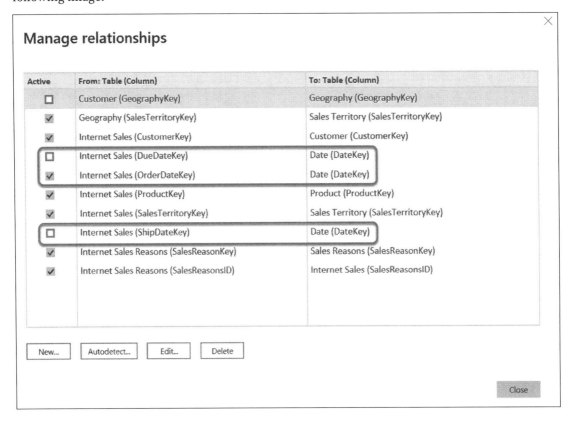

Figure 9.17: The Date table and the Internet Sales table are related via multiple relationships

As the preceding image shows, there are three columns in the **Internet Sales** table participating in the relationships, and all of them are legitimate. Each relationship filters the **Inter Sales** table differently, but we can have only one active relationship between two tables at a time. Currently, the relationship via the **OrderDateKey** column from the **Internet Sales** table and the **DateKey** column from the **Date** table is the active relationship that propagates the filter from the **Date** table to the **Internet Sales** table, which means when we use the **Year** column from the **Date** table and the **Internet Sales** measure from the **Internet Sales** table, and we slice the **Internet Sales** by **order date year**. But what if the business needs to analyze the **Internet Sales** by **Due Date**? What if the business also needs to analyze the **Internet Sales** by **Ship Date**? We obviously cannot physically make a relationship active and inactive to solve this issue. So, we have to programmatically solve the challenge by using the USERELATIONSHIP() function in DAX. The USERELATIONSHIP() function activates an inactive relationship for the duration that the measure is running. So, to meet the requirements, we create two new measures.

The following DAX expression activates the relationship between DueDateKey and DateKey relationship:

```
Internet Sales Due =
    CALCULATE([Internet Sales]
        , USERELATIONSHIP('Internet Sales'[DueDateKey], 'Date'[DateKey])
    )
```

The following DAX expression activates the relationship between ShipDateKey and DateKey:

```
Internet Sales Shipped =
    CALCULATE([Internet Sales]
        , USERELATIONSHIP('Internet Sales'[ShipDateKey], 'Date'[DateKey])
    )
```

Let's use the new measures, side by side, with the **Internet Sales** measure and the **Full Date** column from the **Date** table in a table to see the differences between values:

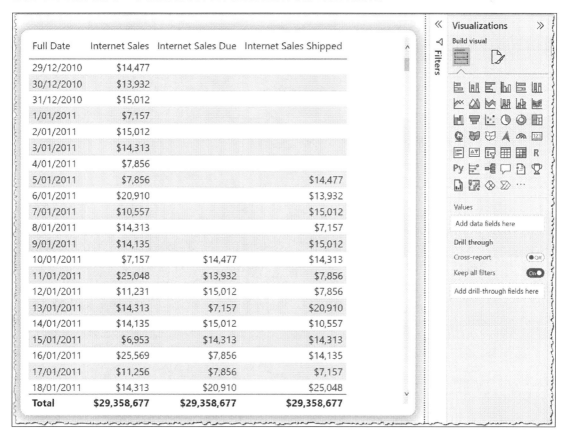

Figure 9.18: Programmatically activating inactive relationships

So, using the USERELATIONSHIP() function makes it possible to have the **Internet Sales, Internet Sales Due,** and **Internet Sales Shipped** measures side by side in a single visual.

Using configuration tables

In many cases, a business wants to analyze some of the business metrics in clusters. Some good examples are analyzing sales by unit price range, analyzing sales by product cost range, analyzing customers by their age range, or analyzing customers by commute distance. In all of these examples, the business does not need to analyze constant values; instead, it is more about analyzing a metric (sales, in the preceding examples) by a range of values.

Some other cases are related to data visualization, such as dynamically changing the color of values when they are in a specific range. An example is to change the values' color to red in all visuals analyzing sales if the sales value for the data points is less than the average sales over time. This is a relatively advanced analysis that can be reused in our reports to keep visualizations' color consistent.

In the preceding examples, we need to define configuration tables. In the latter example, we see how data modeling can positively affect our data visualization.

Segmentation

As stated earlier, there are cases when a business needs to analyze its business metrics by clusters of data. As we analyze the business values in different segments, this type of analysis is commonly known as **segmentation**.

Let's continue with an example. The business needs to analyze **Internet Sales** by **UnitPrice** ranges as shown in the following list:

- **Low**: When the **UnitPrice** is between $0 and $50
- **Medium**: When the **UnitPrice** is between $51 and $450
- **High**: When the **UnitPrice** is between $451 and $1,500
- **Very high**: When the **UnitPrice** is greater than $1,500

At this point, you may think of adding a calculated column to the **Internet Sales** table to take care of the business requirement, but what if the business modifies the definition of unit price ranges in the future? We need to frequently change the calculated column, which is not a viable option. A better approach is to have the definition of unit price ranges in a table. We can store the definitions in an Excel file accessible in a shared **OneDrive for Business** folder. It can be a SharePoint list that is accessible to the business to make any necessary changes. For simplicity, we manually enter the preceding definition as a table using the **Enter data** feature in Power BI.

> We do not recommend manually entering the definition values in Power BI using the **Enter data** feature in real-world scenarios. If the business wants to change the values, we must modify the report in Power BI Desktop and republish it to the Power BI Service.

The following image shows a **Unit Price Ranges** table created in Power BI:

Sort	Price Range	From	To
4	Low	0	50
3	Medium	51	450
2	High	451	1500
1	Very hight	1501	15000

Figure 9.19: Unit Price Ranges table

Now we need to add a calculated column in the **Internet Sales** table. The newly calculated column looks up the **Price Range** value for each **UnitPrice** value within the **Internet Sales** table. To do so, we have to compare the **UnitPrice** value of each row from the **Internet Sales** table with the values of the **From** and **To** columns from the **Unit Price Ranges** table. The following DAX expressions cater to that:

```
Price Range =
    CALCULATE(
        VALUES('Unit Price Ranges'[Price Range])
        , FILTER('Unit Price Ranges'
            , 'Unit Price Ranges'[From] < 'Internet Sales'[UnitPrice]
                && 'Unit Price Ranges'[To] >= 'Internet Sales'[UnitPrice]
        )
    )
```

The following image shows the **Internet Sales by Price Range** analysis when we select **High** and **Medium** from the clustered bar chart:

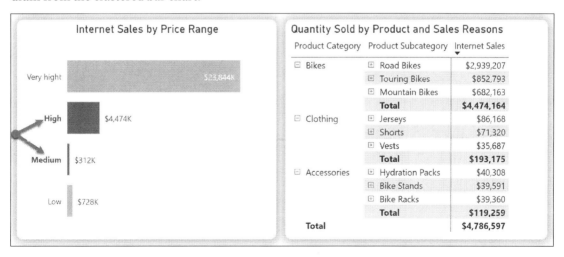

Figure 9.20: Analyzing Internet Sales by price range

As a minor note, look at how the bars are sorted in the bar chart. They are not alphabetically sorted by **Price Range** name nor by the **Internet Sales** values. You already learned how to manage column sorting in the previous chapter, so I will leave this to you to find out how that is possible.

Dynamic color coding with measures

So far, we have discussed many aspects of data modeling, as the primary goal of this book is to learn how to deal with various day-to-day challenges. This section discusses an essential aspect of data visualization, **color coding**, and how data modeling can ease many advanced data visualization challenges. Color coding is one of the most compelling and efficient ways to provide pertinent information about the data. In this section, we make a bridge between data modeling and data visualization.

We could color-code the visuals from early versions of Power BI. However, conditional formatting was not available on many visuals for a long time. Luckily, we can now set conditional formatting on almost all default visuals (and many custom visuals) in Power BI Desktop. Let's continue with a scenario.

A business decided to dynamically use predefined color codes in various visuals so that the visuals' colors are picked depending on the value of the Sales MoM% measure. The Sales MoM% measure calculates the percentage of sales changes, based on the sales values for each year in comparison with the sales values for the previous year. The goal is to visualize Sales MoM% in a **Clustered column chart**. The color for each data point should be calculated based on a config table. The following diagram shows the structure of the config table:

Index	ColourHex	Range%	Description
1	#264653	100%	Divine
2	#287271	90%	Excellent
3	#2A9D8F	80%	Very good
4	#8AB17D	70%	Good
5	#E9C46A	60%	Fine
6	#DA941B	50%	Normal
7	#CB7C15	40%	Keep going
8	#EF7A1A	30%	Low
9	#CB4F15	20%	Very low
10	#7E2711	10%	Critical

Figure 9.21: Config table defining color codes

1. First, we need to enter the data in *Figure 9.21* into a table in Power BI. We name the new table **ConfigColour**.

   The following image shows the **ConfigColour** table in Power BI Desktop:

ColourHex	Index	Range%	Status
#264653	1	100%	Divine
#287271	2	90%	Excellent
#2A9D8F	3	80%	Very good
#8AB17D	4	70%	Good
#E9C46A	5	60%	Fine
#DA941B	6	50%	Normal
#CB7C15	7	40%	Keep going
#EF7A1A	8	30%	Low
#CB4F15	9	20%	Very low
#7E2711	10	10%	Critical

   Figure 9.22: The ConfigColour table

2. Now we need to create a Sales MoM% measure. The following DAX expression calculates sales for the last month (Sales LM):

   ```
   Sales LM =
       CALCULATE([Internet Sales]
           , DATEADD('Date'[Full Date], -1, MONTH)
           )
   ```

3. After we have calculated Sales LM, we just need to calculate the percentage of differences between the **Internet Sales** measures and the Sales LM measure. The following expression caters to that:

   ```
   Sales MoM% = DIVIDE([Internet Sales] - [Sales LM], [Sales LM])
   ```

4. The next step is to create two textual measures. The first measure picks a relevant value from the **ColourHex** column, and the other one picks the relevant value from the **Status** column from the **ConfigColour** table. Both textual measures pick their values from the **ConfigColour** table based on the value of the Sales MoM% measure.

Before we implement the measures, let's understand how the data within the **ConfigColour** table is supposed to work. The following points are essential to understand how to work with the **ConfigColour** table:

- The **ConfigColour** contains 10 rows of data.
- The **ColourHex** contains hex codes for colors.
- The **Range%** contains a decimal number between 0.1 and 1.
- The **Status** column contains a textual description for each color.
- The **Index** column contains the table index.

The preceding points look easy to understand, but the **Range%** column is tricky. When we format the **Range%** column as a percentage, values are between 10% and 100%. Each value, however, represents a range of values, not a constant value. For instance, 10% means all values from 0% up to 10%. In the same way, 20% means all values are between 11% and 20%. The other point to note is when we format the **Range%** values with percentages, each value is divisible by 10 (such as 10, 20, 30,...).

The new textual measures pick the relevant values either from the **ColourHex** column or from the **Status** column, based on the **Range%** column and the **Sales MoM%** measure. So, we need to identify the ranges the `Sales MoM%` values fall in, then compare them with the values within the **ColourHex** column. The following formula guarantees that the `Sales MoM%` values are divisible by 10, so we can later find the matching values within the `ColourHex` column:

```
CONVERT([Sales MoM%] * 10, INTEGER)/10
```

Here is how the preceding formula works:

1. We multiply the value of `Sales MoM%` by 10, which returns a decimal value between 0 and 10 (we will deal with the situations when the value is smaller than 0 or bigger than 10).
2. We convert the decimal value to an integer to drop the digits after the decimal point.
3. Finally, we divide the value by 10.

When we format the results as percentages, the value is divisible by 10. We then check whether the value is smaller than 10%; if so, we return 10%. If it is bigger than 100%, we return 100%.

It is now time to create textual measures. The following DAX expression results in a hex color. We will then use the retrieved hex color in the visual's conditional formatting:

```
Sales MoM% Colour =
var percentRound = CONVERT([Sales MoM%] * 10, INTEGER)/10
var checkMinValue = IF(percentRound < 0.1, 0.1, percentRound)
var checkMaxValue = IF(checkMinValue > 1, 1, checkMinValue)
return
CALCULATE(
    VALUES(ConfigColour[ColourHex])
    , FILTER( ConfigColour
        , 'ConfigColour'[Range%] = checkMaxValue
```

```
        )
    )
```

As you can see in the preceding expression, the `checkMinValue` and `checkMaxValue` variables are adjusting the out-of-range values. The following DAX expression results in a description calculated in a similar way to the previous measure:

```
Sales MoM% Description =
var percentRound = CONVERT([Sales MoM%] * 10, INTEGER)/10
var checkMinValue = IF(percentRound < 0.1, 0.1, percentRound)
var checkMaxValue = IF(checkMinValue > 1, 1, checkMinValue)
return
CALCULATE(
    VALUES(ConfigColour[Status])
    , FILTER( ConfigColour
        , 'ConfigColour'[Range%] = checkMaxValue
        )
    )
```

Now that we have created the textual measures, we can use them to format the visuals conditionally (if supported). The following visuals currently support conditional formatting:

Stacked Column Chart	Clustered Bar Chart	Clustered Column Chart	100% Stacked Bar Chart
100% Stacked Column Chart	Line and Stacked Column Chart	Line and Clustered Column Chart	Ribbon Chart
Funnel Chart	Scatter Chart	Treemap Chart	Gauge
Card	KPI	Table	Matrix

Figure 9.23: Power BI default visuals supporting conditional formatting

The following steps show how to format a clustered column chart conditionally:

1. Put a **Clustered column chart** on a new report page.
2. Choose the **Year-Month** column from the **Date** table from the visual's **Axis** dropdown.
3. Choose the **Sales MoM%** measure from the visual's **Values** dropdown.
4. Choose the **Sales MoM% Description** measure from the **Tooltips** dropdown.
5. Switch to the **Format** tab from the **Visualizations** pane.
6. Expand the **Columns**.
7. Expand **Colors**.
8. Click the **fx** button.
9. Select **Field value** from the **Format by** drop-down menu.
10. Select the **Sales MoM% Colour** measure from the **Based on field** menu.
11. Click **OK**.

The following image shows the preceding steps:

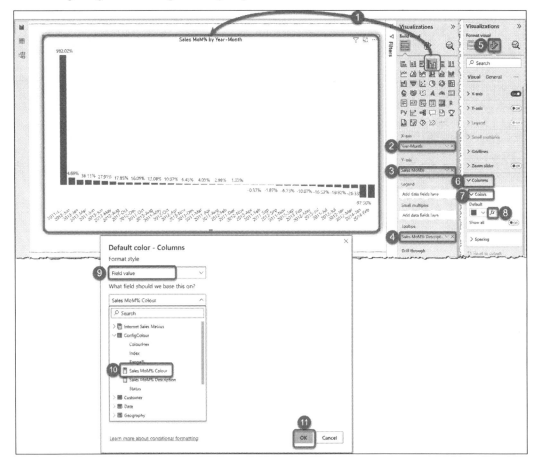

Figure 9.24: Applying dynamic conditional formatting on a clustered column chart

The following image shows the clustered column chart after the preceding settings:

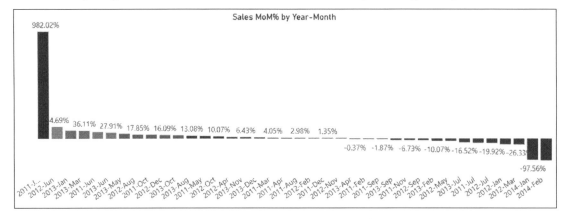

Figure 9.25: The clustered column chart after it has been conditionally formatted

With this technique, we can create compelling data visualizations that can quickly provide many insights about the data. For instance, the following image shows a report page analyzing sales by date. Add a matrix showing **Internet Sales** by Month and Day:

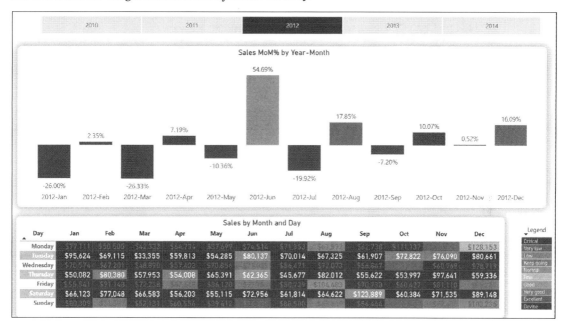

Figure 9.26: Color-coded Sales report

Use the **Sales MoM% Colour** measure to color-code the matrix. Every cell of the matrix shows the sales amount by weekday for the entire month in this report. However, the color of the cell shows the comparison of current sales against the same weekday last month. For instance, if we look at the 2012-Jun sales, we quickly see that the Monday sales were excellent compared to 2011-Jun.

The preceding report page might not be a perfect example of a high-standard data visualization. However, without a doubt, it provides many more insights than a similar report page without color coding. In real-world scenarios, we might have more colors for negative numbers to show the severity of the metric we are analyzing. We will leave this to you as an exercise on how to use this technique to create very professional-looking reports.

Avoiding calculated columns when possible

Creating calculated columns is one of the most essential and powerful features of DAX. Calculated columns, as the name suggests, are computed based on a formula; therefore, the calculated column values are unavailable in the source systems or the Power Query layer. The values of the calculated columns are computed during the data refresh and then stored in memory. It is important to note that the calculated columns reside in memory unless we unload the whole data model from memory, which in Power BI means when we close the file in Power BI Desktop or switch to other content in the Power BI Service. Calculated columns, after creation, are just like any other columns, so we can use them in other calculated columns, measures, calculated tables, or for filtering the visualization layer.

A common approach of developers is to use calculated columns to divide complex equations into smaller chunks. That is why we suggest avoiding the excessive use of calculated columns. The general rules of thumb for using calculated columns are as follows:

- Create a calculated column if you use it in filters.
- Even though you need to use the calculated column in filters, consider creating the new column in the Power Query layer or the source when possible.
- Do not create calculated columns if you can create a measure with the same results.
- Always think about the data cardinality when creating calculated columns. The higher the cardinality, the lower the compression and the higher the memory consumption.
- Always have a strong justification for creating a calculated column, especially when dealing with large models.
- Use the **View Metrics** tool in **DAX Studio** to monitor the calculated column size, which directly translates to memory consumption.

Let's look at an example in this chapter's sample file. The business needs to calculate Gross Profit. To calculate Gross Profit, we must deduct total costs from total sales. We can create a calculated column with the following DAX expression, which gives us Gross Profit for each row of the **Internet Sales** table:

```
Gross Profit = 'Internet Sales'[SalesAmount] - 'Internet Sales'[TotalProductCost]
```

We can then create the following measure to calculate Total Gross Profit:

```
Total Gross Profit with Calc Column = SUM('Internet Sales'[Gross Profit])
```

Let us have a look at the preceding calculated column in **DAX Studio** to get a better understanding of how it performs. Perform the following steps using **View Metrics** in DAX Studio:

1. Click the **External Tools** tab from the ribbon.
2. Click **DAX Studio**.
3. In DAX Studio, click the **Advanced** tab from the ribbon.
4. Click **View Metrics**.
5. Expand the **Internet Sales** table.
6. Find the **Gross Profit** row.

The following image shows the preceding steps:

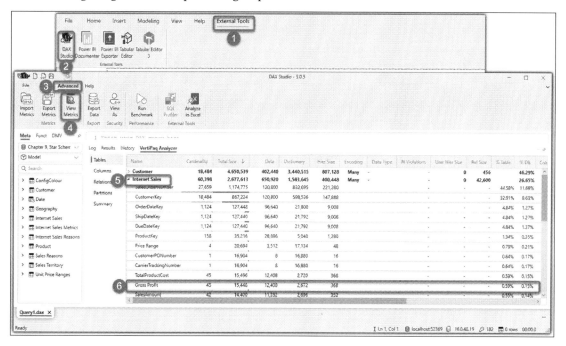

Figure 9.27: View Metrics in DAX Studio

As you see in the preceding image, the **Gross Profit** row size is 15,448 bytes (approximately 15 KB), with the cardinality of 45 consuming 0.31% of the table size. The **Internet Sales** table is a small table with 60,398 rows. So, we can imagine how the column size can grow in larger tables.

While the process of creating a calculated column and then getting the summation of the calculated column is legitimate, it is not the preferred method. We can compute `Total Gross Profit` in a measure with the following DAX expression:

```
Total Gross Profit Measure = SUMX('Internet Sales', 'Internet
Sales'[SalesAmount] - 'Internet Sales'[TotalProductCost])
```

The difference between the two approaches is that the values of the `Gross Profit` calculated row are computed at the table refresh time. It resides in memory, while its measure counterpart aggregates the gross profit when we use it in a visual. So when we use the **Product Category** column from the **Product** table in a **clustered column chart** and the `Total Gross Profit Measure`, the values of the `Total Gross Profit Measure` are aggregated for the number of product categories in memory. The following image shows **Total Gross Profit Measure by Product Category** in a **clustered column chart**:

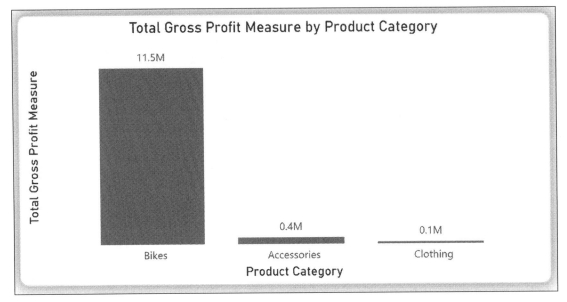

Figure 9.28: Total Gross Profit Measure by Product Category in a clustered column chart

As the preceding image shows, the `Total Gross Profit Measure` is aggregated in the `Product Category` level with only three values, so the calculation is superfast with minimal memory consumption.

Organizing the model

There are usually several roles involved in a Power BI project in real-world enterprise BI scenarios. From a Power BI development perspective, we might have data modelers, report writers, quality assurance specialists, support specialists, and so on. The data modelers are the ones who make the data model available for all other content creators, such as report writers. So, making a model that is as organized as possible is essential. This section looks at several ways to organize our data models.

Hiding insignificant model objects

One way to keep our model tidier is to hide all insignificant objects from the data model. We often have some objects in the data model that are not used elsewhere. However, we cannot remove them from the data model as we may require them in the future. So, the best practice is to hide all those objects unless they are going to serve a business requirement. The following sections discuss the best candidate objects for hiding in our data model.

Hiding unused fields and tables

There are many cases when we have some fields (columns or measures) or tables in the data model that are not used elsewhere. Unused fields are the measures or columns that fulfill the following criteria:

- Are not used in any visuals on any report pages
- Are not used within the **Filters** pane
- No measures, calculated columns, calculated tables, or calculation groups referencing those fields
- No roles within the row-level security reference those fields

If we have some fields falling in all of the preceding categories, it is highly recommended to hide them in the data model. The idea is to keep the data model as tidy as possible so that you can hide some fields that fall into some of the preceding categories, based on your use cases.

Unused tables, on the other hand, are tables with all their fields unused.

While this best practice suggests hiding unused fields and tables, applying it can be time-consuming. If done manually, finding the fields that are not referenced anywhere within the model or are not used in any visuals can be a laborious job. Luckily, some third-party tools can make our lives easier. For instance, we can use **Power BI Documenter**, which can not only find unused tables and fields but also hide all unused tables and fields in one click.

The following image shows how our **Fields** pane looks before and after hiding unused tables with Power BI Documenter:

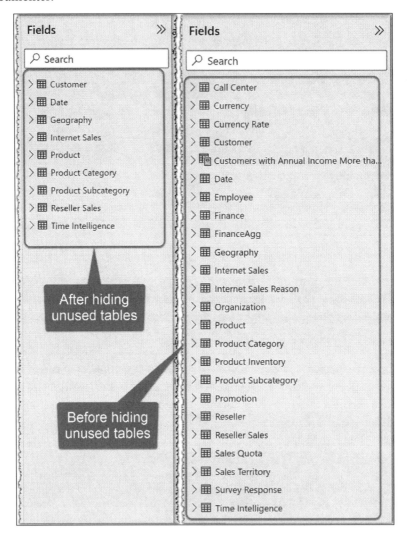

Figure 9.29: Before and after hiding unused tables using Power BI Documenter

The following image shows what the **Internet Sales** table looks like before and after using Power BI Documenter to hide the unused fields:

Chapter 9

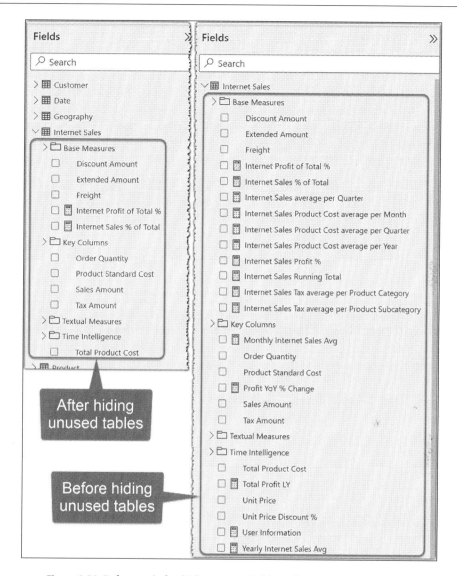

Figure 9.30: Before and after hiding unused tables using Power BI Documenter

To learn more about Power BI Documenter, visit www.datavizioner.com.

Hiding key columns

The other best practice that helps us keep our data model tidy is to hide all key columns. The key columns are Primary Keys and their corresponding Foreign Keys. While keeping the key columns in the data model is crucial, we do not need them to be visible.

Hiding implicit measures

The other items we can hide in our data model are the implicit measures. We discussed implicit and explicit measures in *Chapter 8*, *Data Modeling Components*, in the *Measures* section. Best practices suggest creating explicit measures for all implicit measures required by the business and hiding all the implicit measures in the data model. Hiding implicit measures reduces the confusion of which measure to use in the data visualizations for other content creators, who are not necessarily familiar with the data model.

Hiding columns used in hierarchies when possible

When we create a hierarchy, it is better to hide the base columns from the report view. Having base columns in a table when the same column appears in a hierarchy is somewhat confusing. So, avoiding confusing the other content creators connecting to our data model (dataset) is best.

Creating measure tables

Creating a measure table is a controversial topic in Power BI. Some experts suggest using this technique to keep the model even more organized, while others discourage using it. I think this technique is a powerful way to organize the data model; however, there are some side effects to be mindful of before deciding whether to use this technique. We will look at some considerations in the next section. For now, let's see what a measure table is. A measure table is not a data table in our data model. We only create and use them as the home table for our measures. For instance, we can move all the measures from the **Internet Sales** table to a separate table in our sample report. When a table holds the measures only (without any visible columns), Power BI detects the table as a measure table with a specific iconography (▦). The following steps explain how to create a measure table in Power BI:

1. Click the **Enter Data** button.
2. Leave **Column1** as is with an empty value.
3. Name the table **Internet Sales Metrics**.
4. Click **Load**:

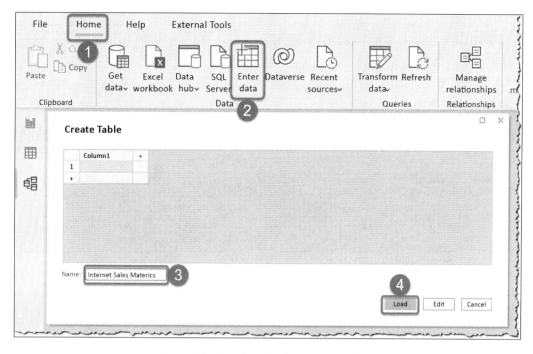

Figure 9.31: Entering data in Power BI Desktop

5. Right-click **Column1** in the **Internet Sales Metrics** table.
6. Click **Hide in report view**:

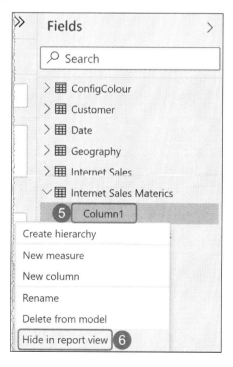

Figure 9.32: Hiding a column

Now we move the measures from the **Internet Sales** table to the **Internet Sales Metrics** table. The following steps show how we can do so from the **Model** view:

7. Right-click the **Internet Sales** table.
8. Click **Select measures** to select all measures within the **Internet Sales** table.

The following image shows the preceding steps:

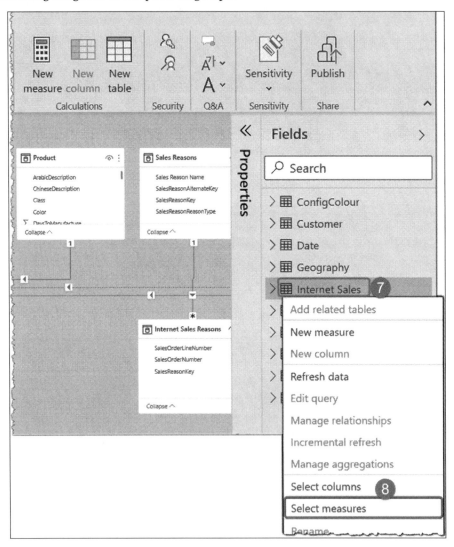

Figure 9.33: Selecting all measures from a table

9. Drag the selected measures and drop them on the **Internet Sales Metrics** table, as shown in the following image:

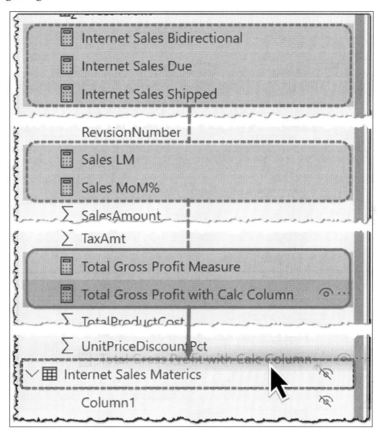

Figure 9.34: Moving multiple measures from one table to another

We now have a measure table keeping all the **Internet Sales** measures. The following image shows the measure table:

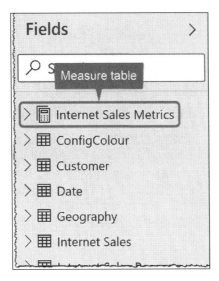

Figure 9.35: The data model after creating the measure table

When Power BI Desktop detects a measure table, it puts it on top of the list of the **Fields** pane. We can create separate measure tables for different business domains to have all relevant measures in the same place. This approach helps to make our model tidier and makes it easier for content creators to understand the model.

While creating measure tables can help keep our data model tidy, some downfalls are associated with this approach. For instance, it does not make too much sense to have a table with an empty column in the model from a data modeling point of view. Having a table in your model that is only used for holding your measures might not sound like a real issue. But one more fundamental problem associated with the measure tables relates to the **featured tables**. As we discussed the concept of featured tables in *Chapter 8*, *Data Modeling Components*, in the *Featured tables* section, we can configure a table within our Power BI data model as a featured table. After we configure a featured table, the columns and measures are available for Excel users across the organization. Therefore, when we move all the measures from a featured table to a measure table, the measures will no longer be available to Excel users. So the key message here is to think about your use cases and then decide whether the measure tables are suitable for your scenarios.

Using folders

Another method to keep our data model tidy is to create folders and put all relevant columns and measures into separate folders. Unlike creating measure tables, creating folders does not have any known side effects on the model. Therefore, we can create as many folders as required. We can create or manage new folders via the **Model** view within Power BI Desktop. This section discusses some tips and tricks for using folders more efficiently.

Creating a folder in multiple tables in one go

A handy way to create folders more efficiently is by creating a folder in multiple tables in a single attempt. This method can be handy in many cases, such as creating a folder in the home tables to keep all the measures or selecting multiple columns and measures from multiple tables and placing them in a folder in various tables. The following steps create a folder to keep all measures in various tables from the **Model** view:

1. Select all tables containing measures.
2. Right-click selected tables and click **Select measures** from the context menu.

    The following image illustrates the preceding steps:

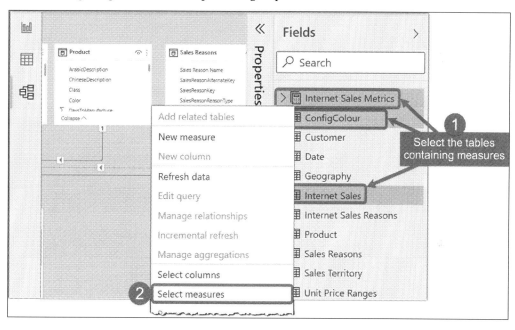

Figure 9.36: Selecting all measures in the model

3. Type a name in **Display folder** (I entered Measures) and press *Enter* on the keyboard.

The following image shows the **Measures** folder created in multiple tables, containing all measures used by those tables:

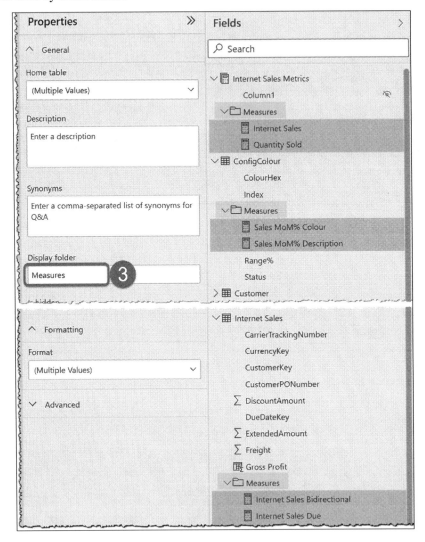

Figure 9.37: Placing all selected measures in a folder within multiple tables

Placing a measure in various folders

Sometimes, you might want to place a measure in multiple folders. A use case for this method is to make a measure more accessible for the contributors or support specialists. In our sample file, for instance, we want to show `Sales LM` and `Sales MoM%` measures in both the **Measures** folder and in a new **Time Intelligence** folder. The following steps show how to do so:

1. Select the Sales LM and Sales MoM% measures.
2. In **Display folder**, add a semicolon after Measures, type in the new folder name, and press *Enter*.

The following image shows the preceding steps:

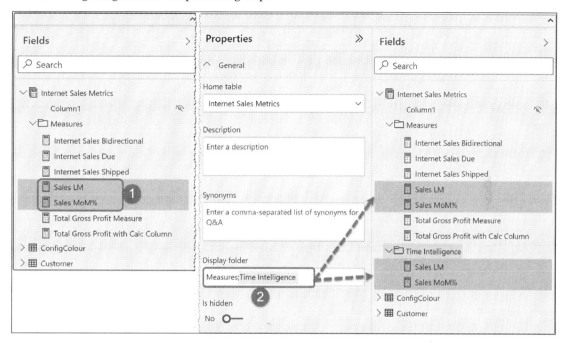

Figure 9.38: Placing measures in multiple folders

To make it clear, the **Display folder** field in the preceding image contains the folder names separated by a semicolon, as follows: Measures;Time Intelligence.

Creating subfolders

Sometimes, we want to create subfolders to make the folders even tidier. For instance, in our sample, we want a subfolder to keep our base measures. The following steps show how to create a subfolder nested in the root folder:

1. Select the desired measure(s).
2. Use a backslash (\) character to create a subfolder, then press *Enter* on the keyboard.

The following image shows the preceding steps:

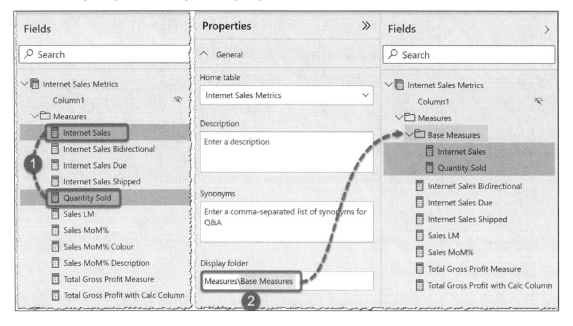

Figure 9.39: Creating subfolders

Reducing model size by disabling auto date/time

When the data is loaded into the data model, Power BI automatically creates some `Date` tables to support calendar hierarchies for all columns in the `DateTime` datatype. This feature is convenient, especially for beginners who do not know how to create a `Date` table or create and manage hierarchies. However, it can consume too much storage, potentially leading to severe performance issues. As mentioned earlier, the auto date/time feature forces Power BI Desktop to create `Date` tables for every single `DateTime` column within the model. The `Date` tables have the following columns:

- `Date`
- `Year`
- `Quarter`
- `Month`
- `Day`

The last four columns create date hierarchies for each `DateTime` column. The `Date` column in the created `Date` table starts from January 1 of the minimum year of the related column in our tables. It ends on December 31 of the maximum number of years for that column. It is a common practice in data warehousing to use 10/01/1900 for unknown dates in the past and 31/12/9999 for unknown dates in the future. Imagine what happens if we have only one column having only one of the preceding unknown date values. To avoid this, it is a best practice to disable this feature in Power BI Desktop. The following steps show how to disable the auto date/time feature:

1. In Power BI Desktop, click the **File** menu.
2. Click **Options and settings**.
3. Click **Options**.

    The following image shows the preceding steps:

    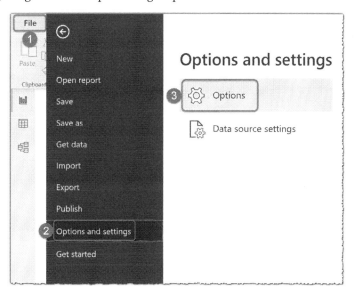

    Figure 9.40: Changing Power BI Desktop options

4. Click **Data Load** from the **GLOBAL** section.
5. Uncheck **Auto date/time for new files**. This will disable this feature globally, whenever you start creating a new file.

The following image shows how to disable the **Auto date/time for new files** feature on a file-by-file basis:

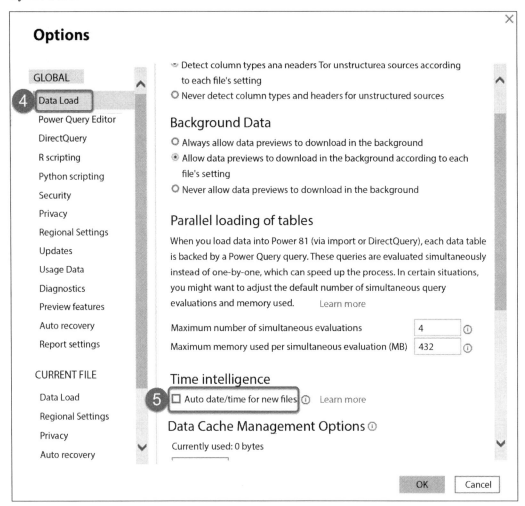

Figure 9.41: Disabling the Auto date/time feature globally

6. Click **Data Load** from the **CURRENT FILE** section.
7. Uncheck **Auto date/time for new files**. This will disable the **Auto date/time for new files** feature only for the current file. So unless you completed the previous steps, the **Auto date/time for new files** feature will be not disabled for new files.

8. Click **OK**:

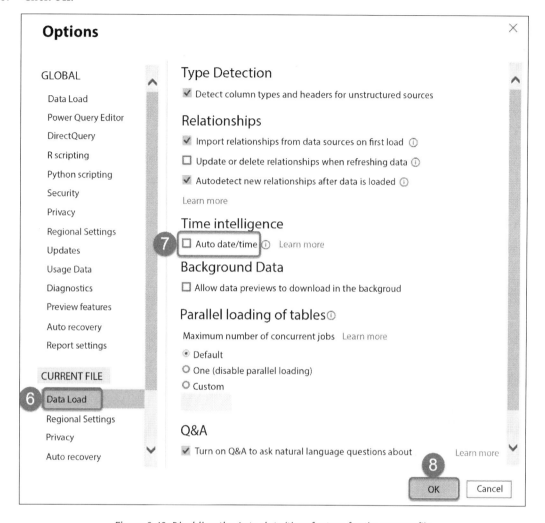

Figure 9.42: Disabling the Auto date/time feature for the current file

Disabling the **Auto date/time for new files** feature removes all the automatically created Date tables, which reduces the file size.

Summary

This chapter taught us some common best practices for working with Star Schema and data modeling. We learned how to implement many-to-many relationships. We also learned how and when to use bi-directional relationships. Then we looked at disabled relationships and how we can programmatically enable them. We also learned about config tables and how they can help us with our data visualization. We then discussed why and when we should avoid using calculated columns. Next, we looked at some techniques to organize the data model. Finally, we learned how we could reduce the model size by disabling the Auto date/time for new files feature in Power BI Desktop.

In the next chapter, *Advanced Modeling Techniques*, we will discuss some exciting data modeling techniques that can boost our Power BI model performance while creating complex models. See you there.

Join us on Discord!

Join The Big Data and Analytics Community on the Packt Discord Server!

Hang out with 558 other members and enjoy free voice and text chat.

`https://packt.link/ips2H`

Section 4
Advanced Data Modeling

This section focuses on advanced data modeling techniques that you may not deal with on a daily basis but are extremely important to know about.

Implementing parent-child hierarchies, dealing with different calculations in a hierarchy, using aggregations, along with the more advanced business requirements to be implemented in a data model are all covered in this section. You need to have a deep understanding of the star schema and DAX, the latter of which we'll cover some new functions for.

Like other parts of this book, the chapters of this section are fully hands-on with real-world scenarios.

This section comprises the following chapters:

- *Chapter 10, Advanced Data Modeling Techniques*
- *Chapter 11, Row-Level and Object-Level Security*
- *Chapter 12, Dealing with More Advanced Data Warehousing Concepts in Power BI*
- *Chapter 13, Introduction to Dataflows*
- *Chapter 14, DirectQuery Connections to Power BI Datasets and Analysis Services in Composite Models*
- *Chapter 15, New Options, Features, and DAX Functions*

10

Advanced Data Modeling Techniques

In the previous chapter, we looked at some data modeling best practices, such as dealing with many-to-many relationships using bridge tables, dealing with inactive relationships, and how to programmatically enable them. We also learned how to use config tables, organize our data model, and reduce the model's size by disabling the auto date/time feature in Power BI Desktop.

This chapter discusses advanced data modeling techniques that can help us deal with more complex scenarios more efficiently. Many techniques require a Power BI Pro license and sometimes a Premium license. We mention the required licensing tier when explaining each technique. This chapter covers the following topics:

- Using aggregations
- Partitioning
- Incremental refresh
- Understanding parent-child hierarchies
- Implementing roleplaying dimensions
- Using calculation groups

We expect you already have a concrete understanding of the basic concepts discussed in the previous chapters. This chapter focuses on more advanced topics and avoids explaining the basics unless they were not previously covered in this book.

Using aggregations

From a data analytics viewpoint, the concept of aggregation tables has been around for a long time. The concept is widely used in SQL Server Analysis Services Multi-Dimensional. Aggregation tables summarize the data at a particular grain and make it available in the data model. While analyzing aggregated data usually performs better at runtime, aggregation typically happens at a higher level of granularity by introducing a new table (or set of tables) containing summarized data.

To enable the users to drill down to a lower grain, we must keep the data in its lowest grain in the data model. We also need to implement a control mechanism to detect the granularity of data the user interacts with in the reporting layer. The calculation happens in the aggregated table if the aggregated data is available in the data model. When the user drills down to the lower grain, the control mechanism runs the calculations in the detail table, which contains more granular data. This approach is intricate, but it works perfectly if we get it right.

Implementing aggregations is useful in almost all data models; it is even more valuable when one of our data sources is big data. For instance, we may have billions of rows hosted in Azure Synapse Analytics. Importing all the data into the data model in Power BI Desktop is utterly impossible. In those cases, using aggregation tables becomes inevitable. Luckily, Power BI Desktop has a **Manage aggregations** feature that detects the grain of data the user interacts with from the report level and automatically handles the calculations either in the aggregate or the detail table. This feature is also known as **User-defines Aggregations** or **Agg Awareness**. Using **Agg Awareness** requires the data source to support DirectQuery.

We discussed the various storage modes in *Chapter 4, Getting Data from Various Sources*, in the *Dataset storage modes* section.

Refer to the following link to find the list of data sources that support DirectQuery: https://learn.microsoft.com/en-us/power-bi/connect-data/power-bi-data-sources?WT.mc_id=DP-MVP-5003466.

While the **Agg Awareness** feature takes care of the complexities of switching the calculations between the aggregate table and the detail table depending on the user interactions with the reports, not all data sources support DirectQuery. Therefore, we might not use the **Agg Awareness** feature. Still, it doesn't mean we cannot implement the aggregation technique. The next few sections discuss two different ways of implementing aggregation tables.

The first method is implementing aggregation tables for non-DirectQuery data sources, such as Excel files. Therefore, not only do we need to implement the aggregation table, but also, we must take care of the control mechanism to switch between the aggregation and the detail table when the user drills down to a different grain of data.

The second method uses the **Manage aggregations** feature for the data sources supporting DirectQuery.

Implementing aggregations for non-DirectQuery data sources

In many real-world scenarios, the data sources may not support DirectQuery mode. Therefore, we cannot use the **Agg Awareness** (**Manage aggregations** feature) in Power BI Desktop. However, we can manually implement aggregations by going through the following process:

1. Summarize the table at a lower grain.
2. Create relationships between the new summary table and the dimensions at the summary grain.
3. Create the desired measures (note that the new measures work at the summary grain).
4. Create another set of new measures that control the level of grain selected by the user.

5. Hide the summary table to make it transparent to the users.

In this section, we use the `Chapter 10, Aggregations on Non-DirectQuery Data Sources.pbix` sample file sourcing data from the `AdventureWorksDW2017.xlsx` Excel file.

You can download the sample file from here:

`https://github.com/PacktPublishing/Expert-Data-Modeling-with-Power-BI-Second-Edition/blob/c946d376871675271055f4b778605691b786cb5c/Samples/Chapter%2010/Chapter%2010%2C%20Aggregations%20on%20Non-DirectQurey%20Data%20Sources.pbix`

The Excel source file is downloadable from here:

`https://github.com/PacktPublishing/Expert-Data-Modeling-with-Power-BI-Second-Edition/blob/c946d376871675271055f4b778605691b786cb5c/Samples/AdventureWorksDW(xlsx)/AdventureWorksDW2017.xlsx`

Implementing aggregation at the Date level

In our sample file, we want to create an aggregate table from the **Internet Sales** table. The **Internet Sales** table contains 60,398 rows. We need to summarize the **Internet Sales** table at the **Date** level only. We name the new summary table **Internet Sales Aggregated**.

> We discussed *Summarization* in *Chapter 5, Common Data Preparation Steps*, in the *Group by* section. Therefore, we skip the data preparation prerequisites and jump straight to the summarization of the **Internet Sales** table.

Summarizing the Internet Sales table

To summarize the **Internet Sales** table at the **Date** level, we must use the **Group by** functionality in Power Query Editor. We want to aggregate the following columns while using a **SUM** or **COUNT** aggregation operation:

- **Order Quantity**: SUM
- **Sales**: SUM
- **Tax**: SUM
- **Freight Costs**: SUM
- **Internet Sales Count**: COUNT

These need to be grouped by the following key columns:

- OrderDateKey
- DueDateKey
- ShipDateKey

The following image shows the **Group By** step within Power Query Editor:

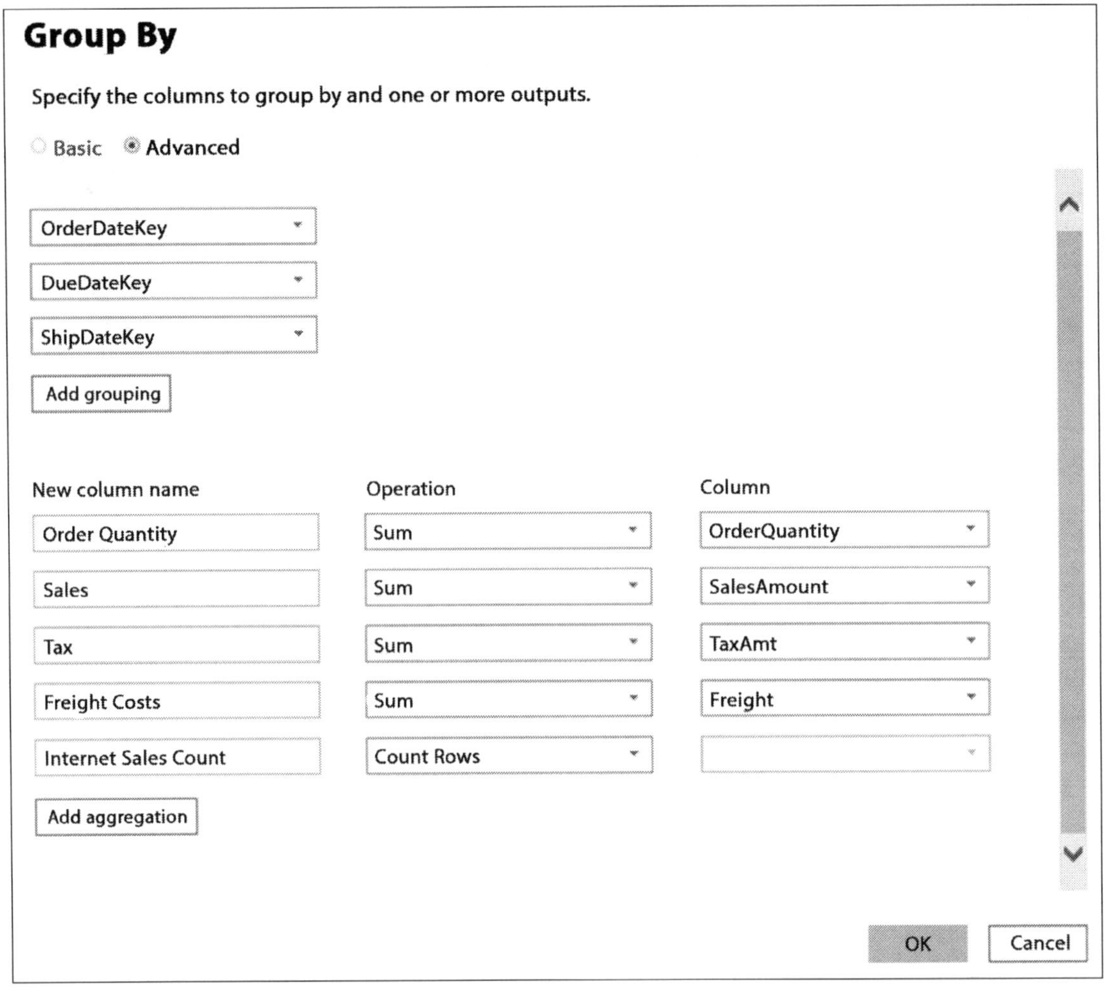

Figure 10.1: Summarizing Internet Sales in Power Query Editor with the Group By functionality

Now that we've summarized the **Internet Sales** table at the **Date** level (the new **Internet Sales Aggregated** table), we can close and apply the changes within Power Query Editor to load the data into the data model.

Creating relationships

At this point, we've loaded the data into the data model. The **Internet Sales Aggregated** table only contains **1,124** rows, which is significantly fewer than the **Internet Sales** table (the detail table). The following image shows the **Internet Sales Aggregated** table after being loaded into the data model:

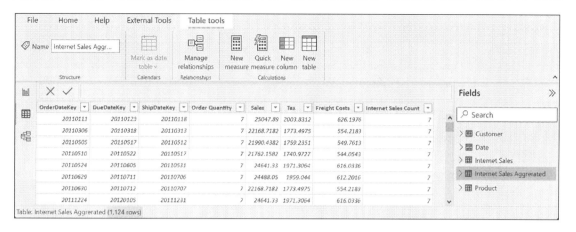

Figure 10.2: The Internet Sales Aggregated table

The next step is to create relationships between the new table and the **Date** table. The following image shows the relationships that have been created:

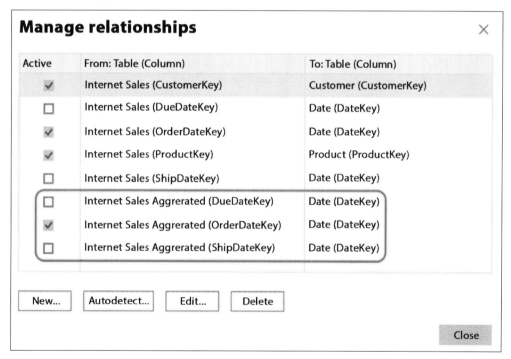

Figure 10.3: Relationships between the Internet Sales Aggregated table and the Date table

The next step is to create a new measure to calculate the **Sales** amount.

Creating new measures in the summary table

Now, it is time to create a new measure within the **Internet Sales Aggregated** table. To keep this scenario simple, we'll create one new measure that calculates the summation of the **Sales** column from the **Internet Sales Aggregated** table. The DAX expression for this is as follows:

```
Sales Agg = SUM('Internet Sales Aggregated'[Sales])
```

The **Sales Agg** measure calculates the sales amount. Remember, the **Internet Sales Aggregated** table is derived from the **Internet Sales** table. Therefore, the **Sales Agg** measure uses the same calculation as the **Internet Sales** measure from the **Internet Sales** table. Here is the DAX expression of the **Internet Sales** measure:

```
Internet Sales = SUM('Internet Sales'[SalesAmount])
```

The main differences between the **Sales Agg** measure and the **Internet Sales** measure are as follows:

- **Sales Agg** calculates the sales amount over a small table (**Internet Sales Aggregated**).
- **Internet Sales** calculates the same in a larger table (**Internet Sales**).
- As a result of the preceding points, the **Sales Agg** measure performs much better than **Internet Sales** when many concurrent users use the report.
- The users can filter the **Internet Sales** values by **Customer**, **Product**, and **Date**, but they can only filter the **Sales Agg** values by **Date**.

Now that we've created the **Sales Agg** measure, we are ready for the next step in our design: creating a new control measure to detect the level of grain selected by the user.

Creating control measures in the base table

This section explains how we create a new control measure to detect the user's selected grain. When a user is in **Date** level, the control measure uses the **Sales Agg** measure (from the summary table). However, if the user selects a column from either the **Product** or **Customer** tables, then the control measure uses the **Internet Sales** measure (from the detail table). We create the control measure in the **Internet Sales** table. We create the control measure in the detail table because we want to hide the summary table in the next step. When it comes to identifying the grain that's been selected by the user, we can use either the IF or SWITCH function to check certain conditions, along with one or a combination of the following DAX functions:

- ISFILTERED
- ISINSCOPE
- HASONEFILTER
- HASONEVALUE

The following DAX expression redirects the calculation to the Internet Sales measure if the user has selected a column from either the **Product** or the **Customer** table, otherwise, it runs the **Sales Agg** measure:

```
Internet Sales Total =
    IF(
```

```
    OR(ISFILTERED('Product'), ISFILTERED('Customer'))
    , [Internet Sales]
    , [Sales Agg]
)
```

Hiding the summary table

The last piece of the puzzle is to hide the **Internet Sales Aggregated** table and the **Internet Sales** measure within the **Internet Sales** table to avoid confusion for other content creators. The following figure shows the model after hiding the **Internet Sales Aggregated** table and the **Internet Sales** measure from the **Internet Sales** table:

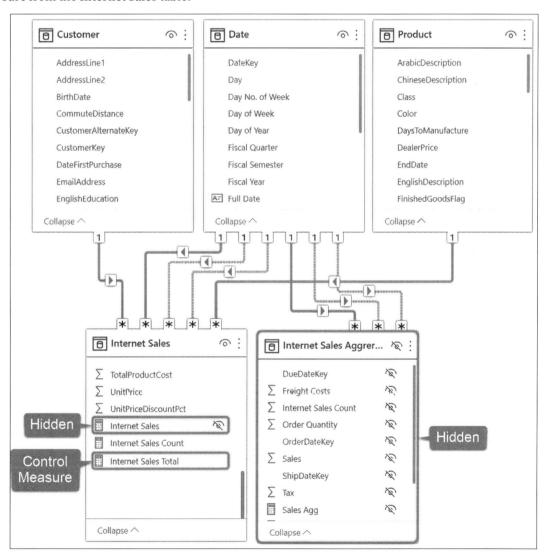

Figure 10.4: The data model after hiding the Internet Sales Aggregated table and the Internet Sales measure

We have everything sorted, so it is time to test the solution in the data visualization layer. We need to ensure that the **Internet Sales** measure and the **Internet Sales Total** measure always result in the same values. We also need to ensure that when the user selects any columns from either the **Product** table or the **Customer** table, the **Internet Sales Total** measure uses the base table (the **Internet Sales** table). In our example, we create a report page that shows the **Internet Sales** and **Internet Sales Total** measures side by side. The following image shows the report page:

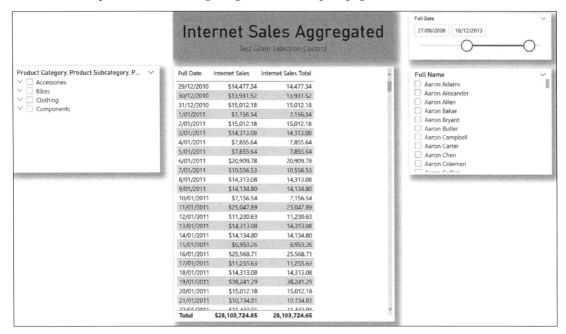

Figure 10.5: Testing the aggregation in data visualization

As the preceding image shows, we have a card visual at the top of the page showing the table used in the calculation within the table visual (in the middle of the report page). We used the following measure in the card visual:

```
Test Grain Selection Control =
    IF(
        OR(ISFILTERED('Product'), ISFILTERED('Customer'))
        , "Internet Sales"
        , "Internet Sales Aggregated"
    )
```

The preceding expression checks if the **Product** or **Customer** tables are filtered. If the result is TRUE, then the **Internet Sales** table is used; otherwise, the **Internet Sales Aggregated** table is used.

The following image shows the same report page when the user selects a **Product Category** from the slicer on the left-hand side of the report:

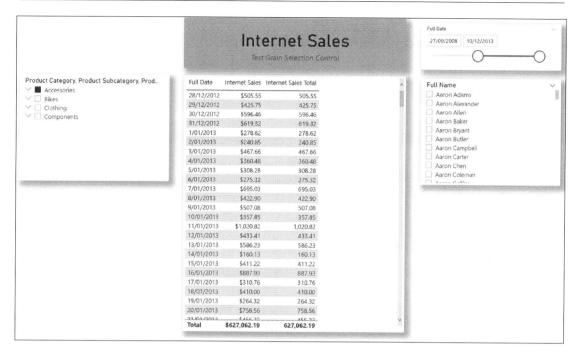

Figure 10.6: The test visuals after selecting a Product Category from the slicer

As the preceding image shows, the aggregation is working correctly.

So far, we've implemented a simple use case for implementing aggregations in Power BI Desktop. But there are many other use cases for aggregations. In the next section, we'll elevate the scenario's complexity.

Implementing aggregation at the Year and Month level

This time, we want to create another summary table that summarizes the **Internet Sales** table at the **Year** and **Month** granular levels based on the **OrderDateKey** column. We also want to include row counts of **Internet Sales** as an aggregated column. The steps for implementing this scenario are the same as in the previous scenario. The only difference is in the data preparation layer summarizing the **Internet Sales** data and changing the granularity of the data from **Date** to **Year** and **Month**. Let's have a closer look at the data preparation layer. To summarize the **Internet Sales** data at the **Year** and **Month** level, we need to aggregate the following columns (with the mentioned aggregation operation):

- Order Quantity: SUM
- Sales: SUM
- Tax: SUM
- Freight Costs: SUM
- Internet Sales Count: Count

Grouped by the following key column:

- OrderDateKey

It is critical to notice that we need to modify **OrderDateKey** so that it is at the **Year** and **Month** level. However, **OrderDateKey** is a number value, not a date value. The other point to note is that we need to create a relationship between the new summary table and the **Date** table using **OrderDateKey** from the summary table and **DateKey** from the **Date** table. Therefore, **OrderDateKey** must remain a number to match the values of the **DateKey** column from the **Date** table. To overcome this challenge, we use the following math:

```
New OrderDateKey = (CONVERT(Integer, ([OrderDateKey]/100)) * 100) + 1
```

The preceding math converts 20130209 into 20130201. You are right if you think **New OrderDateKey** is still at the day level. But we are changing all the dates to the first day of the month, which means when we aggregate the values by **New OrderDateKey**, we are indeed aggregating at the **Year** and **Month** level. So, we only need to replace the **OrderDateKey** values using the **New OrderDateKey** math.

Once we have removed all the unnecessary columns within Power Query Editor, we have to add a step to replace the values of **OrderDateKey** with the following expression:

```
Table.ReplaceValue(
        #"Removed Other Columns"
    ,   each [OrderDateKey]
    ,   each (Int64.From([OrderDateKey]/100) * 100) + 1
    ,   Replacer.ReplaceValue
    ,   {"OrderDateKey"}
)
```

The following image shows these Power Query steps:

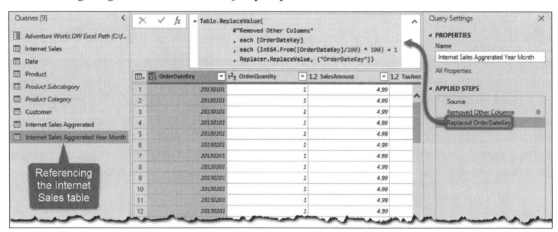

Figure 10.7: Replacing the OrderDateKey values

Chapter 10

The next step is to summarize the results. Remember, we also need to add **Count** of **Internet Sales** as an aggregation. The following image shows the **Group By** step resulting in our summary table:

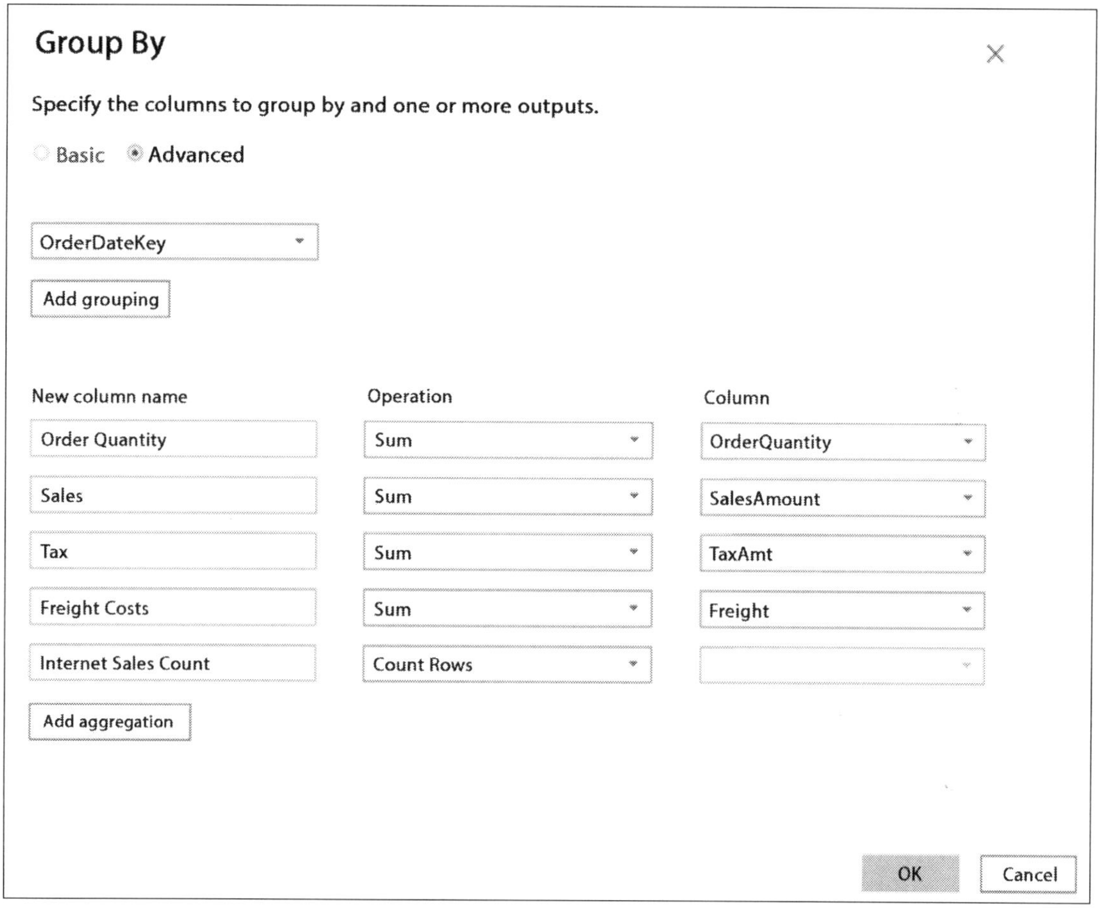

Figure 10.8: Summarizing the Internet Sales table at the Year and Month level

We can now apply the changes within the Power Query Editor window, which adds **Internet Sales Aggregated Year Month** as a new table. Moving forward with our implementation, we must create a relationship between the **Internet Sales Aggregated Year Month** table and the **Date** table. The following image shows the relationship once created:

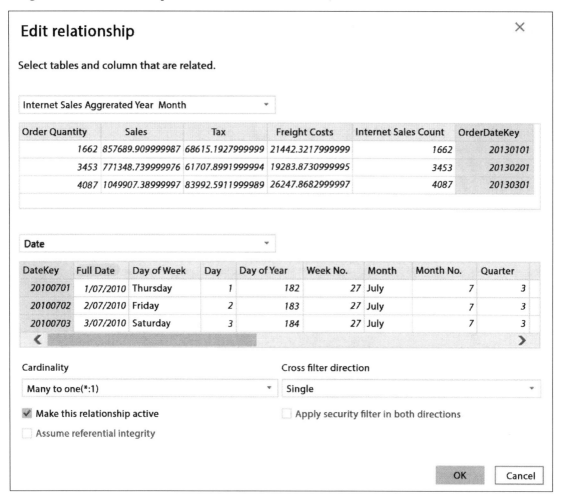

Figure 10.9: Creating a relationship between Internet Sales Aggregated Year Month and Date

We set the relationship's **Cardinality** to **Many to one** and **Cross-filter direction** to **Single**.

When we create the preceding relationship, Power BI automatically detects the relationship as one-to-one. Conceptually, this is correct. Each row of the **Internet Sales Aggregated Year Month** table occurs on the first day of each month related to only one row in the **Date** table. However, we need to change the relationship's cardinality from one-to-one to many-to-one to avoid filter propagation from the **Internet Sales Aggregated Year Month** table to the **Date** table.

The next step is to create a new measure using the following DAX expression in the **Internet Sales Aggregated Year Month** table:

```
Sales Year Month = SUM('Internet Sales Aggregated Year Month'[Sales])
```

Now, we need to create a new control measure to detect the level of detail the user selects, not only at the **Product** and **Customer** levels but also at the Date level in the **Internet Sales** table. The following DAX expression caters to this:

```
Internet Sales Agg =
    IF(
ISFILTERED('Product') ||
ISFILTERED('Customer') ||
ISFILTERED('Date'[Full Date])
        , [Internet Sales]
        , [Sales Year Month]
    )
```

Let us create a test measure that evaluates the IF() function in the preceding expression. The following DAX expression evaluates if either the **Product** and **Customer** tables or the **Full Date** column from the **Date** table are filtered, which results in "Internet Sales" (a text value); otherwise, the output is "Internet Sales Aggregated" (a text value). With the following test measure, we can get a better understanding of how the **Internet Sales Agg** measure works:

```
Internet Sales Agg Test =
    IF(
ISFILTERED('Product') ||
ISFILTERED('Customer') ||
ISFILTERED('Date'[Full Date])
        , "Internet Sales"
        , "Internet Sales Aggregated"
    )
```

The last bit is to test the aggregation on a report page. The following image shows the report page created to test the aggregation results before the user puts any filters on the **Product** or **Customer** tables:

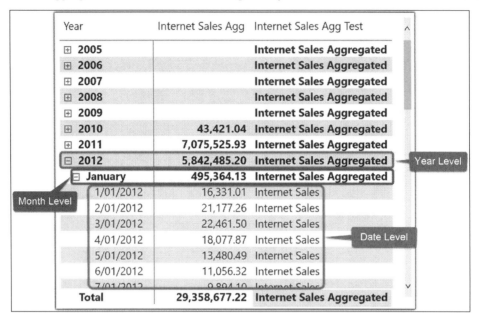

Figure 10.10: Testing the aggregation before filtering by the Product or Customer tables

Note the **Total** value for the **Internet Sales Agg Test** measure **shows Internet Sales Aggregated**. As the preceding image shows, if we do not filter by **Product** or **Customer**, the **Internet Sales Agg** measure calculates the results for the **Year** and **Month** levels. But at the **Date** level, the **Internet Sales** measure calculates the values.

This technique shows its value, especially when many concurrent users use the same report. However, we must be mindful of the following side effects:

- The summary tables will increase memory and storage consumption.
- The summary tables will also increase the data refresh time.
- The development time also increases as we need to create the summary table, create the relationships, and create the measures.

Now that we have implemented aggregations on top of non-DirectQuery data sources, it is time to look at the **Agg Awareness** feature.

Using Agg Awareness

User-defined aggregations or **Agg Awareness** is one of the most significant scalability and data modeling features that unlocks the usage of big data in Power BI. As we know, Power BI compresses and caches data into memory when the query connection mode is Import mode. Imagine a scenario in which we have a reasonably large data source containing billions of rows in an Azure Synapse server (formerly called Azure SQL Data Warehouse) and we want to create an enterprise-grade analytical solution in Power BI.

As stated before, Power BI has a storage limit, especially when we have either the Free or Pro licensing tiers. Even if we have Premium capacity, we are still limited to the amount of dedicated memory available in our Premium capacity. Of course, with Power BI Premium Gen 2, the memory limitation would be less of a concern. Still, if our data model is not designed well enough, the data processing and memory consumption will quickly become a bottleneck. This is where using aggregations comes to the rescue. As we explained in the previous sections, the **Agg Awareness** (**Manage aggregations**) feature is only available for the detail tables sourced from a data source supporting DirectQuery mode.

Supporting DirectQuery mode is a vital point when it comes to data modeling in Power BI Desktop. As discussed in *Chapter 4, Getting Data from Various Sources*, in the *Connection modes* section, when a query is in **Import** mode, we cannot switch it to either DirectQuery mode or **Dual** mode from Power BI Desktop. Therefore, we have to think about implementing aggregations at design time before we start implementing the data model; otherwise, we will end up creating the data model from scratch, which is not ideal.

We can implement aggregations in the following three different approaches. Depending on the data source, we decide which approach is the best fit:

- **Relationship-based aggregation**: In this approach, the data source hosting the detail table is in the Star Schema, so there are relationships between the fact and dimension tables. Therefore, we create relationships between the aggregation table and its dimensions.
- **GroupBy-based aggregation**: In this approach, the data source is big data models avoiding relationships between large tables, so the dimension attributes are denormalized in the fact table. In such scenarios, we implement aggregations using GroupBy columns.
- **Hybrid aggregation**: In this approach, regardless of the data sources' architecture, we denormalize some dimension attributes in the aggregation table. The aggregation table also has relationships with other dimensions. Therefore, we have a mixture of GroupBy and relationship-based aggregation in a single implementation.

With that in mind, the following steps explain the process of implementing user-defined aggregations in Power BI Desktop:

1. Create the aggregation table.
2. Load all the necessary tables in DirectQuery mode.
3. Create relationships between the aggregation table and the dimensions for the relationship-based and hybrid aggregations.
4. Set the storage model of the aggregation and its related dimensions.
5. Configure **Manage aggregation**.
6. Test the aggregation to make sure our queries hit the aggregation.

The preceding process may vary depending on our data platform architecture, but the principles remain the same.

Let us continue with a scenario. The AdventureWorks organization has an existing *Sales Analysis* solution in Power BI that doesn't perform well. The business complains that the automatic data refresh on the Power BI service constantly fails by getting a time-out error. The organization has a data warehouse in SQL Server named AdventureWorksDW2019. The existing solution in Power BI contains a large fact table, **FactInternetSales**, in DirectQuery mode. We want to implement a proof-of-concept to show how aggregations can boost performance. We use the **FactInternetSales** table with the following aggregations:

- **FactInternetSales** row count
- **SalesAmount**
- **OrderQuantity**
- **TaxAmount**
- **Freight**

We need the preceding aggregations at the **EnglishProductName**, **CalendarYear**, and **EnglishMonthName** levels. We also require the **DimCustomer** table for customer analysis to demonstrate the performance when the aggregation isn't hit by the queries.

To implement the proof-of-concept, we have to think about the aggregation approach that can meet the requirements. Let us go through it:

- Relationship-based aggregation: The business needs to analyze the aggregations at the year and month level. So, to implement the aggregation with the relationship-based approach, we need to create the aggregation table containing **ProductKey** and **DateKey** at the year and month level and all aggregation columns mentioned in the scenario. We also have to create an extra **Date** table containing the **DateKey** and other date attributes at the year and month levels. Then we create the relationship between the aggregation table, the new **Date** table, and the **DimProduct** table. It sounds a bit too much. So relationship-based aggregation is not a feasible approach.
- `GroupBy` aggregation: In this approach, we have to denormalize the **CalendarYear**, **EnglishMonthName**, and **EnglishProductName** attributes in the aggregation table, which is fine. We `GroupBy` the aggregation columns by these columns. But what if the user wants to analyze sales by a different product attribute? In that case, the aggregation table does not get hit, instead, the query runs against the detail table, which can lead to poor performance. Therefore, this approach is not feasible either.
- Hybrid aggregation: In this approach, we denormalize the **CalendarYear** and the **EnglishMonthName** attributes and use the **ProductKey** column in the aggregation table. So we `GroupBy` the aggregation columns by the **CalendarYear** and the **EnglishMonthName** attributes and use the **ProductKey** column to create a relationship between the aggregation table and the **DimProduct** table. This approach looks to be the most elegant one.

Now that we have selected the implementation approach, let us go ahead and develop the solution.

To use the AdventureWorksDW2019 SQL Server database as the source, we have to download the SQL Server backup file from Microsoft's website:

```
https://learn.microsoft.com/en-us/sql/samples/adventureworks-install-
configure?view=sql-server-ver15&WT.mc_id=DP-MVP-5003466
```

After downloading the database backup, we need to restore it in an instance of SQL Server. Learn how to restore the database backup here:

```
https://learn.microsoft.com/en-us/sql/samples/adventureworks-install-
configure?view=sql-server-ver15&tabs=ssms&WT.mc_id=DP-MVP-5003466#restore-to-sql-server
```

After restoring the database, we connect to it from Power BI Desktop.

Creating an aggregation table

Depending on our overall data platform architecture, we have a few options to create the aggregation table, as follows:

- Creating a database view or a table on the SQL Server side. This is the most flexible option as we can balance the query load between the cached data in Power BI and SQL Server. We will discuss this more in the *Implementing multiple aggregations* section of this chapter.
- Using a T-SQL statement when connecting to the SQL Server instance from Power Query. This option is also good but is not as flexible as the first one.
- Creating the aggregation table in Power Query Editor. While this is the least desirable option, the first two options are not feasible in some cases. It is best to ensure the query is fully folded.

> The aggregation table is like any other table that can be in **DirectQuery** or **Import** mode. Depending on the scenario and our data platform architecture, we must decide which storage mode to use. If we use DirectQuery mode, it is best to optimize the underlying table in the source database with **columnstore indexes**. Learn more about **columnstore indexes** here:
>
> https://learn.microsoft.com/en-us/sql/relational-databases/indexes/columnstore-indexes-overview?view=sql-server-ver16&WT.mc_id=DP-MVP-5003466
>
> It is important to note that the data types of the columns in the aggregation table must be the same as the corresponding column in the detail table; otherwise, we will not be able to configure the aggregation later.

We'll continue the implementation using the first method. We create the aggregation table as a database view on the SQL Server side using the following T-SQL scripts:

```
CREATE VIEW vw_Sales_Agg AS
SELECT dp.ProductKey
     , dd.CalendarYear
     , dd.EnglishMonthName
     , COUNT(1) Sales_Count
     , SUM(fis.SalesAmount)    AS Sales_Sum
```

```
              , SUM(fis.OrderQuantity) AS OrderQty_Sum
              , SUM(fis.TaxAmt)         AS Tax_Sum
              , SUM(fis.Freight)        AS Freight_Sum
    FROM    FactInternetSales fis
            LEFT JOIN DimDate dd
                ON dd.DateKey = fis.OrderDateKey
            LEFT JOIN DimProduct dp
                ON fis.ProductKey = dp.ProductKey
    GROUP BY dp.ProductKey
              , dd.CalendarYear
              , dd.EnglishMonthName
```

We can now use the preceding database view in Power BI Desktop.

Loading tables in DirectQuery mode

Use Power BI Desktop to connect to the SQL Server instance and get the following tables in DirectQuery mode:

- DimDate
- DimProduct
- DimCustomer
- FactInternetSales
- vw_Sales_Agg

Follow these steps to do so:

1. Use the SQL Server connection to connect to your instance of SQL Server:

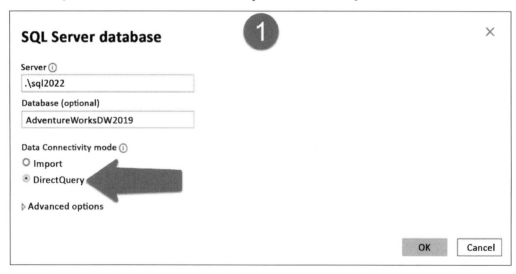

Figure 10.11: Connecting to a SQL Server database in DirectQuery mode

2. Connect to the following tables in DirectQuery mode:
   - **DimDate**
   - **DimCustomer**
   - **DimProduct**
   - **FactInternetSales**
   - **vw_Sales_Agg**

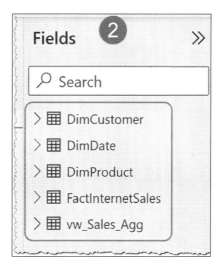

Figure 10.12: Tables loaded in DirectQuery mode

3. Rename **vw_Sales_Agg** to **Sales_Agg**:

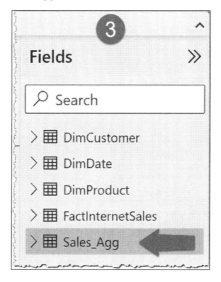

Figure 10.13: Renaming vw_Sales_Agg to Sales_Agg

Creating relationships

Now that we have all tables, we create the relationships between the aggregation table and all the necessary dimensions. In our scenario, we create the relationship between the **Sales_Agg** and **Dim-Product** tables via the **ProductKey** column as follows:

1. Create relationships between the tables:

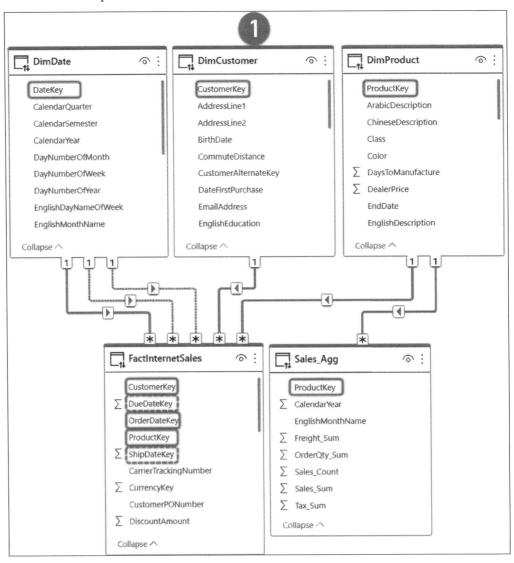

Figure 10.14: Creating relationships in the Model view

Setting the aggregation table and its related dimensions' storage mode

As mentioned earlier, we have to decide to set the aggregation table's storage mode based on our overall data platform architecture. In our scenario, we want to cache the aggregation table in the data model. Therefore, we set the storage mode of the aggregation table to **Import**. By changing the storage mode of the aggregation table to **Import** mode, we get a warning message stating that the storage mode of all related tables must switch to **Dual** mode. We have the option to do it at the same time or later.

1. Change the storage mode of the **Sales_Agg** table to **Import**. Check the **Set the affected tables to dual** option to set the **DimProduct** to **Dual** mode.

   The following image shows the preceding step:

   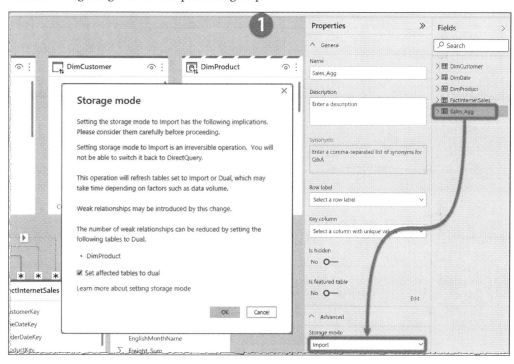

   Figure 10.15: Setting the aggregation table's storage mode to Import

The reason that we change the aggregation table's storage mode to **Import** mode is that we want the queries reaching the aggregation table to run from the cached data that is imported to the model and is available to the xVelocity engine, so the queries are resolved internally. But why must the **DimProduct** be in **Dual** storage mode? The following image shows a simple use case.

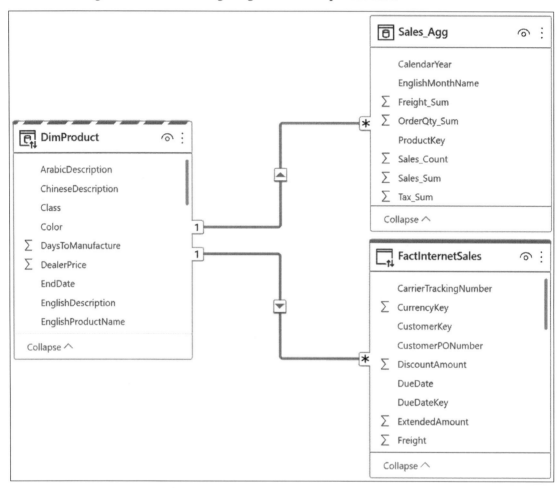

Figure 10.16: Explaining the reason that the DimProduct storage mode is Dual

As the preceding image shows **DimProduct** relates to both **FactInternetSales** and **Sales_Agg** tables. The **FactInternetSale** table is the detail table containing the most granular level of data. So, we set its storage mode to DirectQuery. As explained earlier, we set the **Sales_Agg** storage mode to **Import**. The **DimProduct** table has a one-to-many relationship to the **FactInternetSales** and the **Sales_Agg** table. The interesting point is that both relationships are regular. In the *Dealing with many-to-many relationships* section of *Chapter 9, Star Schema and Data Modeling Common Best Practices*, we discussed the differences between **regular** and **limited** (**weak**) relationships.

Chapter 10

We learned that both tables must have the same storage mode to keep the relationship **regular**; therefore, the **DimProduct** and **FactInternetSales** tables must have the same storage mode. We need to keep the **FactInternetSales** in DirectQuery mode, so the **DimProduct** table must also be in DirectQuery mode. But the **DimProduct** table also has a relationship with the **Sales_Agg** table, and the **Sales_Agg** table's storage is in **Import** mode. Therefore, the only way to avoid limited relationships in the preceding use case is to set the **DimProduct** storage mode to **Dual** mode.

Let us continue implementing the aggregation.

Managing aggregation

Now that we have all the prerequisites, it is time to configure the aggregation table. Follow these steps:

1. Right-click the **Sales_Agg** table and click **Manage aggregations**:

Figure 10.17: Manage aggregations on the Sales_Agg table

2. In the **Manage aggregations** window, do the following:

    a. Ensure that the **Sales_Agg** table is selected in **Aggregation table**.
    b. Leave **Precedence** set to 0.
    c. Set **SUMMARIZATION** for the **Sales_Agg** columns.

d. Click **Apply all**:

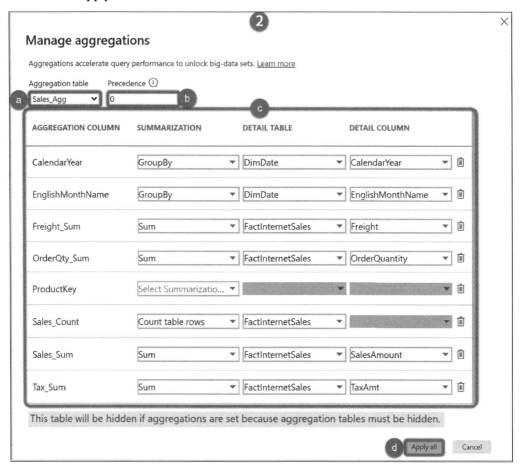

Figure 10.18: Manage aggregations

 When managing the aggregations with the relationship-based aggregation approach, we do not need to set **SUMMARIZATION** for the related columns. Therefore, in our scenario, we do not set **SUMMARIZATION** for **ProductKey**.

After applying the aggregation, the **Sales_Agg** table is hidden.

Switch to the **Model** view to review the data model. The following image shows the data model after managing the aggregation:

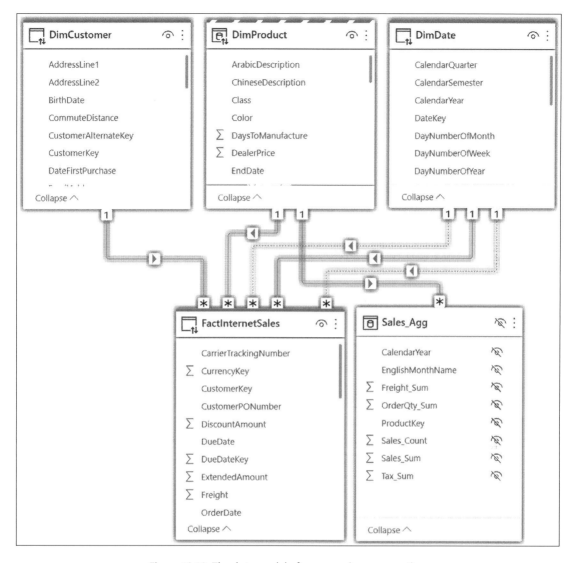

Figure 10.19: The data model after managing aggregations

Here is what we have in the data model after managing aggregations:

- The **FactInternetSales**, **DimCustomer**, and **DimProduct** tables are in **DirectQuery** mode. Note the icon used at the top left of the tables (icon).
- The **DimProduct** table is in **Dual** mode (icon).
- The **Sales_Agg** table is hidden and is in **Import** mode (icon).

Now that we have successfully configured the aggregation from the **FactInternetSales** table, it is time to test it to ensure that the calculations happen on the aggregation table when the queries are at the **Product**, **Year**, or **Month** levels.

Save the report as Chapter 10, User-defined Aggregations (Agg Awareness).pbix.

Testing the aggregation

We have the following options to test the aggregation:

- Performance Analyzer in Power BI Desktop
- DAX Studio
- SQL Server Profiler

The next few sections explain how to use the preceding tools to test the aggregation.

Performance Analyzer

We all know we can create interactive and sophisticated reports in Power BI. Each visual used on a report page generates a query in the background. We can use Performance Analyzer in Power BI Desktop to identify whether the visual's underlying queries hit the aggregation table. Create the following measures in the detail table (**FactInternetSales**):

```
Internet Sales = SUM(FactInternetSales[SalesAmount])

Internet Sales Due =
    CALCULATE(
        [Internet Sales]
        , USERELATIONSHIP(FactInternetSales[DueDateKey], DimDate[DateKey])
        )
```

Follow these steps:

1. From the **Optimize** tab on the ribbon, click **Performance Analyzer**.
2. On the **Performance Analyzer** pane, click the **Start recording** button.
3. Put a **Card** visual on the report canvas and use the **Internet Sales** measure.
4. This adds a **Card** section in the **Performance Analyzer** pane. Expand the **Card** section.

The following image shows the preceding steps:

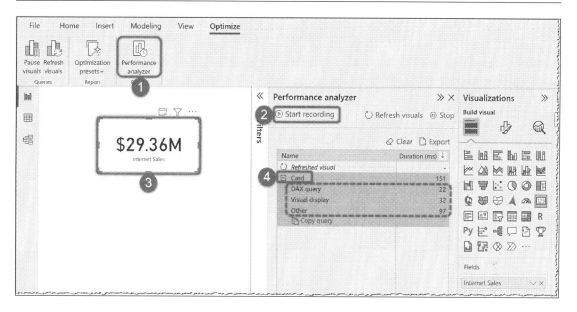

Figure 10.20: Performance Analyzer's results for the Internet Sales Card visual

As the preceding image shows, the results do not include a **Direct query** section, which indicates that the underlying query hit the aggregation table.

Let us add another **Card** visual, use the **Internet Sales Due** measure, and look at the results in Performance Analyzer again. The following image shows the results:

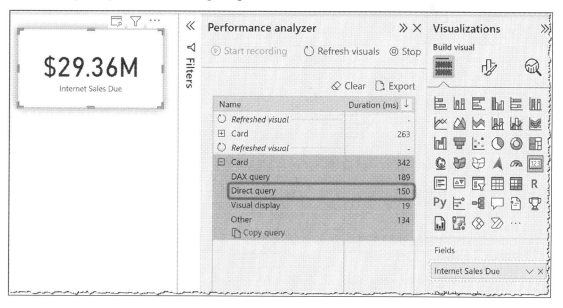

Figure 10.21: Performance Analyzer's results for the Internet Sales Due Card visual

As you can see, this time, the results include a **Direct query** section, taking 150 milliseconds to complete, which means the query did not hit the aggregation table; instead, it reached the detail table, which is in **DirectQuery** mode. The reason for that is the **Internet Sales Due** measure uses the inactive relationship between the **FactInternetSales** and the **DimDate** tables via the **DueDateKey** from the **FactInternetSales** and the **DateKey** from the **DimDate**. Therefore, the underlying query does not hit the aggregation table.

Let us test another scenario:

1. Put a **Table** visual on the report page
2. Put the **EnglishProductName** from the **DimProduct** on the **Table** visual
3. Put the `Internet Sales` measure on the **Table**
4. Expand the **Table** section on the **Performance Analyzer** pane

The following image shows that the underlying query hits the aggregation table as the **Direct query** section does not exist in the Performance Analyzer's results:

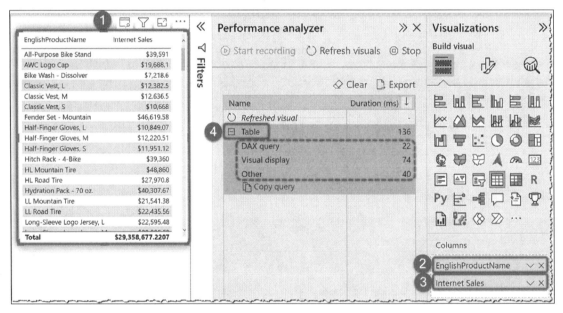

Figure 10.22: Performance Analyzer's results for the Table visual

The next test is an interesting one. We want to see whether, if we use the **CalendarYear** and **EnglishMonthName** columns and the **Internet Sales** measure on a **Matrix** visual, the underlying query hits the aggregation table. Follow these steps:

1. Put a **Matrix** visual on the report page.
2. Select **CalendarYear** under **Rows**.
3. Select the **Internet Sales** measure under **Values**.
4. Expand the **Matrix** section on the Performance Analyzer and observe the results.

The following image shows the preceding steps and the results:

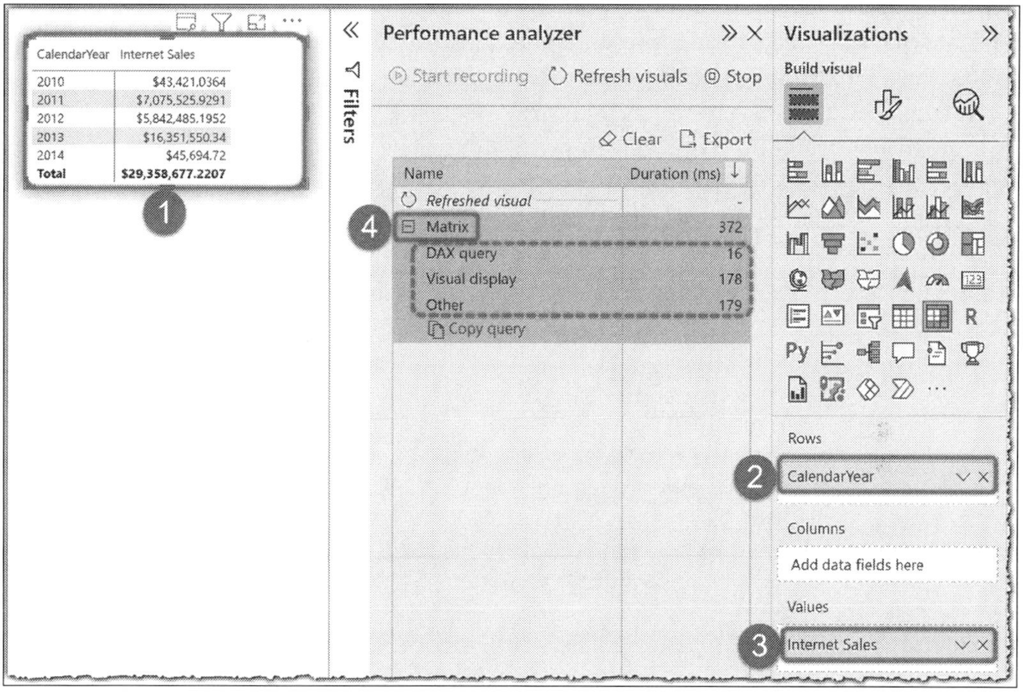

Figure 10.23: Performance Analyzer's results for the Matrix visual

So, the **Matrix** query hits the aggregation, which is what we expect.

5. Select **EnglishMonthName** under **Columns**.
6. Expand the new **Matrix** section on the Performance Analyzer to see the results.

The following image shows the new results:

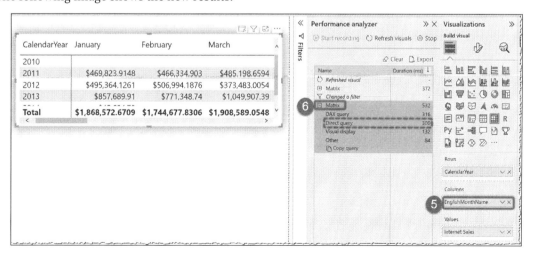

Figure 10.24: Performance Analyzer's new results for the Matrix visual

As the results show, this time the query did not hit the aggregation table. But why? We used the **EnglishMonthName** column in the aggregation. Why doesn't the underlying query hit the aggregation? The reason is that the **EnglishMonthName** column is sorted by the **MonthNumberOfYear** column. So, we need to include the **MonthNumberOfYear** column in the aggregation table as well. To do so, we need to modify the SQL view we created earlier to include the **MonthNumberOfYear** column. Then we have to refresh the **DimDate** table to get the newly added column. Lastly, we manage the aggregation again to add the **MonthNumberOfYear** column to the **GroupBy**. We'll leave those steps for you to complete. The following image shows the Performance Analyzer's results after making the changes:

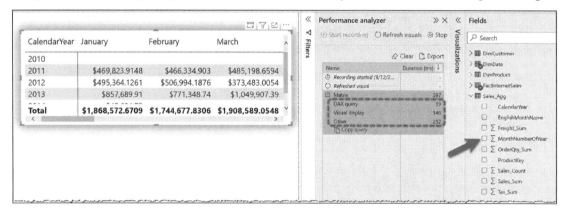

Figure 10.25: Performance Analyzer's results after modifying the aggregation table

 The **Sales_Agg** table is hidden, so to make it visible in the **Report** view, we right-click the table and tick the **View hidden** option.

In this section, we learned how to use Performance Analyzer to indicate if the visuals' queries hit the aggregation table. While using Performance Analyzer is very handy, we cannot use it in more advanced scenarios, such as identifying which aggregation table is hit when we have multiple aggregations in the data model.

In the next section, we'll learn how to use DAX Studio.

DAX Studio

Undoubtedly, DAX Studio is among the most renowned third-party tools used by many Power BI and tabular model developers. It is a free and open-source tool by the SQLBI team. We can download it from its official website: https://daxstudio.org/downloads/. We can use DAX Studio on many occasions. In this section, we'll learn how to use it to indicate the visuals' queries hit the aggregation table. After installing DAX Studio, it appears in the **External Tools** tab on the ribbon in Power BI Desktop.

We'll use the report file built in the previous section. Follow these steps to see how to use DAX Studio to test the aggregation:

Chapter 10

1. Open **Performance Analyzer** again if you closed it and click **Start recording**.
2. Click **DAX Studio** from the **External Tools** tab on the ribbon.
3. In DAX Studio, click the **All Queries** button.
4. Click the **All Queries** tab on the bottom pane.
5. Hover over the **Matrix** visual in Power BI Desktop and click the **Analyze this visual** button that appears.
6. Switch to DAX Studio and look at the **All queries** tab. If you see a black bullet on the right side of the query, then the query hits the aggregation table. If the bullet is white, then it's a miss. We can hover over the bullet to show the tooltip explaining the results.

The following image shows the preceding steps and the results:

Figure 10.26: Using DAX Studio to test the aggregation

In the next section, we'll learn how to use SQL Server Profiler to test the aggregation.

SQL Server Profiler

For those who come from an SQL development or SQL Server administration background, SQL Server Profiler will not be new. We can use it for profiling and monitoring purposes when working with a SQL Server instance, including the database engine, SSAS Tabular, and SSAS Multidimensional. Since Power BI Desktop runs a local instance of the SSAS Tabular model, we can monitor the data model using **SQL Server Profiler** connected to Power BI Desktop. **SQL Server Profiler** is a part of the **SQL Server Management Studio** (**SSMS**) installation package.

You can read more about **SQL Server Profiler** here:

https://learn.microsoft.com/en-us/sql/tools/sql-server-profiler/sql-server-profiler?view=sql-server-ver15&WT.mc_id=DP-MVP-5003466.

We have the following two options for using **SQL Server Profiler:**

- We can register **SQL Server Profiler** as an external tool. Here, we can open **SQL Server Profiler** directly from Power BI Desktop from the **External Tools** tab. With this method, **SQL Server Profiler** automatically connects to our Power BI data model via the **Power BI Diagnostic Port.**

    Read more about registering **SQL Server Profiler** in Power BI Desktop as an external tool here:

    https://www.biinsight.com/quick-tips-registering-sql-server-profiler-as-an-external-tool/

- We can open **SQL Server Profiler** and manually connect to our Power BI data model through the Power BI Desktop Diagnostic Port. To do so, we must find the Diagnostic Port number first, then connect to the data model using the port number.

    Learn more about the different ways to find the Power BI Desktop diagnostic port here:

    https://www.biinsight.com/four-different-ways-to-find-your-power-bi-desktop-local-port-number/

We'll use the first option as it is simpler than the second option. We have to trace the following events within SQL Server Profiler.

If we're using SSMS v17.9 (or later), then we must select the following events:

- **Query Processing\Aggregate Table Rewrite Query**
- **Query Processing\Direct Query Begin**
- **Query Processing\Vertipaq SE Query Begin**

For older versions of SSMS, we must select the following events:

- **Queries Events\Query Begin**
- **Query Processing\DirectQuery Begin**
- **Query Processing\Vertipaq SE Query Begin**

In this section, we'll use the first option. Follow these steps to test the aggregation with SQL Server Profiler:

1. Open **Performance Analyzer** again if you closed it and click **Start recording**
2. Click **SQL Server Profiler** from the **External Tools** tab

3. Click the **Stop** button to stop the current trace
4. Click the **Properties** button to open the **Trace Properties** window
5. Click the **Events Selection** tab
6. Tick the **Show all events** and **Show all columns** options
7. Select the events we mentioned earlier in the **Query Processing** section and deselect all other events
8. Click **Run**
9. Go to Power BI Desktop, hover over the **Matrix** visual, and click the **Analyze this visual** button
10. Switch back to **SQL Server Profiler** and click the **Aggregate Table Rewrite Query** event

The following image shows the preceding steps:

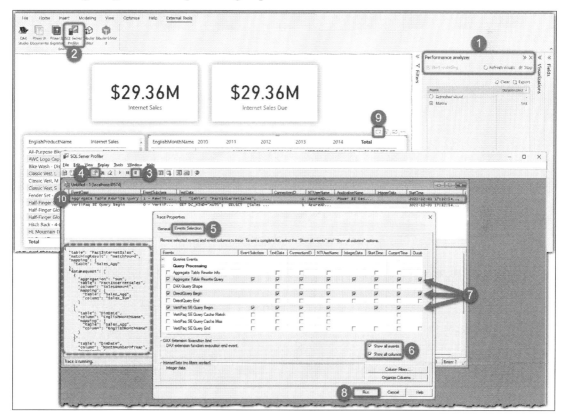

Figure 10.27: Using SQL Server Profiler to test the aggregation

The results are highlighted with dotted lines in the preceding image, revealing much information about the aggregation, as follows:

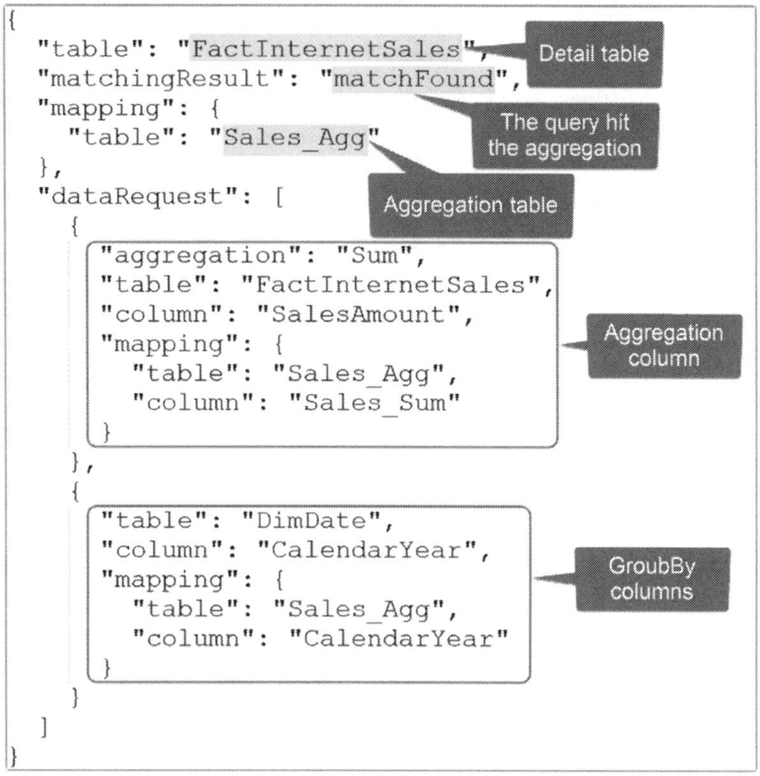

```
{
  "table": "FactInternetSales",            Detail table
  "matchingResult": "matchFound",
  "mapping": {                              The query hit
    "table": "Sales_Agg"                    the aggregation
  },
  "dataRequest": [                          Aggregation table
    {
      "aggregation": "Sum",
      "table": "FactInternetSales",
      "column": "SalesAmount",
      "mapping": {                          Aggregation
        "table": "Sales_Agg",               column
        "column": "Sales_Sum"
      }
    },
    {
      "table": "DimDate",
      "column": "CalendarYear",             GroubBy
      "mapping": {                          columns
        "table": "Sales_Agg",
        "column": "CalendarYear"
      }
    }
  ]
}
```

Figure 10.28: SQL Server Profiler results of testing the aggregation

In the next section, we'll learn how multiple aggregations work and how to implement them.

Implementing multiple aggregations

We learned how to implement user-defined aggregations in the previous section. In this section, we'll take one step further and implement multiple aggregations. The multiple aggregations' implementation is when the detail table is summarized in different aggregation tables. In other words, we create multiple aggregation tables containing the data in different grains. For example, we aggregated the data at the **Year** and **Month** levels in one aggregation table in our previous scenario. Let us expand the scenario and implement another aggregation table keeping the data at the **Year** level. We'll name the new aggregation table **Sales_AggYear**.

So, we expect the queries to hit the **Sales_AggYear** table when we are at the **Year** level and hit the **Sales_Agg** when we are at the **Year** and **Month** level. To implement this scenario, we must go through all the previous steps to implement the aggregation with a small difference. This time, we have to set the value of the **Precedence** option when managing the aggregation. The **Precedence** value tells the engine to consider other aggregation tables. The larger the number, the higher the priority. So, when there are two aggregation tables with 0 and 10 for the precedence values, the engine considers the aggregation table with the higher precedence first. In other words, the xVelocity engine tries to solve the underlying aggregation queries based on their **Precedence** value. We'll use the report file previously created (Chapter 10, User-defined Aggregations (Agg Awareness).pbix). We'll leave the summarization at the **Year** level to you and jump straight to the aggregation implementation. The following image shows the configuration in the **Manage aggregations** window:

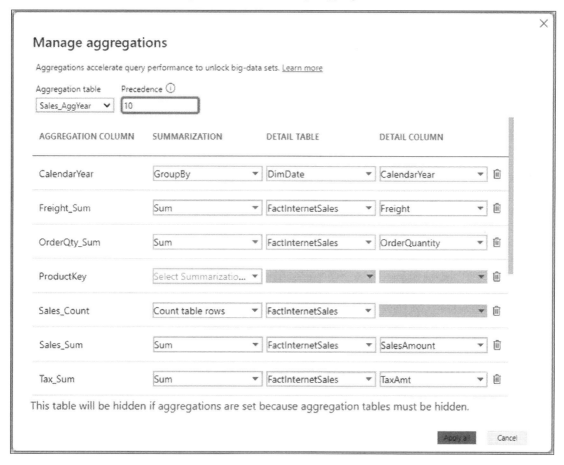

Figure 10.29: Setting the Precedence option of Manage aggregations

Now we'll test the solution using SQL Server Profiler. The following image shows the results of refreshing the table visual (**EnglishProductName** by **Internet Sales**):

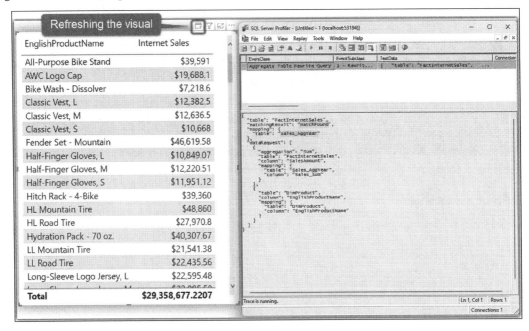

Figure 10.30: Testing multiple aggregations hitting the Sales_AggYear

As the preceding image shows, the visual's query hit the **Sales_AggYear** table instead of the **Sales_Agg**, which is exactly what we expected. In another test, we'll use **CalendarYear** and **EnglishMonthName** in the **Rows** property of a **Matrix** visual and the **Internet Sales** measure for **Values**. The following image shows the results when we are at the **Year** level:

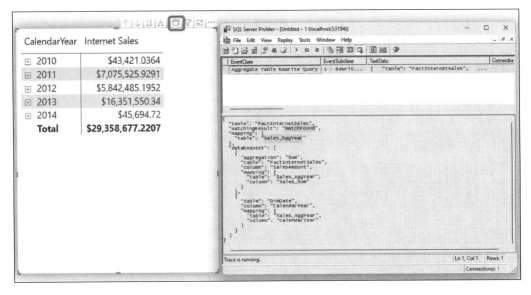

Figure 10.31: Testing multiple aggregations at the Year level hitting the Sales_AggYear

As the preceding image shows, the query hits the **Sales_AggYear** table, which is perfect. Next, we'll drill down to the **Month** level. The following image shows the results:

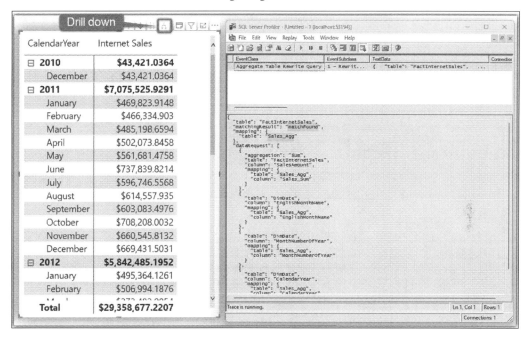

Figure 10.32: Multiple aggregations at the Year and Month levels hitting the Sales_Agg

As the preceding image shows, when we drill down to the **Month** level, the query hits the **Sales_Agg** table. So, we successfully implemented multiple aggregations.

The next section raises some crucial points to note when implementing user-defined aggregations.

Important notes about aggregations

When implementing aggregations, pay attention to the following points:

- The detail table (base table) must be in DirectQuery mode.
- The data types of the aggregation columns from the aggregation table and the corresponding columns from the detail table must be the same; otherwise, we cannot complete the **Manage aggregations**.
- Chained aggregations are not allowed. For example, we cannot create aggregations on Table X when it is the aggregation table for Table Y.
- While configuring the **Manage aggregations** window, we should set **SUMMARIZATION** for each aggregation column. Use the **Count table** rows for the aggregations showing the count rows of the detail table.
- By default, the aggregation tables are hidden.
- Always create measures in the detail table, not in the aggregation table.
- We do not need to **Group By** the aggregation columns from a table with an active relationship with the aggregation table.

- Aggregation for inactive relationships is not supported, even if we use the USERELATIONSHIP() function to activate the relationship.
- User-defined aggregations do not support Dynamic M Query Parameters.
- Power BI ignores aggregation tables with the **Import storage** mode sourced from an SSO-enabled data source for security reasons.

In this section, we discussed various aspects of implementing aggregations in Power BI. The next section focuses on another crucial topic when dealing with large amounts of data in Power BI: incremental refresh and hybrid tables.

Incremental refresh and hybrid tables

Incremental refresh or incremental data loading is a renowned technique for controlling how the data loads into a data store, so we keep the existing data and only load the changes. Let us look at it in more detail.

From a technical standpoint in data movement, there are always two options to transfer the data from location A to location B:

- **Truncation and load**: Transferring the entire data from location A to location B by truncating location B and reloading the entire data from location A to B.
- **Incremental load**: Transferring the data from location A to location B only the first time. The next time, we only load the data changes from A to B. In this approach, we never truncate B. Instead, we only transfer the data that exists in A but not in B.

Incremental refresh detects updated data as deleting the old data and inserting new data.

When we refresh the data in Power BI, if we have not configured an incremental refresh, Power BI uses the first approach, truncation and load. Needless to say, in Power BI, any of the preceding data refresh methods only apply to tables with **Import storage** mode.

Once we've successfully configured the incremental refresh policies in Power BI, depending on our licensing, we have the following three ranges of data:

- The historical range
- The incremental range
- The real-time range

The **historical range** includes all the data that has been processed in the past. Its storage mode is **Import**. The **incremental range** is the current range of data to process. The storage mode of the incremental range is also **Import**. The **real-time range**, as the name resembles, is about capturing the data changes of the source system in Power BI in real time. The storage mode in the real-time range is **DirectQuery**.

Incremental refresh in Power BI always looks for data changes in the **incremental range**, not the **historical range**. Therefore, changes in historical data will not be noticed. As stated earlier, our licensing plan dictates the supported data ranges. We can implement and publish incremental refresh policies excluding the real-time ranges in all licensing plans currently available. The real-time ranges are only available in Premium licenses. After implementing the incremental refresh and publishing the model into the Power BI service, and after refreshing the dataset for the first time, Power BI creates some partitions for the incremental refresh-enabled tables. Based on our incremental refresh configuration on a table, its partitions fall into one of the preceding data ranges as follows:

- Archived partitions represent the historical range
- Incremental partitions represent the incremental range
- Real-time partitions represent the real-time range

The table containing the real-time partition is a **Hybrid Table**, as it stores the archived and incremental partitions in **Import** mode while supporting a real-time partition in **DirectQuery** mode.

Configuring incremental refresh is beneficial for large tables. The following are some benefits of incremental refresh in Power BI:

- The data refreshes much faster because we only transfer the changes, not the entire data
- The data refresh process is less resource-intensive than refreshing the entire data all the time
- The data refresh process is less expensive and more maintainable than non-incremental refreshes over large tables
- On top of the preceding benefits, Hybrid Tables provide real-time data on large tables, which is exceptional

Incremental refresh is inevitable when dealing with massive datasets with billions of rows that do not fit into our data model in Power BI Desktop. Now that we understand incremental refresh and hybrid tables, let's implement them in Power BI.

Configuring incremental refresh policy and hybrid table in Power BI Desktop

We use Power BI Desktop to configure incremental refresh. Once we publish the model into the Power BI service, the first data refresh transfers all data from the data source(s) to the Power BI service. Therefore, the first refresh takes longer. Any future data refreshes are incremental. Configuring incremental refresh in Power BI Desktop is simple. The following steps explain the process:

1. First, we must define two **DateTime** parameters in Power Query Editor, **RangeStart** and **RangeEnd**, which are reserved for defining incremental refresh policies.

Power Query is case sensitive, so the names of the parameters must be **RangeStart** and **RangeEnd**.

2. The next step is to filter the data on either an **Int64** (integer) or **DateTime** column using the **RangeStart** and **RangeEnd** parameters when the value of the **DateTime** column is between **RangeStart** and **RangeEnd**. Therefore, for scenarios where our table has a **Smart Date Key** column instead of **DateTime**, we have to convert the **RangeStart** and **RangeEnd** parameters to **Int64**. The **Int64** or **DateTime** values must have an equal to (=) sign either on **RangeStart** or **RangeEnd**, not both.

A **Smart Date Key** is an integer representation of date values. Using a smart date key is very common in data warehousing to save storage and memory. So, the **20200809** integer value represents the **2020/08/09** date value. Therefore, if the data source is a data warehouse, it will likely have smart date keys in the fact tables instead of dates. For those scenarios, we can use the `Int64.From(DateTime.ToText(RangeStart OR RangeEnd, "yyyyMMdd"))` Power Query expression to generate smart date keys from the query parameters' **DateTime** values.

3. Then we load the data into the data model and configure the incremental refresh. If we have a Premium license, we can configure real-time data processing. In that case, the last partition of data is set to DirectQuery mode.
4. We publish the model to the Power BI service. After publishing and refreshing the dataset for the first time, Power BI creates the partitions.

With the preceding conditions in mind, let's implement incremental refresh with a scenario. In this section, we'll use the `Chapter 10, Incremental Refresh.pbix` sample file. Its data source is the **AdventureWorksDW2019** SQL Server database. We want to refresh the data with the following conditions:

- Archiving ten years of data
- Incrementally refreshing one month of data
- Capturing the last month of real-time data

The sample file is available on GitHub:

`https://github.com/PacktPublishing/Expert-Data-Modeling-with-Power-BI-Second-Edition/blob/c946d376871675271055f4b778605691b786cb5c/Samples/Chapter%2010/Chapter%2010%2C%20Incremental%20Refresh.pbix`

Follow these steps to implement the preceding scenario:

1. In **Power Query Editor**, get the **FactInternetSales** table from **AdventureWorksDW2019** from SQL Server and rename it **Internet Sales**:

Figure 10.33: Getting data from the source

2. Define the **RangeStart** and **RangeEnd** parameters with the **Date/Time** type. As mentioned earlier, **RangeStart** and **RangeEnd** are reserved for configuring incremental refresh. So, the parameter names must match the preceding names. Set **Current Value** for the parameters as follows:

   - Current Value of RangeStart: 1/12/2010 12:00:00 AM
   - Current Value of RangeEnd. 31/12/2010 12:00:00 AM

   Set a **Current Value** setting for the parameters that works for your scenario. Remember that these values are only useful at development time as the **Internet Sales** table will only include the values between the **Current Value** setting of **RangeStart** and **RangeEnd** after defining the filter in the next steps. In our scenario, **Current Value** for **RangeStart** is the first day of the month for the first transaction. The first transaction in **Internet Sales** for the **OrderDate** column is 29/12/2010. Therefore, **Current Value** for **RangeStart** is 1/12/2010, and **RangeEnd** is 31/12/2010.

Figure 10.34: Defining the RangeStart and RangeEnd parameters

3. Filter the **OrderDate** column, as shown in the following image:

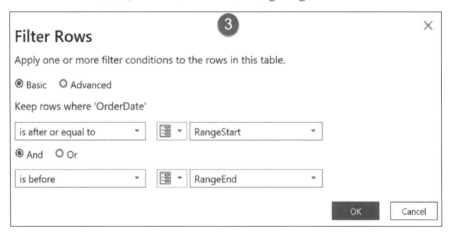

Figure 35: Filtering the OrderDate column by the RangeStart and RangeEnd parameters

4. Click the **Close & Apply** button to import the data into the data model:

Chapter 10

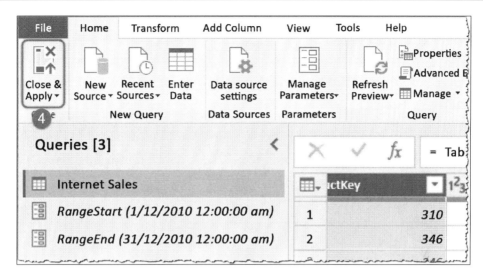

Figure 10.36: Applying changes and loading data into the data model

5. Right-click the **Internet Sales** table and click **Incremental refresh**. The **Incremental refresh** option is available in the context menu of the **Report** view, **Data** view, or **Model** view:

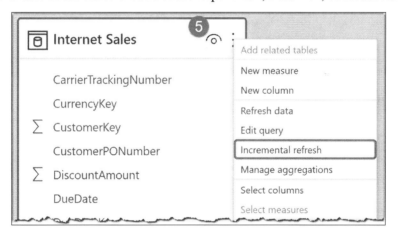

Figure 10.37: Selecting Incremental refresh from the context menu

6. In the **Incremental refresh** window, do the following:

   a. Toggle on **Incrementally refresh this table**
   b. Set the **Archive data starting** setting to **10 Years before refresh date**
   c. Set the **Incrementally refresh data starting** setting to **1 Months before refresh date**
   d. Check **Get the latest data in real time with DirectQuery (Premium only)**
   e. Since we ticked the real-time option, the **Only refresh complete month** option is ticked and disabled
   f. Leave the **Detect data changes** option unchecked
   g. Click **Apply**

The following image shows the preceding steps:

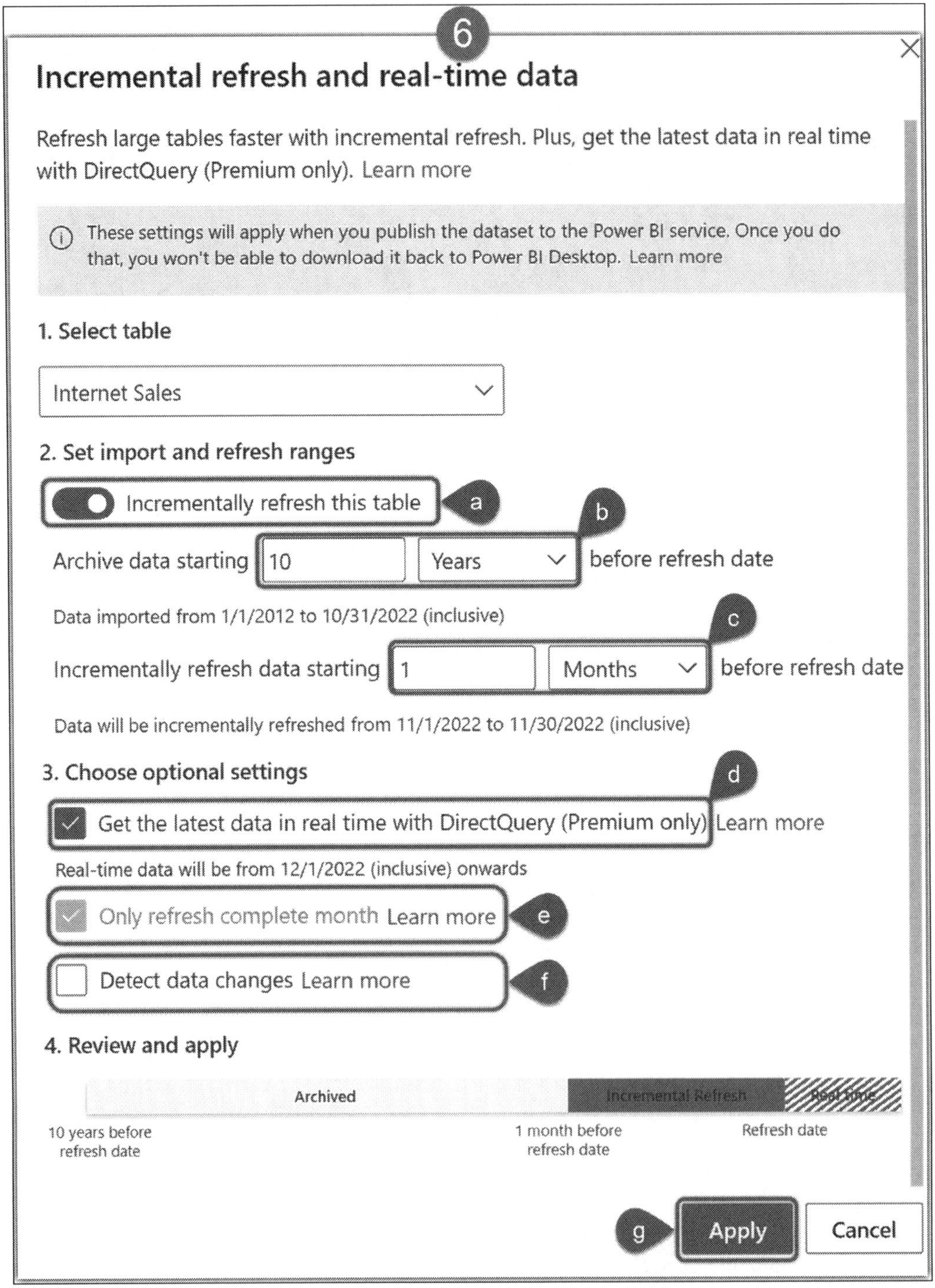

Incremental refresh and real-time data

Refresh large tables faster with incremental refresh. Plus, get the latest data in real time with DirectQuery (Premium only). Learn more

> ⓘ These settings will apply when you publish the dataset to the Power BI service. Once you do that, you won't be able to download it back to Power BI Desktop. Learn more

1. Select table

Internet Sales

2. Set import and refresh ranges

◉ Incrementally refresh this table   (a)

Archive data starting | 10 | Years | before refresh date   (b)

Data imported from 1/1/2012 to 10/31/2022 (inclusive)

Incrementally refresh data starting | 1 | Months | before refresh date   (c)

Data will be incrementally refreshed from 11/1/2022 to 11/30/2022 (inclusive)

3. Choose optional settings

☑ Get the latest data in real time with DirectQuery (Premium only) Learn more   (d)

Real-time data will be from 12/1/2022 (inclusive) onwards

☑ Only refresh complete month Learn more   (e)

☐ Detect data changes Learn more   (f)

4. Review and apply

| Archived | Incremental Refresh | Real-time |

10 years before refresh date   1 month before refresh date   Refresh date

(g) [Apply] [Cancel]

Figure 10.38: Configuring the Incremental refresh and real-time data

> By checking option **d** in the **Incremental refresh and real-time data** window, the **Internet Sales** table becomes a Hybrid Table, which is a **Premium** feature.
>
> The **Only refresh complete month** option depends on the period we select in item **c** in the preceding image. With this option, we can force the incremental refresh only for the complete period. Selecting item **d** in the preceding image deactivates this option.
>
> In data integration and data warehousing processes, we usually add some additional auditing columns to the tables to collect useful metadata, such as **Last Modified At, Last Modified By, Activity, Is Processed,** and so on. If you have a **Date/Time** column indicating the data changes (such as **Last Modified At**), the **Detect data changes** option would be helpful. We do not have any auditing columns in our data source; therefore, we will leave it unchecked.

7. Click the **Publish** button to publish the data model to the Power BI service. Since the **Internet Sales** table is now a Hybrid Table, we can only select **Premium Workspaces**. As the following image shows, the Pro Workspaces are inactive. Click the desired workspace and click **Select**:

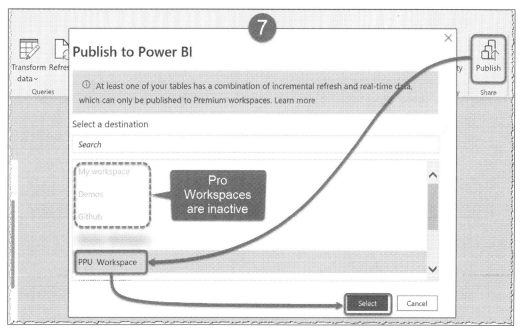

Figure 10.39: Publishing the report to the Power BI service

So far, we've configured the incremental refresh and published the data model to the Power BI service. At this point, a Power BI administrator should take over to complete the **Schedule refresh** settings in the Power BI service. The administrator must also set up an On-premises Data Gateway, pass the credentials, and more. These settings are out of the scope of this book, so we'll leave them to you. We assume Power BI administrators have completed the settings in the Power BI service and refreshed the dataset for the first time. In the next section, we explain how to test the incremental refresh.

Testing the incremental refresh

To visualize the created partitions of a dataset with an incrementally refreshing table and properly test it, we must either have a Premium or an Embedded license to be able to connect the desired workspace in the Power BI service. We must use third-party applications such as **SQL Server Management Studio (SSMS)** or **Tabular Editor** to see the partitions we created for incremental data refresh. We use SSMS to see the created partitions. You can download SSMS from here: https://learn.microsoft.com/en-us/sql/ssms/download-sql-server-management-studio-ssms?view=sql-server-ver16&WT.mc_id=DP-MVP-5003466.

If you do not have a Premium license, you can use a Power BI individual trial to try Power BI **Premium Per User (PPU)** if your Power BI administrators haven't blocked *Allow users to try Power BI paid features* on the Power BI tenant settings. Read more here: https://learn.microsoft.com/en-us/power-bi/fundamentals/service-self-service-signup-for-power-bi?WT.mc_id=DP-MVP-5003466.

But we are still in luck if we have Pro licenses. If you recall, when we implemented the incremental refresh prerequisites in Power Query Editor, we filtered the table's data by the **RangeStart** and **RangeEnd** parameters. So, we expect Power BI to create the partitions after we refresh the dataset for the first time, which means that the dataset must cover the full data range, not only the data filtered by the query parameters in Power BI Editor. Therefore, if the incremental refresh did not go through, we will only see a small portion of the data. We can test it by creating a new report either in Power BI Desktop or the Power BI service (or a new report page if there is an existing report already) *connected live* to the dataset, putting a table visual on the reporting canvas. We'll leave this part to you.

If you already have a Premium license, then follow these steps to connect to a Premium workspace from SSMS:

1. In the Power BI service, navigate to the desired Premium workspace containing a dataset with an incrementally refreshing table.
2. Click **Settings**.
3. Click the **Premium** tab.
4. Copy the **Workspace Connection** URL.

    The following image shows the preceding steps:

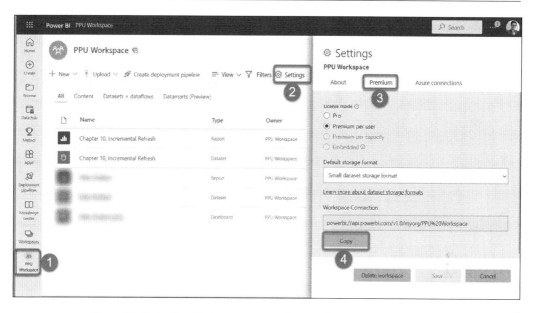

Figure 10.40: Getting Workspace Connection URL from the Power BI service

5. Open **SSMS** and in the **Connect to Server** window, do the following:

    a. Select **Analysis Services** for **Server type**.

    b. Paste the **Workspace Connection** link into the **Server name** box.

    c. Select **Azure Active Directory – Universal with MFA** (if you have MFA enabled in your tenant) for **Authentication**.

    d. Type in your user name.

    e. Click **Connect**:

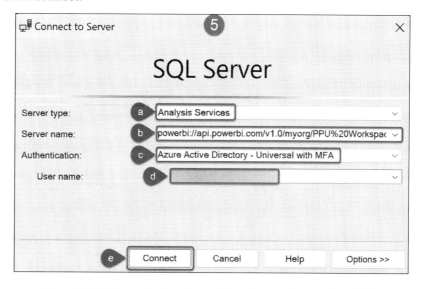

Figure 10.41: Connecting to a Power BI Premium workspace from SSMS

6. We can now see all the datasets contained in the workspace under **Databases** within the **Object Explorer** pane. Expand **Databases**, expand the dataset, and then expand **Tables**.
7. Right-click the **Internet Sales** table.
8. Click **Partitions....**
9. Now, you can view all the partitions that were created by the incremental refresh process, as shown in the following image:

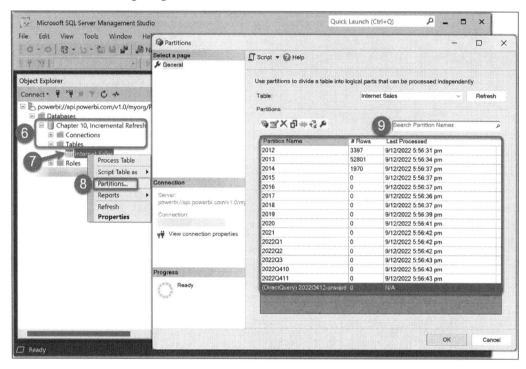

Figure 10.42: Navigating to a table's partitions from SSMS

As you can see, you can see or modify the created partitions directly from SSMS and save the changes back to the Power BI service. This is made possible by the XMLA endpoint read/write capability, which is available in the Power BI Premium and Embedded capacities.

You can read more about *Dataset connectivity with the XMLA endpoint* here: https://learn.microsoft.com/en-us/power-bi/enterprise/service-premium-connect-tools?WT.mc_id=M365-MVP-5003466.

The following image explains the partitions and how they relate to data ranges in more detail:

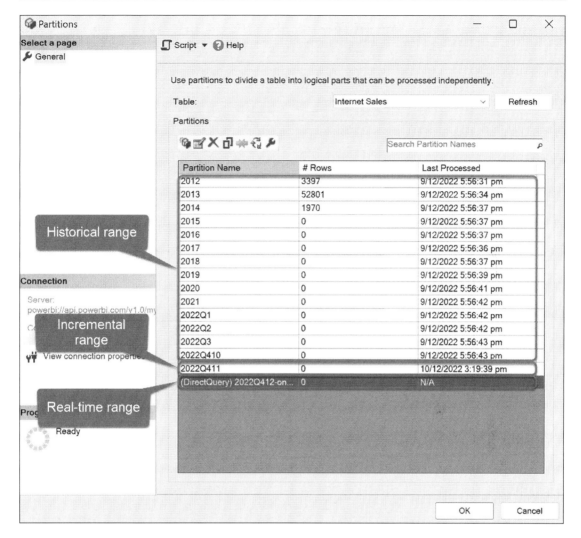

Figure 10.43: Dataset partitions and data ranges

As the preceding image shows, Power BI created partitions at **Year**, **Quarter**, and **Month** levels. This is done based on the incremental refresh configuration, which can be different on a case-by-case basis. Based on how we define our incremental policy, those partitions will be automatically refreshed (if we schedule automatic data to refresh on the service). Over time, some of those partitions will be dropped, and some will be merged with others. For instance, in our sample, when we move to January 2023, the month-level partitions will be merged into the quarter level, and the quarter-level partitions will be merged into the year level.

So far, we have learned how to test the incremental refresh. The next section raises some important points about incremental refresh and hybrid tables.

Important notes about incremental refresh and hybrid tables

Many things can go wrong when we implement a solution in real-world scenarios. In this section, we raise some important notes that become helpful in daily challenges with incremental refresh and hybrid tables.

- Incremental refresh and real-time data (hybrid tables) work best with relational database systems such as SQL Server databases, Azure SQL databases, Synapse Analytics, and so on.
- While incremental refresh works best for the data sources supporting query folding, it also supports file-based data sources and other data sources that do not support query folding. When implementing incremental refresh on data sources that support query folding, it is best to ensure the queries are fully folded.
- As explained earlier, hybrid tables keep the last partition in DirectQuery mode to support real-time data. Therefore, hybrid tables are not available for non-folding data sources.
- When writing this book, the hybrid tables feature was still in public preview, so it is not recommended to implement it in production environments.
- It is best to enable **Automatic page refresh** when visualizing real-time data. Learn more about the **Automatic page refresh** setting here: https://learn.microsoft.com/en-us/power-bi/create-reports/desktop-automatic-page-refresh?WT.mc_id=DP-MVP-5003466.
- Nothing happens in Power BI Desktop when implementing incremental refresh. All the magic happens after publishing the report to the Power BI service after we refresh the dataset for the first time.
- After we refresh the dataset in the Power BI service for the first time, we cannot download the data model (dataset) from the Power BI service anymore. This constraint makes absolute sense. Imagine that we incrementally load billions of rows of data into a table. Even if we could download the file (which we cannot anyways), our desktop machines are not able to handle that much data. That said, we can still download the connected report as a thin report.
- The fact that we cannot download datasets with incrementally refreshing tables from the service raises another concern for Power BI development and future support. If, in the future, we need to make any changes in the data model, we must use third-party tools such as Tabular Editor, ALM Toolkit, or SSMS to deploy the changes to the existing dataset without overwriting it. Otherwise, if we make all changes in Power BI Desktop and publish the changes back to the service and overwrite the existing dataset, all the partitions created on the existing dataset and their data will be gone. To be able to connect to an existing dataset using any of the mentioned tools, we have to use XMLA endpoints, which are available only for Premium users, not Pro. So, be aware of that restriction if you implement incremental refresh with a Pro license.
- When dealing with large data sources, the first data refresh can be tricky. Power BI has **time limit** constraints on the data refresh duration. For Pro licenses, we are limited to 2 hours to complete the data refresh, and for Premium and Embedded, the time limit is 5 hours. The reason is that the data refresh process can consume twice as much memory as a dataset consumes at rest, as Power BI keeps a copy of the existing dataset to answer all the existing queries. At the same time, it refreshes the dataset's data.

Therefore, the time limit constraint can turn into a bottleneck. In those situations, it is best to filter the table with a dummy value, so it does not return any rows. Then we publish the model to the service and perform the first dataset refresh to create all partitions in the dataset. Finally, we use a third-party tool to connect to the dataset via the XMLA endpoint to manually refresh the partitions one by one. That way, we can avoid getting time-outs. This method is only available for Premium datasets.

In this section, we discussed how to implement and test incremental refresh and hybrid tables. The next section explains Parent-Child hierarchy concepts and their implementation.

Parent-Child hierarchies

The concept of a Parent-Child hierarchy is commonly used in relational data modeling. A Parent-Child hierarchy is when the values of two columns in a table represent hierarchical levels in the data. Parents have children; their children have children too, which creates a hierarchical graph. This section explains Parent-Child hierarchies and their implementation in relational data modeling. Then, we'll look at the Parent-Child design in Power BI. The following diagram shows a typical Parent-Child graph. Each node of the graph contains an ID and the person's name:

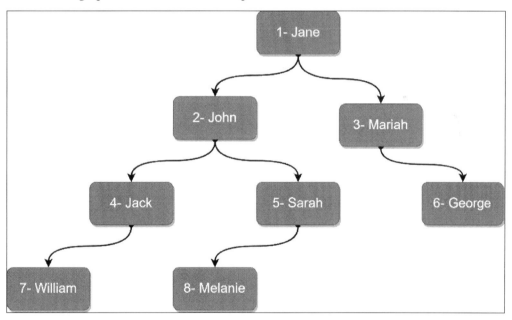

Figure 10.44: A Parent-Child graph

We can represent the preceding graph in a data table, as shown in the following image:

	Parent Child	
ID	Name	ParentID
1	Jane	NULL
2	John	1
3	Mariah	1
4	Jack	2
5	Sarah	2
6	George	3
7	William	4
8	Melanie	5

Figure 10.45: Parent-Child graph representation in a data table

There is a one-to-many relationship between the **ID** and **ParentID** columns. In relational data modeling, we create a relationship between the **ID** and **ParentID** columns that turns the **Parent-Child** table into a self-referencing table, as shown in the following image:

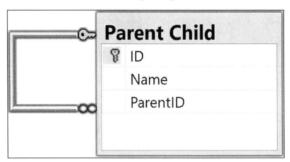

Figure 10.46: The Parent-Child table is a self-referencing table

While data modeling in Power BI is relational, unfortunately, Power BI does not support self-referencing tables, to avoid ambiguity in the data model. However, the good news is that there is a set of DAX functions specifically designed to implement Parent-Child hierarchies in Power BI. Before jumping to the implementation part, let's take a moment to discuss the implementation process:

1. The first step is to identify the depth of the hierarchy. The following diagram shows that our example has four levels, so the depth is 4. The nodes at level 4 are leaves of the hierarchy, so **William** and **Melanie** are leaves:

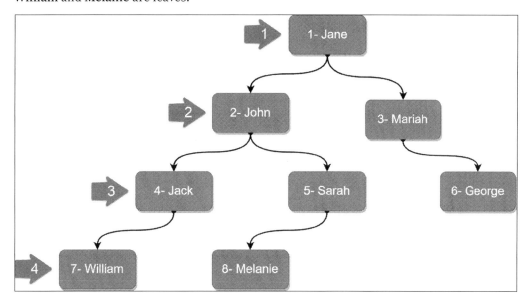

Figure 10.47: Hierarchy depth

2. Then, we create calculated columns for each level of the hierarchy.
3. Finally, we create a hierarchy using the calculated levels.

As you can see, the process is quite simple. Now, let's implement a Parent-Child hierarchy.

Identify the depth of the hierarchy

To identify the depth of a Parent-Child hierarchy, we can use the PATH(ID, ParentID) function. The PATH() function returns a pipe (|) delimited string starting from the parent and ending with the current child. We need to create a new calculated column with the following DAX expression:

```
Path = PATH('Parent Child'[ID], 'Parent Child'[ParentID])
```

The output of the preceding expression provides the path of our hierarchy, as shown in the following image:

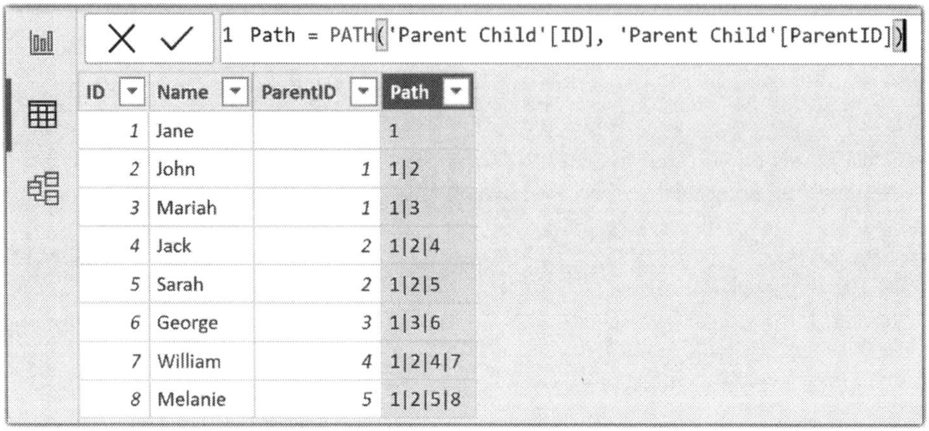
1 Path = PATH('Parent Child'[ID], 'Parent Child'[ParentID])

ID	Name	ParentID	Path
1	Jane		1
2	John	1	1|2
3	Mariah	1	1|3
4	Jack	2	1|2|4
5	Sarah	2	1|2|5
6	George	3	1|3|6
7	William	4	1|2|4|7
8	Melanie	5	1|2|5|8

Figure 10.48: Creating a new calculated column containing the hierarchy path

Here are some considerations in using the `PATH()` function:

- **ID** and **ParentID** must have the same data type, either `integer` or `text`.
- The values of the **ParentID** column must exist in the **ID** column. The `PATH()` function cannot find a parent if the child level does not exist.
- If **ParentID** is null, then that node is the graph's root.
- Each **ID** (child level) can have one and only one **ParentID**; otherwise, the `PATH()` function will throw an error.
- If **ID** is `BLANK()`, then `PATH()` returns `BLANK()`.

Now that we have the values of the **Path** column, we can quickly identify the depth of the hierarchy using the `PATHLENGTH(PathColumn)` function. We need to create another calculated function using the following DAX expression:

```
Path Length = PATHLENGTH('Parent Child'[Path])
```

The following image shows the output of running the preceding expression:

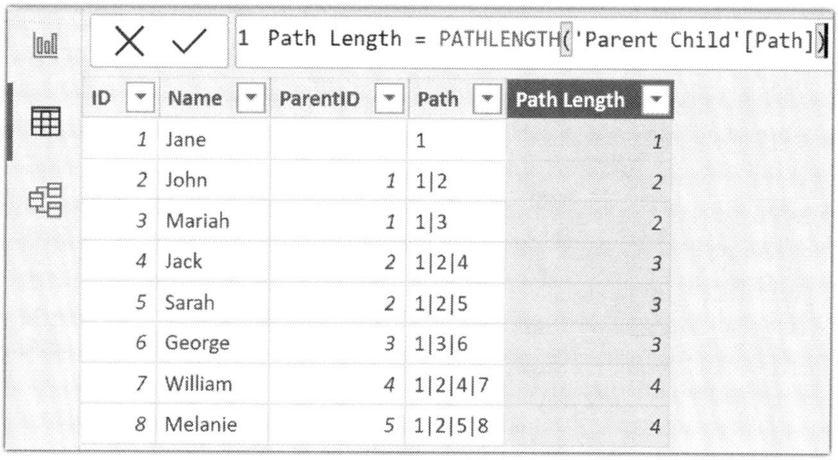

Figure 10.49: Calculating Path Length

Now that we've calculated **Path Length**, we know that the depth value of the hierarchy is **4**. Therefore, we need to create four new calculated columns – one column for each hierarchy level.

Creating hierarchy levels

So far, we have identified the depth of the hierarchy. To implement a Parent-Child hierarchy, in our example, we know that the hierarchy's depth is 4, so we need to create four calculated columns. We can identify these hierarchy levels using the PATHITEM(Path, Path Length, Datatype) function, which returns the item for the specified **Path Length** within the **Path** column. In other words, the PATHITEM() function returns the values of each specified hierarchy level. **Datatype** is an optional operand that defines the data type of the output results, which is either **INTEGER** or **TEXT**. The default **Datatype** is **TEXT**. Let's take a moment to understand how the PATHITEM() function works. For instance, we can read the PATHITEM('Parent Child'[Path], 2, INTEGER) expression as "Return the integer item of **Path** when the hierarchy level is 2." The following image shows the results of running the preceding expression:

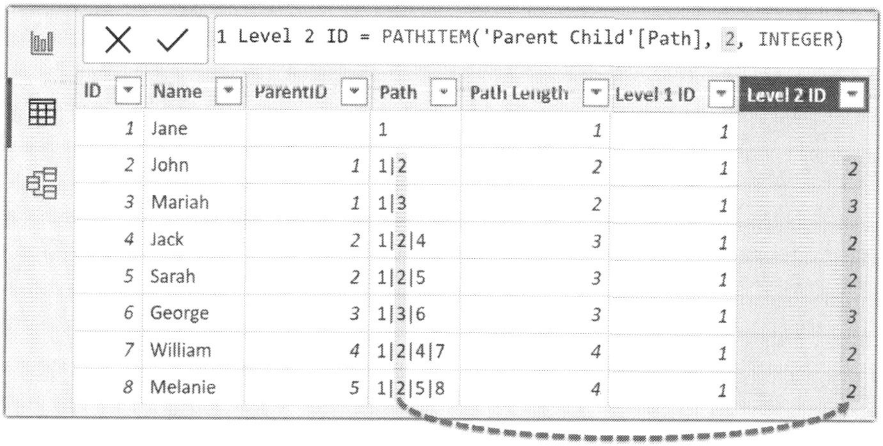

Figure 10.50: The results of running the PATHITEM('Parent Child'[Path], 2, INTEGER) expression

As you can see, `PATHITEM()` returns the IDs of the specified level. But **ID** is not what we are after. We need to return the corresponding value of the **Name** column. To get the corresponding **Name**, we can use the `LOOKUPVALUE(Returning Column, Lookup Column, Lookup Value)` function. For instance, the following expression returns the values from the **Name** column that correspond to the values from the **ID** column where the hierarchy level is 2:

```
Level 2 Name =
    LOOKUPVALUE(
        'Parent Child'[Name]
        , 'Parent Child'[ID]
        , PATHITEM('Parent Child'[Path], 2, INTEGER)
    )
```

Running the preceding expression results in the following output:

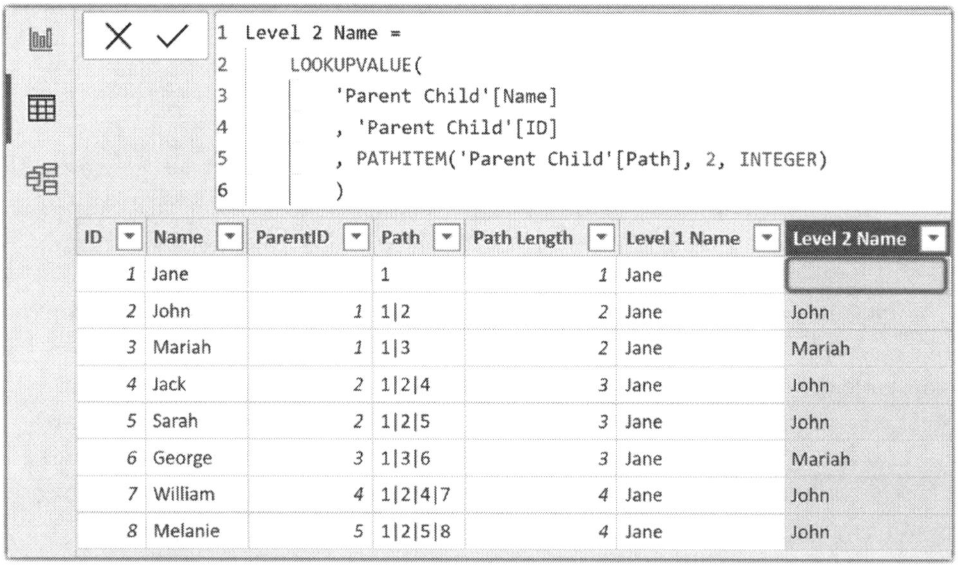

```
Level 2 Name =
    LOOKUPVALUE(
        'Parent Child'[Name]
        , 'Parent Child'[ID]
        , PATHITEM('Parent Child'[Path], 2, INTEGER)
    )
```

ID	Name	ParentID	Path	Path Length	Level 1 Name	Level 2 Name
1	Jane		1	1	Jane	
2	John	1	1|2	2	Jane	John
3	Mariah	1	1|3	2	Jane	Mariah
4	Jack	2	1|2|4	3	Jane	John
5	Sarah	2	1|2|5	3	Jane	John
6	George	3	1|3|6	3	Jane	Mariah
7	William	4	1|2|4|7	4	Jane	John
8	Melanie	5	1|2|5|8	4	Jane	John

Figure 10.51: The results of running the Level 2 Name expression

As you can see, the expression returns nothing (it's blank) for the first value. When we have blank values in a hierarchy, we call it a ragged hierarchy. Ragged hierarchies can confuse the visualization layer as we get `BLANK()` for every hierarchy level. One way to manage ragged hierarchies is to add a filter to avoid `BLANK()` values. The other way is to manage ragged hierarchies in our DAX expressions. We only need to check the value of the **Path Length** column. If it is bigger than or equal to the specified hierarchy level we are looking at, then we return the corresponding value of the **Name** column; otherwise, we return the value of the previous level's **Name** column. Obviously, for the first level of the hierarchy, we do not have null values. Hence, we do not need to check **Path Length**. So, we must create four new calculated columns using the following expressions.

The following expression returns the values of the **Name** column for level 1 of the hierarchy:

```
Level 1 Name =
    LOOKUPVALUE(
        'Parent Child'[Name]
        , 'Parent Child'[ID]
        , PATHITEM('Parent Child'[Path], 1, INTEGER)
    )
```

The following expression returns the values of the **Name** column for level 2 of the hierarchy:

```
Level 2 Name =
    IF(
        'Parent Child'[Path Length] >=2
        , LOOKUPVALUE(
            'Parent Child'[Name]
            , 'Parent Child'[ID]
            , PATHITEM('Parent Child'[Path], 2, INTEGER)
        ) //End LOOKUPVALUE
        , 'Parent Child'[Level 1 Name]
    ) // End IF
```

The following expression returns the values of the **Name** column for level 3 of the hierarchy:

```
Level 3 Name =
    IF(
        'Parent Child'[Path Length] >=3
        , LOOKUPVALUE(
            'Parent Child'[Name]
            , 'Parent Child'[ID]
            , PATHITEM('Parent Child'[Path], 3, INTEGER)
        ) //End LOOKUPVALUE
        , 'Parent Child'[Level 2 Name]
    ) // End IF
```

The following expression returns the values of the **Name** column for level 4 of the hierarchy:

```
Level 4 Name =
    IF(
        'Parent Child'[Path Length] >=4
        , LOOKUPVALUE(
            'Parent Child'[Name]
            , 'Parent Child'[ID]
            , PATHITEM('Parent Child'[Path], 4, INTEGER)
        ) //End LOOKUPVALUE
```

```
        , 'Parent Child'[Level 3 Name]
    ) // End IF
```

The following image shows the results of running the preceding expressions:

ID	Name	ParentID	Path	Path Length	Level 1 Name	Level 2 Name	Level 3 Name	Level 4 Name
1	Jane		1	1	Jane	Jane	Jane	Jane
2	John	1	1|2	2	Jane	John	John	John
3	Mariah	1	1|3	2	Jane	Mariah	Mariah	Mariah
4	Jack	2	1|2|4	3	Jane	John	Jack	Jack
5	Sarah	2	1|2|5	3	Jane	John	Sarah	Sarah
6	George	3	1|3|6	3	Jane	Mariah	George	George
7	William	4	1|2|4|7	4	Jane	John	Jack	William
8	Melanie	5	1|2|5|8	4	Jane	John	Sarah	Melanie

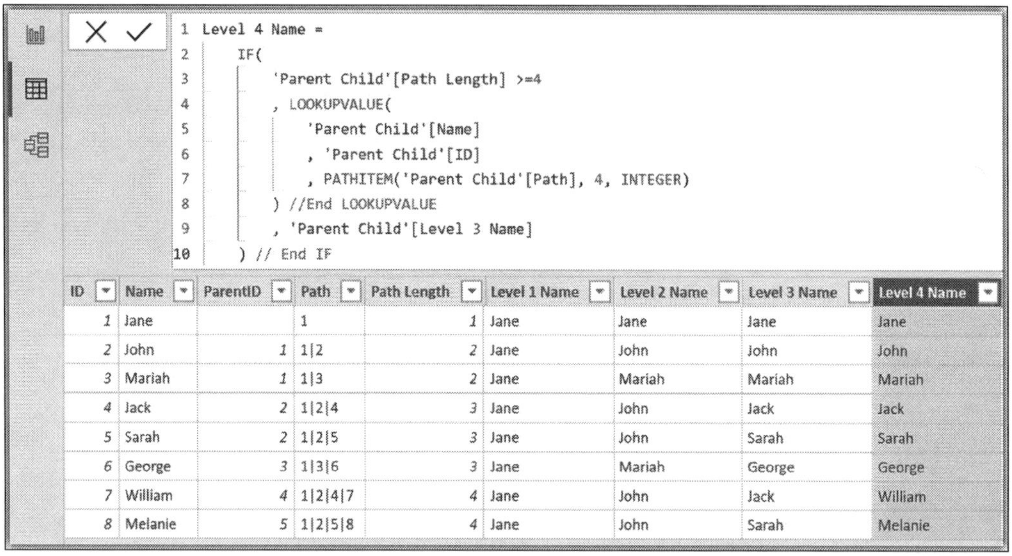

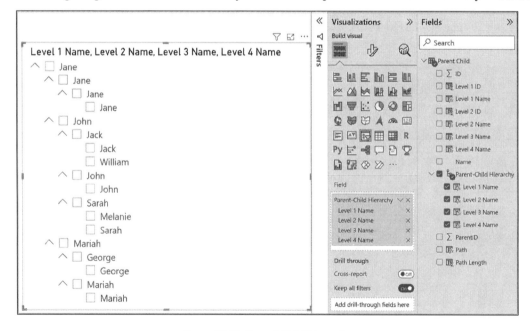

Figure 10.52: Four new calculated columns created returning the hierarchy levels

At this point, we have all the hierarchy levels. Now, we can create a hierarchy using these four levels. The following image shows the new hierarchy and a visual representation of the hierarchy in a slicer:

Figure 10.53: Parent-Child hierarchy

In this section, we discussed how to implement Parent-Child hierarchies. The example we used in this section was a straightforward one, but the principles remain the same. You can use the techniques we discussed in this section to overcome real-world scenarios such as employee hierarchies, organizational charts, and so on. In the next section, we'll discuss roleplaying dimensions and learn how to implement them in Power BI.

Implementing roleplaying dimensions

The roleplaying dimension is one of the most common scenarios we face in data modeling. The term was inherited from multidimensional modeling within the SQL Server Analysis Services Multidimensional. Before jumping to the implementation part, let's take a moment and understand what the roleplaying dimension is. When we create multiple relationships between a fact table and a dimension for logically distinctive roles, we use the concept of a roleplaying dimension. The most popular roleplaying dimensions are the **Date** and **Time** dimensions. For instance, we may have multiple dates in a fact table, such as **Order Date**, **Due Date**, and **Ship Date**, which participate in different relationships with the **Date** dimension. Each date represents a different role in our analysis. In other words, we can analyze the data using the **Date** dimension for different purposes. For instance, we can calculate **Sales Amount** by **Order Date**, which results in different values from the values; that is, either **Sales Amount** by **Due Date** or **Sales Amount** by **Ship Date**. But there is a small problem: the xVelocity engine does not support multiple active relationships simultaneously. However, we can programmatically enable an inactive relationship using the USERELATIONSHIP() function in DAX, which activates the relationship for the calculation duration. We can use the USERELATIONSHIP() function within the CALCULATE() function.

Now that we understand what the roleplaying dimension is, let's implement it in a scenario using the **AdventureWorksDW2017.xlsx** sample file:

1. Open Power BI Desktop, connect to the **AdventureWorksDW2017.xlsx** file, and get data from the **Reseller_Sales** and **Dates** tables:

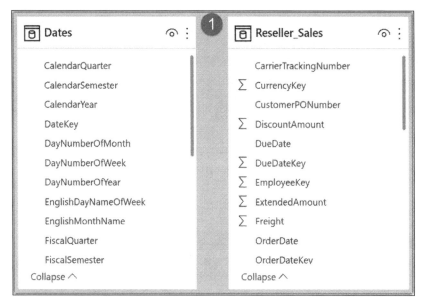

Figure 10.54: Getting data from the Reseller_Sales and Dates tables

2. Create the following relationships between the **Reseller_Sales** and **Dates** tables. Keep the first relationship active:

    a. Reseller_Sales(OrderDateKey) => Dates(DateKey)
    b. Reseller_Sales(DueDateKey) => Dates(DateKey)
    c. Reseller_Sales(ShipDateKey) => Dates(DateKey):

Figure 10.55: Creating relationships between Reseller_Sales and Dates

We now need to create new measures, one for each role, and name the measures appropriately so they resemble the roles.

Keep in mind that the active relationship between the two tables remains the primary relationship. Therefore, all the measures that calculate values on top of the **Reseller_Sales** and **Dates** tables use the active relationship. So, it is essential to keep a relationship active that makes the most sense to the business. In our scenario, **Order Date** is the most important date for the business. Therefore, we will keep the **Reseller_Sales(OrderDateKey) => Dates(DateKey)** relationship active.

We can create the **Reseller Sales by Order Date** measure using the following DAX expression:

```
Reseller Sales by Order Date = SUM(Reseller_Sales[SalesAmount])
```

We can create the **Reseller Sales by Due Date** measure using the following DAX expression:

```
Reseller Sales by Due Date =
    CALCULATE([Reseller Sales by Order Date]
        , USERELATIONSHIP(Dates[DateKey], Reseller_Sales[DueDateKey])
    )
```

We can create the **Reseller Sales by Ship Date** measure using the following DAX expression:

```
Reseller Sales by Ship Date =
    CALCULATE([Reseller Sales by Order Date]
        , USERELATIONSHIP(Dates[DateKey], Reseller_Sales[ShipDateKey])
    )
```

As you can see, we did not use the USERELATIONSHIP() function in the **Reseller Sales by Order Date** measure as the active relationship between the **Reseller_Sales** and **Dates** tables is Reseller_Sales (OrderDateKey) => Dates (DateKey).

Now, we can use the preceding measures in our data visualizations. The following image shows that all the measures that were created to support roleplaying dimensions are used side by side in a matrix:

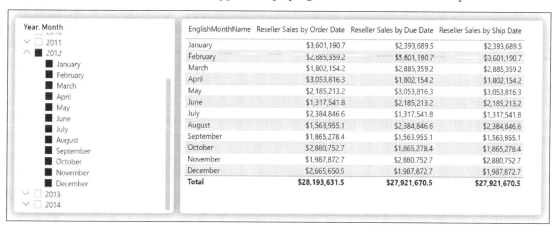

Figure 10.56: Visualizing roleplaying dimensions

If you are coming from a SQL Server Multidimensional background, you may be thinking of creating multiple **Date** tables. While that is another approach to implementing roleplaying dimensions, we do not recommend going down that path. The following are some reasons against creating multiple **Date** tables to handle roleplaying dimensions:

- Having multiple **Date** tables in our model can confuse other content creators, even if we have only two **Date** tables.
- This approach unnecessarily increases the data model size and memory consumption.
- This approach is tough to maintain. We have seen some businesses that have more than 10 roles; having 10 **Date** tables to handle roleplaying dimensions does not sound right.

In this section, we learned about the concept of roleplaying dimensions, and we implemented it in Power BI. In the next section, we'll learn about another advanced topic that solves many daily development challenges: calculation groups.

Using calculation groups

Creating calculation groups is one of the most useful features for Power BI data modelers and developers. It reduces the number of measures you have to create. Calculation groups address the fact that we have to create many measures in larger and more complex data models that are somewhat redundant. Creating those measures takes a lot of development time. For instance, in a **Sales** data model, we can have **Sales Amount** as a base measure. In real-world scenarios, we usually have to create many time intelligence measures on top of the **Sales Amount** measure, such as **Sales Amount YTD**, **Sales Amount QTD**, **Sales Amount MTD**, **Sales Amount LYTD**, **Sales Amount LQTD**, **Sales Amount LMTD**, and so on. We have seen models with more than 20 time intelligence measures created on top of a single measure. In real-world scenarios, we have far more base measures than a business that requires all those 20 time intelligence measures for every single base measure. You can imagine how time-consuming it is to develop all those measures. We only need to create the referencing measures with calculation groups once. Then, we can use them with any base measures. In other words, the measures are then reusable. Calculation groups only used to be available in SQL Server Analysis Services Tabular 2019, Azure Analysis Service, and Power BI Premium. But they are now open to all Power BI licensing plans, including Power BI Free. However, at the time of writing this book, we cannot implement calculation groups directly in Power BI Desktop; we have to use Tabular Editor v.2, a renowned free community tool built by the fantastic Daniel Otykier.

With this brief explanation and before we jump into the development process, let's get more familiar with some requirements and terminologies.

Requirements

As we mentioned earlier, at the time of writing this book, we cannot create calculation groups directly in Power BI Desktop:

- We need to download and install Tabular Editor v.2. You can download it from here: `https://github.com/TabularEditor/TabularEditor/releases/latest`.
- We must have Power BI Desktop July 2020 or later.

- Disable **Implicit Measures** for the entire data model. We covered this in *Chapter 8, Data Modeling Components*, in the *Fields* section.
- The calculation groups do not support implicit measures; therefore, we must have at least one explicit measure in the data model.

Terminology

Let's go through the following terminology involved in calculation groups:

- Calculation Group: A calculation group is indeed a table like any other table that holds calculation items.
- Precedence: Each calculation group has a precedence property that specifies the order of evaluation if there is more than one calculation group. The calculation groups with higher precedence numbers will be evaluated before the calculation groups with lower precedence.
- Calculation Item: We create calculation items within a calculation group using DAX expressions. Calculation items are like template measures that can run over any explicit measures we have in our data model. Each calculation group has two columns: Name with a Text data type and Ordinal with a Whole Number data type. The Name column keeps the names of calculation items. The Ordinal column is a hidden column that keeps the sort order of the Name column. In other words, the Ordinal column sorts the Name column. We can create as many calculation items as required.
- Ordinal: Each calculation item has an Ordinal property. The Ordinal property dictates the order in which the calculation items appear in a visual within the report. When we set the Ordinal property of the calculation items, we are entering the values of the Ordinal column. If the Ordinal property is not set, the calculation items show up in alphabetical order within the report. Setting an Ordinal property does not affect the precedence and the order in which the calculation items get evaluated.
- Sideways Recursion: The term sideways recursion refers to when a calculation item references other calculation items within the same calculation group. Sideways recursion is allowed unless we create infinite loops, such as when calculation item A refers to calculation item B and vice versa. An infinite loop can also occur when a calculation item references an explicit measure that refers to the first calculation item. It is best to avoid sideways recursion.

Now that we are more familiar with the requirements and terminology, it is time to implement calculation groups.

Implementing calculation groups to handle time intelligence

One of the most popular use cases for implementing calculation groups is to handle time intelligence measures. So, let's create a new calculation group and name it **Time Intelligence**. We must then define a series of time intelligence calculation items within the calculation group to meet the business requirements. This section and the next will use the Chapter 10, Calculation Groups.pbix sample file, which sources the data from the AdventureWorksDW2017.xlsx file. We've already loaded the data from the **Internet_Sales** and **Dates** tables. We then took some transformation steps by renaming the tables and columns.

We also removed unnecessary columns from the data model; then, we imported the data into the data model and marked **Date table** as **Date**. We also downloaded and installed Tabular Editor v.2. With that, let's get started:

1. Click **Tabular Editor** from the **External Tools** tab:

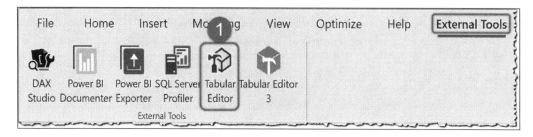

Figure 10.57: Opening Tabular Editor from the External Tools tab

2. In Tabular Editor, right-click the **Tables** node, hover over **Create New**, and click **Calculation Group**. We can also use the *Alt+7* keyboard shortcut:

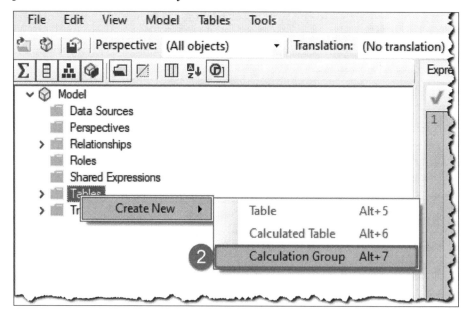

Figure 10.58: Creating a new calculation group in Tabular Editor

3. Name the new calculation group **Time Intelligence**.
4. Set **Calculation Group Precedence** to 10.
5. Rename the **Name** column to **Time Calculations**.

Chapter 10

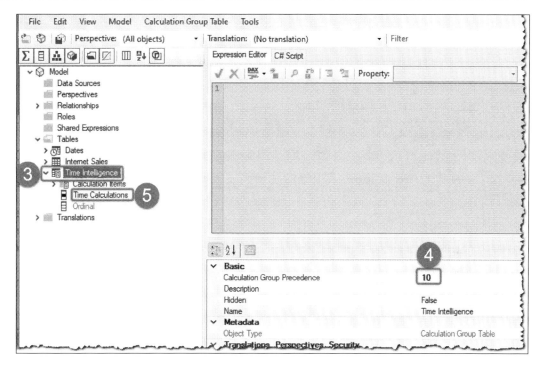

Figure 10.59: Creating a calculation group

6. Right-click the **Calculation Items** node and click **New Calculation Item**:

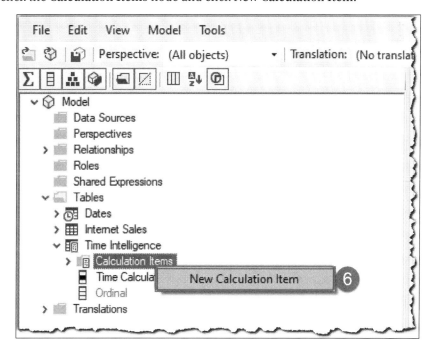

Figure 10.60: Creating calculation items in Tabular Editor

7. Name the new calculation item **Current**. This calculation item will show the current value of a selected measure.
8. Type the SELECTEDMEASURE() expression into the **Expression Editor** box.
9. Set the **Ordinal** property to **0**.
10. Click the **Accept changes** button (✔):

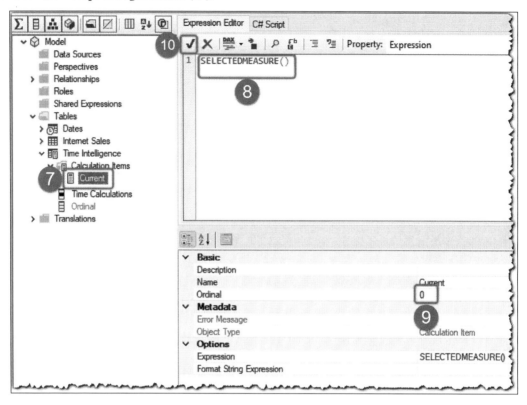

Figure 10.61: Adding a DAX expression for a calculation item

11. Create another calculation item and name it **YTD** with the TOTALYTD(SELECTEDMEASURE(), 'Dates'[Date]) expression, and set its **Ordinal** property to **1**:

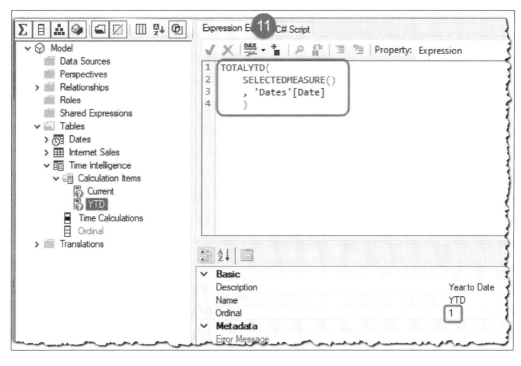

Figure 10.62: Creating another calculation item

12. Click the **Save** (💾) button to save the changes back to our data model in Power BI Desktop:

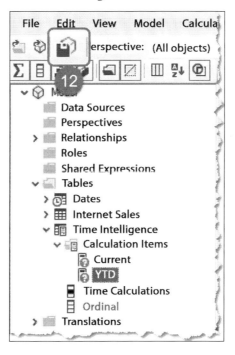

Figure 10.63: Saving the changes from Tabular Editor back to Power BI Desktop

13. Go back to Power BI Desktop and click the **Refresh now** button on the yellow warning ribbon:

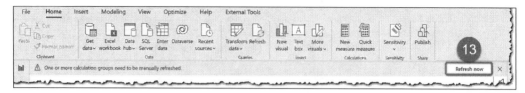

Figure 10.64: Refreshing the calculation group after applying the changes back to Power BI Desktop

We can create as many calculation items as the business requires. In our example, we added seven calculation items, as shown in the following image:

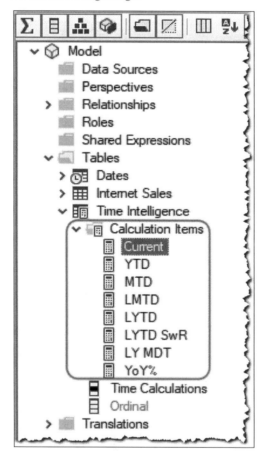

Figure 10.65: Calculation items created in the sample file

Let's look at these expressions. **Ordinal** is used to create the following calculation items:

Calculation Item	DAX Expression	Ordinal	Description
Current	SELECTEDMEASURE()	0	Shows the current values of a selected measure
YTD	TOTALYTD(　SELECTEDMEASURE() 　, 'Dates'[Date])	1	Year to Date
MTD	TOTALMTD(　SELECTEDMEASURE() 　, 'Dates'[Date])	2	Month to Date
LMTD	TOTALMTD(　SELECTEDMEASURE() 　, DATEADD('Dates'[Date], -1, MONTH))	3	Last Month to Date
LYTD	TOTALYTD(　SELECTEDMEASURE() 　, DATEADD('Dates'[Date], -1, YEAR))	4	Last Year to Date
LYTD SwR	CALCULATE(　SELECTEDMEASURE() 　, DATEADD('Dates'[Date], -1, YEAR) 　, 'Time Intelligence'[Time Calculations] = "YTD")	5	Last Year to Date with Sideways Recursion
LY MTD	TOTALMTD(　SELECTEDMEASURE() 　, SAMEPERIODLASTYEAR('Dates'[Date]))	6	Last Year Month to Date
YoY%	var _current = SELECTEDMEASURE() var _ly = 　CALCULATE(　　SELECTEDMEASURE() 　　, DATEADD('Dates'[Date], -1, YEAR) 　) return DIVIDE(_current - _ly, _ly)	7	Year Over Year Change %

Figure 10.66: The expressions and ordinals used to create calculated items in the sample file

Look at the LYTD SwR calculation item in the preceding expressions. The LYTD SwR calculation item is an example of using sideways recursion. The results of the LYTD SwR calculation item are the same as the LYTD calculation item. We just wanted to show what sideways recursion looks like in action. Again, remember to avoid sideways recursion when possible. It can add unnecessary complexities to our code. Besides, sideways recursion can become problematic for report contributors who do not have any context of sideways recursion. Now that we've finished the implementation, let's test it out.

Testing calculation groups

As we mentioned previously, calculation groups only work with explicit measures. So, we must create at least one explicit measure in our sample to make the calculation groups work. We created the following measures in the sample file:

A measure to calculate `SalesAmount`:

```
Total Sales = SUM('Internet Sales'[SalesAmount])
```

A measure to calculate `OrderQuantity`:

```
Quantity Ordered = SUM('Internet Sales'[OrderQuantity])
```

Let's test the calculation group we created to see if it works as expected, as follows:

1. In Power BI Desktop, put a **Matrix** visual on the report page. Put the Year, Month, and Date columns from the **Dates** table into Rows.
2. Put the Time Calculations column from the time intelligence calculation group into Columns.
3. Put the Total Sales measure from the **Internet Sales** table into Values:

Year	Current	YTD	MTD	LMTD	LYTD	LYTD SwR	LY MDT	YoY%
⊞ 2010	$43,421.04	$43,421.04	$43,421.04					
⊞ 2011	$7,075,525.93	$7,075,525.93	$669,431.50	$660,545.81	$43,421.04	$43,421.04	$43,421.04	$161.95
⊟ 2012	$5,842,485.20	$5,842,485.20	$624,502.17	$537,955.52	$7,075,525.93	$7,075,525.93	$669,431.50	-$00.17
⊟ April	$400,335.61	$1,776,176.93	$400,335.61	$373,483.01	$1,923,431.32	$1,923,431.32	$502,073.85	-$00.20
Sunday, 1 April 2012	$15,551.91	$1,391,393.22	$15,551.91	$11,554.46	$1,431,889.01	$1,431,889.01	$10,531.53	$00.48
Monday, 2 April 2012	$12,798.54	$1,404,191.77	$28,350.45	$28,368.59	$1,446,202.09	$1,446,202.09	$24,844.61	-$00.11
Tuesday, 3 April 2012	$5,035.97	$1,409,227.74	$33,386.42	$38,812.46	$1,453,358.63	$1,453,358.63	$32,001.15	-$00.30
Wednesday, 4 April 2012	$12,183.70	$1,421,411.45	$45,570.13	$47,538.71	$1,478,545.78	$1,478,545.78	$57,188.30	-$00.52
Thursday, 5 April 2012	$11,488.65	$1,432,900.10	$57,058.78	$56,526.75	$1,486,198.13	$1,486,198.13	$64,840.66	$00.50
Friday, 6 April 2012	$13,869.53	$1,446,769.62	$70,928.31	$59,753.09	$1,497,632.04	$1,497,632.04	$76,274.56	$00.21
Saturday, 7 April 2012	$6,958.12	$1,453,727.74	$77,886.42	$78,509.01	$1,530,878.11	$1,530,878.11	$109,520.63	-$00.79
Sunday, 8 April 2012	$8,593.79	$1,462,321.53	$86,480.21	$94,442.93	$1,560,000.09	$1,560,000.09	$138,642.61	-$00.70
Monday, 9 April 2012	$15,574.23	$1,477,895.76	$102,054.44	$111,299.03	$1,577,891.44	$1,577,891.44	$156,533.96	-$00.13
Tuesday, 10 April 2012	$17,916.64	$1,495,812.39	$119,971.08	$126,670.25	$1,605,907.76	$1,605,907.76	$184,550.28	-$00.36
Wednesday, 11 April 2012	$24,070.79	$1,519,883.19	$144,041.87	$136,454.20	$1,648,465.44	$1,648,465.44	$227,107.96	-$00.43
Thursday, 12 April 2012	$12,627.81	$1,532,511.00	$156,669.68	$154,916.92	$1,666,699.32	$1,666,699.32	$245,341.85	-$00.31
Friday, 13 April 2012	$10,856.45	$1,543,367.45	$167,526.13	$171,286.76	$1,677,434.13	$1,677,434.13	$256,076.66	$00.01
Saturday, 14 April 2012	$13,687.02	$1,557,054.47	$181,213.15	$180,142.33	$1,684,387.39	$1,684,387.39	$263,029.92	$00.97
Sunday, 15 April 2012	$10,945.13	$1,567,999.60	$192,158.28	$188,404.65	$1,702,571.28	$1,702,571.28	$281,213.81	-$00.40
Total	$29,358,677.22	$45,694.72			$16,351,550.34	$16,351,550.34	$1,874,360.29	$00.00

Figure 10.67: Visualizing calculation groups in a Matrix visual

As highlighted in the preceding image, there is an issue with the format string of **YoY%**. In the next section, we will go through a simple process to fix this issue.

Fixing the format string issue

As shown in the preceding image, all the calculation items we created earlier within the Time Intelligence calculation group are formatted as currency. But we did not set the format string for any of the calculation items. These calculation items inherit the format string from the selected measure. While inheriting the format string from the selected measure is a convenient feature, as highlighted in the preceding image, it may not work for all calculation items, such as **YoY%**.

The format string for **YoY%** must be a percentage, regardless of what the format string carries from the selected measure. We must set the format string for the **YoY%** calculation item to fix this issue, which overrides the selected measure's format string. Here, we must open Tabular Editor again and set the format string of **YoY%** to "0.00%". The following image shows the preceding fix:

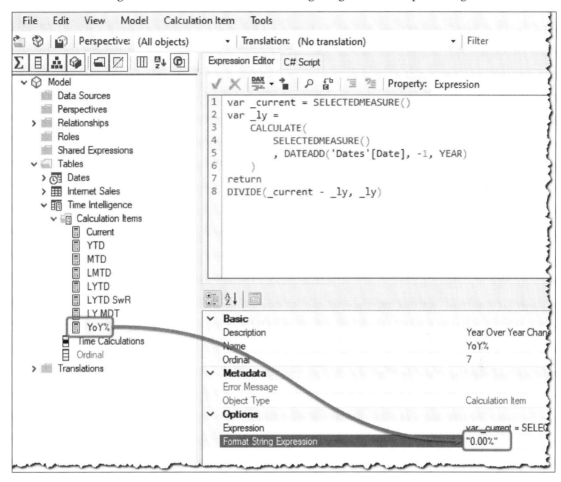

Figure 10.68: Fixing the format string issue in Tabular Editor

 We discussed format strings in *Chapter 8*, *Data Modeling Components*, in the *Fields* section, under the *Custom formatting* subsection.

The following image shows the **Matrix** visual after saving the changes back to the Power BI Desktop model:

Year	Current	YTD	MTD	LMTD	LYTD	LYTD SwR	LY MDT	YoY%
⊞ 2010	$43,421.04	$43,421.04	$43,421.04					
⊞ 2011	$7,075,525.93	$7,075,525.93	$669,431.50	$660,545.81	$43,421.04	$43,421.04	$43,421.04	16195.16%
⊟ 2012	$5,842,485.20	$5,842,485.20	$624,502.17	$537,955.52	$7,075,525.93	$7,075,525.93	$669,431.50	-17.43%
⊟ April	$400,335.61	$1,776,176.93	$400,335.61	$373,483.01	$1,923,431.32	$1,923,431.32	$502,073.85	-20.26%
Sunday, 1 April 2012	$15,551.91	$1,391,393.22	$15,551.91	$11,554.46	$1,431,889.01	$1,431,889.01	$10,531.53	47.67%
Monday, 2 April 2012	$12,798.54	$1,404,191.77	$28,350.45	$28,368.59	$1,446,202.09	$1,446,202.09	$24,844.61	-10.58%
Tuesday, 3 April 2012	$5,035.97	$1,409,227.74	$33,386.42	$38,812.46	$1,453,358.63	$1,453,358.63	$32,001.15	-29.63%
Wednesday, 4 April 2012	$12,183.70	$1,421,411.45	$45,570.13	$47,538.71	$1,478,545.78	$1,478,545.78	$57,188.30	-51.63%
Thursday, 5 April 2012	$11,488.65	$1,432,900.10	$57,058.78	$56,526.75	$1,486,198.13	$1,486,198.13	$64,840.66	50.13%
Friday, 6 April 2012	$13,869.53	$1,446,769.62	$70,928.31	$59,753.09	$1,497,632.04	$1,497,632.04	$76,274.56	21.30%
Saturday, 7 April 2012	$6,958.12	$1,453,727.74	$77,886.42	$78,509.01	$1,530,878.11	$1,530,878.11	$109,520.63	-79.07%
Sunday, 8 April 2012	$8,593.79	$1,462,321.53	$86,480.21	$94,442.93	$1,560,000.09	$1,560,000.09	$138,642.61	-70.49%
Monday, 9 April 2012	$15,574.23	$1,477,895.76	$102,054.44	$111,299.03	$1,577,891.44	$1,577,891.44	$156,533.96	-12.95%
Tuesday, 10 April 2012	$17,916.64	$1,495,812.39	$119,971.08	$126,670.25	$1,605,907.76	$1,605,907.76	$184,550.28	-36.05%
Wednesday, 11 April 2012	$24,070.79	$1,519,883.19	$144,041.87	$136,454.20	$1,648,465.44	$1,648,465.44	$227,107.96	-43.44%
Thursday, 12 April 2012	$12,627.81	$1,532,511.00	$156,669.68	$154,916.92	$1,666,699.32	$1,666,699.32	$245,341.85	-30.75%
Friday, 13 April 2012	$10,856.45	$1,543,367.45	$167,526.13	$171,286.76	$1,677,434.13	$1,677,434.13	$256,076.66	1.13%
Saturday, 14 April 2012	$13,687.02	$1,557,054.47	$181,213.15	$180,142.33	$1,684,387.39	$1,684,387.39	$263,029.92	96.84%
Sunday, 15 April 2012	$10,945.13	$1,567,999.60	$192,158.28	$188,404.65	$1,702,571.28	$1,702,571.28	$281,213.81	-39.81%
Total	$29,358,677.22	$45,694.72			$16,351,550.34	$16,351,550.34	$1,874,360.29	0.16%

Figure 10.69: The Matrix visual after fixing the format string issue

As the preceding image shows, the format string issue has been resolved.

DAX functions for calculation groups

There are many use cases for calculation groups that we haven't covered in this chapter. Therefore, we'll leave the rest for you to investigate. However, it is worthwhile mentioning the DAX functions that are currently available for calculation groups. The following list briefly explains those functions:

- SELECTEDMEASURE(): A reference to an explicit measure used on top of calculation items. You can learn more about the SELECTEDMEASURE() function here: https://learn.microsoft.com/en-us/dax/selectedmeasure-function-dax?WT.mc_id=DP-MVP-5003466.

- ISSELECTEDMEASURE([Measure1], [Measure2], ...): Accepts a list of explicit measures that exist within the data model and then determines if the measure that is currently selected within the visuals is one of the ones mentioned in the input list of parameters. It can be used to apply the calculation logic conditionally. You can learn more about the ISSELECTEDMEASURE([Measure1], [Measure2], ...) function here: https://learn.microsoft.com/en-us/dax/isselectedmeasure-function-dax?WT.mc_id=DP-MVP-5003466.

- SELECTEDMEASURENAME(): Returns the selected measure's name. It can be used to apply the calculation logic conditionally. You can learn more about the SELECTEDMEASURENAME() function here: https://learn.microsoft.com/en-us/dax/selectedmeasurename-function-dax?WT.mc_id=DP-MVP-5003466.

- SELECTEDMEASUREFORMATSTRING(): Returns the format string defined by the selected measure. It can be used to define the format string dynamically based on expressions. You can learn more about the SELECTEDMEASUREFORMATSTRING() function here: https://learn.microsoft.com/en-us/dax/selectedmeasureformatstring-function-dax?WT.mc_id=DP-MVP-5003466.

Summary

In this chapter, we learned about some advanced data modeling techniques, as well as how to implement aggregations using big data in Power BI. We also learned how to configure incremental refresh, which helps deal with the challenges of working with large data sources. Then, we looked at the concept of Parent-Child hierarchies and implemented one in Power BI Desktop. After that, we learned how to deal with roleplaying dimensions in Power BI. Last but not least, we implemented calculation groups.

In the next chapter, *Row-Level Security*, we will discuss a crucial part of data modeling that is essential for organizations that believe the right people must access the right data in the right way.

Join us on Discord!

Join The Big Data and Analytics Community on the Packt Discord Server!

Hang out with 558 other members and enjoy free voice and text chat.

`https://packt.link/ips2H`

11

Row-Level and Object-Level Security

In the previous chapter, we learned advanced data modeling techniques, such as implementing various aggregation types, incremental refresh, parent-child hierarchies, role-playing dimensions, and calculation groups. This chapter discusses an essential aspect of data modeling, **row-level security** and **object-level security** (**RLS** and **OLS** respectively). We will cover the following topics:

- What RLS and OLS mean in data modeling
- Terminology
- Implementation flows
- Common RLS and OLS implementation approaches

We try to cover the preceding topics with real-world scenarios, but remember that each Power BI project may have specific requirements, so it is virtually impossible to cover all possibilities and scenarios in one chapter.

When it comes to Power BI security, many people immediately think it relates to Power BI administration, which is correct to some extent. RLS filters the data within an entire data model to show relevant data to the relevant users. On the other hand, OLS guarantees that only authorized users can access the model objects, such as tables and columns. So, both RLS and OLS are access control mechanisms directly applied to the data model, and their implementation is directly relevant to data modelers. Still, at the end of the day, we publish the data model into the Power BI Service or Power BI Report Server, where the users, depending on their roles, interact with the data model. So, the security settings tasks vary from organization to organization. In some organizations, an administrator's job is to take care of the dataset security-related settings within the Power BI Service or Server. At the same time, some other organizations expect the data modelers to fully support all aspects of RLS and OLS, from development to configuration. The latter is rare, except in small organizations where Power BI developers take care of development, deployment, and administration. Regardless of who supports RLS and OLS within an organization, we cover end-to-end implementation and configuration of both in this chapter.

You can find all resources required in this chapter here: https://github.com/PacktPublishing/Expert-Data-Modeling-with-Power-BI-Second-Edition/tree/ca01add05cfd360fad97cfbf304f66d9c80a8de4/Samples/Chapter%2011.

With that in mind, let's get started.

What RLS and OLS mean in data modeling

As mentioned previously, RLS and OLS are mechanisms to control user access over data or hide data model objects so that the relevant user or group of users can access relevant data or data model objects. This is possible by filtering the data and hiding the objects based on the users' usernames and the role(s) assigned to them by writing simple **Data Analysis Expressions** (**DAX**) or, in more complex scenarios, by making changes in the data model. Therefore, the relationships between tables and their cross-filtering direction are vital. While we predominantly develop RLS within Power BI Desktop, implementing OLS is not available in the desktop itself; instead, we use third-party tools such as Tabular Editor. We publish the report file (PBIX) to the Power BI Service after implementing the data model, including RLS, OLS, or both. When we publish the report file to the Power BI Service, it constructs the PBIX file into two separate objects: a dataset and a report. The dataset encapsulates the Power Query and the data model layers, and the report contains the data visualization. It is important to note that either RLS or OLS kicks in only at the report level and only if:

- The user has the **Viewer** role in the Workspace.
- The report is shared with the user via a **link, direct access**, or an **app**.

 As mentioned earlier, RLS filters data across an entire data model, and OLS hides the data model objects from unauthorized users on the report layer. So, they are not security or permission control configurations over Power BI data models.

Terminology

We should learn some terminology before implementing RLS and OLS. The following sections introduce this terminology.

Roles

A role is a name indicating the characteristic of a security rule over tables in the data model. It is best to pick a meaningful name describing the underlying security rules. We can define roles in Power BI Desktop as follows:

1. Click the **Modeling** tab.
2. Click the **Manage roles** button.
3. Click the **Create** button to add a new role.

The preceding steps are highlighted in the following image:

Figure 11.1: Roles in Power BI Desktop

Rules

Security rules are the DAX expressions ruling the data that a role can see. A DAX expression defining a rule returns a value of true or false. Follow the next steps to add a new rule:

1. Click the **Manage roles** button from the **Modeling** tab of the ribbon.
2. Type in a DAX expression that returns true or false. We can also click the ellipsis button of a table that we want to apply the rule to in order to select a specific column.
3. Click the **Verify DAX expression** button.

The following image shows a rule that filters out the **Currency** table's data to only show sales with a currency of **AUD**. We defined the role under the **AUD Sales Only** role:

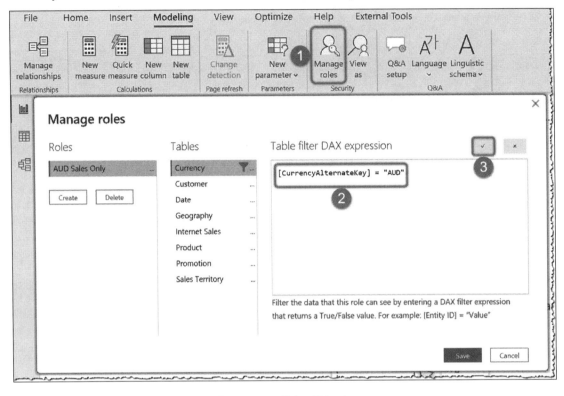

Figure 11.2: Defining RLS rules

Enhanced row-level security editor

In February 2023, Microsoft announced a new row-level security editor that simplifies rule creation. When authoring this book, the enhanced row-level security editor is in public preview. In the new editor, we can toggle between the traditional DAX interface and the new dropdown version. For example, the following image shows the AUD Sales Only role in the new editor:

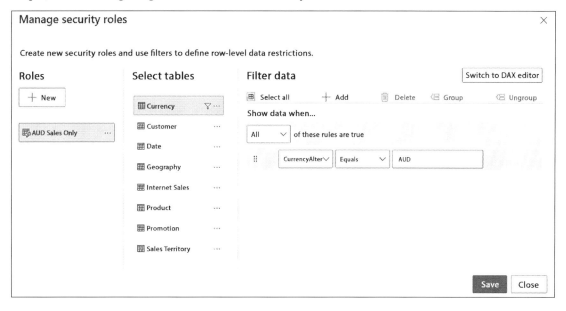

Figure 11.3: Defining RLS rules in the enhanced row-level security editor

As this feature is still in public preview and is subject to change, we use the DAX interface throughout this chapter.

Validating roles

When we create roles and rules, we need to test and validate them. We can validate roles in both Power BI Desktop and the Power BI Service. The following steps show role validation in Power BI Desktop:

1. Click the **View as** button from the **Modeling** tab.
2. Select a role to validate.
3. Click **OK**.

The preceding steps are highlighted in the following image:

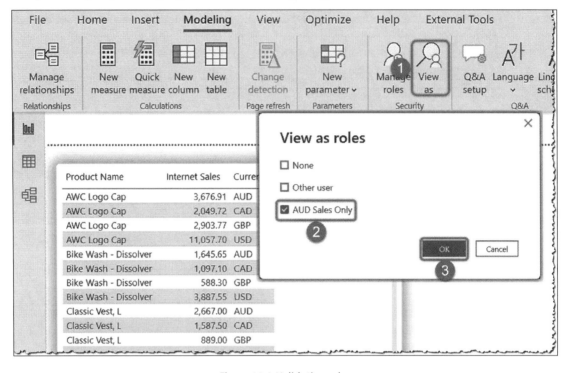

Figure 11.4: Validating roles

The following image shows that the validation results only include **Internet Sales** when the **Currency** is **AUD**. We click the **Stop viewing** button to terminate the validation:

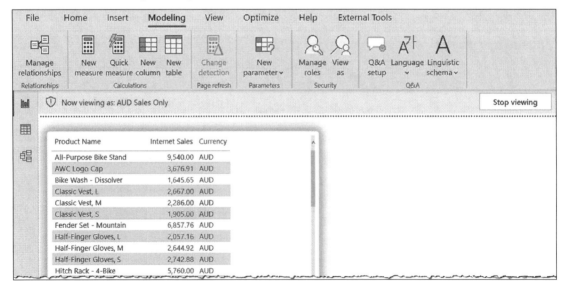

Figure 11.5: Role validation results

Assigning members to roles in the Power BI Service

After implementing security roles, we need to assign users or groups to roles. Managing members is a part of RLS security management within the Power BI Service or Power BI Report Server. The following steps show how to assign members to a role in the Power BI Service and report to a workspace:

1. Navigate to the desired workspace.
2. Hover over the dataset and click the ellipsis button.
3. Click **Security**.
4. Select a role.
5. Type an account or a group and select it.
6. Click the **Add** button.
7. Click the **Save** button.

The preceding steps are highlighted in the following image:

Figure 11.6: Assigning members to RLS roles in the Power BI Service

The next section explains assigning members to a role in Power BI Report Server.

Assigning members to roles in Power BI Report Server

The following steps show how to assign members to a role in Power BI Report Server after publishing a report to the server:

1. Open a web browser and navigate to **Power BI Report Server**.
2. Click the ellipsis button of the desired report from the **Browse** tab.
3. Click **Manage**.

    The preceding steps are highlighted in the following image:

    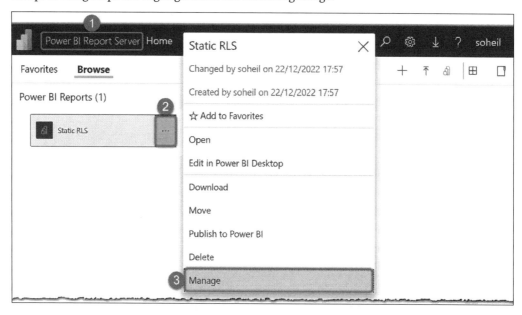

    Figure 11.7: Managing a report in Power BI Report Server

4. Click **Row-level security**.
5. Click the **Add Member** button.
6. Type in a username or group name.
7. Select roles to assign to the user.
8. Click **OK**.

The preceding steps are highlighted in the following image:

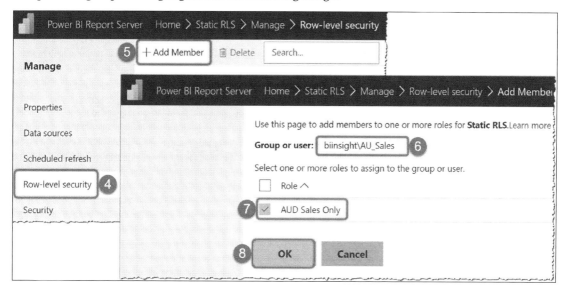

Figure 11.8: Assigning users or groups to roles in Power BI Report Server

After we have assigned users or groups to roles, users can only see the relevant data.

RLS implementation flow

Implementing RLS in Power BI always follows the same flow, which applies to all implementation approaches and all supported storage modes. We implement RLS in the data model; therefore, the dataset's storage mode must be in **Import** mode, **DirectQuery** mode, or **Composite** mode (**Mixed** mode). The following steps explain the RLS implementation flow:

1. Creating security roles.
2. Defining rules within the roles.
3. Validating roles in Power BI Desktop.
4. Publishing the model to the Power BI Service or Power BI Report Server.
5. Assigning members to roles within the Power BI Service or Power BI Report Server.
6. Validating roles in the Power BI Service (role validation is unavailable in Power BI Report Server).

The following diagram illustrates the preceding flow:

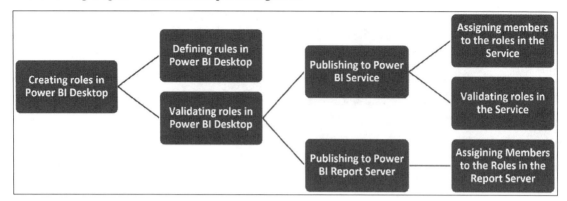

Figure 11.9: RLS implementation flow

In the next section, we look at different RLS implementation approaches.

Common RLS implementation approaches

There are usually two different approaches to implementing RLS in Power BI Desktop: static RLS and dynamic RLS. In the following few sections, we look at both approaches by implementing real-world scenarios.

Static RLS implementation

A static RLS approach is when we define rules that statically apply filters to the data model. For example, in *Figure 11.2*, we created a static RLS rule to filter the **Internet Sales** amounts by currency when the currency equals **AUD**. While static RLS is simple to implement, depending on the scenario, it can get quite expensive to maintain and support. Moreover, static RLS is sometimes just enough to satisfy business requirements.

Let us go through a scenario; Adventure Works is an international organization with a few security groups within **Azure Active Directory** (**Azure AD**) or Microsoft 365, separating users based on their geographical locations. The business wants to implement RLS so that Australian users can see only their **Internet Sales** amount. In contrast, the rest of the world can see all **Internet Sales** amounts *except* Australia's. In this section, we use the Chapter 11, Static RLS.pbix sample file. You can download the sample file from here: https://github.com/PacktPublishing/Expert-Data-Modeling-with-Power-BI-Second-Edition/blob/main/Samples/Chapter%2011/Chapter%2011%2C%20Static%20RLS.pbix.

The following steps show the implementation of the preceding requirement.

Chapter 11

Creating roles and defining rules: Follow these steps to create roles and to define rules:

1. Click the **Manage roles** button from the **Modeling** tab on the ribbon.
2. Click **Create**.
3. Type in **AUD Sales Only** as the role name.
4. Click the ellipsis button of the **Currency** table.
5. Hover over **Add filter....**
6. Click **[CurrencyAlternateKey]**.

The preceding steps are highlighted in the following image:

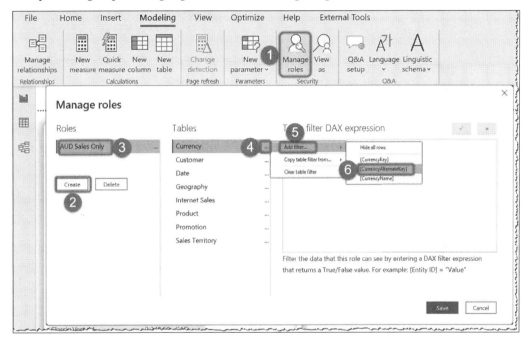

Figure 11.10: Creating an AUD Sales Only RLS role in Power BI Desktop

7. This automatically creates a [CurrencyAlternateKey] = "Value" DAX expression. Replace the **Value** field with **AUD**.
8. Click the **Verify DAX Expression** button.

The preceding steps are highlighted in the following image:

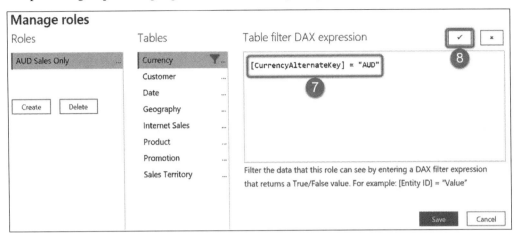

Figure 11.11: Defining a new RLS rule

9. Click the **Create** button again.
10. Type in **Non-AUD Sales** as the role name.
11. Click the ellipsis button of the **Currency** table.
12. Hover over **Add filter…**.
13. Click **[CurrencyAlternateKey]**.
14. Change the generated DAX expression to **[CurrencyAlternateKey] <> "AUD"**.
15. Click the **Validate DAX Expression** button.
16. Click **Save**.

The preceding steps are highlighted in the following image:

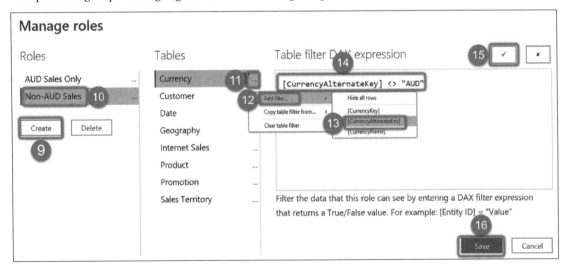

Figure 11.12: Creating a Non-AUD Sales RLS role in Power BI Desktop

Chapter 11

So far, we have created the roles. We now need to validate them.

Validating roles: The following steps explain role validation within Power BI Desktop:

1. Click the **View as** button from the **Modeling** tab.
2. Select a role to validate.
3. Click **OK**.
4. The results of the **Non-AUD Sales** role are visible in the table visual.
5. Click the **Stop viewing** button after finishing with the validation.

The following image shows the validation of the **Non-AUD Sales** role:

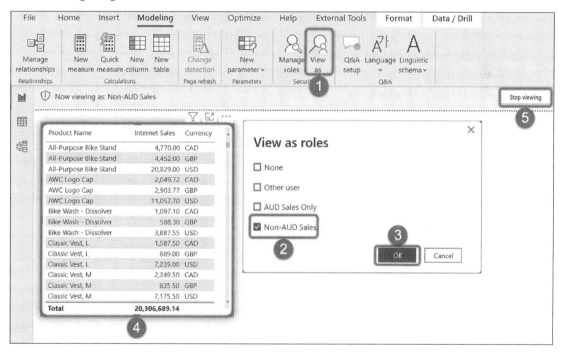

Figure 11.13: Validating the Non-AUD Sales role

The next step is to publish the model to the Power BI Service after ensuring that the roles work as expected and assigning members to the roles.

Publishing a report to the Power BI Service: Follow these next steps to publish a report to the Power BI Service:

1. Click the **Publish** button from the **Home** tab of the ribbon.
2. Select the desired workspace from the list.
3. Click the **Select** button.

The preceding steps are highlighted in the following image:

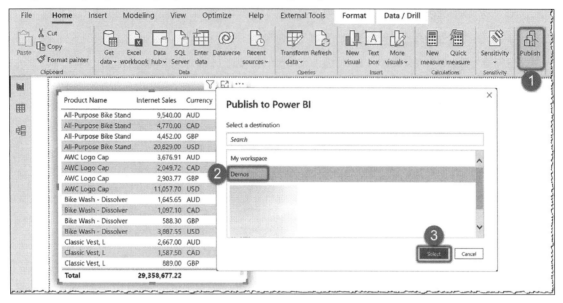

Figure 11.14: Publishing a Power BI report to the Power BI Service

After the report is successfully published, we need to log in to the Power BI Service from a web browser to assign members to roles.

Assigning members to roles: After logging in to the Power BI Service, navigate to the workspace containing the report we published earlier. The following steps show how to assign members to roles:

1. Click the **More options** button of the desired dataset.
2. Click **Security**.
3. Select the desired role.
4. Type in a user or a group; I have two security groups defined in my environment (**AU Users** and **Non-AU Users**), so I assign those two groups to the corresponding roles.
5. Click **Add**.
6. Click **Save**.

The preceding steps are highlighted in the following image:

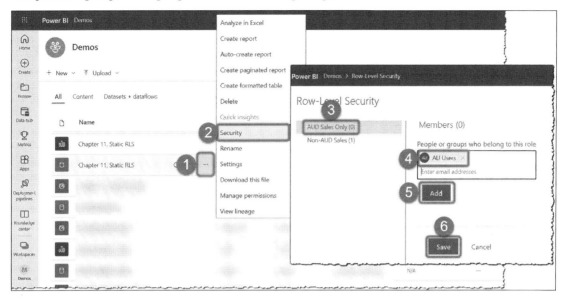

Figure 11.15: Assigning members to roles

 We need to be an **Admin** or a **Member** of the workspace to assign members to security roles or validate roles.

We have now successfully implemented RLS to show sales amounts in **Australian Dollars** (**AUD**) to our Australian users and non-AUD sales to the rest of the world. As mentioned earlier, we can also validate roles in the Power BI Service. To validate roles from the service, we do not need to assign members to roles first. Now, let's validate the roles in the Power BI Service.

Validating roles in the Power BI Service: The following steps will help you to validate roles in the Power BI Service:

1. Click the ellipsis button of a role.
2. Click **Test as role**.

The preceding steps are highlighted in the following image:

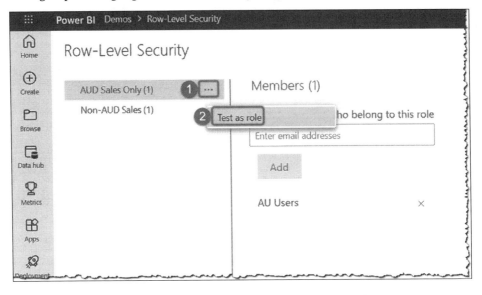

Figure 11.16: Validating RLS roles in the Power BI Service

This opens a report with the selected RLS role-applied filters. The following image shows the validation results for the **AUD Sales Only** role:

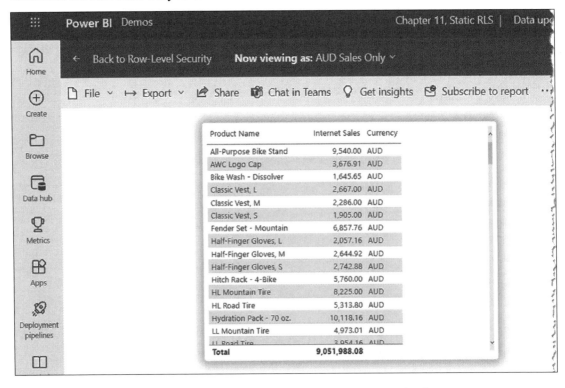

Figure 11.17: The validation results for the AUD Sales Only role

Now that we have learned how to implement a static RLS scenario, let's look at some more complex scenarios that require a dynamic RLS implementation.

Dynamic RLS implementation

In many cases, we need to implement dynamic RLS as static RLS does not cover the requirements. In this section, we look at several real-world scenarios that require implementing dynamic RLS.

Restricting unauthorized users from accessing data

Imagine a scenario where we need to implement RLS for salespersons in a sales data model. Each salesperson must see their sales data only. Implementing static RLS for such a scenario does not work. The reason is that we either have to create one static role per salesperson and assign a member to each role or create a role that works dynamically based on the salesperson's username. This scenario is one of the easiest dynamic RLS implementations yet one of the most common ones. In this section, we use the Chapter 11, Dynamic RLS.pbix sample file supplied with this book. You can download the sample file from here: https://github.com/PacktPublishing/Expert-Data-Modeling-with-Power-BI-Second-Edition/blob/main/Samples/Chapter%2011/Chapter%2011%2C%20Dynamic%20RLS.pbix.

Implementing the preceding scenario is relatively easy. We need to use one of the following DAX functions to retrieve the current username and use it in an RLS role:

- USERNAME(): Returns the current user's login name in the form of DOMAIN_NAME\USER_NAME when used in Power BI Desktop. The USERNAME() function returns the user's User Principal Name (UPN) when published to the Power BI Service and Power BI Report Server.
- USERPRINCIPALNAME(): Returns the user's UPN at connection time. The UPN is in email format.

Implementing RLS in Power BI only makes sense when we publish the model to the service or Power BI Report Server; therefore, using the USERPRINCIPALNAME() function is preferred.

If we embed Power BI reports into a proprietary application and have to use the user login name, we should use the USERNAME() function.

Now, it's time to implement the solution. The steps to create roles and rules, validate roles, publish to the service, and assign members to roles are all the same as we learned before, so we will skip explaining them again. To implement dynamic RLS for this scenario, we need to find the matching value in the **EmailAddress** column from the **Employee** table.

The following steps explain the implementation:

1. Create a **Salespersons Access** role.
2. Create a rule on the **Employee** table in the **EmailAddress** column.
3. Use the [EmailAddress] = USERPRINCIPALNAME() DAX expression.
4. Click **Save**.

The preceding steps are highlighted in the following image:

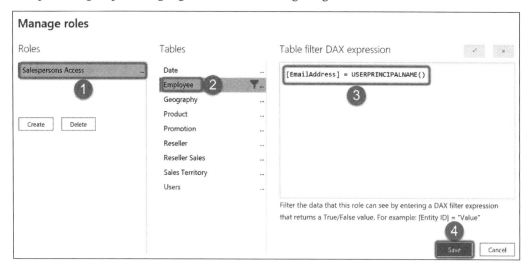

Figure 11.18: Implementing dynamic RLS to filter the data based on the EmailAddress column

 To validate the RLS roles in Power BI Desktop, we do not necessarily have to have data visualizations. We can switch to the **Data** view, select the desired table, and then validate the roles.

5. Switch to the **Data** view.
6. Click the **Employee** table to see the data within the **Data** view.
7. Click the **View as** button from the **Home** tab of the ribbon.
8. Tick the **Other user** option.
9. Type in an email account to test the role.
10. Check the **Salespersons Access** role.
11. Click **OK**.

The following image shows the role validation steps:

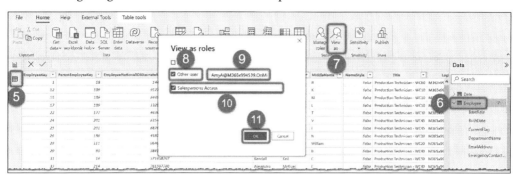

Figure 11.19: Validating dynamic RLS roles within the Data view

The following image shows the results after validating the **Salespersons Access** role:

Figure 11.20: RLS role validation results within the Data view

12. If you would like to see how the data changes in your visuals, click the **Report** view to see the changes, as highlighted in the following image:

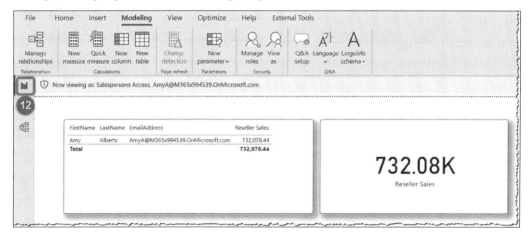

Figure 11.21: Validating RLS roles in the Report view

Now that we are sure that the RLS role works as expected, we publish it to the Power BI Service. If we have the correct RLS security settings in the service, the users must see only their sales data in the report. The following image shows a couple of examples of this:

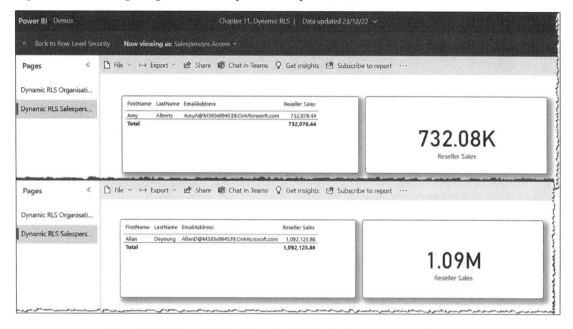

Figure 11.22: Dynamic RLS automatically kicks in when users open the report

As shown in *Figure 11.22*, when **Allan** opens the report he sees his sales data, and **Amy** sees her sales data only.

Now that we know how dynamic RLS works, let's take another step further and look at a more complex scenario. The next section explains dynamic RLS on a sample organizational chart.

Managers can access their team members' data in parent-child hierarchies

So far, we have implemented a straightforward scenario with dynamic RLS to enable salespersons to see the sales data that's relevant to them. But there are many more complex scenarios. Suppose the business started using the report and everyone is happy apart from the sales managers. Their feedback is that they can only see their data, not any of their team members'. Moreover, the **Chief Executive Officer (CEO)** wants to see everyone's sales. The business requires dynamic RLS implementation in which:

- Every salesperson can see their sales data.
- Sales managers can also see their team members' sales.
- The CEO can see everyone's sales.

To implement the preceding scenario, we need to create a parent-child hierarchy based on an existing organizational chart. The **Employee** table in the data model contains the required data to implement the preceding scenario. The **EmployeeKey** and **ParentEmployeeKey** columns contain the supporting data to create a parent-child hierarchy, and the **EmailAddress** column contains the users' UPN supporting the dynamic RLS.

We discussed the parent-child hierarchy implementation in *Chapter 10, Advanced Data Modeling Techniques*.

We create a calculated column with the following DAX expression to identify the parent-child hierarchy path:

```
EmployeePath = PATH(Employee[EmployeeKey], Employee[ParentEmployeeKey])
```

The results of the preceding code snippet are shown in the following image:

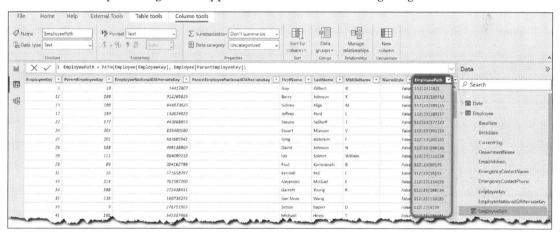

Figure 11.23: Creating the EmployeePath calculated column in the Employee table

The next step is to identify the **EmployeeKey** value based on the **EmailAddress**.

The following DAX expression retrieves caters to that:

```
CALCULATETABLE(
    VALUES(Employee[EmployeeKey])
    , FILTER(Employee, Employee[EmailAddress] = USERPRINCIPALNAME())
    , FILTER(Employee, Employee[Status] = "Current")
)
```

 In the **Employee** table, the **StartDate**, **EndDate**, and **Status** columns keep the employees' employment history. Therefore, to get the current employees, we get the **EmployeeKey** values when the **Status** is **Current**.

To test the preceding code, create a **measure** using the same DAX expression, then validate the RLS role. The following image shows the result of using the same expression in a measure shown in a card visual:

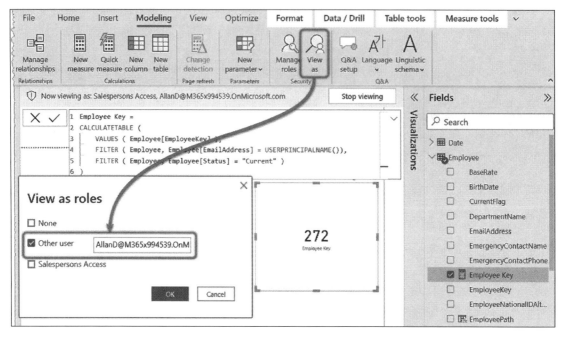

Figure 11.24: Validating DAX expressions for RLS in a measure

We created the **EmployeeKey** measure to test the implementation, so we can remove it after testing. Now that we have retrieved the **EmployeeKey** value, we can use the results to find all rows where an **EmployeeKey** value appears with the **EmployeePath** calculated column. To understand the scenario, let's look closely at the data. The following image shows all salespersons' sales, their **EmployeeKey** values, names, email addresses, and **EmployeePath** values. Please note that the relevant values are marked with filled, dashed, and dotted lines:

EmployeeKey	FirstName	LastName	Title	EmailAddress	EmployeePath	Reseller Sales
272	Allan	Deyoung	North American Sales Manager	AllanD@M365x994539.OnMicrosoft.com	112|277|272	1,092,123.86
290	Amy	Alberts	European Sales Manager	AmyA@M365x994539.OnMicrosoft.com	112|277|290	732,078.44
289	David	Campbell	Sales Representative	DavidC@M365x994539.OnMicrosoft.com	112|277|272|289	3,729,945.35
284	Garrett	Vargas	Sales Representative	GarrettV@M365x994539.OnMicrosoft.com	112|277|272|284	3,609,447.22
291	Jae	Pak	Sales Representative	JaeP@M365x994539.OnMicrosoft.com	112|277|290|291	8,503,338.65
283	Jillian	Carson	Sales Representative	JillianC@M365x994539.OnMicrosoft.com	112|277|272|283	10,065,803.54
288	José	Saraiva	Sales Representative	JoséS@M365x994539.OnMicrosoft.com	112|277|272|288	5,926,418.36
282	Linda	Mitchell	Sales Representative	LindaM@M365x994539.OnMicrosoft.com	112|277|272|282	10,367,007.43
296	Lynn	Tsoflias	Sales Representative	LynnT@M365x994539.OnMicrosoft.com	112|277|294|296	1,421,810.93
281	Michael	Blythe	Sales Representative	MichaelB@M365x994539.OnMicrosoft.com	112|277|272|281	9,293,903.01
286	Pamela	Ansman-Wolfe	Sales Representative	PamelaA@M365x994539.OnMicrosoft.com	112|277|272|286	3,325,102.60
295	Rachel	Valdez	Sales Representative	RachelV@M365x994539.OnMicrosoft.com	112|277|290|295	1,790,640.23
292	Ranjit	Varkey Chudukatil	Sales Representative	RanjitV@M365x994539.OnMicrosoft.com	112|277|290|292	4,509,888.93
287	Shu	Ito	Sales Representative	ShuI@M365x994539.OnMicrosoft.com	112|277|272|287	6,427,005.56
294	Syed	Abbas	Pacific Sales Manager	SyedA@M365x994539.OnMicrosoft.com	112|277|294	172,524.45
293	Tete	Mensa-Annan	Sales Representative	TeteM@M365x994539.OnMicrosoft.com	112|277|272|293	2,312,545.69
285	Tsvi	Reiter	Sales Representative	TsviR@M365x994539.OnMicrosoft.com	112|277|272|285	7,171,012.75
Total						80,450,596.98

Figure 11.25: Salespersons' sales

As the preceding image shows, **Allan**, **Amy**, and **Syed** are sales managers. A sales manager is also a salesperson selling products. The **EmployeePath** column's values reveal that the sales managers are in the third level of the organizational chart, as their employee keys appear in the third position within the **EmployeePath** values. Therefore, they must see all the sales data of their team members. The team members' employee keys appear after the sales managers in the **EmployeePath**. Note that the person with an employee key of **277**, one level below the person with an employee key of **112**, must see all sales data. The employee key of **112** is the CEO's. To implement this scenario, we must find each person's employee key within the **EmployeePath** value for each row. To do so, we use a function in DAX to find values in a parent-child path: PATHCONTAINS(<Path to lookup>,<value to be found within the Path>). The PATHCONTAINS() function returns True if the specified value appears within the path. We already have the path values within the **EmployeePath** column. We also wrote the DAX expression to retrieve the employee key of the current user, which is the value to be found within the path. So, the DAX expression looks like this:

```
VAR _key = CALCULATETABLE (
    VALUES ( Employee[EmployeeKey] ),
    FILTER ( Employee, Employee[EmailAddress] = USERPRINCIPALNAME()),
    FILTER ( Employee, Employee[Status] = "Current" )
)
RETURN
PATHCONTAINS (
        Employee[EmployeePath], _key
)
```

The only remaining part is to create an RLS role and use the preceding expression as a rule. The following image shows a new role, **Sales Team**, with the preceding DAX expression for its rule:

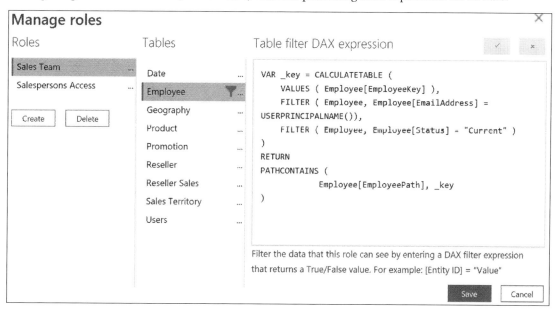

Figure 11.26: Creating a Sales Team role for dynamic RLS

Now, we validate the **Sales Team** role for one of the managers. The following image shows the validation results when **Allan** uses the report:

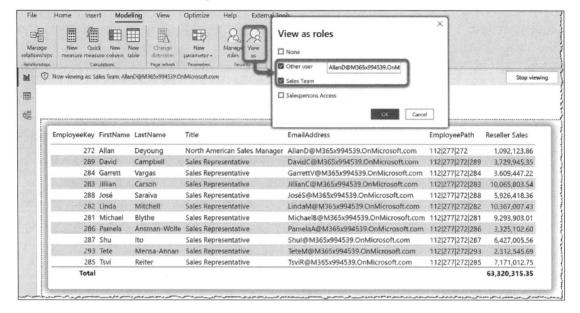

Figure 11.27: Validating dynamic RLS, enabling sales managers to see their team members' sales

We can now publish the report to the service.

 If you are a Power BI administrator, assign the members to the new **Sales Team** role. Otherwise, ask your Power BI administrator to do so.

So far, we have implemented a dynamic RLS enabling the sales managers to see their team members' sales. Now, let's see what the CEO can see after opening the report. As a reminder, the CEO can see everyone's sales data, as illustrated in the following image:

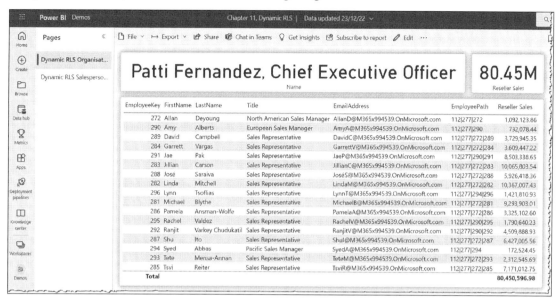

Figure 11.28: The CEO can see everyone's data

While the preceding scenario was more complex than the first one, we may face more challenges in the real world. You must have noted that the **Employee** table contains the users' login data to implement the previous scenarios, such as the **EmailAddress** value. In the next section, we learn how to implement scenarios when the email address data does not exist in the **Employee** table.

Getting the user's login data from another source

Imagine a scenario where the business has the same requirement as outlined previously; however, the source system does not contain the **EmailAddress** column in the **Employee** table. In those cases, we need to get the users' login data from a different source. While the new data source provides users' login data, it may not necessarily have an **EmployeeKey** column to relate employees to their login data. Depending on the source system, we may get different sets of data. In our scenario, we asked the system administrators to give us an extract of the organization's **AD** users. They provided a **JavaScript Object Notation (JSON)** file containing a list of all users' UPNs. You can find it here: https://github.com/PacktPublishing/Expert-Data-Modeling-with-Power-BI-Second-Edition/blob/ca01add05cfd360fad97cfbf304f66d9c80a8de4/Samples/Chapter%2011/Chapter%2011,%20Adventure%20Works,%20AAD%20UPNs.json.

In the real world, we should think about automating the process of generating the JSON file and keeping it up to date.

The generated JSON export from Azure AD contains sensitive data. Therefore, it must be stored in a secured location accessible by a restricted number of users.

For convenience, we use the same Power BI file used in the previous scenario. We just ignore the **EmailAddress** column in the **Employee** table.

The following steps explain how to overcome this challenge:

1. In Power BI Desktop, get the data from the provided **JSON** file, as illustrated in the following image:

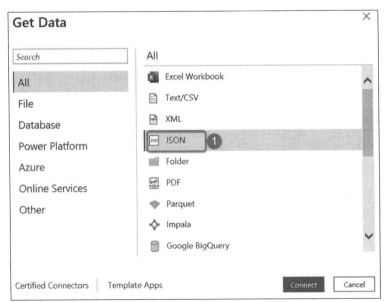

Figure 11.29: Getting data from the JSON file

2. Rename the query as **Users**.
3. Remove the **@odata.context** column.
4. Rename the **value.givenName** column as **First Name**, the **value.surname** column as **Last Name**, and the **value.userPrincipalName** column as **Email Address**. The results look like this:

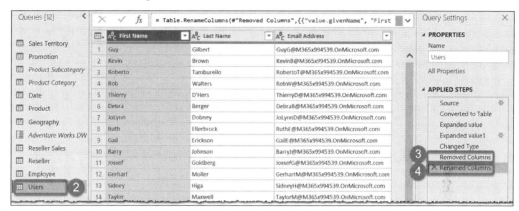

Figure 11.30: Preparing the Users table

As you see, we do not have the **EmployeeKey** column in the **Users** table. However, we can get the **EmployeeKey** value from the **Employee** table by finding the matching values based on the **First Name** and **Last Name** columns. The following steps show how to do this.

5. **Merge** the **Users** table with the **Employee** table on the **First Name** and **Last Name** columns from the **User** and **FirstName** and **LastName** columns from the **Employee** table. Set the **Join Kind** value to **Left Outer (all from first, matching second)**, as illustrated in the following image:

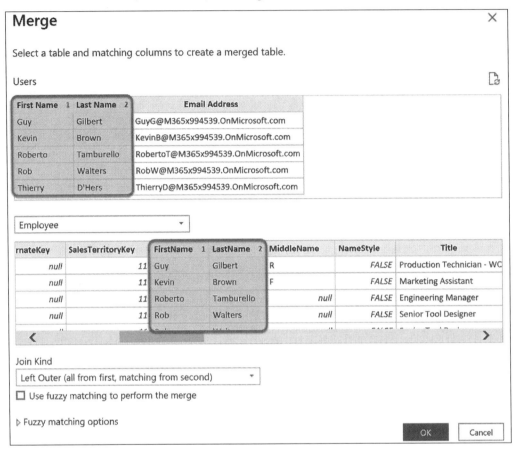

Figure 11.31: Merging the Users table with the Employee table

6. Expand the **Employee** structured column to keep the **EmployeeKey** and **Status** columns, as illustrated in the following image:

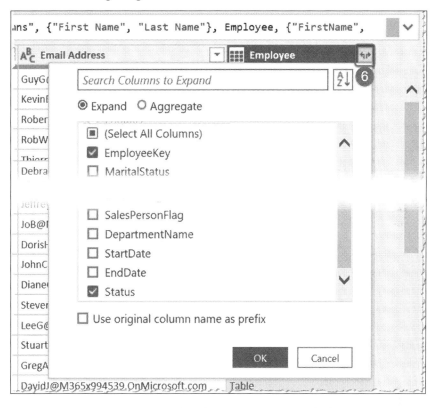

Figure 11.32: Expanding the Employee structured column

 Remember, the **Employee** table keeps the employees' history, which means we can potentially duplicate values. Therefore, we need to keep the **Status** column to make sure all employees' statuses are **Current**.

7. Filter the **Status** column to only show rows with a **Current** status, as illustrated in the following image:

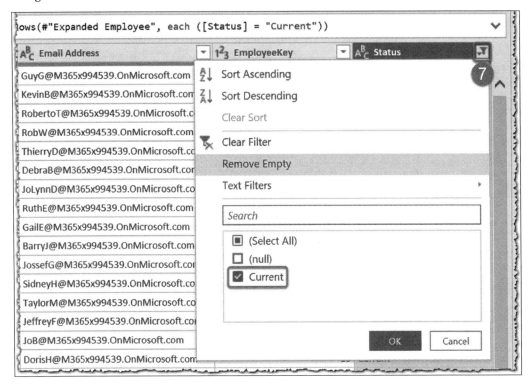

Figure 11.33: Filtering the Employee table to show the rows with a Current status

8. Click the **Close & Apply** button to load the **Users** table into the data model, as illustrated in the following image:

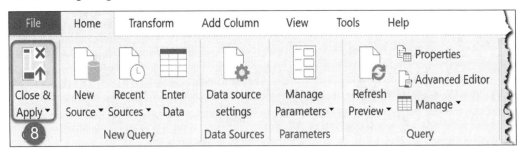

Figure 11.34: Applying the changes and loading the Users table into the data model

9. Create a new relationship between the **Users** table and the **Employee** table if Power BI Desktop has not automatically detected the relationship, as illustrated in the following image:

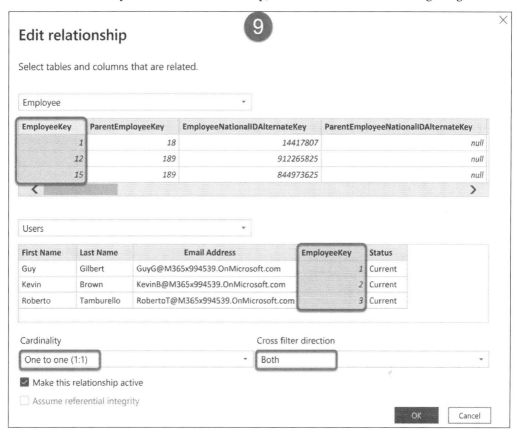

Figure 11.35: Creating a relationship between the Users and Employee tables

As you see in the preceding image, the relationship between the **Users** and the **Employee** tables is a one-to-one relationship, which is precisely what we are after. Now, create a new role on the **Employee** table, as explained in the following steps.

10. Create a new RLS role, **Sales Team AAD**, then create a new rule for the **Employee** table using the following DAX expression, as shown in *Figure 11.36*:

```
VAR _key = CALCULATETABLE (
        VALUES ( Users[EmployeeKey] ),
        FILTER ( Users, Users[Email Address] = USERPRINCIPALNAME())
)
RETURN
PATHCONTAINS (
        Employee[EmployeePath], _key)
```

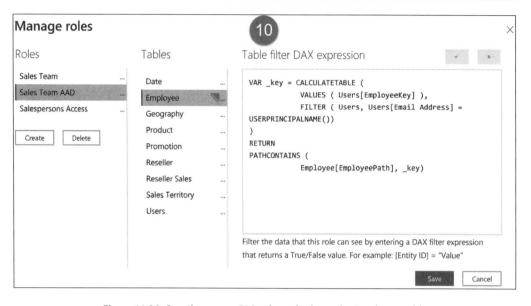

Figure 11.36: Creating a new RLS role and rule on the Employee table

 As we already filtered all rows in the **Users** table to only show the current users, we do not need to add a `FILTER()` function in the `CALCULATETABLE()` code block.

11. Last, but not least, is to validate the role by clicking the **View as** button from the **Modeling** tab of the ribbon, as illustrated in the following image:

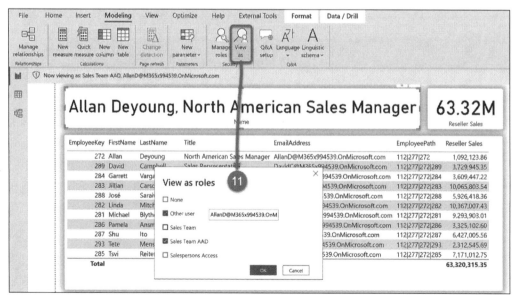

Figure 11.37: Validating the new RLS role

So far, we have learned how to implement various RLS scenarios. We also learned that sometimes we need to change the data model to meet some security requirements. While we covered some common scenarios, there are many more scenarios that we cannot cover in a single chapter, so we leave it to you to investigate more. The next sections explain OLS implementation in Power BI.

Introduction to OLS

In the previous sections, we learned how to control the user's access to data using RLS. In this section, we look at OLS in Power BI. With OLS, we can hide tables and columns that contain sensitive data from the model, such as hiding an entire table or columns for specific users. A more real-world example could be hiding people's salaries, their bank accounts, or any other personal data from the **Employees** table in an HR data model. OLS also secures the metadata. Like RLS, OLS kicks in only in the Power BI Service for the users with the Workspace **Viewer** role and the users with **read** or **build** permissions on the dataset. So, sensitive objects are hidden from them, even though the users with a **build** permission on the dataset can create new reports or use the **Analyse in Excel** feature to connect to the dataset.

The next section explains the implementation flow for OLS.

OLS implementation flow

OLS implementation flow in Power BI is very similar to RLS. The following steps explain the OLS implementation flow:

1. Creating security roles in Power BI Desktop.
2. Securing the objects in third-party tools such as Tabular Editor or SSMS.
3. Saving the changes to the Power BI Desktop model.
4. Validating roles in Power BI Desktop.
5. Publishing the model to the Power BI Service or Power BI Report Server.
6. Assigning members to roles within the Power BI Service or Power BI Report Server.
7. Validating roles in the Power BI Service (role validation is unavailable in Power BI Report Server).

 The OLS restrictions apply to the members assigned to the role.

The following diagram illustrates the preceding flow:

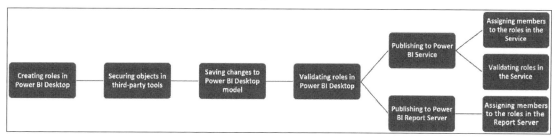

Figure 11.38: OLS implementation flow

Implementing OLS is not currently available in Power BI Desktop, so using third-party tools is inevitable.

OLS implementation

Let's look at OLS implementation with a common scenario. The business wants to make the customers' data visible only to the marketing team and the customers themselves. Therefore, no one who is not working in the marketing team must see the **Customer** table. The business also decided to secure all measures related to the **OrderQuantity** column from the **Internet Sales** table from the marketing team and the customers.

We will use the Chapter 11, OLS.pbix sample file provided with the book. The sample file is accessible here: https://github.com/PacktPublishing/Expert-Data-Modeling-with-Power-BI-Second-Edition/blob/main/Samples/Chapter%2011/Chapter%2011%2C%20OLS.pbix.

In the preceding scenario, we need to have two security groups available. One security group contains all the users except the marketing team members and the customers, and the other is for all the users. The following steps show how to implement the scenario:

1. In Power BI Desktop, create two roles, **Customer Denied** and **OrderQty Denied**, as shown in the following image:

Figure 11.39: Creating two new security roles

We now have to switch to **Tabular Editor** to implement the rest of the scenario. To do this, proceed as follows:

2. Click the **External Tools** tab on the ribbon.
3. Click **Tabular Editor**.

The following image shows the preceding steps:

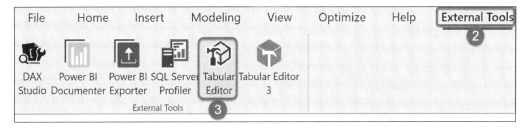

Figure 11.40: Opening Tabular Editor from the External Tools tab

4. In **Tabular Editor**, expand the **Tables** folder.
5. Select the **Customer** table.
6. Expand **Object Level Security** from the **Properties** pane.
7. From the **Internet Sales Denied** drop-down menu, select **None**.

The preceding steps are illustrated in the following screenshot:

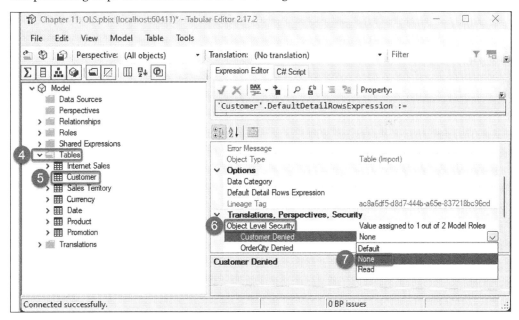

Figure 11.41: Setting up OLS for tables in Tabular Editor

So far, we have set OLS for the **Customer** table, so whoever is a member of the **Customer Denied** role cannot see the **Customer** table, as if it does not exist. In the next few steps, we implement the second part of the requirements within **Tabular Editor**, as follows:

8. Expand the **Internet Sales** table.
9. Click the **OrderQuantity** column.
10. Expand **Object Level Security** from the **Properties** pane.

11. From the **OrderQty Denied** drop-down menu, select **None**.
12. Save the changes to the model.

The preceding steps are highlighted in the following screenshot:

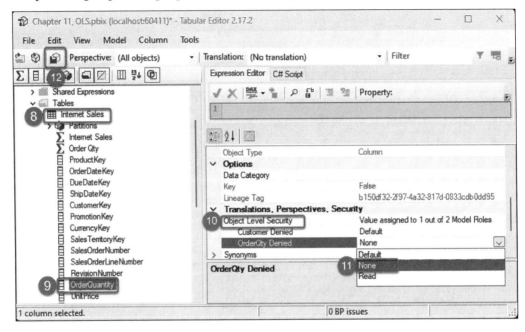

Figure 11.42: Setting up OLS for columns

We have now implemented all OLS settings required by the business. In the next section, we test the roles.

 We cannot restrict measures in OLS. But we can secure the referencing column that consequently hides all dependent measures from unauthorized users.

Validating roles

Role validation for OLS is as same as RLS. The following steps show how to validate roles:

1. In Power BI Desktop, click the **View as** button from the **Modeling** tab.
2. Check the **Customer Denied** role.
3. Click **OK**.

The preceding steps are highlighted in the following screenshot:

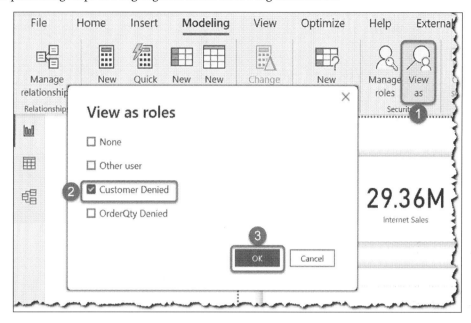

Figure 11.43: Validating the Customer Denied role

The result of the validation is shown in the following image. Note that the **Customer** table has disappeared from the **Fields** pane, and the visual linked to it is broken:

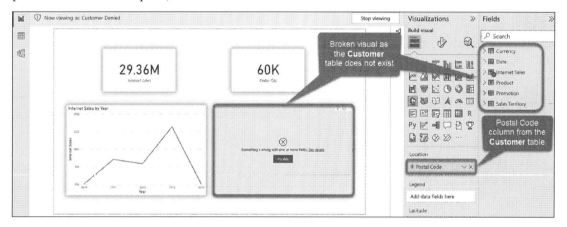

Figure 11.44: Viewing the report as the Customer Denied role

The following image shows the result of the validation of the **OrderQty Denied** role:

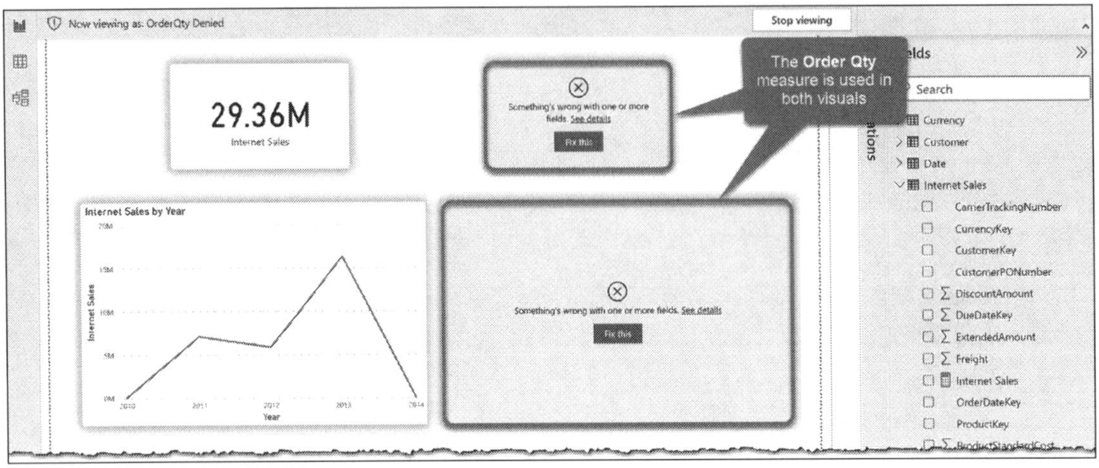

Figure 11.45: Validating the OrderQty Denied role

As the preceding image shows, the visuals linked to the **OrderQuantity** column from the **Internet Sales** table are broken. Here are other things that have happened:

- The **OrderQuantity** column has disappeared from the **Internet Sales** table.
- The **Order Qty** measure linked to the **OrderQuantity** column has also disappeared.

Assigning members and validating roles in the Power BI Service

After implementing OLS, we publish the model to the Power BI Service, assign users or groups to roles, and validate the roles. The steps for assigning members and validating roles are as same as RLS, so we do not repeat them here.

In this section, we learned how to set up OLS in Power BI. In the next section, we look at some applications of RLS and OLS in a single model.

RLS and OLS implementation in a single model

Now that we know how to implement RLS and OLS, let us have a look at a scenario where we need to have both security types in a single data model. While the implementation is very similar, there is a caveat to consider. We cannot have RLS and OLS in different roles, and an error message arises when we do so. Using the previous section's sample file, let's say we want to have a dynamic RLS so that customers can access their data, but we still have to consider the previous requirement to deny everyone's access to the **OrderQuantity** column from the **Internet Sales** table. So, we define an RLS role on the **Customer** table for the **EmailAddress** column, as shown in the following image:

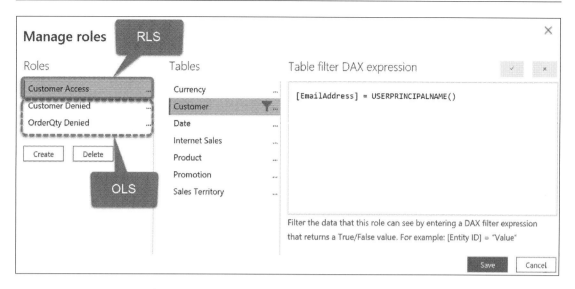

Figure 11.46: Creating an RLS role in an OLS-enabled model

While we can validate each role separately without any issues, if we combine the **OrderQty Denied** and **Customer Access** roles to satisfy the requirement, we get the following error message:

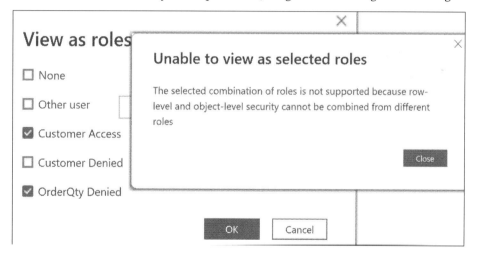

Figure 11.47: An error message is raised when combining RLS and OLS roles

To fix the issue, we must merge the RLS and OLS roles into a single role. In our scenario, the **Customer Denied** role is to secure the customers' data from everyone other than the marketing team members and the customers themselves. So we keep this role, and we merge the **Customer Access** and **OrderQty Denied** roles into the **Customer Access** role, so they can access the customers' data but not any measures referencing the **OrderQuantity** column. Follow these steps in Tabular Editor:

1. Expand the **Internet Sales** table.
2. Select the **OrderQuantity**.
3. Select **None** for **Customer Access** from the **Object Level Security** section.

4. Click **Save**.

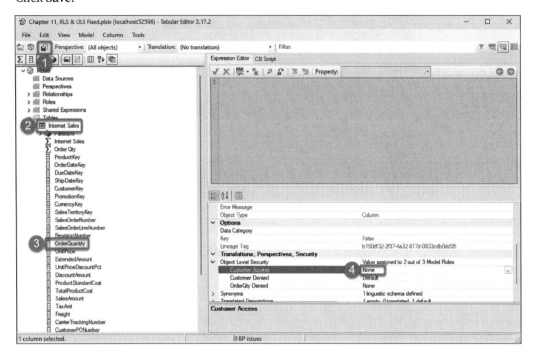

Figure 11.48: Merging RLS and OLS roles

We can now delete the **OrderQty Denied** role. The following image shows validating the roles in the Power BI Service for **Megan**, who is a customer:

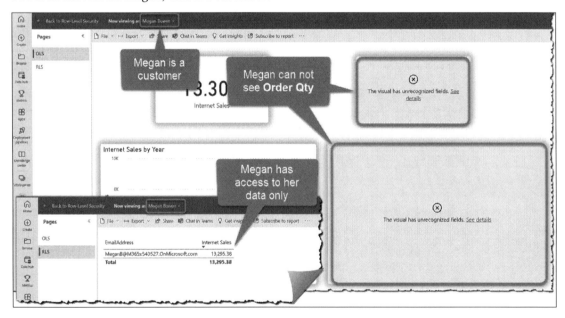

Figure 11.49: Validating roles for a customer

The following image shows role validation in the Power BI Service for Allan, who is not a member of the marketing team, nor is he a customer:

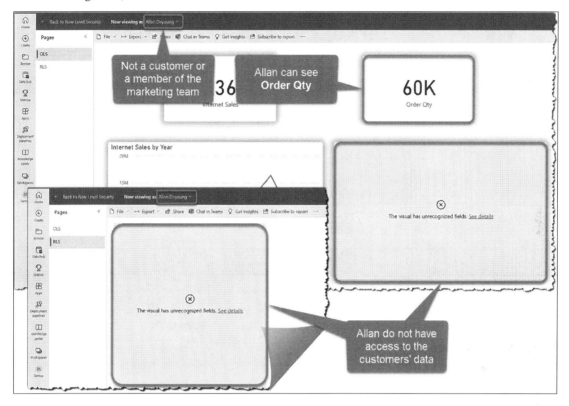

Figure 11.50: Validating roles for the rest of the users

When OLS kicks in, the visuals referencing a secure object break. From a user-friendliness perspective, this is pretty bad. But there are ways to make the visuals user-friendly and, at the same time, have a secure model. One way is to create completely separate thin reports connected live to the same dataset for the users whom OLS must apply to them and for the others. The other way is to have separate report pages for users whom OLS applies and the others. That way, we are required to hide all report pages and use buttons with **Page Navigation**, and control who can access which report page. As this is a data visualization topic, we leave it to you to investigate the ideas. So far, we implemented multiple RLS and OLS scenarios. The next section discusses important points we have to consider when implementing RLS and OLS.

Considerations in using RLS and OLS

As you see, RLS and OLS are powerful security mechanisms that go hand in hand with the data model. Like any other implementation, the first step toward successful and efficient development is to have a design. We saw that in many cases, we are required to modify the data model to implement dynamic RLS. So, paying attention to details when designing the solution, such as how the RLS and OLS implementation may affect the user experience, is crucial. In this section, we put together some considerations to help you design well-thought-out security models:

- As stated at the beginning of this chapter, RLS and OLS implementations require collaboration between developers and administrators. In reality, successful implementation requires a wider group of professionals to collaborate. In real-world scenarios, we do not add user accounts as security role members. Instead, we use security groups. But we need to have a well-thought-out security group construction first. Moreover, the Power BI Administrator role cannot create or manage security groups across an M365 tenant. Therefore, we need to involve the M365 global administrators too. We need to conduct discovery workshops to identify the security requirements and use cases. In the discovery workshops, we need Power BI experts, security experts, and **subject matter experts** (**SMEs**). The outcomes of the discovery workshops must include security group requirements for M365 administrators and data model requirements for Power BI developers.
- Currently, we cannot define security roles and rules in the Power BI Service, so we must define them in Power BI Desktop or third-party tools.
- Both RLS and OLS kick in only for the **Workspace Viewers** or the users with **Read only** or **Read and Build** permissions on the dataset.
- Both RLS and OLS are available only on **DirectQuery**, **Import**, or **Mixed** mode (composite model) connections.
- In OLS, we must be careful when securing tables so that doing so does not break any relationship chains. For instance, in the following data model, securing the **Customer** table breaks the relationship chain between **Geography** and **Internet Sales** tables.

Figure 11.51: Securing tables that break relationship chains is not allowed in OLS

- Securing key columns contributing to relationships works if the table the key columns are in is not secured. For instance, in the preceding image, the **CustomerKey** and **GeographyKey** columns can be secured in the **Customer** table.
- Calculation groups do not support RLS or OLS implementations.
- While we can create multiple roles in RLS, mapping a user into multiple roles may result in incorrect outcomes. Therefore, it is recommended to create the roles in a way that grants all required permissions instead of creating multiple roles. When we map a user to multiple roles, Power BI shows the results of the union of all filters applied by the multiple roles.

Summary

In this chapter, we learned how to implement RLS and OLS in Power BI Desktop and third-party tools. We now know how to manage the roles within the Power BI Service and in Power BI Report Server. We learned what static and dynamic RLS approaches are and how to implement them in our data model to make the relevant data available to authorized users. We also learned how the mixture of RLS and OLS implementation works and what crucial points to note when designing a security model. In the next chapter, *Dealing with More Advanced Data Warehousing Concepts in Power BI*, we look at slowly changing dimensions, and degenerate dimensions.

Join us on Discord!

Join The Big Data and Analytics Community on the Packt Discord Server!

Hang out with 558 other members and enjoy free voice and text chat.

https://packt.link/ips2H

12
Dealing with More Advanced Data Warehousing Concepts in Power BI

In the previous 11 chapters, we learned about various aspects of data modeling to model many different scenarios. This chapter focuses on implementing more advanced data warehousing concepts in Power BI, which become handy in more complex real-world scenarios. This chapter covers the following areas:

- Dealing with **slowly changing dimensions (SCDs)**
- Dealing with **degenerate dimensions**

Dealing with SCDs

The term **slowly changing dimensions**, or in short, **SCD**, is a data warehousing concept introduced by the amazing Ralph Kimball. You can learn more about Ralph Kimball here: https://www.kimballgroup.com/about-kimball-group/.

The SCD concept deals with moving a specific dataset from one state to another. Let us look at SCD in more detail with a scenario.

The **Adventure Works** organization has a **human resources** (**HR**) system in which its data is captured in the organization's data warehouse. **Stephen Jiang** is a **Sales Manager** with 10 sales representatives on his team. The source for this scenario is the AdventureWorksDW2019 database, which you can download from here: https://learn.microsoft.com/en-us/sql/samples/adventureworks-install-configure?view=sql-server-ver16&WT.mc_id=DP-MVP-5003466.

The following image shows the sample data for our scenario:

Full Name	Title	Manager
Stephen Jiang	North American Sales Manager	Brian Welcker
David Campbell	Sales Representative	Stephen Jiang
Garrett Vargas	Sales Representative	Stephen Jiang
Jillian Carson	Sales Representative	Stephen Jiang
José Saraiva	Sales Representative	Stephen Jiang
Linda Mitchell	Sales Representative	Stephen Jiang
Michael Blythe	Sales Representative	Stephen Jiang
Pamela Ansman-Wolfe	Sales Representative	Stephen Jiang
Shu Ito	Sales Representative	Stephen Jiang
Tete Mensa-Annan	Sales Representative	Stephen Jiang
Tsvi Reiter	Sales Representative	Stephen Jiang

Figure 12.1: Stephen Jiang is the sales manager of a team of 10 sales representatives

Brian Welcker, **Stephen**'s manager, resigned in April 2012. **Stephen** applied for the job and got the **Vice President of Sales** role. **Stephen**'s start date is *1st May 2012*. The organization also advertised **Stephen**'s role and hired **Roger Hamilton**, who took over the **North American Sales Manager** role on *1st May 2012*. Here is what is happening:

- We have a resignation, **Brian Welcker**
- A promotion, **Stephen Jiang**
- A new hire, **Roger Hamilton**

The following image shows the changes:

Full Name	Title	Manager
Stephen Jiang	Vice President of Sales	Ken Sánchez
David Campbell	Sales Representative	Roger Hamilton
Garrett Vargas	Sales Representative	Roger Hamilton
Jae Pak	Sales Representative	Amy Alberts
Jillian Carson	Sales Representative	Roger Hamilton
José Saraiva	Sales Representative	Roger Hamilton
Linda Mitchell	Sales Representative	Roger Hamilton
Lynn Tsoflias	Sales Representative	Syed Abbas
Michael Blythe	Sales Representative	Roger Hamilton
Pamela Ansman-Wolfe	Sales Representative	Roger Hamilton
Rachel Valdez	Sales Representative	Amy Alberts
Ranjit Varkey Chudukatil	Sales Representative	Amy Alberts
Shu Ito	Sales Representative	Roger Hamilton
Tete Mensa-Annan	Sales Representative	Roger Hamilton
Tsvi Reiter	Sales Representative	Roger Hamilton
Syed Abbas	Pacific Sales Manager	Stephen Jiang
Roger Hamilton	North American Sales Manager	Stephen Jiang
Stephen Jiang	North American Sales Manager	Stephen Jiang
Amy Alberts	European Sales Manager	Stephen Jiang

Figure 12.2: Stephen's team after he was promoted to Vice President of Sales

We will revisit the preceding scenario in the **SCD type 2** (**SCD 2**) subsection in this chapter for more details.

From a data warehousing standpoint and depending on the business requirements, we have some options to deal with such situations, which leads us to different types of SDC. Keep in mind that the data changes in the source systems before being loaded into the data warehouse (in our examples, the HR system). The source systems are usually transactional. We transform and move the data from the transactional systems via **extract, transform, and load** (**ETL**) processes and land the transformed data into the data warehouse, which is where the concept of SCD kicks in. SCD is about how changes in the source systems reflect the data in the data warehouse. These kinds of changes in the source system are not something that happens very often; hence the term "slowly changing." Many SCD types have been developed over years, which means that covering them is out of the scope of this book, but for your reference, we cover the first three, which are the most common types as follows.

SCD type zero (SCD 0)

With this type of SCD, we ignore all changes in a dimension. So, in our scenario, we ignore all changes in the source system (an HR system, in our example). In other words, we do not change the landing dimension in our data warehouse. SCD type zero is also referred to as **fixed dimensions**, which makes no sense in our scenario.

SCD type 1 (SCD 1)

With SCD type 1, we overwrite the old data with the new. An excellent example of SCD type 1 is when the business does not need to have the employee's employment history and only needs to keep the current employees' data. In some scenarios, we can implement a solution similar to the SCD 1 implementation in Power BI. Let us continue with a scenario.

We have a retail company that releases a list of products in Excel format every year, including list price and dealer price. The product list is released on the first day of July when the financial year starts. We have to implement a Power BI solution that keeps the latest product data to analyze sales transactions. The following image shows the product list for 2013:

ProductNumber	Product Category	Product Sub Category	Product Name	List Price	Dealer Price	Reporting Date
BB-7421	Components	Bottom Brackets	LL Bottom Bracket	53.99	32.394	1/07/2013
BB-8107	Components	Bottom Brackets	ML Bottom Bracket	101.24	60.744	1/07/2013
BB-9108	Components	Bottom Brackets	HL Bottom Bracket	121.49	72.894	1/07/2013
BC-M005	Accessories	Bottles and Cages	Mountain Bottle Cage	9.99	5.994	1/07/2013
BC-R205	Accessories	Bottles and Cages	Road Bottle Cage	8.99	5.394	1/07/2013
BK-M18B-40	Bikes	Mountain Bikes	Mountain-500 Black, 40	539.99	323.994	1/07/2013
BK-M18B-42	Bikes	Mountain Bikes	Mountain-500 Black, 42	539.99	323.994	1/07/2013
BK-M18B-44	Bikes	Mountain Bikes	Mountain-500 Black, 44	539.99	323.994	1/07/2013
BK-M18B-48	Bikes	Mountain Bikes	Mountain-500 Black, 48	539.99	323.994	1/07/2013
BK-M18B-52	Bikes	Mountain Bikes	Mountain-500 Black, 52	539.99	323.994	1/07/2013
BK-M18S-40	Bikes	Mountain Bikes	Mountain-500 Silver, 40	564.99	338.994	1/07/2013
BK-M18S-42	Bikes	Mountain Bikes	Mountain-500 Silver, 42	564.99	338.994	1/07/2013
BK-M18S-44	Bikes	Mountain Bikes	Mountain-500 Silver, 44	564.99	338.994	1/07/2013
BK-M18S-48	Bikes	Mountain Bikes	Mountain-500 Silver, 48	564.99	338.994	1/07/2013
BK-M18S-52	Bikes	Mountain Bikes	Mountain-500 Silver, 52	564.99	338.994	1/07/2013
BK-M38S-38	Bikes	Mountain Bikes	Mountain-400-W Silver, 38	769.49	461.694	1/07/2013
BK-M38S-40	Bikes	Mountain Bikes	Mountain-400-W Silver, 40	769.49	461.694	1/07/2013
BK-M38S-42	Bikes	Mountain Bikes	Mountain-400-W Silver, 42	769.49	461.694	1/07/2013

Figure 12.3: Product list 2013

So each year, we receive a similar Excel file to the preceding image. The files are stored on a SharePoint Online site. As explained earlier, SCD 1 always keeps the current data by updating the old data with the new data. So an **ETL** process reads the data from the source, identifies the existing data in the destination table, inserts the new rows into the destination, updates the existing rows, and deletes the removed rows. Here is why our scenario is similar to SCD 1, with one exception:

- We do not update the data in the Excel files and do not create an **ETL** process to read the data from the Excel files, identify the changes, and apply the changes to an intermediary file.
- We must read the data from the source Excel files and keep the latest data while filtering out the old data and loading the data into the data model.

As you see, while we are taking a different implementation approach than creating **ETL** processes, the results are similar to an SCD 1 implementation with one exception: we do not delete any rows. To implement the solution, we go through the following process:

- Get the data in Power Query Editor using the **SharePoint** folder connector.
- Combine the files.
- Use the **ProductNumber** column to identify the duplicated products.
- Use the **Reporting Date** column to identify the latest dates.
- Keep the latest rows.

Follow these steps to get the data from a **SharePoint Online** folder:

1. Log into **SharePoint Online** and navigate to the site holding the product list Excel files and copy the site URL from the browser.

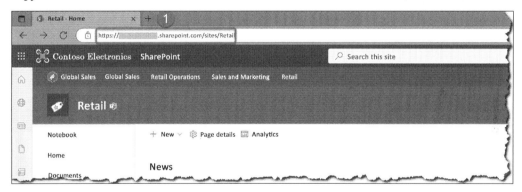

Figure 12.4: Getting the SharePoint Online URL

2. From **Get Data** in the Power BI Desktop, select the **SharePoint folder** connector.

3. Click **Connect**.

Figure 12.5: Connecting to the SharePoint Online folder

4. Paste the site URL copied in *step 1*.
5. Click **OK**.

Figure 12.6: Using the SharePoint Online site URL to connect to a SharePoint Online folder

6. Select the **Microsoft account** section.

7. Click the **Sign in** button and pass your credentials.
8. Click **Connect**.

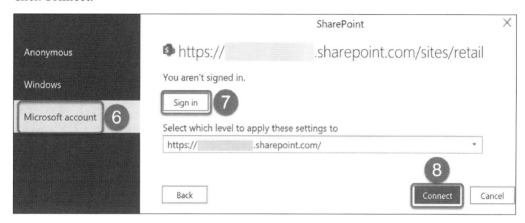

Figure 12.7: Passing Microsoft account credentials to connect to a SharePoint Online folder

9. Click the **Transform Data** button.

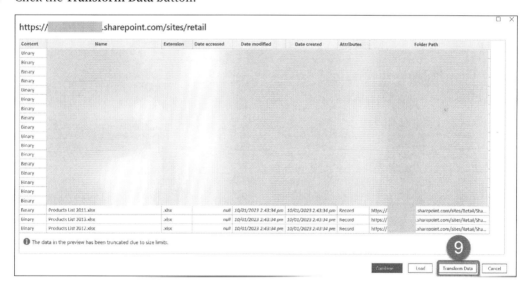

Figure 12.8: Transforming data in Power Query Editor

10. Click the filter dropdown on the **Folder Path** column.
11. Find the **Products List** folder hosting the Excel files and select it.
12. Rename the query to **Product**.

13. Click **OK**.

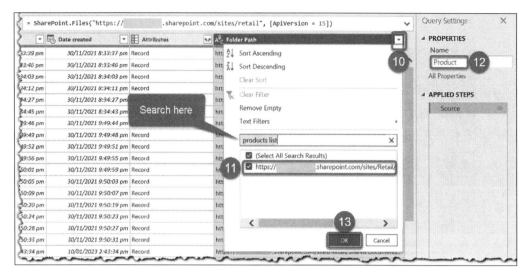

Figure 12.9: Filtering the results to show the Products List folder

So far, we have connected to the SharePoint Online folder. The next step is to combine the Excel files:

14. Click the **Combine Files** button from the **Content** column.

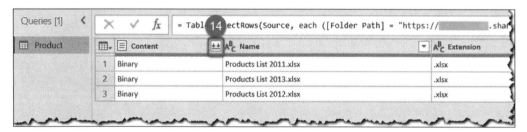

Figure 12.10: Combining Excel files

15. Select the **ProductList** table.

Chapter 12

16. Click **OK**.

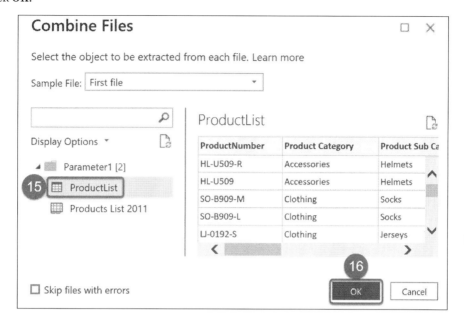

Figure 12.11: Selecting the object to be extracted from each file in the Combine Files window

The above process creates a couple of queries grouped into separate folders, as shown in the following image:

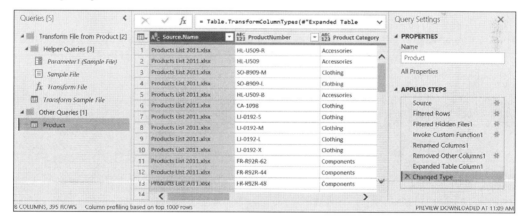

Figure 12.12: The results of combining Excel files

The results of the combined data show a **Source.Name** column that is not necessary and can be removed:

17. Remove the **Source.Name** column:

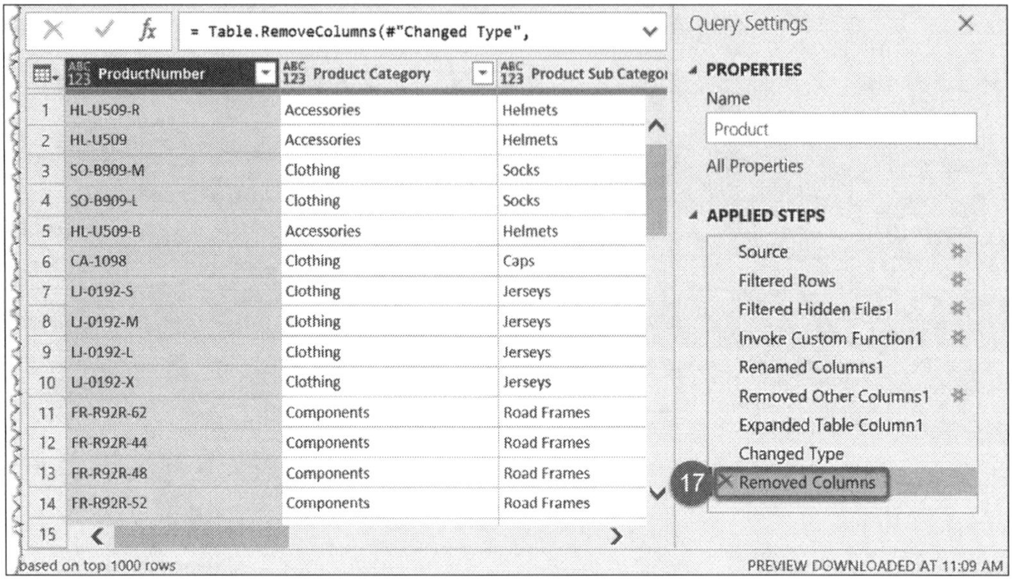

Figure 12.13: The results of removing the Source.Name column

So far, we have successfully combined the Excel files. Now, we want to keep the latest data only. In the next few steps, we implement a mechanism to identify the latest data and load it into the data model. But before we continue, let us take a moment to take a closer look at the data. The results shown in the following image are sorted by **ProductNumber**, and the **Product Category** and **Product Subcategory** columns are removed to better understand how the data changes, but these steps are completely unnecessary and are for demonstration purposes only. The following image shows the results:

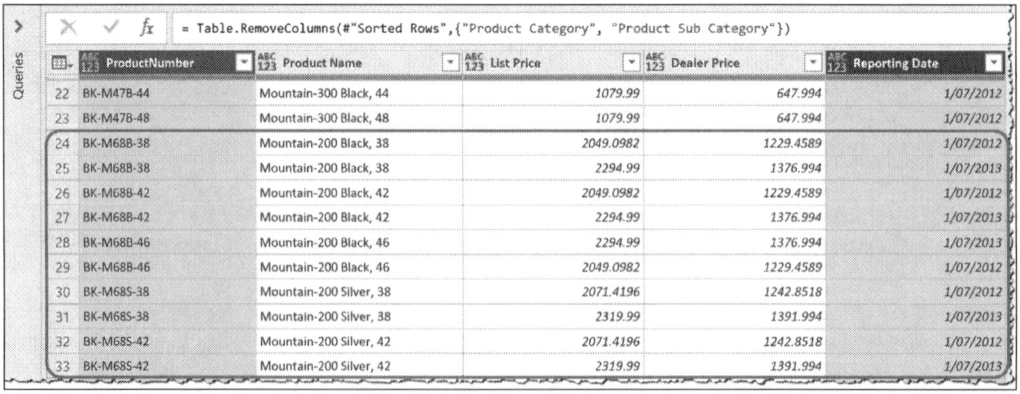

Figure 12.14: Duplicate ProductNumbers with different Reporting Dates

As the preceding image shows, multiple products appear in multiple lists. The goal is to keep the latest product data only based on the **Reporting Date**. So we should get the **ProductNumber** and the maximum of the **Reporting Date**.

To achieve this goal, we use the **Group By** functionality in Power Query Editor. Using **Group By** from the UI uses the `Table.Group()` function in Power Query. Follow these steps:

18. Right-click the **ProductNumber** column.
19. Click the **Group By** column from the context menu.
20. Enter **Reporting Date** for the **New column name**.
21. Select **Max** from the **Operation** dropdown.
22. Select the **Reporting Date** from the **Column** dropdown.
23. Click **OK**.

Figure 12.15: Group By columns in Power Query

The following image shows the results:

	ProductNumber	Reporting Date
1	HL-U509-R	1/07/2013
2	HL-U509	1/07/2013
3	SO-B909-M	1/07/2011
4	SO-B909-L	1/07/2011
5	HL-U509-B	1/07/2013
6	CA-1098	1/07/2013
7	LJ-0192-S	1/07/2013

Figure 12.16: The results of Group By columns

We now have all product numbers with their latest reporting dates. The only remaining piece of the puzzle is to join the results of the **Grouped Rows** step with the data from the previous step. For that, we use the **Merge Queries** option, which runs the `Table.NestedJoin()` function in the background. Follow these steps:

24. Select the **Grouped Rows** step.
25. Click the **Merge Queries** button from the **Home** tab.
26. Select the **Product (Current)** table from the dropdown. Note that we are selecting the current query (**Product**).
27. On the top table, press the *Ctrl* button on your keyboard and select the **ProductNumber** and the **Reporting Date** columns sequentially.
28. Do the same for the bottom table. Note that the sequence of selecting the columns is important.
29. Ensure that the **Join Kind** is **Left Outer (all from first, matching from second)**.
30. Click **OK**.

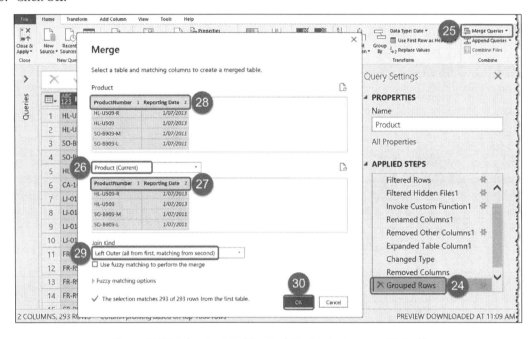

Figure 12.17: Left outer join (Merging) the Product query with itself

In the preceding operation, the **Grouped Rows** is the last transformation step that we joined its results with itself. We already explained how the `Table.NestedJoin()` function works in *Chapter 5, Common Data Preparation Steps*, in the *Merging queries* section. Here is the code generated by Power Query Editor after going through *steps 24 to 30*:

```
Table.NestedJoin(#"Grouped Rows", {"ProductNumber", "Reporting Date"},
#"Grouped Rows", {"ProductNumber", "Reporting Date"}, "Grouped Rows",
JoinKind.LeftOuter)
```

But we want to join the results of the **Grouped Rows** transformation step with the results of the **Removed Columns** step. So we modify the preceding expression as follows:

```
Table.NestedJoin(#"Grouped Rows", {"ProductNumber", "Reporting Date"},
#"Removed Columns", {"ProductNumber", "Reporting Date"}, "Grouped Rows",
JoinKind.LeftOuter)
```

After joining the **Grouped Rows** with the **Removed Columns** step, we need to expand the **Grouped Rows** column. Follow these steps:

31. Click the **Expand** button on the **Grouped Rows** column.
32. Deselect the **ProductNumber** and **Reporting Date** columns to keep the other columns selected.
33. Uncheck the **Use original column name as prefix** option.
34. Click **OK**.

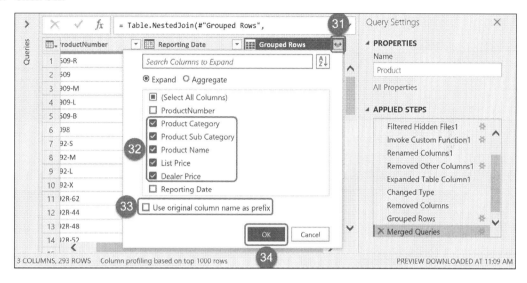

Figure 12.18: Expanding the Grouped Rows column

All done! The following image shows the final results:

Figure 12.19: The final results of implementing SCD 1

We can click the **Close & Apply** button to load the data into the data model, publish it to the Power BI service, and schedule automatic data refreshing. So, when a new Excel file (a new Product list) lands into SharePoint Online, Power BI goes through the above transformation steps to ensure we always have the latest Product data loaded into the data model, which is very similar to the behavior of an SCD 1. The next section explains SCD type 2.

SCD type 2 (SCD 2)

With this type of SCD, we keep the history of data changes in the data warehouse when the business needs to keep the employees' historical and current data. In an SCD 2 scenario, we must maintain historical data based on the business requirements that dictate how we implement this type of SCD. In many cases, we insert a new row of data into the data warehouse whenever a change happens in the transactional system. Inserting a new row of data causes data duplications in the data warehouse, which means that we cannot use the source table's primary key as the primary key of the dimension. Hence, we need to introduce a new set of columns, as follows:

- A new key column that guarantees rows' uniqueness in the **Customers** dimension. This new key column is simply an index representing each row of data stored in the dimension within the data warehouse dimension. The new key is a so-called **surrogate key**. While the surrogate key guarantees the uniqueness of the rows in that dimension, we still need to maintain the source system's primary key. In data warehousing, the source system's primary keys are called **business keys** or **alternate keys**. In other words, the **surrogate key** is a new column added to the dimension as its primary key. This new column does not exist in the data source, so it is different from the primary key in the source system.
- A **Start Date** and an **End Date** column to represent the timeframe during which a row of data is in its current state.
- Another column that shows the status of each row of data.

SCD 2 is the most common type of SCD.

Let's revisit the original scenario we looked at at the beginning of the *Dealing with SCDs* section in this chapter, where **Brian Welcker** hands in his resignation, **Stephen Jiang** is promoted to **Vice President of Sales**, and **Roger Hamilton** is hired as the new **North American Sales Manager**. The preceding activities in the source system translate into the following changes in the data warehouse:

- Update **Brian Welcker**'s last record in the **DimEmployee** table of the data warehouse to add 30th April 2012 as the **End Date**, update the **CurrentFlag** to **0**, and change the value of the **Status** column to **null**.
- Update **Stephen Jiang**'s last record in the **DimEmployee** table of the data warehouse to add 30th April 2012 as the **End Date** column, update the **CurrentFlag** to **0**, and change the value of the **Status** column to **null**.

- Insert a new record for **Stephen Jiang** reflecting his new **Title, BaseRate, ParentEmployeeKey, StartDate** of the new role, **CurrentFlag, SalesPersonFlag,** and **Status**. Please note that some data remains unchanged since **Stephen's** previous record, such as his **HireDate, SalesTerritory,** etc.
- Insert a new record for **Roger Hamilton**.
- Update all employees' **ParentEmployeeKey** where **Stephen** was their manager when he was the **North American Sales Manager** with **Roger's EmployeeID**.
- Update all employees' **ParentEmployeeKey** where **Brian** was their manager when he was the **Vice President of Sales** with **Stephen's** new **EmployeeID**.

An important point to note is that the last two steps depend on the business requirements. If the business needs to keep all changes, we have to add an **EndDate** for the last records of all employees affected by the changes, changing their **CurrentFlag** to 0 and **Status** to **null**. Then we insert new records for all of them with the same data except their **ParentEmployeeKey**.

The latter is not what the business requires in our scenario. Therefore, we only update the last records of the affected employees by updating their **ParentEmployeeKey** values to reflect the new changes. I do not include the T-SQL codes here, as SCD implementation in data warehouses is out of the scope of this book. You can download and use the sample codes mimicking SCD 2 in the **DimEmployee** table from here: https://github.com/PacktPublishing/Expert-Data-Modeling-with-Power-BI-Second-Edition/blob/e570a94df87aeaa9391c7bc8ca38b96d1c6e961a/Samples/Chapter%2012/Mimicking%20SCD2.sql.

The following image shows the data before implementing SCD 2:

EmployeeKey	Full Name	Title	ParentEmployeeKey	Manager	HireDate	Start Date	End Date	CurrentFlag	Status
272	Stephen Jiang	North American Sales Manager	277	Brian Welcker	4/08/2010	4/08/2010		True	Current
277	Brian Welcker	Vice President of Sales	112	Ken Sánchez	15/09/2010	15/09/2010		True	Current
281	Michael Blythe	Sales Representative	272	Stephen Jiang	29/12/2010	29/12/2010		True	Current
282	Linda Mitchell	Sales Representative	272	Stephen Jiang	29/12/2010	29/12/2010		True	Current
283	Jillian Carson	Sales Representative	272	Stephen Jiang	29/12/2010	29/12/2010		True	Current
284	Garrett Vargas	Sales Representative	272	Stephen Jiang	29/12/2010	29/12/2010		True	Current
285	Tsvi Reiter	Sales Representative	272	Stephen Jiang	29/12/2010	29/12/2010		True	Current
286	Pamela Ansman-Wolfe	Sales Representative	272	Stephen Jiang	29/12/2010	29/12/2010		True	Current
287	Shu Ito	Sales Representative	272	Stephen Jiang	29/12/2010	29/12/2010		True	Current
288	José Saraiva	Sales Representative	272	Stephen Jiang	29/12/2010	29/12/2010		True	Current
289	David Campbell	Sales Representative	272	Stephen Jiang	29/12/2010	29/12/2010		True	Current
290	Amy Alberts	European Sales Manager	277	Brian Welcker	15/11/2011	15/11/2011		True	Current
291	Jae Pak	Sales Representative	290	Amy Alberts	29/12/2011	29/12/2011		True	Current
292	Ranjit Varkey Chudukatil	Sales Representative	290	Amy Alberts	29/12/2011	29/12/2011		True	Current
293	Tete Mensa-Annan	Sales Representative	272	Stephen Jiang	30/04/2012	30/04/2012		True	Current
294	Syed Abbas	Pacific Sales Manager	277	Brian Welcker	12/10/2012	12/10/2012		True	Current
295	Rachel Valdez	Sales Representative	290	Amy Alberts	28/12/2012	28/12/2012		True	Current
296	Lynn Tsoflias	Sales Representative	294	Syed Abbas	28/12/2012	28/12/2012		True	Current

Figure 12.20: The employee data before SCD 2 implementation

In the preceding image, the **EmployeeKey** column is the surrogate key of the dimension, the **Start Date** column shows the date **Stephen Jiang** started his job as **North American Sales Manager**, the **End Date** column has been left blank (null), the **CurrentFlag** is **True**, and the **Status** column shows **Current**. Now, let's have a look at the data after implementing SCD 2 reflecting all changes, which is illustrated in the following image:

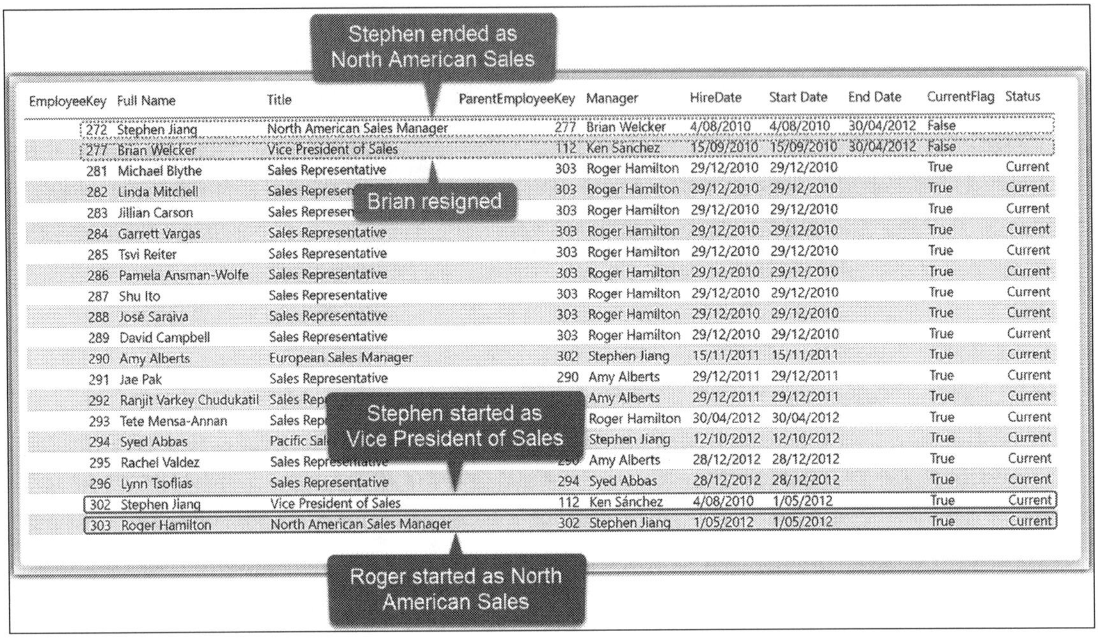

Figure 12.21: The employee data after SCD 2 implementation

The preceding image shows that:

- **Stephan Jiang** started his new role as **Vice President of Sales** on 01/05/2012 and finished his job as **North American Sales Manager** on 30/04/2012.
- **Brian Welcker** finished his work on 30/04/2012.
- **Roger Hamilton** started his new role as **North American Sales Manager** on 01/05/2012.
- All employees who used to report to **Stephen** now report to **Roger**.
- All of **Brian**'s team members are now **Stephen**'s.

Let's see what SCD 2 means when it comes to data modeling in Power BI. The first question is: *Can we implement SCD 2 directly in Power BI Desktop without having a data warehouse?* To answer this question, we have to remember that the data model in Power BI is a semantic layer. The semantic layer, by definition, is a view of the source data (usually a data warehouse), optimized for reporting and analytical purposes.

While the data warehouses host a large collection of historical data, the semantic layer does not necessarily contain the entire data history. The semantic layers usually keep the data for a timeframe that makes sense for to the business users to analyze the data, which helps them in making better decisions. Therefore, the semantic layer does not replace the data warehouse, nor is it another version of the data warehouse. When the business needs to keep the changes' history, we either need to have a data warehouse or find a way to maintain the historical data in the transactional system, such as a **temporal** mechanism. A temporal mechanism is a feature that some relational database management systems like SQL Server offer to provide information about the data kept in a table at any time instead of keeping the current data only. To learn more **temporal tables** in SQL Server, check out the following link: https://learn.microsoft.com/en-us/sql/relational-databases/tables/temporal-tables?view=sql-server-ver15&WT.mc_id=DP-MVP-5003466.

After we load the data into the data model in Power BI Desktop, we have all current and historical data in the dimension tables. Therefore, we have to be careful when dealing with SCD. For instance, the following image shows reseller sales by employee:

EmployeeKey	Full Name	Manager	Sales
290	Amy Alberts	Stephen Jiang	$732,078.4446
289	David Campbell	Roger Hamilton	$3,729,945.3501
284	Garrett Vargas	Roger Hamilton	$3,609,447.2163
291	Jae Pak	Amy Alberts	$8,503,338.6472
283	Jillian Carson	Roger Hamilton	$10,065,803.5429
288	José Saraiva	Roger Hamilton	$5,926,418.3574
282	Linda Mitchell	Roger Hamilton	$10,367,007.4286
296	Lynn Tsoflias	Syed Abbas	$1,421,810.9252
281	Michael Blythe	Roger Hamilton	$9,293,903.0055
286	Pamela Ansman-Wolfe	Roger Hamilton	$3,325,102.5952
295	Rachel Valdez	Amy Alberts	$1,790,640.2311
292	Ranjit Varkey Chudukatil	Amy Alberts	$4,509,888.933
287	Shu Ito	Roger Hamilton	$6,427,005.5556
272	Stephen Jiang	Brian Welcker	$1,092,123.8562
294	Syed Abbas	Stephen Jiang	$172,524.4515
293	Tete Mensa-Annan	Roger Hamilton	$2,312,545.6905
285	Tsvi Reiter	Roger Hamilton	$7,171,012.7514
Total			**$80,450,596.9823**

Figure 12.22: Reseller sales by employees without considering SCD

At first glance, the numbers seem to be right. Well, they may be right; they may be wrong. It depends on what the business expects to see in the report. We did not consider SCD when creating the preceding visual, which means we considered Stephen's sales values (**EmployeeKey 272**). But is this what the business requires? Does the business expect to see all employees' sales without considering the timeframe they are in the current role? For more clarity, let's add the **Start Date**, **End Date**, and **Status** columns to the table. The following image shows the results:

EmployeeKey	Full Name	Manager	Sales	Start Date	End Date	Status
290	Amy Alberts	Stephen Jiang	$732,078.4446	15/11/2011		Current
289	David Campbell	Roger Hamilton	$3,729,945.3501	29/12/2010		Current
284	Garrett Vargas	Roger Hamilton	$3,609,447.2163	29/12/2010		Current
291	Jae Pak	Amy Alberts	$8,503,338.6472	29/12/2011		Current
283	Jillian Carson	Roger Hamilton	$10,065,803.5429	29/12/2010		Current
288	José Saraiva	Roger Hamilton	$5,926,418.3574	29/12/2010		Current
282	Linda Mitchell	Roger Hamilton	$10,367,007.4286	29/12/2010		Current
296	Lynn Tsoflias	Syed Abbas	$1,421,810.9252	28/12/2012		Current
281	Michael Blythe	Roger Hamilton	$9,293,903.0055	29/12/2010		Current
286	Pamela Ansman-Wolfe	Roger Hamilton	$3,325,102.5952	29/12/2010		Current
295	Rachel Valdez	Amy Alberts	$1,790,640.2311	28/12/2012		Current
292	Ranjit Varkey Chudukatil	Amy Alberts	$4,509,888.933	29/12/2011		Current
287	Shu Ito	Roger Hamilton	$6,427,005.5556	29/12/2010		Current
272	Stephen Jiang	Brian Welcker	$1,092,123.8562	4/08/2010	30/04/2012	
294	Syed Abbas	Stephen Jiang	$172,524.4515	12/10/2012		Current
293	Tete Mensa-Annan	Roger Hamilton	$2,312,545.6905	30/04/2012		Current
285	Tsvi Reiter	Roger Hamilton	$7,171,012.7514	29/12/2010		Current
Total			**$80,450,596.9823**			

Figure 12.23: Reseller sales by employees and their status without considering SCD

What if the business needs to only show sales values for employees when their status is **Current**? In that case, we would have to factor the SCD into the equation and filter out **Stephen**'s sales values. Depending on the business requirements, we might need to add the **Status** column as a filter in the visualizations, while in other cases, we might need to modify the measures by adding the **Start Date**, **End Date**, and **Status** columns to filter the results. The following image shows the results when we use visual filters to take out **Stephen**'s sales:

EmployeeKey	Full Name	Manager	Sales	Start Date	End Date	Status
290	Amy Alberts	Stephen Jiang	$732,078.4446	15/11/2011		Current
289	David Campbell	Roger Hamilton	$3,729,945.3501	29/12/2010		Current
284	Garrett Vargas	Roger Hamilton	$3,609,447.2163	29/12/2010		Current
291	Jae Pak	Amy Alberts	$8,503,338.6472	29/12/2011		Current
283	Jillian Carson	Roger Hamilton	$10,065,803.5429	29/12/2010		Current
288	José Saraiva	Roger Hamilton	$5,926,418.3574	29/12/2010		Current
282	Linda Mitchell	Roger Hamilton	$10,367,007.4286	29/12/2010		Current
296	Lynn Tsoflias	Syed Abbas	$1,421,810.9252	28/12/2012		Current
281	Michael Blythe	Roger Hamilton	$9,293,903.0055	29/12/2010		Current
286	Pamela Ansman-Wolfe	Roger Hamilton	$3,325,102.5952	29/12/2010		Current
295	Rachel Valdez	Amy Alberts	$1,790,640.2311	28/12/2012		Current
292	Ranjit Varkey Chudukatil	Amy Alberts	$4,509,888.933	29/12/2011		Current
287	Shu Ito	Roger Hamilton	$6,427,005.5556	29/12/2010		Current
294	Syed Abbas	Stephen Jiang	$172,524.4515	12/10/2012		Current
293	Tete Mensa-Annan	Roger Hamilton	$2,312,545.6905	30/04/2012		Current
285	Tsvi Reiter	Roger Hamilton	$7,171,012.7514	29/12/2010		Current
Total			$79,358,473.1261			

Figure 12.24: Reseller sales by employees considering the SCD

Depending on the business requirements, dealing with SCD is not always as simple as this. For instance, if the business wants to compare the Sales team's performance under **Roger**'s management with the same period while **Stephen** was managing them, then our SCD 2 implementation in the data warehouse does not help as we updated the current employees of **Stephen** to **Roger**. For such scenarios, we need to change the SCD implementation in the data warehouse to align the business requirements and potentially create more complex measures in the Power BI data model. As you can imagine, there are many SCD scenarios depending on the business requirements, which makes it virtually impossible to cover in a single chapter, so we leave it to you to investigate more.

This section explained common types of SCD and how we can implement similar solutions to SCD type 1. We also learned that dealing with SCD type 2 from a data modeling perspective in Power BI does not make sense without having a proper mechanism to maintain the historical data in the source system. The next section focuses on another data warehousing concept that becomes handy to Power BI data modelers: degenerate dimensions.

Dealing with degenerate dimensions

The term "degenerate dimension" was coined by the amazing *Ralph Kimball*. Learn more about the *Kimbal Group* here: https://www.kimballgroup.com/.

The Kimball Group refers to *Webster* to define the meaning of the term "degenerate" as follows:

> *According to Webster, "degenerate" refers to something that's 1) declined from the standard norm, or 2) is mathematically simpler.*

Read the full article here: `https://www.kimballgroup.com/2003/06/design-tip-46-another-look-at-degenerate-dimensions/`.

From a Star Schema standpoint, degenerate dimensions are the dimension key attributes appearing in the fact tables without having their own dimension. In other words, we do not create a separate dimension table for them. But as we know, from a Star Schema perspective, it is not a good practice to put dimension attributes in the fact tables. So a degenerate dimension, according to Webster's definition of the term "degenerate," is an exception outside of the norm of a regular dimension.

The following characteristics define degenerate dimensions:

- The only dimension attributes are the key attributes (primary keys).
- We cannot imagine any other attributes for the dimension.
- There is no other meaningful linkage to any other dimensions.

We briefly looked at degenerate dimensions in *Chapter 6, Star Schema Preparation in Power Query Editor*, under *Creating dimension tables*. Let us continue with the sample file from *Chapter 6*, available here: `https://github.com/PacktPublishing/Expert-Data-Modeling-with-Power-BI-Second-Edition/blob/cb57eb34a28e6bda8b725ca0f5c85200f42c072c/Samples/Chapter%2006/Chapter%206%2C%20Star%20Schema%20Preparation%20in%20Power%20Query%20Editor.pbix`.

The following image shows the **Sales** table after being loaded into the Power BI model:

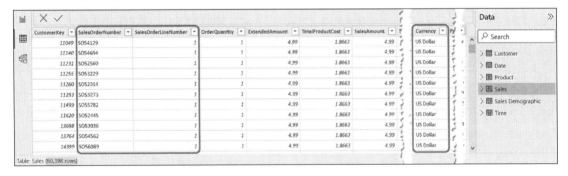

Figure 12.25: Degenerate dimensions in the Sales fact table

As the preceding image shows, the **SalesOrderNumber**, **SalesOrderLineNumber**, and **Currency** are degenerate dimensions in the **Sales** fact table. Let us look at them in more detail.

The **Sales** table has **60,398** rows. Getting the distinct count of the **SalesOrderNumber** and **SalesOrderLineNumber** columns reveals that the combination of the two columns also has **60,398** rows, as shown in the following image:

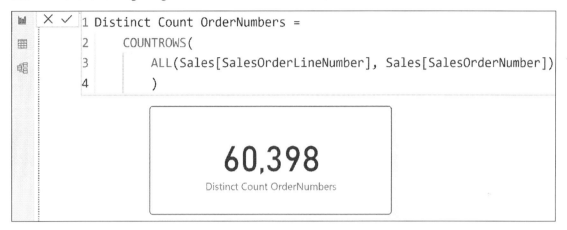

Figure 12.26: Distinct count of the SalesOrderNumber and SalesOrderLineNumber columns

Therefore, the combination of the two columns is indeed the primary key of a hypothetical **Sales Orders** dimension. Let us imagine that we actually create the **Sales Orders** dimension. It must have both **SalesOrderNumber** and **SalesOrderLineNumber** columns. As the xVelocity engine does not support composite keys, we have to add an **Index** column to be used as the primary key of the table. This newly created dimension will have the same amounts of rows as the **Sales** table (the fact table). Therefore, we do not improve the performance of the data model by adding a new dimension. Indeed, we are forcing unnecessary costs, such as the extra development costs of adding an **Index** column to the **Sales Orders** dimension, adding that **Index** column as a foreign key into the **Sales** table, and creating the relationship between the two tables. The overhead development costs aside, we actually degrade the compression of the model and its performance.

Now, let us analyze the necessity of having the **Currency** column in the fact table. Looking at the data reveals that there are no other attributes for the **Currency** column. As the xVelocity engine uses columnstore indexing technology, it best compresses the low cardinality data. Therefore, the fact that the data type of the **Currency** column is **Text** does not hugely affect the data compression and the performance of the data model. So, it does not make sense to create a new dimension for it.

So far, we are convinced that keeping the degenerate dimensions in the **Sales** table is a simpler implementation, which also aligns with the second point of Webster's definition of the term "degenerate." Conceptually, degenerate dimension can be a tricky concept to internalize and apply to real-world scenarios, which some developers get wrong. They put dimensions into the fact tables and name them degenerate dimensions, which can impact performance negatively.

The next chapter focuses on another important data modeling tool available in Power BI: Dataflows.

Summary

In this chapter, we learned about the concept of SCD and how to implement some related scenarios. We also learned more about degenerate dimensions and how to deal with them in our data models in Power BI. The next chapter explains the purely cloud-based data transformation capability in Power BI called Dataflows.

Join us on Discord!

Join The Big Data and Analytics Community on the Packt Discord Server!

Hang out with 558 other members and enjoy free voice and text chat.

`https://packt.link/ips2H`

13

Introduction to Dataflows

In the previous chapter, we learned some more advanced data modeling techniques that are more related to data warehousing: dealing with SCDs and degenerate dimensions. This chapter briefly introduces Dataflows, another available feature in the Power BI platform that can become handy in real-world scenarios. To get the best out of Dataflows, we need to pay attention to numerous technicalities that directly impact our design and implementation, such as the storage mechanism and licensing details making it virtually impossible to cover all in a single chapter. So, this chapter is designed to cover the basics and help you to build robust building blocks for your learning journeys. This chapter covers the following areas:

- Scenarios for using Dataflows
- Dataflow terminology
- Create Dataflows
- Export/import Dataflows
- No-code/low-code experience in Dataflows
- Introduction to composite models
- Query plans in Dataflows

Introduction to Dataflows

In November 2018, Microsoft released Dataflows in public preview. Later on, in April 2019, Dataflows became generally available. Dataflows used to be available in **Premium** licenses only, but it is now available in Power BI Pro with some limitations. The purpose of Dataflows is to support collaborative **self-service data preparation** and **Extract, Transform, and Load** (**ETL**) processes in an organization by leveraging the power of Power Query in the cloud. The Dataflows technology is also known as **Power Query Online**. The Dataflows technology is available in Power Platform either in Power BI or **Power Apps**. The Dataflows store the prepared data in standardized files and folders format known as the **Common Data Model** (**CDM**) folder. If created in **Power Apps**, the resulting tables can be stored in **Dataverse** or an **Azure Data Lake Storage Gen2** (**ADLS Gen 2**). The Power BI Dataflows, however, store the resulting tables in ADLS Gen 2 managed in the Power BI service.

As stated earlier, Dataflows is a wide topic that cannot be completely covered in a single chapter. For more information about the available storage options for Dataflows, check out these resources:

- **Common Data Model (CDM)**: https://learn.microsoft.com/en-us/common-data-model/?WT.mc_id=DP-MVP-5003466
- **Dataverse**: https://learn.microsoft.com/en-us/power-apps/maker/data-platform/data-platform-intro?WT.mc_id=DP-MVP-5003466
- **Azure Data Lake Gen 2**: https://learn.microsoft.com/en-us/azure/storage/blobs/data-lake-storage-introduction?WT.mc_id=DP-MVP-5003466

If we have an ADLS Gen 2 already, we can integrate the workspaces containing Dataflows with the existing ADLS Gen2 to make the prepared data available to various tools and services such as **Azure Machine Learning (Azure ML)**. Moreover, using Dataflows, we can make the prepared data available to other users across the organization. The self-service ETL characteristic of Dataflows technology makes the data preparation processes less dependent on **Information Technology** (IT) departments. Dataflows enable users to use a set of consumption-ready data. As a result, in the long run, Dataflows can decrease development costs by increasing reusability.

The main difference between data preparation in Power Query within Power BI Desktop and Dataflows is that when we use Power BI Desktop to prepare the data, the results are only available within the dataset published to the Power BI service. While we can still access the dataset's tables and data from other datasets in a **composite model** scenario, it is not a good idea to create a composite model for the sake of getting the prepared data into our data model. We will discuss DirectQuery to Power BI datasets in composite models in the next chapter: *DirectQuery to Power BI Datasets and Analysis Services in Composite Models*. For now, we will look at some scenarios for using Dataflows.

Scenarios for using Dataflows

Having a centralized cloud-based self-service data preparation mechanism sounds compelling to some developers to think about moving all data preparation activities to Dataflows instead of Power BI Desktop. Well, that does not sound like a practical idea. The following are some scenarios where using Dataflows makes more sense:

- We do not have a data warehouse in the organization. All Power BI reports get data directly from the source systems, hitting the source systems' performance. Creating Dataflows and scheduling them to automatically refresh the data can help.
- We want to reuse the curated data across the organization. With Dataflows, multiple datasets and reports in Power BI service can benefit the existing prepared data.
- The organization owns ADLS Gen 2, and we want to connect other Azure services to the prepared data.
- We want to prevent business analysts from accessing the source systems. By creating Dataflows, the analysts can access the curated data without needing to connect to underlying disparate data sources.
- We need to prepare data from large data sources at scale, and we own a Power BI **Premium** capacity; Dataflows provide more flexibility and work more efficiently.

- We want to use the prepared data across various technologies in the Power Platform. When we create the Dataflows, we can make them available for other Power Platform products such as Power Apps, Power Automate, Power Virtual Agent, and Dynamics 365.
- We need a self-service data preparation tool that does not require a lot of IT or development background. Indeed, Dataflows' creators only need to have knowledge of Power Query.

Dataflow terminology

As mentioned earlier, Dataflows are also known as **Power Query Online**; therefore, they inherit many Power Query terminologies. The following terminologies are either applicable in Dataflows or are another version of a term that is already available in Power Query:

- **Fields**: Fields are just like columns in Power Query.
- **Tables**: A table (aka entity) consists of a set of fields or columns, similar to what we have in Power Query. There is a difference between a table in Dataflows and a query in Power Query in Power BI Desktop. In Power BI Desktop's Power Query, all tables are queries that result in a table output or those that will be loaded into the data model. But in Dataflows, there are different types of tables, as follows:
- **Regular tables**: The table that is like a table query in Power BI Desktop's Power Query. The icon currently used for regular tables is ⊞.
- **Linked tables**: A linked table is a table that references an existing table in another Dataflow. When we create a linked table, the data will not load into the new Dataflow; only a link to the source Dataflow exists in the new one. For that reason, the linked tables are read-only. As a result, we cannot create any further transformation steps. The icon currently used for linked tables is ⊞.
- **Computed tables**: A computed table is a table that references other tables to take extra transformation steps. In these tables, the data is first processed in the source table; then it flows through the extra transformation steps in the referencing table. The transformed data is stored again for the new table. The icon currently used for computed tables is ⊞.

> Both linked and computed tables are only available in a Power BI **Premium** Workspace. But both tables can be sourced from a Power BI **Pro** Workspace.
>
> The Workspace keeping the linked tables must be a modern workspace (not the classic workspaces linked to Microsoft 365 groups).
>
> We can link to tables in multiple Dataflows in multiple modern workspaces.

Create Dataflows

To create a Dataflow, we must log into our Power BI service in a web browser. The following steps show how to start creating new Dataflow:

1. Select a desired Workspace.
2. Click the **New** button.

3. Click **Dataflow**.

   The preceding steps are highlighted in the following image:

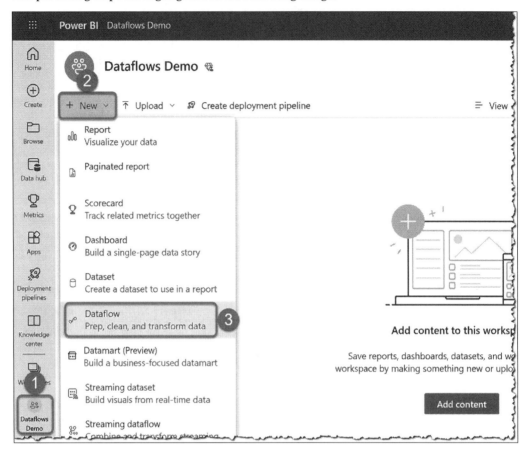

Figure 13.1: Creating Dataflows in the Power BI service

 Dataflows are not available in Personal Workspaces (My Workspace).

We have one of the following options:

- **Define new tables**
- **Link tables from other Dataflows**

- **Import Model**
- Attach a **Common Data Model** folder (preview)

The following image shows the preceding options:

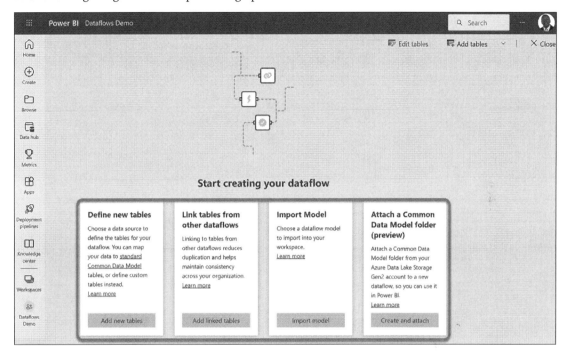

Figure 13.2: Available option to start creating a new Dataflow

As the preceding image shows, all options to create a new Dataflow are available to start creating a new Dataflow; however, if the Workspace is not Premium, we can still create linked tables and computed tables, but we cannot refresh the Dataflow. The following sections show how to create new tables, linked tables, computed tables, and import models. We do not discuss **Attach a Common Data Model folder** because it is in preview and has not been released yet.

Create new entities

So far, we have navigated to the desired Workspace. Now, we want to create tables in the Dataflow. To create a new table from the options available (as shown in *Figure 13.3*), we follow these next steps:

1. Click the **Add new tables** button, as illustrated in the following image:

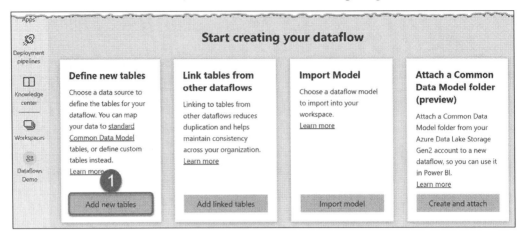

Figure 13.3: Adding new tables within a Dataflow

2. Select any desired data source connector, as illustrated in the following image:

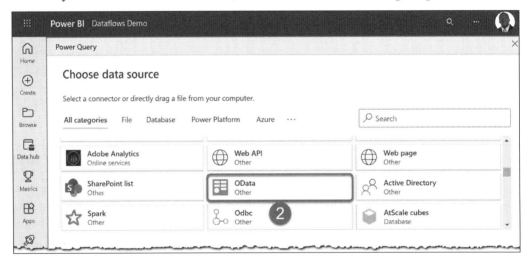

Figure 13.4: Selecting a data source connector

3. Fill in the **Connection settings** fields.
4. Click **Next**.

The preceding steps are highlighted in the following image:

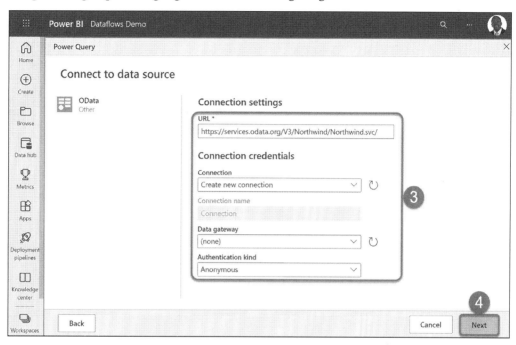

Figure 13.5: Filling in the Connection settings fields

5. Select tables from the **Choose data** pane from the **Power Query** form. Depending on the selected data source, you may see a different form. We used a **Northwind OData** sample available here: https://services.odata.org/V3/Northwind/Northwind.svc.
6. Click **Transform data**.

The preceding steps are highlighted in the following image:

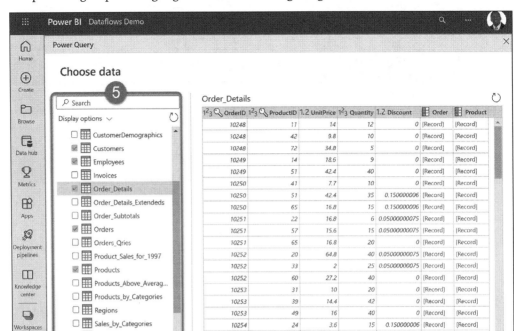

Figure 13.6: Power Query - Choose data form when creating a new Dataflow

If we select an on-premises data source, we need to select an up and running **on-premises Data Gateway**. Installing and configuring the on-premises Data Gateway is out of the scope of this book, but if you are keen to learn more about it, here is a good resource: https://learn.microsoft.com/en-us/data-integration/gateway/service-gateway-onprem?WT.mc_id=DP-MVP-5003466.

We have now navigated to the **Power Query** form, similar to the **Power Query Editor** window in Power BI Desktop. One point to notice in the **Power Query** form is the **warnings** section. As the following image shows, if there are any issues in loading the data from some columns, a warning message shows up in the **warnings** section. We can click on the **warnings** section to see more details:

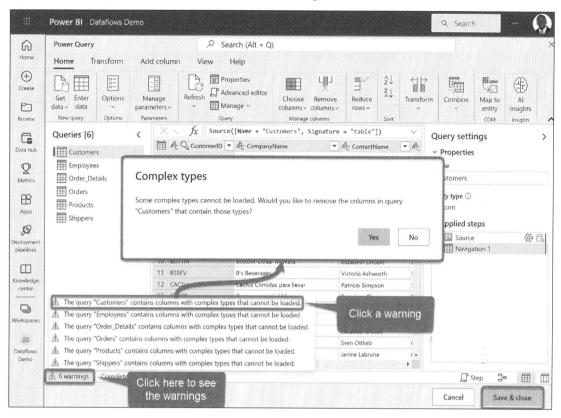

Figure 13.7: Warning messages after getting data from the source

As the preceding image shows, we can click the warning message to take action if necessary. After we have finished all the required transformation steps, we can save the Dataflow by clicking the **Save & close** button.

The next step is to give our Dataflow a name and save it, as shown in the following image:

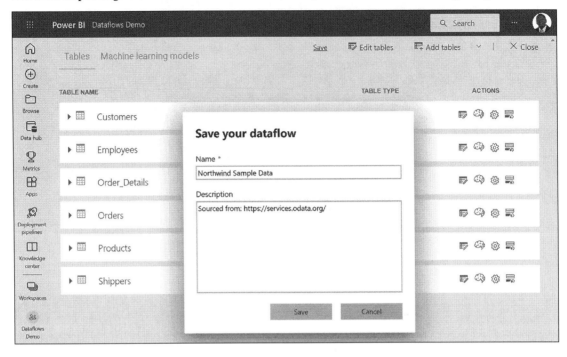

Figure 13.8: Saving the Dataflow

Unlike the Power Query Editor in Power BI Desktop, which loads the data from the source immediately after we click the **Close & Apply** button, Dataflows will not automatically load data from the source. Instead, we have two options: to refresh the data or schedule a data refresh, as shown in the following image:

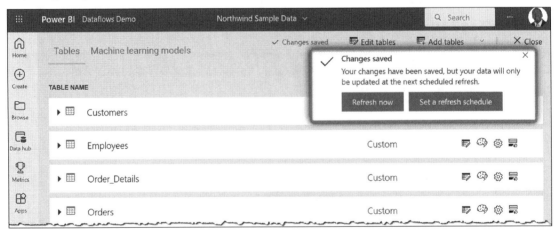

Figure 13.9: Data refresh options after creating a new Dataflow

We can populate the tables by clicking the **Refresh now** button or by setting a schedule to refresh the tables automatically.

Create linked tables from other Dataflows

We can create linked tables (referencing tables from other Dataflows) in a new Dataflow or add a linked table to an existing Dataflow. The following steps show how to add linked tables as a new Dataflow:

1. After navigating to the desired workspace and starting to create your Dataflow, click the **Add linked tables** button, as illustrated in the following image:

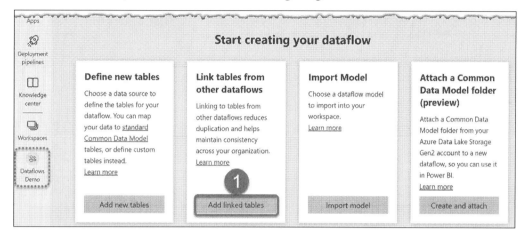

Figure 13.10: Adding linked tables as a new Dataflow

2. Go through **Connection settings**.
3. Click **Next**.

   The preceding steps are highlighted in the following image:

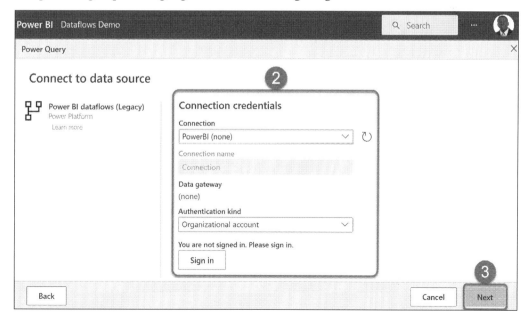

Figure 13.11: Connection settings to create linked tables

4. In the **Power Query** form, expand a workspace.
5. Select any desired Dataflows.
6. Click the desired tables.
7. Click the **Transform data** button.

The preceding steps are highlighted in the following image:

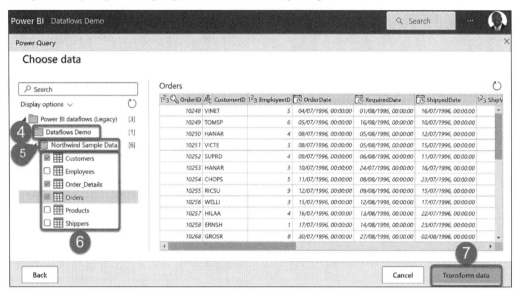

Figure 13.12: Selecting tables from another Dataflow to link

8. Click **Save & close,** as illustrated in the following image:

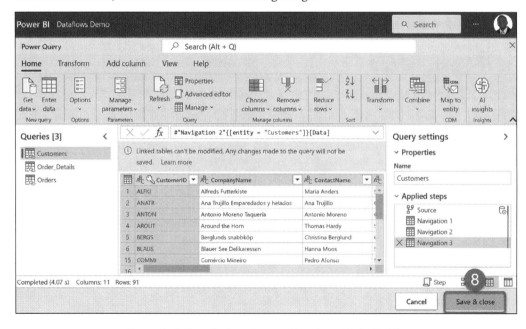

Figure 13.13: Save & close changes for selected linked tables

Chapter 13

9. Type in a name and then click the **Save** button, as illustrated in the following image:

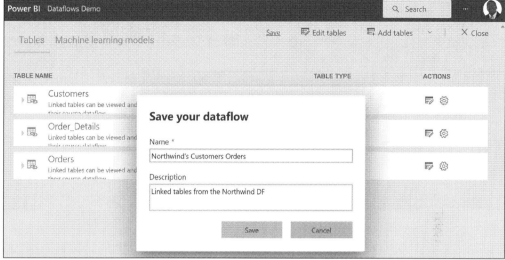

Figure 13.14: Saving linked tables as a new Dataflow

So far, we have learned how to create a new Dataflow with linked tables. In the next subsection, we learn how to create computed tables.

Create computed entities

In this section, we learn how to create computed entities. The most common way to create a computed entity is within an existing Dataflow by referencing another entity. The following steps show how to create a computed entity after navigating to the desired workspace and opening a Dataflow:

1. Click the **Edit tables** button, as illustrated in the following image:

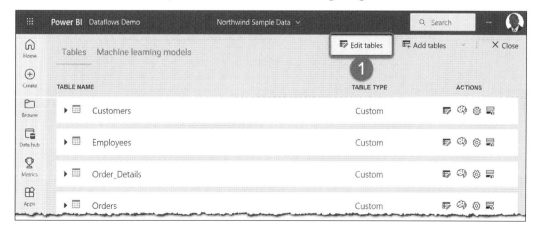

Figure 13.15: Editing entities in a Dataflow

2. Right-click the desired table from the **Queries** pane.

3. Click **Reference**.

The preceding steps are highlighted in the following image:

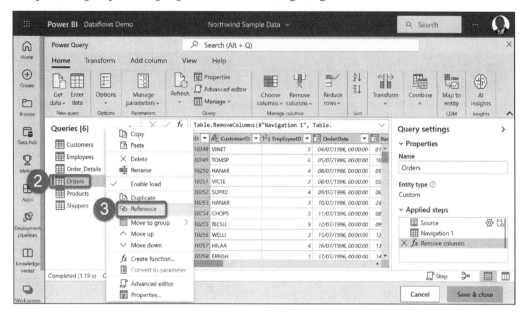

Figure 13.16: Creating a computed table

We created a computed table, as shown in the following image:

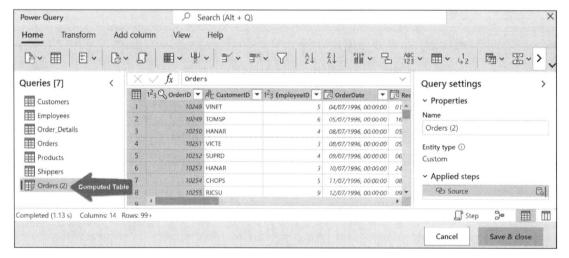

Figure 13.17: Computed table

We can also create a computed table from a linked table by referencing it or adding some transformation steps. The following image shows that the **Date** table is a linked table, and the **Date Comp** table is a computed table referencing it:

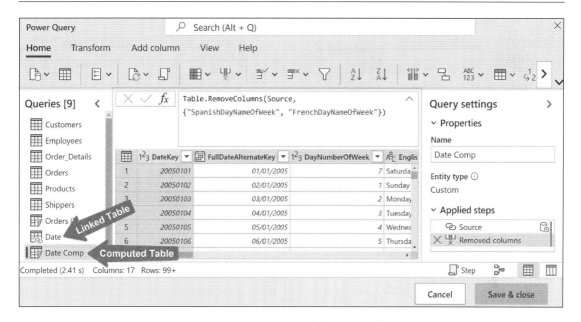

Figure 13.18: Creating a computed table from a linked table

Remember that the linked tables are read-only, and we are not allowed to modify them. If we do so, the Power Query Online engine forces us to roll back the changes.

Configure incremental data refresh in Dataflows

As previously mentioned, one of the use cases for creating Dataflows is to prevent business analysts from accessing the source data. If the source table is large, then we can configure incremental data refresh. We already explained what an incremental refresh is and how to configure it in Power BI Desktop in *Chapter 10, Advanced Data Modeling Techniques*, in the *Incremental refresh and hybrid tables* section; therefore, we do not explain it again. But, there is a minor difference between configuring incremental refresh in the Power BI Desktop and Dataflows. When configuring the incremental refresh in Power BI Desktop, we must first create two query parameters: **RangeStart** and **RangeEnd**. We then use those parameters when defining the incremental refresh policies. But in Dataflows, we must not define the query parameters at all. The engine does it automatically for us.

Let us configure incremental data refresh on the **Orders** table from the **Northwind Sample Data** Dataflow we created earlier. Follow these steps:

1. Navigate to the desired Workspace.
2. Open the Northwind Sample Data Dataflow.
3. Click the **Incremental refresh** (🗔) button of the **Orders** table under the **ACTIONS** section.
4. Toggle the incremental refresh on.
5. Select the **OrderDate** column from the **Choose a DateTime column to filter by** dropdown.
6. Put **30 Years** in the **Store rows from the past** section.
7. Put **1 Month** in the **Refresh rows from the past** section.
8. Click **Save**.

The following image shows the preceding steps:

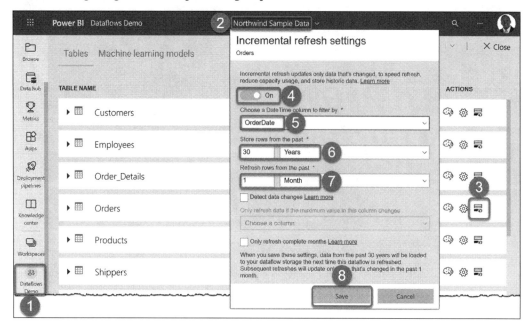

Figure 13.19: Incremental refresh on Dataflows

After saving the changes, edit the Dataflows to see the changes. The following image shows that the **RangeStart** and **RangeEnd** parameters are created, and the **Orders** table is filtered on the **OrderDate** column using the parameters automatically.

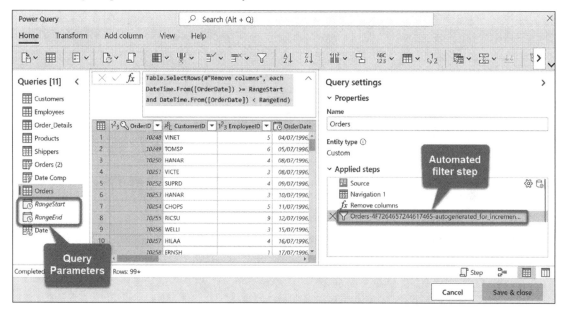

Figure 13.20: Configuring incremental refresh on Dataflows creates query parameters and adds an automated filter step on the corresponding table

Chapter 13

Now that we implemented the Dataflow, let us export its source code for future use.

Export/import Dataflows

It is always a good idea to have a copy of the source code while developing any software solutions and developing Dataflows is not an exception. We can export the Dataflows definitions into JSON format and import them later if required. Please note that exporting and importing are for the Dataflow definitions only, not the data. Let us see how they work.

Export Dataflows

Navigate to the desired workspace, then proceed as follows:

1. Hover over a Dataflow and click the **More options** ellipsis button.
2. From the menu, click **Export.json**.
3. A message shows up when the file is ready.
4. Depending on your browser, the **JavaScript Object Notation (JSON)** file downloads automatically to your local machine.

The preceding steps are highlighted in the following image:

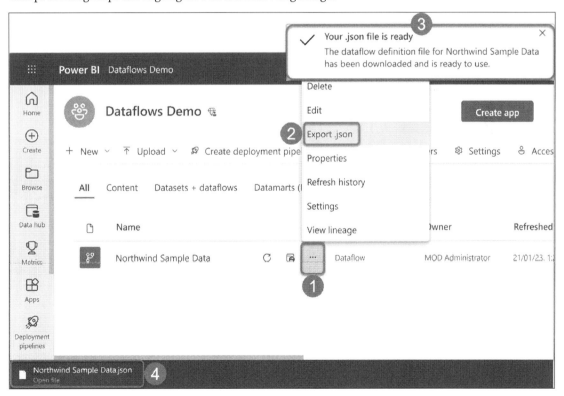

Figure 13.21: Exporting Dataflow definitions in JSON format

Import Dataflows

The following steps show how to import a Dataflow after navigating to the desired workspace:

1. Click the **New** button.
2. Click **Dataflow**.
3. Click the **Import model** option.
4. Select an exported Dataflow definition file (**JSON**).
5. Click **Open**.

The preceding steps are highlighted in the following image:

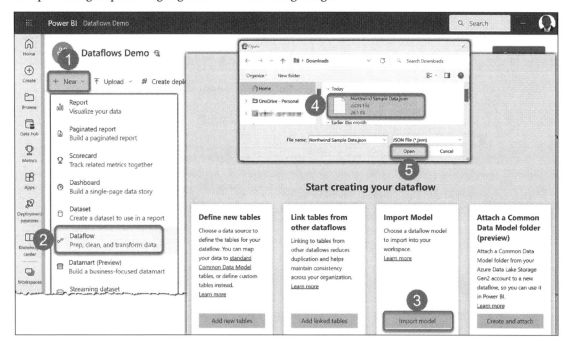

Figure 13.22: Importing a Dataflow

When we go back to the workspace, we see the imported Dataflow. As already mentioned, the export/import process applies to the Dataflow definitions only, not the data. As a result, we need to refresh the data later.

No-code/low-code experience

As mentioned at the beginning of this section, one of the main goals for using Dataflows is to bring self-service data preparation capabilities to the users. If you are an inexperienced user, you might think using Dataflows is a bit tedious.

But Power BI offers no-code/low-code experience in the Dataflows by providing a **Diagram View** of the queries to make it easier to identify the lineage and develop the Dataflows. The **Diagram View** is available in the bottom right of the **Power Query** window, as shown in the following image:

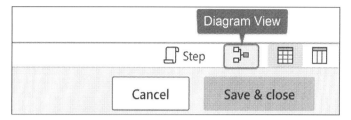

Figure 13.23: Diagram view in Dataflows

After clicking the **Diagram View** button, a visual representation of the queries appears above the **Data View** pane. The following image shows what we see in the **Diagram View** when we select the **Orders** table from the **Queries** pane:

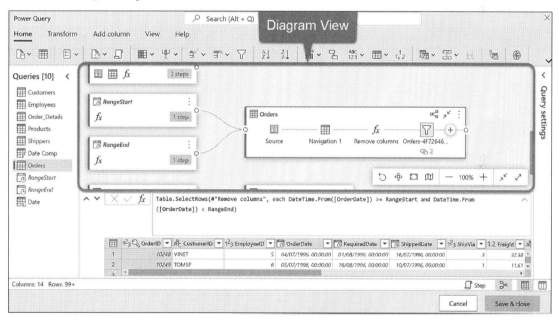

Figure 13.24: Diagram view while selecting the Orders table

We can add new steps by clicking the plus button (+) as the following image illustrates:

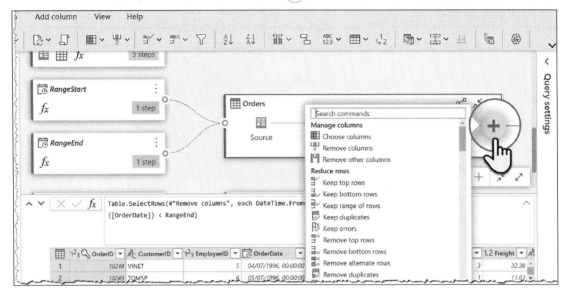

Figure 13.25: Adding new transformation steps to the Orders table from the Diagram View

Furthermore, various query-level actions are available from the context menu by clicking the actions ellipsis button, as shown in the following image:

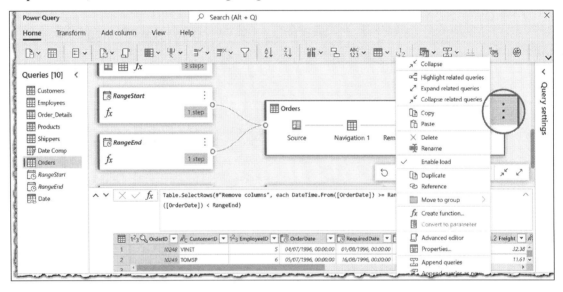

Figure 13.26: Query-level actions available from the Diagram View

In this section, we learned how to create a new Dataflow. After introducing the public preview of the Datamart's feature, you may get a message offering to create a Datamart instead of Dataflow when trying to create a new Dataflow in a Premium Workspace, as shown in the following image:

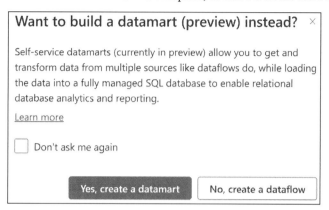

Figure 13.27: A message asking to create a Datamart instead of a Dataflow

While there are similarities between Datamarts and Dataflows, there are some fundamental differences. So we have to decide which option suits our requirements the best. We will discuss Datamarts in *Chapter 15, New Options, Features, and DAX Functions*. For now, we focus on the Dataflows.

Query plans in Dataflows

In May 2021, Microsoft announced the **query plans** for Dataflows that create visual indicators to understand better what happens in the Mashup Engine. This feature, which is still in public preview, is currently available only for data sources supporting query folding. Advanced users can use the query plan to better optimize their queries and fix glitches. We discussed query folding in *Chapter 7, Data Preparation Common Best Practices*, in detail, so we do not discuss the basics again.

We can access the query plan of the transformation steps by right-clicking the step and clicking the **View query plan** option. The following image shows accessing the query plan of the *Change column type* step in a **DimProduct** query sourcing from the AdventureWorksDW2019 database restored on an Azure SQL Database:

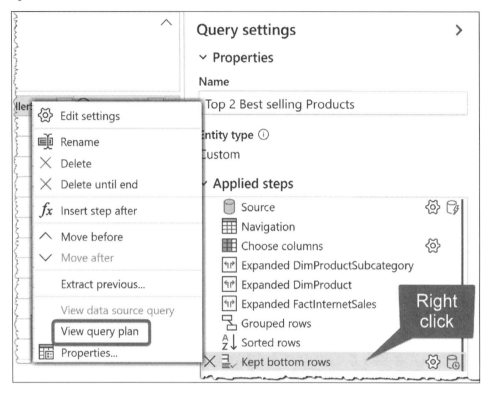

Figure 13.28: Getting the query plan of a transformation step in Dataflows

In the preceding query, I used **DimProductCategory**; I merged it with **DimProductSubcategory**, then with **DimProduct**, then with **FactInternetSales**. I grouped the results by **EnglishProductCategoryName** column and aggregated **SUM** of **SalesAmount**. Then, I sorted the results in ascending order and, lastly, kept the bottom two rows.

The following image shows the query plan of the **Kept bottom rows** step:

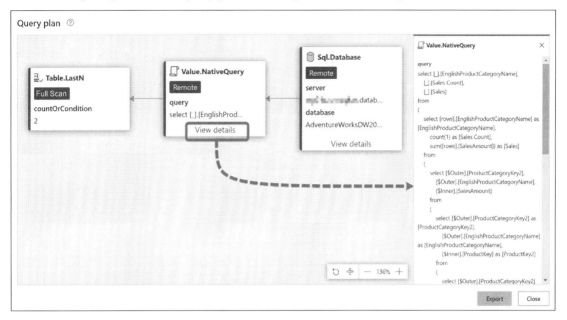

Figure 13.29: The query plan of the selected step

In the query plan shown in the preceding image, the two nodes labeled as **Remote** are folded, but the one labeled as **Full Scan** is not. We can learn more about each node by clicking the **View details** option.

Summary

In this chapter, we learned about Dataflows, what they are, and their terminology. We also learned when and how to create them, along with exporting and importing Dataflows when necessary. As stated at the beginning of this chapter, there is much more to learn about Dataflows than what we discussed in this chapter. So I suggest you read more about this fantastic piece of technology on Microsoft's official website using the following URL: https://learn.microsoft.com/en-us/power-query/dataflows/overview-dataflows-across-power-platform-dynamics-365?WT.mc_id=DP-MVP-5003466.

In the next chapter, we will discuss another advanced data modeling feature: composite models.

Join us on Discord!

Join The Big Data and Analytics Community on the Packt Discord Server!

Hang out with 558 other members and enjoy free voice and text chat.

https://packt.link/ips2H

14

DirectQuery Connections to Power BI Datasets and Analysis Services in Composite Models

In the previous chapter, we learned when and how to use dataflows. This chapter focuses on an advanced data modeling topic, which is expanding composite models by enabling and using DirectQuery connections to Power BI datasets, on-premises SQL Server Analysis Services (SSAS) tabular models, and Azure Analysis Services.

In the previous chapters, we learned about various aspects of data modeling through many different scenarios. This chapter briefly introduces more options available in the Power BI platform that can be handy in real-world scenarios. Each topic discussed in this chapter has extensive technical details, making it virtually impossible to cover in a single chapter. But it is worthwhile having exposure to them. This chapter covers the following areas:

- Introduction to composite models
- Enabling DirectQuery for live connections
- New terminologies

Introduction to composite models

In *Chapter 4*, *Getting Data from Various Sources*, we discussed different storage modes for a dataset. The following is a quick refresher on the datasets' storage modes:

- **Import**: For when we keep the data model in Power BI, and the whole data is cached in the memory. In this mode, all tables are in **Import** storage mode.
- **DirectQuery**: For when we create a data model in Power BI, but the data is NOT cached in the memory. In this mode, all tables are in DirectQuery storage mode.

- **Connect Live:** A specific type of DirectQuery, connecting to a semantic model, not a relational database (data store). When we use **Connect Live**, the data model is hosted elsewhere; therefore, we cannot make any changes to the data model. Instead, we can only get data ready from the data model.
- **Composite** (**Mixed**): When a portion of data is cached in the memory while the rest is not. In this mode, some tables are in **Import** storage mode, and some tables are in **DirectQuery** storage mode or **Dual** storage mode.

The last one is the main topic of this section. Previously, composite models only supported relational databases for DirectQuery but not semantic layers such as **SSAS Tabular models**, **Azure Analysis Services** (**AAS**), and **Power BI datasets**. In December 2020, Microsoft introduced a new generation of composite models for public preview. This new generation of composite model, which is generally available since April 2023, not only supports DirectQuery connections over relational databases such as SQL Server databases but it also supports DirectQuery to SSAS tabular 2022, AAS instances, and Power BI datasets.

This has led to a massive change in how we interact with the data, especially from an analytical perspective. With composite models, we can now connect to multiple semantic layers from a single Power BI data model. We can also import data from other data sources, such as SQL Server or Excel, and create an enterprise-grade self-service semantic layer using Power BI.

Enabling DirectQuery for live connections

To be able to use this feature, we have to have it enabled in the Power BI service and Power BI Desktop. The next subsections explain how to do so.

Allow DirectQuery connections to Power BI datasets in the Power BI service

If you are a Power BI administrator, you need to enable **Allow DirectQuery connections to Power BI datasets** in the admin portal from the Power BI service. If you are not an admin, then you may ask your Power BI administrators to enable it for you. Either way, the following steps show how to enable this feature in the Power BI service:

1. Click the gear button (⚙) located at the top right in the Power BI service.
2. Click **Admin portal**.
3. Expand the **Allow DirectQuery connections to Power BI datasets** setting under the **Export and sharing settings** section.

4. You may enable this feature for **The entire organization** or just **Specific security groups** depending on your organizational data governance policies.
5. Click **Apply**.

The following image shows the preceding steps:

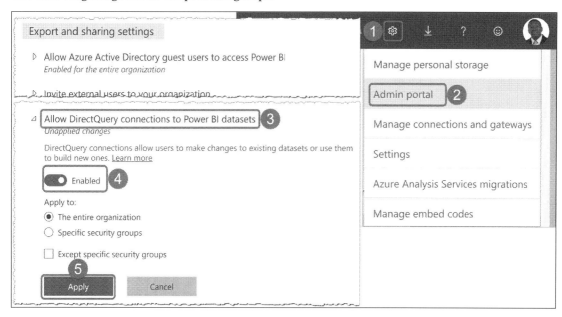

Figure 14.1: Enabling DirectQuery connections to Power BI datasets in the Power BI service

Now that we've enabled this feature, it is time to learn some new terminologies.

New terminologies

The new generation of composite models comes with new terminologies. Understanding these terms helps us to resolve more complex scenarios more efficiently and with fewer issues. In the following few subsections, we will learn about these new terms.

Chaining

Chaining is a new terminology introduced with the new composite model. When a Power BI report or dataset is based on some other semantic model hosted in SSAS tabular, AAS, or Power BI datasets, we create a chain; in other words, chaining is about the dependencies between semantic layers used in composite models. So, when we create a dataset on top of other datasets, the new dataset depends on a series of other datasets.

Chain length

When we create a chain, its length refers to the number of semantic layers the current dataset depends on. Let's implement a scenario to understand these terminologies better.

The business has a semantic model hosted in an AAS dataset that is still under development. The AAS developers have a massive backlog and future tasks to implement. The business has an urgent requirement for reporting. The business needs to define banding for the **UnitPrice** column on the **FactInternetSales** table as follows:

- **Low:** When the unit price is smaller than $100
- **Medium:** When the unit price is between $101 and $1,000
- **High:** When the unit price is between $1,001 and $3,000
- **Very high:** When the unit price is greater than $3,001

Let's look at the scenario in more detail. First, we have a semantic model in AAS, but the developers are too busy with their day-to-day tasks to respond to an urgent request from the business. The business can have many urgent daily requests, but our AAS developers cannot stop their development tasks to meet business requirements. As a Power BI data modeler, we can help to solve this issue very quickly.

The following steps show how to meet the preceding requirement in Power BI Desktop:

1. Select **Connect live** when connecting to the AAS instance from Power BI Desktop, as illustrated in the following image:

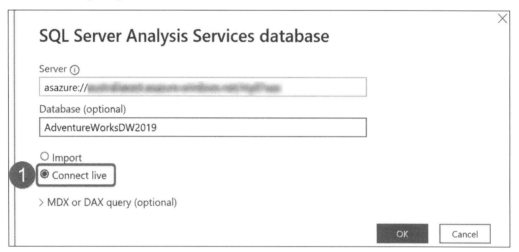

Figure 14.2: Connecting live to AAS

2. After inputting your credentials and connecting to AAS, click the **Model** tab to see the current AAS data model, as illustrated in the following image:

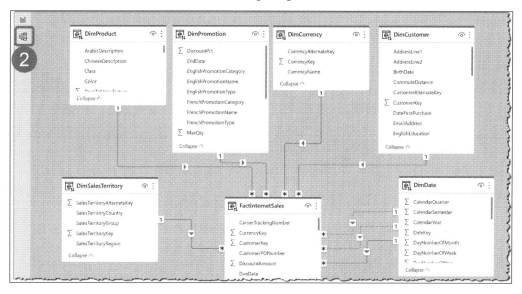

Figure 14.3: Current data model in AAS (connection mode: Connect live)

3. Click the **Make changes to this model** button from the **Home** tab. This changes the connection mode from Connect Live to DirectQuery:

Figure 14.4: Changing the connection mode from Connect Live to DirectQuery in top of an AAS model

4. Click **Add a local model**, as illustrated in the following image:

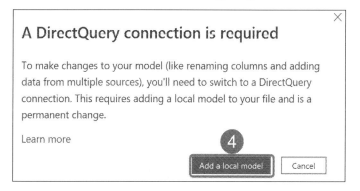

Figure 14.5: Confirming to add a local model

5. Tick the **Include tables added later** option if necessary and click the **Submit** button:

Figure 14.6: Submitting the selected tables

6. As the following image shows, all tables are now turned to DirectQuery mode. We can hover over the tables to see more details:

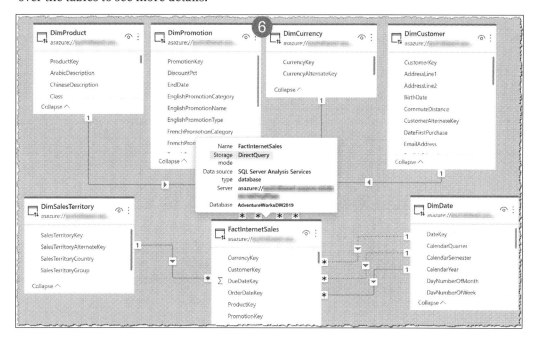

Figure 14.7: The look and feel of the Model view after turning the connection mode to DirectQuery

7. Switch back to the **Report** view and create a new **calculated** column using the following DAX expression:

```
Unit Price Range Band =
    SWITCH(
            TRUE()
           , 'FactInternetSales'[Unit Price] <= 100, "Low"
           , AND('FactInternetSales'[Unit Price] >= 101,
'FactInternetSales'[Unit Price] <= 1000), "Medium"
           , AND('FactInternetSales'[Unit Price] >= 1001,
'FactInternetSales'[Unit Price] <= 3000), "High"
           , "Very High"
    )
```

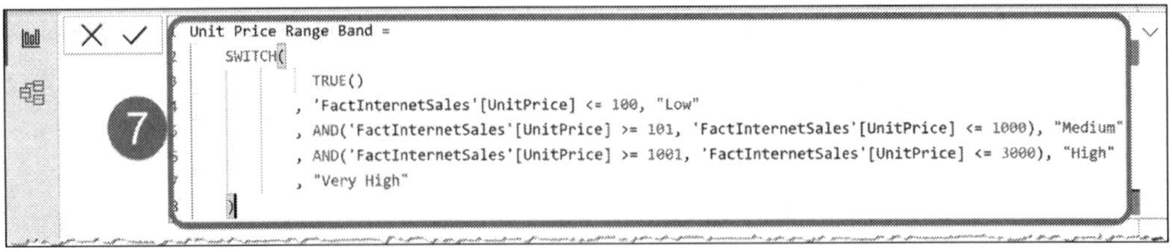

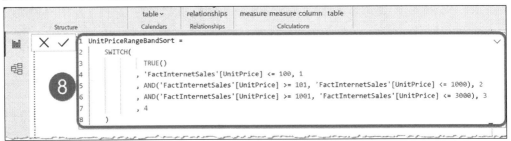

Figure 14.8: Creating a Unit Price Range Band calculated column

8. Create another calculated column using the following DAX expression to sort the **Unit Price Range Band** column:

```
UnitPriceRangeBandSort =
    SWITCH(
            TRUE()
            , 'FactInternetSales'[UnitPrice] <= 100, 1
            , AND('FactInternetSales'[UnitPrice] >= 101,
'FactInternetSales'[UnitPrice] <= 1000), 2
            , AND('FactInternetSales'[UnitPrice] >= 1001,
'FactInternetSales'[UnitPrice] <= 3000), 3
            , 4
    )
```

Figure 14.9: Creating a UnitPriceRangeBandSort calculated column

9. Sort the **Unit Price Range Band** column by the **UnitPriceRangeBandSort** column, as illustrated in the following image:

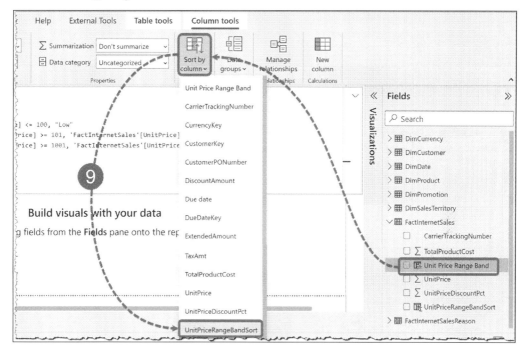

Figure 14.10: Sorting a column by another column

As you can see, the **Data** view is not available as the dataset is now in **DirectQuery** mode. Therefore, to see the changes we make, we have to use a table visual. The following image shows a table visual with the new calculated columns we built:

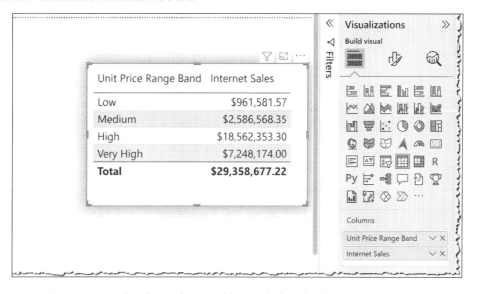

Figure 14.11: Testing the results in a table visual when the dataset is in DirectQuery

Now that we've met the business requirements, we can visualize the data as desired, but the last piece of the puzzle is to publish the report to the service. The following image shows a lineage view of the report after it is published to the Power BI service:

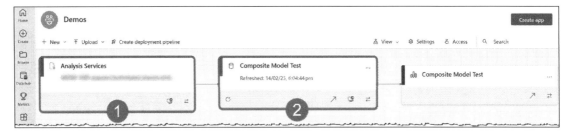

Figure 14.12: Lineage view of a published report in the Power BI service

Now, let's revisit the new terminologies. We are running DirectQuery on a semantic model hosted in **Analysis Services**, which is the first chain, from the **Composite Model Test** dataset, which is the second chain. So, the chain length in our scenario is 2. If we create another dataset on top of the **Composite Model Test**, then the chain length will be 3.

 When writing this book, the maximum chain length allowed is 3; therefore, we cannot create a composite model with a chain length of 4.

So far, we've learned the basics of using DirectQuery on live connections. The next section focuses on RLS in composite models with DirectQuery on live connections.

RLS in composite models with DirectQuery to Power BI datasets

Now that we have a better understanding of how composite models work with a DirectQuery connection to Power BI datasets, SSAS tabular, or AAS models, it is time to take this another step further and discuss more technical scenarios that include RLS. We'll use the **AdventureWorksDW2019** database for this scenario.

The business has an **Internet Sales** dataset published to the Power BI service. The following image shows the **Internet Sales** data model:

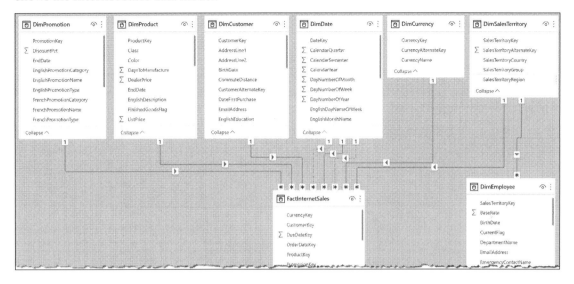

Figure 14.13: Internet Sales data model

Note the one-to-many relationship between the **DimSalesTerritory** and **DimEmployee** tables. The developer created a dynamic RLS so each salesperson can see only their relevant territory's sales values. To ensure the **DimEmployee** table always shows the data that is relevant to the report users, we have to use the following DAX expression to create a rule on the **DimEmployee** table:

```
[EmailAddress] = USERPRINCIPALNAME()
```

We also use the following expression to create a rule on **DimSalesTerritory** that caters to that:

```
VAR __SalesReps =
CALCULATETABLE(
    VALUES(DimEmployee[SalesTerritoryKey]),
    TREATAS( {USERPRINCIPALNAME()}, DimEmployee[EmailAddress] )
)
RETURN
DimSalesTerritory[SalesT0erritoryKey] in __SalesReps
```

The following image shows what Rachel Valdez, a salesperson active in Germany, can see in the report:

Figure 14.14: Dynamic RLS implemented for salespersons

The sample file for the preceding report is Chapter 14, Dynamic RLS Internet Sales.pbix, which you can download from here: https://github.com/PacktPublishing/Expert-Data-Modeling-with-Power-BI-Second-Edition/blob/28e2af1762336ab5236a3b3961c41e9020de8200/Samples/Chapter%2014/Chapter%2014,%20Dynamic%20RLS%20Internet%20Sales.pbix.

The business now requires including **Resellers Sales** in a new report, so when salespersons open the report, they only see their own data. The **Resellers Sales** data is currently kept in the organizational data warehouse. We want to create a new composite model with DirectQuery to the existing dataset in Power BI and add **DimReseller** and **FactResellerSales** tables from the data warehouse. The following image shows a part of the data model after connecting in **DirectQuery** mode to the existing Power BI dataset and creating the relationships:

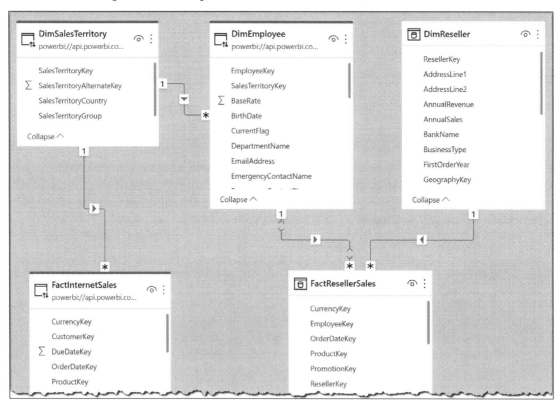

Figure 14.15: Reseller Sales data added to the Power BI dataset

So, the new data model contains the tables from the remote dataset and two imported tables from the data warehouse. The remote dataset in the Power BI service has RLS implemented, so we expect RLS to propagate to the new data model. The new report file is Chapter 14, Composite Model Internet Sales.pbix, which can be downloaded from here: https://github.com/PacktPublishing/Expert-Data-Modeling-with-Power-BI-Second-Edition/blob/28e2af1762336ab5236a3b3961c41e9020de8200/Samples/Chapter%2014/Chapter%2014,%20Composite%20Model%20Internet%20Sales.pbix.

As discussed in *Chapter 11*, *Row-Level and Object-Level Security*, RLS kicks in only when the user has the **Viewer** role on the containing workspace or the report is shared with the user via a link, direct access, or an app. So, I published the new report to the Power BI service and made a desired security group **Viewer** role on the workspace. The following image shows the lineage view of the new report published to the Power BI service:

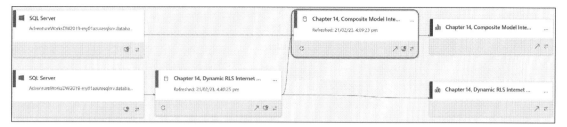

Figure 14.16: Composite model's lineage view

As the preceding image shows, the chain length of the composite model is 2. The following image shows what happens when a user that is a member of the security group logs in to Power BI and runs the report:

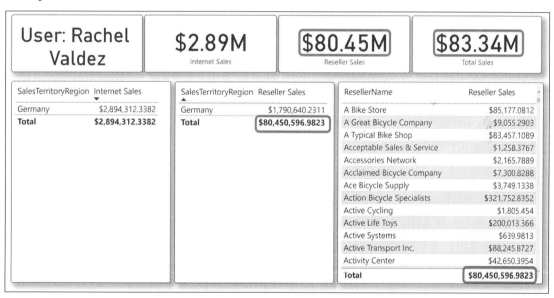

Figure 14.17: Composite model Internet Sales report

As the preceding image shows, the RLS implemented on the first chain kicked in and identified that Rachel logged in, and it also worked as expected on the **Internet Sales** measure in the first chain dataset. But, something strange happened in the **Reseller Sales**, and consequently, the **Total Sales**, which is `[Internet Sales] + [Reseller Sales]`. While the only SalesTerritoryRegion is Germany, which is correct, the total is completely wrong. In fact, Rachel sees all **Reseller Sales** instead of **Germany's** sales. The reason is that the relationship between the **DimEmployee** and **FactResellerSales** tables is a limited relationship, as shown in *Figure 14.16*.

In fact, all relationships between the DirectQuery tables and the imported tables are limited relationships. We touched on limited relationships in *Chapter 9, Star Schema and Data Modeling Common Best Practices*, in the *Dealing with many-to-many relationships* section, where we discussed the two relationship evaluation types: regular and limited. As a quick reminder, the relationship between two tables is regular when both have the same storage mode, and the relationship between the two is not many-to-many. If we violate any of the two conditions, the relationship between tables is limited.

When a relationship is limited, **table expansion** does not happen. Table expansion happens on the tables of the **many** side of a **many-to-one** relationship or the tables with a **one-to-one** relationship. Table expansion means that the columns of the table on the **one** side of the relationship are reachable by the table on the **many** side. Look at *Figure 14.16*, for instance; you can imagine a wide **FactResellerSales** that also contains all columns from the **DimReseller** table. It is like reaching to the **DimReseller** columns from the **FactResellerSales** table using the `RELATED()` function.

That is why when the relationship is limited, the `RELATED()` function is not supported. When the relationship is limited, the filter propagation from the **one** side to the **many** side of the one-to-many relationship does not work as expected. Therefore, when Rachel opens the report, she sees all reseller sales and not only hers. To fix the issue, we add another RLS rule on the **FactResellerSales** table to enforce the filter on the **SalesTerritoryKey** column using the following DAX expression:

```
VAR __SalesReps =
CALCULATETABLE(
    VALUES(DimEmployee[EmployeeKey]),
    TREATAS( {USERPRINCIPALNAME()}, DimEmployee[EmailAddress] )
)
RETURN
FactResellerSales[EmployeeKey] in __SalesReps
```

In composite models with DirectQuery for Power BI datasets or Azure Analysis Services, the remote tables are not available to create RLS rules. But we can still run DAX expressions to filter the imported tables. For instance, as the following image shows, **DimEmployee** (remote table) is not available in the **Manage roles** window. Still, we can filter **FactInternetSales** by running DAX expressions on the remote table:

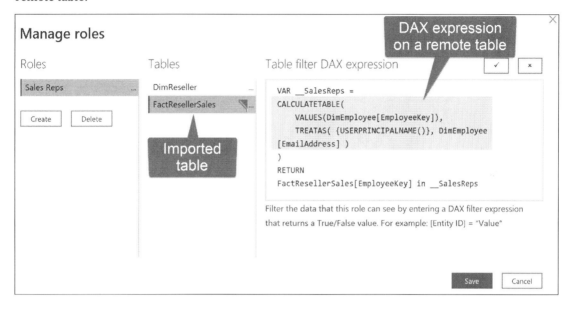

Figure 14.18: Creating new RLS roles in composite models

The following image shows the results of the report for Rachel after the new RLS role is added to the composite model:

Figure 14.19: Composite model with RLS run by Rachel

When Pamela opens the same report, she sees only her data, which is exactly how we expect the report to work. The following image shows the report run by Pamela:

Figure 14.20: Composite model with RLS run by Pamela

As we see, limited relationships make RLS work slightly differently in composite models with DirectQuery for Power BI datasets than the regular models. That aside, we understand that the RSL applied to different dataset chains always flows downstream, which means that the RLS in the chain 1 dataset filters the data in the chain 2 dataset. This affects how we implement further reports on the datasets from a permission perspective. For instance, think about a situation where we want to enable the contributors to create reports with a composite model dataset structure with DirectQuery for a Power BI dataset. We will discuss this in the next section.

Setting dataset permissions for contributors (report writers)

As we all know, the implemented RLS on a dataset kicks in only for users who access the report via a **shared link**, have **read-only direct access** to the report, or have a **Viewer** role on the workspace. The report writers should have **Build** permission on the referenced dataset(s) to connect to the datasets in Power BI Desktop to create **thin reports**. A thin report is a report we build upon an existing dataset. In other words, thin reports do not have data models but a data visualization only. Follow these steps to grant **Build** permission to contributors after navigating to a desired workspace:

1. Hover over the first chain dataset and click the **more options** ellipsis button.
2. Click the **Manage permissions** option.
3. Hover over a user account or security group and click the **More options** ellipsis button.
4. Click **Add build**.

The following image shows the preceding steps:

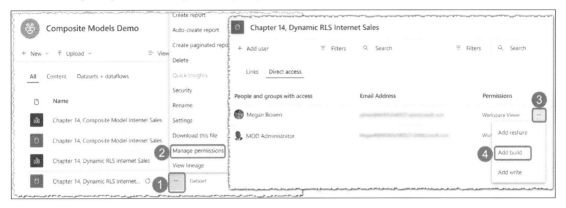

Figure 14.21: Grant build permission on a chained dataset for contributors

While the composite model scenarios we implemented in this chapter are not overly complex, they are real-world scenarios that can help us solve more challenging implementations. This feature is newly made generally available (April 2023), so its capabilities will improve over time. So I strongly suggest keeping an eye on Microsoft's official website to monitor the changes, limitations, and considerations. Here is Microsoft's official documentation: https://learn.microsoft.com/en-us/power-bi/connect-data/desktop-directquery-datasets-azure-analysis-services?WT.mc_id=DP-MVP-5003466.

Summary

In this chapter, we learned about new terminologies for composite models in Power BI and how to enable DirectQuery connections to Power BI datasets on Power BI Desktop and the Power BI service, and implemented simple but pragmatic scenarios to build solid foundations for future implementations and more complex scenarios. In the next chapter, we will look at other new features and capabilities for data modeling in Power BI.

Join us on Discord!

Join The Big Data and Analytics Community on the Packt Discord Server!

Hang out with 558 other members and enjoy free voice and text chat.

https://packt.link/ips2H

15

New Options, Features, and DAX Functions

In *Chapter 14*, *DirectQuery Connections to Power BI Datasets and Analysis Services in Composite Models*, we learned how to use a DirectQuery connection to Power BI datasets, Azure Analysis Services, and SQL Server Analysis Services tabular models in a composite model. We also discussed some design challenges, especially when datasets include RLS. In this chapter, which is the book's last chapter, we look into some newly released features, options, and DAX functions. This chapter covers the following topics:

- Fields parameters
- Introduction to Datamarts
- New DAX functions

Field parameters

Microsoft announced the **field parameters** feature in May 2022 for Power BI Desktop. At the time of writing, this feature is still in public preview. The field parameters feature helps Power BI developers to create data models that support more dynamic reports, where users can switch between different fields (measures and columns) in a slicer that affects other linked visuals. The field parameters feature is different from the query parameter and is accessible via the **Report** view, on the **Modeling** tab from the ribbon.

We already implemented a solution in *Chapter 2*, *Data Analysis eXpressions and Data Modeling*, under the *Implementing Dynamic Measure Selection with Field Parameters* subsection, to dynamically select between two measures, so we do not need to explain how to use field parameters again. Instead, we use the sample file to extend the solution and discuss what happens in the background in more detail. The sample file is accessible here: `https://github.com/PacktPublishing/Expert-Data-Modeling-with-Power-BI-Second-Edition/blob/cb57eb34a28e6bda8b725ca0f5c85200f42c072c/Samples/Chapter%2002/Chapter%202%2C%20Time%20Intelligence.pbix`.

The following image shows what we currently have in the report:

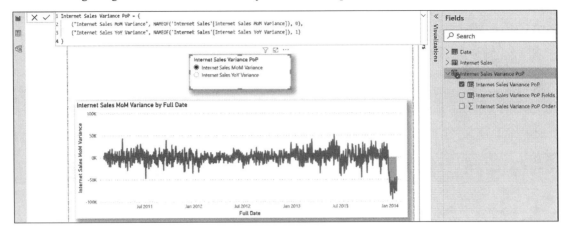

Figure 15.1: Dynamic measures with field parameters

As the preceding image shows, using the field parameters feature creates a new calculated table. After configuring the field parameters, there is no way back to modify it in the UI, but we can modify the automatically generated DAX expressions. Power BI uses a new DAX function, NAMEOF(), which accepts a measure or a column name returning the field's fully qualified name. The calculated table generated by the field parameters is like any other calculated table, so we can modify it and add columns or measures. For instance, we used the following DAX expression to add a new measure to the calculated table that retrieves the fully qualified name of the [Internet Sales] measure:

```
Internet Sales Field Name = NAMEOF([Internet Sales])
```

The following image shows the results:

Figure 15.2: Using the NAMEOF() function

Or we can modify the calculated table's DAX expression as follows to add another field to it:

```
Internet Sales Variance PoP = {
    ("Internet Sales MoM Variance", NAMEOF('Internet Sales'[Internet Sales MoM Variance]), 0),
    ("Internet Sales YoY Variance", NAMEOF('Internet Sales'[Internet Sales YoY Variance]), 1),
    ("Internet Sales LY", NAMEOF([Internet Sales LY]), 2)
}
```

The following image shows the results:

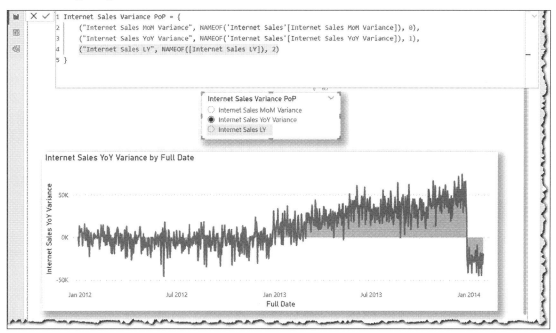

Figure 15.3: Modifying the calculated table created by field parameters

Let us configure another field parameter to enable users to dynamically select the **X-axis** of another **Area** chart between the **Year**, **Month**, and **Full Date** columns. The new field parameters create a new calculated table named **Date Fields**.

 We renamed the **CalendarYear** column to **Year** and the **EnglishMonthName** to **Month** and saved the file as `Chapter 15, Field Parameters.pbix`.

As the steps are similar to the scenario we explained in *Chapter 2*, *Data Analysis eXpressions and Data Modeling*, we skip the step-by-step explanation. The following image shows the configuration:

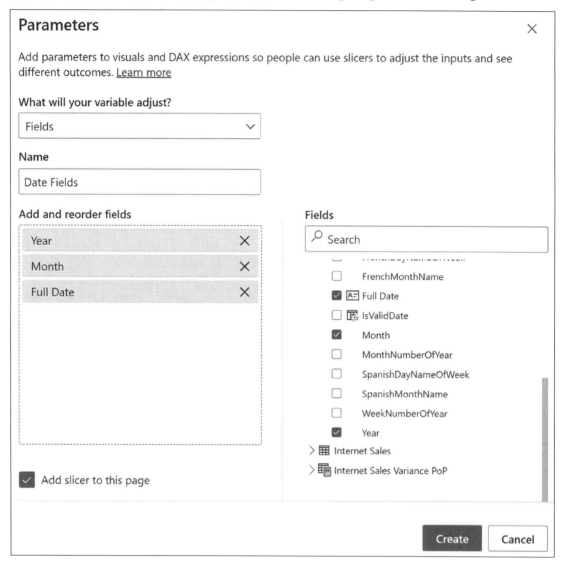

Figure 15.4: Configuring new field parameters

Now we make a copy of the existing **Area** chart and change its **X-axis** to the **Date Fields** column from the newly calculated table. The following image shows the results where the user selects the Internet Sales LY measure from the first slicer and **Month** from the second:

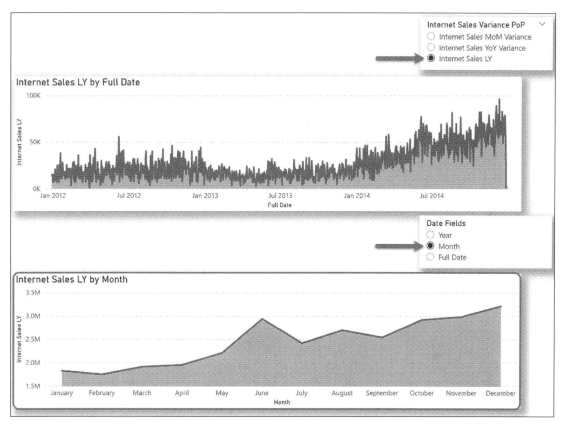

Figure 15.5: Using the Date Fields in a new Area chart

As the preceding image shows, the highlighted **Area** chart shows the **Internet Sales LY** by **Month**. But what if the business wants to have date hierarchies in the slicer, one to show **Year** and **Month** levels and another for the **Full Date**? To do so, we only need to add a new column to the **Date Fields** table that categorizes the **Year** and **Month** columns as **Year-Month** and the **Full Date** as **Date**. So we modify the DAX expressions as follows:

```
Date Fields = {
    ("Year", NAMEOF('Date'[Year]), 0, "Year-Month"),
    ("Month", NAMEOF('Date'[Month]), 1, "Year-Month"),
    ("Full Date", NAMEOF('Date'[Full Date]), 2, "Date")
}
```

The preceding expression adds a new **Value4** column to the **Date Fields** table. The following image shows the results:

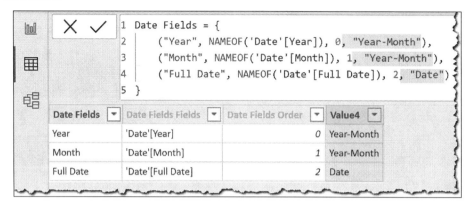

Figure 15.6: Adding a new column to the Date Fields calculated table

Rename the **Value4** column **Date Hierarchy**, then add it to the **Date Fields** slicer as shown in the following image:

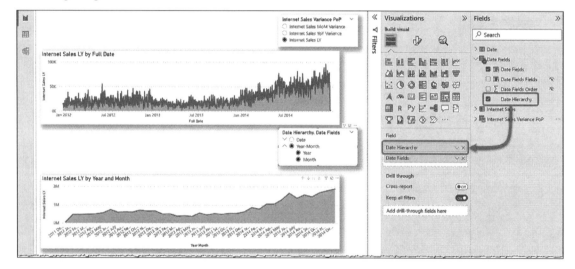

Figure 15.7: Adding Date Hierarchy to the Date Fields slicer

As the preceding image shows, we now have a hierarchy in the slicer, so when the user selects the **Year-Month** level, the second **Area** chart shows the **Year** and **Month** as a hierarchy so the user can drill down or up through its levels. With field parameters, we can add more flexible data models that support more dynamic data visualization. We can leverage the power of field parameters in a thin report after publishing the data model, with field parameters implemented into the Power BI Service.

 A thin report is a Power BI report connected live to a published Power BI dataset in the Power BI Service.

Last but not least, the field parameters are not visible in Excel when using the **Analyze in Excel** feature in Power BI.

The next section focuses on another powerful feature in Power BI: Datamarts.

Introduction to Power BI Datamarts

Microsoft announced the public preview availability of **Datamarts** in May 2022. When authoring this chapter, Datamarts are still in preview, so using them in production environments is not recommended. The Datamarts capability opens endless possibilities for organizations to achieve their data analytics goals on the Power BI platform. Before we look into the Power BI Datamarts, let us take a step back and understand the meaning of a Datamart.

What is a Datamart?

A quick search on the Internet provides multiple definitions by technology-leading companies such as IBM, Amazon, and Oracle. They all agree that a Datamart is a subject-oriented subset of a data warehouse focusing on a particular business unit, department, subject area, or business functionality. The Datamart's data is usually stored in databases containing a moving frame required for data analysis, not the full history of data. For instance, organizations store the historical and current data of various business sectors, such as sales, inventory, marketing, finance, etc., in an enterprise data warehouse. They then create a Datamart for social marketing for the past 5 years. The following diagram shows a simplistic architecture of Datamarts of top of an enterprise data warehouse:

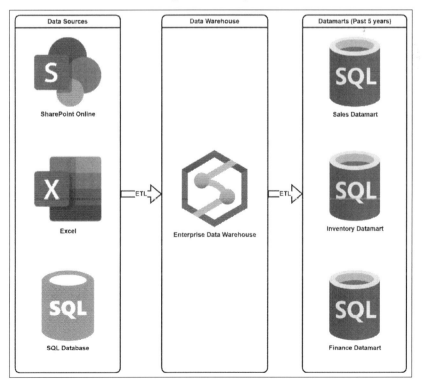

Figure 15.8: A simple business intelligence architecture containing Datamarts

In the preceding diagram, the first ETL arrow (the left arrow) shows the processes of extracting the data from the source systems, transforming and loading it into an enterprise data warehouse that keeps a full history of data. Then we have some other ETL processes to constantly land the past 5 years of data into the Datamarts.

In the real world, the **Business Intelligence** (BI) or the **Information Technology** (IT) departments are responsible for implementing and maintaining the ETL processes, the enterprise data warehouse and Datamarts, which often take a reasonably long time to deliver the solution to the end users. This lengthy process usually leads the end-users to try to solve the problem themselves by creating Datamart-like solutions, often created in Excel files stored in their personal space. From a data governance perspective, this is a massive risk to organizations by exposing them to the whole laundry of privacy and security breaches.

Now that we have a better understanding of a Datamart and its challenges, let us look at it through the Power BI lens.

What is Power BI Datamarts?

As mentioned earlier, one of the weaknesses of traditional data warehousing and building datamarts is that they require a lot of knowledge to create and maintain, making the process lengthy and costly. The industry answer to this challenge was self-service BI, which usually suffers from a lack of governance. As we all know, one of the many strengths of Power BI is the ability to package self-service BI capabilities and governance altogether. With the Power BI Datamarts technology, Microsoft provides a governed self-service datamart capability in the Power BI Service. Power BI Datamarts provide no-code/low-code datamart capabilities using Azure SQL Database technology in the background. The Power BI Datamarts support sensitivity labels, endorsement, discovery, and **Row-Level Security** (**RLS**), which help protect and manage the data according to the business requirements and compliance needs. Therefore, the whole process of data integration, transformation, preparation, storage, modeling, and visualization is governed by the organization. To recap, Power BI Datamarts can be used in any or all of the following scenarios:

- Creating self-service solutions with fully managed relational database capability, backed by Azure SQL Database without requiring an Azure subscription.
- No-code/low-code experience using a diagram view in the data preparation layer similar to Dataflows.
- Building business-focussed semantic layers in the cloud (the Power BI Service) with data modeling capabilities, such as managing relationships, creating measures, defining incremental refresh, and creating and managing RLS.

Now that we have a good understanding of what Datamarts are in Power BI, let us see what they are not.

Demystifying Power BI Datamart misunderstandings

Whenever we start using a new tool, we first have to understand what it is and in what situations it is meant to be used. The same principle applies to Power BI Datamarts. So far, we have learned what Power BI Datamarts are, but it is also important to know what they are not. This subsection aims to demystify some misunderstandings and misconceptions. A Power BI Datamart is not:

- A replacement for Dataflows. As we learned in the previous section, a Dataflow is a self-service ETL and data preparation layer connecting to various data sources, transforming the data and storing the results in CSV format in **Azure Data Lake Gen 2** (**ADLS Gen2**). A Datamart is a self-service BI solution containing a self-service data preparation (or ETL) layer and a data model (or semantic layer). While the Datamart includes the data preparation layer, the results are stored in an Azure SQL database for different requirements than Dataflows. The Dataflows will still be used across the organization for self-service data preparation and enabling organizational users to reuse the results. Therefore, Datamarts are not a replacement for Dataflows.

- A replacement for datasets. While Datamarts contain datasets, we cannot consider them as a replacement for datasets. As mentioned earlier, there are currently many data modeling restrictions in Datamarts. We will discuss the Datamart's current restrictions in a separate subsection, but just to name some, we cannot currently create calculated columns or calculated tables in a Datamart. We also cannot define aggregations or define Object-level security.

- A replacement for or an alternative to data warehouses. As discussed earlier, a datamart is a business-centric subset of a data warehouse that does not contain the full history of data. Indeed, data warehouses are the best candidates to be used as a source for a Power BI Datamart; therefore, they are not meant to replace data warehouses.

Lastly, the Datamart Editor, which we will cover next, is not a replacement for Power BI Desktop. While we can implement data preparation and data model in a Datamart, this capability is not mature enough to replace the need to develop solutions in Power BI Desktop. At the time of writing this book, there are so many restrictions, especially for data modeling, making the Datamart capability far behind Power BI Desktop. Besides, this capability is a Premium feature, while Power BI Desktop is free. Moreover, Power BI Desktop supports much more data sources than Datamarts. Therefore, they are not replacing Power BI Desktop.

Now that we know what Power BI Datamarts are and what they are not, let us get familiar with the Datamart Editor, the development tool in the Power BI Service.

The Datamart Editor

The **Datamart Editor** is a visual designer tool to implement Power BI Datamarts in the Power BI Service. The Datamart Editor provides data preparation with Power Query as well as data modeling capabilities. However, it does not include reporting capabilities. So report writers must create reports outside of the Datamart Editor. The Datamart Editor also provides the ad-hoc querying capability to analyze the data in two flavors: **Visual query** and **SQL query**. While the Datamart Editor is similar to Power BI Desktop, it has a long way to go to get to the point that Power BI Desktop is at today. The following image shows the current version of the Datamart Editor:

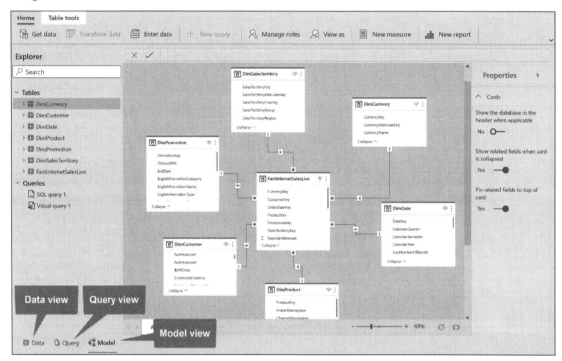

Figure 15.9: The Datamart Editor

As the preceding image shows, the Datamart Editor has three views: The **Data**, **Query**, and **Model** views. Each view provides different capabilities. The **Data** and **Model** views are similar to their counterparts in Power BI Desktop with lesser capabilities. But the **Query** view is new. It allows us to analyze the data. The **Query** view currently supports two different querying methods. The **Visual query** uses the Power Query's visual diagram providing no-code experience to those unfamiliar with **Transact SQL (T-SQL)** language. The **SQL query**, on the other hand, is made for more seasoned developers familiar with T-SQL. In the next few subsections, we will discuss the different capabilities the Datamart Editor has to offer.

Create a simple Power BI Datamart

The Power BI Datamarts are available in Power BI Service in a Premium Workspace. So, organizations with either Premium or Embedded capacity or **Premium Per User** (**PPU**) licensing plans can leverage the power of Datamarts.

The business requires a fully managed and governed copy of its Internet Sales from an existing enterprise data warehouse, keeping the last calendar year of data. We will use the AdventureWorksDW2019 sample database available for download using the following URL: https://learn.microsoft.com/en-us/sql/samples/adventureworks-install-configure?view=sql-server-ver16&WT.mc_id=DP-MVP-5003466.

For demonstration purposes and to be able to show the last two calendar years of data, I created a new table named **FactInternetSalesLive** and populated it with more than 10 million rows of random data, but you do not need to do so. Instead, you can use the **FactInternetSales** table. With that, let's begin.

Load the data into the Datamart

Log into your Power BI Service and navigate to the desired Workspace. Remember that it must be a Premium Workspace. Follow these steps:

1. Click the **New** dropdown button and click the **Datamart (Preview)** from the menu.
2. Enter a name for the Datamart and click the **Create** button.
3. Click the **Get Data** button.

    Click the SQL Server database or Azure SQL database, depending on where you restored the AdventureWroksDW2019 database.

4. Enter the Server and Database names. If you use an op-premises SQL database, you must have installed and configured the on-premises Data Gateway and select the gateway here. Read more about the On-premises Data Gateway using this URL: https://learn.microsoft.com/en-us/power-bi/connect-data/service-gateway-onprem?WT.mc_id=DP-MVP-5003466.
5. Click **Next**.

The following image shows the preceding steps:

Graphical user interface, application

Description automatically generated:

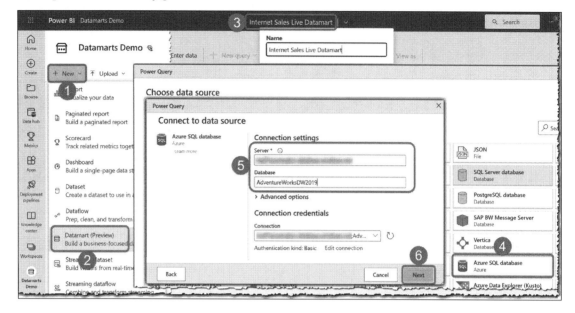

Figure 15.10: Creating a Datamart from an Azure SQL DB

1. Select the desired table; in my example, I select the **FactInternetSalesLive** table.
2. Click the **Select related tables** button.
3. Click the **Transform data** button.

The following image shows the preceding steps:

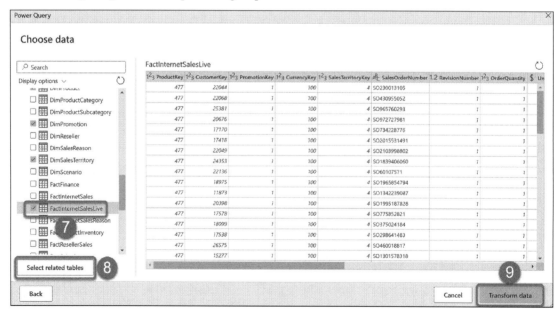

Figure 15.11: Selecting a table and its related tables when creating a Datamart

Chapter 15

We can now perform the required transformation steps to filter the **FactInternetSalesLive** data to show the last two years of data. If we do not add the filter, we load the entire 10 million rows of data into the Datamart, which is not what we require.

1. Select the **FactInternetSalesLive** table.
2. Filter the OrderDateKey to be greater than or equal to the 1st Jan for the last two years using the following Power Query expression:

   ```
   Int64.From(Date.ToText(Date.From(DateTime.LocalNow()), "yyyy0101")) - 20000
   ```

3. Click the **Save** button.

The following screenshot shows the preceding steps:

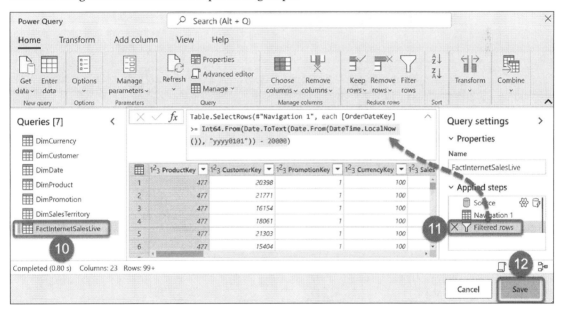

Figure 15.12: Filtering the results and saving the transformation steps

At this point, the Datamart starts creating the ETL rules and piping the data from the source into the underlying Azure SQL DB. If you do not want to wait till the process is done you can click the **Go to workspace** button, or wait while it is done, and it automatically navigates you to the Datamart.

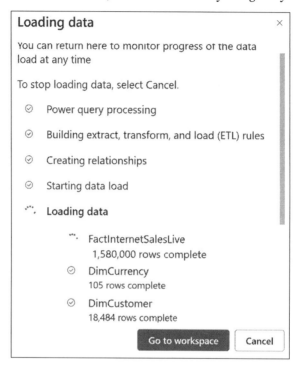

Figure 15.13: Loading data when creating the Datamart

As mentioned earlier, one of the differences between Dataflows and Datamarts is that Dataflows load data into ADLS Gen2, while Datamarts load data into an Azure SQL DB. So far, we have created the data transformation layer using Power Query Online, and the data is loaded into an Azure SQL DB. The other thing that automatically happens in the background is that a new dataset is created in the Workspace, which brings us to the next step—to build the data model.

Build the data model in Datamarts

The Datamart Editor currently provides limited data modeling capabilities such as creating measures, creating and managing relationships, configuring incremental data load, and creating RLS.

Let us continue with our scenario. So far, we have prepared the data and loaded the results into the database. The Datamart Editor automatically creates a dataset behind the scenes. The dataset contains a raw data model in the DirectQuery storage model of the underlying Azure SQL DB. Therefore, we are limited to modeling activities supported in DirectQuery mode.

 As the created dataset is currently in DirectQuery mode, the data preparation layer only supports foldable Power Query transformations.

We have learned all these capabilities throughout this book so we will avoid explaining them again.

The next step is to create and manage relationships. Let us see how it works in Datamarts.

Create and manage relationships

We can create new relationships or manage the existing ones within the Datamart Editor via the **Model** view. To create a new relationship, drag and drop the key column from the table of the **Many** side of the relationship to the key column of the table of the **One** side of the relationship. The following image shows the **Create Relationship** window, where we can create relationships between the **FactInternetSalesLive** table and the **DimCustomer** table via the **CustomerKey** column on both tables:

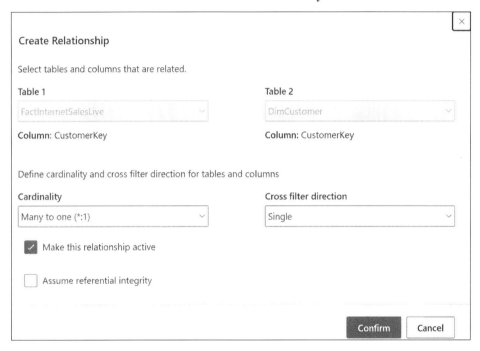

Figure 15.13: Creating a new relationship in the Datamart Editor

As the preceding image shows, we have the option to **Assume referential integrity**. Let us see what this option means.

Relationship option: Assume referential integrity

The term **Referential Integrity** comes from relational databases to guarantee the consistency of the key columns (primary key and foreign key) participating in a relationship in both related tables. For instance, if we update a primary key in a table, we want to ensure that the related foreign key of the related table is kept up to date with the changes. The **Assume referential integrity** option in the **Create Relationship** window comes from the same concept, where the values of the column of the **One** side of a **One-to-Many** relationship are never null or blank, and there is always a matching value found on the **Many** side of the relationship for each value on the **One** side. This option is only available when the storage mode of the tables participating in the relationship is **DirectQuery**.

Enabling this option allows us to run more efficient queries against the source systems by generating **INNER JOIN** statements instead of **OUTER JOIN**, which improves the query performance. In the data warehousing world, referential integrity is not respected as much as in transactional systems because of its downsides. For instance, bulk loading the data and data loading parallelism are vital characteristics of ETL processes in data warehousing. Putting referential integrity constraints on tables can degrade the data loading performance, and in some cases, it leads the data loading process to fail. The concept of **Inferred Dimensions** is another scenario where referential integrity becomes problematic. An inferred dimension is a foreign key of a dimension table appearing in the fact table without having a match in the dimension table. This is a common scenario, where the data in the fact table is loaded while the related dimensions are not fully populated.

For those reasons, it is not recommended to use this option while creating the relationships in the Datamart Editor unless you are sure about the integrity of your data in the data source. If this option is selected but the integrity of the underlying data is not up to the standards, you will get unexpected or incorrect results without any error messages.

Analyze Datamarts in the Datamart Editor

As mentioned earlier, the Datamart Editor provides **Visual query** and **SQL query** capabilities that can be used by two groups of users. The **Visual query** is a self-service no-code querying mechanism for data analysts who are unfamiliar with SQL language. On the other hand, the SQL query capability can be used by developers who have loved and used T-SQL to analyze data for many years. Both the **Visual query** and **SQL query** options are available in the **Query** view in the Datamart Editor.

No-code experience with the Visual query

Imagine a case where a business analyst who has access to an existing datamart needs to analyze the data further. For instance, imagine a case where a business analyst unfamiliar with T-SQL wants to analyze the products sold in our previous scenario. The following steps explain the process:

1. Click the **Query** view.
2. Click the **New query** dropdown button.
3. Click the **New visual query** option.
4. Drag and drop the **DimProduct** table onto the Visual query canvas.
5. Drag and drop the **FactInternetSalesLive** table onto the canvas.

Chapter 15

The following image shows the preceding steps:

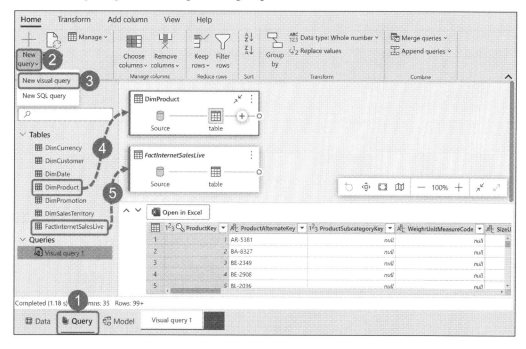

Figure 15.15: Creating a new Visual query in the Datamart Editor

6. Click the **Actions** ellipsis button on the **DimProduct**.
7. Click **Merge queries as new**.
8. Select the **FactInternetSalesLive** from the **Right table for merge** dropdown.
9. Select the **ProductKey** from the **DimProduct** table.
10. Select the **ProductKey** from the **FactInternetSalesLive** table.
11. Keep the **Join kind** as **Left outer**.
12. Click **OK**.

The following image shows the preceding steps:

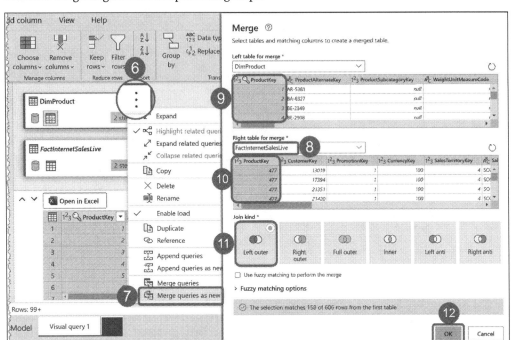

Figure 15.16: Merging tables in the Visual query in the Datamart Editor

13. On the data preview pane, scroll to the right and click the expand button of the **FactInternetSalesLive** column.
14. Select the **SalesAmount** column.
15. Click **OK**.

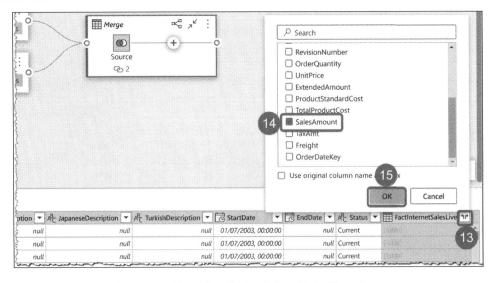

Figure 15.17: Expanding the FactInternetSalesLive column

Chapter 15

16. Select the new **Merge** table from the canvas and click the plus button (+).
17. Click the **Choose columns** from the context menu.
18. Select the **ProductKey**, **EnglishProductName**, and **SalesAmount** columns.
19. Click **OK**.

The following image shows the preceding steps:

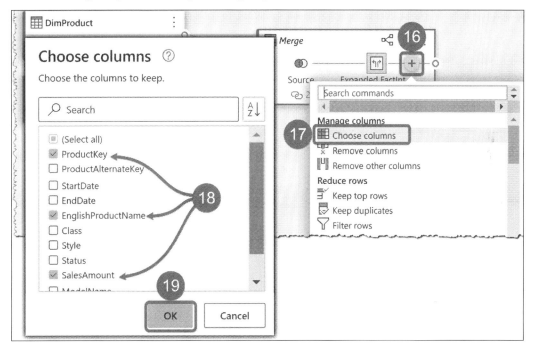

Figure 15.18: Choosing columns in the diagram view in Datamarts

20. Click the plus button (+) one more time and click the **Group by** transformation.
21. Click the **Advanced** option.
22. Click the **Add grouping** button.
23. Ensure that you selected the **ProductKey** and **EnglishProductName** on the **Group by** section.
24. Type in **Sold Products Count** as the name for the first aggregation with the Count rows operation.
25. Click the **Add aggregation** button.
26. Type in **Internet Sales** for the **New column** name, select **Sum** as the operation, and select the **SalesAmount** from the **Column** dropdown.
27. Click **OK**.

The following image shows the preceding steps:

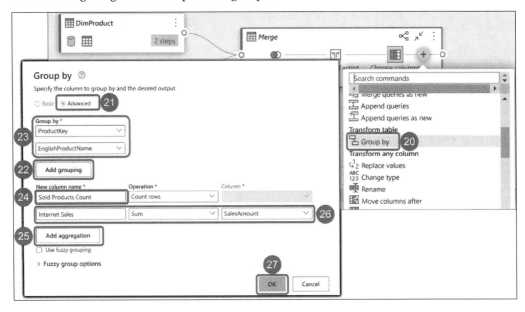

Figure 15.19: Using the Group by operation in the diagram view in Datamarts

As you can see, we created a summary table without writing even a line of code. We can now double-click the **Visual query 1** tab to rename it **Products Sold Summary**. The following image shows the results:

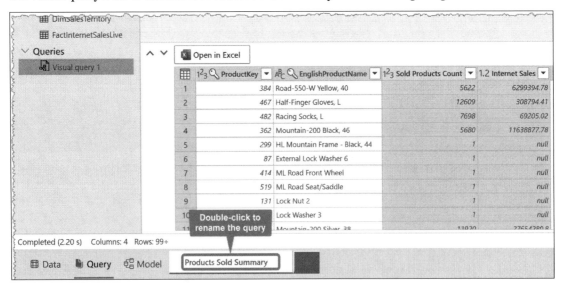

Figure 15.20: Renaming visual queries in Datamarts

Click the **Open in Excel** button to download the query as an Excel file. The Excel file contains a Power Query query connecting to the underlying Azure SQL DB, using the native query generated from the preceding Visual query. The following image shows the results being loaded into Excel after passing my credentials:

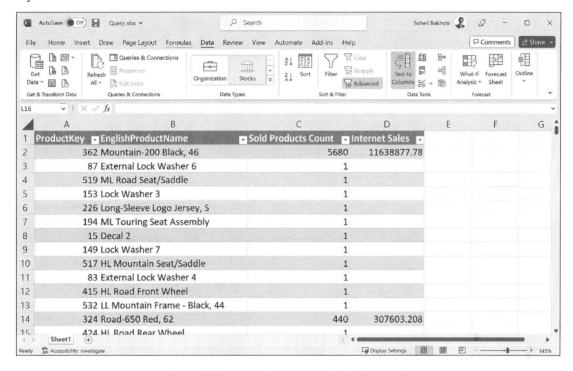

Figure 15.21: Renaming visual queries in Datamarts

We can get the native query from the visual diagram, which takes us to the next subsection.

Get the underlying native query

We can easily get the native query generated by each transformation step from the diagram view in the Datamarts by right-clicking the step, then clicking the **View data source query** from the context menu. The following image shows the preceding steps and the generated native query:

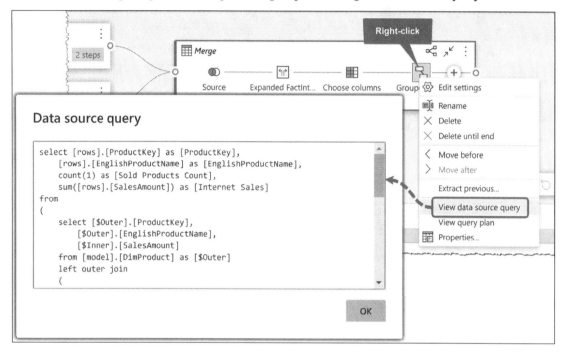

Figure 15.22: Getting a native query from the diagram view in Datamarts

One of the use cases for the generated native query is to reuse it later to create new tables or SQL queries.

As we can see in the preceding image, we can look at the query plans to investigate the queries in more detail. The next section explains how.

View query plan

One of the coolest new features available for public preview in 2023 for Power Query Online is named **View query plan**. This feature provides more details about the query evaluation, which can be used for query performance tuning and seeing where things went wrong from a query folding perspective. We can get to the query plan by right-clicking a transformation step and clicking the **View query plan** option from the context menu, as shown in the following image:

Chapter 15

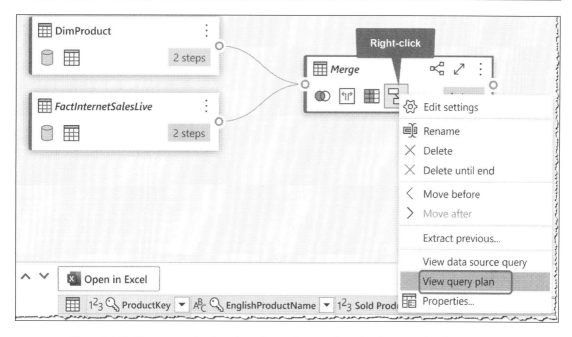

Figure 15.23: View query plan for a transformation step from the diagram view in Datamarts

This opens the **Query plan** window where we can click the **View details** to see more about the selected node:

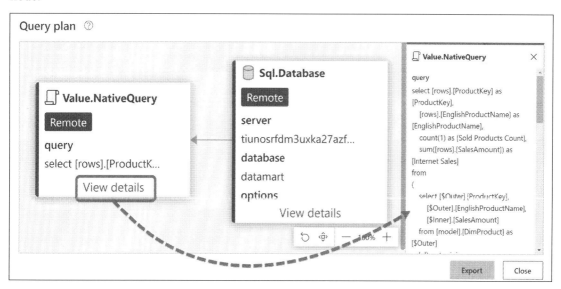

Figure 15.24: View details of a node in the query plan in Datamarts

We can click the **Export** button to export the query plan in JSON format. We will leave this for you to test.

SQL query experience

If you are a seasoned SQL developer and you want to analyze the Datamart running T-SQL statements, then this subsection is for you. Follow these steps to run your queries against the underlying SQL database hosting your Datamart's data:

1. Switch to the **Query** view in the Power BI Datamart Editor.
2. Click the **New query** dropdown.
3. Click the **New SQL query** from the menu. This creates the **SQL query 1** under the **Queries** section in the **Explorer** pane.
4. Type a SQL statement.
5. Click the **Run** button.

The following image shows the preceding steps:

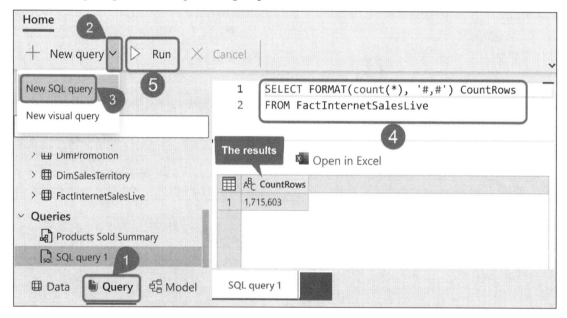

Figure 15.25: SQL query experience for analyzing Datamarts

Analyze Datamarts in SQL client tools

As mentioned earlier, the Power BI Datamarts load the prepared data into an Azure SQL database. We can connect to the underlying database using **SQL client tools** such as **SQL Server Management Studio (SSMS)** or **Azure Data Studio**. The following steps explain how to use SSMS to connect to the SQL endpoint of the Datamart we created earlier:

1. In the Power BI Service, hover over the desired Datamart and click the **More options** ellipsis button.
2. Click **Settings**.
3. Expand **Server settings**.
4. Click the **Copy** button to copy the connection string.

   The following image shows the preceding steps:

   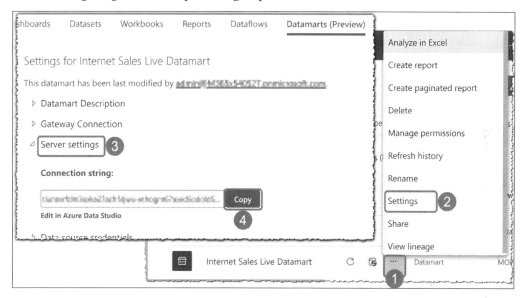

   Figure 15.26: Copying the connection string of a Datamart

5. In SSMS, click the **Connect** dropdown button.
6. Click the **Database Engine** option.
7. Paste the copied connection string in the **Server name** textbox.
8. Select **Azure Active Directory – Universal with MFA** from the **Authentication** dropdown.
9. Click **Connect**.

The following image shows the preceding steps:

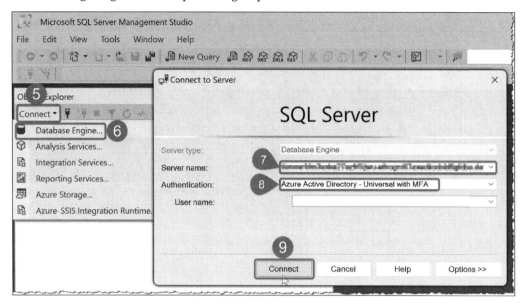

Figure 15.27: Connecting to the Datamart's SQL endpoint from SSMS

After passing our credentials, we connect to the Azure SQL database, and we can run SQL statements. The following image shows the results:

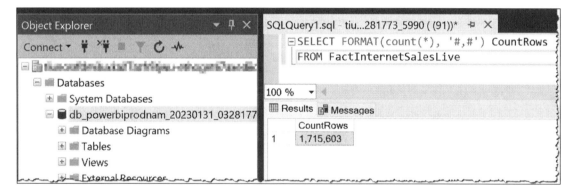

Figure 15.28: Running SQL statements in SSMS against the Datamart's database

RLS in Datamarts

We can implement RLS in Datamarts to control users' access. In *Chapter 11, Row-Level and Object-Level Security*, we learned that RLS kicks in only for users with the **Viewer** role in the Workspace. That principle remains the same here. In Datamarts, the implemented RLS automatically propagates to downstream objects, including the automatically generated datasets and reports. It is interesting to know that the RLS applies to the Azure SQL database too. Let us implement a simple RLS scenario to understand how it works.

The business requires restricting the users' access so that North American users can only access their region's sales. We implement the scenario on the existing Datamart created before. Let us look at the data model again to better understand the RLS implementation. As the following image shows, the **DimSalesTerritory** table has a **one-to-many** relationship with the **FactInternetSalesLive** table:

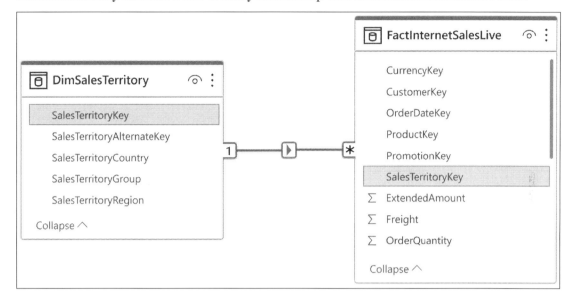

Figure 15.29: One-to-many relationship between DimSalesTerritory and FactInternetSalesLive

So applying RLS to **DimSalesTerritory** filters the **FactInternetSalesLive** table. The following image shows **DimSalesTerritory**'s data:

	SalesTerritoryKey	SalesTerritoryAlternateKey	SalesTerritoryRegion	SalesTerritoryCountry	SalesTerritoryGroup
1	1	1	Northwest	United States	North America
2	2	2	Northeast	United States	North America
3	3	3	Central	United States	North America
4	4	4	Southwest	United States	North America
5	5	5	Southeast	United States	North America
6	6	6	Canada	Canada	North America
7	7	7	France	France	Europe
8	8	8	Germany	Germany	Europe
9	9	9	Australia	Australia	Pacific
10	10	10	United Kingdom	United Kingdom	Europe
11	11	11	0	NA	NA	NA

Figure 15.30: DimSalesTerritory's data

As the preceding image shows, by applying RLS to the **SalesTerritoryGroup** column we achieve the goal.

Implementing RLS in Datamarts is possible via the Datamart Editor from either the **Data** or the **Model** views. Follow these steps to implement the scenario:

1. Click the **Manage roles** button from the **Home** tab.
2. Click the **New** button under the **Roles** section.

3. Name the new role North Americans.
4. Select the **DimSalesTerritory** table.
5. Click the **Add** button from the **Filter data** section.
6. Select the **SalesTerritoryGroup** column from the dropdown, use the **Equals** operator, and type in North America for the filter.
7. Click **Save**.

The following image shows the preceding steps:

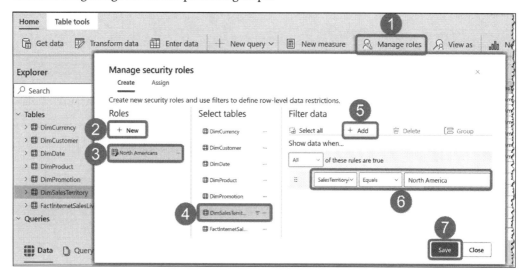

Figure 15.31: Implementing RLS in Datamarts

So far, we have created a new RLS role and added a new rule to it. The next step is to assign members to the role. Follow these steps to do so:

8. From **Manage security roles**, click the **Assign** tab.
9. Select the **North Americans** role.
10. Type in the account names or security groups that you want to apply the role to and select them. I have a security group named **North American Users** that I select.
11. Click the **Add** button.
12. Click the **Save** button to apply the changes.
13. Click **Close**.

The following image shows the preceding steps:

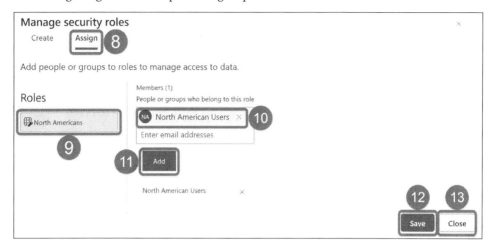

Figure 15.32: Assigning members to RLS roles in Datamarts

Now that we have assigned members to the RLS role, it is time to test the role to see if it works as expected. Follow these steps:

1. Click the **View as** button.
2. Select the **North Americans** role.
3. Click **OK**.

The following image shows the preceding steps and the results:

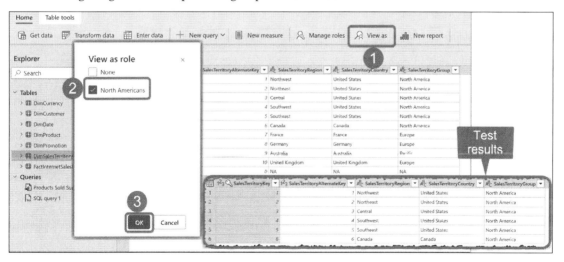

Figure 15.33: Testing RLS roles in Datamarts

As the preceding image shows, the **DimSalesTerritory** table only shows the rows where the value of the **SalesTerritoryGroup** column is North America. This filter propagates to the **FactInternetSalesLive** table via the relationship between the two, which is exactly what we want.

As mentioned earlier, defining RLS in Datamarts applies it to the underlying Azure SQL database. We use SSMS to connect to the underlying Azure SQL DB. The underlying base SQL tables are not exposed to us; instead, there are SQL views created for each table. We can use SSMS to script the views to observe the construction of the views. The following image shows the scripts of the **model.DimSalesTerritory** view. The highlighted part of the code is where RLS is applied:

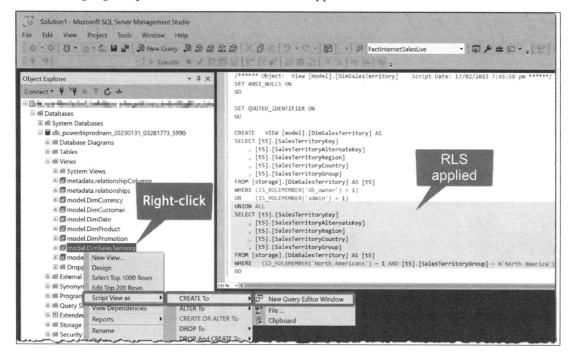

Figure 15.34: Scripting SQL views to see how RLS is applied at the database level in Datamarts

In this section, we learned what Datamarts are, and how to implement and work with them. While writing this chapter, the Datamarts feature is still in public preview and has not generally been available. Therefore, it may differ from what is available when reading this book. In the next section, we discuss some new DAX functions.

New DAX functions

As we all know, Microsoft constantly adds new features, options, and functions to Power BI. While writing this book, Microsoft introduced 11 new DAX functions. This section briefly covers the new functions that I personally find more interesting and have many use cases. This section does not explain the syntax of the new functions; instead, we will refer to Microsoft's official documentation website and explain the trickier points.

This section uses the `AdventureWorksDW2019` SQL Server database as our sample data source, which can be downloaded from the following URL: `https://learn.microsoft.com/en-us/sql/samples/adventureworks-install-configure?view=sql-server-ver16&WT.mc_id=DP-MVP-5003466`.

NETWORKDAYS()

This function is very useful in calculating the number of working days by considering weekends and public holidays. We could calculate the number of working days before this function became available, but this function offers another level of convenience to Power BI developers. The syntax for this function, as per Microsoft's official documentation website, is as follows:

```
NETWORKDAYS(<start_date>, <end_date>[, <weekend>, <holidays>])
```

See Microsoft's official documentation here: https://learn.microsoft.com/en-us/dax/networkdays-dax?WT.mc_id=DP-MVP-5003466.

As you see, the function accepts a start date and an end date as required parameters, but the weekend and holidays are optional. The **holidays** parameter must be a list of public holidays in date format. For instance, the business wants to calculate adding working days from AdventureWorksDW2019, considering the 1st to the 5th of January each year is a public holiday. To achieve the requirement, import the **DimDate** table into Power BI Desktop and use the following DAX expression to add a new calculated column to the table:

```
Is Public Holiday =
    AND(
        DimDate[EnglishMonthName] = "January"
        , AND(
            DimDate[DayNumberOfMonth] >=1
            , DimDate[DayNumberOfMonth] <= 5
        )
    )
```

The following image shows the results after filtering the values of the **Is Public Holiday** calculated column to **True**:

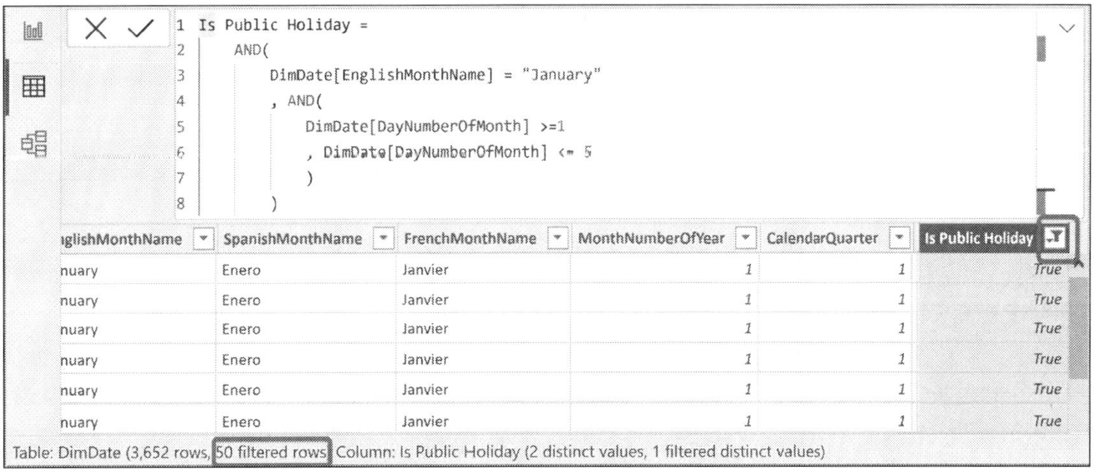

Figure 15.35: Considering the 1st to the 5th of January each year as a public holiday

Now we create a measure using the following DAX expression to calculate the number of working days when the weekends in our sample are Saturday and Sunday; hence, the weekend parameter is 1:

```
Working Days =
NETWORKDAYS(
        FIRSTDATE(DimDate[FullDateAlternateKey])
        , LASTDATE(DimDate[FullDateAlternateKey])
        , 1
        , CALCULATETABLE (
            VALUES (DimDate[FullDateAlternateKey])
            , DimDate[Is Public Holiday] = TRUE
        )
)
```

The following image shows the results in a **Card** visual:

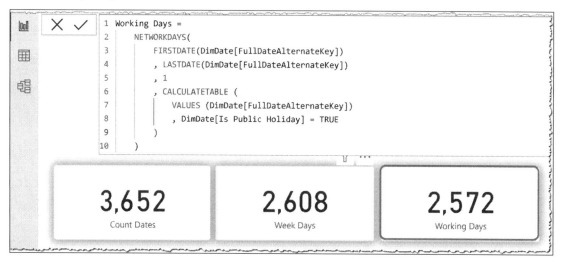

Figure 15.36: Calculating working days using the NETWORKDAYS() function

We can have a separate table containing the public holidays to use in the `NETWORKDAYS()` function.

You can download the `Chapter 15, NETWORKDAYS.pbix` sample from here: https://github.com/PacktPublishing/Expert-Data-Modeling-with-Power-BI-Second-Edition/blob/28e2af1762336ab5236a3b3961c41e9020de8200/Samples/Chapter%2015/Chapter%2015,%20NETWORKDAYS.pbix.

EVALUATEANDLOG()

The `EVALUATEANDLOG()` function was revealed by DAX maestro Jeffrey Wang for the first time through his blogpost in August 2022: https://pbidax.wordpress.com/2022/08/16/introduce-the-dax-evaluateandlog-function/. The `EVALUATEANDLOG()` function is useful for debugging DAX code, especially when evaluating virtual tables.

As we all know, previously, there weren't any options in Power BI Desktop to see the results of the virtual tables if we used some third-party tools such as DAX Studio. With the EVALUATEANDLOG() function, we still require third-party tools, but we are not required to deconstruct the DAX code to get the subsequent results of each part of the code. Make no mistake—the EVALUATEANDLOG() function is useful for debugging all kinds of DAX code, not just virtual tables. Nevertheless, I mostly find it helpful with virtual tables. We can use this function by adding it to our existing DAX code.

The syntax of the function is as follows:

```
EVALUATEANDLOG(<Value>, [Label], [MaxRows])
```

The Value parameter accepts any scalar or table DAX expression. We can add a label by specifying the Label optional parameter and setting the maximum number of retrieving rows, by specifying the MaxRows optional parameter.

You can read more on Microsoft's official documentation web page here: https://learn.microsoft.com/en-us/dax/evaluateandlog-function-dax?WT.mc_id=DP-MVP-5003466.

Whenever the xVelocity engine sees the EVALUATEANDLOG() function in code, it runs the DAX expressions of the Value parameter to be shown in the Power BI Desktop visuals. It also sends the results in JSON format to the DAXEvaluationLog event of the event log. We can then capture the results using either SQL Server Profiler or a new community tool built by Jeffrey Wang: DAX Debug Output. We use the latter in this section. The **DAX Debug Output** tool is available for download here: https://github.com/pbidax/DAXDebugOutput.

Now, let us evaluate the Working Days measure created in the previous section's sample file, Chapter 15, NETWORKDAYS.pbix. We only need to change the DAX expression we previously wrote to the following:

```
NETWORKDAYS(
        EVALUATEANDLOG(FIRSTDATE(DimDate[FullDateAlternateKey]), "StartDate")
        , EVALUATEANDLOG(LASTDATE(DimDate[FullDateAlternateKey]), "EndDate")
        , 1
        , EVALUATEANDLOG(SUMMARIZECOLUMNS(
            DimDate[FullDateAlternateKey]
            , TREATAS({TRUE}, DimDate[Is Public Holiday])
        ), "VirtualTable", 10)
    )
```

As you see, I added the EVALUATEANDLOG() to three parts of the code to capture the results. The third one captures the top 10 rows of the virtual table. Now I run the **DAX Debug Output** tool and connect the currently running Power BI report file to capture the DAXEvaluationLog event.

The following image shows the results of the first `EVALUATEANDLOG()` in the DAX Debug Output tool:

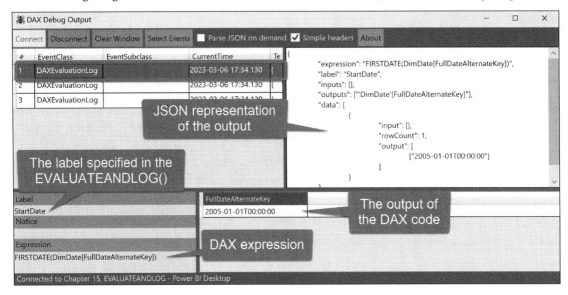

Figure 15.37: The results of the first EVALUATEANDLOG() in the DAX Debug Output tool

The following image shows the results of the second `EVALUATEANDLOG()` in the DAX Debug Output tool:

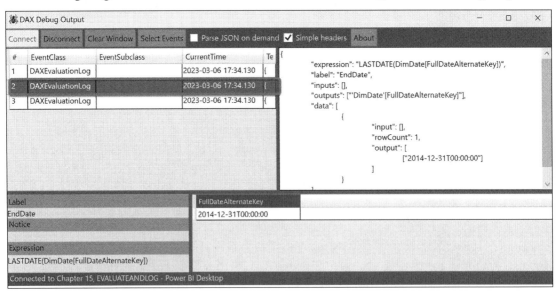

Figure 15.38: The results of the second EVALUATEANDLOG() in the DAX Debug Output tool

The following image shows the results of the third `EVALUATEANDLOG()` in the DAX Debug Output tool:

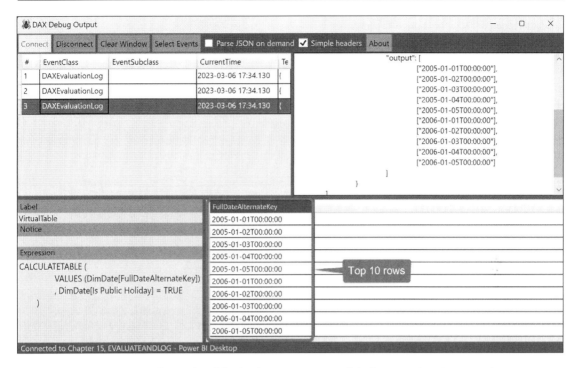

Figure 15.39: The results of the third EVALUATEANDLOG() in the DAX Debug Output tool

The code that includes the EVALUATEANDLOG() function runs as if it does not contain the EVALUATEANDLOG() function in Power BI Desktop, as the following image shows:

Figure 15.40: The results of running a measure containing EVALUATEANDLOG() in Power BI Desktop

Removing the EVALUATEANDLOG() function from our code after we finish debugging is crucial.

As you see, there are endless debugging and DAX performance tuning scenarios where the EVALUATEANDLOG() function becomes handy. You can download the Chapter 15, EVALUATEANDLOG.pbix sample file from here: https://github.com/PacktPublishing/Expert-Data-Modeling-with-Power-BI-Second-Edition/blob/28e2af1762336ab5236a3b3961c41e9020de8200/Samples/Chapter%2015/Chapter%2015,%20EVALUATEANDLOG.pbix.

Window functions

The **window functions** in DAX help solve complex calculations such as rolling averages elegantly and efficiently. With window functions, we can divide the rows of a specific table into logical windows of data, separated by the values of certain columns. These windows of data are called **partitions**. To define the partitions, we specify the required columns in the PARTITIONBY() function. In some calculations, such as ranking the data, we need to sort the data in a specific order and use the ORDERBY() function.

Both the PARTITIONBY() and ORDERBY() functions must be used only within other window functions as optional parameters. The window functions work upon the current partition or the current row. The current row is determined either by its **absolute position** or **relative position**.

The absolute position is when we specifically specify the position in the window functions, such as the first row, but the relative position is the one that must be calculated based on the position of the current row, such as the fifth row before the current. Some window functions, such as the INDEX() function, require the absolute position, some accept the relative position such as OFFSET(), and some accept both absolute and relative positions, such as the WINDOW() function.

The following window functions are currently available in Power BI, but we can expect to see more window functions being added to DAX in the future:

- PARTITIONBY()
- ORDERBY()
- INDEX()
- OFFSET()
- WINDOW()

While these functions are released and ready for us to use, we are all still learning the advantages and disadvantages of this feature. The Power BI team also adds new features and functionalities to the existing functions and introduces more window functions over time.

One interesting feature in all window functions in DAX is that the optional parameters are skippable. So if we do not specify the PartitionBy parameter in one of the preceding window functions, the function still works. In that case, there is one single partition of data. Conversely, when the PartitionBy parameter is defined using the PARTITIONBY() function, the calculations reset for each partition. For instance, if we want to calculate the rolling average of sales over partitions of years, the equation resets the calculation at the beginning of each year.

PARTITIONBY()

The values of specified columns in the `PARTITIONBY()` function are used to partition the table rows in the window functions. Its syntax is as follows:

```
PARTITIONBY ( <partitionBy_columnName>[, partitionBy_columnName [, …] ] )
```

For instance, we can imagine the `PARTITIONBY(DimDate[Year], DimDate[Month], DimDate[MonthOrder])` function resulting in creating partitions, as the following image shows:

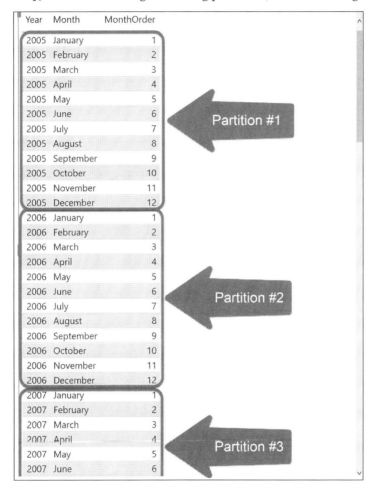

Figure 15.41: How the PARTITIONBY() function works in Power BI

As mentioned earlier, the `PARTITIONBY()` function is not useful on its own and must be used as the PartitionBy parameter of the other window functions. The PartitionBy parameter in the window functions is optional, so the data has only one partition if omitted. If the PartitionBy parameter is specified, the calculation using the window function iterates through each partition and resets the equation when it gets to the next partition. For instance, if we use a window function in an `AVERAGEX()` function to calculate the rolling average over the partitions defined in the preceding image, the average equation resets when it gets to the first row (January) in each partition.

ORDERBY()

The specified columns in the ORDERBY() function are used to specify the sort order of the partition's columns used in the window functions. The ORDERBY() function's syntax is as follows:

```
ORDERBY ( <orderBy_columnName>[, <order>][, orderBy_columnName [, <order>]] [, …] )
```

The order parameter is optional when only one column is specified. It is also optional for the last column when multiple columns are specified. The order parameter can be ASC, 1, or TRUE to show ascending order or, DESC, 0 (zero), or FALSE for descending. The ascending order is the default when the order parameter is omitted. The ORDERBY() function is also not useful and must be used as the OrderBy parameter of the other window functions.

> The ORDERBY() function is different from the ORDER BY statement. The ORDERBY() function manipulates the sort order of the partitions' columns in window functions, while the ORDER BY statement defines the sort order of DAX query results. In Power BI Desktop, we do not write DAX queries; we write DAX expressions. Therefore, we do not use any DAX statements. Here are some resources for your reference:
>
> Read about DAX statements here: https://learn.microsoft.com/en-us/dax/statements-dax?WT.mc_id=DP-MVP-5003466.
>
> Read about DAX queries here: https://learn.microsoft.com/en-us/dax/dax-queries?WT.mc_id=DP-MVP-5003466.

INDEX()

The INDEX() function returns a row at an absolute position over a sorted data partition. Its syntax is as follows:

```
INDEX(<position>[, <relation>][, <orderBy>][, <blanks>][, <partitionBy>])
```

The following are brief explanations of the parameters used in the preceding syntax:

- The position parameter is the only mandatory parameter that can be either an absolute 1-based position or a DAX expression returning a scalar value. The position parameter can be either positive or negative. A positive number, such as 1, means the first row, and a negative number, such as -2, means the second last row.
- The relation parameter is optional. When specified, the columns of the orderBy and PartitionBy parameters must come from the relation table. If omitted, all columns in the orderBy and PartitionBy parameters must come from a single table. We must also explicitly define the orderBy parameter. In addition, the default is ALLSELECTED() of all columns used in the orderby and PartitionBy parameters.

- We use the ORDERBY() function to define the optional orderBy parameter. If the relation parameter is specified, the columns used in the orderBy parameter must come from the relation table. If the orderBy parameter is omitted, the relation parameter must be explicitly specified, and the default sort order is by the columns in the relation parameter that are not specified in the PartitionBy parameter.
- blanks is an optional parameter defining how to deal with the blank values while sorting. The only accepted value is currently KEEP, which is also the default value.
- We use the PARTITIONBY() function to define the optional PartitionBy parameter. If the relation parameter is specified, the columns used in the PartitionBy parameter must come from the **relation** table. If omitted, the relation parameter acts as a single partition.

Let us see how it works in action. We want to get the best-selling product. The following measure caters to that:

```
Index, Best Selling Product =
VAR __ProductSale =
    ADDCOLUMNS (
        SUMMARIZE (FactInternetSales
, DimProduct[Product])
        , "ProductSales", [Sales]
    )
VAR __BestSeller =
    INDEX(1
        , __ProductSale
        , ORDERBY([ProductSales], DESC)
    )
RETURN
    CONCATENATEX(
        __BestSeller
        , 'DimProduct'[Product] & ": " & FORMAT([ProductSales], "$#,#.#")
    )
```

In the preceding code, we first defined a virtual table containing products' sales (__ProductSale). Then we used it in the INDEX() function's relation parameter, which is sorted in descending (DESC) order in the ORDERBY() function, and we asked for the first row of the results. Last but not least, we concatenated the values of the resulting columns. As you may have noticed, the preceding calculation has only one data partition.

The following image shows how the preceding code works when we run its different parts in DAX Studio:

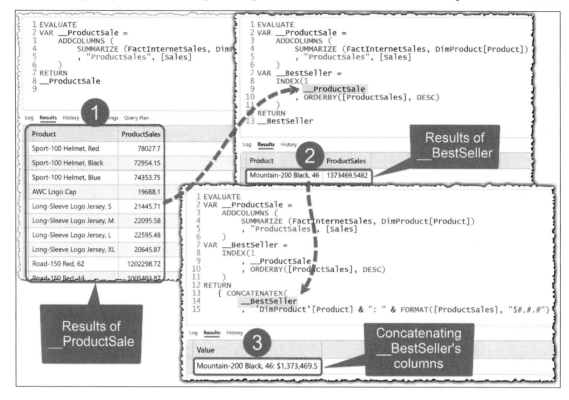

Figure 15.42: How the INDEX() function works in DAX Studio

The following image shows when the Index, Best Selling Product measure is used in a Power BI report:

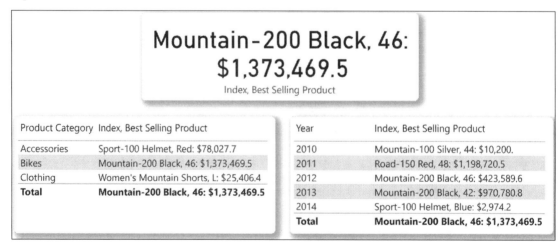

Figure 15.43: Using the Index, Best Selling Product measure in Power BI

In this example of using the INDEX() function, we did not use the partition parameter; therefore, the INDEX() function considers only one partition. Let us implement a sample that requires data partitioning.

We want to get the current month's sales difference as a percentage compared to the current year's best-selling month. In other words, the maximum monthly sales each year are the target sales of the year. We compare each month's sales with the yearly target. The following measure caters to that:

```
Index, % of Best Selling Month =
VAR __YearMonthSales =
    FILTER(
        ADDCOLUMNS(
            ALL(
                DimDate[Year]
                , DimDate[Month]
                , DimDate[MonthOrder]
            )
            , "__Sales", [Sales])
        , [__Sales] > 0)
VAR __BestSellingMonthSales =
    INDEX(
        1
        , __YearMonthSales
        , ORDERBY([__Sales], DESC)
        , PARTITIONBY(DimDate[Year])
    )
VAR __Result =
        DIVIDE(
            [Sales]
            , MAXX(
            __BestSellingMonthSales
                , [__Sales]
            )
        )
RETURN
    IF(HASONEVALUE(DimDate[Year]), __Result, BLANK())
```

The preceding code might look daunting to less-experienced developers, so I will explain how it works. In the preceding code:

- We defined the __YearMonthSales table variable to calculate the sales at the year and month levels.

- We define another table variable, __BestSellingMonthSales. This table variable accepts the __YearMonthSales variable as the INDEX() function's relation parameter. We sort the results of the __YearMonthSales variable by the [__Sales] column in descending order. So the maximum number of sales always shows in the first row. We partition the data by the DimDate[Year] column of the __YearMonthSales variable. We pick the first row of each partition and show it as the output of the __BestSellingMonthSales variable.
- We define another variable, __Result, which divides the [Sales] measure by the maximum of [__Sales] for the current row.
- We omit the totals, as calculating the percentage in our sample for totals does not make sense.

I used the EVALUATEANDLOG() function to validate the results. The following is the DAX expression after adding the EVALUATEANDLOG() function:

```
Index, % of Best Selling Month EVALUATEANDLOG =
VAR __YearMonthSales =
    EVALUATEANDLOG(
        FILTER(
            ADDCOLUMNS(
                ALL(
                    DimDate[Year]
                    , DimDate[Month]
                    , DimDate[MonthOrder]
                )
                , "__Sales", [Sales])
            , [__Sales] > 0)
    , "__YearMonthSales")
VAR __BestSellingMonthSales =
    EVALUATEANDLOG(
        INDEX(
            1
            , __YearMonthSales
            , ORDERBY([__Sales], DESC)
            , PARTITIONBY(DimDate[Year])
        )
    , "__BestSellingMonthSales")
VAR __Result =
    EVALUATEANDLOG(
        DIVIDE(
            [Sales]
            , MAXX(
                __BestSellingMonthSales
```

```
            , [__Sales]
            )
        )
    , "__Result")
RETURN
    IF(HASONEVALUE(DimDate[Year]), __Result, BLANK())
```

The following image shows the results in the DAX Debug Output tool after using the Index, % of Best Selling Month EVALUATEANDLOG measure in a table visual:

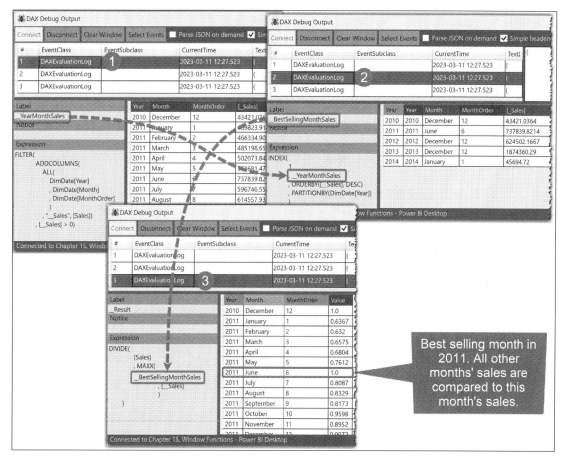

Figure 15.44: Evaluating the Index, % of Best Selling Month EVALUATEANDLOG measure in the DAX Debug Output tool

The numbers in the preceding image show:

1. The results of the __YearMonthSales variable.
2. The results of the __BestSellingMonthSales variable.
3. The results of the __Result variable.

The following image shows the `Sales` and `Index, % of Best Selling Month` measures used side by side in a table visual in Power BI:

Year	Month	Sales	Index, % of Best Selling Month
2010	December	$43,421.0364	100.00%
2011	January	$469,823.9148	63.68%
2011	February	$466,334.903	63.20%
2011	March	$485,198.6594	65.76%
2011	April	$502,073.8458	68.05%
2011	May	$561,681.4758	76.13%
2011	June	$737,839.8214	100.00%
2011	July	$596,746.5568	80.88%
2011	August	$614,557.935	83.29%
2011	September	$603,083.4976	81.74%
2011	October	$708,208.0032	95.98%
2011	November	$660,545.8132	89.52%
2011	December	$669,431.5031	90.73%
2012	January	$495,364.1261	79.32%
2012	February	$506,994.1876	81.18%
2012	March	$373,483.0054	59.80%
2012	April	$400,335.6145	64.10%
2012	May	$358,877.8907	57.47%
2012	June	$555,160.1428	88.90%
2012	July	$444,558.2281	71.19%
2012	August	$523,917.3815	83.89%
2012	September	$486,177.4502	77.85%
2012	October	$535,159.4846	85.69%
2012	November	$537,955.517	86.14%
2012	December	$624,502.1667	100.00%
2013	January	$857,689.91	45.76%
2013	February	$771,348.74	41.15%
2013	March	$1,049,907.39	56.01%
2013	April	$1,046,022.77	55.81%
Total		$29,358,677.2207	

Figure 15.45: Sales and Index, % of Best Selling Month measures in Power BI

As the preceding image shows, the best selling months in each year show 100% as the **Sales** value is compared to itself. All other months' values are compared to the best-selling month of each year.

This subsection taught us how the INDEX() function works. Microsoft's official documentation can be found here: https://learn.microsoft.com/en-us/dax/index-function-dax?WT.mc_id=DP-MVP-5003466.

Next, we will look at the OFFSET() function.

OFFSET()

The OFFSET() function retrieves a row calculated based on the relative position of the current row. The relative position can be a negative value to calculate the number of rows before the current row, or a positive value for the rows after the current one. With this function, we can retrieve the value of the n rows before the current row or after the current one. Its syntax is:

```
OFFSET ( <delta>[, <relation>][, <orderBy>][, <blanks>][, <partitionBy>] )
```

The parameters are very similar to the parameters in the INDEX() function, the only difference is the delta parameter, which is the relative position to the current row. It can be a DAX expression returning a scalar value. This parameter is mandatory. We use a negative value to calculate rows before the current row and a positive-value for the rows after the current one. For example, the following measure calculates the previous month's sales:

```
Offset, Previous Month Sales =
CALCULATE(
    [Sales]
    , OFFSET(
        -1
        , ORDERBY(DimDate[Year], ASC, DimDate[MonthOrder], ASC, DimDate[Month])
    )
)
```

We used DimDate[MonthOrder], because the DimDate[Month] column is sorted by DimDate[MonthOrder] in the data model.

The following image shows the results in Power BI:

Year	Month	Sales	Offset, Previous Month Sales
2010	December	$43,421.0364	
2011	January	$469,823.9148	$43,421.0364
2011	February	$466,334.903	$469,823.9148
2011	March	$485,198.6594	$466,334.903
2011	April	$502,073.8458	$485,198.6594
2011	May	$561,681.4758	$502,073.8458
2011	June	$737,839.8214	$561,681.4758
2011	July	$596,746.5568	$737,839.8214
2011	August	$614,557.935	$596,746.5568
2011	September	$603,083.4976	$614,557.935
2011	October	$708,208.0032	$603,083.4976
2011	November	$660,545.8132	$708,208.0032
2011	December	$669,431.5031	$660,545.8132
2012	January	$495,364.1261	$669,431.5031
2012	February	$506,994.1876	$495,364.1261
2012	March	$373,483.0054	$506,994.1876
2012	April	$400,335.6145	$373,483.0054

Figure 15.46: Calculating the previous months' sales using the OFFSET() function

This was a simple example of what we can do with the OFFSET() function. As you know, we could calculate the exact same equation using time intelligence or combinations of other DAX functions.

In this subsection, we looked at a simple example of using the OFFSET() function. Microsoft's official documentation can be found here: https://learn.microsoft.com/en-us/dax/offset-function-dax?WT.mc_id=DP-MVP-5003466.

The WINDOW() function comes next.

WINDOW()

The WINDOW() function retrieves multiple rows calculated based on the given position range. The range is calculated based on the mandatory parameters: from, from_type, to, and to_type. The from and to positions can be either ABS (absolute) or REL (relative), which are defined by the from_type and to_type parameters. The from parameter, depending on the from_type, indicates the first row from the current row, and the to parameter indicates the last row based on the to_type parameter.

The syntax of this function is:

```
WINDOW ( from[, from_type], to[, to_type][, <relation>][, <orderBy>][,
<blanks>][, <partitionBy>] )
```

All parameters other than the first four are similar to the INDEX() parameters in the preceding syntax. The WINDOW() function can be used to solve some scenarios that would be complex to overcome without the WINDOW() function, such as calculating moving averages. For instance, the following measure calculates the running total of sales by Product Category and Product Subcategory:

```
Window, RT Sales by Product Category and Subcategory =
CALCULATE(
    [Sales]
    , WINDOW(
        1, ABS
        , 0, REL
        , ORDERBY(DimProduct[Product Category], ASC, DimProduct[Product Subcategory], ASC)
    )
)
```

The following image shows the results in a **Table** visual:

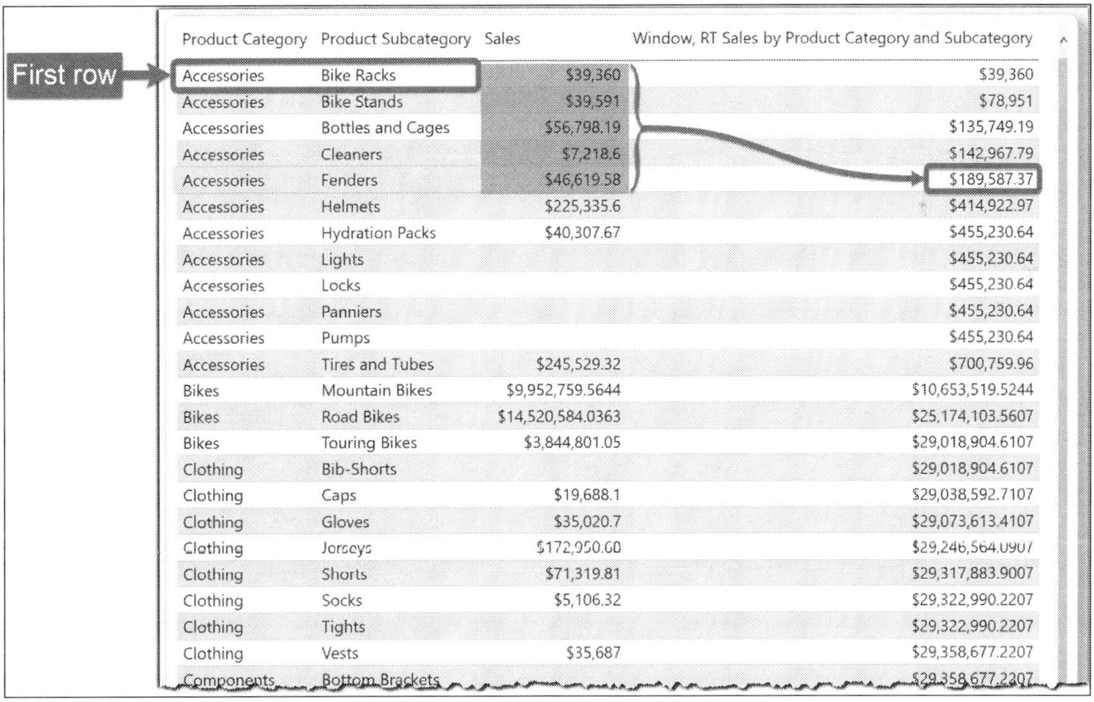

Product Category	Product Subcategory	Sales	Window, RT Sales by Product Category and Subcategory
Accessories	Bike Racks	$39,360	$39,360
Accessories	Bike Stands	$39,591	$78,951
Accessories	Bottles and Cages	$56,798.19	$135,749.19
Accessories	Cleaners	$7,218.6	$142,967.79
Accessories	Fenders	$46,619.58	$189,587.37
Accessories	Helmets	$225,335.6	$414,922.97
Accessories	Hydration Packs	$40,307.67	$455,230.64
Accessories	Lights		$455,230.64
Accessories	Locks		$455,230.64
Accessories	Panniers		$455,230.64
Accessories	Pumps		$455,230.64
Accessories	Tires and Tubes	$245,529.32	$700,759.96
Bikes	Mountain Bikes	$9,952,759.5644	$10,653,519.5244
Bikes	Road Bikes	$14,520,584.0363	$25,174,103.5607
Bikes	Touring Bikes	$3,844,801.05	$29,018,904.6107
Clothing	Bib-Shorts		$29,018,904.6107
Clothing	Caps	$19,688.1	$29,038,592.7107
Clothing	Gloves	$35,020.7	$29,073,613.4107
Clothing	Jerseys	$172,950.60	$29,246,564.0907
Clothing	Shorts	$71,319.81	$29,317,883.9007
Clothing	Socks	$5,106.32	$29,322,990.2207
Clothing	Tights		$29,322,990.2207
Clothing	Vests	$35,687	$29,358,677.2207
Components	Bottom Brackets		$29,358,677.2207

Figure 15.47: Calculating the running total of sales by Product Category and Product Subcategory using the WINDOW() function

The preceding code calculates the running total of sales based on the first absolute row to the current relative one. We are also aware that there is only one partition. So the calculation always starts from the first row and goes up to the current position. For instance, if the current position is the **Accessories** and **Fenders** row, the equation starts from the first row up to the current. Now, let us take a further step. If we want to calculate the running totals by **Product Category** and **Product Subcategory**, but we want the running total to be specific to each **Product Category**, then we need to partition the data like the following DAX expression:

```
Window, RT Sales by Product Category and Subcategory Partitioned =
CALCULATE(
    [Sales]
    , WINDOW(
        1, ABS
        , 0, REL
        , ORDERBY(DimProduct[Product Category], ASC, DimProduct[Product Subcategory], ASC)
        , PARTITIONBY(DimProduct[Product Category])
    )
)
```

The following image shows the results:

Product Category	Product Subcategory	Sales	Window, RT Sales by Product Category and Subcategory Partitioned
Accessories	Bike Racks	$39,360	$39,360
Accessories	Bike Stands	$39,591	$78,951
Accessories	Bottles and Cages	$56,798.19	$135,749.19
Accessories	Cleaners	$7,218.6	$142,967.79
Accessories	Fenders	$46,619.58	$189,587.37
Accessories	Helmets	$225,335.6	$414,922.97
Accessories	Hydration Packs	$40,307.67	$455,230.64
Accessories	Lights		$455,230.64
Accessories	Locks		$455,230.64
Accessories	Panniers		$455,230.64
Accessories	Pumps		$455,230.64
Accessories	Tires and Tubes	$245,529.32	$700,759.96
Bikes	Mountain Bikes	$9,952,759.5644	$9,952,759.5644
Bikes	Road Bikes	$14,520,584.0363	$24,473,343.6007
Bikes	Touring Bikes	$3,844,801.05	$28,318,144.6507
Clothing	Caps	$19,688.1	$19,688.1
Clothing	Gloves	$35,020.7	$54,708.8
Clothing	Jerseys	$172,950.68	$227,659.48
Clothing	Shorts	$71,319.81	$298,979.29
Clothing	Socks	$5,106.32	$304,085.61
Clothing	Tights		$304,085.61
Clothing	Vests	$35,687	$339,772.61
Total		**$29,358,677.2207**	**$29,358,677.2207**

Figure 15.48: Calculating the running total of sales by Product Category and Product Subcategory using the WINDOW() function for each Product Category

We can handle calculations similar to time-intelligent functions using a similar pattern over partitioned data. For instance, we can calculate year-to-date using PARTITIONBY(DimDate[Year]). The following measure caters to that:

```
Window, Sales YTD =
CALCULATE(
    [Sales]
    , WINDOW(
        1, ABS
        , 0, REL
    , ORDERBY( DimDate[Year], ASC, DimDate[MonthOrder], ASC, DimDate[Month])
    , PARTITIONBY(DimDate[Year])
    )
)
```

In the preceding code, we have to use DimDate[MonthOrder] first and then DimDate[Month] in the ORDERBY() function. The following image shows the results:

Figure 15.49: Calculating Sales YTD using the WINDOW() function

So far, we have learned how the WINDOW() function works when the from_type parameter is ABS (*absolute*) and the to_type parameter is REL (*relative*) to calculate the running total on a single partition of data. Now let us take one step further and calculate a three-month moving average of sales. As the moving average must be calculated on a moving window over the data, both the from_type and to_type parameters must be REL (*relative*). Run the following measure:

```
Window, 3M Moving Avg =
AVERAGEX(
```

```
    WINDOW(
        -2, REL
        , 0, REL
        , ORDERBY(DimDate[Year], ASC, DimDate[MonthOrder], ASC, DimDate[Month])
    )
    , [Sales]
)
```

In the preceding code, -2 moves back from the current row, which is 0 (zero); therefore, we always calculate the 3-monthly average. The following image shows the results:

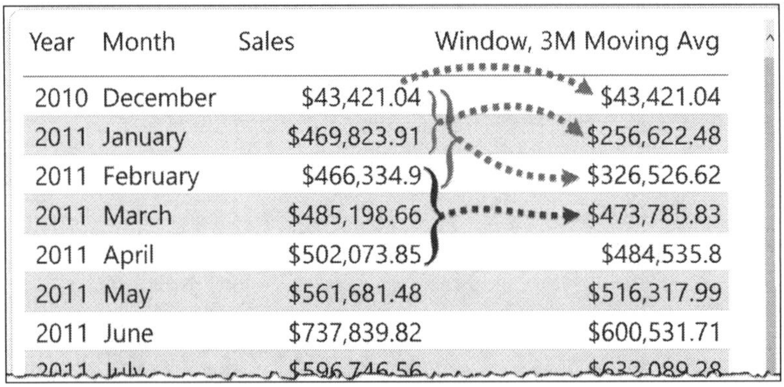

Year	Month	Sales	Window, 3M Moving Avg
2010	December	$43,421.04	$43,421.04
2011	January	$469,823.91	$256,622.48
2011	February	$466,334.9	$326,526.62
2011	March	$485,198.66	$473,785.83
2011	April	$502,073.85	$484,535.8
2011	May	$561,681.48	$516,317.99
2011	June	$737,839.82	$600,531.71
2011	July	$596,746.56	$632,089.28

Figure 15.50: Calculating 3-month moving average using the WINDOW() function

In the preceding image, the dotted lines show how the moving 3-month average is calculated.

In this subsection, we looked at a couple of scenarios implemented using the WINDOW() function. You can download the Chapter 15, Window Functions.pbix sample file containing all window functions here: https://github.com/PacktPublishing/Expert-Data-Modeling-with-Power-BI-Second-Edition/blob/28e2af1762336ab5236a3b3961c41e9020de8200/Samples/Chapter%2015/Chapter%2015,%20Window%20Functions.pbix.

Microsoft's official documentation can be found here: https://learn.microsoft.com/en-us/dax/window-function-dax?WT.mc_id=DP-MVP-5003466.

Since all window functions are newly released, the official Microsoft documentation website has plenty of room for improvement. But if you are interested in diving deep, the amazing Jeffrey Wang wrote a comprehensive blog explaining how the window functions work in DAX; I strongly suggest that you read his blog: https://pbidax.wordpress.com/2022/12/15/introducing-dax-window-functions-part-1/.

While we covered most of the new functions, Microsoft will continue to expand the functionalities of the window functions and other new functions. Microsoft has a specific web page for the new functions, so I recommend keeping an eye on it: https://learn.microsoft.com/en-us/dax/new-dax-functions?WT.mc_id=DP-MVP-5003466.

Summary

This chapter taught us about new data modeling options, features, and DAX functions. We looked closer at field parameters and how they become handy in making more dynamic reports. We also learned about Datamarts by implementing some simple samples. We connected to the underlying SQL endpoint from SSMS and looked closer at RLS implementation in Datamarts. Last but definitely not least, we implemented some scenarios using the new DAX functions.

This is the last chapter of this book; I hope you enjoyed reading it and that you learned some new techniques and ideas to deal with data modeling in Power BI. For more details about the topics discussed in this book—and future updates—keep an eye on my website: www.biinsight.com. I share the tech topics that I find interesting on social media; you can follow me on Twitter (https://twitter.com/_SoheilBakhshi) and LinkedIn (https://www.linkedin.com/in/bakhshi/).

Happy data modeling!

Join us on Discord!

Join The Big Data and Analytics Community on the Packt Discord Server!

Hang out with 558 other members and enjoy free voice and text chat.

https://packt.link/ips2H

packt.com

Subscribe to our online digital library for full access to over 7,000 books and videos, as well as industry leading tools to help you plan your personal development and advance your career. For more information, please visit our website.

Why subscribe?

- Spend less time learning and more time coding with practical eBooks and Videos from over 4,000 industry professionals
- Improve your learning with Skill Plans built especially for you
- Get a free eBook or video every month
- Fully searchable for easy access to vital information
- Copy and paste, print, and bookmark content

At www.packt.com, you can also read a collection of free technical articles, sign up for a range of free newsletters, and receive exclusive discounts and offers on Packt books and eBooks.

Other Books You May Enjoy

If you enjoyed this book, you may be interested in these other books by Packt:

Mastering Microsoft Power BI, Second Edition

Greg Deckler, Brett Powell

ISBN: 9781801811484

- Build efficient data retrieval and transformation processes with the Power Query M language and dataflows
- Design scalable, user-friendly DirectQuery, import, and composite data models
- Create basic and advanced DAX measures.
- Add ArcGIS Maps to create interesting data stories
- Build pixel-perfect paginated reports
- Discover the capabilities of Power BI mobile applications
- Manage and monitor a Power BI environment as a Power BI administrator
- Scale up a Power BI solution for an enterprise via Power BI Premium capacity

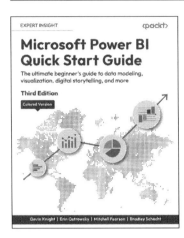

Microsoft Power BI Quick Start Guide, Third Edition

Devin Knight, Erin Ostrowsky, Mitchell Pearson, Bradley Schacht

ISBN: 9781804613498

- Connect to data sources using import, DirectQuery, and live connection options
- Use Power Query Editor for data transformation and data cleansing processes, and write M and R scripts and dataflows to do the same in the cloud
- Design effective reports with built-in and custom visuals to optimize user experience
- Implement row-level and column-level security in your dashboards
- Administer a Power BI cloud tenant for your organization
- Use built-in AI capabilities to enhance Power BI data transformation techniques
- Deploy your Power BI Desktop files into Power BI Report Server

Packt is searching for authors like you

If you're interested in becoming an author for Packt, please visit `authors.packtpub.com` and apply today. We have worked with thousands of developers and tech professionals, just like you, to help them share their insight with the global tech community. You can make a general application, apply for a specific hot topic that we are recruiting an author for, or submit your own idea.

Share your thoughts

Now you've finished *Expert Data Modeling with Power BI, Second Edition*, we'd love to hear your thoughts! Scan the QR code below to go straight to the Amazon review page for this book and share your feedback or leave a review on the site that you purchased it from.

https://packt.link/r/1803246243

Your review is important to us and the tech community and will help us make sure we're delivering excellent quality content.

Index

A

absolute position 630
Access 128
Advanced Editor 102
AdventureWorksDW2019 database 586
Adventure Works organization 531
Agg Awareness 414
   aggregation, managing 435-437
   aggregation table, creating 429, 430
   aggregation table, setting 433-435
   approaches 427
   dimensions storage mode, setting 433-435
   relationships, creating 432
   tables, loading in DirectQuery mode 430, 431
   using 426-428
aggregation, at Date level
   control measures, creating in base table 418
   Internet Sales table, summarizing 415, 416
   new measures, creating in summary table 418
   relationships, creating 416, 417
   summary table, hiding 419-421
aggregations
   implementing, at Date level 415
   implementing, at Year and Month level 421-426
   implementing, for non-DirectQuery data sources 414
   important notes 449, 450
   managing 435-437
   testing 438
   using 413, 414
aggregation, testing options
   DAX Studio 442, 443
   Performance Analyzer 438-442
   SQL Server Profiler 443-446
alternate keys 544
Area Char 56
artificial intelligence (AI) algorithms 196
Assume referential integrity 609, 610
Azure Active Directory (Azure AD) 496
Azure Analysis Services (AAS) 23, 82, 167-170, 578
Azure Data Factory (ADF) 82
Azure Data Lake Gen 2 (ADLS Gen2) 603
   reference link 554
Azure Data Lake Storage Gen2 (ADLS Gen 2) 553
Azure Data Studio 618
Azure Machine Learning (Azure ML) 554
Azure SQL Database 25

B

base table
   control measures, creating 418
bidirectional relationships 360-363, 376
   avoiding 376-379
Binary data 331

Boyce-Codd normal form 27
bridge table
 hiding 376
 using, in many-to-many relationship 369-375
Bronze data sources 175
Business Intelligence (BI) 177, 602
business keys 544

C

calculated columns
 avoiding 391-394
calculated tables 323-328
 creating 30-35
 creating, in Power BI Desktop 35
calculation groups
 DAX functions 484
 format string issue, fixing 482-484
 implementing, to handle time intelligence 475-481
 requirements 474
 terminology 475
 testing 482
 using 474
carriage return (CR) 137
chaining 579
chain length 580-586
color coding 386
Column by Delimiter
 splitting 191-194
column distribution 107-109
column profile 110
column quality 104, 105
columns
 adding, from examples 199-201
 duplicating 201-203
 merging 194, 195
comma-separated values (CSV) files 128, 134-139

Common Data Model (CDM) 553
 Dataverse 554
 reference link 554
Common Data Services (CDS) 82, 173
Composite Key 312
 handling 350-354
composite models 577
 working, with DirectQuery for Power BI datasets 586-592
composite primary keys 255
configuration tables
 dynamic color coding with measures 386-391
 segmentation 384, 385
 using 384
connection modes
 Connect Live mode 177
 Data Import mode 176
 DirectQuery mode 177
 working with 175
connection, types
 Connect Live 167
 DirectQuery 167
 Import 167
 report-level measures 167
Connect Live mode 177
 applications 178
 limitations 178
Currency column 256
custom columns
 adding 196-199
custom connectors software development kit (SDK) 81
Customer Relationship Management (CRM) 170
Customer table 256-259
custom functions 118-123
 recursive function 124, 125
custom types 90

Index 655

D

data
  loading, into Datamarts 605-608
  obtaining, from common data sources 127, 128
Data Analysis Expressions (DAX) 29, 82, 488
  time dimension, creating with 74-76
  used, for generating date dimension 66-69
  versus Power Query 267
Dataflows 25, 553, 554
  computed entities, creating 565-567
  computed tables 555
  creating 555, 556
  entities, creating 557-562
  exporting 569
  in Power BI 7, 8
  fields 555
  importing 570
  incremental data refresh, configuring 567, 568
  linked tables 555
  linked tables, creating from 563-565
  no-code/low-code experience 570-573
  query plans 573-575
  regular tables 555
  tables 555
  terminologies 555
  using, scenarios 554
Data Import mode 176
  applications 176
  limitations 176
Datamart Editor 604
  Datamarts, analyzing 610
Datamarts 25, 162-164, 601, 602
  analyzing, in Datamart Editor 610
  analyzing, in SQL client tools 618-620
  data, loading into 605-608
  data model, building 608
  relationships, creating 609
  relationships, managing 609
  RLS, implementing 620-624

Datamarts, in Datamart Editor
  no-code experience, with Visual query 610-617
  SQL query experience 618
Datamarts, relationships
  Assume referential integrity 609, 610
data modeling
  in Power BI 9
  in Power BI Desktop 317, 318
  RLS and OLS 488
  time intelligence 48
data model layer, Power BI 3
  Data view 4
  Model view 6
data models
  building, in Datamarts 608
  building, in Power BI 10, 11
  folder, using 402
  insignificant objects, hiding 395
  measure tables, creating 398-402
  organizing 394
  size, reducing by auto date/time disable 406-409
data, obtaining from data sources
  AAS 167
  CSV files 134-139
  Dataverse 173, 174
  Excel 140
  folder 128-133
  OData Feed 170-173
  Power BI dataflow 160-162
  Power BI Datamarts 162-164
  Power BI datasets 152-160
  SQL Server 164, 165
  SSAS 167
  TSV files 134-139
  TXT files 134-139
data preparation, best practices
  case sensitivity, in Power Query 283
  data type conversion 296

key columns, defining in queries 312
naming conventions, using 313, 314
proportion of data, loading 280-282
queries, organizing in Power Query Editor 294-296
query folding 283
query parameters, using 309
query size, optimizing 307

data preparation layer, Power BI 3

Data Quality Bar 104

dataset permissions for contributors
setting 592
Composite (Mixed) 578

dataset storage modes 179, 180
Composite (Mixed) mode 179, 578
Connect Live 578
DirectQuery storage mode 179, 577
Import storage mode 179, 577

data source certification 174
Bronze data sources 175
Silver data sources 175

data type conversion 183-191

data type conversion best practices 296
affecting, data modeling 296-303
columns, avoiding 304
including 305, 306
one data type, considering 306

data type facets 296

Dataverse 82, 173, 174
reference link 554

Data view 4

Data View pane 99-101

data visualization layer, Power BI
Model view 6
Report view 6, 7

Data warehouse in SQL Server 11

Date
dealing with 225-230

date dimension 262-265
creating 267
generating, with DAX 66-69
valid dates, detecting 48-56

Date level
aggregation, implementing at 415

Date table
marking, as data table 69-74

DateTime
dealing with 225-230

DateTimeZone
dealing with 225-230

DAX Debug Output tool 627

DAXEvaluationLog event 627

DAX functions 67, 624
EVALUATEANDLOG() function 626-630
for calculation groups 484
NETWORKDAYS() 625, 626
Window functions 630

DAX Studio 442, 443
download link 302
using 36

degenerate dimension 252, 256
dealing with 549-551
reference link 550

denormalization 14-22

Development (Dev) 113

dimensional modeling 11

dimension tables 12, 237, 242
creating 246

dimension tables, business requirement perspective
Currency column 256
Customer table 256-259
Date dimensions 262-265
Geography dimension 247-250
Product dimension 252-255
Sales Demographic 260-262

sales order 250-252
Time dimension 265-267

DirectQuery 160
composite models, working for Power BI datasets 586-592

DirectQuery for live connections
allowing, to Power BI datasets in Power BI service 578
enabling 578

DirectQuery for PBI datasets and AS
enabling, in Power BI Desktop 579

DirectQuery mode 23, 177
applications 177
limitations 177
tables, loading 430, 431

dynamic measure selection
implementing, with Fields Parameters 63-66

dynamic RLS implementation 503
team members data, accessing by managers in parent-child hierarchies 506-511
unauthorized users, restricting from accessing data 503-506
user's login data, obtaining from another source 512-519

E

enhanced row-level security editor 491

Enter data feature 384

Enterprise Resource Planning (ERP) 128, 170, 280

EVALUATEANDLOG() function 626-630

Excel 10, 128, 140

Excel file
stored, in local drive 140-146
stored, in SharePoint Online 147

Excel file on SharePoint Online, methods
Excel file path, obtaining directly from SharePoint 151, 152

Excel file path, obtaining from Excel desktop app 147-150

explicit measures 346

expressions 83

External Tools 442

Extract part 218

extract, transform, and load (ETL) 25, 218, 533-535, 553

extract, transform, and load (ETL) tool 128
Azure Data Factory 291
SQL Server Integration Services (SSIS) 291

F

facets 301

factless fact tables 370

Factorial calculation 124

fact tables 12, 237, 242
creating 268-276

featured tables 322, 323

field parameters feature 595-601

fields 329
columns 334
custom formatting 331-333
data types 329-331
hierarchies 342, 343
measures 343

fields, columns
binning 334-337
calculated columns 334
grouping 334-337
properties 337-342

fields, measures
explicit measures 346
implicit measures 344-346
textual measure 346-348

Fields Parameters 56
dynamic measure selection, implementing with 63-66

filtering rows 204-207
filter propagation 358-360
fixed dimensions 534
folder
   creating, in multiple tables 403
   measure, placing in multiple tables 404, 405
Folder data source 128-133
foreign key 350
function value 88

G

Geography dimension 247-250
globally unique identifier (GUID) 82
Gold/Platinum data sources 175
Group By functionality
   working with 207-210

H

hybrid tables 23, 450, 451
   configuring, in Power BI Desktop 451-457
   important notes 462, 463

I

implicit measures 344-346
Import mode 23
inactive relationship
   dealing with 379
   multiple direct relationship, with tables 381-383
   via multiple filter path 380, 381
incremental load 450
incremental refresh 450, 451
   important notes 462, 463
   policy, configuring in Power BI Desktop 451-457
   testing 458-461

INDEX() function 632-639
Inferred Dimensions 610
Information Technology (IT) 554, 602
insignificant objects
   columns, hiding 398
   implicit measures, hiding 398
   key columns, hiding 397
   unused fields and tables, hiding 395-397
Internet Sales Last Month (LM) 56
Internet Sales Last Month to Date (LMTD) 48
Internet Sales Last Year (LY) 56
Internet Sales Last Year Month to Date (LY MTD) 48
Internet Sales Last Year to Date (LYTD) 48
Internet Sales Month-over-Month (MoM) variance 57
Internet Sales Month to Date (MTD) 48
Internet Sales table
   summarizing 415, 416
Internet Sales Year-over-Year (YoY) variance 57
Internet Sales Year to Date (YTD) 48
iterative data modeling, approach 25, 26
   business logic, demonstrating in data visualizations 27
   business logic, testing 27
   data modeling 27
   data preparation based on business logic 26
   discovery workshops, conducting 26
   professional data modelers, thinking 27, 28

J

JavaScript Object Notation (JSON) 128

K

Kimball Group
   URL 531

Index

L

limited relationship 367
lineage 37
line feed (LF) 137
list value 84
Load part 218

M

machine learning (ML) 196
many-to-many relationship 355-357
   dealing with 365-369
   with bridge table 369-375
measure tables
   creating 398-402
Microsoft documentation
   reference link 174
Model view 6
Multi-Dimensional eXpressions (MDX) 23
multiple aggregations
   implementing 446-449

N

native query
   underlying 616
NETWORKDAYS() function 625, 626
new terminologies 579
   chaining 579
   chain length 580-586
no-code experience
   with Visual query 610-615
non-DirectQuery data sources
   aggregations, implementing 414
Notepad++
   download link 137
number facets 301

numbers, from text
   extracting 222-224

O

object-level security (OLS) 519
   implementation flow 519, 520
   in data modeling 488
OData data source tables 282
OFFSET() function 639, 640
OLS implementation 520-522
   in single model 524-527
   members, assigning 524
   roles, validating 522-524
   roles, validating in Power BI Service 524
   using, conserations 527, 528
one-to-one relationship 355
on-premises Data Gateway 560
Open Data Protocol (OData) 10, 170-173, 280
ORDERBY() function 632

P

Parent-Child hierarchies 463-465
   depth, identifying 465-467
   levels, creating 467-471
   team members data, accessing by
      managers 506-511
PARTITIONBY() function 631
partitions 630
Performance Analyzer 438-442
period-over-period calculations 56-63
Platform-as-a-Service (PaaS) 167
Portable Document Format (PDF) 128
Power BI
   data model, building 10, 11
   flow of data 7, 8
   in data modeling 9

Power BI dataflow 160-162, 267, 312
Power BI Datamarts 601, 602
  creating 605
  misunderstandings, demystifying 603
  usage, scenarios 602
Power BI datasets 152-160
  composite models, working with DirectQuery 586-592
  DirectQuery for live connections, allowing in Power BI service 578
Power BI Desktop 2
  calculated tables, creating 35
  data modeling 317, 318
  DirectQuery for PBI datasets and AS, enabling 579
  hybrid table, configuring 451-457
  incremental refresh policy, configuring 451-457
  roles 488
Power BI Desktop Report file (PBIX) 9, 308
Power BI Diagnostic Port 444
Power BI Documenter 395
Power BI feature
  comparing 22
Power BI layers 2, 3
  data model layer 3
  data preparation layer/Power Query 3
  data visualization layer 6
Power BI licensing, considerations 22
  calculation groups 23, 24
  Dataflows 25
  Datamart 25
  hybrid tables 23
  incremental data load 23
  maximum size, of individual dataset 23
  shared dataset 24
Power BI Pro Workspace 555
Power BI Report Server
  members, assigning to roles 494, 495

Power BI Service
  DirectQuery for live connections, allowing to Power BI datasets 578
  members, assigning to roles 493, 494
Power BI tools and apps
  download link 2
Power Pivot 9
Power Query
  case-sensitive 82
  expression 83
  query 83
  types 89
  values 83
  versus DAX 267
  working, with Pivot tables 230-235
Power Query Diagnostics tool 292
Power Query Editor 90-92
  Advanced Editor 102
  Data View pane 99-101
  Queries pane 92
  Query Settings pane 94
  status bar 101, 102
Power Query Editor, Queries pane
  custom functions 92
Power Query features, for data modelers 103
  column distribution 107-109
  column profile 110
  column quality 104, 105
Power Query, functionalities
  column, adding from examples 199-201
  column, duplicating 201-203
  columns, merging 194, 195
  custom column, adding 196-199
  data type conversion 183-191
  dealing, with Date 225-230
  dealing, with DateTime 225-230
  dealing, with DateTimeZone 225-230
  filtering rows 204-207

numbers from text, extracting 222-225
queries, appending 210-214
queries, duplicating and referencing 218, 219
queries, merging 215-218
Split Column by Delimiter 191-194
values, replacing 219-222
working, with Group By 207-210

Power Query M formula language
in Power BI 81

Power Query Online 25, 553-555

Premium licenses 553

Premium Per User (PPU) 160, 458, 605

primary key 350

primitive types 89

primitive values 84

Product dimension 252-255

Production (Prod) 113

Project Web App (PWA) 170

Q

queries
appending 210-214
duplicating and referencing 218, 219
merging 215-218

queries, join
types 217

Queries pane
constant values 92
custom functions 92
groups 93
query parameters 92
tables 92

query folding 283
best practices 285
data preparation, pushing to source system 291
data sources 284

DirectQuery or Dual storage modes 284
disabled View Native Query 292, 293
enabling, for native queries 288-290
indications 285
SQL statements, using 286-288

query parameters 8, 63, 111-118
connections, parameterizing 309
defining 111
row counts, restricting in development for large tables 309-312
using 309

query plans
in Dataflows 573-575

Query Settings pane 94
Applied steps 97, 98
Query Properties 95, 96

query size optimization
query load, disabling 309
summarization (group by) 308, 309
unnecessary columns, removing 308
unnecessary rows, removing 308

R

record value 85

recursive function 124, 125

regular relationship 367

relationships
bidirectional relationships 360-363
cardinalities 355
composite keys, handling 350-354
creating 416, 417, 432
filter propagation behavior 358-360
foreign key 350
primary key 350
using 348-350

relationships, cardinalities
many-to-many relationships 355-357
one-to-many relationships 355
one-to-one relationships 355

relative position 630
Replacer function 219
Report view 6, 7
RLS and OLS, terminologies 488
  enhanced row-level security editor 491
  roles 488
  roles, validating 491, 492
  rules 489, 490
RLS implementation
  in single model 524-527
  using, conserations 527, 528
RLS implementation flow 495
RLS implementation flow, approaches 496
  dynamic RLS implementation 503
  static RLS implementation 496-503
roleplaying dimensions
  implementing 471-474
Row-Level Security (RLS) 602
  implementing, in Datamarts 620-624
  in data modeling 488

S

Sales Demographic 260, 261
sales order 250, 252
SAP Business Warehouse (SAP BW) 175
SCD 0 type 534
SCD 1 type 534-543
SCD type 2 533, 544-549
segmentation 384
self-service data preparation 553
semantic model 9
Server Management Studio (SSMS) 618
Silver data sources 175
slowly changing dimensions (SCDs)
  dealing with 531-533
  types 534-549

Smart Date Key 227, 452
snowflaking 14
Splitter.SplitTextByCharacterTransition() function
  reference link 121
SQL client tools
  Datamarts, analyzing 618-620
SQL query 604
SQL query experience 618
SQL Server 164, 165
SQL Server Analysis Services Multi-Dimensional (SSAS MD) 23
SQL Server Analysis Services (SSAS) 2, 9, 167, 168, 577, 578
SQL Server Analysis Services Tabular models (SSAS Tabular) 82
SQL Server Integration Services (SSIS) 82
SQL Server Management Studio (SSMS) 443, 458
SQL Server Profiler 443-446
Star Schema 11, 12
  business requirements 238
  dimensions and facts 237
  dimensions and facts, defining 242
Star Schema, business requirements
  linkages, between existing tables 239
  lowest required grain of Date and Time, searching 240-242
  number of tables, in data source 238, 239
Star Schema, dimensions and facts
  potential dimensions, determining 243
  potential facts, determining 243-246
star schema modeling
  versus transactional modeling 11, 12
static RLS implementation 496-503
  requirement 496-502
status bar 101, 102

Index 663

storage modes
  DirectQuery mode 178
  Dual mode 178
  Import mode 178
  working with 178, 179

Structured Column 17

structured values 84
  function value 88
  list value 84
  record value 85
  table value 86-88

subfolders
  creating 405, 406

Subject Matter Experts (SMEs) 27, 173, 244, 280, 528

summary table
  hiding 419-421
  measures, creating 418

surrogate key 544

T

tables 318
  calculated tables 323-328
  featured tables 322, 323
  pivoting 230-235
  properties 319-322

table value 86-88

tab-separated values (TSV) files 134-139

Tabular Editor 458

temporal tables
  reference link 547

text file (TXT) 128, 134-139

textual measure 346-348

time dimension 265-267
  creating 267
  creating, with DAX 74-76

time intelligence, in data modeling 48
  period-over-period calculations 56-63
  valid dates, detecting in date dimension 48-56

transactional modeling
  versus star schema modeling 11, 12

Transact SQL (T-SQL) language 604

truncation and load 450

type number facets 301

type value 89

U

Uniform Resource Locators (URLs) 112

Universal Time Coordinate (UTC) 228

User Acceptance Testing (UAT) 113

User-defines Aggregation 414

user's login data
  obtaining, from another source 512-519

V

values 83
  primitive values 83, 84
  replacing 219-222
  structured values 83, 84

variables 83

View query plan 616, 617

virtual relationship 37

virtual tables 29, 30
  calculated tables, creating 30-35
  calculated tables, creating in Power BI Desktop 35
  DAX Studio, using 36
  relationships 37-48
  results, displaying visually 35

Visual query 604
  no-code experience with 610-615

W

weak relationship 367
WINDOW() function 630, 640-644
Window functions, in DAX
  INDEX() function 632-639
  OFFSET() function 639, 640
  ORDERBY() function 632
  PARTITIONBY() function 631
  WINDOW() function 640-644

X

XMLA endpoint 9
  reference link 9
xVelocity 301, 308
xVelocity engine 9

Y

Year and Month level
  aggregation, implementing at 421-426

Download a free PDF copy of this book

Thanks for purchasing this book!

Do you like to read on the go but are unable to carry your print books everywhere? Is your eBook purchase not compatible with the device of your choice?

Don't worry, now with every Packt book you get a DRM-free PDF version of that book at no cost.

Read anywhere, any place, on any device. Search, copy, and paste code from your favorite technical books directly into your application.

The perks don't stop there, you can get exclusive access to discounts, newsletters, and great free content in your inbox daily

Follow these simple steps to get the benefits:

1. Scan the QR code or visit the link below

https://packt.link/free-ebook/9781803246246

1. Submit your proof of purchase
2. That's it! We'll send your free PDF and other benefits to your email directly

Made in the USA
Middletown, DE
06 January 2024